INDUSTRIAL
CONTROL
ELECTRONICS

INDUSTRIAL CONTROL ELECTRONICS

APPLICATIONS AND DESIGN

J. MICHAEL JACOB
Purdue University

PRENTICE HALL, Englewood Cliffs, New Jersey 07632

Library of Congress Cataloging-in-Publication Data

Jacob, J. Michael.
  Industrial control electronics.

  Includes index.
  1. Electronic control. 2. Industrial electronics.
I. Title.
TK7881.2.J33 1988   621.8'043   88–15266
ISBN 0–13–459306–5

Cover design: 20/20 Services, Inc.
Manufacturing buyer: Robert Anderson

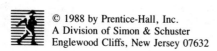 © 1988 by Prentice-Hall, Inc.
A Division of Simon & Schuster
Englewood Cliffs, New Jersey 07632

Printed in the United States of America
10 9 8 7 6 5 4 3 2 1

ISBN 0-13-459306-5

Prentice-Hall International (UK) Limited, *London*
Prentice-Hall of Australia Pty. Limited, *Sydney*
Prentice-Hall Canada, Inc., *Toronto*
Prentice-Hall Hispanoamericana, S.A., *Mexico*
Prentice-Hall of India Private Limited, *New Delhi*
Prentice-Hall of Japan, Inc., *Tokyo*
Simon & Schuster Asia Pte. Ltd., *Singapore*
Editora Prentice-Hall do Brasil, Ltda., *Rio de Janeiro*

To my parents,
Don and Louise

Contents

Preface

The use of electronics to control industrial manufacturing processes is key to the economic success of any company; indeed, to any country. Properly applied electronic controls improve the precision, accuracy, speed, and economy of a manufacturing procedure. This, in turn, lowers the cost of the product, while providing higher quality.

The latest movement in industrial automation is computer-integrated manufacturing (CIM). The plant's computer systems are tied together with the proper hardware and software. Orders entered by the sales department automatically initiate the production process. Networked computers schedule and oversee the ordering and routing of materials, part production, component assembly, finished product testing, and shipment to the customer. Successful integration to this extent requires that the elements used in production be well controlled, accurate, and highly reliable. So the entire CIM system depends on the quality of the electronics used to control the manufacturing processes.

Industrial control electronics also find applications in fields far removed from manufacturing. The same circuits used to assure proper motor speed can be used in the monitoring of blood flow and the detection of blood clots in an artificial kidney. The electronics used in a cascaded controller to assure correct level in a drug processing vat can be used to linearize the performance of a 60-V 100-A dc power supply. Industrial control electronics can be quite useful in many fields outside a manufacturing facility.

The control of a system is traditionally broken into two segments. The control engineer is taught optimal control theory. His or her skills are based on Laplace mathematics and involve such things as matrix operations, multivariable disturbances, the s domain, poles and zeros, z transforms, and probability and sampling theories. The other segment is the control technician or electrician. He or she is skilled in installation, calibration, troubleshooting, relay ladder diagrams, and the *National Electrical Code®*.

These two people, jointly charged with the job of implementing a functional control system, too often do not even speak the same language. This book is designed to bridge that gap. It provides the information to allow the control engineer to translate the Laplace domain control equation into working hardware, practical in the environment of an industrial manufacturing plant. Similarly, an instrumentation technician, given the task to "make this work," will find in this book the details and subtleties central to the success of any closed-loop control system. The mathematical "magic" is explained and related to the required circuit components and performance.

Initially, this book was designed for electrical engineering technology (EET) associate-degree sophomore courses and bachelor-degree junior or senior courses. It teaches how to *implement* those automated data acquisition and controls techniques learned in the traditional control theory courses. For this reason the manuscript has also been used in continuing education and in-plant technician and engineering training.

The approach is based heavily on electronics. It is expected that the reader is familiar with discrete and integrated analog and digital circuits. The first chapter provides an overview of the nature, structure, and purpose of an industrial control system, using dedicated and computer controls. Then the reader is taken around the loop, studying the requirements, circuits, industrial implementation, and evaluation of each element. Included are circuits to sense the process variable, signal condition it, encode, transmit, isolate, and protect that signal in a manufacturing environment, compute (either with analog or digital electronics) a correction signal, and finally, to proportionally convert that low-level voltage into line-driven, kilowatt power. The final chapter examines the effects this feedback has on the system's performance.

The electronics and system behavior is rigorously, mathematically supported. The reader is expected to be fluent in algebra and to be familiar with the concepts of differentiation and integration. A one-semester introduction to calculas is adequate. The use of Laplace-based mathematics has been placed in an appendix. This allows sophomore-level courses to use the text with a good sense of continuity, while junior- or senior-level courses can explore the Laplace foundations of the more sophisticated concepts.

The book includes several features that are unique among controls and industrial electronics texts. There is a significant use of manufacturers' applications and notes. This provides the reader with the latest, most authoritative source of information. Throughout the book, servo control and process control are given comparable treatment, assuring a more balanced view of the controls field than is found in many books. Signal voltage conversion to current or frequency for transmission is absolutely necessary in a manufacturing environment, but often omitted in textbooks. This is presented in Chapter 4, along with isolation, shielding, and grounding techniques. Controllers based around analog electronics, microprocessors, and programmable controllers (PLC) all find valid use in industry. Each is presented, in depth, in Chapters 5 and 6. Proportional control of power is typically omitted in controls texts and given a rather one-sided presentation in books on industrial electronics. Chapter 7 provides the reader with the information needed to design and implement practical power circuits using power op amps, pulse-width modulation, thyristor time proportioning, and phase-angle firing.

This book is the product of a rather extended development cycle. The manuscript, in one form or another, has been used by over 200 students. Readers have been diverse, ranging from students in EET associate-degree programs, EET bachelor-degree programs, technician continuing education, engineering continuing education, and engineering and science graduate schools. Each iteration has seen modifications based on technical updates and on corrective feedback from the students who used it.

A complete treatment of all the material presented here requires two semesters. Several techniques have been successful. If the text is to be used for a required two-course sequence, then a direct approach is fine. The material can be split near the middle of Chapter 5 (analog controllers). Laplace operations and process transfer functions (Appendixes A and B) should be presented before undertaking the more complex controllers or system response (Chapter 8) in the second course.

Few schools can afford the luxury of two required controls courses. A more vertically integrated approach has also been used successfully. The introductory course covers Chapters 1 through 3 in detail. The concepts of signal conditions for zero and span and current transmission are extracted from Chapter 4. However, commercial modules are used as examples rather than the build-your-own approach of the remainder of Chapter 4. On/off and proportional control from Chapter 5 are presented along with the principles of P-I and PID. However, circuit implementation and more advanced control schemes are omitted. Power interfaces are restricted to thyristor-based circuits (Section 7–3). The course closes with an overview of Laplace operations (Appendix A), closed-loop system performance (Section 8–1), and controller tuning (Sections 8–4.2 and 8–4.3).

The follow-up course (advanced instrumentation and controls) fills in those areas omitted in the first, broad-brush course. Laplace math is used more often (Appendix B and well as Appendix A). The details of circuit design, isolation, cabling, advanced analog controllers, digital control, power ICs, switch mode servo amps, and Bodé plots are supported with numerous, open-ended, realistic problems.

As with any such effort, many people contribute to the quality of the final product. First, I must express my sincere appreciation to my students. They really wrote this book. I have just put it down on paper. Their patient suffering through the early versions of the manuscript and their (constant, negative) feedback are largely responsible for the quality of this book. Greg Burnell, my editor, has been more patient than anyone deserves. I trust that tolerance is now rewarded. Finally, and foremost, I thank my wife, Jean. Her faith in me and her understanding of all of the stolen hours has kept me writing, day after day.

J. Michael Jacob

INDUSTRIAL CONTROL ELECTRONICS

1

Introduction to Industrial Control

To control is "to verify . . . by comparison with a standard . . . to regulate" [1]. There are a wide variety of control systems all around, and within, you. The body's temperature, chemical balance, sensory perception, and movement are all under complex automatic biological controls. Similarly, the production and movement of industrial energy and products are, today, under increasingly complex automatic electronic controls. These control systems are largely responsible for the high-quality, low-cost, efficient products that shape your daily life. In fact, much of what is taken for granted could not be produced at all without automatic electronic controls. In areas as diverse as farming, housing, transportation, medicine, energy, and even entertainment, automatic electronic controls are employed extensively.

In this chapter you will look closely at what automatic controls are supposed to do. The elements necessary to provide control are presented. These are often arranged by *how* they control, either open loop or closed loop. Examples of each are given. Control systems are also classified by *what* they control. Servomechanism control systems (control of movement) and process control systems (control of temperature, flow, pressure, etc.) are both illustrated.

OBJECTIVES

After studying this chapter you should be able to do the following:

1. Explain the purpose of automatic controls.
2. Draw the block diagram of a control loop and describe each element.

3. Describe, in detail, three examples of open-loop control and three examples of closed-loop control.
4. Explain the difference between a servomechanism control system and a process control system, giving a detailed example of each.
5. Describe digital supervisory control, direct digital control, and distributed computer control. Explain the advantages and disadvantages of each. Illustrate an example of each.

1–1 PURPOSE OF AUTOMATIC CONTROL

There are several ways in which industrial production benefits from the use of automatic controls. Things can be done that are beyond normal human ability. Tremendous forces and temperatures are accurately manipulated in the rolling of a sheet of steel. At the other extreme, very precise placement of leads and components is achieved during integrated-circuit manufacturing.

Cost of production is reduced through the use of automatic controls. This is because much tighter tolerances can be obtained. Figure 1–1a shows the variation in quality for production without automatic controls. A certain level of performance (Q) is expected of the product. Quality control standards allow no more than N (percent) of the output from manufacturing to fall below this minimum. To meet this target, most of production must far exceed the required performance. However, with automatic controls, there is significantly less variation in the product's quality. This is illustrated in Figure 1–1b. This manufacturing process can be tuned so that an acceptable reject level is maintained while most of the products just exceed the required performance level. This results in savings in energy, materials, labor, facilities, and money.

Automatic controls also allow for operation in extreme and hazardous conditions. Application to vehicle control has allowed fast, safe travel from the environmental extremes of space to those of the ocean floor. High-speed operation, whether for improved maneuverability of fighter jets or for rapid parts assembly by robot, can also be achieved.

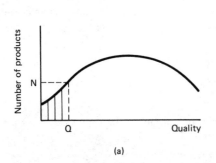
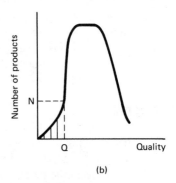

Figure 1–1   Product quality distribution (a) without and (b) with automatic controls.

Operator safety is improved by placing the automatic equipment controls near the hazardous environment and allowing the operator to be remotely located.

These benefits, and more, are obtained because the automatic control system is designed to keep certain important process parameters at or near their desired value without significant human intervention.

1–2 OPEN-LOOP CONTROL

The simplest form of control is open loop. Its block diagram is given in Figure 1–2. Energy is applied to the process through an actuator. The calibrated setting on the actuator determines precisely how much energy is applied. The process uses this energy to produce its output. Changing the actuator's setting changes the energy into the system and the resulting output of the process as well.

A tank heating system is an example of this simple, open-loop control. It is illustrated in Figure 1–3. The product to be heated enters the tank at the top and is withdrawn from the bottom. Surrounding the tank is a steam jacket. The amount of steam that enters the jacket, and therefore how much heat is transferred to the product, are controlled by a valve. For a given steam temperature and pressure, tank level, and incoming liquid temperature, the position of the valve will determine the outlet liquid temperature. The valve can be calibrated. If a different temperature is required, you simply move the valve to another position on its calibrated scale.

For reasonably stable conditions, the open-loop control scheme works adequately. Its simplicity leads to several advantages. Little equipment is needed. This makes the system inexpensive to purchase and install, and much less prone to breakdown.

However, what happens if there is a disturbance in any of the input parameters? Changes in steam temperature will directly affect the product's temperature. An increase in steam pressure (across the valve) will cause more steam to flow into the jacket, adding more heat to the liquid. If the level in the tank goes down (by either an increased outlet drain or decreased input), the remaining liquid will absorb more heat. Finally, if the liquid comes in at a higher temperature, it will leave at a higher temperature. All of these variations affect the liquid's temperature. But the calibrated valve setting assumes that these (and other) input parameters do not change. Clearly, if there are any variations or disturbances, the open-loop control system will not keep the output parameter (temperature in this example) at the desired value.

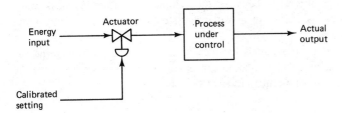

Figure 1–2 Open-loop control.

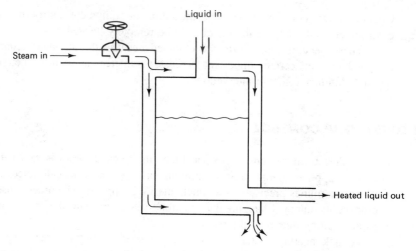

Figure 1–3   Tank temperature open-loop control.

1–3 CLOSED-LOOP CONTROL

Open-loop control cannot guarantee the desired output from a process subject to even mild disturbances. Some technique is necessary to monitor the actual output, compare it to the desired value, and reposition the actuator to eliminate any error. This is the essence of automatic control. In its simplest form, an operator watches a gage, slightly adjusting the valve as experience has taught is needed. More realistically, a collection of instruments and electronics is used.

1–3.1 Elements of a Closed-Loop Control System

A typical automatic closed-loop control system is shown in Figure 1–4. Whether you are controlling the direction of a spacecraft or the temperature of your house, virtually all automatic control systems have these elements. The *actual output*, which you are attempting to control, is sampled by a sensor, conditioned, and transmitted to the controller. The controller may be a computer, an electronic circuit, a collection of pneumatic tubes and orifices, or it may be as simple as a single lever. A second input, called the *set point*, is also applied to the controller. It indicates what the *desired output* should be. The controller takes the difference between these inputs to determine how much *error* there is. It then alters its output in a way calculated to bring the actual output back in line with the set point.

    The controller's signal is transmitted to the actuator. The actuator governs the application of energy to the process. Changing the energy into the system causes the actual process output to change (hopefully, to track the set point).

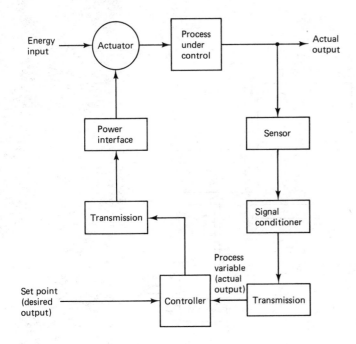

Figure 1–4   Automatic control system.

Figure 1–5 illustrates closed-loop control of the tank's temperature that you saw earlier. First the actual heated liquid's temperature must be measured. This is often done with a thermocouple inside a protective sheath. The output from the thermocouple is only a few millivolts at best and is strongly dependent on the ambient (as well as measured) temperature. The ice-point compensation and transmitter is a circuit that compensates for ambient temperature, amplifies and shifts the millivolt signal, and converts it to the industrial transmission standard. Properly adjusted, when the liquid is at its minimum temperature, the transmitter outputs 4 mA. When maximum temperature is reached, 20 mA is outputted.

This analog current is transmitted over a twisted, shielded pair of wires to the controller. Often this controller is in a central control room, hundreds of meters or more from where the measurement was taken. The controller compares the process variable (i.e., temperature measurement) with the position of the set-point control. A new output is calculated and transmitted, again as a 4- to 20-mA current to the actuator. This signal is amplified and used to drive a motor. The motor, in turn, changes the position of the valve, adjusting the amount of steam flowing into the jacket.

Should a disturbance in steam pressure or temperature, liquid inlet temperature, or tank level cause the outlet temperature to rise, the thermocouple's voltage difference will increase. This will cause current out of the transmitter to increase, driving up the process variable pointer in the controller. The controller, in response, will alter its output current. This will cause the motor to close the valve a bit, cutting back on the amount of steam entering the jacket. The liquid will cool.

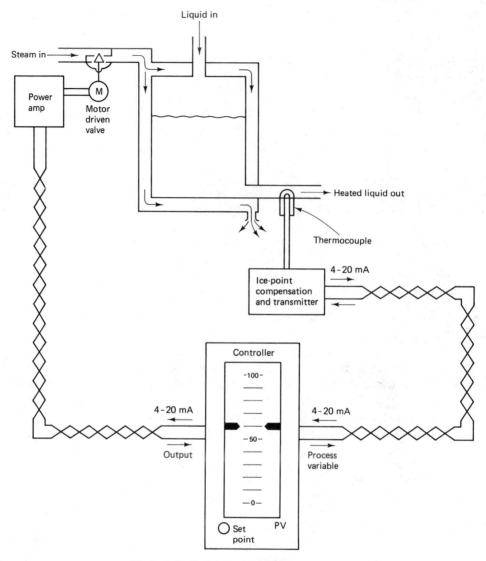

Figure 1-5   Tank temperature closed-loop control.

1-3.2 Servomechanism Control Systems

Control systems are often divided into two major groups, process control and servomechanism control. In servo control the position, speed, or acceleration of an object is made to follow closely the set-point command. Of course, there must be some regulation to reduce the effects that a disturbance has on the object's movement. However, analysis and design of servo systems are carried out primarily from the viewpoint of how well the output responds to a change in set point, given a constant load. This response is fast, often completed within a second or less. Since movement is the desired response, you can identify a servo system by its actuator. For small systems the actuator is often an electric motor. Systems requiring more force may use a hydraulic cylinder as the actuator.

A position control servo system is shown in Figure 1–6. The actuator is the permanent-magnet dc motor shown in the center. Through a series of pullies and belts (or perhaps gears) the motor drives the cog along the rack. Rotation is again geared down and moves the wiper on a potentiometer. Proper connection assures that movement of the cog from the extreme left to the extreme right will rotate the potentiometer precisely through its 300° arc, from stop to stop. The potentiometer is the sensor portion of the automatic control system shown in Figure 1–4. The voltage on its wiper is an indication of position. This is fed back to the differential amplifier. There it is subtracted from the set-point voltage, and the difference (the error) is amplified. The differential amplifier is the controller, as illustrated in Figure 1–4. The power of the controller output is boosted and drives the motor.

When the signal from the position feedback potentiometer (the sensor) equals the signal from the set-point control, the system is at rest. There is no output from the differential amplifier, since there is no error. The power amplifier provides no signal to the motor. The motor does not move.

If you want to move the drive to the right, the set-point voltage must be increased. This produces a positive error out of the differential amplifier and, subsequently, out of the power amplifier to the motor. The motor begins to rotate clockwise, driving the cog clockwise, moving the system to the right. As the cog moves clockwise, so does the potentiometer. This feeds a larger signal back to the differential amplifier. The error becomes smaller; a lower voltage is fed to the power amplifier and to the motor. The motor runs more slowly. Eventually, the feedback signal from the position potentiome-

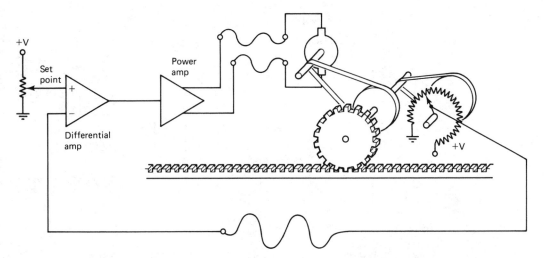

Figure 1–6 Position control servo system.

ter will match the set-point signal. The error has been reduced to zero. The system comes to rest.

The control of velocity is also classified as servomechanism control. Figure 1–7 is a simple velocity control system. The purpose of the control system is to provide constant tension on the film (or paper, plastic, cloth, etc.). Driving the take-up roll at a constant speed, however, will cause the tension to increase as the diameter of the roll increases.

The rider roll is the key. It sits on the film and is free to turn as the film passes under it. It may also move up in response to increasing tension in the film, or down if the film's tension slackens. Mechanically coupled to the rider roll is the wiper of a potentiometer. Together, the rider roll and the potentiometer form a tension transducer, outputting a dc voltage proportional to the tension in the film.

When the tension is correct, the voltage from the rider roller's potentiometer matches the set-point voltage. The difference amplifier outputs zero volts. This effectively grounds the voltage divider at the input of the power amplifier. The voltage from the divider then drives the power amplifier, causing the motor to run at the nominal speed.

As the film on the take-up reel builds, the tension will try to increase. This, in turn, causes the rider to begin to move up. The potentiometer wiper is pulled up, causing the inverting input of the difference amplifier to become larger than the set point on the noninverting input. The output of the differential amplifier goes negative.

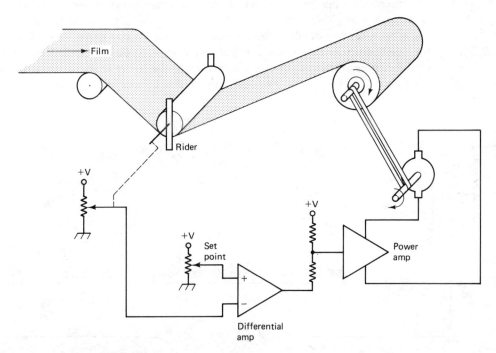

Figure 1–7 Take-up roll speed control. [From Richard W. Miller, *Servomechanisms, Devices and Fundamentals* (Reston, Va.: Reston Publishing Co., 1977).]

Pulling the bottom of the voltage divider below ground lowers the input voltage to the power amplifier. The power amplifier decreases the power it is driving into the motor and the motor runs more slowly. Slowing the motor reduces the tension in the film.

One of the most intense users of servomechanism control is the industrial robotic arm, as shown in Figure 1–8. Such arms are revolutionizing manufacturing. Their speed, accuracy, precision, durability, and flexibility are lowering production costs while increasing output and quality. Industrial robots typically have three or more joints. Each joint may have three degrees of freedom (ways of moving): roll, pitch, and yaw. To provide rapid, smooth, well-coordinated movement of the tool being manipulated, the position and often velocity and acceleration of each degree of freedom of each joint must be controlled *simultaneously*.

Coordinated control of position, velocity, and acceleration of all of the degrees of freedom is best accomplished with a microprocessor or minicomputer. A position sensor (potentimeter, optical encoder, ultrasonic detector, etc.) monitors the position of each degree of freedom and transmits this information to an interface circuit. Here it is converted to the digital format needed by the computer. Upon request from the computer, this position information is presented. By knowing the current position and the previous position of the part, the computer can determine the velocity and the acceleration. Control equations within the computer's program use this information, as well as data on the desired position of the part, to calculate a proper output. This

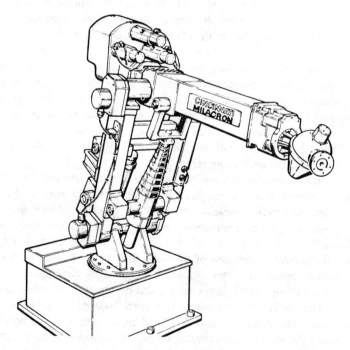

Figure 1–8   Industrial robotic arm. (Courtesy of Cincinnati Milacron.)

output (digital number) is converted by a second interface board to the necessary voltage or series of pulses to drive the actuator for that particular degree of freedom. Actuators may be stepper motors, dc motors, ac motors, hydraulic motors, or cylinders. This series of readings, conversions, calculations, and corrections is occurring thousands of times a second for all of the robot's degrees of freedom. This is truly an impressive example of servomechanism control.

1–3.3 Process Control Systems

You saw in Section 1–3.2 that servomechanism control was one of the two major groups of industrial control systems. The other major type of control is process control. In process control the variables which are manipulated are those used most often in manufacturing. These include temperature, liquid and solid level, flow rate, pressure, force, composition, pH, humidity, viscosity, and density.

The primary objective of a process control system is to *regulate* one or more of these variables, keeping them at a constant value (the set point). This regulation must compensate for changes in the system's load and other disturbances introduced. Of course, if the set point is changed, the variable under control should follow it. However, unlike servo control (in which significant, rapid variations in set point were the rule), in process control set-point changes occur only occasionally and are usually less than 10% of full scale. Therefore, analysis and design of process control systems are carried out primarily from the viewpoint of how well the output responds to a change in load, given a constant set point. Response rates are slow, often on the order of minutes or hours. This is much longer than typical for servo systems.

Process control systems may be subdivided into two categories, batch and continuous processes. Batch processing involves the timed sequencing of operations performed on the material being processed. Heating to a given temperature for a given time, adding a prescribed amount of a second ingredient, and stirring for a given time are examples of operations performed in a batch process. At the end of the sequence of time steps, the material is often passed on to another batch station for further processing and the sequence begun again with new materials. Following a recipe to make a cake involves a series of batch processing steps.

In a continuous process, one or more characteristics of the material being processed are manipulated as the material passes through that part of the process. Material is continuously entering and leaving the process. Producing film is an example of a continuous process. A liquid is continuously poured onto a rotating drum, where it cools into a sheet. The sheet is pulled off, heated, and stretched in both length and width. This sets the correct dimensions of thickness and width. Depending on the film's final use, additional processing, coating, and drying stages are applied as the film passes by. Casting, heating, stretching, coating, and drying are all continuous processes.

The control of temperature is a prime example of process control. You saw this illustrated in Figure 1–5 and described in Section 1–3.1. The electronics shown are standard for most process control loops, independent of the parameter being measured or manipulated. A transducer converts the physical parameter to a low-level electrical signal. This is sent to a transmitter, which conditions it and converts it into a 4- to 20-mA (0 to 100%) current. This standard signal is sent over a pair of twisted wires to the indicator and controller. This unit is often quite a distance from the process, in a control room. A correction signal is produced by the controller, and sent over another 4- to 20-mA current loop to the actuator's electronics. Generally, the actuator is a valve, pump, motor, or heater.

To simplify the schematic, much of the standard electronics is omitted. Look at Figure 1–9. The precise types of temperature transducer and signal conditioner are not shown. The circle labeled *TT* is the temperature transmitter, which includes the ice-point compensation and/or other signal conditioners. Similarly, the temperature indicator/controller is shown as a circle labeled *TIC*. The valve electronics are not drawn. As the temperature of the outlet flow varies, the transducer and temperature transmitter

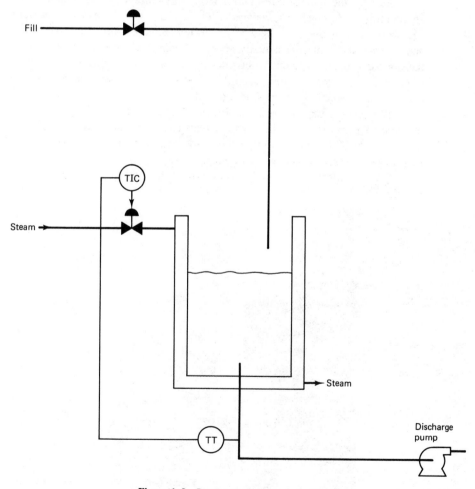

Figure 1–9 Process temperature control loop.

sense the change and vary the 4- to 20-mA signal to the controller proportionally. The controller changes its output signal, sending the valve to a new setting. This changes the amount of steam allowed into the jacket around the tank. Properly done, the temperature of the product stabilizes.

To assure a properly heated product to the next stage at a controlled rate, a flow control loop must be used to drive the discharge pump. There is a wide spectrum of flow transducers available. Many of these will be discussed in Chapter 3. One of the simplest is a paddle wheel, illustrated in Figure 1–10. A small magnet is embedded in the end of each blade, and a coil is built into the upper body. As each blade passes the magnet, a pulse is produced in the coil. These pulses are coupled to a circuit which outputs a current between 4 and 20 mA, proportional to the frequency of the pulses. This is the flow transmitter, shown as a circle labeled *FT* in Figure 1–11.

As with the temperature control loop, this current is transmitted to an indicator and controller. Although it is labeled *FIC*, in fact it may be exactly the same piece of equipment as that used for the *TIC* in the temperature loop. The 4- to 20-mA output current from the controller actually goes to the drive electronics, which in turn powers the discharge pump. Although not shown, this electronics may be as simple as a pair of transistors or may require several cabinets of heavy-duty, high-power electronics comprising a variable-frequency ac motor drive.

The process, as illustrated in Figure 1–11, has a major problem. It is entirely possible to pump the tank dry, which may cause the steam system to overheat and burn out. Or if the outlet flow is too slow, the tank may overflow. A level control loop must be added, as shown in Figure 1–12.

Several different level transducers will be discussed in Chapter 3. Pressure at the bottom of the tank is directly proportional to the level in the tank. So a pressure transducer,

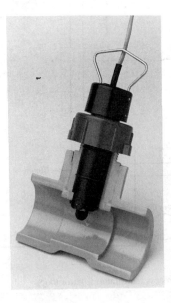

Figure 1–10   Paddle wheel flow transducer. (Courtesy of Signet Scientific.)

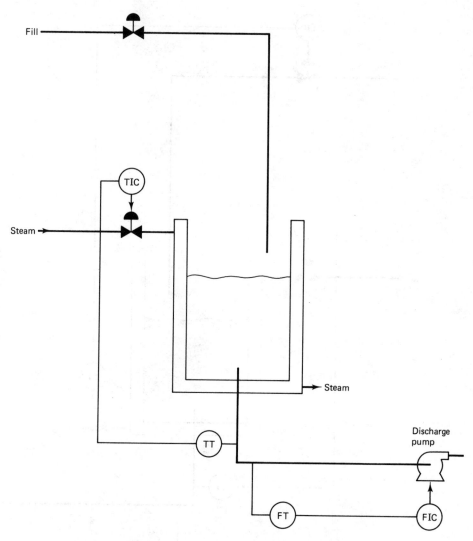

Figure 1–11   Process with flow control loop added.

such as shown in Figure 1–13, gives a direct measure of the tank's level. The output from this transducer varies from 0 V to 100 mV at full pressure. The transmitter (signal conditioner) used must output 4 mA when the transducer outputs 0 V, and 20 mA when it receives 100 mV from the transducer. The level indicator and controller, *LIC*, and the valve and valve actuator electornics may be very similar to those used for the temperature control loop.

With this level control loop in place, changes in outlet flow rate will be reflected in changes in inlet flow. Not only does this assure that the tank neither overflows nor is pumped dry, but since a constant volume of liquid is maintained in the tank, the

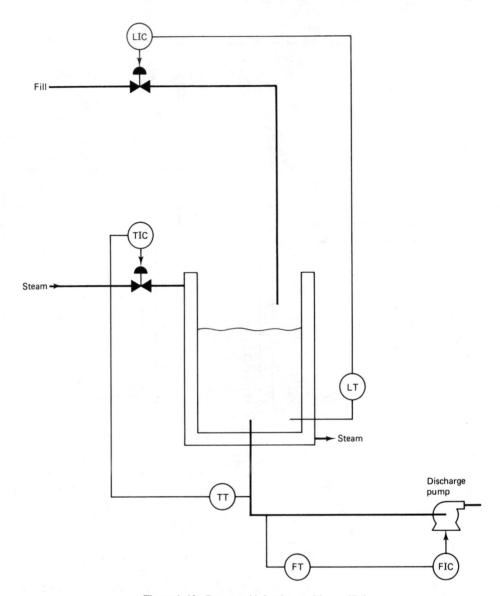

Figure 1–12 Process with level control loop added.

temperature control system does not see major variations in the amount of liquid to be heated. Tighter temperature control may be a by-product of the level control system.

It may also be desirable, or necessary, to alter the chemical composition of the material in the vat. This can be done by adding a second fill pipe, valve, a transducer sensitive to the additive, and appropriate composition transmitter (transducer signal conditioners) and controller. An agitator to assure proper mixing may be needed (see Figure

RANGE	0–6, 15, 25, 50 PSIG	0–100, 200, 500, 1000, 2000, 3000, 5000 PSIS	0–10000, 15000, 20000 PSIS

PHYSICAL

Overload	2× rated pressure without damage	2× rated pressure without damage	2× rated pressure without damage. (30,000 max.)
	5× rated pressure without bursting	5× rated pressure without bursting	5× rated pressure without bursting. (50,000 max.)
Case Material	316L stainless steel	15-PH stainless steel	15-PH stainless steel
Shock & Vibration	Undamaged by 50 Gs Meets MIL-STD 810 B	Undamaged by 50 Gs Meets MIL-STD 810 B	Undamaged by 50 Gs Meets MIL-STD 810 B
Weight	2 oz. (56.5 g) less cable and adapter	2 oz. (56.5 g) less cable and adapter	2 oz. (56.5 g) less cable and adapter

ELECTRICAL

Excitation Voltage	5 Vac or Vdc 6 Vac or Vdc max.	5 Vac or Vdc 6 Vac or Vdc max.	5 Vac or Vdc 6 Vac or Vdc max.
Signal Output	100 mV at rated pressure ± 1%	100 mV at rated pressure ± 1%	100 mV at rated pressure ± 1%
Sensitivity	20 mV/v	20 mV/v	20 mV/v
Zero Balance	± 5 mV at 70°F (21.5°C)	± 5 mV at 70°F (21.5°C)	± 5mV at 70°F (21.5°C)
Bridge Resistance	Input, 150 ± 50 ohms Output, 115 ± 25 ohms	Input, 150 ± 50 ohms Output, 115 ± 25 ohms	Input, 150 ± 50 ohms Output, 115 ± 25 ohms
Electrical Connection	4 conductor shielded cable, 3' (910 mm) long	4 conductor shielded cable, 3' (910 mm) long	4 conductor shielded cable, 3' (910 mm) long

PERFORMANCE

Accuracy	± 0.50% from best fit straight line	± 0.25% from best fit straight line	± 0.50% from best fit straight line .
Operating Temperature	−60°–200°F (−51°–93°C)	−60°–200°F (−51°–93°C)	−60°–200°F (−51°–93°C)
Compensated Temperature	30°–160°F (−1.5°–71°C)	30°–160°F (−1.5°–71°C)	30°–160°F (−1.5°–71°C)
Thermal Effect On Zero	Less than ± 1% of full scale per 100°F (55°C) over compensated range	Less than ± 1% of full scale per 100°F (55°C) over compensated range	Less than ± 1% of full scale per 100°F (55°C) over compensated range
Thermal Effect On Sensitivity	Less than ± 1% of reading per 100°F (55°C) over compensated range	Less than ± 1% of reading per 100°F (55°C) over compensated range	Less than ± 1% of reading per 100°F (55°C) over compensated range
Resolution	Infinite	Infinite	Infinite
OPTIONS	1, 3, 4, 5, 7	3, 4, 5, 7	3, 4, 5, 7

PRINTED IN USA 10K3 8SCP   Item 1061300   SPECIFICATIONS SUBJECT TO CHANGE WITHOUT NOTICE.

Options

For applications requiring improved performance, optional features can be incorporated into the Model AB High Performance transducers at additional cost. The options are designated by the following numerical codes.

OPTION 1
Absolute pressure version available in 0–15, 25, and 50 PSIA.

OPTION 3
Barbed fitting for attaching protective hose around cable.

OPTION 4
Slice longer cable onto standard 3 ft. (910 mm) cable.

OPTION 5
Install longer continuous cable.

OPTION 7
Extend operating temperature range to 300°F (148.9 C°). Not applicable for 6 and 15 PSI. Includes Bendix PTIH-10-6P electrical connector with extended case. (Mating connector not included.)

Pin and Wire Codes
A+ Excitation (Red) B+ Signal (Green)
C− Signal (White)   D− Excitation (Black)
E and F not used

For easy installation, the Model AB High Performance can be mounted with an adapter.

Dimensions

For more information about our full line of pressure transducers, contact:
Data Instruments, Inc.
4 Hartwell Place
Lexington, MA U.S.A. 02173
(617) 861-7450, Telex 200081

Figure 1–13   Pressure transducer used for measuring liquid level. (Courtesy of Data Instruments.)

1–14). If the volume of additive is very small, as compared to the primary fluid (from fill *A*), this control scheme may work adequately. However, the level sensor and control loop manipulate fill *A*, which affects not only level but also the percentage mixture. Similarly, any changes in fill *B* by the composition controller will affect level but to a much smaller degree.

A feedforward loop based on the inlet flow of fill *A* could be added. This would

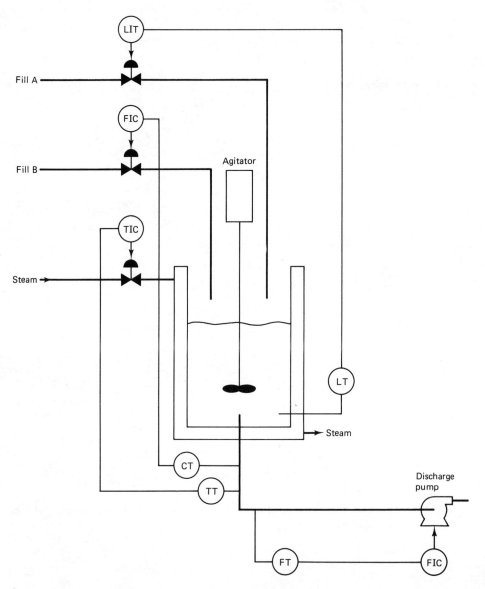

Figure 1–14 Process with chemical composition loop added.

allow the composition controller to anticipate changes in fill *A*. It could then manipulate fill *B* proportionally, long before the composition sensor had noticed a change. This is illustrated in Figure 1–15. Of course, the composition controller must be a bit more sophisticated than the simple, single-input controllers used on the other loops.

Operation of this process is beginning to get pretty complicated. Add to this the fact that changes in fill *B* really will affect level. Also add the necessity to make smooth,

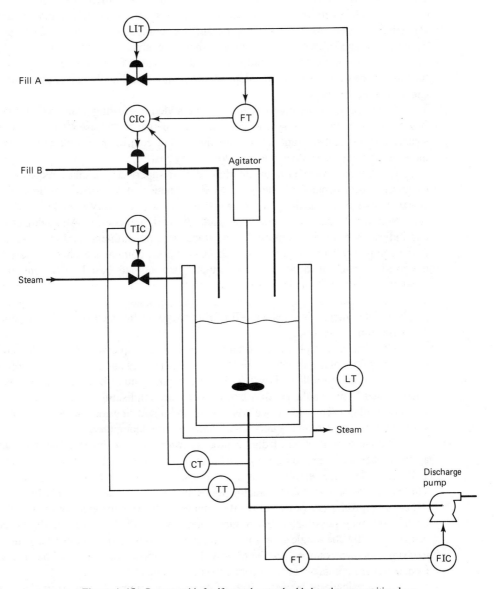

Figure 1–15 Process with feedforward control added to the composition loop.

coordinated changes in all four of the controlled parameters simultaneously. Manual adjust of the system with the set-point knobs on each of the controllers (see Figure 1–5) is a poor way to operate. Computer control can be added.

Digital supervisory control is illustrated in Figure 1–16. The existing analog control equipment is kept intact. The signal from each transmitter is sent to the computer's input as well as to the controllers. Most controllers have a remote set-point option. This allows the controller to receive its set point from a 4- to 20-mA signal rather than from the knob on its front panel. So the outputs from the computer manipulate these set points. Under direction of the program, the computer can display high-resolution dynamic displays of the process's current status or of the history of any variable. Coordinated set-point adjustments of all loops can be made. Feedforward compensation as well as compensation for the interdependence of fill A and fill B, level, and composition can all be accounted for.

Digital supervisory control can easily be added to existing analog control systems. If the computer fails, the system continues to operate at its last set point and can be switched to manual operation. Because the analog controllers handle the dynamics of the loop, the computer does not have to be very fast.

Conversely, for a new installation, digital supervisory control requires a lot of electronic instrumentation. The ultimate performance of the system is limited by the characteristics of the analog controllers. This system is not very flexible.

Figure 1–17 shows a second approach, direct digital control. All analog controllers and indicators have been removed. The transducer transmitters send their signals only to the computer. The computer reads all these inputs, compares each with the set points previously entered at the keyboard, calculates new outputs based on current status and previous outputs, and manipulates the actuators directly. Data are stored for later reanalysis, alarms sound and messages print out if appropriate, and the high-resolution color graphics CRT display is updated. All of this happens, for each of the loops controlled, 10 to 100 times a second.

Many more complex control techniques can be implemented when the computer has direct control of the actuator. This should provide significant performance improvement over the analog controller. However, if the computer fails, the entire process is totally uncontrolled. This could be disastrous. Also, accomplishing all the tasks associated with controlling each loop, as well as storing and displaying information and interfacing with the operator, requires a very fast, expensive minicomputer.

The latest generation of digital process control is distributed computer control. It appears, at first glance, to be very similar to digital supervisory control. Look at Figure 1–18. Each loop has its own transducer, transmitter, indicator/controller, and actuator. This is just as it was for the analog loops in Figures 1–15 and 1–16. However, the indicator/controller is a powerful microcomputer. The complex calculation and modeling control schemes possible in the minicomputer of Figure 1–17 (direct digital control) can be done by the single-loop microcomputer controller. It may also have the ability to change its own control equation to provide optimum performance without intervention from the main computer or the operator. This is called self-tuning.

Communications between each of the microcomputer-based controllers and the

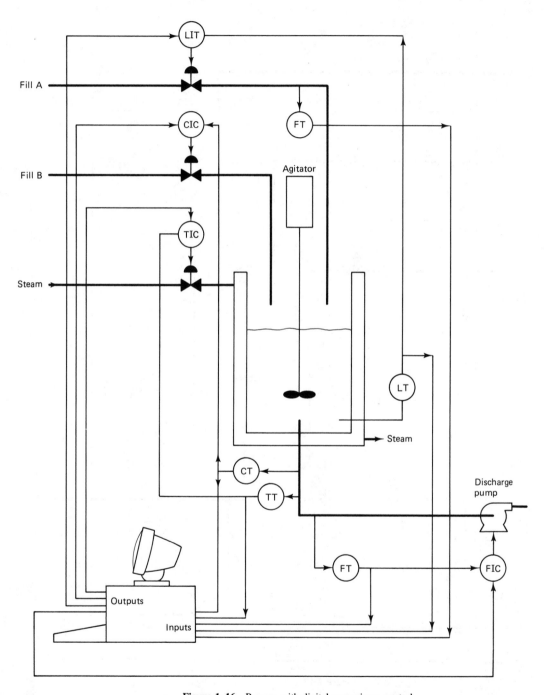

Figure 1–16 Process with digital supervisory control.

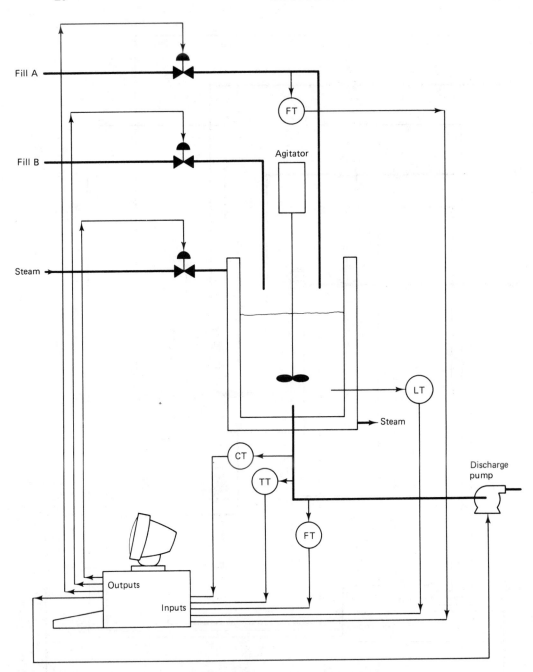

Figure 1–17 Process with direct digital control.

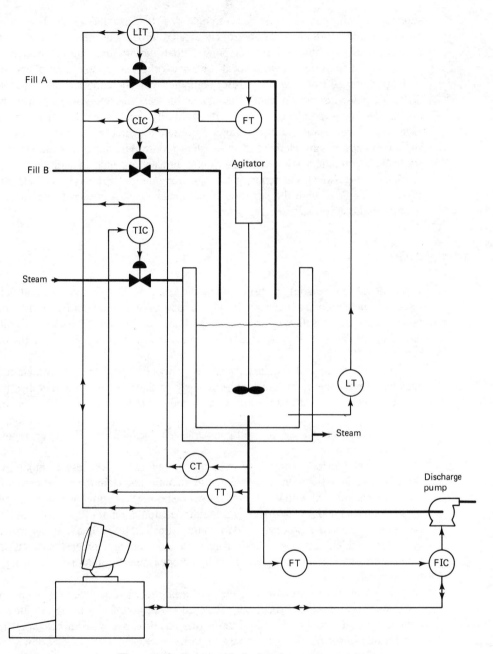

Figure 1–18 Process with distributed computer control.

supervisory computer is over a radio-frequency (often coaxial) cable. This single cable may be shared by hundreds of controllers located throughout the plant. Data concerning actual process variable values, set points, controller tuning, alarms, and so on, are passed back and forth over this local area network. The remote controllers may even be reprogrammed from the supervisory computer over the communication network.

Distributed computer control combines the best of supervisory control and direct digital control. A computer, with all its flexibility and computational power, controls each loop. System status can be monitored and operation directed from a central supervisory station. Failure of any element in the system (controller, network communications, or supervisory computer) will not bring the entire process to a halt. In addition, sophisticated graphics, diagnostics, and report generation for hundreds of loops (perhaps the entire plant) can be done with the supervisory computer since it does not *constantly* have to monitor and control each separate loop.

SUMMARY

There are several reasons for using automatic controls. Both very large and very small forces can be manipulated accurately. Operations under extreme or hazardous conditions can be carried out safely. Variation in product quality can be reduced significantly, providing a more reliable product to the customer at lower production cost to the manufacturer.

Open-loop control requires that an experienced operator directly manipulate the actuator. The actuator, in turn, applies energy to the process. This modifies the result of the process. By inspecting this output and through experience, the operator can decide where to set the actuator. Firing a rifle is an example of an open-loop control system. Such control is simple and comparatively inexpensive. However, regulation of disturbances is poor.

In a closed-loop control system, the output of the process is monitored by a sensor, conditioned, and then transmitted to a controller. Here the actual output (process variable) is compared with the desired output (set point). A correction signal is generated by the controller and sent to drive the actuator. Manipulation of the actuator, and therefore the product from the process, is done automatically, in such a way as to cause the output to track the set point. Disturbances in input energy, process characteristics, or load on the outlet of the process can all be compensated for automatically using closed-loop control.

Control systems are also classified according to what they control. In servomechanism control the position, speed, or acceleration of an object is made to follow the set-point command closely. How well the actual position, speed, or acceleration responds to a change in set point is of primary importance. Response rates of a few seconds or less are normal. Electric motors and hydraulic motors and cylinders are often the actuators.

Process control systems control the temperature, force, level, flow, pressure, chemical composition, pH, humidity, density, and so on, of a product. The primary object is to regulate one or more of these variables, keeping them at the set point, independent of changes in input energy, process characteristics, or output load. Response (or lack of response) to a change in load is the main measure of the quality of the process control system. Response rates are often on the order of minutes or even hours.

Process control systems are further divided into batch processing and continuous processing. To coordinate large, interactive manufacturing processes, computer control is often needed. Digital supervisory control, direct control, and distributed computer control offer varying degrees of computer automation.

REFERENCE

1. *Webster's New World Dictionary of the American Language*. Chicago: World Publishing Company.

PROBLEMS

1–1. (a) List three automatic control systems in an automobile.
   (b) State whether they are open-loop or closed-loop control.
   (c) Briefly explain how each works, identifying the controlled variable and explaining how the system performs to assure that it tracks the set point.

1–2. List three reasons why automatic controls are used in industry and explain each.

1–3. (a) Explain the difference between open-loop and closed-loop control.
   (b) Give an example of each not discussed in the chapter.
   (c) List the major advantage of closed-loop control over open-loop control.
   (d) List the major advantage of open-loop control over closed-loop control.

1–4. The diagram of a level control system is given in Figure 1–19.
   (a) Match each of the items with the blocks of a general automatic control system as shown in Figure 1–4.
   (b) Explain how the system in Figure 1–19 compensates if the outlet valve is opened further.

1–5. Compare servomechanism control and process control. For each, discuss
   (a) parameters being controlled.
   (b) speed of response.
   (c) purpose of control. (Is the controlled variable to track a set point or is the controlled variable to remain fixed despite changes in load?)

1–6. The speed of a shaft is often an important parameter to control. The speed can be sensed by connecting a dc generator to the shaft.
   (a) Draw a diagram similar to Figure 1–6 of the complete speed control system.
   (b) Match each of the items in your drawing with the blocks of a general automatic control system as shown in Figure 1–4.
   (c) Explain how the system increases the shaft's speed if the set-point potentiometer is increased.

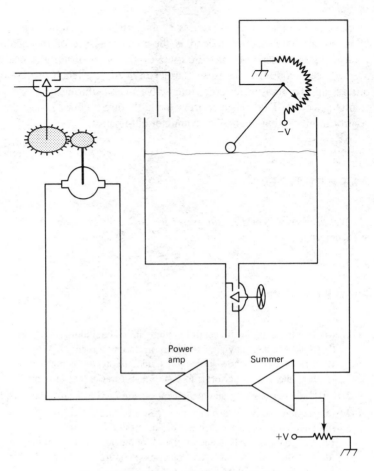

Figure 1–19   Level control system (Problem 1–4).

1–7. The purpose of a plotter is to move a pen precisely from one place to another over a page. Closed-loop controls are used to ensure accuracy and improve the speed of response.
   (a) Is this servomechanism control or process control? Explain.
   (b) An optical encoder is often used as the sensor. Such an encoder is shown in Figure 1–20. Explain how the encoder is used to measure position. Does the encoder tell about actual position or only a change in position? Explain.
   (c) The controller may be a microcomputer. Explain how the microcomputer can determine both absolute position of the pen and speed of the pen using only the signal from the optical encoder.
   (d) Explain why knowing both pen position and current pen speed would allow the microcomputer to move the pen more rapidly and more precisely to a new location.

1–8. Complete Figure 1–21 to produce a complete closed-loop control system that uses the spring-loaded telescoping arm to sense the profile of a pattern and to position a cutting torch. The torch should cut a profile similar to the one across which the arm travels.

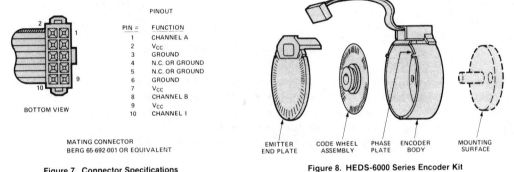

PINOUT

PIN =   FUNCTION
1   CHANNEL A
2   V_{CC}
3   GROUND
4   N.C. OR GROUND
5   N.C. OR GROUND
6   GROUND
7   V_{CC}
8   CHANNEL B
9   V_{CC}
10   CHANNEL I

BOTTOM VIEW

MATING CONNECTOR
BERG 65-692-001 OR EQUIVALENT

Figure 7. Connector Specifications

EMITTER   CODE WHEEL   PHASE   ENCODER   MOUNTING
END PLATE   ASSEMBLY   PLATE   BODY   SURFACE

Figure 8. HEDS-6000 Series Encoder Kit

SETSCREW
2-56
HOLLOW OVAL
POINT

18.0
(0.71)

25.4
(1.00)

50.5
(1.99) DIA.

8.48 ± 0.51
(0.334 ± 0.020)

UNITS mm (INCHES)

Figure 9. Code Wheel

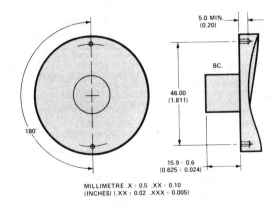

5.0 MIN.
(0.20)

B.C.

46.00
(1.811)

15.9 ± 0.6
(0.625 ± 0.024)

180°

MILLIMETRE .X ± 0.5 .XX ± 0.10
(INCHES) (.XX ± 0.02 .XXX ± 0.005)

Figure 10. Mounting Requirements

Figure 1–20   Optical encoder. (Courtesy of Hewlett-Packard.)

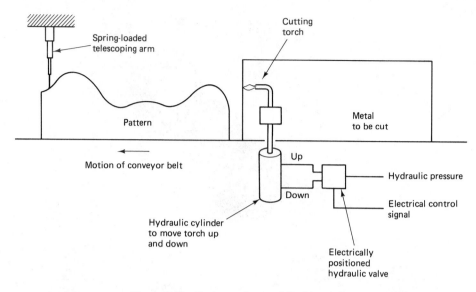

Figure 1–21 Cutting torch control (Problem 1–8).

1–9. **(a)** Explain the difference between continuous process control and batch process control.

(b) Give an example of each (not discussed in the chapter).

1–10. **(a)** It is necessary to control the temperature inside a furnace. Complete Figure 1–22 to show how the fuel flow can be controlled.

(b) Identify each of the items in your block as related to Figure 1–4.

1–11. **(a)** Draw a diagram similar to Figure 1–5 to indicate how outlet flow from a holding pond *up* into a processing tank would be controlled.

(b) Identify each item in your drawing in terms of the blocks in Figure 1–4.

1–12. Tank *A* has a temperature control loop with a steam jacket. There is no effort to control level. Tank *B* has a cold water inlet from the tap and a hot water inlet from tank *A*. Draw a control diagram similar to Figure 1–11 through 1–15 indicating how to

(a) control temperature at the outlet of tank *B*.

(b) control level of tank *B*.

(c) control level of tank *A*.

(d) add feedforward control to the tank *B* level control loop based on the required inlet flow from tank *A*.

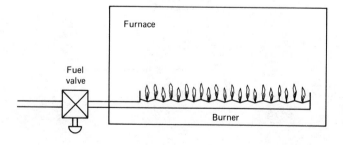

Figure 1–22 Furnace temperature control (Problem 1–10).

(e) add feedforward control to the tank *A* level control based on the temperature requirement in tank *B*.

1–13. (a) Describe the differences among digital supervisory control, direct digital control, and distributed computer control.

(b) List one advantage of each of the types of computer control above, as compared to the other two types.

1–14. Draw a diagram similar to Figure 1–16 showing how you would use digital supervisory control added to the system you drew for Problem 1–12.

1–15. Draw a diagram showing how to replace the digital supervisory control of Problem 1–14 with direct digital control.

1–16. Draw a diagram showing how to replace the digital supervisory control of Problem 1–14 with distributed computer control.

2

Process Element Characteristics

In Chapter 1 you saw that a typical industrial control system consists of several elements. These were illustrated in Figure 1–4. The output of the process is monitored by a transducer. Its signal is transmitted to a controller where a correction signal is generated. This signal is transmitted to an actuator and power electronics which manipulate the input of the process.

Each of these process elements has its own performance characteristics. In Appendix A you will see how to describe these characteristics mathematically using differential equations. These are solved using Laplace transform techniques. The response of *each* element in the system (the process itself, the transducer, the electronics, and the actuator) can be described with a relationship in the Laplace domain.

Fortunately, practically all of the different industrial processes, transducers, electronics, and actuators can be described with a small set of standard relationships. There are six major categories. With reasonable accuracy, all of the elements you see can be placed in one of these categories. For each, the math has already been done. You do not have to write any differential equations, solve any Laplace transforms, or plot any time-domain equations. It has all been done. The performance is described by a few key parameters and a family of normalized response plots.

In this chapter the transfer function of an element will be defined. Then, using that transfer function, each of the six standard categories of element response will be described. These categories are gain, integral, first order, dead time, first order with dead time, and second order. For each category, the Laplace and time-domain equations will be given, responses to a step and other key inputs plotted, and major parameters defined and related to the equations and plots.

OBJECTIVES

After studying this chapter you should be able to do the following:

1. Define the transfer function.
2. List the six major categories of element response.
3. For *each* of these six categories:
   a. Define the key parameters.
   b. Sketch the response to a step input.
   c. Given values for the parameters, denormalize its response plot.
   d. Compare this response type to others.
4. Describe the performance of higher-order elements.

2–1 TRANSFER FUNCTION

When working with any of the elements in a process, you need a simple, concise, but complete way of describing that element's performance. An equation of the output will not work, since the output of an element depends on its input. So the ratio of output to input is used. Then, given any input, you can predict its output. This ratio of output signal to input signal of an element is called its *transfer function*.

2–2 GAIN OR SPAN

In Section 2–1 you saw that simple elements such as amplifiers and potentiometers have transfer functions which are only a single number, the *gain*. In process control, gain will also be called *span*. The transfer function is simple and Laplace transforms are not needed because the output of these elements *immediately* track changes at the input. However, in reality, no element's output immediately follows changes at its input. So must you always write and use transfer functions using Laplace terms? Look at Example 2–1.

EXAMPLE 2–1

A motor-driven valve is used to fill a tank. It is desired to control the level in the tank. The valve requires 10 revolutions to go from full off to full open. The motor runs at 100 r/min. When open, 50 liters/min flow through the valve. Should you consider the response time of the valve if the tank's volume is

(a) 800 liters?
(b) 10 liters?

Solution   To go 10 revolutions at 100 r/min will take the valve

$$t_{valve} = \frac{10 \text{ revolutions}}{100 \text{ r/min}} = 0.1 \text{ min}$$

So, watching the valve, you will be able to see it turning for 6 s.

When fully open, the flow rate is 50 liters/min. To fill an 800-liter tank will take

$$t_{tank} = \frac{800 \text{ liters}}{50 \text{ liters/min}} = 16 \text{ min}$$

(a) Out of the 16 min it takes for the tank to fully respond, the 6 s of valve response time can be ignored. However, for a 10-liter tank

$$t_{tank} = \frac{10 \text{ liters}}{50 \text{ liters/min}} = 0.2 \text{ min}$$

(b) The smaller tank will fill in 12 s, given full flow. However, when you command full flow, it takes the valve 6 s to respond. As compared to the 12-s tank response time, this is significant, and you must take it into consideration.

From Example 2–1 you can deduce that when the response time of an element is small compared to the other elements in a system, its transfer function may be expressed as simple gain.

It is usual to think of gain as being unitless. This is certainly true for the amplifier and the attenuator. However, many industrial control elements have gains with mixed units. Both sensors and actuators are examples.

The potentiometer can be used to convert rotation of its shaft into voltage. When used like this, it is a rotational position transducer whose input is position (measured in degrees) and whose output is voltage. Its transfer function then must be

$$\frac{V_o}{\text{degrees of rotation}}$$

Actuators may also have simple gain which must be expressed with mixed units. A pneumatically controlled valve will be closed with 3 psi or less applied, and fully open with 15 psi or more. The manufacturer specifies the flow rate through the valve, when it is fully open, for various input pressures. For this process element, the input is air pressure (psi) and the output is flow (gallons per minute or liters per minute or cubic feet per minute). Assuming that the valve responds faster than anything else in the system, its transfer function then is expressed in

$$\frac{\text{gal/min}}{\text{psi}}$$

2–3 INTEGRAL PROCESS ELEMENT

The simplest process element has a transfer function that can be expressed as a single constant, gain. Its output depends directly on its input. The integral process element is only slightly more complicated. For an integral process, the *rate of change* of its output depends directly on its input.

Mathematically, this means that

$$\frac{dv_o}{dt} = Kv_i$$

$$dv_o = Kv_i\, dt$$

Integrating both sides gives you

$$\int dv_o = \int Kv_i\, dt$$

$$v_o = K \int v_i\, dt \qquad\qquad (2\text{–}1)$$

So, stated a second way, the output of an integral process depends on the integral of its input.

There are three standard test signals which are routinely used when evaluating a process element's response. They are the step, the pulse, and the ramp. The most common is the step.

$$v_o = K \int A\, dt$$

where K is the integral constant and A is the amplitude of the step.

$$v(t) = KAt \qquad\qquad (2\text{–}2)$$

which is the equation for a ramp. The slope, or rate of increase of the output, is KA per second.

It is very important that you be aware of the implications of equation 2–2. If you introduce a step change at the input of an integral process element, its output will begin to increase, and will continue to increase until the limits of the system are reached. For electronics, this means that the element will go into saturation, driven hard up against the supply voltage. For a liquid-level tank with an integral type of response, the level will rise until the tank overflows.

The response of an integral type of process to a pulse is more easily understood

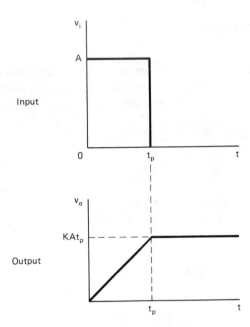

Figure 2–1 Integral process response to a discrete pulse.

using Figure 2–1. Since there are two discrete parts to the input, equation 2–1 is easier to use in determining the output.

$$v_o = K \int v_i \, dt \qquad\qquad (2\text{–}1)$$

$$= K \int_0^{t_p} A \, dt + K \int_{t_p}^{\infty} 0 \, dt$$

$$= KAt \Big|_0^{t_p}$$

The first integral is for the step $t = 0$ to $t = t$ and produces a ramp. This is just like the result you obtained for the step input in equation 2–2. When the input returns to zero, the output holds at

$$v_o = KAt_p$$

A pulse input will cause the output of the integral type process element to ramp up during the pulse and to hold that value after the pulse has gone to zero.

The circuit in Figure 2–2 is an example of an integral type of process element. The voltage across the capacitor is

$$v_c = \frac{1}{C} \int i \, dt$$

If you apply a constant current to a capacitor (i.e., a step), the capacitor will charge up linearly until its voltage equals the current source's maximum available voltage.

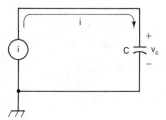

Figure 2–2 Integral-type circuit.

At that point, the circuit is in saturation. This is precisely the behavior predicted for an integral type of element in response to a step input.

A second example of an integral element is the liquid-level process shown in Figure 2–3. The outlet flow is fixed by the positive-displacement pump. So it does not change as the height of liquid in the tank goes up and down. When inlet flow (q_{in}) equals outlet flow (q_{out}) the height in the tank does not change. However, if the q_{in} goes up at all, the height will ramp up and the tank will eventually overflow. Conversely, if q_{in} falls below q_{out}, the height will ramp down and the tank will be pumped dry.

Mathematically, a change in height is caused by a difference in flow rates.

$$\Delta h = \frac{q_{in} - q_{out}}{A} \Delta t$$

where A is the cross-sectional area of the tank. In terms of derivatives,

$$dh = \frac{q_{in} - q_{out}}{A} dt$$

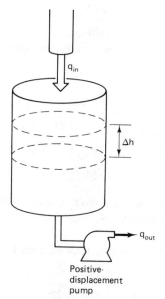

Positive-
displacement
pump

Figure 2–3 Liquid-level process with constant outlet flow.

Let

$$q_{\text{diff}} = q_{\text{in}} - q_{\text{out}}$$

$$dh = \frac{1}{A} q_{\text{diff}} \, dt$$

Integrating both sides gives

$$\int dh = \frac{1}{A} \int q_{\text{diff}} \, dt$$

$$h = \frac{1}{A} \int q_{\text{diff}} \, dt$$

2–4 FIRST-ORDER PROCESS ELEMENT

In Section 2–3 you saw that integral process elements must be handled with care. A change in input will cause the output to ramp until it overflows or saturates. Fortunately, most industrial elements do not behave this way. Many are termed *self-regulating*. A step at the input causes the output to rise *exponentially* until a new, stable level is reached. These *self-regulating* process elements are also called *first-order* elements.

Each of these processes produces a relationship between its input and output which looks like

$$v_o(t) = A_1 A_2 (1 - e^{-t/\tau}) \tag{2–3}$$

where A_1 is the circuit's steady-state gain and A_2 is the amplitude of an applied step.

At the first instant in time following the step input

$$t = 0$$

equation 2–3 becomes

$$v_{o_{t=0}} = A_1 A_2 (1 - e^0)$$

$$= A_1 A_2 (1 - 1)$$

$$= 0$$

This points out a very important fact about first-order elements. Their outputs cannot change instantaneously. First-order elements tend to absorb or smooth out (filter out) spikes.

As times goes on, the exponential term decreases from 1 toward 0. Eventually as $t \to \infty$,

$$v_{o_{t \to \infty}} = A_1 A_2 (1 - e^{-\infty/\tau})$$

TABLE 2–1 EXPONENTIAL RESPONSE OF A FIRST-ORDER SYSTEM

t	$e^{-t/\tau}$	$1 - e^{-t/\tau}$	Percent remaining
0	1	0	100
1τ	0.3679	0.6321	36.79
2τ	0.1353	0.8647	13.53
3τ	0.0498	0.9502	4.98
4τ	0.0183	0.9817	1.83
5τ	0.0067	0.9933	0.67

But $e^{-\infty} = 0$, so

$$v_{o_t \to \infty} = A_1 A_2$$

This states that in the steady state, the output from a first-order element in response to a step will just be the steady-state gain of the element (A_1) times the height of the step (A_2). Said another way, eventually a first-order element responds like a simple gain element.

How the first-order element responds between the application of the step ($t = 0$) and when it reaches its steady-state output [$v_o = A_1 A_2$] is what makes it unique. Equation 2–3 indicates that the response is exponential. How rapidly that exponential term changes is controlled by τ, the time constant. This is illustrated in Table 2–1. After the first time constant, the output has risen to within 36.79% of its final value. At the end of 3τ, the output is within 5% of its final value. After 4τ the element's response has risen to within 2%. And after 5τ the response is virtually complete. So, how accurately you want the output to reflect its steady-state value will determine how many time constants you must wait.

Table 2–2 illustrates a second way to think about the time constant. During any one time constant, the output will change by 63.21% of its maximum possible change.

TABLE 2–2 ONE TIME CONSTANT PRODUCES 63.21% OF MAXIMUM POSSIBLE CHANGE

t	$1 - e^{-t/\tau}$	Δ_{max}	$\Delta_{actual} = $ $63.21\% \times \Delta_{max}$	Output after next τ
0	0	1	0.6321	$0 \quad + 0.6321 = 0.6321$
1τ	0.6321	$1 - 0.6321 = 0.3679$	0.2325	$0.6321 + 0.2325 = 0.8646$
2τ	0.8647	$1 - 0.8647 = 0.1353$	0.0855	$0.8647 + 0.0855 = 0.9502$
3τ	0.9502	$1 - 0.9502 = 0.0498$	0.0315	$0.9502 + 0.0315 = 0.9817$
4τ	0.9817	$1 - 0.9817 = 0.0183$	0.0116	$0.9817 + 0.0116 = 0.9933$
5τ	0.9933			

TABLE 2-3 COMMON INDUSTRIAL ELEMENTS TIME CONSTANTS

(a) Thermowell and Thermocouple Assembly Time Constants

Fluid type[a]	Fluid velocity (ft/s)	Annular clearance (in.)	Annular fill	Time constants (s)
Gas	5	0.04	Air	107 and 49
	50	0.04	Air	93 and 14
	152	0.04	Air	92 and 8
	300	0.04	Air	92 and 5
	152	0.04	Oil	22 and 7
	152	0.04	Mercury	17 and 8
	152	0.02	Air	52 and 9
	152	0.005	Air	17 and 8
Liquid	0.01	0.01	Air	62 and 17
	0.1	0.01	Air	32 and 10
	1	0.01	Air	26 and 4
	10	0.01	Air	25 and 2
	10	0.01	Oil	7 and 2
	10	0.01	Mercury	2 and 0.2
	10	0.055	Air	228 and 1
	10	0.005	Air	4 and 1

(b) Miscellaneous Electronic Transmitter Time Constants

Transmitter type	Manufacturer and model	Time constant (s)
Differential pressure	Rosemount 1151DP	0.2–1.7[b]
Gage pressure	Rosemount 1151GP	0.2–1.7[b]
Absolute pressure	Rosemount 1151AP	0.2–1.7[b]
Flange-mounted level	Rosemount 1151LL	0.2–1.7[b]
Differential pressure	Foxboro 823DP	0.2–1.6[c]
Gage pressure	Foxboro 823GM	0.2–1.6[c]
Absolute pressure	Foxboro 823AM	0.2–1.6[c]
Flange-mounted level	Foxboro E17	0.3
Diaphragm seal dip	Foxboro E13DMP	1.6 (M capsul)
	Foxboro E13DMP	0.5 (H capsul)
Turbine flow meter	Foxboro 81A	0.03 maximum
Transmitting rotameter	Wallace & Tiernan	0.2
Speed (magnetic pickup)	Dynalco SS	0.04 (~2000 Hz)
	Dynalco SS	0.2 (~400 Hz)
	Dynalco SS	0.8 (~80 Hz)
	Dynalco SS	3.5 (~15 Hz)
Vortex flowmeter	Fischer & Porter 10LV2	2.5
Nuclear density gage	Texas Nuclear SGH	15–300[b]
	Kay-Ray	2.2–26[b]
Nuclear level gage	Kay-Ray	0.4–13[b]

[a] The gas is saturated steam and the liquid is organic.

[b] Time constant is adjustable.

[c] Time constant is selected by three-position jumper.

Source: Instrument Society of America.

Look at the second row. At the end of the first τ, the output has risen to 0.6321. This leaves a maximum possible *change* (Δ_{max}) of 0.3679. During the next τ the output will actually change by

$$\Delta_{actual} = 63.21\% \times 0.3679 = 0.2325$$

So at the end of that τ the output will be

$$\text{output}\bigg|_{2\tau} = \text{output}\bigg|_{1\tau} + 0.2325 = 0.6321 + 0.2325$$

$$= 0.8646$$

This number is consistent with

$$\text{output}\bigg|_{2\tau} = 1 - e^{-2\tau/\tau} = 0.8647$$

This same concept also holds true for the exponential decrease, which is a first-order element's response to a step down.

Table 2–3 is a listing of the time constants you can expect from many of the more common industrial elements. This table can be used along with Figures 2–4 and 2–5 to plot the expected response of any of these first-order elements.

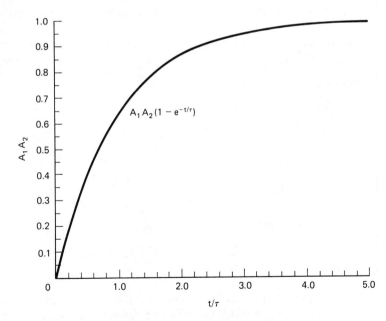

Figure 2–4   Normalized response of a first-order element to a step up.

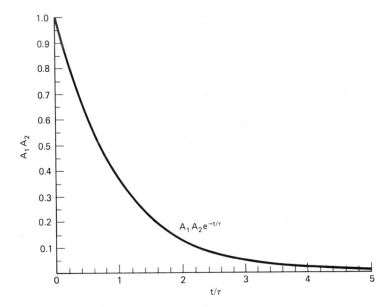

Figure 2–5 Normalized response of a first-order element to a step down.

EXAMPLE 2–2

A ¼-in.-long resistance temperature detector (RTD) with a steady-state gain of 0.3925 Ω/°C and a 5.5-s time constant experiences a 75°C step change in temperature. Before the temperature change, the RTD had a stable 100Ω resistance. Write the time-domain equations for the resistance of the RTD. Draw the response curve.

Solution

$$T_{\text{nominal}} = 100 \ \Omega$$

$$A_1 = 0.3925 \ \Omega/°C$$

$$A_2 = 75°C \qquad \text{(step height)}$$

$$\tau = 5.5 \ s$$

$$T_{\text{out}} = A_1 A_2 (1 - e^{-t/\tau})$$

To this must be added the initial conditions

$$T_{\text{out}} = A_1 A_2 (1 - e^{-t/\tau}) + T_{\text{nominal}}$$

$$= 29.44 \ \Omega (1 - e^{-t/5.5 \ s}) + 100 \ \Omega$$

To get a plot of this you could substitute t into this equation, make a table of values, and then plot these. Or you could *denormalize* Figure 2–4. First, multiply the horizontal axis

$$\frac{t}{\tau} \times 5.5 \text{ s}$$

Second, multiply the vertical axis

$$A_1A_2 \times 29.44 \; \Omega$$

Third, offset the vertical origin by $T_{nominal}$. The result is shown in Figure 2–6.

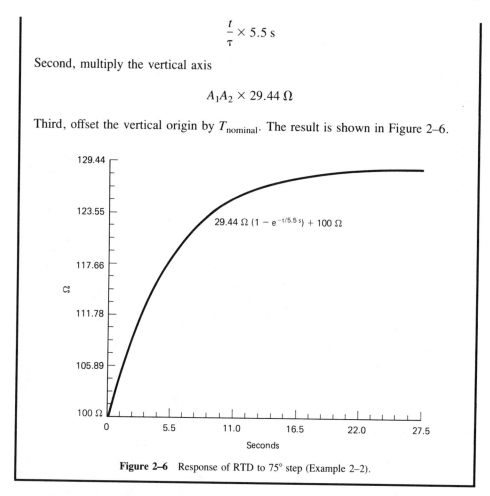

Figure 2–6   Response of RTD to 75° step (Example 2–2).

Figures 2–4, 2–5, and 2–6 and Example 2–2 all dealt with the response of a first-order element to a step. The second standard test signal is a ramp.

$$v_o(t) = A_1A_2\tau \left(e^{-t/\tau} + \frac{t}{\tau} - 1 \right) \tag{2–4}$$

The normalized plot of Equation 2–4 is given in Figure 2–7. Notice that the output initially lags the input. But after 5τ, the exponential term falls out. Then the output tracks the input. It will have a slope of A_1A_2. Because Figure 2–7 is normalized, it appears that the steady-state output parallels the input but lags by 1τ. However, the slope of the input is A_1, while the slope of the output is A_1A_2. If $A_2 > 1$, the output will be steeper than the input. This will eventually allow the output to catch and pass the input. Conversely, if $A_2 < 1$, the output slope is smaller than the input. The output will rise more slowly than the input and the two will get farther apart.

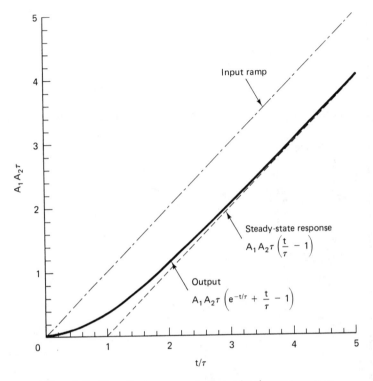

Figure 2–7   Normalized response of a first-order element to a ramp.

The third standard input is the pulse or impulse.

$$v_o(t) = \frac{A}{\tau} e^{-t/\tau} \tag{2-5}$$

This is the same as the response to a step down, as shown in Figure 2–5. Actually, the impulse is rather unrealistic. It is defined as having no width and infinite height. The response of a first-order element to a more practical pulse input is shown in Example 2–3.

EXAMPLE 2–3

The RTD of Example 2–2 is monitoring the temperature of liquid flowing through a pipe. A cell of liquid which is 75°C hotter than the surrounding liquid passes the RTD. It takes 3 s for the cell of superheated liquid to pass. Plot the RTD's output.

Solution   From Example 2–2 you found that the response to the increased temperature was

$$T_{\text{out}} = 29.44 \ \Omega(1 - e^{-t/5.5 \text{ s}}) + 100 \ \Omega$$

However, instead of solving this, you simply denormalize Figure 2–4. This is plotted in Figure 2–6. So for the first 3 s the RTD's output will follow the plot in Figure 2–6. The pulse is then gone. The output falls exponentially as shown in Figure 2–5. You denormalize the horizontal axis of Figure 2–5 by multiplying by the 5.5-s time constant of the RTD. Also, multiply the vertical axis by 12.38, which is the value of RTD had reached when the pulse passed. The composite output is shown in Figure 2–8.

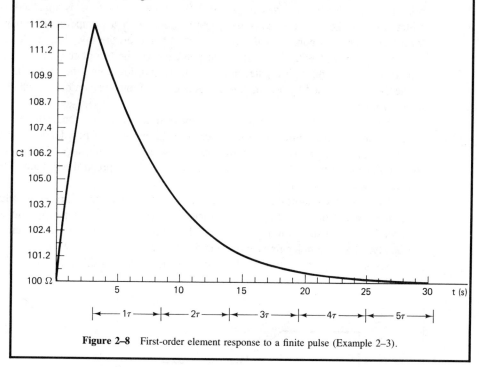

Figure 2–8   First-order element response to a finite pulse (Example 2–3).

2–5 DEAD TIME

So far you have seen three types of process elements: gain, integral, and first order. All of these at least *begin* to respond as soon as an input is applied.

There are elements, however, whose outputs are delayed. A change at the input does not affect the output until after some delay or *dead time*. Appropriately enough, these are called dead-time process elements.

Most dead-time elements are associated with some form of transportation delay. Actually, you have to deal with a dead-time process every day. When you first turn on the hot water in your shower or bath, there is a delay while the hot water is transported from the heater to you. The farther this distance, the longer the dead time.

For simple dead-time processes, once the delay has expired, the output tracks the input. That is, after the delay, the dead time exhibits gain. Figure 2–9 shows the response of a simple dead-time element.

Many real processes exhibit both dead-time and first-order response. When a step is applied to a first-order plus dead-time process, the output does not respond until after the transportation delay is over. Then it rises exponentially, taking 5 time constants to complete its response. This is shown in Figure 2–10.

The chemical composition mixture system in Figure 2–11 is an example of a first-order-plus-dead-time process [1, p. 191]. Inlet liquid flow is matched with the outlet flow of the mixture. This is probably done with a pump on the outlet and a level transducer and controller driving a control valve on the inlet liquid. A vat of the powder to be mixed with the liquid is suspended near the top of the tank. The powder falls from the vat, through a gate, along a shoot, and down into the tank. The position of the gate is governed by a cylinder. The stirrer is a motor-driven blade, which assures uniform mixture.

A step change in the gate positioner, made in an effort to change the composition of the outlet mixture, will immediately change the amount of powder leaving the vat. However, this change must fall down the shoot and into the tank. That is the dead time. Once in the tank, the powder must dissolve and be spread throughout. That is an exponential, or first-order, process.

There are two additional comments to be made concerning first-order-plus-dead-time processes. Complex, high-order processes often exhibit a step response which is very similar to that shown in Figure 2–10. These processes, therefore, are often modeled and analyzed as a simpler first-order-plus-dead-time process [1, p. 190].

Second, a significantly long dead time can make it very difficult to establish good,

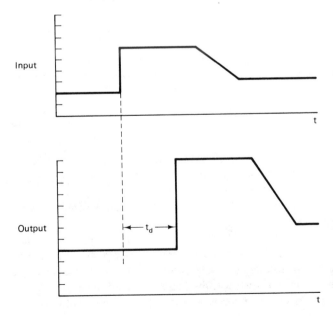

Input

Output

Figure 2–9 Response of a simple dead-time element.

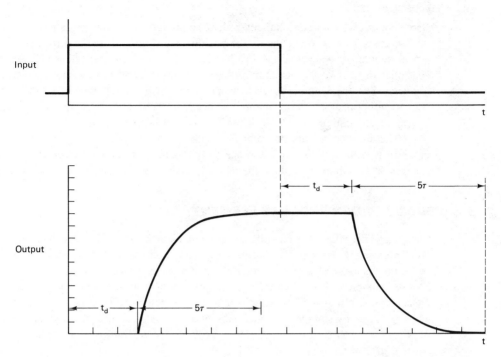

Figure 2–10   Response of a first-order-plus-dead-time process to a step.

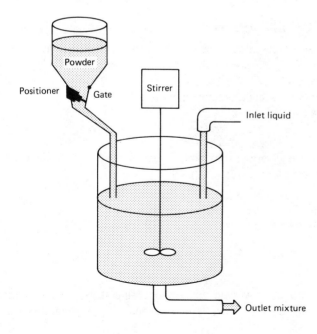

Figure 2–11   Composition mixture system example of a first-order-plus-dead-time process.

stable control with a traditional controller. To produce a change in the process's output, the controller moves the actuator (the positioner in Figure 2–11) and then monitors the process output to determine the result. However, absolutely no effect appears. So the controller may drive the actuator further, and further, and further, until the dead time is over. Then the output begins to respond, actually far too much. So the controller begins cutting back on the actuator. But because of the dead time, no effect is noticed. Therefore, the controller cuts back further, and further, and further.

The solution to this problem is to place a microcomputer in the controller and program it with a model of the process. It can then anticipate the dead time, timing changes at its output to produce the desired results once the dead time has expired.

2–6 SECOND-ORDER PROCESS ELEMENT

Mathematically, the most complicated process element you will see here is the second-order element. However, by carefully adjusting each of its three parameters, you can shape the response of a second-order element to fit your needs.

"Examples are mechanical systems possessing both potential and kinetic energies and electrical circuits with energy contained in both magnetic and electric fields. In addition to energy storage elements, second order systems invariably include some form of energy absorption or damping. This might be viscous friction in a mechanical system or resistance in an electric circuit" [2].

The second-order element is described by three parameters.

$$A = \text{steady-state gain}$$

$$\omega_n = \text{natural or resonant frequency}$$

$$\zeta = \text{damping coefficient}$$

The precise shape of the response is determined by the damping coefficient, ζ. You will see much more on this later. If you set ζ to zero, the element will oscillate. The frequency of that oscillation is ω_n.

Also, the time constant of a second-order element is defined as

$$\tau = \frac{1}{\omega_n}$$

The amplitude of the response is determined by both the system gain, A, and the natural frequency, ω_n. So a second gain term is often defined:

$$\text{element gain} = K_p = A\omega_n^2$$

2–6.1 Overdamped Response

A second-order element is said to be *overdamped* if

$$\zeta > 1$$

In relative terms, this means that the system will respond sluggishly. You may have seen a spring-loaded swinging door or gate. It is a second-order system. Placing a very heavy grease in the spring mechanism will slow its response. When you pull it back and let go, it *slowly* returns to its center position without swinging too far. Under these conditions, the door is overdamped.

Cascading two first-order elements with different time constants produces an overdamped second-order system. You would see this if it were necessary to place a simple *RC* filter after the output of a bare RTD temperature probe and transmitter (electronic signal conditioner). The *RC* filter is a first-order element, as in the probe.

$$\omega_n^2 = \frac{1}{\tau_1 \tau_2}$$

$$\omega_n = \frac{1}{\sqrt{\tau_1 \tau_2}} \tag{2–6}$$

$$\tau_{system} = \frac{1}{\omega_n} = \sqrt{\tau_1 \tau_2} \tag{2–7}$$

$$k_p = \frac{A_1 A_2}{\tau_1 \tau_2} \tag{2–8}$$

$$\zeta = \frac{\tau_1 + \tau_2}{2 \sqrt{\tau_1 \tau_2}} \tag{2–9}$$

As far as the damping is concerned, this means that if $\tau_t \ll \tau_2$, then ζ becomes large. The element is heavily damped, and it behaves like a first-order element with $\tau = \tau_2$. This holds true for all inputs, steps, ramps, or pulses. However, if the time constant for each term is comparable ($\tau_1 \approx \tau_2$), the exponentials die out at similar rates. So you must consider both terms.

EXAMPLE 2–4

Determine the damping of two cascaded first-order elements when $\tau_1 = 1$ s and
(a) $\tau_2 = 10$ s.
(b) $\tau_2 = 1.5$ s.

Solution   From Equation 2–9,

$$\zeta = \frac{\tau_1 + \tau_2}{2 \sqrt{\tau_1 \tau_2}}$$

(a) $\zeta = \dfrac{1 \text{ s} + 10 \text{ s}}{2 \sqrt{(1 \text{ s})(10 \text{ s})}}$ **(b)** $\zeta = \dfrac{1 \text{ s} + 1.5 \text{ s}}{2 \sqrt{(1 \text{ s})(1.5 \text{ s})}}$

$= \dfrac{11 \text{ s}}{2 \times 3.16 \text{ s}}$ $= \dfrac{2.5 \text{ s}}{2 \times 1.225 \text{ s}}$

$= 1.74$ $= 1.021$

2–6.2 Critically Damped Response

A second-order element is said to be *critically* damped if

$$\zeta = 1$$

In relative terms, this means that the system will respond rapidly. If the swinging door discussed in Section 2–6.1 were critically damped, pulling it back and letting it go would cause it to move smoothly to its stop. Its travel would be as rapid as possible without causing the door to overshoot and swing past the stop into the next room.

Cascading two first-order elements with equal (or nearly equal) time constants produces a critically damped second-order system. Compare this to the parameter derivation of Section 2–6.1.

$$\omega_n^2 = \frac{1}{\tau^2}$$

$$\omega_n = \frac{1}{\tau}$$

$$\tau_{\text{system}} = \frac{1}{\omega_n}$$

$$k_p = A\omega_n^2 = \frac{A_1 A_2}{\tau^2}$$

$$\zeta = \frac{\tau + \tau}{2\sqrt{\tau\tau}} = 1$$

2–6.3 Underdamped Response

A second-order element is said to be *underdamped* if

$$\zeta < 1$$

In relative terms, this means that the system will overshoot. If the swinging door discussed in previous sections were underdamped, pulling it back and letting it go would cause it to swing past the stop into the next room, stop, swing back again, perhaps swinging back and forth past the stop several times before settling down.

When a step is applied to an underdamped element,

$$v_o(t) = A\left[1 + \frac{e^{-\zeta\omega_n t}}{\sqrt{1 - \zeta^2}} \cdot \sin\left(\omega_n\sqrt{1 - \zeta^2}\, t - \psi\right)\right]$$

The plot of that response is given in Figure 2–12. Look very carefully at both the plot and the equation. The output rises quickly but overshoots and then oscillates back and forth sinusoidally with a decaying amplitude.

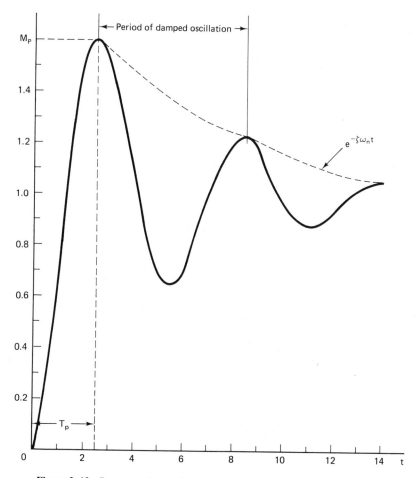

Figure 2–12 Response of an underdamped second-order element to a step input.

There are several parameters that are important. The sinusoidal part of the response
is

$$\sin \left(\omega_n \sqrt{1 - \zeta^2}\, t - \psi \right)$$

The standard way of expressing a sine wave is

$$\sin \left(\omega_d t + \psi \right)$$

where ω_d is the frequency of the oscillation. Comparing these two expressions, then,
gives the frequency of the sinusoidal oscillation part of the step response,

$$\omega_d = \omega_n \sqrt{1 - \zeta^2} \qquad (2\text{–}10)$$

The oscillation frequency depends both on the resonant frequency ω_n and the damping.
The closer the damping is to critical ($\zeta = 1$), the lower the frequency. The more

lightly the system is damped, the closer the oscillation frequency is to the resonant frequency.

The amplitude of this oscillation dies off exponentially. The traditional expression of a sine wave is

$$A \sin(\omega_d t + \psi)$$

The underdamped second-order response is, in part,

$$e^{-\zeta \omega_n t} \sin(\omega_d t + \psi)$$

For the first-order system, you saw an exponential response of

$$e^{-t/\tau}$$

Comparing these expressions, the exponential decay time constant for an underdamped second-order element can be defined as

$$\tau_d = \frac{1}{\zeta \omega_n} \tag{2-11}$$

For the systems that are critically damped, $\zeta = 1$ and $\tau = 1/\omega_n$, which is precisely what you saw in Section 2–6.2. As the damping gets smaller, τ becomes longer and the oscillations continue for much more time.

As with the first-order, exponential responses, it is useful to know how long it takes before the system settles to within 5% of its final value. Five percent settling requires three time constants, 2% settling requires 4τ, and after 5τ the response is within 0.5% of its final value.

2–6.4 Normalized Responses

In the preceding sections of this chapter you have seen the response of first- and second-order elements. Deriving this response requires several steps. First you have to determine the proper transfer function of the element. Then you multiply it by the Laplace transform of the input. Next you find the inverse transform in the table. Finally, you calculate a set of values for output versus time, which are plotted.

The families of normalized responses provide a much simpler approach. Figure 2–13 is a collection of responses of first- and second-order elements to a step input. In Figure 2–14 are the responses to an impulse and in Figure 2–15 are the responses to a ramp. The vertical axes have been scaled with $A = 1$. This is most obvious in Figure 2–13 since all the responses settle out to a steady-state value of 1. The horizontal axis is a bit more complicated. Instead of plotting time on the horizontal axis, $\omega_n t$ has been plotted. This is equivalent to setting $\omega_n = 1/s$. This makes the horizontal axis unitless.

To use these figures to obtain plots that are of some real-world value, you must *denormalize* the axes. You scale the vertical axis by *multiplying* it by the factor in Table 2–4. For step responses and most responses to a ramp this means just multiply the vertical axis by the overall gain. However, for the response to an impulse, the

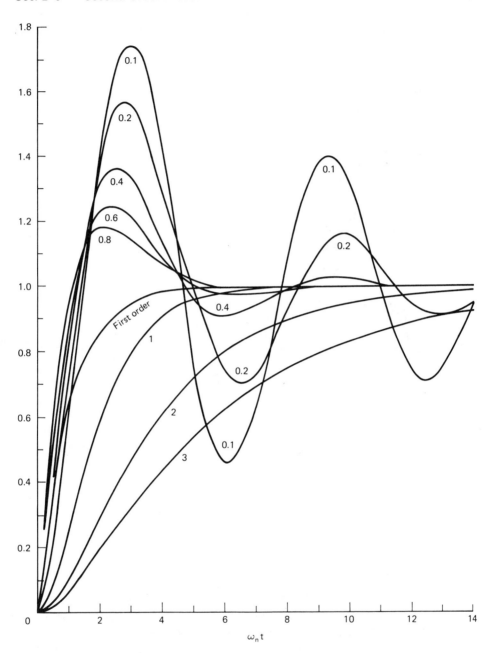

Figure 2–13 Normalized response to a step input.

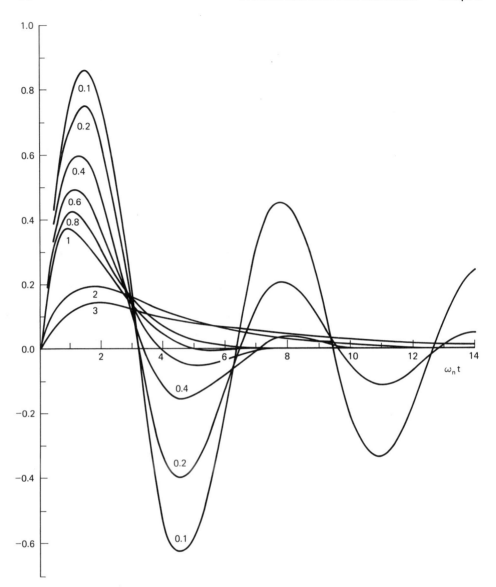

Figure 2–14 Normalized response to an impulse input.

denormalization factor is a bit more complicated. The horizontal axis is denormalized by dividing by ω_n. This converts the $\omega_n t$ to time in seconds.

So, to obtain the response plot of a first- or second-order element you do not have to perform any Laplace math, equation solving, data creation, or plotting. Just determine ζ, A, and ω_n. The ζ specifies which curve to use. The proper denormalization factor from Table 2–4 *multiplies* the vertical axis and ω_n *divides* the horizontal axis. That's it. Just select the proper curve and rescale the axes.

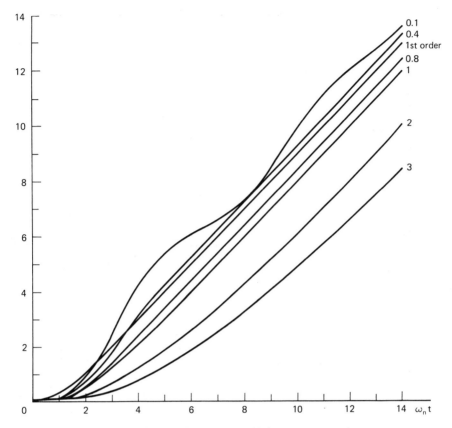

Figure 2–15   Normalized response to a ramp input.

TABLE 2–4   VERTICAL-AXIS DENORMALIZATION FACTORS

	First order	Second order $\zeta > 1$	$\zeta = 1$	$\zeta < 1$
Impulse	$\dfrac{A}{\tau}$	$\dfrac{A}{\tau_1 - \tau_2}$	$\dfrac{A}{\tau}$	$A\omega_n$
Step	A	A	A	A
Ramp	$A\tau$	A	A	A

EXAMPLE 2–5

Given a second-order, critically damped element, plot the response to an impulse using the normalized curves.

$$A = 2 \times 10^{-8}$$

$$\tau = 6.33 \ \mu s$$

Solution

$$\omega_n = \frac{1}{\tau} = 1.58 \times 10^5$$

This means that you rescale the horizontal axis of Figure 2–14 by dividing by 1.58×10^5. So 2 becomes

$$\frac{2}{1.58 \times 10^5} = 12.7 \ \mu s$$

and 10 becomes

$$\frac{10}{1.58 \times 10^5} = 63.3 \ \mu s$$

To scale the vertical axis, look at Table 2–4. For an impulse input into a critically damped system, the vertical denormalization factor is

$$\frac{A}{\tau} = \frac{2 \times 10^{-8}}{6.33 \ \mu s} = 3.16 \times 10^{-3}$$

The denormalized plot is shown in Figure 2–16.

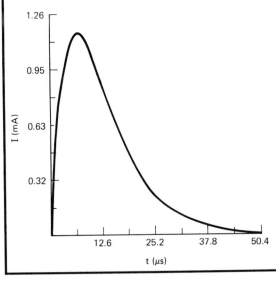

Figure 2–16 Denormalized response for Example 2–5.

2–7 HIGHER-ORDER PROCESS ELEMENT

Practical, industrial processes may cascade many first-order elements. In fact, in a petroleum distillation process, 50 or more elements may be cascaded. How do you handle something of this order?

Just such a process is illustrated in Figure 2–17a. N first-order elements have been cascaded, each with a time constant that equals τ/N. The result of applying a step input to these cascaded elements is shown in Figure 2–17b. As the number of first-order elements in cascade goes up, there appears to be a longer and longer delay before the output responds. However, the more first-order elements that are cascaded, the steeper the response becomes, once it starts. With enough first-order elements, the response appears to be like a dead-time element. Fewer cascaded stages can be approximated as a dead-time-plus-first-order or dead-time-plus-second-order element [3].

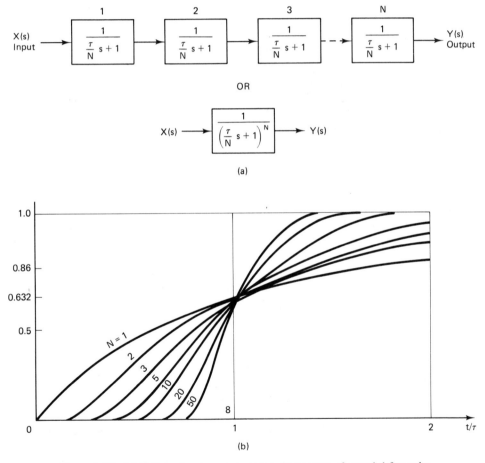

Figure 2–17   (a) N first-order elements in series; (b) response of cascaded first-order lags. (Courtesy of Instrumentation Society of America.)

SUMMARY

Each element in an industrial process can be described by its transfer function. This provides a simple, concise, but complete way of describing that element's performance. The transfer function is the ratio of the element's output to its input, expressed in the Laplace domain.

The simplest transfer function is gain (also called span). It consists of a single number. Output tracks input well. It is usual to think of gain as being unitless. However, sensors and actuators in particular input one type of quantity while outputting something entirely different. So gain transfer functions may be expressed with mixed units.

For an integral process, the *rate of change* of its output depends directly on the magnitude of its input. Mathematically, this means that

$$v_o = k \int v_i \, dt$$

Any change at the input of an integral element will cause its output to ramp. As long as this unbalancing step is maintained at the input, the output will continue to change. Eventually, electronics will saturate, a tank will overflow. So have care when working with integral processes.

In contrast to the integral process, first-order processes are self-regulating. A step change at the input of a first-order element will cause the output to change exponentially to a new level. For a step input

$$v_o = A_1 A_2 (1 - e^{-t/\tau})$$

The time constant τ specifies the speed of the element's response. During one time constant, the output will change by 63.2% of the maximum possible change. Since as the output changes this maximum possible change decreases, the actual response must also decrease. This illustrates the exponential nature of a first-order element. Following this same line of reasoning, you can conclude that the output can never reach its full response. However, after 3τ it is within 5% of its final value, after 4τ it is within 2%, and after 5τ the actual response is within 0.5% of its final value. A spike is a very short duration input. Since the amount of response from a first-order element depends on the length of time you give the element to respond, spikes tend to be absorbed by first-order elements.

Dead-time processes are normally associated with transportation delays. A change at the input will be duplicated at the output after the dead time has expired. Dead-time delays may also be associated with first-order elements. In such a dead-time-plus-first-order system, a step at the input will cause no change at the output until the delay has expired. Following that delay, the output will rise (or fall) exponentially, as a normal first-order element. Because of this delay, traditional control tends to make dead-time processes oscillate. Some intelligence should be incorporated into the controller to anticipate the effects of this dead time.

Second-order elements have two energy storage mechanisms. Because of the exchange of energy among the input, these two storage devices, and the load, three classes of response are possible. The key to the class of response a particular element will follow is ζ, the damping coefficient.

For $\zeta > 1$, the element is overdamped. This means that cascading two first-order elements with different time constants will produce an overdamped second-order system. These elements behave relatively sluggishly.

For $\zeta = 1$, the element is critically damped. This means that cascading two first-order elements with the same time constants produces a critically damped second-order system. These elements respond more rapidly than overdamped elements. However, their response is still slower than a first-order element.

Reducing ζ to less than 1 causes the element to be underdamped. The response of an underdamped element to a step input is indeed faster than a critically damped element. However, the output overshoots the final value, oscillating above and below that final value. The amplitude of these oscillations die out exponentially.

Normally, to determine the response of an element to one of the three standard test inputs (step, impulse, or ramp) you must solve the inverse Laplace transform of the element's transfer function, determine proper scaling, tabulate values of output versus time, and then plot those data. Instead, you can use Figure 2–13, 2–14, or 2–15. These are normalized plots of first- and second-order elements' responses to the three standard inputs. Given the parameters of the element, A, τ, ζ, and ω_n, you simply pick the proper curve and divide the horizontal axis by ω_n and multiply the vertical axis by the proper factor from Table 2–4.

Cascading many first-order elements produces a system that begins to behave like a dead-time or dead-time-plus-first-order element (see Figure 2–17). This allows reasonably simple modeling of very complex industrial processes.

REFERENCES

1. ROBERT BATESON, *Introduction to Control System Technology* 2nd ed. Columbus, Ohio: Charles E. Merrill Publishing Company, 1973.

2. ROBERT C. WEYRICK, *Fundamentals of Automatic Control.* New York: McGraw-Hill Book Company, 1975, p. 164. Material reproduced with permission of McGraw-Hill/Gregs Division.

3. PRADEEP B. DESHPANDE and RAYMOND H. ASH, *Elements of Computer Process Control with Advanced Control Applications.* Research Triangle Park, N.C.: Instrument Society of America, 1981, pp. 12–15.

PROBLEMS

2–1. A potentiometer can be used to measure rotational position. If it can rotate a maximum of 300° and is attached to a 10-V dc source, write the transfer function for the potentiometer where angular position of the shaft (in degrees) is the input and the voltage between the wiper and ground is the output. Also, draw the schematic.

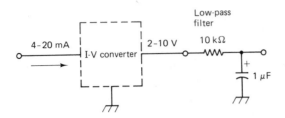

Figure 2–18   Low-pass filter (Problem 2–3).

2–2. A transducer transmitter produces an output signal that varies from 4 mA at the lowest value of the process variable to 20 mA at the highest value. It is desired to convert this signal to a voltage that goes from 2 to 10 V.
   (a) What is the gain or span of that element?
   (b) What units must be associated with it?
   (c) Draw the schematic of the current-to-voltage converter.

2–3. The circuit in Figure 2–18 must be added to the *I–V* converter of Problem 2–2. It is a low-pass filter used to reduce the 60-Hz noise which may have been introduced into the transmitted current signal.
   (a) What is the steady-state gain of this element?
   (b) How long does it take for this filter to respond fully to an input step?
   (c) If the process variable that is being measured has a time constant of 5 s, do you have to consider the transfer function of the filter? Why or why not?
   (d) Repeat part (c) for a process time constant of 20 ms.

2–4. Consider the *RC* low-pass filter of Figure 2–18.
   (a) How long does it take this element to settle to within 5% of its final value in response to a step input?
   (b) How long does it take for this element to respond fully to a step input?
   (c) Given that the input steps from 8 V down to 5 V, plot the output of this element.

2–5. (a) Describe in detail a dead-time process not illustrated in this chapter.
   (b) Describe in detail a first-order-plus-dead-time process not illustrated in this chapter.

2–6. The chemical composition system of Figure 2–11 has a steady-state gain of 0.002% solution/ 1% opening of gate, a dead time of 1.7 s, and a time constant of 4.0 s.
   (a) Calculate the output (percent solution) assuming that the gate is at 30% open and has been at that position for a long time.
   (b) Plot the output (percent solution) assuming that the gate is stepped from 30% open to 50% open. Denormalize the proper curve to help you.
   (c) How long does it take the output to reach steady state (i.e., to stabilize)?

2–7. (a) Repeat Problem 2–6 with a dead time of 0.3 s.
   (b) What do you conclude about the response of a first-order-plus-dead-time element when $t_d \ll \tau$?

2–8. The circuit in Figure 2–19 is a second-order low-pass Sallon–Key equal-component filter.

$$A_o = 2.23$$

$$\zeta = 0.39$$

$$\omega_n = 6313 \text{ rad/s}$$

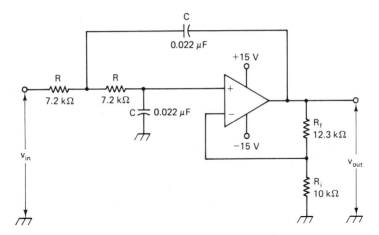

Figure 2–19   Schematic (Problem 2–8).

(a) Calculate the frequency (in hertz) of the damped oscillations that occur at the output in response to a step input.

(b) Calculate the length of time it takes those oscillations to settle to within 5% of the final value.

2–9. Using the information that you calculated in Problem 2–8, accurately sketch the response of the circuit in Figure 2–19 to a 1-V step input.

2–10. For the RC low-pass filter of Problem 2–4 and Figure 2–18, plot the circuit's response to a ramp by denormalizing the standard response plots.

2–11. For the second-order filter of Problem 2–8, use the standard response plots to obtain the output voltage versus time graph with an input voltage which is

(a) a ramp.

(b) an impulse.

(c) a 1-V step.

3

Transducers

In Chapter 1 you saw that the purpose of a control system is to assure close correlation between the actual output of a system and the desired output. The actual output was called the process variable and the desired output was called the set point. Figure 1–4 showed the many blocks typically used. Much effort (mathematical and electronic) and money are expended to assure proper system performance. However, no matter how good the mathematical design or the electronic implementation, the final control can be no better than the system's *perception* of the process variable. The quality of the measurement of the variable being controlled sets the bottom line on overall system performance. It is indeed important to understand the physical principles that allow a transducer to convert a parameter (heat or force or position) into an electrical quantity. But just as important is your ability to read and interpret the manufacturer's specifications. Of primary concern is that you match the transducer's accuracy, resolution, linearity, repeatability, and response speed to the system requirements. A poorly specified transducer can doom the performance of a system. You just cannot control something more accurately than you can measure it. On the other hand, selecting a temperature transducer with a range of −100 to +400°F and an accuracy of +0.01°F cannot be justified when you are trying to control the temperature of your house.

To begin this chapter you will learn the definitions of the parameters used to specify how well and how quickly the transducer converts what it is measuring into its electrical output. You must be certain that you are interpreting these parameters the same way that the manufacturer is presenting them. The bulk of the chapter presents a description of the commonly used process and servo control transducers. Displacement, force, motion, fluid, and temperature transducers are all discussed. The physical measurement techniques are explained and time will be spent interpreting manufacturers' specifications and application examples.

OBJECTIVES

After studying this chapter you should be able to do the following:

1. Define each of the following terms, give an example, and calculate the effect on transducer output.
   a. Accuracy
   b. Resolution
   c. Repeatability
   d. Linearity
   e. Hysteresis
   f. Response rate
2. List three ways to measure displacement.
3. Explain and illustrate two techniques for connecting potentiometers as displacement transducers.
4. Sketch an LVDT and explain its operation and signal conditioning.
5. Describe incremental, quadrature, and absolute optical encoders.
6. Define stress, strain, Young's modulus, and the stress–strain curve.
7. Calculate applied force given gage parameters, beam parameters, and ΔR.
8. Illustrate and calculate temperature effects and temperature compensation techniques on a strain gage.
9. Define a load call and illustrate proper gage interconnection.
10. Calculate applied forces on a load call.
11. Explain the operation and list advantages and disadvantages of a dc generator, alternator, magnetic pickup, optical encoder, strain gage accelerometer, mass and spring accelerometer, and piezoelectric accelerometer.
12. Explain the operation and list advantages and disadvantages of a manometer, bellows, Bourdon tube, diaphragm, float, pressure-to-level converter, conductivity-capacitance, orifice plate (ΔP), vane, and turbine.
13. Explain the operation and list advantages and disadvantages of a thermistor, RTD, thermocouple, temperature–voltage integrated circuit, and temperature–current integrated circuits.

3–1 TRANSDUCER SPECIFICATIONS

The purpose of a transducer is to convert a physical quantity into an electrical signal. The most common quantities measured by transducers are position, force, velocity, acceleration, pressure, level, flow, and temperature. The transducer's output may typically be voltage, current, resistance, capacitance, or frequency. How well and how quickly the transducer changes its output in response to a change in the physical parameter at its input is key to the success of your control system.

Transducer performance is described (guaranteed) by the manufacturer in two sets of specifications. Static specifications describe the *steady-state* correlation between the physical input and the electrical output. Accuracy, resolution, repeatability, linearity, and hysteresis are all static specifications. How *quickly* the output changes in response to changes at the input is described by the dynamic performance specifications. Rise time, time constant, dead time, frequency response and the second-order parameters of damping, resonant frequency, settling time, and percent overshoot may be used by manufacturers to describe the dynamic performance of their transducers.

3–1.1 Static Specifications

To determine the static specifications of a transducer, the manufacturer performs a calibration. This is "a test during which known values of the measurand are applied to a transducer and corresponding output readings are recorded" [1, p. 30]. A calibration may be performed on each transducer produced and the results (either in a table or a curve) provided to the customer. Or, calibration may be performed by the quality control department on a statistical sample of the transducers produced.

There are two other points to be made about calibration. First, the applied input must be known to be true. Generally, this means that it has been calibrated and there is documentation to show that its value can be traced to the standards at the National Bureau of Standards. Second, unless specifically indicated, calibration is static. An input is applied and the output monitored until it has stopped changing. Only when the output has fully responded to a change at the input and is stable can the output value be recorded.

Accuracy is perhaps the most widely used and misused of the static specifications. Actually, accuracy is specified in terms of the percent error. Error is the difference between the true (correct) output from the transducer and the actual output. But accuracy is expressed in *percent* error. The big question is, "percentage of what?"

There are three different answers. Accuracy may be expressed as percent of the full-scale output, as percent of the reading, or in absolute terms of the input.

EXAMPLE 3–1

A load cell is a transducer used to measure weight. A calibration record (table of values) is given in Table 3–1. Plot the calibration curve.

TABLE 3–1   CALIBRATION RECORD
FOR EXAMPLE 3–1

	Output (mV)	
Load (kg)	Increasing	Decreasing
0	0.08	0.06
5	0.45	0.88
10	1.02	2.04
15	1.71	3.10
20	2.55	4.18
25	3.43	5.13
30	4.48	6.04
35	5.50	7.02
40	6.53	8.06
45	7.64	9.35
50	8.70	10.52
55	9.85	11.80
60	11.01	12.94
65	12.40	13.86
70	13.32	14.82
75	14.35	15.71
80	15.40	16.84
85	16.48	17.92
90	17.66	18.70
95	18.90	19.51
100	19.93	20.02

Solution   The input is plotted on the horizontal and is scaled from 0 to 100 kg (Figure 3–1). The output is plotted on the vertical and is scaled from 0 to 20 mV. Notice that the actual data points and the direction of the test (first increasing, then decreasing) are indicated in the plot.

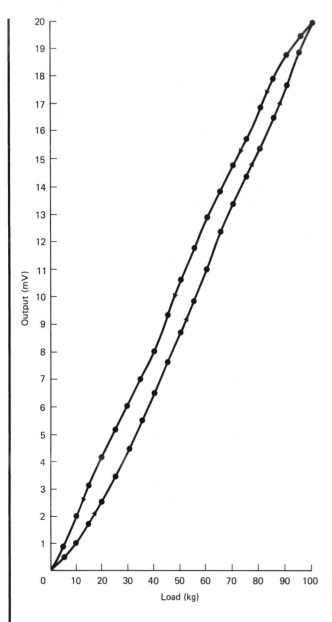

Figure 3–1 Calibration curve (Example 3–1).

EXAMPLE 3–2

Determine the accuracy of the transducer whose calibration record is given in Table 3–1. Express your answer in both % FSO (percent of full-scale output) and % of reading.

Solution   There are several steps to solving this problem. First you must determine what the true output should be. Assuming a desired linear relationship between output is

$$v_{true} = \frac{v_{full\ scale}}{load_{full\ scale}} \times load \tag{3–1}$$

$$= \frac{20\ mV}{100\ kg} \times load$$

$$= 0.2\ \frac{mV}{kg} \times load$$

Next, at each point on the calibration record you calculate and record the true output, the error, the accuracy as % FSO, and the accuracy as % of true reading. This has been done in Table 3–2. Finally, you report the largest of these errors. The largest error as a percent of full scale is 7.85% at 25 kg (increasing). As a percent of reading, there is a 60% error at 5 kg (decreasing).

TABLE 3–2 ACCURACY FOR EXAMPLE 3–2

	True output (mV)	Actual output (mV)	Error (mV)	Accuracy	
				% FSO	% reading
0	0	0.08	−0.08	−0.4	a
5	1.00	0.45	0.55	2.75	55.00
10	2.00	1.02	0.98	4.90	49.00
15	3.00	1.71	1.29	6.45	43.00
20	4.00	2.55	1.45	7.25	36.25
25	5.00	3.43	1.57	7.85	31.40
30	6.00	4.48	1.52	7.60	25.33
35	7.00	5.50	1.50	7.50	21.43
40	8.00	6.53	1.47	7.35	27.01
45	9.00	7.64	1.36	6.80	15.11
50	10.00	8.70	1.30	6.50	13.00
55	11.00	9.85	1.15	5.75	10.45
60	12.00	11.01	0.99	4.95	8.25
65	13.00	12.40	0.60	3.00	2.77
70	14.00	13.32	0.68	3.40	7.14
75	15.00	14.35	0.65	3.25	4.33
80	16.00	15.40	0.60	3.00	3.75
85	17.00	16.48	0.52	2.60	3.06
90	18.00	17.66	0.34	1.70	1.89
95	19.00	18.90	0.10	0.50	0.53
100	20.00	19.93	0.07	0.35	0.35
100	20.00	20.02	−0.02	−0.10	−0.10
95	19.00	19.51	−0.51	−2.55	−2.68
90	18.00	18.70	−0.70	−3.50	−3.89
85	17.00	17.92	−0.92	−4.60	−5.41
80	16.00	16.84	−0.84	−4.20	−5.25

TABLE 3–2 (continued)

	True output (mV)	Actual output (mV)	Error (mV)	Accuracy	
				% FSO	% reading
75	15.00	15.71	−0.71	−3.55	−4.73ɨ
70	14.00	14.82	−0.82	−4.10	−5.86
65	13.00	13.86	−0.86	−4.30	−6.62
60	12.00	12.94	−0.94	−4.70	−7.83
55	11.00	11.80	−0.80	−4.00	−5.82
50	10.00	10.52	−0.52	−2.60	−5.20
45	9.00	9.35	−0.35	−1.75	−3.89
40	8.00	8.06	−0.06	−0.30	−0.75
35	7.00	7.02	−0.02	−0.10	−0.29
30	6.00	6.04	−0.04	−0.20	−0.67
25	5.00	5.13	−0.13	−0.65	−2.60
20	4.00	4.18	−0.18	−0.90	−4.50
15	3.00	3.10	−0.10	−0.50	−16.67
10	2.00	2.04	−0.04	−0.20	−10.00
5	*1.00*	*0.88*	*0.12*	*0.60*	*60.00*
0	0	0.06	−0.06	−0.30	a

[a] Not defined since division by zero is illegal.

Obviously, there is a significant difference between the results these two specifications produce. It is critical to understand which the manufacturer is using. What you really want to know is how much uncertainty there is in the measured value of the input. The *absolute error* is expressed in the units of the input parameter. Accuracy in terms of % FSO will allow you to determine the absolute error. Percent of reading specifications will not.

EXAMPLE 3–3

A load cell has a full-scale rating of 20 mV at 100 kg. Calibration indicates a +7.85% FSO accuracy. What is the absolute error?

Solution   The error is +7.85% of 100 kg or +7.85 kg. The output may be off by +7.85% of 20 mV or +1.57 mV.

Compare this to the calibration record in Table 3–2. At 25 kg (increasing) the actual value of the output is 3.43 mV. According to the calculations above, the true output is within +1.57 mV of that reading. So the true reading is between

$$3.43 \text{ mV} + 1.57 \text{ mV} = 5.00 \text{ mV}$$

and

$$3.43 \text{ mV} - 1.57 \text{ mV} = 1.86 \text{ mV}$$

According to Table 3–2, the true value is 5.00 mV.

This type of analysis and a determination of the absolute error cannot be done with accuracy, specified as percent of reading. There is one other, often very serious mistake made when using accuracy expressed in percent of full scale and percent of reading.

EXAMPLE 3–4

It is necessary to measure the torque applied by a hydraulic motor to a shaft. An accuracy of 0.1 ft-lb is desired. The maximum torque to be applied is 20 ft-lb. A transducer with a full-scale rating of 100 ft-lb and 0.2% accuracy is available. Can the transducer be used?

Solution   The absolute error of the transducer is 0.2% of 100 ft-lb, or 0.2 ft-lb. The required absolute error is 0.1 ft-lb. So the available transducer will *not* work. It is very tempting to use the % FSO specification as if it were percentage of reading. This would have given an error of 0.2% of 20 ft-lb or 0.04 ft-lb. This is *wrong*.

Be careful to interpret and use the accuracy specifications as intended by the manufacturer.

Resolution is the smallest change at the input of the transducer that will result in a change in the output. It tells you how closely you can measure the input. The optical encoder in Figure 3–2 has four holes. Each time the shaft rotates $\frac{1}{4}$ of a revolution the beam is completed briefly. This produces a pulse that can be counted. The count indicates how much the shaft has been rotated. In this simple illustration, the shaft must turn 90° before the output (the displayed count) changes. So this encoder has a 90° resolution. Industrial-grade optical encoders provide between 100 and 1000 pulses per revolution.

Computers are widely used in industrial control. The number of bits produced by the analog-to-digital (A/D) converter places a bottom line on the resolution of the measurement. The resolution of an A/D converter is

$$\text{resolution} = 2^n$$

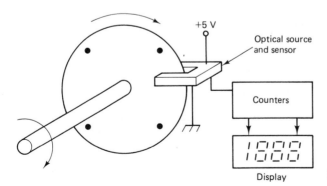

+5 V

Optical source and sensor

Counters

Display   **Figure 3–2**   Simple optical encoder.

EXAMPLE 3–5

A 2.5-m-long vane is rotated slowly in a circle. The motor and gears attach to the vane at its center. It is necessary to know the position of the vane within 2 cm. What must be the resolution of the optical encoder attached to the shaft that positions the vane? (Assume that the encoder is attached directly to the shaft without gearing.)

Solution   The circumference of a circle with a diameter of 2.5 m is

$$c = \pi d$$

$$= \pi (2.5 \text{ m})$$

$$= 7.854 \text{ m}$$

Using ratio and proportion gives us

$$\frac{\text{arc}}{360°} = \frac{2 \text{ cm}}{785.4 \text{ cm}}$$

$$\text{arc} = \frac{(360°)(2 \text{ cm})}{785.4 \text{ cm}} = 0.917°$$

So your encoder must be able to resolve 0.917°. The encoder must have

$$\frac{360°}{0.917°} = 392.6 \text{ pulses per revolution}$$

Of course, an encoder with more pulses per revolution will give finer resolution. So choose an encoder with 392.6 pulses per revolution or more.

---

where n is the number of bits in the binary word. So an 8-bit converter can resolve 1 part in 2^8 or 256. A 10-bit converter divided the analog signal into 1024 parts. Twelve bits gives 4096 resolution.

EXAMPLE 3–6

A temperature transducer that outputs 10 mV/°C is used to measure the temperature in a chamber that goes from 0 to 100°C. Can an 8-bit A/D converter with a 5-V full-scale input be used to produce a 1°C resolution?

Solution   An 8-bit A/D converter has a resolution of 1 part in 2^8 or 256. So for 5-V full-scale input, each bit is worth

$$\frac{5 \text{ V}}{256} = 19.5 \text{ mV}$$

A 1°C causes only a 10-mV input change. It appears that the converter does not have enough resolution. At maximum temperature, the transducer outputs

$$\frac{10 \text{ mV}}{°C} \times 100°C = 1 \text{ V}$$

This is nowhere near the full-scale input of the converter. So the solution is to amplify the transducer output by 5. Then 100°C produces 5 V, which matches the full-scale input of the converter. One degree Celsius now produces

$$V = 1°C \times 10 \text{ mV/°C} \times 5 = 50 \text{ mV}$$

Since the A/D converter's resolution is 19.5 mV, it can now resolve 0.39°C.

Repeatability is a measure of how well the output returns to a given value when the same precise input is applied several times. Be careful not to confuse repeatability with accuracy. These two specifications are compared to Example 3–7.

EXAMPLE 3–7

Three load cells similar to the one used in Example 3–1 are tested for repeatability. The same 50-kg weight is placed on each load cell 10 times. The resulting data are given in Table 3–3. Plot these data and discuss the repeatability and accuracy of each transducer.

TABLE 3–3 REPEATABILITY TEST FOR EXAMPLE 3–7

Trial no.	Load cell output (mV)		
	A	B	C
1	10.02	11.50	10.00
2	10.96	11.53	10.03
3	11.20	11.52	10.02
4	9.39	11.47	9.93
5	10.50	11.42	9.92
6	10.94	11.51	10.01
7	9.02	11.58	10.08
8	9.47	11.50	10.00
9	10.08	11.43	9.97
10	9.32	11.48	9.98
Maximum	11.20	11.58	10.08
Average	10.09	11.49	9.99
Minimum	9.02	11.42	9.92

Solution   The three load cells' tests are plotted in Figure 3–3. Load cell A has readings scattered widely about. The average of these readings is very near the proper value, but there is a wide distribution among the readings. Load cell A is accurate (sort of) but not repeatable. Load cell B has all of its readings tightly grouped, but grouped about the wrong average. This transducer is repeatable but not accurate. The readings for load cell C are tightly grouped about the correct reading. This is what you want. This transducer is both repeatable and accurate.

A transducer that is repeatable but not overly accurate may still be quite usable in a measurement or control application. As long as the transducer is repeatable, you will get consistent results. You can condition this wrong number with an amplifier or attenuator to correct any offset and scaling error. This electronic adjustment (called zero and span) will then produce a signal that is both repeatable and accurate. There is some disagreement over how to specify repeatability numerically. Some sources define repeatability as

$$\text{repeatability} = \frac{\text{maximum} - \text{minimum}}{\text{full scale}} \times 100\% \qquad (3\text{–}2)$$

Others say that

$$\text{repeatability} = \frac{\text{largest deviation} - \text{average}}{\text{full scale}} \times 100\% \qquad (3\text{–}3)$$

where the largest deviation is the reading farthest from the average, either above or below. When you use repeatability specifications, be sure you know how the manufacturer has calculated the number give.

Hysteresis is also an indication of the reproducibility of a transducer's output. A given input value when reached by increasing the input may produce an output that is different when reached by decreasing the input. This is the reason for two calibration runs, one increasing and one decreasing.

Look at Figure 3–4. Approaching 55 kg from below, by adding weight to the load cell, results in an output of 9.85 mV. However, after having run the load cell to full scale and then lowering the weight, at 55 kg, the transducer outputs 11.80 mV.

To calculate the hysteresis, you take the difference between the output on the decreasing run and the output on the increasing run at each point in the calibration record (Table 3–1). Report the largest of these as a percentage of the full-scale output.

Hysteresis is caused by the physical mechanism of the transducer taking some "set" as a result of its history (the inputs previously applied). So the amount of hysteresis exhibited depends on the magnitude of the previous inputs. In testing, you should run the input all the way to full scale before beginning the decrease. In practice, if the input the transducer is measuring does not make it to full scale, the resulting hysteresis will be less than specified.

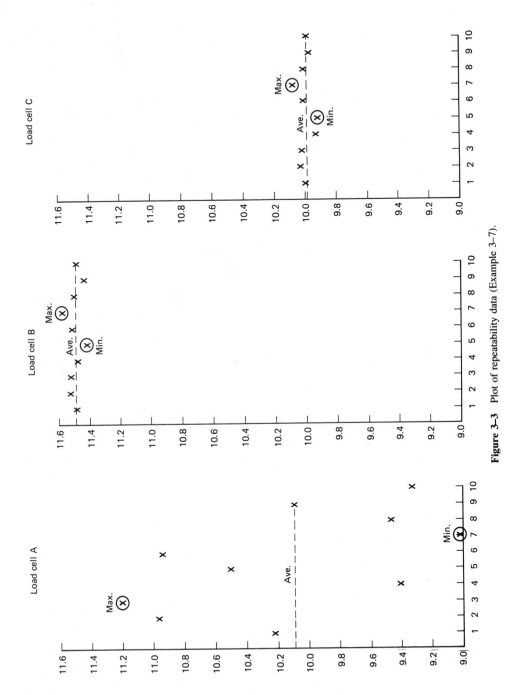

Figure 3–3 Plot of repeatability data (Example 3–7).

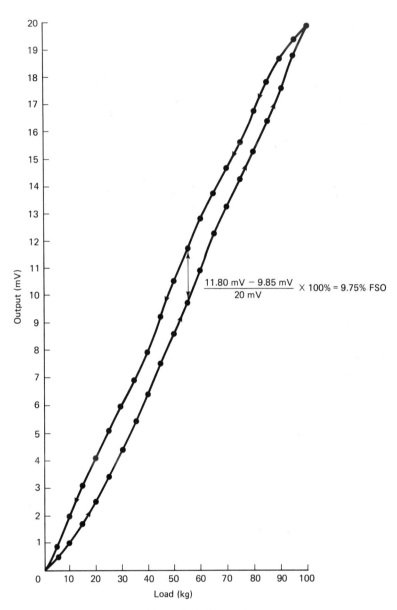

$$\frac{11.80 \text{ mV} - 9.85 \text{ mV}}{20 \text{ mV}} \times 100\% = 9.75\% \text{ FSO}$$

Figure 3–4 Hysteresis.

Also, remember that hysteresis is a *static* specification. Data are taken one point at a time, and then only after the transducer's output has stabilized. Inertia, or friction, will cause an effect that appears very similar to hysteresis. If you sweep the input, not allowing the output to settle before going to the next input value, inertia or friction may cause the output to lag. The resulting transducer transfer curve (input versus output) looks just like a hysteresis plot. The effect will become worse if you increase the input sweep rate. This is *not* hysteresis.

Ideally, the transfer curve of a transducer is a straight line. A given change in the input will have the same effect on the output, whether the output is at 25% of full-scale output or 75% of full-scale output.

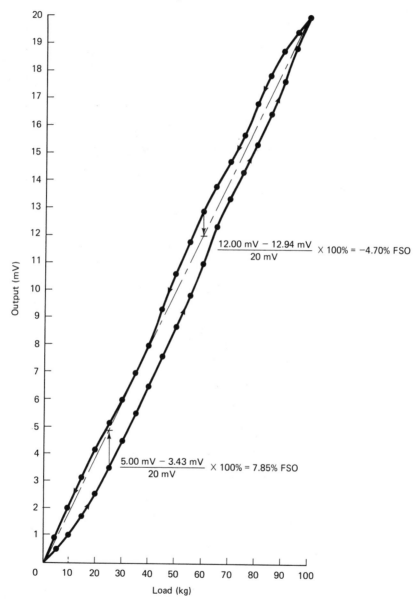

Figure 3–5 Endpoint linearity.

Linearity may be specified several different ways. Three of the more popular techniques are endpoint linearity, independent straight-line linearity, and least-squares (also called best-fit or linear regression) linearity.

For endpoint linearity, a straight line is drawn between the two endpoints of the calibration curve. If the theoretical value of zero and full-scale input and output are

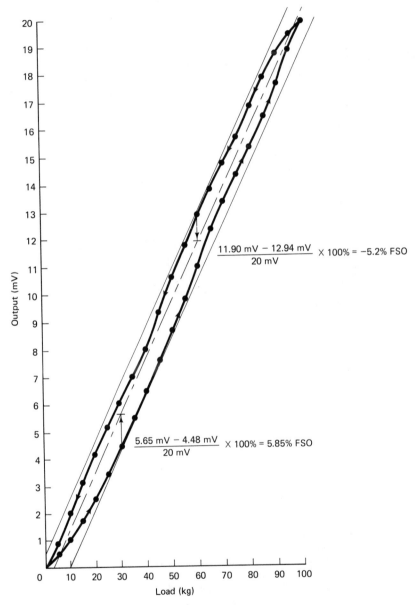

Figure 3–6 Independent straight-line linearity.

used, the resulting number is called the theoretical shape linearity. You then determine the maximum deviation both above and below that straight line. These are reported as +____% and −____% of full-scale output [1, pp. 33–34]. Look at Figure 3–5 and Table 3–2. To determine independent straight-line linearity, you draw two parallel straight lines which just enclose the calibration curve. The independent straight line is drawn halfway between these two boundaries. You then determine and report the maximum deviation from this single, centered straight line as +____%, −____% of full-scale output [1, pp. 33–34]. Refer to Figure 3–6.

Least-squares linearity is measured from a statistically derived straight line. "This is the straight line which the sum of the squared distances (error) is least or at a minimum" [2]. Given a set of *x*, *y* pairs, which is the calibration data (input value on the *x* axis, output on the *y*) you can calculate the equation of the straight line that yields minimum error [2].

$$x = \text{input values}$$

$$y = \text{output values}$$

$$m = \text{slope of straight line}$$

$$b = y \text{ intercept of the straight line}$$

$$n = \text{number of data points}$$

$$m = \frac{n \, \Sigma \, (xy) - \Sigma \, x \, \Sigma \, y}{n \, \Sigma \, (x^2) - (\Sigma \, x)^2} \tag{3-4}$$

$$b = \frac{\Sigma \, y}{n} - m \frac{\Sigma \, x}{n} \tag{3-5}$$

The calculation of the slope and the intercept of this best-fit (least-squares) straight line can get a bit tedious. Many calculators have this routine built in, or can be programmed to calculate *m* and *b* after you enter all the data points.

EXAMPLE 3–8

For the transducer data in Table 3–1, determine the least-squares (best-fit) line, plot it, and calculate the linearity.

Solution   Since the calibration curve has 21 points increasing and 21 points decreasing, there are really 42 points to be entered. Entering these points yields

$$m = 0.2079$$

$$b = -0.6368 \text{ mV}$$

The *y* intercept is plotted on Figure 3–7. Then the slope is used to determine a second point. The desired straight line can then be drawn between two points. The equation for this line is

$$v_{\text{out}} = \left(0.2079 \frac{\text{mV}}{\text{kg}}\right) \times l_{\text{input}} - 0.6368 \text{ mV}$$

To determine the linearity, you compute the straight-line value for each data point in Table 3–1 and compare these to the actual values. The largest deviations are at 40 kg input and 60 kg input. So

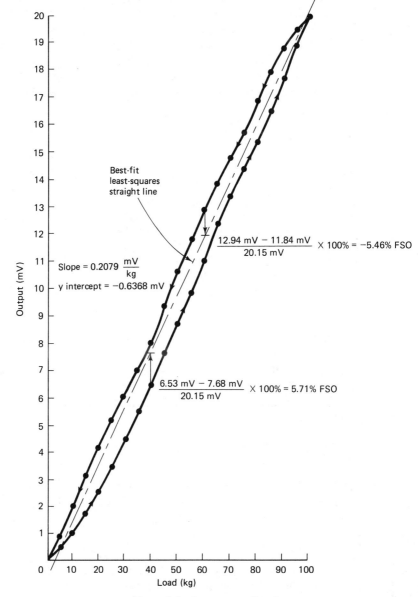

Figure 3–7 Least-squares linearity.

$$\% \text{ linearity} = \frac{+1.15\,\text{mV}}{20.15\,\text{mV}} \times 100\% = 5.71\%$$

and

$$\% \text{ linearity} = -\frac{1.10\,\text{mV}}{20.15\,\text{mV}} \times 100\% = -5.46\%$$

$$= 5.71\%, -5.46\% \text{ FSO}$$

3–1.2 Dynamic Specifications

All of the specifications presented in Section 3–1.1 were static. An input was applied to the transducer, the system allowed to respond and stabilize fully, and then the output was measured. In fact, if the transducer had not fully responded when its output was recorded, erroneous data would result. However, rarely is a transducer used in a static situation. The purpose of the transducer is to sense *changes* in its input and pass these along to a controller which can direct the system's performance. Therefore, how well the transducer responds to *changes* in its input is important to know. These are called dynamic specifications.

The dynamic performance of a transducer may be described two ways. The transducer's response to a step change at the input is specified by rise time, time constant, and dead time. If the transducer is second order (Section 2–6), the damping coefficient (ζ), resonant frequency (ω_n), settling time, or percent overshoot may be given. The second type of dynamic specification describes the transducer's response to a sinusodial input. A frequency response plot and the high-frequency cutoff may be specified.

The responses of first-order and second-order elements to a step were described in Chapter 2. However, the key parameters will be repeated here. The *rise time* is the length of time it takes the output to reach 10 to 90% of full response when a step is applied to the input. This is illustrated in Figure 3–8.

The *time constant* is used primarily to describe a first-order element. As described in Chapter 2, it is the time for the output to change by 63.2% of its maximum possible change. In Table 2–2 you saw that the element had responded 63.2% at the end of the first time constant. After three time constants, the response was within 5% of its final value. Four time constants put you within 2%. Response is considered complete after five time constants. This is illustrated in Figure 3–9.

Dead time is the length of time from the application of a step change at the input of the transducer until the output *begins* to change. The response of a transducer with both dead time and a time constant (first order) is shown in Figure 3–10. The mathematics, consequences, and precautions for handling an element with dead time are discussed more fully in Section 2–5.

First-order elements are characterized by their time constant (as in Figure 3–9). The dynamic response of transducers with second-order transfer function is defined by its damping *coefficient* (ζ) and its *resonant frequency* (ω_n). These concepts are discussed

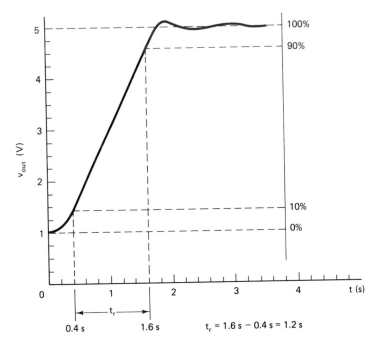

Figure 3–8 Rise time.

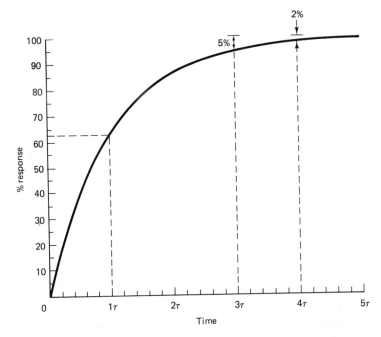

Figure 3–9 Time constant.

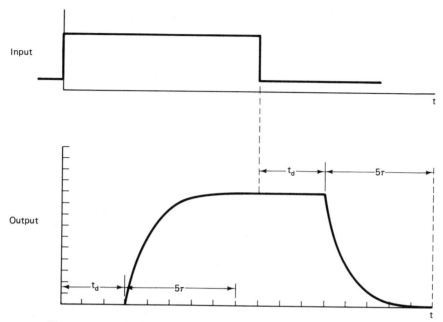

Figure 3–10   Response of a transducer with both dead time and a time constant.

in detail in Section 2–6. Damping coefficient and resonant frequency determine the shape and response time of a second-order transducer's response to a step input.

Look at Figure 3–11. This is the same as Figure 2–12. The vertical axis is % response. All curves eventually settle into 1.0 (100%). The horizontal axis is presented in units of $\omega_n t$. To scale that axis in seconds, divide each number by the natural resonance frequency specification of the transducer (ω_n). Each curve represents a different damping coefficient (ζ). If the transducer is

Overdamped	then	$\zeta > 1$
Critically damped	then	$\zeta = 1$
Underdamped	then	$\zeta < 1$

Overshoot occurs for underdamped transducers. The *percent overshoot* is a measure of the initial peak, as compared to the steady-state value.

$$\% \text{ overshoot} = \frac{m_p - \text{steady state}}{\text{steady state}} \times 100\%$$

It is strictly dependent on the damping coefficient:

But how long do you have to wait until the transducer is giving you a good output? *Settling time* will tell you. The 2% settling time is the time it takes from the application of the input step until the output has settled (for the last time) within a band ±2% of its final value. This is illustrated in Figure 3–12.

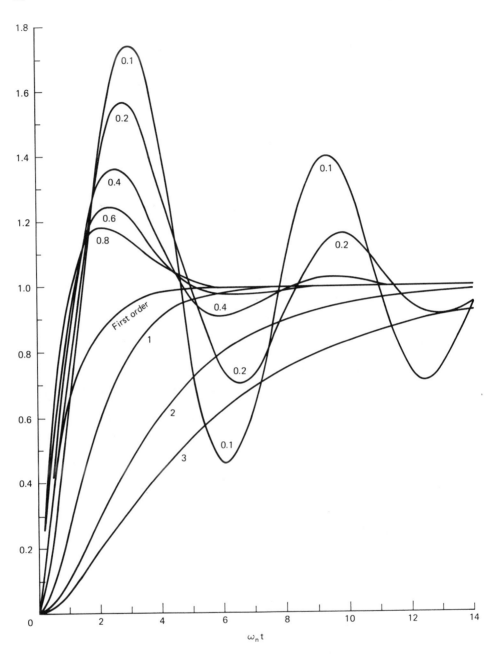

Figure 3–11 Normalized response to a step.

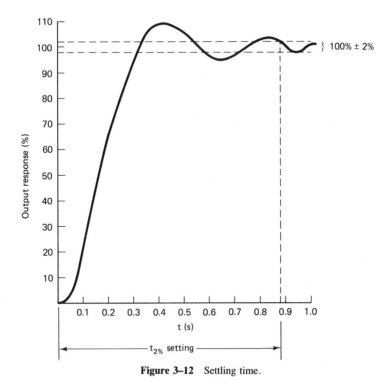

Figure 3–12   Settling time.

Frequency response and the high-frequency cutoff are the two specifications that describe the response of a transducer to a sine wave at its input. For a reasonably linear transducer, a sine wave in will yield a sine wave out. As the frequency of the input goes up, the transducer is required to respond more and more quickly. Eventually, the transducer can no longer respond as rapidly as its input is changing. So the output of the transducers becomes smaller. As the input frequency increases, the output amplitude continues to fall. This roll-off of output amplitude with an increase of input frequency is the frequency response. It is illustrated in a frequency response plot such as Figure 3–13. The vertical axis is the gain of the transducer. This may simply be the output/input ratio. However, often the gain is plotted in decibels.

$$dB = 20 \log \frac{output}{input}$$

The horizontal axis is logarithmic, not linear. This allows a wider frequency range to be displayed.

The high-frequency cutoff (f_h) is that frequency at which the transducer's gain has fallen to 0.707 of the value it had at its stable low frequency. If the vertical axis is scaled in decibels, f_h occurs when the gain does decreased by -3 dB.

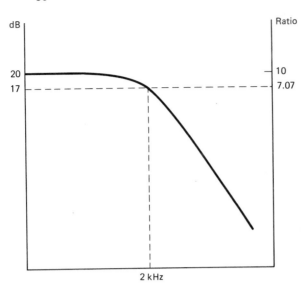

Figure 3–13 Frequency response plots.

EXAMPLE 3–9

Determine the high-frequency cutoff of the transducer whose frequency response is plotted in Figure 3–13.

Solution The transducer's low-frequency gain is 20 dB. This corresponds to a ratio of 10. The high-frequency cutoff is the frequency where that gain has fallen by −3 dB (or a ratio reduction of 0.707). This gives a decible gain of 17 dB and a ratio gain of 7.07. The intersection of the 17-dB line with the frequency response plot occurs at 2 kHz.

Since a transducer rarely has a sinusoid for an input, is there any real value in knowing the high-frequency cutoff? The high-frequency cutoff can be related to the rise time by

$$t_r = \frac{0.35}{f_h}$$

So even if the transient response specifications are not given, you can determine the speed of a transducer from its high-frequency cutoff.

3–2 POSITION TRANSDUCERS

The location of an item is of primary concern in many servo control systems. Automated assembly using robots demands precise positioning. Milling, shaping, and drilling of machine parts as well as the movement of the head on a computer's disk drive or the pen on a plotter require the control (and therefore measurement) of position. Thickness control of film or the effects of thermal expansion on a part require measurement of position with resolution to the fraction of a millimeter. Surveying for the foundation of a multistory building demands displacement measurements with equal accuracy, but with a range of hundreds of meters. Throughout the technical world, location is an important parameter to know.

Techniques for measuring position are diverse. You will see three here. Potentiometers are inexpensive and easy to use. Linear variable differential transformers (LVDTs) allow you to measure very small displacements. Optical encoders are rugged and easily interfaced to a computer.

3–2.1 Potentiometers

Potentiometers used to measure displacement appear very similar to those you may have used to make adjustments in any basic electrical or electronic circuit. However, much more attention and effort are given to all of the details in displacement potentiometer manufacturing.

Linear potentiometers for straight-line displacement and angular potentiometers for rotary displacement measurements are available. The basic outlines are shown in Figure 3–14. Full-scale angular displacement as small as 10° is available. A full single-

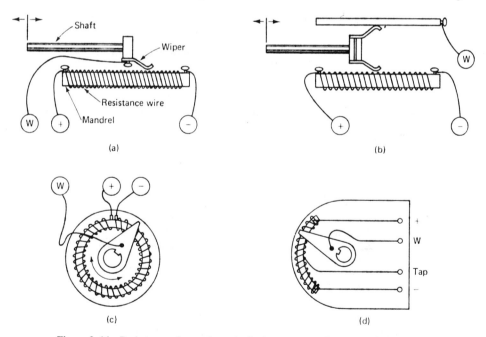

Figure 3–14   Basic types of potentiometric displacement transducers: (a) linear (basis); (b) linear (with wiper bus); (c) angular (single turn); (d) angular (sector, tapped). [From Harry N. Norton, *Sensor and Analyzer Handbook* (Englewood Cliffs, N.J.: Prentice-Hall, Inc., 1982), p. 100.]

turn potentiometer may provide accurate measurement up to 357°. Multiturn potentiometers may measure up to 3500° of rotation. This is done by using a helically shaped resistive body. The wiper moves around and up the helix as it is turned [1, pp. 100–101].

The resistive body of potentiometers may be wirewound. A very thin (0.01 mm diameter) wire of platinum or nickel alloy is carefully wound on a form [1, pp. 100–101]. As the wiper is moved from winding to winding the resistance between it and either end varies. The smallest change in position that can be detected (i.e., the resolution) occurs when the wiper moves from one turn to the next. So numerically, the resolution is

$$\text{resolution} = \frac{\text{full-scale displacement}}{\text{number of turns of wire}}$$

EXAMPLE 3–10

It is necessary to measure the position of a panel. It moves 0.8 m. Its position must be known within 0.1 cm. Part of the mechanism which moves the panel is a shaft that rotates 250° when the panel is moved from one extreme to the other. A control potentiometer has been found which is rated at 300° full-scale movement. It has 1000 turns of wire. Can this be used?

Solution   The shaft provides a

$$\frac{250°}{0.8 \text{ m}} = 312.5°/\text{m or } 3.125°/\text{cm}$$

conversion. A resolution of 0.1 cm at the panel translates into

$$0.1 \text{ cm} \times 3.125°/\text{cm} = 0.3125°$$

required resolution for the potentiometer. The potentiometer actually has a resolution of

$$\frac{300°}{1000} = 0.300°$$

The potentiometer can detect a change of 0.3°, which is finer than the required 0.3125°. So the available potentiometer *will* work.

If the shape of the body that the wire is wound on is kept accurately uniform, there will be a linear relationship between the position of the wiper and the output voltage. However, varying the body shape will cause a prescribed, nonlinear transfer function. This is illustrated in Figure 3–15.

There are many standard functions available, or custom position-to-voltage relationships that can be produced. This nonlinear relationship may be used to compensate for a nonlinearity in the item being measured or to introduce a special function into the control scheme without having to resort to special mathematics electronics or a computer.

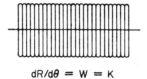

$$dR/d\theta = W = K$$

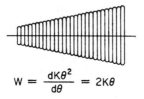

$$W = \frac{dK\theta^2}{d\theta} = 2K\theta$$

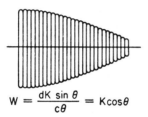

$$W = \frac{dK\,\sin\,\theta}{c\theta} = K\cos\theta$$

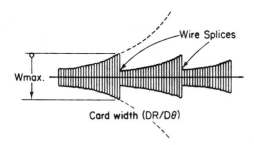

Wire Splices

Wmax.

Card width (DR/Dθ)

Figure 3–15   Typical card shapes.
(Courtesy of Bourns, Inc.)

Standard functions are shown in Figure 3–16. As you look at these diagrams, remember that what you are seeing is the output voltage as the potentiometer is rotated continuously from one extreme to the other.

Continuous potentiometers have a body made of carbon film, metal film, conductive plastic, or ceramic metal ("cermet"). These potentiometers have several advantages over those that are wirewound. First, the resolution may be much higher, since it is no longer limited by the number of turns that can be wrapped onto the body. Since the wiper moves across a smooth surface (not bouncing from turn to turn), wear, bounce, and the resulting failures are decreased. The maximum speed that a wirewound potentiometer may be turned is about 300 r/min. Above that, the noise created as the wiper bounces from turn to turn becomes significant. A continuous potentiometer may be turned at speeds of 2000 r/min [3, pp. 20, 24].

"It is essential to know a number of different electrical characteristics in order to understand and specify potentiometers. These include: resolution (travel, voltage, theoretical), linearity/conformity (terminal-based, zero based, independent), resistance tolerance, tap location, power rating, noise, starting and running torque, moment of inertia, ac characteristics, and electrical overtravel" [3, p. 16]. You have already read about resolution and linearity in Section 3–1. Since most potentiometers are used to produce a voltage, the exact total body resistance is not nearly as important as the accuracy of the voltage supplying the potentiometer. However, you should observe the power rating,

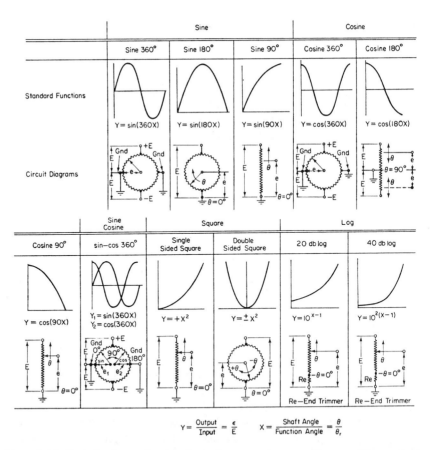

Figure 3–16   Typical resistance functions for nonlinear potentiometers. (Courtesy of Bourns, Inc.)

ambient temperature, and self-heating carefully. The interplay of these parameters is shown in Example 3–11.

EXAMPLE 3–11

A control potentiometer is rated as

150 Ω

1 W (derate at 10 mW/°C above 60°C)

30°C/W thermal resistance

Can it be used with a 10-V supply at 80°C ambient temperature?

Solution   The power dissipated by the potentiometer is

$$P = \frac{E^2}{R} = \frac{(10 \text{ V})^2}{150 \text{ } \Omega}$$
$$= 667 \text{ mW}$$

The actual temperature of the potentiometer depends on the ambient temperature and the rise in temperature caused by the power the potentiometer is dissipating (self-heating).

$$T_{\text{pot}} = T_{\text{ambient}} + P\Theta$$
$$= 80°C + (667 \text{ mW})(30°C/W)$$
$$= 80°C + 20°C$$
$$= 100°C$$

The allowable power dissipation must be derated (decreased) by 10 mW for each degree above 65°C.

$$P_{\text{allowed}} = P_{\text{rated}} - (T_{\text{pot}} - 65°C)(10 \text{ mW}/°C)$$
$$= 1 \text{ W} - (100°C - 65°C)(10 \text{ mW}/°C)$$
$$= 1 \text{ W} - 350 \text{ mW}$$
$$= 650 \text{ mW}$$

At first glance it would appear that the potentiometer is well below the 1-W rated power dissipation. However, when you derate for temperature and account for self-heating, the maximum power dissipation is 650 mW, below the actual 667 mW. This potentiometer will fail.

Noise can be generated by the material of the potentiometers. Several mechanisms combine, however. All are directly proportional to either temperatures or current. So to minimize self-generated noise, keep the supply voltage as low as practical. Noise is also produced as the wiper bounces along. Continuous potentiometers can be turned more rapidly and produce less noise than wirewound potentiometers.

Wirewound potentiometers also exhibit series inductance and capacitance between windings. At 60 Hz this reactance may be in the megohm range. But if you excite the potentiometer with a 10-kHz sine wave, this reactance may drop into the kilohms. If you are using ac excitation, keep both the frequency and the basic resistance as low as practical.

Electrical overtravel refers to the fact that the terminals may not be at the exact end of the body. This means that once the wiper reaches the terminal, the shaft may be turned more but the output voltage will not change [3, pp. 16–24].

There are several ways to connect potentiometers into a control system. The simplest is to drive one end with a ground-referenced voltage, and ground the other end. This is shown in Figure 3–17a. This causes zero volts out when the wiper has been driven all the way to the bottom, and V_{supply} out when the wiper is at the top. See Figure 3–17b. This configuration is useful if the wiper is not driven to the extremes of the potentiometer. The zero adjustment allows you to place zero volts at whatever position on the potentiometer you desire. Similarly, the full-scale adjustment lets you calibrate

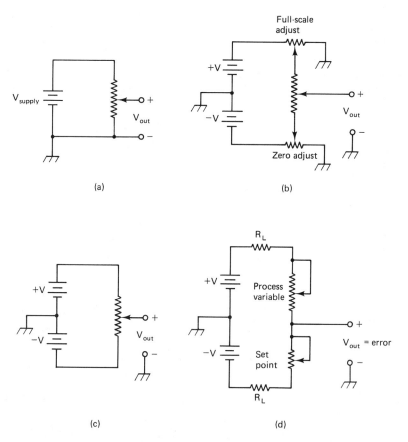

Figure 3–17 Potentiometer connections: (a) simple; (b) adjustable; (c) double-ended; (d) error output.

the output voltage to some convenient value when the wiper has been driven as far up as it will be. Several iterations of increasing finer adjustment will be necessary, since these two adjustments are interdependent.

Driving both ends of the potentiometer places zero volts in the center of the potentiometer. This is shown in Figure 3–17c. A modification of this can be used to produce a ground-referenced error signal for use by a controller. Look at Figure 3–17d. The set point is a potentiometer located on a control panel. The process variable is driven by the parameter being measured. Error is defined as

$$\text{error} = \text{SP} - \text{PV}$$

If the set point and process variable are at the same location (same resistance), there is no error and the output voltage is at zero. If the wiper on the set point is moved up, its resistance is raised. This makes V_{out} go positive. The process should then respond by moving the wiper on the process variable potentiometer up proporportionally. V_{out} is returned to zero volts. The opposite happens if the set point is lowered. Resistors R_L are added to limit current flow when the set point is moved all the way down.

All of the discussion to this point has assumed no loadings. However, in reality, each position potentiometer transducer must drive a load. This load can produce a nonlinearity several orders of magnitude worse than the transducer itself. Look at Figure 3–18. The desired output (assuming no loading) is

$$V_{\text{desired}} = \frac{R_1}{R_1 + R_2} V_{\text{in}}$$

However, R_L parallels R_1, so its effect must be considered.

$$V_{\text{actual}} = \frac{[R_1 R_L/(R_1 + R_L)] \, V_{\text{in}}}{[R_1 R_L/(R_1 + R_L)] + R_2}$$

Algebraic simplification yields

$$V_{\text{actual}} = \frac{R_1 R_L}{R_1 R_L + R_1 R_2 + R_2 R_L} V_{\text{in}} \tag{3–6}$$

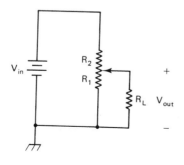

Figure 3–18 Potentiometer loading.

EXAMPLE 3–12

Plot the transfer curve and determine endpoint linearity of a 1-kΩ potentiometer driving a 5-kΩ load, powered from a 10-V source.

Solution   The desired and actual values are presented in Table 3–4. These are obtained at 50-Ω steps of the wiper (R_1). Even if the load is five times the resistance of the potentiometers, more than 2.5% error is produced by the load (Figure 3–19).

TABLE 3–4 NONLINEARITY OF A POTENTIOMETER CAUSED BY LOADING FOR EXAMPLE 3–12

R_1 (Ω)	R_2 (Ω)	$V_{desired}$ (V)	V_{actual} (V)	% Deviation of full scale
0	0	0.0	0	0
50	950	0.5	0.4953	0.05
100	900	1.0	0.9823	0.18
150	850	1.5	1.4627	0.37
200	800	2.0	1.9380	0.62
250	750	2.5	2.4096	0.90
300	700	3.0	2.8791	1.21
350	650	3.5	3.3477	1.52
400	600	4.0	3.8168	1.83
450	550	4.5	4.2878	2.12
500	500	5.0	4.7619	2.38
550	450	5.5	5.2406	2.59
600	400	6.0	5.7252	2.75
650	350	6.5	6.2171	2.83
700	300	7.0	6.7179	2.82
750	250	7.5	7.2289	2.71
800	200	8.0	7.7519	2.48
850	150	8.5	8.2886	2.11
900	100	9.0	8.8409	1.59
950	50	9.5	9.4106	0.89
1000	0	10.0	10.0000	0

You can use a computer to solve equation 3–6 over and over, each time for different values of R_1 and R_2, each time determining the worst-case endpoint nonlinearity. You then repeat this procedure for different values of R_L. The results of all these iterations are shown in Table 3–5. The first column gives the endpoint nonlinearity caused by load (as a percent of full scale). The second column is the ratio of load resistance to full resistance of the potentiometer necessary to achieve that nonlinearity.

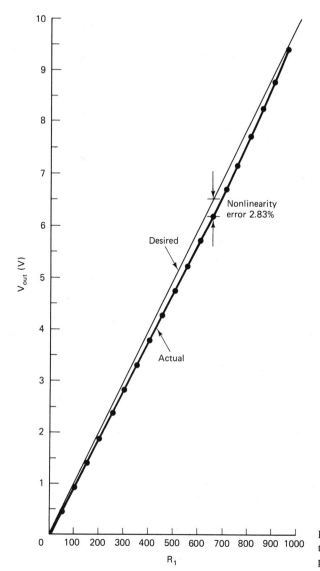

Figure 3–19 Nonlinearity of a potentiometer caused by loading (Example 3–12).

TABLE 3–5
LOADING EFFECTS ON
THE NONLINEARITY OF
A POTENTIOMETER

Error (%)	$\dfrac{R_L}{R_p}$
10	1.263
5	2.742
1	14.59
0.5	29.41
0.1	147.9
0.05	296.1

EXAMPLE 3-13

A position measurement may have a nonlinearity of no more than 0.5% when driving a 10-kΩ load resistance. What size potentiometer should you use?

Solution   From Table 3-5, for a nonlinearity of 0.5%,

$$\frac{R_L}{R_p} = 29.41$$

So

$$R_p = \frac{R_L}{29.41}$$
$$= \frac{10\ k\Omega}{29.41}$$
$$= 340\ \Omega$$

You must choose a potentiometer with a resistance *less* than 340 Ω.

3-2.2 Linear and Rotary Variable Differential Transformers*

"The LVDT (linear variable differential transformer) is an electromechanical device that produces an electrical output proportional to the displacement of a separate movable core. It consists of a primary coil and two secondary coils symmetrically spaced on a cylindrical form. A free-moving rod-shaped magnetic core inside the coil assembly provides a path for the magnetic flux linking the coils. A cross section of the LVDT and a plot of its operating characteristics are shown in Figures 3-20 and 3-21.

"When the primary coil is energized by an external ac source, voltages are induced in the two secondary coils." Look at the schematic in Figure 3-22. "These are connected in series opposing so the two voltages are opposite polarity. Therefore, the net output of the transducer is the difference between these voltages, which is zero when the core is at the center or null position. When the core is moved from the null position, the induced voltage in the coil toward which the core is moved increases, while the induced voltage in the opposite coil decreases. This action produces a differential voltage output that varies linearity with changes in core position. The phase of this output voltage changes abruptly by 180° as the core is moved from one side of null to the other."

Typical specifications of a general-purpose LVDT transducer are given in Figure 3-23. Notice that full scale ranges from 0.050 to 10.00 in. With a 0.25% full-scale linearity, this allows measurements down to 0.000125 in. However, the dynamic response (which is not clearly specified) must be considerably slower than the 2.5-kHz excitation signal.

---

* The quoted material in Section 3-2.2 is from Ref. 4.

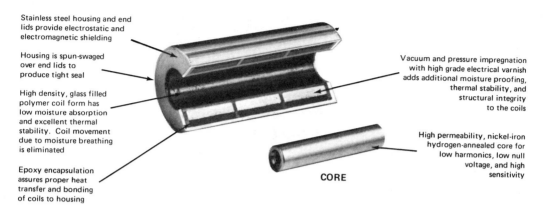

Stainless steel housing and end lids provide electrostatic and electromagnetic shielding

Housing is spun-swaged over end lids to produce tight seal

High density, glass filled polymer coil form has low moisture absorption and excellent thermal stability. Coil movement due to moisture breathing is eliminated

Epoxy encapsulation assures proper heat transfer and bonding of coils to housing

Vacuum and pressure impregnation with high grade electrical varnish adds additional moisture proofing, thermal stability, and structural integrity to the coils

High permeability, nickel-iron hydrogen-annealed core for low harmonics, low null voltage, and high sensitivity

CORE

Figure 3–20   Cutaway view of the Schaevitz AC LVDT. (Courtesy of Schaevitz Engineering.)

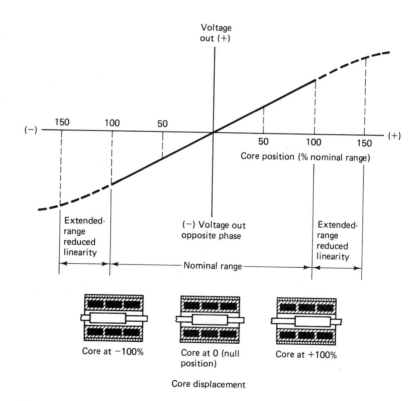

Figure 3–21   LVDT output voltage and phase as a function of core position. (Courtesy of Schaevitz Engineering.)

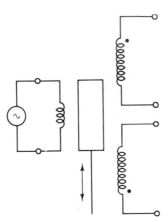

Figure 3–22 LVDT schematic.

"The LVDT has many commendable features that make it useful for a wide variety of applications. Some of these features are unique to the LVDT and are not available in any other transducers (element). The features arise from the basic fact that the LVDT is an electrical transformer with a separable noncontacting core.

"Ordinarily, there is no physical contact between the movable core and coil structure, which means that the LVDT is a frictionless device. This permits its use in critical measurements that can tolerate the addition of the low-mass core but cannot tolerate friction loading. Two examples of such applications are dynamic deflection or vibration tests of delicate materials and tensile or creep tests on fibers or other highly elastic materials.

"The absence of friction and contact between the coil and core of an LVDT means that there is nothing to wear out. This gives an LVDT essentially infinite mechanical life. This is a paramount requirement in applications such as the fatigue-life testing of materials and structures. The infinite mechanical life is also important in high-reliability mechanisms and systems found in aircraft, missiles, space vehicles, and critical industrial equipment.

"The frictionless operation of the LVDT combined with the induction principle by which the LVDT functions is truly infinite resolution. This means that the LVDT can respond to even the most minute motion of the core and produce an output. The readability of the external electronics represents the only limitation on resolution.

"The separation between LVDT core and LVDT coil permits the isolation of media such as pressurized, corrosive, or caustic fluids from the coil assembly by a nonmagnetic barrier interposed between the core and the inside of the coil. It also makes the hermatic sealing of the coil assembly possible and eliminates the need for a dynamic seal on the moving member. Only a static seal is necessary to seal the coil assembly within the pressurized system.

"The fact that the LVDT is a transformer means that there is complete isolation between excitation input (primary) and output (secondaries). This makes an LVDT an effective analog computing element without the need for buffer amplifiers. It also facilitates the isolation of the signal ground from excitation ground in high-performance measurement and control loops.

HR SERIES—GENERAL APPLICATIONS

- OPTIMUM PERFORMANCE FOR THE MAJORITY OF APPLICATIONS

- LARGE CORE-TO-BORE CLEARANCE — 1/16 INCH (1.6 mm) RADIAL

The HR high reliability series of LVDT's is suitable for most general applications. The HR series features large core-to-bore clearance, high output voltage over a broad range of excitation frequencies, and a magnetic stainless steel case for electromagnetic and electrostatic shielding.

GENERAL SPECIFICATIONS

Input Voltage . . . . . 3 V rms (nominal)
Frequency Range . . . 50 Hz to 10 kHz
Temperature Range . . −65°F to +300°F
(−55°C to +150°C)
Null Voltage . . . . . . Less than 0.5% full scale output
Shock Survival . . . . . 1000 g for 11 milliseconds

Vibration Tolerance . . 20 g up to 2 kHz
Coil Form Material . . . High density, glass- filled polymer
Housing Material . . . AISI 400 series stainless steel
Lead Wires . . . . 28 AWG, stranded copper, Teflon-insulated, 12 inches (300 mm) long (nominal)

PERFORMANCE SPECIFICATIONS AND DIMENSIONS (2.5 kHz)

LVDT MODEL NUMBER	NOMINAL LINEAR RANGE	LINEARITY ±PERCENT FULL RANGE				SENSITIVITY mV Out/ Volt In Per	IMPEDANCE Ohms		PHASE SHIFT	WEIGHT Grams		DIMENSIONS	
												A (Body)	B (Core)
	Inches	50	100	125	150	.001 In.	Pri.	Sec.	Degrees	Body	Core	Inches	Inches
050 HR	±0.050	0.10	0.25	0.25	0.50	6.3	430	4000	−1	32	4	1.13	0.80
100 HR	±0.100	0.10	0.25	0.25	0.50	4.5	1070	5000	−5	48	6	1.81	1.30
200 HR	±0.200	0.10	0.25	0.25	0.50	2.5	1150	4000	−4	60	8	2.50	1.65
300 HR	±0.300	0.10	0.25	0.35	0.50	1.4	1100	2700	−11	77	10	3.22	1.95
400 HR	±0.400	0.15	0.25	0.35	0.60	0.90	1700	3000	−18	90	15	4.36	2.95
500 HR	±0.500	0.15	0.25	0.35	0.75	0.73	460	375	−1	109	18	5.50	3.45
1000 HR	±1.000	0.25	0.25	1.00	1.30*	0.39	460	320	−3	126	21	6.63	4.00
2000 HR	±2.000	0.25	0.25	0.50*	1.00*	0.24	330	330	+5	168	27	10.00	5.30
3000 HR	±3.000	0.15	0.25	0.50*	1.00*	0.27	115	375	+11	225	28	12.81	5.60
4000 HR	±4.000	0.15	0.25	0.50*	1.00*	0.22	275	550	+1	295	36	15.64	7.00
5000 HR	±5.000	0.15	0.25	1.00*	—	0.15	310	400	+3	340	36	17.88	7.00
10000 HR	±10.00	0.15	0.25	1.00*	—	0.08	550	750	−5	580	43	30.84	8.50

*Requires reduced core length

ORDERING INFORMATION

(Fold out page 32 for instructions on how to use this chart.)

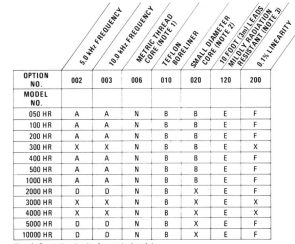

OPTION NO.	002	003	006	010	020	120	200
MODEL NO.							
050 HR	A	A	N	B	B	E	F
100 HR	A	A	N	B	B	E	F
200 HR	A	A	N	B	B	E	F
300 HR	X	X	N	B	B	E	X
400 HR	A	A	N	B	B	E	F
500 HR	A	A	N	B	B	E	F
1000 HR	A	A	N	B	B	E	F
2000 HR	D	D	N	B	X	E	F
3000 HR	X	X	N	B	X	E	X
4000 HR	X	X	N	B	X	E	X
5000 HR	D	D	N	B	X	E	F
10000 HR	D	D	N	B	X	E	F

Note 1: See outline drawing for metric thread size
Note 2: Consult factory for mass, dimensions, and thread size
Note 3: Withstands 10^{12} NVT total integrated flux

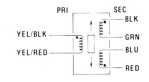

CONNECT GRN TO BLU FOR DIFFERENTIAL OUTPUT

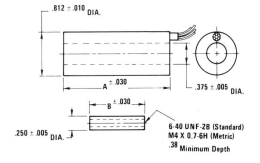

Figure 3–23 LVDT specifications. (Courtesy of Schaevitz Engineering.)

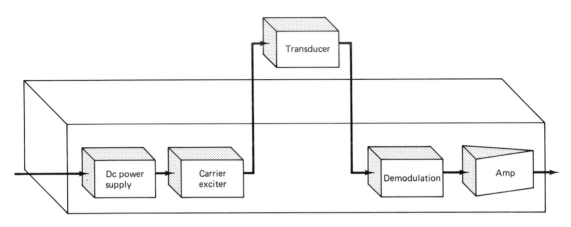

Figure 3–24 LVDT transducer instrumentation. (Courtesy of Schaevitz Engineering.)

"The instrumentation used with an LVDT-type transducer must fulfill several functions at one time if the transducer is to operate properly. The block diagram illustrates these functions for any measurement involving LVDT-type transducers." See Figure 3–24. "An LVDT requires a constant amplitude ac voltage at a frequency not readily available. This means that an oscillator of the appropriate frequency must be connected to an amplifier with amplitude regulation in its output.

"An LVDT's output is usually too low-level to operate ordinary readouts, so it is necessary to amplify the output of the LVDT. Sometimes this is done in two steps, using an ac carrier amplifier prior to demodulation and a dc amplifier after demodulation.

"Most readouts are dc-operated devices, so the amplified ac output must be converted into filtered dc before it can be used with ordinary dc-type readout devices. Furthermore, to take advantage of the phase polarity of an LVDT requires the use of a synchronous demodulator. Most demodulators are followed by one or more stages of low-pass filtering. All of the electronic circuits require stable dc voltages for proper operation."

Fortunately, you do not have to build this instrumentation from scratch. There are several commercial LVDT instrumentation packages. Figure 3–25 is an example of one of these. If you prefer to package your own systems, Signetics manufactures the NE/SE5520. It is a single monolithic integrated circuit which provides a variable-frequency sine-wave generator, primary booster amplifier, secondary signal amplification, synchronous demodulation, and demodulated dc amplification. The basic specifications are given in Figure 3–26. Figure 3–27 shows a typical application.

"The rotary variable differential transformer is a device for producing a voltage whose magnitude varies linearly with the angular position of the shaft. A specially shaped ferromagnetic rotor simulates the linear displacement of the straight cylindrical core of a linear differential transformer. There are no slip rings to produce mechanical friction or induce electrical noise because the coupling between the stationary windings and the rotor is electromagnetic only. The miniture precision ball bearings which support the operating shaft are the only friction-producing elements.

"Although an RVDT is capable of continuous rotation, most RVDTs operate

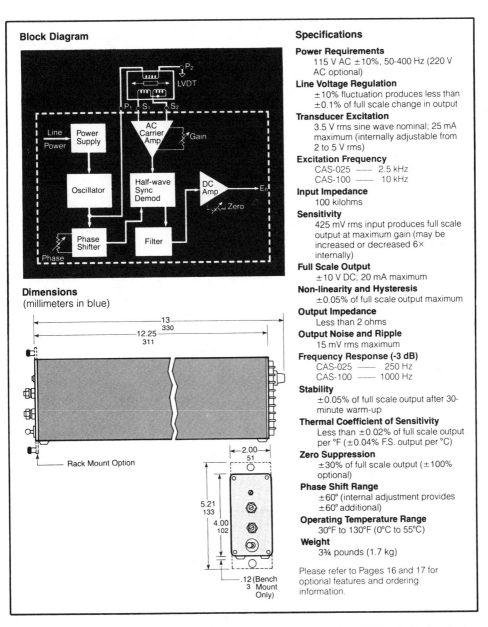

Block Diagram

Dimensions
(millimeters in blue)

Rack Mount Option

Specifications

Power Requirements
115 V AC ±10%, 50-400 Hz (220 V AC optional)

Line Voltage Regulation
±10% fluctuation produces less than ±0.1% of full scale change in output

Transducer Excitation
3.5 V rms sine wave nominal; 25 mA maximum (internally adjustable from 2 to 5 V rms)

Excitation Frequency
CAS-025 ——— 2.5 kHz
CAS-100 ——— 10 kHz

Input Impedance
100 kilohms

Sensitivity
425 mV rms input produces full scale output at maximum gain (may be increased or decreased 6× internally)

Full Scale Output
±10 V DC; 20 mA maximum

Non-linearity and Hysteresis
±0.05% of full scale output maximum

Output Impedance
Less than 2 ohms

Output Noise and Ripple
15 mV rms maximum

Frequency Response (-3 dB)
CAS-025 ——— 250 Hz
CAS-100 ——— 1000 Hz

Stability
±0.05% of full scale output after 30-minute warm-up

Thermal Coefficient of Sensitivity
Less than ±0.02% of full scale output per °F (±0.04% F.S. output per °C)

Zero Suppression
±30% of full scale output (±100% optional)

Phase Shift Range
±60° (internal adjustment provides ±60° additional)

Operating Temperature Range
30°F to 130°F (0°C to 55°C)

Weight
3¾ pounds (1.7 kg)

Please refer to Pages 16 and 17 for optional features and ordering information.

Figure 3–25   LVDT instrumentation package. (Courtesy of Schaevitz Engineering.)

DESCRIPTION

The NE/SE5520 is a signal conditioning circuit for use with Linear Variable Differential Transformers (LVDT). The chip includes a low distortion amplitude stable sine wave oscillator with programmable frequency to drive the primary of the LVDT; a synchronous demodulator to convert the LVDT output amplitude and phase to position information; and an output amp to provide gain and filtering.

FEATURES

- Oscillator frequency: 1kHz to 20kHz
- Low distortion <5%
- Capable of ratiometric operation
- Single supply operation 5 to 25V or dual supply ±5 to ±12V
- Low power consumption

APPLICATIONS

- LVDT signal conditioning
- RVDT signal conditioning

PIN CONFIGURATION

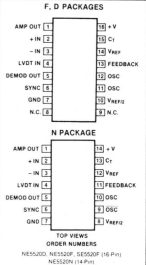

ABSOLUTE MAXIMUM RATINGS

PARAMETER	RATING	UNIT
Supply voltage	+30	V
Split supply voltage	(±15)	V
Operating temperature range		
SE5520	−55 to +125	°C
NE5520	0 to +70	°C
Storage temperature range	−65 to 150	°C

BLOCK DIAGRAM

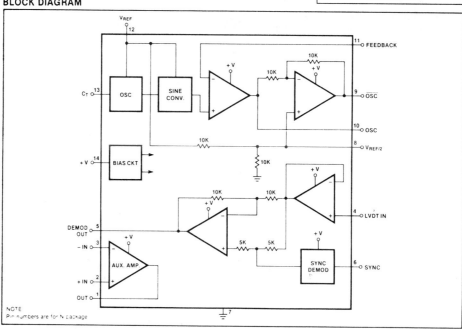

Figure 3–26   Signetics NE/SE 5520 with a LVDT. (Courtesy of Signetics.)

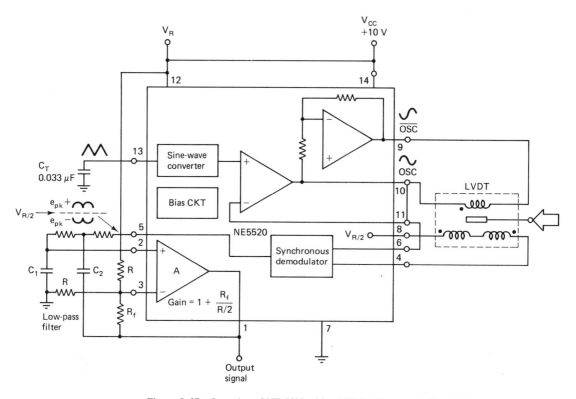

Figure 3–27   Operation of NE 5520 with a LVDT. (Courtesy of Signetics.)

within a range of $\pm 40°$. Within this range, linearity is better than $\pm 0.5\%$ of full scale displacement. However, over small angular displacements, linearity improves substantially. For example, the linearity for a displacement angle of $\pm 5°$ is better than 0.1% of full scale.

The practical upper limit of an RVDT's angular displacement is approximately $\pm 60°$. Resolution, on the other hand, is essentially infinite. For small angular displacements, resolutions to a very small fraction of a degree are quite common." The output curve of an RVTD is given in Figure 3–28.

"In practice, only one of the two linear regions is calibrated at the factory. The null position corresponding to this factory-calibrated region is identified by appropriate marks on both the body and shaft. As with the LVDT, the RVDT's output voltage characteristic shifts $180°$ in phase around a null or zero shaft angle position.

"The ac-operated RVDTs require an ac voltage to energize their primary coil. They produce an ac voltage from their secondary (output) coils directly proportional to shaft position. The dc-operated RVDT accepts a dc input voltage that is internally converted to an ac carrier for exciting the primary coil. An integral demodulator and filter convert the secondary coil voltage into a smooth dc output signal which is subse-

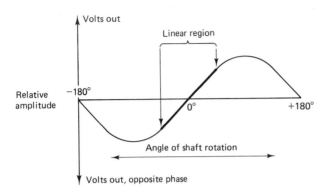

Figure 3–28 RVDT output curve.
(Courtesy of Schaevitz Engineering.)

quently amplified. Thick-film/thin-film circuitry is utilized." Typical specifications are given in Table 3–6.

3–2.3 Optical Encoders*

"There are two basic generic styles of optical encoders: incremental and absolute." The incremental encoder provides a pulse each time the shaft has rotated a defined distance. "An absolute encoder provides a 'whole world' output with a unique code pattern representing each position."

The absolute encoder is represented in Figure 3–29. The output "code is derived from independent tracks on the encoder disk corresponding to individual photodetectors. The output from these detectors would then be high or low depending on the code disk pattern for that particular position.

"Absolute encoders are used in applications where a device is inactive for long periods of time or moves at slow rates, such as flood control, telescopes, cranes, etc.

"Absolute encoders are capable of using many thousands of different codes but the most common are Gray, natural binary, and binary-coded decimal (BCD).

"The incremental encoder creates a series of equally spaced signals corresponding to the mechanical increment required; ie to divide a shaft rotation into 1000 parts, an encoder could be selected to supply 1000 square wave cycles per revolution. By using a counter to count those cycles, we could tell how far the shaft rotated. 100 counts would equal 36°, 150 counts 54°, etc. We are limited only by the counter's register capacity. The number of cycles per revolution is limited by physical line spacing and quality of light transmission." Figure 3–30 gives an exploded view of an incremental encoder.

The simpler type of incremental encoder is the tachometer encoder. Its output waveform and code track on the disk are shown in Figure 3–31. "A tachometer encoder is sometimes called a single track incremental encoder because it has only one output and cannot detect direction. The output is usually a square wave.

"Velocity information is available by looking at the time interval between pulses

---

* The quoted material in Section 3–2.3 is from Ref. 5.

TABLE 3–6 RVDT SPECIFICATIONS

GENERAL SPECIFICATIONS — AC-RVDT'S

Input voltage . . . . . . 3 V rms (nominal)
Input frequency . . . . . 400 Hz to 20 kHz
Operating
temperature . . . . –65°F to +300°F
(–55°C to +150°C)

Bearings . . . . ABEC class 7
Temperature coefficient
of sensitivity . . . . . . .02%/°F (.04%/°C)over range
20°F to 160°F
(–5°C to 75°C)

ELECTRICAL SPECIFICATIONS

RVDT MODEL	LINEARITY PERCENT OF RANGE			SENSITIVITY mV/V/°	IMPEDANCE		PHASE ANGLE Degrees
	±30°	±40°	±60°		Pri.	Sec.	
(@ 2.5 kHz)							
R30A	0.25	0.5	1.5	2.3	125	500	+35
R36A	0.5	1.0	3.0	1.1	750	2000	+4
(@ 10 kHz)							
R30A	0.25	0.5	1.5	2.9	370	1300	+3
R36A	0.5	1.0	3.0	1.7	2500	5400	–17

GENERAL SPECIFICATIONS — DC-RVDT'S

Input voltage . . . . . . ±15 V DC, 30 ma
Operating
temperature . . . . . . 0°F to 160°F
(–18°C to +75°C)

Survival temperature . –65°F to 300°F
(–55°C to +150°C)
Temperature
coefficient . . . . .04%/°F (.08%/°C)
Bearings . . . . ABEC class 7

ELECTRICAL SPECIFICATIONS

RVDT MODEL	LINEARITY PERCENT OF RANGE			SCALE FACTOR mV/degree	IMPEDANCE Ohms	-3dB RESPONSE Hz
	±30°	±40°	±60°			
R30D	0.25	0.5	2.0	125	<100	500

MECHANICAL SPECIFICATIONS

RVDT MODEL	MOMENT OF INERTIA Pound-Inch-Second²	MAXIMUM TORQUE Inch-Ounces		MAXIMUM LOAD Pounds		WEIGHT Grams	SERVO MOUNT BU-ORD
		Unbalance	Friction	Radial*	Axial		
R30A	0.53 X 10⁻⁶	.004	.015	8	10	36	11
R30D	0.53 X 10⁻⁶	.004	.015	8	10	53	11
R36A	1.62 X 10⁻⁶	.012	.015	25	25	255	15

*Shaft end

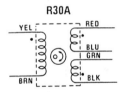

R30A

CONNECT GRN TO BLU FOR DIFFERENTIAL OUTPUT

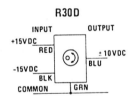

R30D

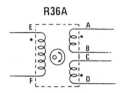

R36A

CONNECT (B) TO (C) FOR DIFFERENTIAL OUTPUT

Source: Schaevitz Engineering.

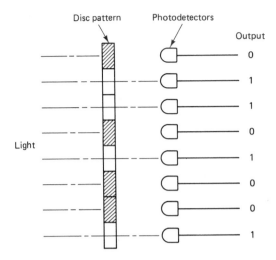

Figure 3–29 Eight-bit absolute encoder (left) and disk (right). (Courtesy of BEI Industrial Encoder Division.)

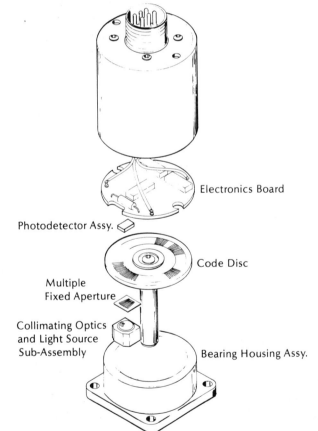

Figure 3–30 Incremental optical encoder. (Courtesy of BEI Industrial Encoder Division.)

Output waveform

Code track on disk

Figure 3–31 Tachometer encoder output and code track. (Courtesy of BEI Industrial Encoder Division.)

or at the number of pulses within a time period. When using the interval between pulses, the encoder should provide good edge-to-edge accuracy. Any inaccuracy will cause the servo system to constantly correct 'errors' caused by disc pattern irregularities.

"Most incremental systems use two output channels in quadrature for position sensing." The output waveforms and code tracks on the disc for a quadrative encoder are shown in Figure 3–32. "This allows us to count the transitions and to view the state of the opposite channel during these transitions. Using this information we can determine if A leads B, and thus derive direction.

"It is important to have this direction information available due to the vibration inherent in almost any system. An error in count will occur should the encoder using a single-channel (tachometer type) stop on a transitional edge. As vibration forces the unit back and forth across this edge, the counter will up-count with each transition even though the system seems to be stopped. By utilizing quadrature detection on a two-channel encoder and viewing the transition in its relationship to the state of the opposite channel, we can generate reliable direction information.

"Once the quadrature signal is decoded we can generate pulses of fixed duration at selected transitions within a cycle. These pulses can be fed via clockwise and counter-clockwise output lines to an up-down counter or programmable controller input port. Many counter and PC manufacturers include a quadrature detection circuit [also called antijitter] as part of their electronics. This allows the use of a two-channel quadrative input without further conditioning."

An antijitter circuit is shown in Figure 3–33. The condition of A (when B occurs) determines whether B causes a count up or a count down. The Z input is used to reset the counter to zero once a cycle.

Carefully review the manufacturer's literature before making connections to any optical encoder. You must provide dc power and ground to the encoder. The outputs

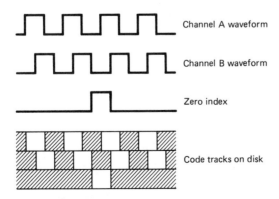

Channel A waveform

Channel B waveform

Zero index

Code tracks on disk

Figure 3–32 Quadrature encoder outputs and code tracks. (Courtesy of BEI Industrial Encoder Division.)

 **HEWLETT PACKARD** | **QUADRATURE DECODER/ COUNTER INTERFACE IC** | **HCTL-2000**

Description

The HCTL-2000 is an HCMOS IC that performs the quadrature decoder, counter, and bus interface function. The HCTL-2000 is designed to improve system performance in digital closed loop motion control systems and digital data input systems. It does this by shifting time intensive quadrature decoder functions to a cost effective hardware solution. The HCTL-2000 consists of a 4x quadrature decoder, 12 bit binary up/down state counter, and 8 bit bus interface. The use of Schmitt triggered CMOS inputs and a 3 bit state delay filter allows reliable operation in noisy environments. The HCTL-2000 provides LSTTL compatible tri-state output buffers. Operation is specified for a temperature range from -40 to +85° C at clock frequencies up to 3.9 mHz.

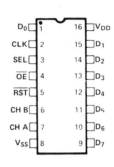

PINOUT

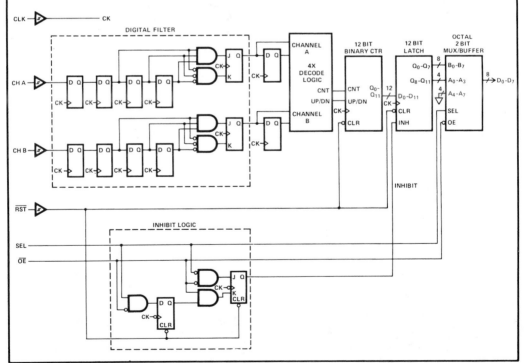

Figure 3–33 Antijitter circuit for quadrature encoder. (Courtesy of Hewlett-Packard.)

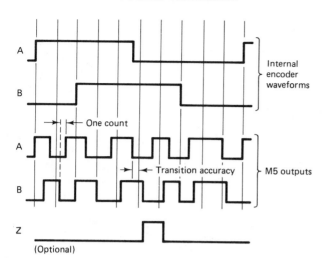

Figure 3–34   Count multiplication. (Courtesy of BEI Industrial Encoder Division.)

from the encoder are usually open collector. A logic low is a short to ground. A high is an open. You must connect a properly sized pull-up resistor from each output to a voltage which will provide logic level compatability with whatever counter, PC, or computer is to use the signals.

Count multiplication can also be provided either by external or (occasionally) internal logic. "With quadrature detection we have the ability to derive 1X, 2X, or 4X the basic code disk resolution. 10,000 pulses per turn can be generated from a 2500-cycle two channel encoder. With a quality disk and a properly phased encoder, this 4X signal will be accurate to better than $\frac{1}{2}$ count." This is accuracy of better than 0.018°.

This multiplication is illustrated in Figure 3–34. The decode electronics must not only sense direction but must also provide an output pulse on each edge of one or both inputs.

3–2.4 Synchros and Resolvers[*]

A synchro is an angular position transducer. It consists of a primary wound on the rotor and three secondaries placed 120° apart on the stator. The magnitude and phase of the voltage induced into each stator winding depends on the position of and voltage applied to the rotor. So, for a known primary voltage, the secondary voltages *uniquely* define the rotor's position. The primary is usually connected to the line (115 ac rms at 60 Hz) producing maximum voltages on the secondaries of generally 11.8 or 90 V. The resolver is similar to the synchro, except there are two secondaries on the stator, placed 90° apart. The physical and electrical performance of a synchro and a resolver are illustrated in Figure 3–35.

The synchro has several advantages over the other position transducers you have

---

[*] The quoted material in Section 3–2.4 is from Ref. 6.

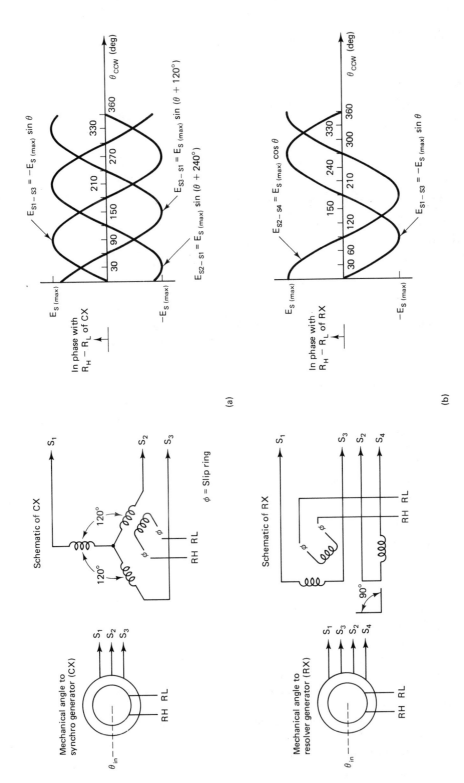

Figure 3-35 (a) Synchro and (b) resolver physical and electrical characteristics. (Courtesy of ILC Data Device Corporation.)

seen so far. It is an absolute position encoder. Should power be cycled to the processing circuitry, the synchro still indicates the position of the shaft. This is similar to the absolute optical encoder. However, synchro converter resolution is typically 12 to 14 bits.

The input power to a synchro or resolver may be 115 V ac rms, 60 Hz (although other voltages and frequencies are available). This makes powering the transducer simple, convenient, and inexpensive since a separate dc excitation supply is not required. The output from the synchro (or resolver) is high-level ac, and the position information is contained in the *ratio* of each of the stator winding voltage with the reference (primary) voltage. Any noise induced into these signals or any losses caused by long wiring runs will be common to both the stator signals and the reference rotor signal and small as compared to the signals. Since you must divide the stator voltage by the rotor voltage to get the position information, these common errors are eliminated.

These are all significant advantages. But how do you convert these sinusoidal signals into an indication of position? The original answer was to use a receiver synchro. When wired as shown in Figure 3–36, the shaft of the receiver synchro will rotate to align itself with the shaft of the transmitter synchro. A pointer could be attached to the shaft of the receiver synchro to indicate the position of the transmitter synchro's shaft. When used to move a pointer, the receiver synchro must be capable of delivering some torque.

A receiver synchro can also be used to produce an output voltage. The rotor is fixed, not free to turn as it was in Figure 3–36. Also, the receiver synchro's rotor is not connected to the source used to power the transmitter synchro's rotor. Instead, a voltage is induced across the receiver synchro's rotor, which is a measure of the difference in the angular position of these two rotors.

$$v_{\text{receiver rotor}} = (E_{\text{pk}} \sin \omega t) \cos \theta \qquad (3-7)$$

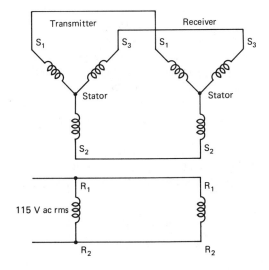

Figure 3–36 Transmitter and receiver synchro wiring.

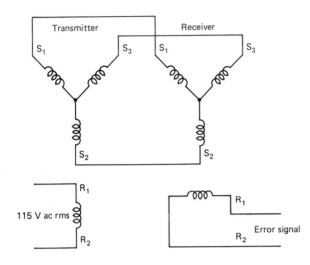

Figure 3–37 Transmitter and receiver synchro wiring to produce an error signal.

This is shown in Figure 3–37. In fact, if you move the shaft of the receiver to point at the desired position of the shaft you are controlling, the output from its rotor is an indication of the error (desired position − actual position).

As you can see from equation 3–7, the output from the receiver synchro is not linear. In fact, it is not unique. There are two angles, as the shaft is rotated through a complete circle, which will produce the same output. A more convenient solution is offered by the synchro-to-digital (S/D) or resolver-to-digital converter. The S/D converter is a hybrid analog integrated circuit. It uses the S_1, S_2, S_3, and R_1 and R_2 signals from the transmitter synchro to produce a binary word. The relationship of angle and the value of the binary bit position is illustrated in Table 3–7.

"The SDC1740, SDC1741, and SDC1742 are hybrid, continuous tracking synchro or resolver to digital converters which employ a type 2 servo loop and contain three-state latches on the digital output." They are pictured in Figure 3–38.

"The input signal can either be three-wire synchro plus reference or four-wire resolver plus references format depending on the option; and the outputs are presented in TTL-compatible parallel natural binary buffered by three state latches. An outstanding feature of these converters is that although the profile is only 0.28 in. (7.1 mm) they contain internal transformers which provide for true isolation on the signal and reference inputs."

Figure 3–39 gives the functional diagram for these converters. "If the unit is a synchro-to-digital converter the three-wire synchro output will be connected to S_1, S_2, and S_3 on the unit and the Scott T transformer pair will convert these signals into resolver format

$$V_1 = KE_0 \sin \omega t \sin \theta$$

$$V_2 = KE_0 \sin \omega t \cos \theta$$

TABLE 3–7 ANGULAR VALUE FOR THE BINARY
BITS OF A S/D CONVERTER

Bit no.	Degrees	Degrees,	minutes	Radians
1	180	180	0	3.141593
2	90	90	0	1.570796
3	45	45	0	0.785398
4	22.5	22	30	0.392699
5	11.25	11	15	0.196349
6	5.625	5	37.5	0.098175
7	2.8125	2	48.75	0.049087
8	1.40625	1	24.38	0.024544
9	0.70312	0	42.19	0.012272
10	0.35156	0	21.09	0.006136
11	0.17578	0	10.55	0.003068
12	0.08789	0	5.27	0.001534
13	0.04395	0	2.64	0.000767
14	0.02197	0	1.32	0.000383
15	0.01099	0	0.66	0.000192
16	0.00549	0	0.33	0.000096

Source: Analog Devices.

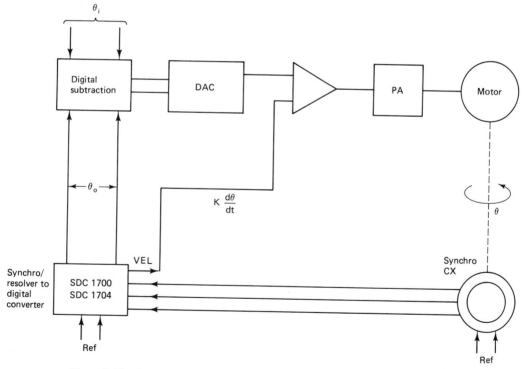

Figure 3–38 Control loop using both the SDC digital output and analog velocity output. (Courtesy
of Analog Devices.)

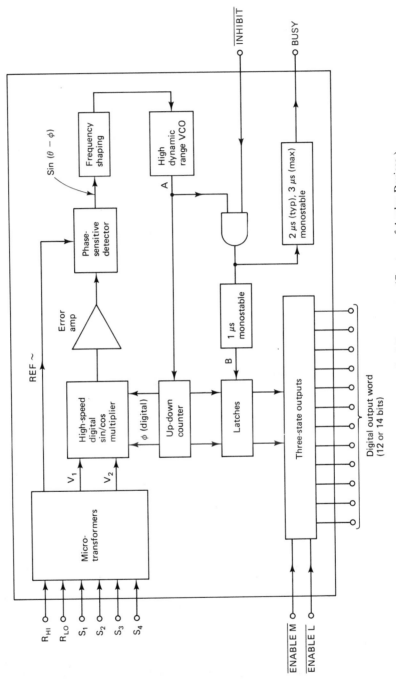

Figure 3-39 Functional diagram of a S/D converter. (Courtesy of Analog Devices.)

where θ is the angle of the synchro shaft. If the unit is a resolver-to-digital converter, the four-wire resolver output will be connected to S_1, S_2, S_3, and S_4 on the unit and the transformers will act purely as isolators.

"To understand the conversion process, assume that the current word state of the up-down counter is ϕ. Then V_1 is multiplied by $\cos \phi$ and V_2 is multiplied by $\sin \phi$ to give

$$KE_0 \sin \omega t \sin \theta \cos \phi$$

and

$$KE_0 \sin \omega t \cos \theta \sin \phi$$

These signals are subtracted by the error amplifier to give

$$KE_0 \sin \omega t (\sin \theta \cos \phi - \cos \theta \sin \phi)$$

or

$$KE_0 \sin \omega t \sin (\theta - \phi)$$

A phase-sensitive detector, integrator, and voltage-controlled oscillator (VCO) form a closed-loop system which seeks to null $\sin (\theta - \phi)$.

"When this is accomplished, the word state of the up-down counter (ϕ) equals, within the rated accuracy of the converter, the synchro shaft angle θ.

"Assuming that the $\overline{INHIBIT}$ is at a logic high state, then the digital word will be strobed into the latches 1 μs after the up-down counter has been updated. If the three-state $\overline{ENABLE}$ is at a logic low, then the digital output word will be presented to the output pins of the unit." The *BUSY* signal is provided by the converters to indicate that a conversion is taking place. Data will not be valid until *BUSY* goes low. This is illustrated in Figure 3-40.

"A feature of these converters is that the signals and reference inputs can be resistively scaled to accommodate any range of input signal and reference voltages."

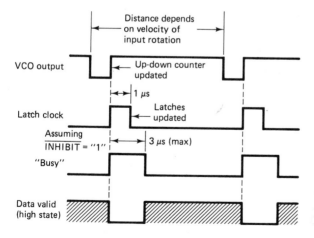

Figure 3-40 Timing diagram for the SDC/RDC 1740, 1741, 1742 S/D converters. (Courtesy of Analog Devices.)

There are several related support modules available as well. There are synchro/resolver input modules which output BCD instead of natural binary. These are easy to connect to a display. There are complementary modules which take a digital input and synthesize the corresponding synchro or resolver S_1, S_2, S_3, S_4, R_1, and R_2 signals (D/A converters). The SAC1763 inputs synchro signals, but outputs an analog voltage linearity proportional to the shaft position.

3–3 FORCE TRANSDUCERS*

In servo and process control the measurement of force is very important. An entire engineering discipline (experimental stress analysis) has been established to evaluate the forces applied to various parts of a machine or a vehicle. Accurately measured forces allow the design of machinery (including cars and spacecraft) that is lighter, more efficient, more reliable, less expensive, and which provides higher performance.

Also, being able to measure force allows you to obtain indirectly the value of parameters which are difficult to measure directly. In a constant gravitational field, force is a measure of the quantity of material present (its mass). So force transducers can be used to measure both weight and the amount of material in a tank (level). Pressure is a key parameter in pneumatics and hydraulics. It is just force per unit area. So force measurement techniques are often needed to measure pressure. The pressure across an opening is an indication of the rate that a fluid is flowing through the opening. Force transducers are used in measuring flow. Knowing the force applied to a defined mass tells you the acceleration being experienced by the mass. So measuring force tells you about acceleration of a vehicle.

$$F = ma$$

$$a = \frac{dv}{dt}$$

or

$$v = \int a \, dt$$

Velocity is the integral of acceleration. And

$$v = \frac{dx}{dt}$$

or

$$x = \int v \, dt$$

* The quoted material in Section 3–3 is from Ref. 7.

Position is the integral of velocity. With an accelerometer (a device that measures the force applied to a known mass) and a computer, you can determine the acceleration, velocity, and position of a vehicle. This is the essence of inertia guidance. Finally, the force exerted by a spring is directly proportional to how much it has been stretched.

$$F = kx$$

where k is the spring constant. Measurement of the force exerted on (or by) the spring is a nonintrusive way to measure the displacement in a spring–mass–damper system.

3–3.1 Stress and Strain

''The relationship between stress and strain is one of the most fundamental concepts from the study of mechanics of materials and is of paramount importance to the stress analyst. When a force is applied to a body, the body deforms. In the general case this information is called strain. . . . We will . . . define the term *strain* to mean deformation per unit length or fractional change in length and give it the symbol ϵ. . . . Strain may be either tensile (positive) or compressive (negative).'' Look at Figure 3–41. ''When written in equation form,

$$\epsilon = \frac{\Delta L}{L} \tag{3–8}$$

We see that strain is a ratio and therefore dimensionless. To maintain the physical significance of strain, it is often written with units of inch/inch. For most metals the strains measured in experimental work are typically less than 0.005000 in./in. Since practical strain values are so small, they are often expressed in microstrain, which is $\epsilon \times 10^6$ (note this is equivalent to parts per million or ppm) and has the symbol $\mu\epsilon$. . . . For example: 0.005 in./in. = 5000 $\mu\epsilon$ = 0.5%.

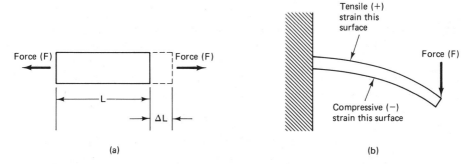

Figure 3–41   (a) Strain with a unilateral force applied; (b) cantilever in bending. (Courtesy of Hewlett-Packard.)

"While forces and strains are measurable quantities used by the designer and stress analyst, stress is the term used to compare the loading applied to a material with its ability to carry the load. Since it is usually desirable to keep machines and structures as small and light as possible, the parts should be stressed, in service, to the highest permissible level. *Stress* refers to force per unit area on a given plane with a body. . . . Expressed in equation form,

$$\sigma = \frac{F}{A} \qquad (3-9)$$

and has units of force per unit area.

"Now that we have defined stress and strain we need to explore the stress–strain relationship, for it is this relationship that allows us to calculate stresses from the measured strains. If we have a bar made of mild steel and incrementally load it in uniaxial tension and plot the strain versus the normal stress in the direction of the applied load, the plot will look like the stress–strain diagram in Figure 3–42."

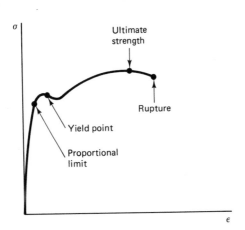

Figure 3–42 Stress-strain diagram in mild steel. (Courtesy of Hewlett-Packard.)

From Figure 3–42 "we see that up to a point, called the proportional limit, there is a linear relationship between stress and strain. Hooke's law describes this relationship. The slope of this straight-line portion of the stress–strain diagram is the *modulus of elasticity* or Young's modulus for the material. The modulus of elasticity, E, has the same units as stress (force per unit area) and is determined experimentally for materials. Written in equation form this stress–strain relationship is

$$\sigma = E \cdot \epsilon \qquad (3-10)$$

"There are two other points of interest on the stress–strain diagram . . . , the yield point and the ultimate strength value of stress. The yield point is the stress level at which strain will begin to increase rapidly with little or no increase in stress. If the material is stressed beyond the yield point, and then the stress is removed, the material will not return to its original size but will retain a residual offset or strain. The ultimate strength is the maximum stress developed in the material before rupture.''

3–3.2 Strain Gage

''Probably the most important electrical characteristic which varies in proportion to strain is that of electrical resistance. Devices whose output depends on this characteristic are the piezoresistive or semiconductor gage, the carbon-resistor gage, and the bonded metallic wire and foil resistance gages. The carbon and resistor gage is the forerunner of the bonded resistance wire strain gage. It is low cost, can have a short gage length, and is very sensitive to strain. A high sensitivity to temperature and humidity are the disadvantages of the carbon-resistor strain gage.

''The semiconductor strain gage is based on the piezoresistive effect in certain semiconductor materials such as silicon and germanium. Semiconductor gages have elastic behavior and can be produced to have either positive or negative resistance changes when strained. They can be made physically small while still maintaining a high nominal resistance. The strain limit for these gages is in the 100 μ to 10,000 $\mu\epsilon$ range with most tested to 3000 $\mu\epsilon$ in tension. Semiconductor gages exhibit a high sensitivity to strain but the change in resistance with strain is nonlinear. Their resistance and output are temperature sensitive and the high output, resulting from changes in resistance as large a 10 to 20%, can cause measurement problems when using the devices in a bridge circuit.

''The bonded resistance strain gage is by far the most widely used strain measurement tool for today's experimental stress analyst. It consists of a grid of very fine wire, or more frequently of thin metallic foil, bonded to a thin insulating backing called a carrier matrix. The electrical resistance of this grid material varies linearly with strain. In use the carrier matrix is attached to the test specimen with an adhesive. When the specimen is loaded, the strain on its surface is transmitted to the grid material by the adhesive and carrier system. The strain in the specimen is found by measuring the change in the electrical resistance of the grid material.'' Figure 3–43 is a picture of a bonded resistance strain gage with a constantan foil grid and polyimide carrier material.

The bonded resistance strain gage is low in cost, can be made with a short gage length, is only moderately affected by temperature changes, has small physical size and low mass, and has fairly high sensitivity to strain. It is suitable for measuring both static and dynamic strains.''

''When a metallic conductor is strained its undergoes a change in electrical resistance, and it is this change that makes the strain gage a useful device. The measurement of this resistance change with strain is *gage factor* (GF). Gage factor is defined as the ratio of the fractional change in resistance to the fractional charge in length (strain) along the axis of the gage. Gage factor is a dimensionless quantity and the larger the value, the more sensitive the strain gage. Gage factor is expressed in equation form as

$$\text{GF} = \frac{\Delta R/R}{\Delta L/L} = \frac{\Delta R/R}{\epsilon}\text{''} \tag{3–11}$$

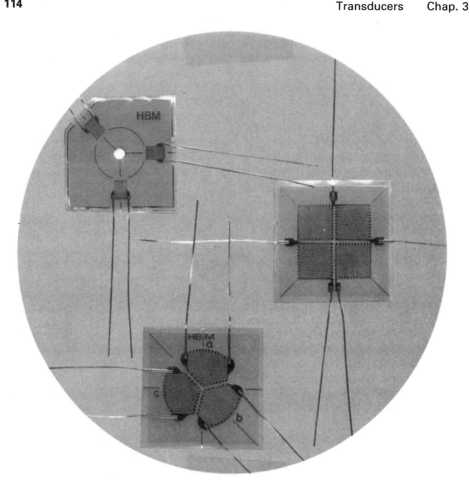

Figure 3–43 Foil bonded resistance strain gages. (Courtesy of Hewlett-Packard.)

EXAMPLE 3–14

A strain gage is bonded to a steel beam which is 10.00 cm long and has a cross-sectional area of 4.00 cm. Young's modulus of elasticity for steel is 20.7×10^{10} N/m^2. The strain gage has a nominal (unstrained) resistance of 240 Ω and a gage factor of 2.20. When a load is applied, the gage's resistance changes by 0.013 Ω. Calculate the change in length of the steel beam and the amount of force applied to the beam.

Solution   From equation 3–11,

$$\text{GF} = \frac{\Delta R/R}{\Delta L/L}$$

or

$$\frac{\Delta R}{R} = GF \left(\frac{\Delta L}{L} \right)$$

or

$$\Delta L = \frac{\Delta R}{R} \frac{L}{GF}$$

$$= \frac{0.013 \ \Omega}{240 \ \Omega} \times \frac{0.1 \ m}{2.20} = 2.46 \times 10^{-6} \ m$$

From equation 3–10,

$$\sigma = E \cdot \epsilon$$

But

$$\sigma = \frac{F}{A}$$

and

$$\epsilon = \frac{\Delta L}{L}$$

So

$$\frac{F}{A} = E \frac{\Delta L}{L}$$

or

$$F = E \frac{\Delta L}{L} A$$

To keep units consistant, the area must be converted from cm² to m².

$$A = 4 \ cm^2 \times \frac{1 \ m^2}{10^4 \ cm^2} = 4 \times 10^{-4} \ m^2$$

$$F = 20.7 \times 10^{10} \frac{N}{m^2} \times \frac{2.46 \times 10^{-6} \ m}{0.1 \ m} \times 4 \times 10^{-4} \ m^2$$

$$= 2.037 \times 10^3 \ N$$

In pounds,

$$F = 2.037 \times 10^3 \ N \times \frac{1 \ lb}{4.482 \ N} = 454 \ lb$$

"Ideally we would prefer the strain gage to change resistance only in response to the stress-induced strain in the test specimen, but the resistivity and the strain sensitivity of all known strain sensitive materials vary with temperature. Of course that means the gage resistance and the gage factor will change when the temperature changes."

In simple terms, the resistance of a conductor at a given temperature, T, is

$$R_T = R_{T0}(1 + \alpha_0 \, \Delta T) \tag{3-12}$$

where R_T = resistance at T
R_{T0} = resistance at a reference temperature T_0
α_0 = temperature coefficient
ΔT = change in temperature from T_0

This new resistance consists of the original resistance R_0 at T_0 and the change in that resistance ΔR caused by the change in temperature ΔT. Some algebraic manipulation of equation 3-12 should produce

$$\Delta R = \alpha_0 \, \Delta T \, R_{T_0} \tag{3-13}$$

EXAMPLE 3–15

Calculate the change in resistance caused by a 1°C change in temperature for the strain gage in Example 3–14. The temperature coefficient (α_0) for most metals is

$$\alpha_0 = 0.003925/°C$$

Solution   Substituting the required values into equation 3–13 yields

$$\Delta R = (0.003925/°C)(1° \text{ C})(240 \; \Omega)$$
$$= 0.942 \; \Omega$$

But the stress applied by the load in Example 3–14 caused only a 0.013-Ω change in the strain gage's resistance. So 1°C change in the temperature of the strain gage caused a change in resistance

$$\frac{\Delta R_{\text{temp}}}{\Delta R_{\text{stress}}} = \frac{0.942 \; \Omega}{0.013 \; \Omega} = 72.5$$

72.5 times larger than the 454-lb load produced!

From Example 3–15 you should see that it is absolutely necessary to compensate for temperature effects on the strain gage.

3–3.3 Wheatstone Bridge Circuit

"Because of its outstanding sensitivity, the Wheatstone bridge circuit is the most frequently used circuit for static strain measurements." The simple bridge is shown in Figure 3–

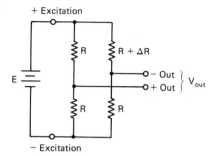

Figure 3–44 Simple strain gage Wheatstone bridge.

44. With no stress $\Delta R = 0$, all four resistors are equal, $+$out $= -$out, so $V_{out} = 0$. When stress is applied, the strain gage changes its resistance by ΔR.

$$V_{out} = \frac{R}{R + R} E - \frac{R}{R + (R + \Delta R)} E$$

$$= \frac{1}{2} E - \frac{RE}{2R + \Delta R}$$

$$= \frac{(2R + \Delta R)E - 2RE}{2(2R + \Delta R)}$$

$$= E \frac{\Delta R}{4R + 2\,\Delta R} \tag{3–14}$$

Since ΔR, the effect of the stress, is in both the numerator and the denominator of equation 3–14, the output of the bridge changes *nonlinearity* with applied force. However, R is several hundred ohms, while ΔR is typically $0.01\ \Omega$, a factor of 10,000 times smaller. So since

$$4R \gg 2\,\Delta R$$

Equation 3–14 can be rewritten, dropping the $2\,\Delta R$ from the denominator,

$$V_{out} = \frac{\Delta RE}{4R} \tag{3–15}$$

Keep in mind that V_{out} is differential. It is not ground referenced. Also, it will be very small and will come from a source whose output impedance is $R/2$, which may still be a hundred ohms or more. This signal must be amplified by a circuit with a very large input impedance and the ability to output a ground referenced signal which depends solely on the *difference* between its two inputs ($+$out and $-$out of the bridge).

So what is the advantage of using a Wheatstone bridge? By making both resistors on one side of the bridge strain gages the effects of temperature can be eliminated.

Look at Figure 3–45. One strain gage is mounted so that the applied force will cause it to elongate. This is the *active* gage. The second gage is placed transverse to the stress. There is no significant stress in line with this gage, so the applied force does not cause it to elongate. This is the *dummy* gage. The applied force will affect only the active gage, unbalancing the bridge. However, any change in temperature

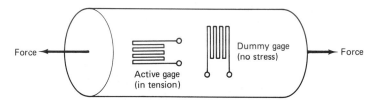

Figure 3–45 Placement of active and dummy gages for temperature compensation.

EXAMPLE 3–16

Determine V_{out} in Figure 3–44 given that $R_0 = 240\ \Omega$, $E = 10$ V, and
(a) stress causes the upper resistor (the active gage) on the right to increase by 0.013 Ω.
(b) temperature causes both resistors on the right (both active and passive) to increase by 9.4 Ω.
(c) stress causes the active gage to increase by 0.013 Ω *and* temperature causes both resistors to increase by 9.4 Ω.

Solution   **(a)** Use equation 3–15.

$$V_{out} = \frac{\Delta R E}{4R}$$

$$= \frac{(0.013\ \Omega)(10\text{ V})}{4(240\ \Omega)} = 0.13 \text{ mV}$$

The stress produces a rather small signal.
(b) Using the voltage-divider law gives us

$$V_{out} = \frac{(240\ \Omega)(10\text{ V})}{240\ \Omega + 240\ \Omega} - \frac{(249.4\ \Omega)(10\ \Omega)}{249.4\ \Omega + 249.4\ \Omega}$$

$$= 5\text{ V} - 5\text{ V} = 0\text{ V}$$

The use of a dummy gage eliminates the effect of temperature.
(c) With both a temperature and a stress-induced resistance change,

$$V_{out} = \frac{(240\ \Omega)(10\text{ V})}{240\ \Omega + 240\ \Omega} - \frac{(249.4\ \Omega)(10\text{V})}{249.4\ \Omega + (249.4\ \Omega + 0.013\ \Omega)}$$

$$= 5\text{ V} - \frac{(249.4\ \Omega)(10\text{ V})}{498.813\ \Omega}$$

$$= 5\text{ V} - 4.99987\text{ V}$$

$$= 0.13 \text{ mV}$$

So even in the presence of both stress and temperature resistance changes, the use of a dummy gage eliminates the effects of the temperature change.

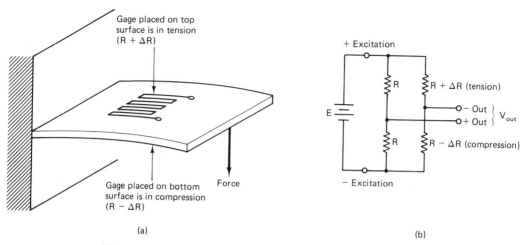

Figure 3–46 Two active strain gages: (a) physical placement; (b) bridge configuration.

will affect both gages in the same way. Identical changes in resistance by both resistors on one side of the bridge will *not* unbalance the bridge. The voltage at −out does not change, so the effects of temperature are eliminated.

If you are going to the trouble and expense of placing two gages on the beam, you might as well make both of them active. By connecting both active gages on one side of the bridge, temperature-induced effects are eliminated. By having one gage in tension (its resistance increases with load) and the other in compression (its resistance decreases with load), the output voltage for a given load doubles when compared to the single active gage bridge (see Figure 3–46).

$$V_{\text{out}} = \frac{\Delta RE}{2R} \tag{3–16}$$

To implement the circuit in Figure 3–46, you must, to make the left side of the bridge, provide two resistors which are within a hundredth of an ohm of each other and which thermally track each other. Or you could use two more strain gages. A four-active-strain-gage bridge is shown in Figure 3–47. The output from the bridge with four active strain gages is twice as large for a given load as the output from the

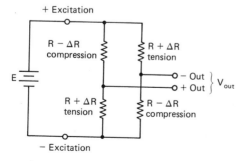

Figure   3–47 Four-active-strain-gage bridge.

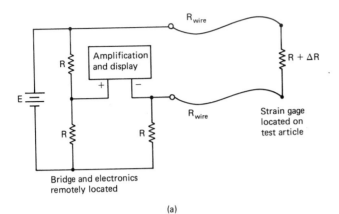

(a)

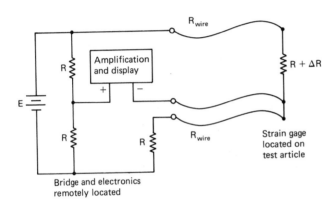

(b)

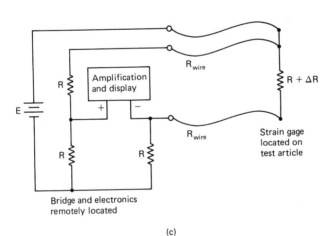

(c)

Figure 3–48 Strain gage connection to a remote bridge: (a) two-wire (incorrect); (b) three-wire (correct); (c) alternate three-wire (correct).

bridge with two active strain gages and four times larger than the output from the single strain gage bridge.

$$V_{out} = \frac{\Delta R E}{R} \tag{3–17}$$

Proper wiring to the strain gage, the excitation supply, and the signal conditioning electronics is important. This is especially true when part of the bridge is located on the test article and part is located remotely in an instrument. The key point is that exactly the same length and type wire exist in each leg of one side of the bridge or in the same leg on both sides of the bridge. This way the additional resistance added by the wiring to one resistor will be balanced by an identical amount of resistance added by the wiring to the other resistor. Correct and incorrect wiring are shown in Figure 3–48. These correct techniques also compensate for changes in the wiring resistance (R_{wire}) caused by changes in temperature.

3–3.4 Load Cells

Proper, reliable results using strain gages can be obtained only if the gages are correctly applied. They must be perfectly aligned with the force, the adhesive must faithfully transmit the force between gage and beam, the beam must provide equal compression and tension to opposite legs of the bridge, the physical characteristics of the beam must be known, and the solder connections to the strain gages must have equal, negligible resistance. All of this sounds like a pretty tall order.

The usual solution is to buy a load cell. A load cell is a transducer specifically designed to measure force. It consists of a beam with properly mounted strain gages (usually four). Beam geometry and stress–strain parameters are matches with the strain gages. All you have to do is provide the excitation supply and the amplification and display electronics. Several different load cells are shown in Figure 3–49. Although you see many specifications associated with the load cells of Figure 3–49, the one of central importance is the output at rated capacity (also called the sensitivity). It is expressed in mV/V. This is the differential output voltage from the bridge caused by *full-scale* load, for each volt of the excitation supply.

EXAMPLE 3–17

A GSE5353 load cell has a full-scale rating of 500 lb.
(a) What is the recommended excitation voltage?
(b) Using that excitation, what is the output voltage per pound?
(c) What is the nonlinearity in pounds?
(d) What is the zero shift (in pounds) if the temperature varies across its rated range?
(e) If used to weigh a tank, must the tank be hung from the cell, or placed on top of the cell? Why?

Solution   Refer to Figure 3–49.

(a) The manufacturer recommends a 10-V dc excitation.

(b) $V_{out(max)}$ = (output at rated capacity)($V_{excitation}$)

$\qquad\qquad$ = (2 mV/V)(10 V) = 20 mV

But this is for 500 lb:

$$V_{out/lb} = \frac{V_{out(max)}}{\text{full-scale load}}$$

$$= \frac{20 \text{ mV}}{500 \text{ lb}} = 40 \text{ }\mu\text{V/lb}$$

This means that your electronics must be able to *clearly* and accurately amplify differential signals of 40 μV or less if you expect to resolve and display 1-lb increments.

(c) Nonlinearity is $\pm 0.05\%$ FS.

$$\text{nonlinearity} = (\pm 0.05\%)(500 \text{ lb}) = \pm 0.25 \text{ lb}$$

So no matter how good your electronics, there will be a ± 0.25-lb uncertainty in your answer. So trying to display your results with more resolution than $\frac{1}{2}$ lb is pointless, and misleading.

(d) The temperature range is +25 to +125°F. This represents a 100°F shift. The zero shift with temperature is +0.002% FS/°F.

$$\text{zero shift} = (+0.002\%/°\text{F})(100°\text{F})(500 \text{ lb})$$

$$= +1 \text{ lb}$$

This is four times as great as the nonlinearity. So if the transducer experiences significant changes in temperature, you must readjust the zero.

(e) The note at the bottom of the specifications indicates that "specifications are for tension loading." So you must mount the load so that it is suspended from the load cell.

3–4 MOTION TRANSDUCERS

The measurement of the relative motion of a piece of equipment has many uses. By knowing how *fast* a tool is moving, it can be positioned more quickly and with less overshoot than if simple *position* control were used alone. Control of the speed of conveyor belts, wind-up rolls, and so on, is critical to accurate manufacturing. Endurance and shock testing of parts demands the measurement of the movement to which those parts are subjected. Accurate navigation of aircraft, missiles, and spacecraft now relies on measurement of their motion.

Motion measurements are divided into several categories. Linear velocity, v, is the rate of change of position, x.

$$v = \frac{dx}{dt}$$

It is expressed in in./s, cm/s, m/s, mi/h, or km/h. Angular velocity is a measure of how rapidly the point of interest is revolving about a center. Most often this is shaft rotation. Angular velocity is expressed in rad/s, deg/s, or r/min. Acceleration is the rate of change of velocity.

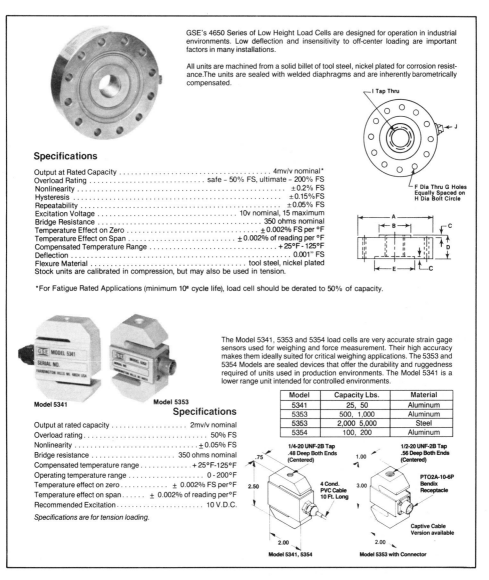

Figure 3–49   Load cells. (Courtesy of GSE.)

$$a = \frac{dv}{dt}$$

or

$$a = \frac{d^2x}{dt^2}$$

Jerk is the rate of change of acceleration, which makes it the third derivative of position:

$$\text{jerk} = \frac{da}{dt}$$

or

$$\text{jerk} = \frac{d^3x}{dt^3}$$

It is of interest in shock and vibration studies and in the psychological studies of movement produced discomfort in people.

All of these parameters are vector quantities. They each have a direction as well as a magnitude. So motion transducers must be able to detect the direction of the motion and somehow encode that information along with the magnitude signal. Generally, this means that the transducer will sense motion along only one axis, indicating either + or − travel along that axis. Sensitivity to off-axis motion is a parameter you must carefully evaluate.

3–4.1 Velocity Transducers

There are two major classes of velocity transducers, those that measure movement *along* an axis (linear) and those that measure movement about or around an axis (angular). Each will be presented in separate parts of this section.

Linear velocity can be measured in several rather different ways. For motion that will have a limited overall displacement, the electromagnetic linear velocity transducer works well. Longer movement can be accommodated with an integrating accelerometer. If no connection to the moving part is allowed, Doppler radar or laser systems may be used.

The electromagnetic linear velocity transducer is illustrated in Figure 3–50. It is also referred to as a coil and bobbin type of velocity pickup. All electromagnetic velocity transducers operate on the fact that the voltage induced into a coil by a magnetic field is directly proportional to rate of change of the magnetic field.

$$v = -N\frac{d\phi}{dt}$$

The core of the electromagnetic linear velocity transducer is a permanent magnet. The voltage induced into the coil depends on how fast the core is pulled. Reversing

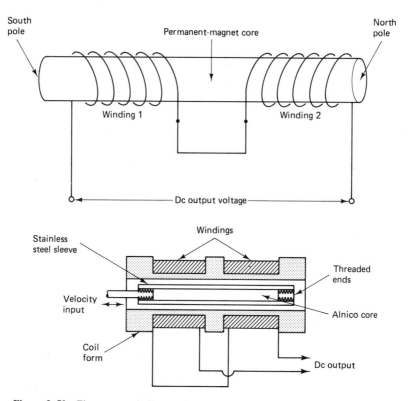

Figure 3–50   Electromagnetic linear velocity transducer. (Courtesy of Schaevitz Engineering.)

the direction of the motion reverses the polarity of the induced voltage. Of course, with this configuration, the magnet must not be pulled out of the core, so this limits the total travel of the part whose velocity you are trying to measure.

Less restrictive is the integrating accelerometer velocity transducer. Its output voltage is derived from a piezoelectric acceleration transducer (discussed in Section 3–4.2). Since

$$a = \frac{dv}{dt}$$

$$dv = a\, dt$$

$$v = \int a\, dt + V_0$$

you can calculate the velocity at any instant in time by integrating the acceleration signal and adding the initial velocity (V_0). This integration and offset are done by electronics built within the transducer. Product data and specifications are given in Figure 3–51.

There are times when a transducer cannot be attached to the item whose velocity

Piezoelectric Velocity Transducer

Model 793VS   Model 793V

The Model 793V Velocity Transducer is a rugged vibration sensor for wide range velocity measurements. Combined in a small housing is a piezoelectric accelerometer, a low-noise amplifier and an integrator which converts the signal from acceleration to velocity. The solid piezoelectric construction and the low-noise signal conditioning allow the measurement of vibration over a wide frequency and amplitude range.

The low noise performance is made possible by the unique integration within the transducer which is superior to external integration of an accelerometer signal. In addition, the physical construction minimizes erroneous signals from thermal transients, base strain, transverse motion and magnetic fields. This solid unit offers significant advantages over the coil-and-magnet type velocity pickups, primarily in the areas of reliability, frequency range, and phase accuracy. Available with standardized sensitivities of 100 mV/in/sec or 500 mV/in/sec. Waterproof molded cable, explosion proof housing, or internal temperature sensor optional.

Applications:

- Machinery Monitoring
- Structural Analysis
- Fan Monitoring
- General Vibration Measurement
- Dynamic Balancing
- Test Cell Application
- Low Frequency Monitoring

Features:

- ☐ Wide Frequency Range
- ☐ Three Models
  - 793V   100 mV/in/sec, 2.5 Hz to 3500 Hz
  - 793V-1   100 mV/in/sec, 10 Hz to 3500 Hz
  - 793V-5   500 mV/in/sec, 10 Hz to 3500 Hz
- ☐ No Moving Parts to Fatigue
- ☐ Increased Reliability
- ☐ "Drop-Proof" Protection
- ☐ Mounts in any Orientation
- ☐ Low Magnetic Sensitivity
- ☐ Small Size and Weight
- ☐ Inherently Attenuates High Frequencies
- ☐ No Critical Alignment Requirement
- ☐ Increased Dynamic Range
- ☐ Low Noise
- ☐ Small and Predictable Phase Shifts at Very Low Frequencies

Powering the Piezo-Velocity Transducer

The internal amplifier requires an external DC power source to operate. Proper operation can be obtained by applying a DC voltage (+18 to +30 VDC) to the center conductor of the cable through a constant current diode (1 to 10 mA) as shown in Figure 1.

A blocking capacitor is required in series with the output signal if the readout instrument is DC coupled. The Wilcoxon Research P700 Series Power Units will supply power to any of the 700 Series Accelerometers. A typical set-up for a vibration measurement is shown in Figure 2.

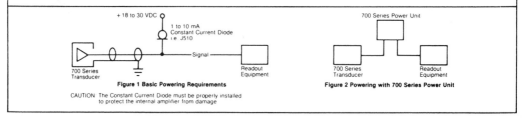

Figure 1 Basic Powering Requirements

CAUTION The Constant Current Diode must be properly installed to protect the internal amplifier from damage

Figure 2 Powering with 700 Series Power Unit

Figure 3–51   Integrating acceleration velocity transducers. (Courtesy of Wilcox Research.)

you are trying to measure. Perhaps the mass of the transducer would slow down the motion of the part, or perhaps it is a vehicle or target you are trying to track. Doppler radar or lasers are used.

The Doppler effect relies on a shift in frequency, which is proportional to relative velocity. You experience this if you stand beside a road and are passed by a car that is blowing its horn. As the car approaches, the horn sounds as if it were at a high pitch. When the car passes you and is receding, the sound shifts to a lower pitch. The received frequency of a stationary observer is

$$f_{\text{received}} = f_0 + f_v$$

where f_0 is the emitted frequency and f_v is a linear function of velocity. It is positive if the emitter is approaching the observer and negative when the emitter is receding.

In Doppler radar or laser units, either a continuous wave (CW) or a series of pulses (pulsed) is projected toward the object whose velocity is to be measured. The beam is bounced back from the target and its frequency is shifted according to its relative velocity. This echo is received and its timing and frequency compared with the transmitted signal. The length of time it takes for the signal to reach the target and return is a measure of the distance to the target. The frequency of the echo is compared with the transmitted frequency. The shift (f_v) indicates the velocity of the target.

Of course, the most familiar example of this form of velocity transducer is the radar used by police to detect speeders. However, systems working on the same principles are used in missile targeting and in tracking and navigation of spacecraft. The motion of the test bed shown in Figure 3–52 is monitored by a laser Doppler velocimetry system. Travel over a 10-in. range is monitored with $+1$ μm (i.e., 10^{-6} m) accuracy.

Angular velocity transducers are usually divided into two groups: those that output a *voltage* as a function of rotational speed, and those whose output *frequency* depends on the rate of rotation. The most common angular velocity transducer is the dc electromagnetic tachometer. The field is established by permanent magnets or separately excited electromagnet windings on the stator. The rotor is made of a series of coils. When rotated through the magnetic field voltage is induced into the coils. The magnitude of the induced EMF in the coils is directly proportional to how rapidly the rotor spins. By connecting several coils in series and rotating these through multiple fields, a large, reasonably ripple-free output is obtained. This signal is coupled from the rotating coils to the outside world through communtators and brushes. These also assure that the output is dc. A reversal in direction causes the output voltage to change polarity.

There are several reasons that dc tachometers are so popular. They are easy to use, outputting a relatively high level dc output voltage that requires little or no additional signal conditioning. Tachometers using permanent magnets typically output 3 to 7 V per 1000 r/min while those with electromagnet windings on the stator output 10 to 20 V per 1000 r/min. Direction of rotation is directly indicated by the polarity of the output voltage. Accuracies of 0.1 to 0.25% FSO can be obtained.

However, the commutator and brushes needed to couple the output from the rotor cause significant problems. Good routine (preventive) maintenance is necessary. Any

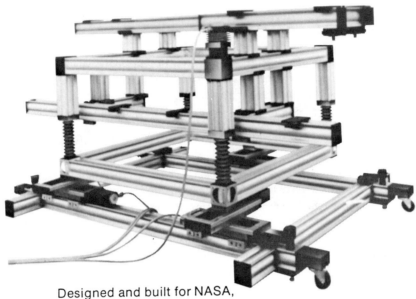

Designed and built for NASA,
this system provides XYZ motion
over 10 inches of travel for wind
tunnel experiments, utilizing Laser Doppler
velocimetry measurements. Accuracy ± 1 micron.

Figure 3–52 High-resolution positioning system using laser Doppler velocimetry measurement. (Courtesy of Klinger Scientific.)

arcing at the brushes produces radio-frequency interference (RFI) from which the rest of the control system must be protected.

For those applications where the brush-related problems are unacceptable, consider the ac induction tachometer. Also called the ac permanent magnet tachometer or drag cup tachometer, this rotational velocity transducer has no brushes. It consists of primary and secondary windings placed at right angles on the stator. The rotor is squirrel-cage or cup shaped and made of a high-conductance metal.

When a 60-Hz signal is connected to the primary, an eddy current at right angles to this coil is induced in the rotor. When the rotor is stationary, the magnetic field produced by the eddy currents in the rotor is at right angles to the secondary. The secondary is not cut, so no signal is coupled into the secondary. However, when you rotate the rotor, this field is moved across the secondary, inducing an output voltage. The more rapidly you rotate the rotor, the faster the field induced into the rotor cuts the secondary and the larger the resulting output induced in the secondary.

The output is ac, so you must rectify and filter it to produce a useful signal. Since the primary and secondary are at right angles, the output is 90° out of phase with the excitation voltage. When rotated in one direction, the output leads the excitation supply. Reversing the direction causes the output to shift 180°, now lagging the excitation by 90°. So to determine direction you must detect this phase relationship.

The ac induction tachometer overcomes the problems introduced by the brushes of the dc tachometer. However, you must provide phase-sensitive rectification and filtering to obtain a useful signal.

If *continuous* rotation is not necessary, or if the entire processing and display electronics are to be rotated (such as in aircraft), the Watson angular rate sensor may be a valid choice. It is shown in Figure 3–53. "The patented sensing mechanism consists of piezoelectric bender elements mounted to a rigid base in a 'tuning fork' configuration. The two drive elements are resonately driven in opposite directions. When a rotation exists, Coriolis forces transfer momentum to the perpendicular plane and cause bending of the sense elements. The sense elements vibrate 180° out of phase with angular motion but vibrate in phase when linear acceleration or vibration is present. A sophisticated electrical circuit to drive the elements and subtract the sensing signals results in an angular motion response output with almost total rejection of linear motion [8].

Parameters of major importance for angular velocity transducers include the range in r/min (formerly rpm), starting and running torque, and the sensitivity (in mV per r/min). Errors are introduced by the *IR* losses caused by loading the output coils; variation in temperature, which changes magnetic coupling characteristics; and shaft vibration, which changes spacing and results in output shifts.

The angular velocity transducers you have seen so far output a voltage. Another group of transducers output a signal whose *frequency* depends on the speed of rotation. The amplitude of this signal may or may not vary.

The ac permanent-magnet tachometer uses a rotor with several permanent-magnet poles. A single coil on the stator is cut repeatedly as the rotor's magnets are swept past the coil. A pulse of one polarity is produced when a north pole passes the coil, while the opposite polarity pulse occurs when the south pole passes. The amplitude of these pulses and their rise time vary with the speed of the shaft. So signal conditioning is necessary to convert these pulses into TTL- or CMOS-compatible levels for counting or timing.

A Hall effect device provides a saturated transistor when in the presence of an adequately strong magnetic field. When the field falls below a specified threshold, the transistor opens. The coil in the ac permanent-magnet tachometer can be replaced with a Hall effect device. The output could then by "pulled up" to +5 V through a resistor and counted directly.

The toothed-rotor tachometer places a single permanent magnet and sensor in a unit on the frame (stator). The rotor is gear-shaped and made of a low-reluctance metal. As a tooth rotates beneath the magnet and sensor, coupling between magnet and sensor is enhanced, causing the magnetic field to cut the sensor. One output pulse is produced as each tooth rotates under the sensor. Depending on the gear and sensor design, the output may vary in shape from TTL square waves to positive and negative pulses to almost pure sinusoids.

Incremental optical encoders, discussed in Section 3–2.3, output a fixed number

ANGULAR RATE SENSOR SPECIFICATIONS
ONE AXIS UNITS
Models ARS-C121-1A, ARS-C131-1A, ARS-C141-1A

•Power supply requirements:	+15 VDC ±5% 20 mA maximum −15 VDC ±5% 20 mA maximum
•Output:	0 VDC at zero angular rate ±10 VDC at full scale angular rate
•Sensitivity:	ARS-C121-1A ± 30°/second full scale ARS-C131-1A ±100°/second full scale ARS-C141-1A ±300°/second full scale
Output current:	±10 mA maximum
•System frequency:	280 Hz nominal
Resolution:	Limited by noise
Linearity:	<0.1% full scale
Hysteresis:	Not measurable
Temperature offset:	.5% full scale/°C maximum
•Frequency response:	DC-55 Hz
•Output noise:	15mV RMS maximum
•Operating and storage temperature range:	−20°C to +50°C
Storage and operating altitude:	Unlimited
•Shock:	200 G
Life:	No wear-out mode
•Dimensions:	
•Weight:	110 grams (4 oz.)

•Custom units with variation in these parameters are available.

Note: Above units optionally available with digital output.

Specifications subject to change without notice.

Figure 3–53 Angular rate sensor. (Courtesy of Watson Industries, Inc.)

of pulses per revolution. So the frequency of these pulses is a measure of the angular velocity of the shaft.

Most of the rotational speed transducers you have seen so far require that you attach the shaft of the transducer to the shaft to be measured. This may present significant mechanical problems. It may be impossible to fit the transducer where you want to measure. Gears, belts, and shafts all flex and introduce errors. The inertia of the transducer may load down the system you are trying to measure.

All of these problems are overcome by a reflective optical sensor. Narrow strips of reflective tape (usually, six) are carefully placed on a nonreflective shaft or coupling. A reflective optical source and sensor are placed in a convenient location where the infrared beam from the transmitter can fall on the rotating shaft. When the strip of reflective tape rotates past, the light is bounced back to the sensor, which outputs a pulse (often a saturated, open-collector transistor). Should it be difficult to locate the optical source and sensor near the shaft, light can be carried to and from the shaft with a fiber optic cable. A reflective optical sensor set up for shaft velocity measurement is illustrated in Figure 3–54.

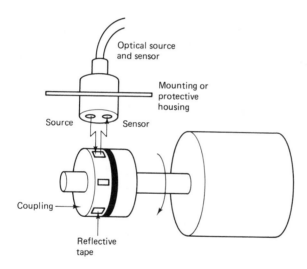

Figure 3–54 Reflective angular sensing for angular velocity.

EXAMPLE 3–18

A dc motor that drives a conveyor belt has a maximum speed of 1720 r/min. It is necessary to monitor the speed with a resolution of 1 r/min and provide a new number every 100 ms.

(a) How many pulses per revolution are required?

(b) If it were necessary to use a 6-pulse/revolution reflective optical sensor, describe the degradation in preformance.

Solution   **(a)** The revolutions per second are

$$\text{speed} = 1720 \frac{\text{r}}{\text{min}} \times \frac{1 \text{ min}}{60 \text{ s}}$$

$$= 28.67 \frac{\text{r}}{\text{s}}$$

In 100 ms, the allowed counting time

$$\text{speed} = 28.67 \frac{\text{r}}{\text{s}} \times \frac{0.1 \text{ s}}{\text{counting period}}$$

$$= 2.867 \frac{\text{r}}{\text{counting period}}$$

However, you must get 1720 counts during the counting period.

$$\text{pulses per revolution} = \frac{1720 \text{ counts}}{2.867 \text{ revolution}}$$

$$= 600 \text{ counts/revolution}$$

A transducer with 600 pulses/revolution would yield a 1-to-1 correlation between the counts accumulated in 0.1 s and the actual r/min speed of the shaft. Any transducer with more than 600 pulses/revolution will exceed the minimum revolution specifications.

(b) If you are forced to use a 6-pulse/revolution reflective optical sensor, you will be off by 100. You would have to count for 100 s to get the same resolution. But a 0.1-s counting time is about as long as most control applications can tolerate. You could convert the frequency to a voltage with a V/F converter and then amplify the voltage. But the minimum response rate and ripple output will still cause problems. One other option is to use a phase-locked loop (PLL) with a 100 counter in its feedback. This makes the oscillator of the PLL run 100 times faster to maintain the lock. At the oscillator output you have essentially multiplied the transducer frequency by 100.

3–4.2 Acceleration

You saw at the beginning of Section 3–4 that

$$v = \frac{dx}{dt} \quad \text{and} \quad a = \frac{dv}{dt}$$

Conversely,

$$v = \int a \, dt \quad \text{and} \quad x = \int v \, dt$$

So if you can measure the acceleration a vehicle is undergoing, the velocity and position can be calculated. Navigation as well as motion studies on machinery employ this principle.

Also, the force that a part experiences is directly related to its acceleration:

$$F = ma$$

The measurement of the acceleration of a machine part allows you to determine not only its motion, but also the stresses it must endure.

Acceleration is measured in units of

$$\frac{\text{length}}{\text{time}^2}$$

that is, m/s^2, cm/s^2, $in./s^2$, or ft/s^2. However, it is traditional to express this in terms of the acceleration that a freely falling body experiences at sea level. This is the gravitational constant, g.

$$1g = \frac{9.81 \text{ m}}{s^2} = 32.2 \frac{\text{ft}}{s^2}$$

Most acceleration measurement techniques use some variation of the mass–spring–damper system. This is shown in Figure 3–55. Under a steady acceleration, a constant f_m will be exerted on the mass. There will be no input force f_i. The mass will move, stretching or compressing the spring until the force exerted by the spring, f_k, balances the force due to acceleration. With offsetting forces, the mass is in static balance, and therefore comes to rest. Since the damper's force is dependent on velocity and the mass is no longer moving, $f_R = 0$.

At rest, then,

$$f_m = f_k$$
$$ma = kx \tag{3–18}$$
$$a = \frac{k}{m} x$$

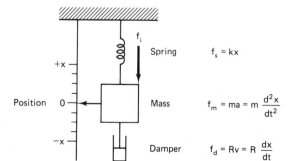

Position   0

Spring $f_s = kx$

Mass $f_m = ma = m \dfrac{d^2 x}{dt^2}$

Damper $f_d = Rv = R \dfrac{dx}{dt}$

Figure   3–55 Classical mass–spring–damper system.

Measuring the position at which the seismic mass comes to rest tells you the acceleration that the mass is experiencing. So the measurement of steady acceleration is just a displacement problem.

However, this mass–spring–damper system is second order. As you saw in Chapter 2, there is a damping coefficient and resonant frequency associated with it. For equation 3–18 to be valid, the seismic mass must be at rest. So accelerometers are slightly underdamped to allow the mass to move rapidly to the new steady-state position dictated by a change in acceleration. Damping coefficients of

$$\zeta = 0.7 \pm 0.1$$

are usual.

The other specification of a second-order system is the resonance frequency ω_n. Take the Laplace domain system equation developed in Appendix A for the mass–spring–damper and compare it to the general underdamped second-order transfer function. A little algebra will show you that

$$\omega_n = \sqrt{\frac{k}{m}}$$

So what? If you drive a second-order system above its resonance frequency, it will not respond. As the frequency of the driving force (the acceleration you are trying to measure) approaches the resonance frequency, the response becomes oscillatory. Only well below the resonance frequency does the system properly track the input. A good rule of thumb is [9]

$$f_n = \frac{\omega_n}{2\pi}$$

$$f = \frac{f_n}{2.5}$$

As was illustrated by equation 3–18,

$$a = \frac{k}{m}x$$

the mass–spring–damper system converts the measurement of acceleration into a measurement of the displacement of the seismic mass. You saw in Section 3–2 many ways to measure position. Five techniques are popular in accelerometers. These include the use of a potentiometer, strain gage, variable reluctance (both variable inductance and LVDT), capacitance, and a piezoelectric crystal.

An accelerometer using a potentiometer to sense the displacement of the seismic mass is shown in Figure 3–56. Potentiometric accelerometers have the advantages of providing a large easily used output, and of being relatively inexpensive. However, because of the large mass needed to overcome the inertia and friction of the potentiometer, the resonance frequency is less than 60 Hz. Remember, this means that the usable frequency is considerable below that. So you will see these accelerometers used to measure slowly varying or steady-state acceleration.

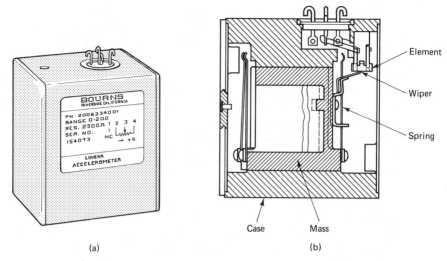

Figure 3–56   Accelerometer using a potentiometer. (Courtesy of Bourns, Inc.)

Strain gage accelerometers, also called piezoresistive, use a mass attached to a cantilever beam. Acceleration of the seismic mass causes stress in the beam, which is measured by strain gages bonded to the beam. A strain gage accelerometer is illustrated in Figure 3–57. Semiconductor strain gages are used because of their high sensitivity (gage factor). In fact, the same configuration can be placed in a silicon wafer using monolithic integrated-circuit fabrication techniques. This produces an extremely small, light, and responsive accelerometer.

Capacitance is inversely proportional to the distance between the plates making up the capacitor. In a capacitive accelerometer, the acceleration forces closer together

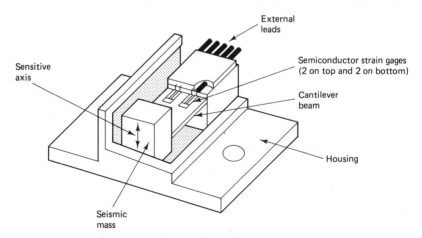

Figure 3–57   Strain gage accelerometer. (Courtesy of Entran Devices, Inc., Fairfield, N.J.)

the plates that are perpendicular to the motion. This, in turn, raises the capacitance. Placed in an ac bridge, this causes an imbalance, outputting an ac whose amplitude is an indication of the acceleration. Another way to detect the change in capacitance is to allow the capacitor to control the frequency of an oscillator or timer. For most oscillators the period or time interval out is directly proportional to the size of the timing capacitor.

The same concept can be used to vary the inductance of a coil. The seismic mass is a low-reluctance core which is partially engaged within the coil of an inductor. Acceleration in one direction moves the core farther into the coil, raising the inductance. Acceleration in the opposite direction moves the core out of the coil, lowering the inductance. An ac bridge is the usual way of converting the change in inductance to an electrical signal. However, as RF oscillator may also be created with the accelerometer's inductance as part of a tank circuit.

A second technique for measuring acceleration with an inductor is to replace the low-reluctance core by a permanent magnet. As long as the acceleration is constant, the magnet is stationary and there is no voltage induced in the coil. Any *change* in acceleration will cause the seismic mass magnet to move to a new location. *Movement* of the magnet causes it to induce a voltage in the coil. So the output is a voltage directly dependent on the rate of change of the magnet (and therefore the rate of change of acceleration). Although the resonance frequency is under 100 Hz, this type of transducer is normally used only in vibration testing.

The final inductive type of accelerometer uses the seismic mass as the core of a LVDT. This is shown in Figure 3–58. The core is suspended within the two secondary windings by the two cantilever springs. Acceleration along the sensitive axis causes the core to move to a new location. This, in turn, couples more ac into one coil than the other, causing an ac output proportional to core displacement, and therefore to acceleration. Resonance frequency is generally less than 80 Hz. You must drive the primary of the LVDT and detect the output from the secondaries as you would with any other LVDT. The frequency of the excitation signal should be at least one order of magnitude greater than the accelerometer's resonance frequency.

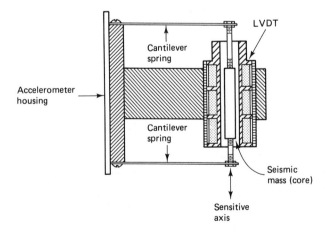

Figure 3–58 Accelerometer using an LVDT. (Courtesy of Schaevitz Engineering.)

Perhaps the most popular type of accelerometer uses a piezoelectric crystal to convert acceleration into an electrical output. During the manufacturing of quartz crystals a large dc potential is placed along one axis of the crystal. This must be done while the crystal is still hot. This polarizing field causes the crystal to become permanently thicker in the direction of the electric field. Later, if the crystal is compressed along this polarizing axis, a proportional charge is produced between the electrodes used for polarization. This is

$$q = DF$$

where q = induced charge
$\quad\;F$ = applied force
$\quad\;D$ = piezoelectric strain constant

However, placing two electrodes on parallel faces of an insulator produces a capacitance. So piezoelectric crystals also exhibit capacitance. An unbalanced charge on a capacitor causes (or is caused by) an electric potential:

$$e = \frac{q}{C}$$

so

$$e = \frac{DF}{C} \tag{3–19}$$

A piezoelectric accelerometer is illustrated in Figure 3–59. The crystal is preloaded, so that acceleration in one direction increases the force on the crystal, increasing the

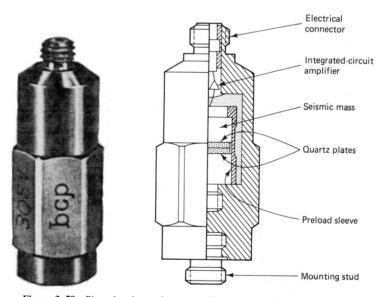

Electrical connector

Integrated-circuit amplifier

Seismic mass

Quartz plates

Preload sleeve

Mounting stud

Figure 3–59   Piezoelectric accelerometer. (Courtesy of PCB Piezotronics, Inc.)

output. Acceleration in the opposite direction counteracts some of the preload on the crystal, decreasing the force on the crystal and lowering the output.

There are three major advantages of a piezoelectric accelerometer compared to the other acceleration transducers you have seen. The operating temperature of the piezoelectric unit extends up to the temperature where the polarization was originally introduced. Upper limits of over 800°C have been produced. Second, because of the simple mechanical configuration, piezoelectric accelerometers can be made very small. This smaller size improves the speed of response of the transducer and lowers the effect the transducer has on the system it is trying to measure. A subminiature piezoelectric accelerometer is shown in Figure 3–60. But perhaps the overriding advantage of the piezoelectric accelerometer is its *useful* frequency range (as opposed to the resonance frequency). Flat response is available from a low-frequency cutoff of a few hertz to an upper frequency limit of 10 kHz [1, pp. 66–67].

Balancing these advantages are two major problems. The output voltage is a sensitive function of *all* the capacitance across the crystal. Look back at equation 3–19. Any increase in capacitance across the crystal will lower the output voltage. To complicate matters further, the output impedance of the crystal itself is high. This makes the piezoelectric accelerometer sensitive to resistive as well as capacitive loading. The connector, coaxial cable, and signal-conditioning electronics all add capacitance across the crystal. Even if you calibrate the system, any change in cable length, amplifier, or even humidity will alter the response significantly. Trying to charge and discharge this capacitance through the high impedance of the crystal also slows down its response.

Figure 3–60 Subminiture piezo-electric accelerometer. (Courtesy of Endevco.)

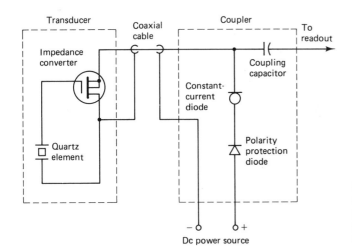

Figure 3–61 Schematic of a piezo-electric accelerometer with an integrated amplifier (Piezotron System). (Courtesy of Kistler Instrument Corp.)

The solution to this problem is a charge amplifier (impedance converter) integrated inside the transducer itself. This was shown in Figure 3–59. A typical schematic is given in Figure 3–61. The MOS transistor provides a fixed, known capacitive load across the crystal and virtually no resistive loading. It also drives its output voltage from a low source impedence. This effectively isolates the cable and processing electronics capacitance from the crystal.

3–5 FLUID TRANSDUCERS

Fluid transducers are divided into three groups according to the parameter being measured: pressure, level, or flow. Manufacturing that involves a liquid must be able to measure one or more of these parameters. You will see fluid transducers in the food-processing industry, in drug and chemical manufacturing, and along the entire line of oil production, from exploration, through drilling, pumping, transportation, refining, to sales. The monitoring and control of all sorts of engines rely on fluid transducers. Hydraulic systems employed in automated production (such as industrial-grade robots) require strict control of pressure, flow, and level. Fluid transducers are used extensively, throughout the industrial world.

3–5.1 Pressure Transducers*

Pressure is defined as the force exerted by a fluid against a given area. So it is expressed in terms of force per unit area. Pressure is normally measured in comparison to a reference. One reference is a *perfect vacuum*. At a perfect vacuum, the pressure is zero. So pressure measured with vacuum as its reference is called *absolute pressure*.

---

* The quoted material in Section 3–5.1 is from Ref. 10.

The other major way to express pressure is *gage pressure*. Gage pressure uses the ambient pressure (whatever that happens to be at the moment) as its reference.

All pressure measurements require two ports, one for the measurement and one for the reference. Absolute pressure devices seal the reference port to a chamber containing a vacuum. Gage pressure devices open the reference port to the surrounding local pressure. A third alternative allows you to connect the reference port to a second pressure (of your choice). Since the difference in pressure between two points in a system is important in many measurement and control problems, *differential pressure* transducers are also widely used.

The pressure at the bottom of a column of liquid depends on the height of the column and the density of the liquid:

$$p = \rho g h$$

where ρ = liquid's density
  g = constant for converting mass to weight, 980.665 cm/s^2
  h = height of the column

This pressure is referred to as the *head*.

Pressure is force per unit area. In metric terms this is newtons/meter^2, which is called a pascal (Pa). The English unit is lb/in.^{2}. This is abbreviated psia for absolute pressure, psig for gage pressure, or psid for differential pressure. For conversions,

$$1 \text{ psi} = 6.8948 \times 10^3 \text{ Pa} \tag{3–20}$$

The height of a column of mercury or water that would yield a certain head pressure is also used as a unit of measure for that pressure.

$$1 \text{ in. of mercury (Hg)} = 3.386 \times 10^3 \text{ Pa} \tag{3–21}$$

$$1 \text{ mm Hg} = 133.32 \text{ Pa} \tag{3–22}$$

The head pressure created by 1 millimeter of mercury is also called a *torr*. It is used extensively in measuring vacuums.

$$1 \text{ torr} = 1 \text{ mm Hg} = 133.32 \text{ Pa} \tag{3–23}$$

Since water is so much less dense than mercury, it produces a lower head pressure.

$$1 \text{ in. of water (H}_2\text{O)} = 2.491 \times 10^2 \text{ Pa} \tag{3–24}$$

Standard atmospheric pressure is defined at sea level as

$$\begin{aligned} 1 \text{ atm} &= 760 \text{ mm Hg} \\ &= 1.01325 \times 10^5 \text{ Pa} \end{aligned} \tag{3–25}$$

Barometric pressure, in weather reporting, is measured in bar or millibar:

$$1 \text{ bar} = 1 \times 10^5 \text{ Pa} \tag{3–26}$$

These equations are summarized in Table 3–8.

TABLE 3–8 PRESSURE CONVERSION CHART

to obtain ↓ by ↘	multiply no. of →										
	atm	bar	dyn/cm²	in. Hg (0°C)	in. H²O(4°C)	kg/m²	lb/in.² (psi)	lb/ft²	mm Hg (torr)	μm	newtons/meter²
atm		9.86923×10^{-1}	9.86923×10^{-7}	3.34207×10^{-2}	2.458×10^{-3}	9.678×10^{-5}	0.068046	4.7254×10^{-4}	1.316×10^{-3}	1.316×10^{-6}	9.869×10^{-6}
bar	1.01325		10^{-6}	3.3864×10^{-2}	2.491×10^{-3}	9.8067×10^{-5}	6.8948×10^{-2}	4.788×10^{-4}	1.333×10^{-3}	1.333×10^{-6}	$\times 10^{-5}$
dyn/cm²	1.01325×10^{6}	10^{6}		3.386×10^{4}	2.491×10^{3}	98.067	6.8948×10^{4}	478.8	1.333×10^{3}	1.333	10
in. Hg (0°C)	29.9213	29.53	2.953×10^{-5}		7.355×10^{-2}	2.896×10^{-3}	2.036	0.014139	0.03937	3.937×10^{-5}	2.953×10^{-4}
in. H²O(4°C)	406.8	401.48	4.0148×10^{-4}	13.60		3.937×10^{-2}	27.68	0.1922	0.5354	5.354×10^{-4}	4.014×10^{-3}
kg/m²	1.033227×10^{4}	1.0197×10^{4}	1.0197×10^{-2}	354.3	25.40		703.06	4.882	13.59	13.59×10^{-3}	1.019×10^{-1}
lb/in.² (psi)	14.695595	14.504	1.4504×10^{-5}	0.4912	3.6126×10^{-2}	1.423×10^{-3}		6.9444×10^{-3}	1.934×10^{-2}	1.934×10^{-5}	1.450×10^{-4}
lb/ft²	2116.22	2088.5	2.0885×10^{-3}	70.726	5.202	0.2048	144.0		2.7844	2.7844×10^{-3}	2.089×10^{-2}
mm Hg (torr)	760	750.06	7.5006×10^{-4}	25.400	1.868	7.3558×10^{-2}	51.715	0.35913		10^{-3}	7.502×10^{-3}
μm	760×10^{3}	750.06×10^{3}	0.75006	2.54×10^{4}	1.868×10^{3}	73.558	51.715×10^{3}	359.1	1×10^{3}		7.502
newtons/meter²	1.01325×10^{5}	1×10^{5}	10^{-1}	3.386×10^{3}	2.491×10^{2}	9.8067	6.8948×10^{3}	4.788×10^{1}	1.333×10^{2}	1.333×10^{-1}	

Source: Kulite Semiconductor Products, Inc.

Pressure transducers use some form of mechanical device that stretches proportionally in response to an applied pressure. Strain gages, LVDTs, potentiometers, variable inductance, or capacitance convert this displacement into an electrical signal.

One major class of pressure transducers uses a diaphragm to flex in response to pressure and a strain gage(s) to measure this strain. The diaphragms may be made from stainless steel or from silicon. The strain gage may also be either a foil grid or a semiconductor.

"Pressure applied to the diaphragm through the pressure port produces a minute deflection which introduces strain to the gages. The strain produces an electrical resistance change proportional to the pressure. Four gages (or two gages with fixed resistor) form a Wheatstone bridge." A diaphragm and strain gage pressure transducer is shown in Figure 3–62.

"The differential resistance is measured by applying a constant voltage to the bridge. Diaphragm deflection results in an analog (millivolt) output which is proportional to pressure.

"Fixed resistors are used for bridge completion (in half bridge units), temperature compensation, zero balance, and to achieve full scale output.

"Various output voltages can be provided through amplifier or other signal conditioning circuits internal or external to the transducer. Also other supply voltages are accommodated by using appropriate internal circuitry.

"In addition to relative low cost and good accuracy, the pressure transducers (with foil strain gage on a stainless steel diaphragm) have good temperature stability and can be bonded to corrosive resistant materials. They do, however, have a low output (about 3 mV/V), which makes more amplification necessary.

"Semiconductor gage characteristics provide overall accuracy and performance. They are manufactured from pure silicon wafers which are processed through steps of oxidation, wafer alignment, photo etching, and diffusion. Gold wire welded to the gage ends is used as a conductor to the solder tabs to provide maximum conductivity and thus constant resistance value.

"The initial resistance values as manufactured are measured and closely controlled. Then the resistance at 70, 30, and 130°F is measured. The gages are assembled in sets which have thermal characteristics within close tolerances. This controlled procedure is important in order to provide the strain gage characteristics necessary to consistently produce transducers that meet catalog specifications.

"The strain gages" (either metal foil or semiconductor) "are epoxy bonded to a precision metal diaphragm, the thickness of which determines the pressure range of the transducer. . . . The flat stainless steel diaphragm (designed for low stress levels) has minute movement. This results in exceptional long life and excellent linearity. The diaphragm is either part of a single piece construction or part of an assembly which is election-beam welded to the body. Thus the strain gages are isolated from the media and the diaphragm is protected from external strains. No other devices are needed to protect the strain gages and electronics from the media.

"The diaphragm and body materials have thermally matched temperature coefficients. This minimizes thermal strains due to ambient temperature changes."

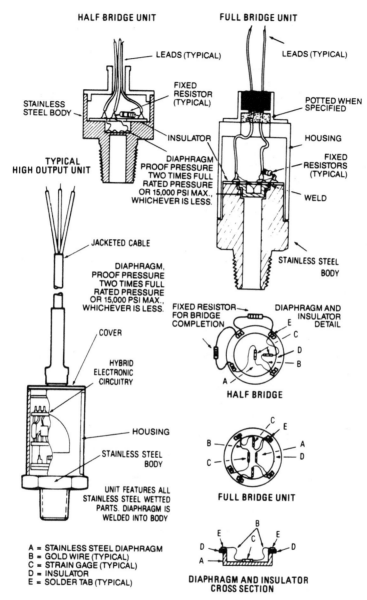

Figure 3-62 Diaphragm with strain gage pressure transducer. (Courtesy of Omega Engineering, Inc., Stamford, CT.)

An alternative to a stainless steel diaphragm to which you must bond some form of strain gage is a piezoresistive (silicon) diaphragm. The semiconductor strain gages are diffused into a silicon diaphragm. This yields several advantages.

"The high sensitivity, or gage factor, is perhaps 100 times that of wire strain gages. Piezoresistors are diffused into a homogeneous single crystalline silicon medium. The diffused resistors are thus integrated into the silicon force sensing member. Typically, other types of strain gages are bonded to force sensing members of dissimilar material, resulting in thermoelastic strain and complex fabrication processes. Most strain gages are inherently unstable due to degradation of the bond, as well as temperature sensitivity and hysteresis caused by the thermoelastic strain.

"Silicon is an ideal material for receiving the applied force. Silicon is a perfect crystal and does not become permanently stretched. After being strained, it returns to the original shape. Silicon wafers are better than metal for pressure sensing diaphragms, as silicon has extremely good elasticity within its operating range. Silicon diaphragms normally fail only by rupturing.

"The sensing element consists of four nearly identical piezoresistors buried in the surface of a thin circular silicon diaphragm. Gold pads attached to the silicon diaphragm surface provide connection to the piezoresistors, and serve as pads for probe-type resistance measurements, or for bonding wire leads. The thin diaphragm is formed by chemically etching a circular shaped cavity into the surface opposite the piezoresistors. The unetched portion of the silicon slice provides a rigid boundary constraint for the diaphragm and a surface for mounting to some other member." Figure 3–63 "is a cross-sectional view of the sensing element with wire leads bonded to the metal contact. A pressure causes the thin diaphragm to bend, inducing a stress or strain in the diaphragm and also in the buried resistor. The resistor values will change depending on the amount of strain they undergo, which depends on the amount of pressure applied to the diaphragm. Hence, a change in pressure (mechanical input) is converted to a change in resistance (electrical output). The sensing element converts (transducers) energy from one form to another.

"The resistors can be connected in either a half-bridge or a full Wheatstone bridge arrangement. . . . All four resistors will change by approximately the same value. Note that two resistors increase and two decrease depending on their orientation with respect to the crystalline direction of the silicon material.

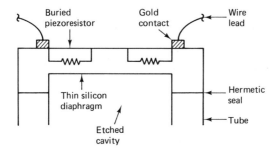

Figure 3–63 Cross-sectional view of a piezoresistive pressure transducer sensing element. (Courtesy of Omega Engineering, Inc., Stamford, CT.)

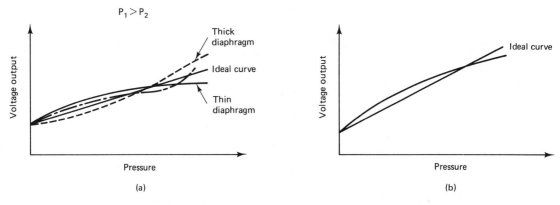

Figure 3–64   Silicon diaphragm nonlinearity: (a) $P_1 > P_2$; (b) $P_1 < P_2$.

"Diaphragms of different thicknesses produce different transducer output curve shapes, when the diaphragm is deflected by a pressure greater at P_1 than P_2." This is shown in Figure 3–64a. Diaphragms deflected at the opposite direction ($P_1 < P_2$) exhibit nonlinearity curves of one shape only, regardless of diaphragm thickness. . . .

"Zero pressure ($P_1 = P_1$) does not produce zero output. There is some voltage through the unit, even with zero scale reading. This is called the null offset or null voltage, and represents the beginning point of the transducer response graph.

"Pressure may be applied to both sides of the sensing chip. P_1 is the termination side and only clean dry gases such as air are recommended as measurands on this side. Few restrictions apply to the P_2 side, except that media incompatible with polyester, silicon, or silicon-based adhesive should not be used.

"In absolute devices, P_2 is sealed with a vacuum representing a fixed reference. The difference in pressure between the vacuum reference and the measurand applied at P_1 causes the deflection of the diaphragm, producing the output voltage change. Differential and gage devices measure one pressure with respect to another. In differential devices, measurands are applied to the P_2 port."

Instead of sensing strain in the diaphragm, you could sense how much it moves in response to an applied pressure. Since this movement is typically a fraction of a millimeter, the displacement to electrical signal converter must be very sensitive. This may be done by allowing the diaphragm to be one plate in a capacitor. Variations in diaphragm position (in response to pressure) cause a change in the capacitance. A capacitive absolute-pressure transducer is shown in Figure 3–65. Of course, as with all the other capacitance output devices you have seen, significant signal conditioning is required. This is usually either an ac bridge (with rectifier and amplifier electronics) or an RF oscillator (with frequency-to-voltage conversion).

There are two other techniques popular for converting pressure to displacement. The capsule and bellows are both sealed chambers made of metal. When the pressure inside the chamber exceeds the pressure outside, the chamber expands. The capsule

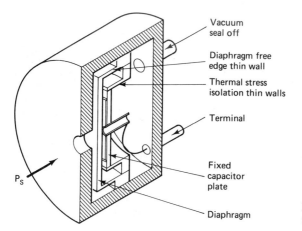

Figure 3–65   Capacitive absolute-pressure transducer. (Courtesy of Rosemount, Inc.)

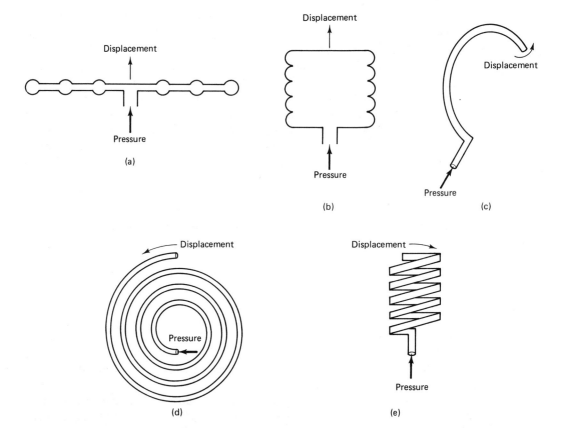

Figure 3–66   Pressure-to-displacement transducers: (a) capsule; (b) bellows; (c) simple Bourdon tube; (d) spiral; (e) helix.

has a single convolution, while the bellows has many. These are shown in Figure 3–66.

The final often-used type of pressure transducer is a Bourdon tube. The tube is bent in a gentle curve of over 180°. This places a greater area on the outer surface of the curve than on the inner. Applying pressure inside the tube places greater force on this outer surface, causing the tube to straighten. The amount of this movement is proportional to the pressure. To get a rotational rather than a linear movement, the Bourdon tube may be coiled into a spiral or a helix. Also, the more turns in the coil, the farther the tube moves for a given pressure. Look at Figure 3–66.

The Bourdon tube converts pressure to displacement. Originally, this displacement was indicated by a needle and scale, attached to the tube. To produce an electrical output, however, you must let the tube drive a position transducer. The curved tube, bellows, or capsule may be connected to the core of an LVDT. This is illustrated in Figure 3–67.

High-output-level pressure transducers have the force available to rotate the wiper of a potentiometer. By connecting the wiper to a helical Bourdon tube, enough range of motion can be generated to move the wiper from minimum to maximum. A potentiometric pressure transducer is shown in Figure 3–68.

There are several specifications common to pressure transducers no matter how the pressure is sensed or how it is converted to an electrical output. In the final analysis, these are the numbers you will have to deal with. They include initial null (or zero) balance, thermal zero effect, and thermal sensitivity effect as well as the nonlinearity, repeatability, and hysteresis discussed at the beginning of this chapter. These effects are illustrated in Example 3–19.

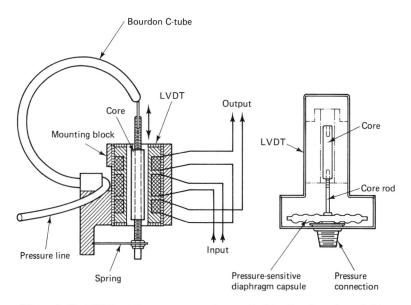

Figure 3–67   LVDT sensing pressure transducer with (a) a Bourdon tube and (b) a capsule. (Courtesy of Schaevitz Engineering.)

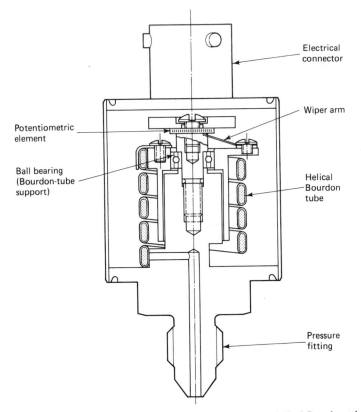

Figure 3–68 Potentiometer sensing pressure transducer with a helical Bourdon tube. (Courtesy of Bourns, Inc.)

EXAMPLE 3–19

A pressure transducer has the following specifications:

> Input pressure: 0–100 psi
> Full-scale output: 100 mV
> Zero accuracy: ±1 mV
> Accuracy: ±1% FS
> Zero balance: 0.02% FS/°F (balance set at 75°F)
> Thermal sensitivity effect: 0.02% FS/°F (difference from 75°F)

Assuming that the transducer is used at 95°F, calculate the error introduced by accuracies, thermal zero effect, and the thermal sensitivity effect.

Solution   Accuracy produces an error that *may* be as large as

$$\text{error} = \pm 0.01 \times 100 \text{ psi} = \pm 1 \text{ psi}$$

The zero accuracy is ± 1 mV or ± 1 psi. The transducer was factory calibrated for zero output with 0 psi at 75°F. Using it at 95°F will cause a shift in both the zero and the full scale.

$$\text{error} = \pm 0.0002/°F \times 100 \text{ psi} \times (95°F - 75°F)$$
$$= \pm 0.4 \text{ psi}$$

Looking at all three effects together, you may see as much as a ± 1.4 psi (or ± 1.4 mV) reading when there is no pressure applied (zero accuracy + zero balance). At any other point, the error may be as much as ± 1.4 psi (or ± 1.4 mV) off (accuracy + thermal sensitivity).

3–5.2 Flow Transducers

Flow tells you how fast material is moving. It can be expressed in three ways: volumetric flow, mass flow, and the velocity of flow. Volumetric flow (Q) indicates the volume of a fluid moving past a point per unit time. Its units are m^3/s or gal/min. Mass flow (Q_m) is in units of mass per unit time (i.e., kg/s). The velocity of the material is called the velocity flow (Q_v) and expressed in m/s. These three quantities are related by

$$Q = \text{volumetric flow}$$

$$Q_m = \text{mass flow} = \rho Q$$

$$Q_v = \text{velocity of flow} = \frac{Q}{A}$$

where ρ is the density of fluid and A is the cross-sectional area of the pipe.

Flow may also be described as being either *laminar* or *turbulent*. In laminar flow, the fluid moves parallel to the walls of the pipe, sliding smoothly, in a single uniform direction. In turbulent flow, the fluid tumbles and swirls. At any particular point, or at any *instant* in time, the flow rate may vary radically. Whether the flow is laminar or turbulent will affect the type of transducer used. The transducer may also, to some degree, introduce turbulence in the flow. Quantitatively, the degree of turbulence is indicated by the Reynolds number:

$$N = \frac{Q_v d \rho}{\mu}$$

where N = Reynolds number
  Q_v = velocity of flow
  d = diameter of the pipe
  ρ = density
  μ = viscosity

For $N > 4000$ the flow is turbulent and for $N < 2000$ the flow is laminar.

The type of material whose flow you are measuring strongly affects the transducer selection. The density may vary from a powder or other solid moving along a conveyor belt, to a pure, dry stream of an inert gas. It may be homogeneous or it may have large chunks. It may be a good electrical insulator or a conductor. It could be caustic or inert.

This diversity of material properties is responsible for the large selection of flow transducer types. In general, flow transducers are divided into two groups. One group introduces an obstruction and uses the energy in the flow to produce a measurable effect. Obstruction transducers include pressure differential units (orifice, venturi, Pitot tubes), turbines and paddle wheels, cantilever vanes and floats. Nonintrusive measuring transducers include electromagnetic and ultrasonic techniques.

Placing an obstruction in the line of flow will have two effects. It will cause a pressure drop across the obstruction. The pressure on the upstream side will go up, while the pressure on the downstream side will drop. Second, the flow will be lowered. This is just like placing a resistor in a series circuit. The current (i.e., flow) causes a voltage drop (i.e., pressure drop) across the resistor (i.e., restriction) and the total current in the circuit goes down.

The orifice plate is the simplest of the pressure differential obstructions. A plate with a hole in it is placed in line with the flow. The pressure drop across the plate is measured using a differential pressure transducer. This is shown in Figure 3–69a.

Bernoulli's equation is fundamental to fluid mechanics. It establishes the relationship of kinetic and potential energy at any two points in the flow of a noncompressible fluid. From this comes the relationship between flow and the pressure dropped across the orifice:

$$Q = k \sqrt{p_2 - p_1} \qquad (3\text{--}27)$$

where Q = flow
  k = constant that is set by the geometry of the orifice and the units of measure used
  p_2 = high-side pressure
  p_1 = low-side pressure

Notice that the flow is proportional to the *square root* of the pressure drop. So you must condition the output of the pressure transducer with a module called a square-root extractor to produce a signal that varies linearly with flow.

The orifice plate has several advantages. It is simple to design, build, and install. This simplicity also yields low maintenance requirements. It can be used for most fluids as long as the flow is reasonably free of particles. However, there are also several disadvantages. The output (Δp) is nonlinear. Remember that you must use a square-root extractor. The larger the output you require, the more pressure drop you must produce. This increasingly loads the system, lowering the very flow you were trying to measure. Because of its abrupt obstruction, the orifice plate may tend to plug up.

The venturi is shown in Figure 3–69b. Instead of an abrupt barrier in the line of

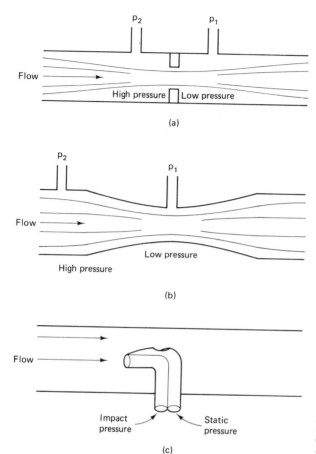

Figure 3–69   Differential pressure obstruction flow sensors: (a) orifice plate; (b) venturi; (c) Pitot tube.

flow, the diameter of the tube is gently narrowed, and then widened. The relationship between flow and pressure difference is the same as with the orifice plate (equation 3–27). However, since there is no sudden stop, there is a much lower tendency to plug up. Also, the pressure on the outlet side of the tube is very near the inlet pressure (p_2). So flow measurement error due to pressure loading is much lower for a venturi than for an orifice plate. Look at the physical construction of both the orifice plate and the venturi in Figure 3–69. The orifice is simply a plate or plug, with a hole, bolted between two flanges. The venturi is much more complex in shape and therefore more expensive and requires some extension in the length of the flow line.

Placing a tube facing into the flow will produce a pressure within the tube (called the impact pressure) which is higher than the pressure in the surrounding flow (the static pressure). As the velocity (flow) of the fluid goes up, the impact pressure increases, although the static pressure does not. The difference between the impact pressure and the static pressure is a measure of the flow (velocity). Equation 3–27 also applies for the Pitot tube, with p_2 being the impact pressure and p_1 the static pressure.

The Pitot tube works well for gas flow. In fact, it has long been used as the sensor in some aircraft airspeed indicators. It also is used in biomedical applications to measure blood flow. However, in an industrial environment, it may plug or be sheared off if the flow contains any particles.

Fluid moving through a tube exerts a force on any obstruction it meets. This force is proportional to the flow. You can measure this force to obtain a reading of the flow. This principle is used in both the cantilever beam flow meter and the rotameter.

The cantilever beam flow meter is shown in Figure 3–70a. Flow causes a force on the target, producing a deflection. This small deflection is sensed by strain gages bonded to the beam and can be measured and displayed with traditional strain gage electronics. To compensate for temperature variation of the fluid, four active strain gages should be used. Flow in either direction can be sensed and the direction is indicated by the polarity of the dc voltage out. (The ability to measure flow in either direction is unusual among flow transducers.) Disadvantages associated with other obstruction-type flow sensors also plague the cantilever beam transducer. There is a pressure drop across the beam, although not as severe as with an orifice. The target encourages clogging and may be damaged by particles. In addition, the strain gage leads must be brought out through the wall of the tube. This requires extra effort in sealing the transducer.

In the variable-area rotameter, shown in Figure 3–70b, the flow pushes on a target, compressing a spring. The target comes to rest at a position where the force from the spring balances the force from the fluid flow. Since the compression force of a spring is proportional to its displacement, measuring how far the target has been pushed tells you about the flow. If placed vertically, the force of gravity can replace the spring. This type of transducer produces a noticeable pressure drop (therefore lowering

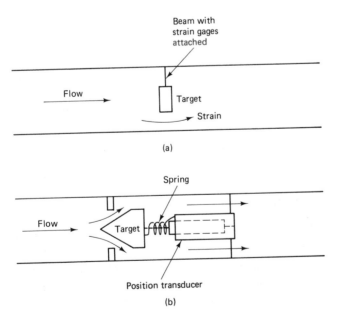

Figure 3–70 Deflection-type flow transducers: (a) cantilever beam; (b) variable-area rotameter.

flow and introducing error) and may be nonlinear. Also, you must bring out the leads from the potentiometer or LVDT used to measure displacement.

Instead of producing a linear movement, the flow may be used to spin a sensor. Then when you measure the rotational velocity of the sensor, you know the flow. The simpler version uses a paddle wheel with one blade extending into the flow. The higher the flow rate, the faster the paddle wheel spins. Look at Figure 3–71a. Embedded in the end of each paddle is a permanent magnet. In the body of the transducer is a Hall effect transistor. It saturates each time a blade rotates pass. The output is pulses. The frequency of these pulses is proportional to the flow. Paddle wheel flow transducers came in an integral unit that can be screwed directly into the flow through a standard fitting.

The paddle wheel flow transducer produces very little pressure drop, so loading is not a problem. The output signal can easily be made to be compatible with whatever logic, microprocessor, or programmable controller you are using. However, since you only get four pulses per revolution, at low flows you must either measure the time between pulses or lose resolution.

Greater resolution can be obtained by adding more blades. Drag is reduced by going to a turbine configuration instead of a paddle wheel. This is shown in Figure 3–71b. The magnets are removed from the blade tips. Instead, the blade is made of a low-reluctance material and a magnetic pickup is used (refer to Section 3–4.1). Another option uses a photoreflective optical sensor to detect rotation of the blade tips. This type of unit eliminates any electromagnetic drag produced by the magnetic pickup. As with the paddle wheel, the output is frequency. Calibration, which relates the frequency out to the flow rate, is also dependent on the temperature and viscosity of the fluid, the pressure drop, and the turbulence of the flow. Often, flow straighteners are needed upstream, as well as a screen to protect the turbine blades from particles in the fluid. Turbines are used most often in hydraulic systems where the fluid has an inherent lubrication effect.

All of the obstruction-type flow meters you have seen here work by using some of the energy in the flow to produce a measurable effect. But removing energy from the flow must cause it (to some degree) to slow down. That is, measurement of flow with any of these devices lowers the flow.

Nonintrusive measurement techniques do not load the system, lowering flow. If you are measuring the flow of a liquid that is mildly conductive (even water will work), the electromagnetic flow meter may be used. The principle is illustrated in Figure 3–72. A nonconductive section of pipe is required. Lining a metal pipe with a nonconductive material will work. Which material to use is determined largely by the temperature and corrosiveness of the liquid. An electromagnetic field is placed at right angles to the flow. The generator rule states that a conductor cutting a magnetic field will induce a voltage that is at right angles to both the electromagnetic field and the direction of motion. Electrodes are placed so as to sense this induced EMF. This induced voltage is linearly proportional to the velocity of flow, the strength of the magnetic field, and the diameter of the pipes.

This type of transducer has the obvious advantage of producing no pressure drop

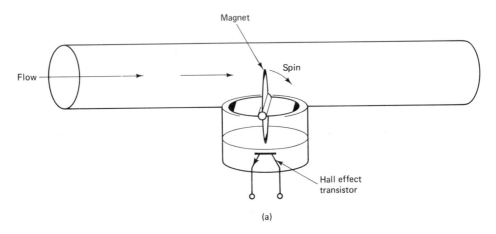

(a)

(b)

Figure 3–71 Spin-type flow transducers: (a) paddle wheel; (b) flow turbine. [(a) Courtesy of Fischer & Porter Co.; (b) courtesy of Ametek Cox Instruments.]

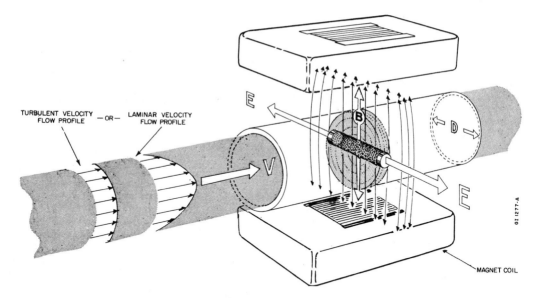

Figure 3–72   Electromagnetic flow meter. (Courtesy of Fischer & Porter Co.)

to load down the flow. Flow reversals can easily be detected. Also, there is nothing to clog up or break off. However, the fluid must be consistently conductive, a special section of pipe is required, and the output is in the microvolt range. Finally, driving the electromagnets may be a problem. Using a dc may cause low-conductance fluids to polarize the areas around the electrical pickup, lowering their effectiveness. An ac excitation may be used, but this produces an ac output and allows capacitive effects associated with the fluid to degrade the output. Pulsed dc has been used, although more sophisticated drive and sense circuitry is required.

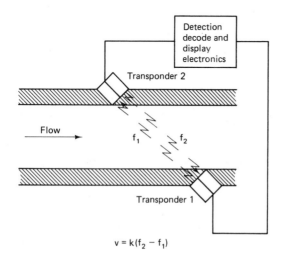

Figure 3–73   Ultrasonic flow transducers.

The other nonintrusive flow transducer uses the propagation of ultrasonic waves through the fluid. One configuration is shown in Figure 3–73. The transducers are piezoelectric crystals capable of both receiving and transmitting ultrasonic signals. They may be operated into the megahertz range. These transducers are placed at 45° to the flow. Each transmits a frequency. The signal traveling with the flow will arrive at a higher frequency than that at which it was transmitted. The signal traveling against the flow will have its frequency lowered. This difference in arrival frequencies is directly proportional to the velocity of the fluid.

Ultrasonic flow transducers may be used on nonconductive fluids or on gases. It provides absolutely no obstruction or loading to the flow. In fact, there are flow transducers that may be clamped onto the outside of a pipe for occasional temporary measurement of the flow within. The disadvantage to ultrasonic flow measurement is the cost of the associated electronics.

3–5.3 Level Transducers

Knowing how much material there is in a tank or vat is important in many manufacturing processes. Overflowing the tank can cause an expensive, perhaps very dangerous accident. Conversely, pumping a tank dry may spoil the process that was scheduled to receive the material from the now dry tank. Or it may damage the empty vessel if the process requires a certain amount of material to absorb heat. Also, in chemical and food production, the proper final result of a step often requires mixing and processing ingredients according to a precise recipe. Accurate measurement of the quantity of material is critical.

The material whose level you are measuring is not necessarily a homogeneous liquid. Depending on the process, it may be a powder, beads, or flakes. It may be intended for food or be highly corrosive. It may pile up against the sides of the vat or it may slosh producing waves. All these properties should influence your choice of a level transducer.

Level transducers are divided into two major classes, continuous and discrete. Continuous transducers indicate the precise level, proportionally along the entire height of the tank. They will be discussed in more detail later in this section. On the other hand, it may only be necessary to have an indication (or alarm) when the tank reaches a prescribed level or if the tank is in danger of overflowing or being emptied. For these applications, a simple switch closure or voltage step is adequate. In fact, such discrete transducer outputs are much simpler for the controller to handle than is the output from a continuous transducer.

The float switch is shown in Figure 3–74a. It comes in either normally open or normally closed configuration. The contacts are similar to those used in relays. They are spring loaded open and are made of a ferromagnetic material. When a magnet moves above them the magnetic field pulls the contacts closed. These contacts are sealed inside a nonferrous tube. A permanent magnet(s) is embedded inside the float. This travels up and down the tube in response to the level you are measuring. Retainer rings restrict the range of motion of the float. These contacts will handle either dc or ac up to 115 V ac. So you can easily configure a float switch to input to some logic

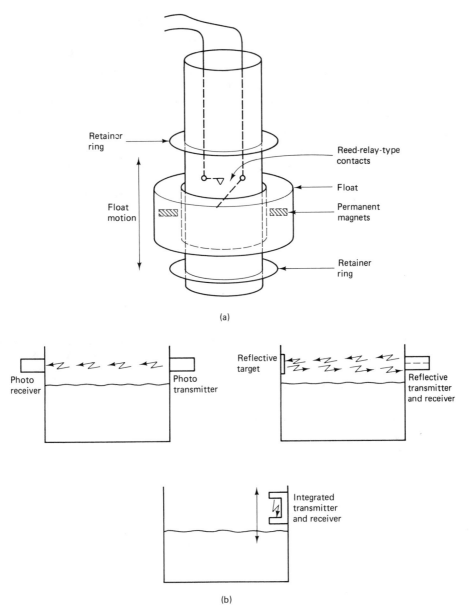

Figure 3–74   Discrete level transducers: (a) float switch; (b) photoelectric.

circuitry, to drive a programmable controller, or to directly power an alarm or other actuator.

Photo detection can be used to sense level if the optical properties of the material will reliably block the transmission of light. Several possible configurations are illustrated in Figure 3–74b. The transmitter is usually an infrared light-emitting diode with appropriate lenses and beam collimation. The receiver is a photosensitive transistor with optical filters to pass only the wavelength of the light being transmitted. This minimizes errors from ambient lighting. When the level is below the sensor, light reaches the receiver, and the phototransistor saturates, giving you a logic low. When the level in the tank blocks the light, the phototransistor goes off. In addition to dc power, you may have to provide an external pull-up resistor connected between the phototransistor's open collector and whatever voltage you want for a logic-high level. There are also receivers available that use a light-sensitive thyristor rather than a phototransistor. These receivers output 115 V ac when hit by the beam.

The reflective transmitter and receiver is easier to install than the units with separate transmitter and receiver. Only one set of wires is required, and as long as the target is large enough, alignment is not critical. The integrated transmitter and receiver provide added flexibility. By mounting it on a rod, it can be raised or lowered, allowing you easily to select the alarm level.

Photodetectors are more durable than float switches since there are no mechanical parts to fail. However, the photodetector requires that the material block the transmission of light. This somewhat limits their application.

The measurement of heat transfer can also be used to detect the presence of material in a tank. A resistive temperature sensor is driven hard enough to cause it to self-heat. The heat radiated into the air from this sensor is low, causing the sensor to detect a relatively high temperature. When immersed in a liquid, heat is more rapidly conducted away from the sensor. The temperature of the sensor drops noticeably as soon as it is covered by the liquid. An external signal conditioner is necessary to drive the sensor and to convert its output into a useful signal. This technique will have problems if the temperature of the liquid is near the sensor's self-heating temperature (in air) or if the temperature of the liquid varies much.

In some applications it is enough to know that the liquid is above or below a given level. That is all that a discrete level transducer can tell you. However, much process control requires a precise, linear indication of the amount of material in the tank. This demands a continuous level transducer. There are a wide variety of ways to produce a signal that tracks the amount of material in a tank. Five will be presented. The pressure at the bottom of the tank depends linearly on the level of the liquid in the tank. Whether liquid or solid, the weight of the tank is a measure of the amount it contains. Floats and levers can be used to track the top of the liquid and move a potentiometer or valve. For electrically insulating liquids or solids, the tank and an electrode can be turned into a giant capacitor. Ultrasonic detectors, like those used in the automatic range finder and focus of some cameras, will easily find the distance to the surface of the liquid.

In Section 3–5.1 you saw that the pressure at the bottom of a column of liquid is defined as the head and is proportional to the height of the column.

$$p = \rho g h$$

where p = head (pressure)

ρ = density of the liquid

h = height of the column

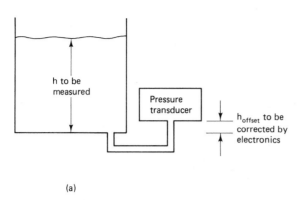

(a)

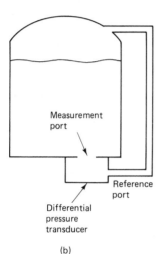

(b)

Figure 3–75   Level measurement by sensing pressure with (a) an offset transducer and (b) a sealed tank.

So you can measure the level of liquid in a tank by measuring the pressure at the bottom of the tank.

However, this technique makes several assumptions of which you should be aware. First, for the results to be consistent, the liquid must be uniform. Really all this says is that the density must be a constant. Second, the height resulting from the pressure reading is from the transducer up. So if you cannot mount the pressure transducer at the bottom of the tank, your signal-conditioning electronics must add or subtract some offset to get the zero point right. This is shown in Figure 3–75a.

The final consideration when using pressure to indicate level is the pressure at the top of the tank. If the tank is open to atmospheric pressure, the basic head equation works, and you can use a transducer that measures gage pressure (pressure with respect to atmospheric pressure). However, if the tank is sealed, the pressure at the bottom of the tank depends not only on the head, but also on the pressure at the top:

$$p_{\text{bottom}} = \rho g h + p_{\text{top}}$$

or

$$h = \frac{p_{\text{bottom}} - p_{\text{top}}}{\rho g}$$

To perform this calculation automatically you can use a differential pressure transducer with the reference port plumbed into the top of the tank. This is shown in Figure 3–75b.

A true measure of how much is in a tank is its weight. This works whether the tank is holding a liquid, a solid, or something in between. The tank should be fully supported by load cells. If it is necessary to use more than one, you must either assure that the weight is evenly distributed, or you must provide some form of circuitry that will add the loads indicated by each cell. Finally, the signal-conditioning electronics must be adjusted to give a zero output when the load cells are supporting an empty tank. All of this need not be as complicated as it sounds. In many installations, an active and dummy gage can be bonded to an existing support beam. Then you just run a calibration record (and curve) by filling and emptying the tank, measuring the amount you add and the resulting stress.

Perhaps the most widely used level transducer and control system is the float and valve arrangement inside the tank of a residential toilet. Its principle of operation is illustrated in Figure 3–76. A float moves up and down on the top of the water in the tank. Through a pivot arrangement (simplified in the drawing), a valve is positioned. The valve location is proportional to level. When the level is low, the float falls, opening the valve. As the level rises, the float comes up, pushing down on the valve to close it. The lever arm and pivot also mechanically amplify the force applied by the float to the valve by a factor of l_1/l_2.

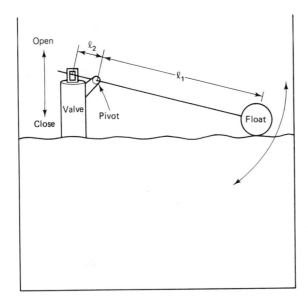

Figure 3–76 Float-driven level control system.

For more sophisticated controls applications, the valve can be replaced with the slider arm of a linear potentiometer. As the level varies, the float goes up and down, moving the arm on the potentiometer. Gearing can be added to convert the vertical motion of the lever arm, l_2, to a circular motion, to turn the shaft of a rotory potentiometer.

This float and potentiometer system for measuring level has several advantages over the other transducers that you will see. The output signal may be a high-level dc voltage. This probably needs no further signal conditioning and is easy for the controller and display electronics to use. Second, the system is simple. So it will be both relatively inexpensive and reliable.

However, there are several disadvantages. The float has a rather limited range of motion. The mechanism must be inserted inside the tank, and properly positioned and supported. In many applications, placing something *inside* the tank is impossible. Also, the potentiometer may have to be carefully sealed and protected from being submerged in the liquid.

The capacitance of a parallel-plate capacitor is

$$C = \frac{A\epsilon}{d}$$

where C = capacitance
A = area of the plates
ϵ = dielectric constant
d = distance separating the plates

The dielectric constant of air is approximately 1.0, water has a constant more like 80, while some solids may have dielectric constants of 10,000 or more. This radical variation in dielectric constant can be exploited to measure level. Look at Figure 3–77. Concentric probes are placed into the tank. As the level rises, the average dielectric constant also goes up linearly. The capacitance is then a measure of the level in the tank. To increase the capacitive effect, several concentric electrodes can be used. Wiring alternate layers together increases the area. As with the other capacitance transducers shown in this chapter, the level capacitance transducer must be followed by signal-conditioning electronics which convert the capacitance to a more easily used signal. With an ac bridge, the magnitude of the capacitance determines the magnitude of the ac signal out of the bridge. Using the level-sensitive capacitance to set the frequency of an oscillator provides a frequency that is related directly to the level in the tank.

If the tank is conductive, it is possible to insert only one electrode and use the tank itself as the other plate of the capacitor. However, consider the restrictions carefully. For safety reasons the metal tank must be tied to earth. This may be inconvenient as far as your signal-conditioning electronics are concerned. Also, any electrical noise, ground loops, or accidents may inject misleading (perhaps damaging) signals onto the tank, and therefore into the control circuitry.

If the liquid whose height you are measuring is conductive, resistance rather than capacitance can be used. The concentric, highly conductive probes in Figure 3–77 are replaced by two lengths of resistive wire. It is necessary to use wire with a high,

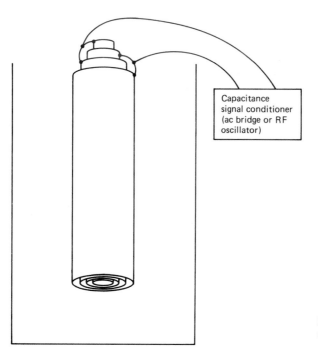

Figure 3–77 Capacitance level transducer.

stable, well-defined resistance per unit length. As the level rises, more and more of the wire is shorted out, lowering the resistance. The resistance, then, is inversely proportional to the level. This technique is popular when trying to determine the height of a column of mercury in a manometer or traditional blood pressure cuff transducer.

With the advent of automatic focusing on consumer cameras has come an accurate, inexpensive, easy-to-use, modular, ultrasonic range detector. To measure level with an ultrasonic range detector module, you mount the module above the tank, looking down at the surface. A pulse must be applied to the module to initiate a measurement. When the ultrasonic signal is transmitted, the module outputs a pulse. When the echo is received, another pulse is outputted from the module. Using an external counter you must measure the time between the transmit pulse and the echo-received pulse. Since the ultrasonic signal is traveling at the speed of sound, the time between transmission and echo received is a measure of the distance to the surface. Distances to be measured should be between 0.5 and 10 m.

$$d = 0.5vt$$

where d = distance to the surface
$\quad v$ = velocity of sound
$\qquad$ = 331.5 m/s at sea level and 0°C
$\quad t$ = total time to the surface and back

Mounting the ultrasonic range detector above the tank looking down is convenient. It is easy to get at, installation is simple, and the unit does not have to be sealed against the effects of the material in the tank. However, as the tank fills up, the distance from the sensor to the surface becomes smaller. This produces a smaller transit time and a lower count on the external timer. That is, as the level goes up, the data gathered provide a lower number. There are two options. One is to use an ultrasonic detector which will work in the material in the tank. Place the module at the bottom of the tank. The beam will reflect off the surface, providing a longer transit time as the level moves up. The other possibility is to provide additional data manipulation with the counters to correct the data obtained from the top-mounted ultrasonic detector.

EXAMPLE 3-20

Determine the block diagram and appropriate equations to use an ultrasonic range detector to determine the level in a tank that is 5 m deep. There should be 0 output when the tank is empty, and 1000 when the tank is full.

Solution   The block diagram is given in Figure 3-78. The ultrasonic detector is mounted 0.5 m above the full point of the tank. When the tank is empty the wave must travel 5.5 m and return. This will take

$$t_{empty} = \frac{5.5 \text{ m}}{(0.5)(331.5 \text{ m/s})}$$
$$= 33.183 \text{ ms}$$

When the tank is full, the wave must travel 0.5 m and return. This will take

$$t_{full} = \frac{0.5 \text{ m}}{(0.5)(331.5 \text{ m/s})}$$
$$= 3.017 \text{ ms}$$

The time difference between empty and full is

$$t_{diff} = 33.183 \text{ ms} - 3.017 \text{ ms}$$
$$= 30.167 \text{ ms}$$

This difference in time is supposed to produce a count difference of 1000. So the time for each count is

$$t_{per\ count} = \frac{30.167 \text{ ms}}{1000}$$
$$= 30.167 \text{ μs}$$

This count signal can be provided with a clock that runs at

$$f_{clock} = \frac{1}{30.167 \text{ μs}}$$
$$= 33.15 \text{ kHz}$$

Now look more carefully at the block diagram in Figure 3-78. The timing and control block begins a measurement by issuing a pulse to the transducer and to the presettable counter. The counter loads in the value 1100. When the transducer emits a sound wave, it provides a pulse on the transmitted line. This opens the gate. The counter begins to count the clock, beginning at 1100 and *decrementing* once every 30.17 μs. If the tank is full, after 3.017 ms the received line will be pulsed and the gate will close. During this time, the counter will have decremented 100 times, leaving a count of 1000. If the tank is empty, it will take 33.183 ms for the received pulse to occur, closing the gate. During this time, the counter will decrement 1100 times, leaving a count of 0.

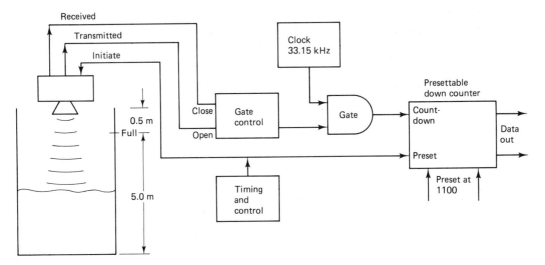

Figure 3–78   Top-mounted ultrasonic level sensor (Example 3–20).

3–6 TEMPERATURE TRANSDUCERS*

"Synthetic fuel research, solar energy conversion and new engine development are but a few of the burgeoning disciplines responding to the state of our dwindling natural resources. As all industries place new emphasis on energy efficiency, the fundamental measurement of temperature assumes new importance. The purpose of this application note is to explore the more common temperature monitoring techniques and introduce procedures for improving their accuracy.

"We will focus on the four most common temperature transducers: the thermocouple, the RTD, the thermistor and the integrated circuit sensor." The general response, advantages, and disadvantages of these are given in Table 3–9.

"Galileo is credited with inventing the thermometer, circa 1592. In an open container filled with colored alcohol he suspended a long narrow-throated glass tube, at the upper end of which was a hollow sphere. When heated, the air in the sphere expanded and

---

*The quoted material in Section 3–6 is from Ref. 11 except where noted otherwise.

TABLE 3–9 COMMON TEMPERATURE TRANSDUCERS

Thermocouple	RTD	Thermistor	I.C. Sensor
Advantages ☐ Self-powered ☐ Simple ☐ Rugged ☐ Inexpensive ☐ Wide variety ☐ Wide temperature range	☐ Most stable ☐ Most accurate ☐ More linear than thermocouple	☐ High output ☐ Fast ☐ Two-wire ohms measurement	☐ Most linear ☐ Highest output ☐ Inexpensive
Disadvantages ☐ Non-linear ☐ Low voltage ☐ Reference required ☐ Least stable ☐ Least sensitive	☐ Expensive ☐ Current source required ☐ Small ΔR ☐ Low absolute resistance ☐ Self-heating	☐ Non-linear ☐ Limited temperature range ☐ Fragile ☐ Current source required ☐ Self-heating	☐ T <200°C ☐ Power supply required ☐ Slow ☐ Self-heating ☐ Limited configurations

Source: Omega Engineering.

bubbled through the liquid. Cooling the sphere caused the liquid to move up the tube. Fluctuations in the temperature of the sphere could then be observed by noting the position of the liquid inside the tube. This 'upside-down' thermometer was a poor indicator since the level changed with barometric pressure and the tube had no scale. Vast improvements were made in temperature measurement accuracy with the development of the Florentine thermometer, which incorporated sealed construction and a graduated scale.

"In the ensuing decades, many thermometric scales were conceived, all based on two or more fixed points. One scale, however, wasn't universally recognized until the early 1700s, when Gabriel Fahrenheit, a Dutch instrument maker, produced accurate and repeatable mercury thermometers. For the fixed point on the low end of his temperature scale, Fahrenheit used a mixture of ice water and salt (or ammonium chloride). This was the lowest temperature he could reproduce, and he labeled it 'zero degrees.' For the high end of his scale, he chose human blood temperature and called it 96°.

"Why 96 and not 100°? Earlier scales had been divided into 12 parts. Fahrenheit, in an apparent quest for more resolution divided his scale into 24, then 48 and eventually 96 parts.

"The Fahrenheit scale gained popularity primarily because of the repeatability and quality of the thermometers that Fahrenheit build.

"Around 1742, Anders Celsius proposed that the melting point of ice and the boiling point of water be used for the two benchmarks. Celsius selected zero degrees as the boiling point and 100° as the melting point. Later, the end points were reversed and the centigrade scale was born. In 1948 the name was officially changed to the Celsius scale.

"In the early 1800 William Thomson (Lord Kelvin), developed a universal thermodynamic scale based upon the coefficient of expansion of an ideal gas. Kelvin established the concept of absolute zero and his scale remains the standard for modern thermometry.

"The conversion equations for the four modern temperature scales are:

$$°C = 5/9(°F - 32) \qquad °F = 9/5°C + 32$$

$$°K = °C + 273.15 \qquad °R = °F + 459.67$$

"The Rankine scale (°R) is simply the Fahrenheit equivalent of the Kelvin scale, and was named after an early pioneer in the field of thermodynamics, W. J. M. Rankine."

3–6.1 Thermocouple

"When two wires composed of dissimilar metals are joined at both ends and one of the ends is heated, there is a continuous current which flows in the thermoelectric circuit. Thomas Seebeck made this discovery in 1821." See Figure 3–79a. "If this circuit is broken at the center, the net open circuit voltage (the Seebeck voltage) is a function of the junction temperature and the composition of the two metals" (Figure 3–79b).

"We can't measure the Seebeck voltage directly because we must first connect a voltmeter to the thermocouple, and the voltmeter leads themselves create a new thermoelectric circuit. Let's connect a voltmeter across a copper–constantan (type T) thermocouple and look at the voltage output." This is shown in Figure 3–80.

"We would like the voltmeter to read only V_1, but by connecting the voltmeter

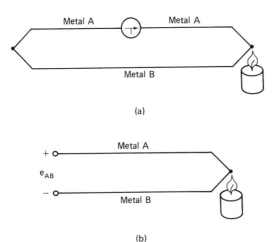

(a)

(b)

Figure 3–79 Seebeck effect: (a) current in a closed circuit; (b) voltage across an open circuit. (Courtesy of Omega Engineering, Inc., Stamford, CT.)

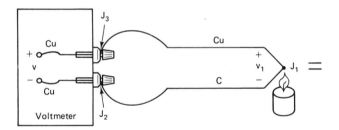

Equivalent circuits:

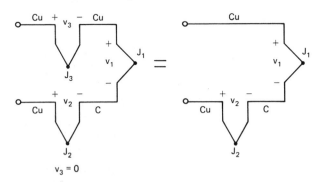

Figure 3–80 Measuring junction voltage with a DVM. (Courtesy of Omega Engineering, Inc., Stamford, CT.)

in an attempt to measure the output of junction J_1, we have created two more metallic junctions: J_2 is a copper-to-constantan junction which will add an EMF (V_2) in opposition to V_1. The resultant voltmeter reading V will be proportional to the temperature difference between J_1 and J_2. This says that we can't find the temperature of J_1 unless we first find the temperature of J_2.

"One way to determine the temperature of J_2 is to physically put the junction into an ice bath, forcing its temperature to be 0°C and establishing J_2 as the reference junction. Since both voltmeter terminal junctions are now copper–copper, they create no thermal EMF and the reading V on voltmeter is proportional to the temperature difference between J_1 and J_2." Look at Figure 3–81.

"Now the voltmeter reading is

$$V = V_1 - V_2 = t_{j1} - t_{j2}$$

If we specify T_{j1} in degrees Celsius:

$$T_{j1}(°C) + 273.15 = t_{j1}$$

$$V = V_1 - V_2 = (T_{j1} + 273.15) - (T_{j2} + 273.15)$$

$$= T_{j1} - T_{j2} = T_{j1} - 0$$

$$= T_{j1}$$

We use this protracted derivation to emphasize that the ice bath junction output, V_2, is not zero volts. It is a function of absolute temperature.

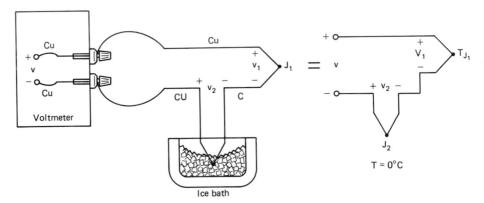

Figure 3–81 Thermocouple measurement using an external reference. (Courtesy of Omega Engineering, Inc., Stamford, CT.)

"By adding the voltage of the ice-point reference junction we have now referenced the reading V to 0°C. This method is very accurate because the ice point temperature can be precisely controlled. The ice point is used by the National Bureau of Standards (NBS) as the fundamental reference point for their thermocouple tables, so we can now look at the NBS tables and directly convert from voltage V to temperature T_{j1}.

"A thermistor, whose resistance R_T is a function of temperature, provides us with a way to measure the absolute temperature of the reference junction." Look at Figure 3–82. "Junctions J_3 and J_4 and the thermistor are all assumed to be at the same temperature, due to the design of the isothermal block. Using a digital multimeter under computer control, we simply:

1. Measure R_T to find T_{ref} and convert T_{ref} to its equivalent reference junction voltage, V_{ref}.
2. Measure V and subtract V_{ref} to find V_1, and convert V_1 to temperature T_{j1}.

"This procedure is known as software compensation because it relies upon the software of a computer to compensate for the effect of the reference junction. The

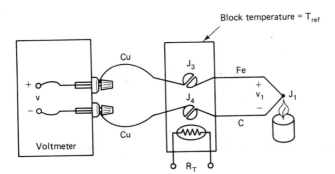

Figure 3–82 External reference junction with no ice bath. (Courtesy of Omega Engineering, Inc., Stamford, CT.)

isothermal terminal block temperature sensor can be any device which has a characteristic proportional to absolute temperature: an RTD, a thermistor, or an integrated circuit sensor.

"It seems logical to ask: If we already have a device that will measure absolute temperature (like an RTD or thermistor) why do we even bother with a thermocouple that requires reference junction compensation? The single most important answer to this question is that the thermistor, the RTD, and the integrated circuit transducer are only useful over a certain temperature range. Thermocouples, on the other hand, can be used over a range of temperatures, and optimized for various atmospheres. They are much more rugged than thermistors, as evidenced by the fact that thermocouples are often welded to a metal part or clamped under a screw. They can be manufactured on the spot, either by soldering or welding. In short, thermocouples are the most versatile temperature transducer available and since the measurement system performs the entire task of reference compensation and software voltage-to-temperature conversion, using a thermocouple becomes as easy as connecting a pair of wires.

"Thermocouple measurement becomes especially convenient when we are required to monitor a large number of data points. This is accomplished by using the isothermal reference junction for more than one thermocouple element." Look at Figure 3–83. "A reed relay scanner connects the voltmeter to the various thermocouples in sequence. All of the voltmeter and scanner wires are copper, independent of the type of thermocouple chosen. In fact, as long as we know what each thermocouple is, we can mix thermocouple types on the same isothermal junction block (often called a zone box) and make the appropriate modifications in software. The junction block temperature sensor, R_T, is located at the center of the block to minimize errors due to thermal gradients.

"Software compensation is the most versatile technique we have for measuring thermocouples. Many thermocouples are connected on the same block, copper leads

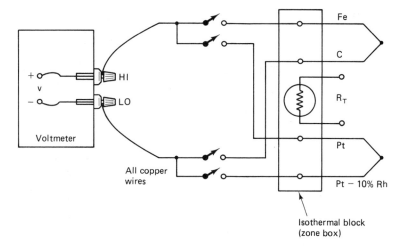

Figure 3–83 Scanning many thermocouples. (Courtesy of Omega Engineering, Inc., Stamford, CT.)

are used throughout the scanner, and the technique is independent of the types of thermo-couples chosen. In addition, when using a data acquisition system with a built-in zone box, we simply connect the thermocouple as we would•a pair of test leads. All of the conversions are performed by the computer. The one disadvantage is that the computer requires a small amount of additional time to calculate the reference junction temperature. For maximum speed we can use hardware compensation.

"Rather than measuring the temperature of the reference junction and computing its equivalent voltage as we did with software compensation, we could insert a battery to cancel the offset voltage of the reference junction. The combination of this hardware compensation voltage and the reference junction voltage is equal to that of a 0°C junction.

"The compensation voltage, e, is a function of the temperature sensing resistor, R_T. The voltage V is now referenced to 0°C, and may be read directly and converted to temperature by using the NBS tables.

"Another name for this circuit is the electronic ice point reference. These circuits are commercially available for use with any voltmeter and with a wide variety of thermo-couples. The major drawback is that a unique ice point reference circuit is usually needed for each individual thermocouple type." Figure 3–84 illustrates the principle.

"The advantage of the hardware compensation circuit or electronic ice-point refer-ence is that we eliminate the need to compute the reference temperature. This saves us two computation steps and makes a hardware compensation temperature measurement somewhat faster than a software compensation measurement."

"The AD594/AD595 (from Analog Devices) is a complete instrumentation amplifier and thermocouple cold junction compensator on a monolithic clip. It combines an ice point reference with a precalibrated amplifier to produce a high level (10 mV/°C) output directly from a thermocouple signal. Pin strapping options allow it to be used as a linear amplifier-compensator or as a switch output set-point controller using either fixed

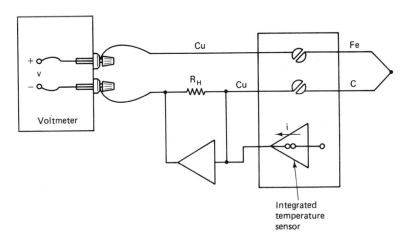

Figure 3–84 Electronic ice-point compensation. (Courtesy of Omega Engineering, Inc., Stamford, CT.

or remote set-point control. It can be used to amplify its compensation voltage directly, thereby converting it to a stand-alone Celsius transducer with a low-impedance voltage output'' [12].

"The AD594/AD595 includes a thermocouple failure alarm that indicates if one or both thermocouple leads become open. The alarm output has a flexible format which includes TTL drive capability'' [12].

"The AD594/AD595 can be powered from a single-ended supply (including +5 V) and by including a negative supply, temperatures below 0°C can be measured. To minimize self-heating, an unloaded AD594/AD595 will typically operate with a total supply current of 160 μA, but is also capable of delivering in excess of +5 mA to a load'' [12].

"The AD594 is precalibrated by laser wafer trimming to match the characteristic of type J (iron–constantan) thermocouples and the AD595 is laser trimmed for type K (chromal–alumel) inputs. The temperature transducer voltages and gain control resistors are available at the package pins so that the circuit can be recalibrated for other thermocouple types by the addition of two or three resistors. These terminals also allow more precise calibration for both thermocouple and thermometer applications'' [12].

A typical circuit configuration is shown in Figure 3–85. Three points must be made. First, the connection of the iron (or chromal) lead and pin 1 of the IC to circuit common is *not* optional. This point must be tied to common to properly bias the input of the instrumentation amplifier. Second, the output is taken from pins 8 and 9. Third, the output is nonlinear, just as the thermocouple is. It has just been amplified to *approximately* 10 mV/°C. The precise outputs are given in Table 3–10.

"We have used hardware and software compensation to synthesize an ice-point reference. Now all we have to do is to read the digital voltmeter and convert the voltage reading to a temperature. Unfortunately, the temperature-versus-voltage relationship of a thermocouple is not linear. The National Bureau of Standards Thermocouple Table for a J-type thermocouple is given in Table 3–11.

"We could store these look-up table values in a computer, but they would consume an inordinate amount of memory. A more viable approach is to approximate the table values, using a power series polynomial:

$$T = a_0 + a_1 x + a_2 x^2 + a_3 x^3 + \cdots + a_n x^n$$

where T = temperature

x = thermocouple voltage

a = polynomial coefficients unique to each thermocouple

n = maximum order of the polynomial

"As n increases, the accuracy of the polynomial improves. A representative number is $n = 9$ for ± 1°C accuracy. Lower-order polynomials may be used over a narrow temperature range to obtain higher system speed.

"Table 3–12 is an example of the polynomials used in conjunction with system software compensation packages for a data acquisition system. Rather than directly calculating the exponentials, the computer is programmed to use the nested polynomial

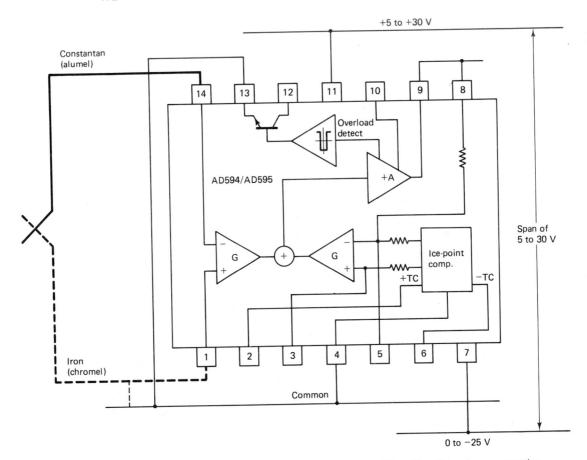

Figure 3–85 AD594/AD595 monolithic thermocouple amplifier with cold junction compensation. (Courtesy of Analog Devices.)

form to save execution time. The polynomial fit rapidly degrades outside the temperature range shown and should not be extrapolated outside those limits.

"All the foregoing procedures assume the thermocouple voltage can be measured accurately and easily. . . . Examine the requirements of the system voltmeter" shown in Table 3–13.

"Even for the common type K thermocouple, the voltmeter must be able to resolve 4 μV to detect a 0.1°C change. The magnitude of this signal is an open invitation for noise to creep into any system. For this reason instrument designers utilize several fundamental noise rejection techniques, including tree switching, normal mode filtering, integration, and guarding.

TABLE 3-10 OUTPUT VOLTAGE VERSUS TEMPERATURE FOR THE AD594/595

Thermocouple temperature (°C)	Type J voltage (mV)	AD594 output (mV)	Type K voltage (mV)	AD595 output (mV)	Thermocouple temperature (°C)	Type J voltage (mV)	AD594 output (mV)	Type K voltage (mV)	AD595 output (mV)
-200	-7.890	-1,523	-5.891	-1,454	500	27.388	5,300	20.640	5,107
-180	-7.402	-1,428	-5.550	-1,370	520	28.511	5,517	21.493	5,318
-160	-6.821	-1,316	-5.141	-1,269	540	29.642	5,736	22.346	5,529
-140	-6.159	-1,188	-4.669	-1,152	560	30.782	5,956	23.198	5,740
-120	-5.426	-1,046	-4.138	-1,021	580	31.933	6,179	24.050	5,950
-100	-4.632	-893	-3.553	-876	600	33.096	6,404	24.902	6,161
-80	-3.785	-729	-2.920	-719	620	34.273	6,632	25.751	6,371
-60	-2.892	-556	-2.243	-552	640	35.464	6,862	26.599	6,581
-40	-1.960	-376	-1.527	-375	660	36.671	7,095	27.445	6,790
-20	-0.995	-189	-0.777	-189	680	37.893	7,332	28.288	6,998
-10	-0.501	-94	-0.392	-94	700	39.130	7,571	28.128	7,206
0	0	3.1	0	2.7	720	40.382	7,813	29.965	7,413
10	0.507	101	0.397	101	740	41.647	8,058	30.799	7,619
20	1.019	200	0.798	200	750	42.283	8,181	31.214	7,722
25	1.277	250	1.000	250	760	—	—	31.629	7,825
30	1.536	300	1.203	300	780	—	—	32.455	8,029
40	2.058	401	1.611	401	800	—	—	33.277	8,232
50	2.585	503	2.022	503	820	—	—	34.095	8,434
60	3.115	606	2.436	605	840	—	—	34.909	8,636
80	4.186	813	3.266	810	860	—	—	35.718	8,836
100	5.268	1,022	4.095	1,015	880	—	—	36.524	9,035

120	6.359	1,233	4.919	1,219	900	—	—	37.325	9,233
140	7.457	1,445	5.733	1,420	920	—	—	38.122	9,430
160	8.560	1,659	6.539	1,620	940	—	—	38.915	9,626
180	9.667	1,873	7.338	1,817	960	—	—	39.703	9,821
200	10.777	2,087	8.137	2,015	980	—	—	40.488	10,015
220	11.887	2,302	8.938	2,213	1,000	—	—	41.269	10,209
240	12.998	2,517	9.745	2,413	1,020	—	—	42.045	10,400
260	14.108	2,732	10.560	2,614	1,040	—	—	42.817	10,591
280	15.217	2,946	11.381	2,817	1,060	—	—	43.585	10,781
300	16.325	3,160	12.207	3,022	1,080	—	—	44.349	10,970
320	17.432	3,374	13.039	3,327	1,100	—	—	45.108	11,158
340	18.537	3,588	13.874	3,434	1,120	—	—	45.863	11,345
360	19.640	3,801	14.712	3,641	1,140	—	—	46.612	11,530
380	20.743	4,015	15.552	3,849	1,160	—	—	47.356	11,714
400	21.846	4,228	16.395	4,057	1,180	—	—	48.095	11,897
420	22.949	4,441	17.241	4,266	1,200	—	—	48.828	12,078
440	24.054	4,655	18.088	4,476	1,220	—	—	49.555	12,258
460	25.161	4,869	18.938	4,686	1,240	—	—	50.276	12,436
480	26.272	5,084	19.788	4,896	1,250	—	—	50.633	12,524

Source: Analog Devices.

TABLE 3–11 TYPE J [IRON VERSUS COPPER–NICKEL (CONSTANTAN)] THERMOCOUPLE OUTPUT (ABSOLUTE mV) REFERENCE JUNCTION AT 0°C

°C	0	1	2	3	4	5	6	7	8	9	10
−210	−8.096										
−200	−7.890	−7.912	−7.934	−7.955	−7.976	−7.996	−8.017	−8.037	−8.057	−8.076	−8.096
−190	−7.659	−7.683	−7.707	−7.731	−7.755	−7.778	−7.801	−7.824	−7.846	−7.868	−7.890
−180	−7.402	−7.429	−7.455	−7.482	−7.508	−7.533	−7.559	−7.584	−7.609	−7.634	−7.659
−170	−7.122	−7.151	−7.180	−7.209	−7.237	−7.265	−7.293	−7.321	−7.348	−7.375	−7.402
−160	−6.821	−6.852	−6.883	−6.914	−6.944	−6.974	−7.004	−7.034	−7.064	−7.093	−7.122
−150	−6.499	−6.532	−6.565	−6.598	−6.630	−6.663	−6.695	−6.727	−6.758	−6.790	−6.821
−140	−6.159	−6.194	−6.228	−6.263	−6.297	−6.331	−6.365	−6.399	−6.433	−6.466	−6.499
−130	−5.801	−5.837	−5.874	−5.910	−5.946	−5.982	−6.018	−6.053	−6.089	−6.124	−6.159
−120	−5.426	−5.464	−5.502	−5.540	−5.578	−5.615	−5.653	−5.690	−5.727	−5.764	−5.801
−110	−5.036	−5.076	−5.115	−5.155	−5.194	−5.233	−5.272	−5.311	−5.349	−5.388	−5.426
−100	−4.632	−4.673	−4.714	−4.755	−4.795	−4.836	−4.876	−4.916	−4.956	−4.996	−5.036
−90	−4.215	−4.257	−4.299	−4.341	−4.383	−4.425	−4.467	−4.508	−4.550	−4.591	−4.632
−80	−3.785	−3.829	−3.872	−3.915	−3.958	−4.001	−4.044	−4.087	−4.130	−4.172	−4.215
−70	−3.344	−3.389	−3.433	−3.478	−3.522	−3.566	−3.610	−3.654	−3.698	−3.742	−3.785
−60	−2.892	−2.938	−2.984	−3.029	−3.074	−3.120	−3.165	−3.210	−3.255	−3.299	−3.344
−50	−2.431	−2.478	−2.524	−2.570	−2.617	−2.663	−2.709	−2.755	−2.801	−2.847	−2.892
−40	−1.960	−2.008	−2.055	−2.102	−2.150	−2.197	−2.244	−2.291	−2.338	−2.384	−2.431
−30	−1.481	−1.530	−1.578	−1.626	−1.674	−1.722	−1.770	−1.818	−1.865	−1.913	−1.960
−20	−0.995	−1.044	−1.093	−1.141	−1.190	−1.239	−1.288	−1.336	−1.385	−1.433	−1.481
−10	−0.501	−0.550	−0.600	−0.650	−0.699	−0.748	−0.798	−0.847	−0.896	−0.945	−0.995
0	0.000	−0.050	−0.101	−0.151	−0.201	−0.251	−0.301	−0.351	−0.401	−0.451	−0.501
0	0.000	0.050	0.101	0.151	0.202	0.253	0.303	0.354	0.405	0.456	0.507
10	0.507	0.558	0.609	0.660	0.711	0.762	0.813	0.865	0.916	0.967	1.019
20	1.019	1.070	1.122	1.174	1.225	1.277	1.329	1.381	1.432	1.484	1.536
30	1.536	1.588	1.640	1.693	1.745	1.797	1.849	1.901	1.954	2.006	2.058
40	2.058	2.111	2.163	2.216	2.268	2.321	2.374	2.426	2.479	2.532	2.585
50	2.585	2.638	2.691	2.743	2.796	2.849	2.902	2.956	3.009	3.062	3.115
60	3.115	3.168	3.221	3.275	3.328	3.381	3.435	3.488	3.542	3.595	3.649
70	3.649	3.702	3.756	3.809	3.863	3.917	3.971	4.024	4.078	4.132	4.186
80	4.186	4.239	4.293	4.347	4.401	4.455	4.509	4.563	4.617	4.671	4.725
90	4.725	4.780	4.834	4.888	4.942	4.996	5.050	5.105	5.159	5.213	5.268
100	5.268	5.322	5.376	5.431	5.485	5.540	5.594	5.649	5.703	5.758	5.812

(table continues)

175

TABLE 3-11 (continued)

°C	0	1	2	3	4	5	6	7	8	9	10
110	5.812	5.867	5.921	5.976	6.031	6.085	6.140	6.195	6.249	6.304	6.359
120	6.359	6.414	6.468	6.523	6.578	6.633	6.688	6.742	6.797	6.852	6.907
130	6.907	6.962	7.017	7.072	7.127	7.182	7.237	7.292	7.347	7.402	7.457
140	7.457	7.512	7.567	7.622	7.677	7.732	7.787	7.843	7.898	7.953	8.008
150	8.008	8.063	8.118	8.174	8.229	8.284	8.339	8.394	8.450	8.505	8.560
160	8.560	8.616	8.671	8.726·	8.781	8.837	8.892	8.947	9.003	9.058	9.113
170	9.113	9.169	9.224	9.279	9.335	9.390	9.446	9.501	9.556	9.612	9.667
180	9.667	9.723	9.778	9.834	9.889	9.944	10.000	10.055	10.111	10.166	10.222
190	10.222	10.277	10.333	10.388	10.444	10.499	10.555	10.610	10.666	10.721	10.777
200	10.777	10.832	10.888	10.943	10.999	11.054	11.110	11.165	11.221	11.276	11.332
210	11.332	11.387	11.443	11.498	11.554	11.609	11.665	11.720	11.776	11.831	11.887
220	11.887	11.943	11.998	12.054	12.109	12.165	12.220	12.276	12.331	12.387	12.442
230	12.442	12.498	12.553	12.609	12.664	12.720	12.776	12.831	12.887	12.942	12.998
240	12.998	13.053	13.109	13.164	13.220	13.275	13.331	13.386	13.442	13.497	13.553
250	13.553	13.608	13.664	13.719	13.775	13.830	13.886	13.941	13.997	14.052	14.108
260	14.108	14.163	14.219	14.274	14.330	14.385	14.441	14.496	14.552	14.607	14.663
270	14.663	14.718	14.774	14.829	14.885	14.940	14.995	15.051	15.106	15.162	15.217
280	15.217	15.273	15.328	15.383	15.439	15.494	15.550	15.605	15.661	15.716	15.771
290	15.771	15.827	15.882	15.938	15.993	16.048	16.104	16.159	16.214	16.270	16.325
300	16.325	16.380	16.436	16.491	16.547	16.602	16.657	16.713	16.768	16.823	16.879
310	16.879	16.934	16.989	17.044	17.100	17.155	17.210	17.266	17.321	17.376	17.432
320	17.432	17.487	17.542	17.597	17.653	17.708	17.763	17.818	17.874	17.929	17.984
330	17.984	18.039	18.095	18.150	18.205	18.260	18.316	18.371	18.426	18.481	18.537
340	18.537	18.592	18.647	18.702	18.757	18.813	18.868	18.923	18.978	19.033	19.089
350	19.089	19.144	19.199	19.254	19.309	19.364	19.420	19.475	19.530	19.585	19.640
360	19.640	19.695	19.751	19.806	19.861	19.916	19.971	20.026	20.081	20.137	20.192
370	20.192	20.247	20.302	20.357	20.412	20.467	20.523	20.578	20.633	20.688	20.743
380	20.743	20.798	20.853	20.909	20.964	21.019	21.074	21.129	21.184	21.239	21.295
390	21.295	21.350	21.405	21.460	21.515	21.570	21.625	21.680	21.736	21.791	21.846
400	21.846	21.901	21.956	22.011	22.066	22.122	22.177	22.232	22.287	22.342	22.397
410	22.397	22.453	22.508	22.563	22.618	22.673	22.728	22.784	22.839	22.894	22.949
420	22.949	23.004	23.060	23.115	23.170	23.225	23.280	23.336	23.391	23.446	23.501

430	23.501	23.556	23.612	23.667	23.722	23.777	23.833	23.888	23.943	23.999	24.054
440	24.054	24.109	24.164	24.220	24.275	24.330	24.386	24.441	24.496	24.552	24.607
450	24.607	24.662	24.718	24.773	24.829	24.884	24.939	24.995	25.050	25.106	25.161
460	25.161	25.217	25.272	25.327	25.383	25.438	25.494	25.549	25.605	25.661	25.716
470	25.716	25.772	25.827	25.883	25.938	25.994	26.050	26.105	26.161	26.216	26.272
480	26.272	26.328	26.383	26.439	26.495	26.551	26.606	26.662	26.718	26.774	26.829
490	26.829	26.885	26.941	26.997	27.053	27.109	27.165	27.220	27.276	27.332	27.388
500	27.388	27.444	27.500	27.556	27.612	27.668	27.724	27.780	27.836	27.893	27.949
510	27.949	28.005	28.061	28.117	28.173	28.230	28.286	28.342	28.398	28.455	28.511
520	28.511	28.567	28.624	28.680	28.736	28.793	28.849	28.906	28.962	29.019	29.075
530	29.075	29.132	29.188	29.245	29.301	29.358	29.415	29.471	29.528	29.585	29.642
540	29.642	29.698	29.755	29.812	29.869	29.926	29.983	30.039	30.096	30.153	30.210
550	30.210	30.267	30.324	30.381	30.439	30.496	30.553	30.610	30.667	30.724	30.782
560	30.782	30.839	30.896	30.954	31.011	31.068	31.126	31.183	31.241	31.298	31.356
570	31.356	31.413	31.471	31.528	31.586	31.644	31.702	31.759	31.817	31.875	31.933
580	31.933	31.991	32.048	32.106	32.164	32.222	32.280	32.338	32.396	32.455	32.513
590	32.513	32.571	32.629	32.687	32.746	32.804	32.862	32.921	32.979	33.038	33.096
600	33.096	33.155	33.213	33.272	33.330	33.389	33.448	33.506	33.565	33.624	33.683
610	33.683	33.742	33.800	33.859	33.918	33.977	34.036	34.095	34.155	34.214	34.273
620	34.273	34.332	34.391	34.451	34.510	34.569	34.629	34.688	34.748	34.807	34.867
630	34.867	34.926	34.986	35.046	35.105	35.165	35.225	35.285	35.344	35.404	35.464
640	35.464	35.524	35.584	35.644	35.704	35.764	35.825	35.885	35.945	36.005	36.066
650	36.066	36.126	36.186	36.247	36.307	36.368	36.428	36.489	36.549	36.610	36.671
660	36.671	36.732	36.792	36.853	36.914	36.975	37.036	37.097	37.158	37.219	37.280
670	37.280	37.341	37.402	37.463	37.525	37.586	37.647	37.709	37.770	37.831	37.893
680	37.893	37.954	38.016	38.078	38.139	38.201	38.262	38.324	38.386	38.448	38.510
690	38.510	38.572	38.633	38.695	38.757	38.819	38.882	38.944	39.006	39.068	39.130
700	39.130	39.192	39.255	39.317	39.379	39.442	39.504	39.567	39.629	39.692	39.754
710	39.754	39.817	39.880	39.942	40.005	40.068	40.131	40.193	40.256	40.319	40.382
720	40.382	40.445	40.508	40.571	40.634	40.697	40.760	40.823	40.886	40.950	41.013
730	41.013	41.076	41.139	41.203	41.266	41.329	41.393	41.456	41.520	41.583	41.647
740	41.647	41.710	41.774	41.837	41.901	41.965	42.028	42.092	42.156	42.219	42.283
750	42.283	42.347	42.411	42.475	42.538	42.602	42.666	42.730	42.794	42.858	42.922
760	42.922										

Source: Omega Engineering.

TABLE 3-12 NATIONAL BUREAU OF STANDARDS POLYNOMIAL COEFFICIENTS[a]

	Type E: nickel-10% chromium(+) versus constantan(−), −100 to 1000°C ±0.5°C, 9th order	Type J: iron(+) versus constantan(−), 0 to 760°C ±0.1°C, 5th order	Type K: nickel-10% chromium(+) versus nickel-5%(−) (aluminum silicon), 0 to 1370°C ±0.7°C, 8th order	Type R: platinum-13% rhodium(+) versus platinum(−), 0 to 1000°C ±0.5°C, 8th order	Type S: platinum-10% rhodium(+) versus platinum(−), 0 to 1750°C ±1°C, 9th order	Type T: copper(+) versus constantan(−), −160 to 400°C ±0.5°C, 7th order
a_0	0.104967248	−0.048868252	0.226584602	0.263632917	0.927763167	0.100860910
a_1	17189.45282	19873.14503	24152.10900	179075.491	169526.5150	25727.94369
a_2	−282639.0850	−218614.5353	67233.4248	−48840341.37	−31568363.94	−767345.8295
a_3	12695339.5	11569199.78	2210340.682	$1.90002E+10$	8990730663	78025595.81
a_4	−448703084.6	−264917531.4	−860963914.9	$-4.82704E+12$	$-1.63565E+12$	−9247486589
a_5	$1.10866E+10$	2018441314	$4.83506E+10$	$7.62091E+14$	$1.88027E+14$	$6.97688E+11$
a_6	$-1.76807E+11$		$-1.18452E+12$	$-7.20026E+16$	$-1.37241E+16$	$-2.66192E+13$
a_7	$1.71842E+12$		$1.38690E+13$	$3.71496E+18$	$6.17501E+17$	$3.94078E+14$
a_8	$-9.19278E+12$		$-6.33708E+13$	$-8.03104E+19$	$-1.56105E+19$	
a_{09}	$2.06132E+13$				$1.69535E+20$	

[a] Temperature conversion equation: $T = a_0 + a_1 x + a_2 x^2 + \cdots + a_n x^n$; nested polynomial form: $T = a_0 + x(a_1 + x(a_2 + x(a_3 + x(a_4 + a_5 x))))$ (5th order).

Source: Omega Engineering.

178

TABLE 3–13 REQUIRED DVM SENSITIVITY

Thermocouple type	Seebeck coefficient ($\mu V/°C$)	DVM sensitivity for 0.1°C (μV)
E	62	6.2
J	51	5.1
K	40	4.0
R	7	0.7
S	7	0.7
T	40	4.0

Source: Omega Engineering.

"In summary, the integrity of a thermocouple system may be improved by following these precautions:

1. Use the largest wire possible that will not shunt heat away from the measurement area.

2. If small wire is required, use it only in the region of the measurement and use extension wire for the region with no temperature gradient.

3. Avoid mechanical stress and vibration which could strain the wires.

4. When using long thermocouple wires, connect the wire shield to the DVM guard terminal and use twisted pair extension wire.

5. Avoid steep temperature gradients.

6. Try to use the thermocouple wire well within its temperature rating.

7. Use a guarded integrating A/D converter.

8. Use extension wire only at low temperatures and only in regions of small gradients.

9. Keep an event log and a continuous record of thermocouple resistance."

3–6.2 RTD

"The same year that Seebeck made his discovery about thermoelectricity, Sir Humphry Davy announced that the resistivity of metals showed a marked temperature dependence. Fifty years later, Sir William Siemens proffered the use of platinum as the element in a resistance thermometer. His choice proved most propitious, as platinum is used to this day as the primary element in all high-accuracy resistance thermometers. In fact, the platinum resistance temperature detector, or PRTD, is used today as an interpolation standard from the oxygen point ($-182.96°C$) to the antimony point ($630.74°C$).

"Platinum is especially suited to this purpose, as it can withstand high temperatures while maintaining excellent stability. As a noble metal, it shows limited susceptibility to contamination.

"All metals produce a positive change in resistance for a positive change in temperature. This, of course, is the main function of an RTD. As we shall soon see, system error is minimized when the nominal value of the RTD resistance is large. This implies a metal wire with a high resistivity. The lower the resistivity of the metal, the more material we will have to use.

"Because of their lower resistivities, gold and silver are rarely used as RTD elements. Tungsten has a relatively high resistivity, but is reserved for very high temperature applications because it is extremely brittle and difficult to work.

"Copper is used occasionally as an RTD element. Its low resistivity forces the element to be longer than a platinum element, but its linearity and very low cost make it an economical alternative. Its upper temperature limit is only about 120°C.

"The most common RTDs are made of either platinum, nickel, or nickel alloys. The economical nickel derivative wires are used over a limited temperature range. They are quite nonlinear and tend to drift with time. For measurement integrity, platinum is the obvious choice.

"The common values of resistance for a platinum RTD range from 10 Ω for the bird-cage model to several thousand ohms for the film RTD. The single most common value is 100 Ω at 0°C. The DIN 43760 standard temperature coefficient of platinum wire is $\alpha = 0.00385$. For a 100-Ω wire this corresponds to +0.385 $\Omega/°C$ at 0°C. This value for α is actually the average slope from 0°C to 100°C. The more chemically pure platinum wire used in platinum resistance standards has a value of +0.00392 $\Omega/\Omega/°C$.

"Both the slope and the absolute value are small numbers, especially when we consider the fact that the measurement wires leading to the sensor may be several ohms or even tens of ohms. A small lead impedance can contribute a significant error to our temperature measurement." This is the same problem encountered with a remote strain gage. The solution was a three-wire connection, shown in Figure 3–48. Look back at these again, now. By correctly using a three-wire connection to the RTD, the wiring resistances are split, half placed in each of two legs of the bridge. This way the wiring resistance effect is eliminated.

"The technique of using a current source along with a remotely sensed digital voltmeter alleviates many problems associated with the bridge. The output voltage read by the DVM is directly proportional to RTD resistance, so only one conversion equation is necessary. The three bridge-completion resistors are replaced by one reference resistor. The digital voltmeter measures only the voltage dropped across the RTD and is insensitive to the length of the lead wires." Refer to Figure 3–86.

"The one disadvantage of using four-wire ohms is that we need more extension wire than the three-wire bridge. This is a small price to pay if we are at all concerned with the accuracy of the temperature measurements.

"The same practical precautions that apply to thermocouples also apply to RTDs, i.e., use shields and twisted-pair wire, use proper sheathing, avoid stress and steep gradients, use large extension wire, keep good documentation and use a guarded integrating DVM. In addition, the following precautions should be observed.

"Due to its construction, the RTD is somewhat more fragile than the thermocouple and precautions must be taken to protect it.

"Unlike the thermocouple, the RTD is not self-powered. A current must be passed

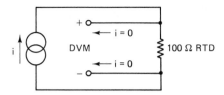

Figure 3–86 Four-wire resistance measurement of an RTD. (Courtesy of Omega Engineering, Inc., Stamford, CT.)

through the device to provide a voltage that can be measured. The current causes Joule (R^2) heating with the RTD, changing its temperature. This self-heating appears as a measurement error. Consequently, attention must be paid to the magnitude of the measurement current supplied by the ohmmeter. A typical value for self-heating error is $\frac{1}{2}$°C per milliwatt in free air. Obviously, an RTD immersed in a thermally conductive medium will distribute its Joule heat to the medium and the error due to self-heating will be smaller. The same RTD that rises 1°C per milliwatt in free air will rise only $\frac{1}{10}$°C per milliwatt in air which is flowing at the rate of 1 meter per second.

"To reduce self-heating errors, use the minimum ohms measurements current that will still give the resolution you require, and use the largest RTD you can that will still give good response time. Obviously, there are compromises to be considered.

"Thermal shunting is the act of altering the measurement temperature by inserting a measurement transducer. Thermal shunting is more a problem with RTDs than with thermocouples, as the physical bulk of an RTD is greater than that of a thermocouple.

"The platinum-to-copper connection that is made when the RTD is measured can cause a thermal offset voltage."

3–6.3 Thermistor

"Like the RTD, the thermistor is also a temperature-sensitive resistor. While the thermocouple is the most versatile temperature transducer and the PRTD is the most stable, the word that best describes the thermistor is "sensitive." Of the three major categories of sensors, the thermistor exhibits by far the largest parameter change with temperature.

"Thermistors are generally composed of semiconductor materials. Although positive temperature coefficient units are available, most thermistors have a negative temperature coefficient (TC); that is, their resistance decreases with increasing temperature. The negative TC can be as large as several percent per degree Celsius, allowing the thermistor circuit to detect minute changes in temperature which could not be observed with an RTD or thermocouple circuit.

"The price we pay for this increased sensitivity is loss of linearity. The thermistor is an extremely nonlinear device which is highly dependent upon process parameters. Consequently, manufacturers have not standardized thermistor curves to the extent that RTD and thermocouple curves have been standardized." Figure 3–87 gives a comparison of the range and linearity of the thermistor, RTD, and thermocouple.

"An individual thermistor curve can be very closely approximated through use of the Steinhart–Hart equation:

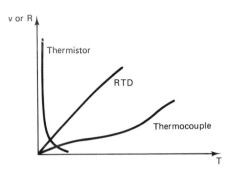

Figure 3–87 Relative response of thermistor, RTD, and thermocouple. (Courtesy of Omega Engineering, Inc., Stamford, CT.)

$$\frac{1}{T} = A + B \ln R + C(\ln R)^3$$

where T = degrees Kelvin

      R = resistance of the thermistor

A, B, C = curve-fitting constants

"A, B, and C are found by selecting three data points on the published data curve and solving the three simultaneous equations. When the data points are chosen to span no more than 100°C within the nominal center of the thermistor's temperature range, this equation approaches a rather remarkable ±0.02°C curve fit.

"Somewhat faster computer execution time is achieved through a simpler equation:

$$T = \frac{B}{\ln R - A} - C$$

where A, B, and C are again found by selecting three (R, T) data points and solving the three resultant simultaneous equations. This equation must be applied over a narrower temperature range in order to approach the accuracy of the Steinhart–Hart equation.

"A great deal of effort has gone into the development of thermistors which approach a linear characteristic. These are typically two- or four-leaded devices requiring external matching resistors to linearize the characteristic curve. The modern data acquisition system with its computing controller has made this kind of hardware linearization unnecessary.

"The high resistivity of the thermistor affords it a distinct measurement advantage. The four-wire resistance measurement is not required as it is with RTDs. For example, a common thermistor value is 5000 Ω at 25°C With a typical TC of 4%/°C, a measurement lead resistance of 10 Ω produces only a 0.05°C error. This error is a factor of 500 times less than the equivalent RTD error.

"Because they are semiconductors, thermistors are more susceptible to permanent decalibration at high temperatures than are RTDs or thermocouples. The use of thermistors is generally limited to a few hundred degrees Celsius.

"Thermistors can be made very small, which means they will respond quickly to temperature changes. It also means that their small thermal mass makes them especially susceptible to self-heating errors.

"Thermistors are a good deal more fragile than RTDs or thermocouples and they must be carefully mounted to avoid crushing or bond separation."

3–6.4 Integrated-Circuit Temperature Transducers

Each of the three temperature transducers you have seen so far has had some significant limitation. The thermocouple outputs a very small signal that varies nonlinearly with temperature. It also must have some form of reference correction. The RTD outputs a change in resistance with changing temperature, but it is *very* small. The thermistor's output is quite nonlinear.

For each of these transducers you must add electronics to compensate for these shortcomings. Also, additional circuitry may be needed to produce a reasonably large output voltage or current. Usually, this electronics takes the form of monolithic integrated circuits. The next logical step, then, is to combine the temperature-sensing element and the signal-conditioning electronics into a single monolithic integrated-circuit package.

That is what has been done with the three integrated-circuit (IC) temperature sensors presented in this section. The LM335 outputs 10 mV/°K. The LM34 provides a more convenient 10 mV/°F. The AD592 outputs current at the rate of 1 μA/°K.

The LM335 is a temperature-sensitive zener diode. When reverse biased into its breakdown region, it outputs

$$V_z = \frac{10\,\text{mV}}{°\text{K}}\,T$$

Recall that the size of the degree Kelvin and the degree Celsius are the same, and there is 273° offset.

$$0°\text{C} = 273°\text{K}$$

So the output of the LM335 becomes

$$V_z = 2.73\,\text{V} + \left(\frac{10\,\text{mV}}{°\text{C}}\right)T$$

where T is expressed in °C.

The three temperature ranges available are listed in Table 3–14. Notice that none of these come close to having the range of a thermocouple or RTD. This is inherent in the silicon material of the integrated circuit.

TABLE 3–14 LM135/235/335
TEMPERATURE RANGES

Device	Range (°C)	Use
LM135	−55 to +150	Military
LM235	−40 to +125	Industrial
LM335	−40 to +100	Commercial

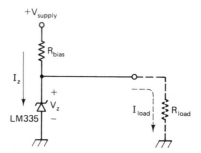

Figure 3–88 Simple temperature transducer using a LM335.

The simplest circuit using a LM335 is shown in Figure 3–88. Since the LM335 is a zener diode, you must provide a reverse bias voltage and zener current. The current should be limited to

$$5 \text{ mA} > I_z > 400 \text{ } \mu\text{A}$$

The manufacturer's testing is done at

$$I_z = 1 \text{ mA}$$

so this seems a reasonable choice. At higher currents the LM335 will heat itself up due to the $I_z V_z$ power it must dissipate. At current levels below 1 mA, accuracy appears to fall off.

To determine the proper size of the series limiting resistor in Figure 3–88, first calculate the voltage across the zener at the nominal temperature over which it will be used. Then set

$$R_{\text{bias}} = \frac{V_{\text{supply}} - V_{\text{nominal}}}{1 \text{ mA}}$$

For linear results it is important that the load current be small compared to the minimum current that will actually flow through the zener. So be sure that the load current

$$I_{\text{load}} \ll I_{z \min}$$

$$\frac{V_{\max T}}{R_L} \ll \frac{V_{\text{supply}} - V_{\max T}}{R_{\text{bias}}}$$

The rated linearity of a LM335 is $\pm 1°\text{C}$. However, it would be nice to be able to adjust the transducer so that you get maximum accuracy over the range you are measuring. Also, that 2.73-V offset is a nuisance. Ideally, $0°\text{C}$ would produce 0 V dc. The circuit in Figure 3–89 provides you with a two-point calibration capability. Initially, adjust the zero potentiometer to give -2.73 V at its wiper and set the 10-kΩ potentiometer to midrange. Place the sensor at the lowest temperature for your application. Adjust the zero potentiometer to remove *half* of the error. Place the sensor at the maximum temperature that you will use and adjust the 10-kΩ potentiometer to remove *half* of this upper point error. Alternately place the sensor at its two extremes, adjusting out

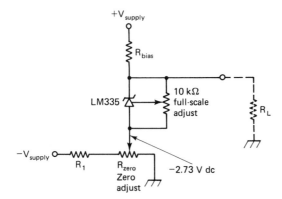

Figure 3–89 Two-point calibration for a LM335 temperature sensor.

half of the error each time. Use the zero adjust at the bottom and the 10-kΩ adjust at the top. Do not forget to give the sensor time to stabilize at its new temperature each time before making an adjustment. Also, be sure to keep R_{zero} small as compared to R_{bias} so that adjusting R_{zero} will not affect the I_z.

EXAMPLE 3–21

Design a circuit using a LM335 to cover a range of -10 to $+50°C$ with a nominal temperature of 20°C. Assume a supply voltage of ± 5 V dc. Also, calculate the minimum recommended load resistance.

Solution Use the circuit in Figure 3–89. At the nominal temperature

$$V_z = 2.73 \text{ V} + (10 \text{ mV/°C})(20°C)$$
$$= 2.93 \text{ V}$$

But since the anode of the zener was at -2.73 V, the output voltage will be

$$V_{out} = V_z + V_{offset}$$
$$= 2.93 \text{ V} - 2.73 \text{ V} = 200 \text{ mV}$$

To select R_{bias},

$$R_{bias} = \frac{5 \text{ V} - 0.2 \text{ V}}{1 \text{ mA}} = 4.8 \text{ k}\Omega$$

So pick $R_{bias} = 4.7$ kΩ.

To minimize the effects of adjusting R_{zero} on I_{bias}, select $R_{zero} \ll R_{bias}$. Pick $R_{zero} = 500$ Ω.

To check load resistance, solve the inequality for R_L:

$$R_L \gg \frac{V_{\max T} R_{bias}}{V_{supply} - V_{\max T}}$$

To get $V_{\max T}$,

$$V_z = 2.73 \text{ V} + \left(\frac{10 \text{ mV}}{°\text{C}}\right)(50°\text{C}) = 3.23 \text{ V}$$

$$V_{\max T} = 3.23 \text{ V} - 2.73 \text{ V} = 0.5 \text{ V}$$

$$R_L \gg \frac{(0.5 \text{ V})(4.7 \text{ k}\Omega)}{5 \text{ V} - 0.5 \text{ V}} = 522 \ \Omega$$

If all of this still seems to be a lot of trouble, consider the LM34 series sensors from National Semiconductor. "The LM34 series are precision integrated-circuit temperature sensors, whose output voltage is linearly proportional to the Fahrenheit temperature. The LM34 thus has an advantage over linear temperature sensors calibrated in degrees Kelvin, as the user is not required to subtract a large constant voltage from its output to obtain convenient Fahrenheit scaling. The LM34 does not require any external calibration or trimming to provide typical accuracies of $\pm\frac{1}{2}°$F at room temperature and $\pm1\frac{1}{2}°$F over a full -50 to $+300°$F temperature range. Low cost is assured by trimming and calibration at the wafer level. The LM34's low output impedence, linear output, and precise inherent calibration make interfacing to readout or control circuitry especially easy. It can be used with single power supplies or with plus and minus supplies. As it draws only 70 μA from its supply, it has very low self-heating, less than 0.2°F in still air. The LM34 is rated to operated over a -50 to $+300°$F temperature range, while the LM34C is rated for a -40 to $+230°$F range (0°F with improves accuracy). The LM34 series is available packaged in hermetic TO-46 transistor packages, while the LM34C is also available in the plastic TO-92 transistor package" [13].

"The LM34 can be applied easily in the same way as other integrated-circuit temperature sensors. It can be glued or cemented to a surface and its temperature will be within about 0.02°F of the surface temperature. The TO-46 metal package can also be soldered to a metal surface or pipe without damage. Of course in that case, the V_ terminal of the circuit will be grounded to that metal. Alternatively, the LM34 can be mounted inside a sealed-end metal tube, and can then be dipped into a bath or screwed into a threaded hole in a tank. As with any IC, the LM34 and accompanying wiring and circuits must be kept insulated and dry, to avoid leakage and corrosion. This is especially true if the circuit may operate at cold temperatures where condensation can occur. Printed-circuit coatings and varnishes such as Humi-seal and epoxy paints or dips are often used to ensure that moisture cannot corrode the LM34 or its connections" [13].

Several circuits for using the LM34 are given in Figure 3–90. The simplest, Figure 3–90a, requires no extra components. It output varies from 50 mV to 3.00 V dc, indicating temperatures from +5 to +300°F. If you want to measure temperatures below 0°F, you must provide the IC with a source of negative power. This is shown in Figure 3–90b. For this circuit, 300°F produces +3.00 V dc of output; −50°F yield −500 mV dc.

Often it is necessary to locate the sensor more than a few centimeters from the support electronics. For this, there are two additional requirements. Only two leads

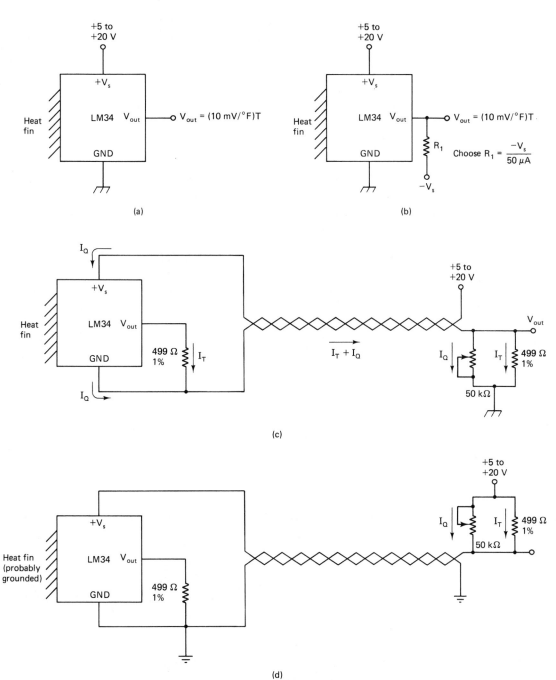

Figure 3–90 Typical applications of the LM34: (a) simplest; (b) negative temperatures; (c) remote sensing; (d) remote sensing with a grounded sensor. (Courtesy of National Semiconductor.)

should be run to the sensor (not three). The signal returned by the sensor should be current, not voltage. This eliminates the effects of series resistance in the wiring. The circuits in Figure 3–90c and d meet these requirements. Use Figure 3–90d if it is necessary to ground the sensor. In either circuit, the output voltage produces a current I_T. This combines with the quiescent bias current needed to run the chip (70 μA) and flows through the twisted pair of wires.

$$I_T = \frac{V_{out}}{499 \ \Omega}$$

At the processing electronics the bias current is split off and flows through the 50-kΩ potentiometer (when you set it correctly). So I_T goes through the 499-Ω resistor to recover the original voltage. Also notice that when the remote sensor is grounded, the output voltage must be taken *differentially* between +V and the signal returned from the sensor. Be aware, too, that the temperature coefficient of the 499-Ω resistors must be kept as low as possible. This is because I_T changes not only with changes in V_T, but also with any changes in the 499-Ω resistor induced by temperature. The LM35 is the Celsius complement to the LM34. Otherwise, the two integrated circuits perform similarly.

If you do have to transmit the signal any significant distance, a current signal is not affected by series wiring resistance. The AD590 or AD592 from Analog Devices may be a better choice then the voltage output LM34. The current out of the AD590 and AD592 is

$$I_{out} = \left(\frac{1 \ \mu A}{\degree K} \right) T$$

where T is in °K or

$$I_{out} = 273 \ \mu A + \left(\frac{1 \ \mu A}{\degree C} \right) T$$

where T is in °C. The AD590 provides an accuracy of ±0.5°C over its entire range of −55 to +150°C. The AD592 is considerably lower in cost. Its range is −25 to +105°C, but the accuracy of 0.5°C is specified at 25°C with 0.2°C linearity over 0 to 70°C.

Two typical applications of the AD590 or AD592 are shown in Figure 3–91. In Figure 3–91a a single potentiometer has been selected to convert the current to a voltage. This single-point calibration will assure correct readings at the calibration point. So be sure to set the potentiometer at the temperature that is most critical.

Like the LM335, the AD590 and AD592 sense absolute temperature. This means that if you want to work in degrees Celsius or degrees Fahrenheit, there is a large offset. The zero offset can be removed with the zero potentiometer of Figure 3–91b. Adjustment of the zero and span potentiometers should be done just as was described for the LM335 circuit in Figure 3–89.

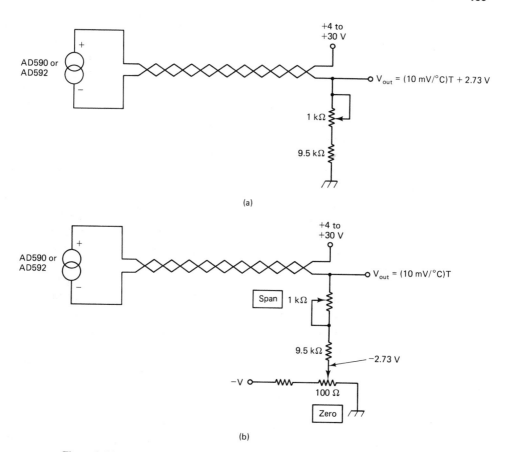

Figure 3–91   Temperature sensing and conversion with the AD590/AD592: (a) single-point calibration; (b) two-point zero and span. (Courtesy of Analog Devices.)

SUMMARY

The quality of a control system can be no better than its perception of that system's performance. For that reason, the selection and proper application of transducers are fundamental to a control system's success.

   Transducers specifications define how accurately the transducer converts the physical parameter it is measuring into an electrical signal. They are divided into static and dynamic specifications. Static specifications are obtained from a calibration record and include accuracy, absolute error, resolution, repeatability, hysteresis, and linearity. Dynamic specifications indicate how quickly the transducer responds to a change in its input. Rise time, time constant, dead time, damping coefficient and resonant frequency, percent overshoot, settling time, and frequency response are all dynamic specifications.

Position is central to servo control. But displacement can also be an indication of temperature, force, pressure, acceleration, and level. The simplest position transducer is a potentiometer. The LVDT and RVDT are considerably more sensitive, but more difficult to use. Optical position encoders may be incremental or absolute. Incremental encoders require additional circuitry but may have high resolution. Synchros and resolvers have been and are still being used for the high-resolution pointing of large machinery (i.e., artillery and satellite tracking antenna). Hybrid integrated circuits are used to convert their ac signals into position data.

Force measurements are key to stress analysis. But they are also used in determining the amount of material present, the acceleration of an item, the pressure on a surface, and the flow and level of a fluid. The strain gage is the most often used force transducer. Its stress–strain characteristics allow forces to produce minute changes in length and therefore changes in resistance. This change in resistance is so small, however, that special measurement and temperature-compensation techniques are necessary. Load cells provide the beam(s), properly mounted gages, and compensation circuitry in an easily applied package.

Measurement of velocity may be either linear or angular. Velocity resulting in a very limited overall displacement can be measured with an electromagnetic transducer (a variation of the LVDT). Longer-range motion may use an integrating accelerometer, or Doppler radar or lasers. There are a wide variety of angular velocity transducers. The dc electromagnetic tachometer and the ac induction tachometer output a voltage proportional to rotational speed. Other transducers, such as the ac permanent-magnet tachometer, tooth-rotor tachometer, and optical encoders all output a signal whose frequency indicates angular velocity.

Acceleration is useful in both stress and vibration analysis and in navigation. Some form of mass–spring–damper system is used to sense acceleration, and the resulting displacement is measured. So resonant frequency and damping coefficient are important specifications of these transducers. A piezoelectric crystal outputs a charge (voltage) proportional to the force exerted on it by a mass. This is also a direct measure of the acceleration the mass is undergoing. Although parasitic capacitance, loading, and low signal levels are a problem here, crystal accelerometers provide the fastest response.

Pressure is always measured with respect to some reference. It may be a complete vacuum (psia) or ambient pressure (psig) or differential. A pressure difference across a surface will cause the surface to bend. This motion is a measure of the pressure. Steel and silicon wafers are used as diaphragms. Strain gages are used to sense the flex. More movement is possible with a capsule or bellows. Capacitance or a LVDT can sense this motion. The greatest range of movement comes with a Bourdon tube. Its displacement in response to an applied pressure may be sensed with a potentiometer or LVDT.

Obstruction and nonintrusive techniques are used to measure flow. The pressure dropped across a barrier is proportional to the flow through the barrier. Differential pressure ways of measuring flow include the orifice, venturi, and Pitot tube. The force exerted on a barrier is also determined by the flow. Cantilever beams and rotometers measure this force. The force is converted to a spin by paddle wheel and turbine transducers. However, obstruction techniques lower the flow they are trying to measure. Nonintrusive techniques do not. Electromagnetic and ultrasonic transducers are available.

The level in a tank can be sensed either discretely or continuously. Discrete level sensors include float switches and photoelectric and thermal sensing. For a linear signal you can use a pressure sensor placed at the bottom of the tank, weigh the tank, use probes to measure a variation in capacitance or resistance, or mount an ultrasonic module to measure the distance to the surface.

Thermocouples are the most widely used temperature transducer. But they are nonlinear, require an ice-point compensation, and output a low-level voltage. RTDs are more linear than thermocouples but change their resistance a very small amount for a change in temperature. The thermistor has a large change in resistance, but it is very nonlinear and has a limited temperature range. Integrated-circuit temperature sensors work over a small temperature range. But they output reasonably sized voltage or current signals very linearly.

REFERENCES

1. HARRY N. NORTON, *Sensor and Analyzer Handbook*, © 1982, pp. 30, 33, 100, 101. Reprinted by permission of Prentice-Hall, Inc., Englewood Cliffs, New Jersey.

2. DONALD ARY and LUCY CHESTER JACOBS, *Introduction to Statistics: Purpose and Procedures*. New York: Holt, Rinehart and Winston, pp. 203–207.

3. RICHARD W. MILLER, *Servomechanisms: Devices and Fundamentals*, © 1977, pp. 16–24. Adapted by permission of Prentice-Hall, Inc., Englewood Cliffs, New Jersey.

4. *LVDT and RVDT Linear Angular Displacement Transducers*, Technical Bulletin 1002A. Pennsauken, N.J.: Schweitz.

5. *Optical Encoder Design Guide*. Goleta, Calif.: BEI Electronics, Inc., Industrial Encoder Division.

6. *Data-Acquisition Data Book*. Norwood, Mass.: Analog Devices, 1982.

7. *Practical Strain Gage Measurements*, Application Note AN290–1. Palo Alto, Calif.: Hewlett-Packard Company.

8. *Data Sheet*. Eau Claire, Wis.: Watson Industries, Inc.

9. CURTIS D. JOHNSON, *Process Control Instrumentation Technology*. New York: John Wiley & Sons, Inc., 1982, p. 176.

10. *Pressure and Strain Measurement Handbook and Encyclopedia*. Stamford, Conn.: Omega Engineering, Inc.

11. TEMPERATURE MEASUREMENT HANDBOOK AND ENCYCLOPEDIA. Stamford, Conn.: Omega Engineering, Inc.

12. *Data Handbook*, Vol. 1, *Integrated Circuits*. Norwood, Mass.: Analog Devices, 1984, pp. 8–31.

13. *Preliminary Specifications*. Santa Clara, Calif.: National Semiconductor (October 1984).

PROBLEMS

3–1. The calibration record for a pressure transducer is given in Table 3–15. Using it, do the following:
  (a) Plot the calibration curve.
  (b) Determine the accuracy in % FSO and % of reading.
  (c) Determine the absolute error.
  (d) Calculate hysteresis and mark the point you used on the calibration curve.
  (e) Replot the calibration record and add the endpoint linearity line. Indicate the value of the endpoint linearity and its location on the curve.
  (f) Repeat part (e) for independent straight-line linearity.
  (g) Repeat part (e) for least-squares linearity.

3–2. An antenna used to track a satellite must be able to be pointed very accurately. As the satellite passes overhead, the dish must be moved through a 180° arc. A resolver measures the angular position of the dish and sends its position signal to a 19-bit resolver-to-digital converter, where it is decoded for a computer. What is the resolution, in degrees, of this position-measuring system?

3–3. A control system is used to accurately tighten bolts on an assembly line. The bolts should be run in to 18 ft-lb of torque with full-scale torque of 25 ft-lb. The results for a sample run of three machines are given in Table 3–16. Calculate the repeatability of each machine two ways.

3–4. The response of a transducer to a step input is given in Figure 3–92. Calculate the following values.
  (a) Dead time.
  (b) Time constant.

TABLE 3–15 CALIBRATION RECORD FOR PROBLEM 3–1

Pressure (psig)	Actual output (mV)	Desired output (mV)
0	0.6	0
2	15.3	26.7
4	44.7	53.3
6	72.3	80.0
8	100.0	106.7
10	129.5	133.3
12	158.8	160.0
14	187.9	186.7
12	162.5	160.0
10	137.9	133.3
8	112.2	106.7
6	86.1	80.0
4	57.3	53.3
2	28.2	26.7
0	6.1	0

TABLE 3–16 REPEATABILITY DATA FOR
PROBLEM 3–3

Run	Machine A	Machine B	Machine C
1	17.63	18.05	17.53
2	18.29	17.94	17.59
3	18.38	17.83	17.51
4	17.04	18.15	17.49
5	17.89	18.04	17.46
6	18.05	18.19	17.52
7	18.98	17.89	17.56
8	19.42	17.93	17.51
9	17.95	18.04	17.48
10	16.82	18.13	17.46
11	18.14	17.96	17.41
12	18.36	17.86	17.43
13	17.49	17.99	17.52
14	17.38	18.10	17.54
15	18.21	18.04	17.50

   (c) Rise time.

   (d) High-frequency cutoff.

3–5. It is necessary to measure a linear displacement of 10 cm with a resolution of at least 0.02 mm. Explain how this can be done using a 10-turn potentiometer (3000° of movement full scale) with a total of 5000 turns of wire.

3–6. A 10-kΩ potentiometer has a 5.7-kΩ load attached to the wiper. Complete Table 3–17 to determine the effects of this loading. Calculate the absolute error and endpoint nonlinearity. Discuss the implication of this on sizing potentiometer loads.

3–7. From Figure 3–23, select an LVDT to replace the potentiometer of Problem 3–5.

   (a) Indicate the most sensitive model that will work.

   (b) What is the absolute error (in cm) due to nonlinearity?

   (c) What excitation voltage is recommended?

   (d) For a 0.02-mm movement, what output change do you expect?

3–8. An optical encoder is to replace the potentiometer of Problem 3–5. (Remember than an optical encoder is only a single turn of 360°.) Assume that the proper gearing is provided to assure 360° revolution of the encoder from one end of the linear displacement to the other.

   (a) Calculate the pulses per revolution needed.

   (b) Can you use an absolute encoder? Explain.

3–9. Design a quadrature encoder ×4 multiplier that will produce the output shown in Figure 3–93.

3–10. For the synchro shown in Figure 3–35, assume that the rotor is driven by a 115-V ac sine wave.

   (a) Calculate E_{S1-S3}, E_{S2-S1}, and E_{S3-S1} at rotor angles of 0°, 45°, 90°, 180°, 270°, and 330°.

   (b) Do you get a unique set of numbers? Explain how they are used to detect the rotor's position.

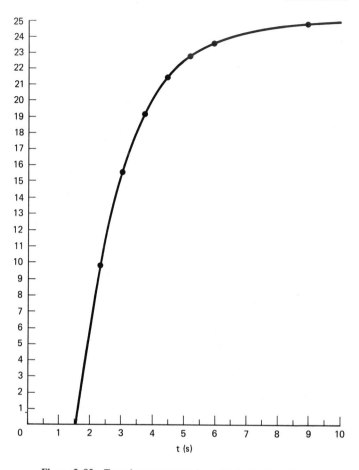

Figure 3–92   Transducer response time plot for Problem 3–4.

TABLE 3–17   POTENTIOMETER LOADING FOR PROBLEM 3–7

Wiper position (% FSO)	Desired output (% FSO)	Loaded output (% FSO)	Absolute error (%)
0	0		
10	10		
20	20		
30	30		
40	40		
50	50		
60	60		
70	70		
80	80		
90	90		
100	100		

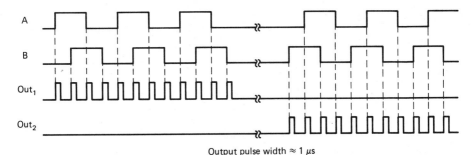

Output pulse width ≈ 1 μs

Figure 3–93   Desired multiplier output for Problem 3–9.

3–11. It is necessary to hit within ± 200 ft of a target 2 mi away. Assume that the only variable is the accuracy with which you can point the gun.
  (a) Calculate the allowable error in positioning angle of the gun.
  (b) Calculate the required S/D converter resolution.

3–12. A force of 18 lb is applied to a steel beam that is 6 in. long and has a cross-sectional area of 0.1 in.^{2}. The strain gage bonded to the beam has a nominal resistance of 350 Ω and a gage factor of 1.96. Calculate the change in resistance of the strain gage and the change in length of the steel beam.

3–13. Assuming that the strain gage of Problem 3–12 experiences a 10°C temperature change, calculate the change in its resistance caused by the temperature change. Compare this (numerically) to the change in resistance due to stress from Problem 3–12.

3–14. Determine V_{out} in Figure 3–47 given that $R_0 = 350$ Ω, $E = 20$ V, and
  (a) stress causes $\pm \Delta R = \pm 0.022$ Ω.
  (b) temperature causes all resistors to increase by 12.6 Ω.
  (c) stress causes $\pm \Delta R = \pm 0.022$ Ω *and* temperature causes all resistor to increase by 12.6 Ω.

3–15. A GSE4650 load cell (see Figure 3–49) is rated at 1000 lb full scale. Determine the following values.
  (a) Recommended excitation voltage.
  (b) Output voltage at 1000 lb load.
  (c) Output voltage per pound of load.
  (d) Absolute error (i.e., in pounds) of nonlinearity, hysteresis, and repeatability.
  (e) Assuming that the electronics were adjusted to show proper zero and full-scale readings when the load cell was 20°C, calculate the absolute zero error and the absolute span error if the load cell temperature changes to 50°C.

3–16. It is necessary to control both the position and velocity of a sled that moves back and forth over a bed at speeds up to 100 cm/s.
  (a) Explain how you can use a piezoelectric velocity transducer (Figure 3–51) to obtain both velocity and position feedback signals.
  (b) At maximum sled velocity, what is the transducer's output?
  (c) Discuss the advantage of using this transducer over other possible choices of position and velocity transducers.
  (d) Discuss factors that contribute to measurement accuracy.

3–17. A permanent-magnet dc tachometer has a sensitivity of 4 V/1000 r/min, 5000 r/min full scale, and an accuracy of ±0.2% FSO. Testing shows a brush noise of 400 mV p-p. Calculate the absolute error (in r/min) caused by

    (a) % accuracy.

    (b) noise.

    (c) total uncertainty.

3–18. The full-scale output of the ARC-C141-1A Watson angular rate sensor (Figure 3–53) is specified as 300°/s, and the frequency response is 55 Hz. Convert these two specifications to r/min.

3–19. For the problem in Example 3–18, if a 1500-pulse/revolution optical encoder were available, together with a ×4 pulse multiplying antijitter circuit, how often could you receive a new count (full scale of 1720 r/min)?

3–20. The sled of Problem 3–16 must be accelerated linearly from a standstill to maximum velocity in 0.1 s. Can the piezoelectric velocity transducer of Figure 3–51 withstand that acceleration?

3–21. Construct a table of acceleration transducers listing type, frequency range, advantages, and disadvantages.

3–22. What pressure does an 18-in.-high column of water produce in psig, psia, Pa, mm Hg, and atm?

3–23. Calculate the pressure in psig of a perfect vacuum.

3–24. A pressure transducer is rated for 30 mm of vacuum to +185.3 psig. The output voltage swings from +1 V to +5 V. Calculate the pressure indicated by the following output voltages: 1.5 V, 2 V, 2.5 V, 3 V, 4 V.

3–25. A sensitive pressure transducer with a Bourdon tube may be sensitive to the direction in which you mount it, whereas a silicon diaphragm type of transducer is not. Explain.

3–26. Construct a table of flow transducers listing type, a brief description of measurement technique, advantages, and disadvantages.

3–27. An orifice type of flow transducer is used to measure the flow of water into an open tank. At 0.5 gal/min, the high-side pressure is 0.8 psig.

    (a) Calculate k.

    (b) Calculate the flow when the high-side pressure is 15.0 psig.

3–28. The sensitivity of flow turbines and paddle wheels is expressed in Hz/gal per minute. Explain why measuring frequency at low flow is unacceptable. Also, explain how you could get high-resolution readings at low flow.

3–29. Explain two specific applications in which discrete level transducers are sufficient and two in which you must use a continuous transducer.

3–30. The drawing of a float-type level transducer in Figure 3–76 is overly simple. Draw an accurate, detailed sketch of a float level transducer that *rotates* a potentiometer as the level goes up and down.

3–31. Two rectangular electrodes 5 cm wide by 50 cm long are placed 1.0 mm apart and placed in a 50-cm-deep tank of water. Calculate the capacitance between the electrodes when the tank is empty, 20% full, 50% full, 80% full, and completely full.

3–32. Convert the block diagram for the ultrasonic level detector of Figure 3–78 into a complete schematic using TTL components. Indicate all component values used, and select and specify all ICs. Indicate pin numbers, typical waveforms, and power supply voltage and current requirements.

3–33. Most industrial electronics will function over an ambient temperature (i.e., temperature right next to the chip) from −25 to +125°C. Test specifications are generated at 25°C. Convert these three temperatures into Fahrenheit, Kelvin, and Rankine.

3–34. A temperature is measured with a J-type thermocouple and DVM as shown in Figure 3–80. Ambient temperature is 28°C and the voltmeter indicates 10.933 mV. What is the actual temperature of the thermocouple?

3–35. The noncompensated thermocouple measurement of Problem 3–34 is replaced by the AD594 thermocouple amplifier with cold junction compensation of Figure 3–85.
(a) What must be done to assure that the output will indicate temperatures accurately below 0°C?
(b) What is done to compensate for the fact that the IC is at 28°C?
(c) What output would you get from the AD594 for a thermocouple temperature of 177°C?

3–36. Use the polynominal (Table 3–12) to calculate the temperature that would produce a 9.501-mV output from a J-type thermocouple with a correct ice-point reference.

3–37. A RTD is placed in a bridge just like the three-wire strain gage bridge of Figure 3–48b. The three-bridge completion resistors are 100.000 Ω and the RTD is 100.000 Ω at 20°C.
(a) What is the voltage across the bridge when the RTD is placed in a 200°C oven?
(b) How can you adjust the bridge to cause the output to go to 0 V at 0°C? Give a specific, numerical answer.

3–38. Suppose that the power supply for the circuit in Problem 3–37 is 1.5 V dc.
(a) Calculate the current through the RTD at 20°C.
(b) Calculate the power dissipated by the RTD.
(c) Assuming a typical value of self-heating error $\frac{1}{2}$°C per milliwatt, calculate the absolute error and % reading error introduced by self-heating at 20°C and at 200°C.

3–39. A thermistor has the following three calibration points:

$$T = 0°C \qquad R = 16.32 \text{ k}\Omega$$

$$T = 50°C \qquad R = 1800 \ \Omega$$

$$T = 100°C \qquad R = 339.2 \ \Omega$$

(a) Calculate the three coefficients A, B, and C for the approximation

$$T = \frac{B}{\ln (RA)} - C$$

(b) Use your coefficients to determine the temperature indicated by R = 9951 Ω, 5000 Ω, 2663 Ω, 1000 Ω.

3–40. For the circuit in Figure 3–89, select appropriate values for R_{bias}, R_L, R_{zero}, given $+V_{supply}$ = ±15 V. The temperature range is 20 to 70°C with a nominal value of 40°C. Also, calculate the minimum recommended load resistance.

3–41. (a) For the circuit in Figure 3–90c, given that the supply voltage is +15 V and the temperature is 115°F, calculate V_{out} LM34, I_T, value of 50-kΩ potentiometer for I_Q = 70 μA, V_{out}.
(b) Repeat part (a) for the circuit in Figure 3–90d with I_Q = 90 μA.

3–42. Repeat Problem 3–41a for the circuit in
(a) Figure 3–91a.
(b) Figure 3–91b.

4

Signal Conditioners and Transmission

In Chapter 3 you saw a host of transducers, with which you were able to convert the parameters of interest in a manufacturing process into an electrical signal. Unfortunately, this signal may be much too small, go down instead of up, have an undesired dc offset, or be nonlinear.

The instrumentation amplifier is a special-purpose integrated circuit that utilizes several operational amplifiers (op amps). It is far superior to a single op amp circuit in applications requiring you to recover a very small difference in potential between two lines when there is a large unwanted voltage common to both lines. This is typical of most bridge circuits. So you will see instrumentation amplifers used in strain gage and RTD signal conditioning.

Now you have a clean, high-level, linear signal. It is an accurate measure of what is happening in the process under control. Generally, this signal is physically located near the transducer. Unfortunately, in most modern manufacturing the display of this process variable signal and its use by the controller must occur several meters to several kilometers away (as the electron flows). On its way to the control and display electronics the signal you so carefully measured, amplified, linearized, compensated, and filtered will run into a few problems.

Series resistance in the wiring and connectors will lower the signal value. Interference from power sources will introduce 60-Hz and RFI noise. This interference is random and often several times larger than the signal itself. Failures, faults, and installation errors may introduce several hundred volts into the signal. This could destroy both the signal measurement electronics and the display and control circuits. Differences in earth ground potential at the transducer, the controller, and the power supplies can also cause erroneous readings several times larger than the signal. All of these problems combine to make virtually useless the signal that arrives at the display and controller.

Fortunately, each of these problems has a solution. In this chapter you will see proper signal conversion, transmission, isolation, and shielding. Current transmission (rather than voltage) eliminates the effects of series resistance. Encoding the information in the *frequency* of the signal, rather than its amplitude, removes the impact of 60-Hz and RFI interference. Isolation amplifiers and couplers protect circuiting from fault voltages of several thousand volts. Proper shielding and grounding break ground loops.

OBJECTIVES

After studying this chapter you should be able to do the following:

1. For both the instrumentation amplifier and the zero and span converter:
   a. Draw the schematic.
   b. Qualitatively describe the operation.
   c. Analyze a given circuit to determine performance.
   d. Design a circuit to meet given performance specifications.
   e. Discuss specific applications.
   f. State limitations.
2. Explain with an example why signals should be transmitted as current rather than voltage.
3. For each of the following voltage-to-current converters—floating, floating boosted, floating offset, grounded, and dedicated IC:
   a. Describe its operation, listing precautions or limitations.
   b. Analyze a given circuit, calculating all significant voltages and currents.
   c. Design a converter to meet given specifications.
4. Explain how signal transmission as current can minimize the effects of noise pickup.
5. Design a floating current-to-ground referenced voltage converter to meet given specifications.
6. Analyze a given current-to-voltage converter, calculating all significant voltages and currents.
7. Given the block diagram of a voltage-to-frequency converter IC:
   a. Configure a circuit to perform voltage-to-frequency conversion and explain its operation.
   b. Configure a circuit to perform frequency-to-voltage conversion and explain its operation.
8. Discuss applications requiring an isolation amplifier.
9. For the transformer-coupled amplifier, optically coupled amplifier, and the digital optical coupler:

   a. Compare it to the other two isolation techniques.

   b. Describe its theory of operation.

   c. Analyze a given circuit, calculating all significant voltages and currents.

10. Describe sources of electrostatic and electromagnetic noise.

11. Explain how proper shielding eliminates these noise signals.

12. Demonstrate proper shield connection to the transducer, electronics, and controller.

13. Demonstrate proper grounding of signal shields, power supplies, signal sources, amplifiers, processor, and loads.

4–1 INSTRUMENTATION AMPLIFIERS

The instrumentation amplifier integrated circuit is a dedicated differential amplifier with extremely high input impedence. Its gain can be precisely set by a single internal or external resistor. The high common-mode rejection makes this amplifier very useful in recovering small signals buried in large common-mode offsets or noise.

The instrumentation amplifier (IA) is *not* a general-purpose building block, like the operational amplifier. The IA is a *closed-loop* device with carefully set gain. The op amp itself is an open-loop device with some very large (but widely variable) gain. This allows the IA to be optimized for its role as a signal conditioner of low-level (often dc) signals in large amounts of noise. The op amp, in contrast, can be used to build a wide variety of circuits but does not make as good a difference amplifier as does the IA.

Instrumentation amplifiers consist of two stages. The first stage offers very high input impedance to both input signals and allows you to set the gain with a single resistor. The second stage is a difference amplifier with the output, negative feedback, and ground reference connections all brought out.

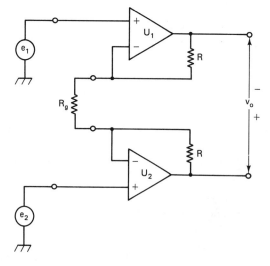

Figure 4–1   Instrumentation amplifier input stage.

The input stage is shown in Figure 4–1. It consists of two carefully matched op amps. Each input voltage (e_1 and e_2) is applied directly to the noninverting input of its op amp. This op amp (configured as a voltage follower) produces the IA's very high input impedance. The outputs of the op amps are connected together through a string of resistors. The two R resistors are internal to the integrated circuit, while R_g is the gain-setting resistor. It may be internal or connected externally. The output voltage is taken between the two outputs of the op amps.

$$V_o = (e_2 - e_1)\left(1 + \frac{2R}{R_g}\right) \tag{4–1}$$

You can derive equation 4–1 by first noting that there can be no difference in potential between the inverting and noninverting inputs of the op amps. This means that e_1 is at the top of R_g and e_2 is at the bottom of R_g. That is, the voltage across R_g is

$$v_{Rg} = e_2 - e_1$$

$$I_{Rg} = \frac{e_2 - e_1}{R_g}$$

This current must flow through all three resistors because none of the current can flow into the op amps' inputs. So the output voltage, V_o, is

$$V_o = I_{Rg} \times (2R + R_g)$$

$$= \frac{e_2 - e_1}{R_g}(2R + R_g) \tag{4–2}$$

$$= (e_2 - e_1)\left(1 + \frac{2R}{R_g}\right)$$

Changing R_g will inversely alter the output voltage. To increase gain, you lower R_g. This decreases the effects of offset currents.

The second stage of the instrumentation amplifier is a unity-gain difference amplifier. The full IA schematic (both stages) is shown in Figure 4–2. Three terminals are brought out. The sense terminal gives you access to the negative feedback loop. The reference terminal allows you to establish the dc reference (ground) potential of the output. For normal operation, connect the sense terminal directly to the output (completing the negative feedback loop), and tie the reference terminal to ground. This configures the output as a standard difference amplifier.

Correct use of the sense and reference terminals will increase the accuracy and flexibility of your circuits. If the load being driven by the instrumentation amplifier is any distance from the amplifiers, the wire resistance will drop part of the output. A solution to this problem is shown in Figure 4–3. The output voltage is divided between R_{wire} and R_{load}, reducing the voltage to the load.

By connecting the sense and reference terminals to the load, that same amount of resistance is added into the gain equation for the difference amplifier:

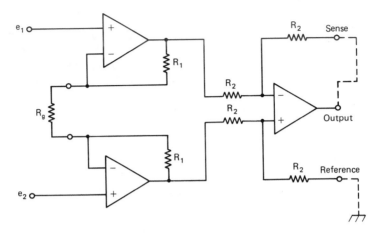

Figure 4–2   Instrumentation amplifier full schematic.

$$G = \frac{R_2 + R_{\text{wire}}}{R_2}$$

The gain goes up precisely enough to compensate for losses in the wire.

Should the IA be unable to provide adequate load current, you can place boost transistors inside the negative feedback loop of the output difference amplifier. This is shown in Figure 4–4. Again, by connecting the sense terminal at the load, any nonlinearity and offsets between the output pin and the load are eliminated.

The output dc level of the IA can be shifted as shown in Figure 4–5. A dc reference voltage is applied to the reference terminal. This shifts the output of the IA by the same amount. You can verify this by analyzing the difference amplifier using superposition. The voltage follower assures that the lower R_2 is being driven from an ideal voltage source (zero impedence) to keep the second amplifier's gain correct and

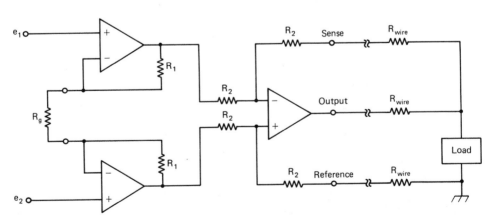

Figure 4–3   Driving a remote load.

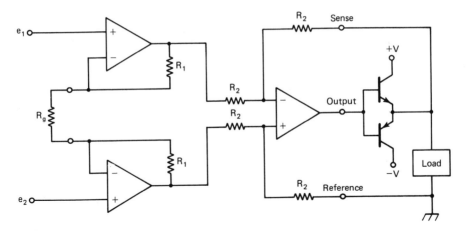

Figure 4–4 Current boosting an instrumentation amplifier.

balanced. This output offset control allows you to compensate for the amplifier's offset and to shift the sensor's signal to a different zero point (more on that later).

Use of the sense and reference terminals gives you some flexibility in using the instrumentation amplifier. They can compensate for wire losses in driving remote loads, allow you to current boost the IA without offset or linearity losses, and alter the output dc level. There are other uses. The common-mode rejection can be tuned for optimum performance. You can also cause the IA to output a current rather than a voltage.

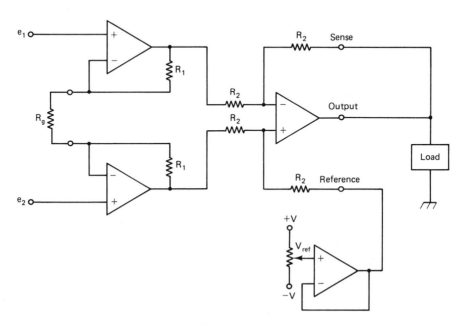

Figure 4–5 Output offset control.

TABLE 4-1 AD524 SPECIFICATIONS[a]

Parameter	AD524A Min.	AD524A Typ.	AD524A Max.	AD524B Min.	AD524B Typ.	AD524B Max.	AD524C Min.	AD524C Typ.	AD524C Max.	AD524S Min.	AD524S Typ.	AD524S Max.	Units
Gain													
Gain equation (external resistor gain programming)		$\left(\dfrac{40,000}{R_G}+1\right)\pm20\%$			$\left(\dfrac{40,000}{R_G}+1\right)\pm20\%$			$\left(\dfrac{40,000}{R_G}+1\right)\pm20\%$			$\left(\dfrac{40,000}{R_G}+1\right)\pm20\%$		
Gain range (pin programmable)	1 to 1000			1 to 100			1 to 1000			1 to 1000			
Gain error													
$G=1$			±0.05			±0.03			±0.02			±0.05	%
$G=10$			±0.25			±0.15			±0.1%			±0.25	%
$G=100$			±0.5			±0.35			±0.25			±0.5	%
$G=1000$			±2.0			±1.0			±0.5			±2.0	%
Nonlinearity													
$G=1$			±0.01			±0.005			±0.003			±0.01	%
$G=10, 100$			±0.01			±0.005			±0.003			±0.01	%
$G=1000$			±0.01			±0.01			±0.01			±0.01	%
Gain vs. temperature													
$G=1$			5			5			5			5	ppm/°C
$G=10$			15			10			10			10	ppm/°C
$G=100$			35			25			25			25	ppm/°C
$G=1000$			100			50			50			50	ppm/°C
Voltage offset (may be nulled)													
Input offset voltage			250			100			50			100	μV
vs. temperature			2			0.75			0.5			2.0	μV/°C
Output offset voltage			5			3			2.0			3.0	μV
vs. temperature			100			50			25			50	μV/°C
Offset referred to the input vs. supply													
$G=1$	70			75			80			75			dB
$G=10$	85			95			100			95			dB
$G=100$	95			105			110			105			dB
$G=1000$	100			110			115			110			dB
Input current													
Input bias current		±100	±50		±100	±25		±100	±15		±100	±50	nA
vs. temperature		±100			±100			±100			±100		pA/°C
Input offset current		±100	±35		±100	±15		±100	±10		±100	±35	nA
vs. temperature		±100			±100			±100			±100		pA/°C
Input													
Input impedance													
Differential resistance		10^9			10^9			10^9			10^9		Ω
Differential capacitance		10			10			10			10		pF
Common-mode resistance		10^9			10^9			10^9			10^9		Ω
Common-mode capacitance		10			10			10			10		pF
Input voltage range													
Max. differ. input linear, V_D		±10			±10			±10			±10		V
Max. common mode linear, V_{CM}		$12V-\left(\dfrac{G}{2}\times V_D\right)$			$12V-\left(\dfrac{G}{2}\times V_D\right)$			$12V-\left(\dfrac{G}{2}\times V_D\right)$			$12V-\left(\dfrac{G}{2}\times V_D\right)$		V

Parameter					Units
Common-mode rejection dc					
to 60 Hz with 1-kΩ source imbalance					
G = 1	**70**	**75**	**80**	**70**	dB
G = 10	**90**	**95**	**100**	**90**	dB
G = 100	**100**	**105**	**110**	**100**	dB
G = 1000	**110**	**115**	**120**	**110**	dB
Output rating,					
V_{out}, R_L = 2 kΩ	±10	±10	±10	±10	V
Dynamic response					
Small signal, −3 dB					
G = 1	1	1	1	1	MHz
G = 10	400	400	400	400	kHz
G = 100	150	150	150	150	kHz
G = 1000	25	25	25	25	kHz
Slew rate	5.0	5.0	5.0	5.0	V/μs
Settling time to 0.01%, 20-V step					
G = 1 to 100	15	15	15	15	μs
G = 1000	75	75	75	75	μs
Noise					
Voltage noise, 1 kHz					
R.T.I.	7	7	7	7	nV/√Hz
R.T.O.	90	90	90	90	nV/√Hz
R.T.I. 0.1 to 10 Hz					
G = 1	15	15	15	15	μV p-p
G = 10	2	2	2	2	μV p-p
G = 100,1000	0.3	0.3	0.3	0.3	μV p-p
Current noise,					
0.1 to 10 Hz	60	60	60	60	pA p-p
Sense input					
R_{in}	20	20	20	20	kΩ ± 20%
I_{in}	15	15	15	15	μA
Voltage range	±10	±10	±10	±10	V
Gain to output	1	1	1	1	%
Reference input					
R_{in}	**40**	**40**	**40**	**40**	kΩ ± 20%
I_{in}	15	15	15	15	μA
Voltage range	±10	±10	±10	±10	V
Gain to output	1	1	1	1	%
Temperature range					
Specified performance	−25/+85	−25/+85	−25/+85	−55/+125	°C
Storage	−65/+150	−65/+150	−65/+150	−65/+150	°C
Power supply					
Power supply range	±6/±15/±18	±6/±15/±18	±6/±15/±18	±6/±15/±18	V
Quiescent current	3.5/5.0	3.5/5.0	3.5/5.0	3.5/5.0	mA

[a] At V_S = ±15 V, R_L = 2 kΩ, and T_A = +25°C unless otherwise specified. Specifications subject to change without notice. Specifications shown in boldface are tested on all production units at final electrical test. Results from those tests are used to calculate outgoing quality levels. All min. and max. specifications are guaranteed, although only those shown in boldface are tested on all production units.

Source: Analog Devices.

The specifications for an instrumentation amplifier look a bit different from those of an op amp. There are several that you should review carefully. They will allow you to determine the amount of error the IA introduces. Table 4–1 lists the specifications of the AD524, a low-cost monolithic instrumentation amplifier. Its schematic is shown in Figure 4–6.

The gain may be set with an external resistor, R_g connected between RG_1 and RG_2. Using R_g allows you to adjust the gain, according to

$$G = \frac{40,000}{R_g} + 1$$

But notice in Table 4–1 that this equation is only $\pm 20\%$ accurate. So use R_g if you plan to tweak the gain.

For much more accurate gain without any external components, pin strapping is provided. Look again at Figure 4–6. Three laser-trimmed resistors are provided within the IC. These closely matched to the 20-kΩ resistors used elsewhere. Since they respond to temperature precisely the same as the 20-kΩ resistors, gain changes very little as the temperature of the IC changes. To set the gain, simply place a jumper between RG_2 and the gain resistor you want.

However, this equation does not hold perfectly true for all values of input, output, or temperature. The gain error (an error from the equation) indicates the maximum deviation from the equation, while the gain temperature coefficient indicates the variation of the gain as a function of temperature.

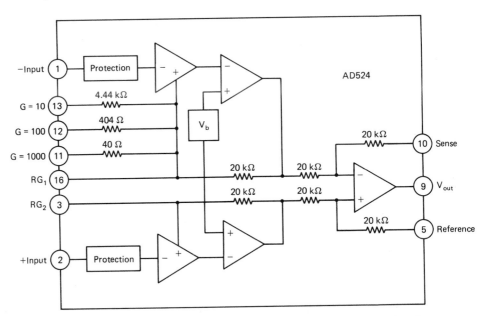

Figure 4–6 AD524 instrumentation amplifier functional diagram. (Courtesy of Analog Devices.)

Nonlinearity describes the variation of the gain versus resistance curve from a straight line. Beware. The straight line to which the percent deviation is compared is the line that gives the manufacturer the "best fit." It is probably not a straight line drawn from the minimum point to the maximum point. It is whatever straight line will yield the smallest nonlinearity specifications.

Common-mode inputs are a major factor with instrumentation amplifiers. The voltage out of each side of a balanced bridge will be equal, but definitely nonzero. This voltage (very often $\frac{1}{2} V_{supply}$) must be rejected by the instrumentation amplifier, resulting in a zero output. Example 4–1 illustrates this further.

EXAMPLE 4–1

For the circuit in Figure 4–7, calculate V_a, V_b, and V_{out}.

Solution

$$V_b = \tfrac{1}{2}V_{supply} = 5 \text{ V}$$

$$V_a = \left(\frac{349\ \Omega}{350\ \Omega + 349\ \Omega}\right) 10 \text{ V} = 4.99285 \text{ V}$$

$$V_{out} = G(V_a - V_b)$$
$$= 100(4.99285 \text{ V} - 5 \text{ V}) = -715 \text{ mV}$$

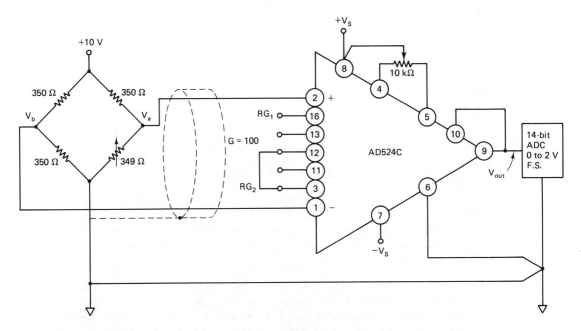

Figure 4–7   AD524 used as a bridge amplifier. (Courtesy of Analog Devices.)

The amplifier must amplify a signal of 7.15 mV by 100 while completely ignoring the 5-V dc level that is output by both sides of the bridge. How effective the amplifier is at amplifying the difference between its inputs while ignoring (rejecting) the same signals at each input is indicated by the common-mode rejection ratio.

$$\text{CMRR} = 20 \log \frac{G}{A_c} \qquad (4\text{--}3)$$

where

$$A_c = \frac{V_{\text{out(common mode)}}}{e_{\text{common mode}}}$$

Notice that the CMRR goes up with gain. Common-mode signals are not amplified by the input stage, while the differential signal is.

EXAMPLE 4–2

For the problem of Example 4–1, calculate the effect on the output of the 5-V common-mode signal.

Solution   For a gain of 100,

$$\text{CMRR} = 100 \text{ dB}$$

$$100 \text{ dB} = 20 \log \frac{G}{A_c}$$

$$5 = \log \frac{G}{A_c}$$

$$10^5 = \frac{G}{A_c}$$

$$A_c = \frac{G}{10^5} = \frac{100}{10^5}$$

$$= 0.001 \times 5 \text{ V} = 5 \text{ mV}$$

For the 715-mV output, the common-mode error is

$$\frac{5 \text{ mV}}{715 \text{ mV}} \times 100\% = 0.7\%$$

EXAMPLE 4–3

"To illustrate how instrumentation amplifier specifications are applied, we will now examine a typical case where an AD524 is required to amplify the output of an unbalanced transducer." Figure 4–7 "shows a differential transducer, unbalanced by 100 Ω, supplying a 0- to 20-mV signal to an AD524C. The output of the IA feeds a 14-bit A-to-D converter with a 0- to 2-V input voltage range. The operating temperature range is -25 to $+85°C$. Therefore, the largest change in temperature T within the operating range is from ambient to $+85°C$: $(85°C - 25°C) = 60°C$'' [1]. Determine the effect that errors have on the signal with respect to full-scale input. This is called the error budget.

Solution   Errors can be divided into three groups. First are errors that occur at ambient temperature and can be nulled out, or zeroed. Second are terms caused by drift. Finally, are errors that cannot be tuned out and are independent of temperature. These are irreducible errors. ''In many applications differential linearity and resolution are of prime importance. This would be so in cases where the absolute value of a variable is less important than changes in value. In these applications, only the irreducible errors are significant. Furthermore, if a system has an intelligent processor monitoring the A/D output, the addition of an auto-gain/auto-zero will remove all reducible errors and may eliminate the requirement for initial calibration'' [1]. The final error budget is given in Table 4–2. Since each individual error term is so small, each has been shown in parts per million (ppm).

$$1 \text{ ppm} = 0.0001\%$$

Without any effort to adjust the circuit, at 25°C, there is a maximum possible error of 6656.5 ppm or 0.666% of full scale. You can eliminate this by careful zeroing. Once zeroed at 25°C, if the temperature rises to 85°C, there will be a 10,516.5 ppm or 1.052% of full-scale error. Computer-controlled auto cal and auto zero can software-compensate for this. So only 45 ppm or 0.0045% of full-scale error is left.

In addition to the error budget, there are several other factors that you must consider to get optimum performance from an instrumentation amplifier. The source impedance has been mentioned several times. The source impedence effects are illustrated in Figure 4–8. Current to bias the input transistors must flow from the sources, through the source impedences, and into the amplifier. The input voltage at the inverting input then becomes

$$e_1 - I_{R1}R_{S1}$$

and the voltage at the noninverting input is

$$e_2 - I_{R2}R_{S2}$$

The bias current is the average of I_{R1} and I_{R2}. This bias current produces a voltage drop across the two source impedances. If the two impedances are equal,

$$R_{S1} = R_{S2}$$

the bias currents will have exactly the same effect at each input. That is a common-mode signal and will be rejected by the CMRR. So to minimize the effect of bias

TABLE 4-2 ERROR BUDGET ANALYSIS OF AD524CD IN BRIDGE APPLICATION

Error source	AD524C specifications	Calculation	Effect on absolute accuracy at $T_A = 25°C$ (ppm)	Effect on absolute accuracy at $T_A = 85°C$ (ppm)	Effect on resolution (ppm)
Gain error	±0.25%	±0.25 = 2500 ppm	2500	2500	—
Gain instability	25 ppm	(25 ppm/°C)(60°C) = 1500 ppm	—	1500	—
Gain nonlinearity	±0.003%	±0.003% = 30 ppm	—	—	30
Input offset voltage	±50 µV, RTI	±50 µV/20 mV = ±2500 ppm	2500	2500	—
Input offset voltage drift	±0.5 µV/°C	(±0.5 µV/°C)(60°C) = 30 µV / 30 µV/20 mV = 1500 ppm	—	1500	—
Output offset voltage[a]	±2.0 mV	±2.0 mV/20 mV = 1000 ppm	1000	1000	—
Output offset voltage drift[a]	±25 µV/°C	(±25 µV/°C)(60°C) = 1500 µV / 1500 µV/20 mV = 750 ppm	—	750	—
Bias current—source imbalance error	±15 nA	(±15 nA)(100 Ω) = 1.5 µV / 1.5 µV/20 mV = 75 ppm	75	75	—
Bias current—source imbalance drift	±100 pA/°C	(±100 pA/°C)(100 Ω)(60°C) = 0.6 µV / 0.6 µV/20 mV = 30 ppm	—	30	—
Offset current—source imbalance error	±10 nA	(±10 nA)(100 Ω) = 1 µV / 1 µV/20 mV = 50 ppm	50	50	—
Offset current—source imbalance drift	±100 pA/°C	(100 pA/°C)(100 Ω)(60°C) = 0.6 µV / 0.6 µV/20 mV = 30 ppm	—	30	—
Offset current—source resistance—error	±10 nA	(10 nA)(175 Ω) = 3.5 µV / 3.5 µV/20 mV = 87.5 ppm	87.5	87.5	—
Offset current—source resistance—drift	±100 pA/°C	(100 pA/°C)(175 Ω)(60°C) = 1 µV / 1 µV/20 mV = 50 ppm	—	50	—
Common mode rejection 5 V dc	115 dB	115 dB = 1.8 ppm × 5 V = 8.8 µV / 8.8 µV/20 mV = 444 ppm	444	444	—
Noise, RTI (0.1–10 Hz)	0.3 µV p-p	0.3 µV p-p/20 mV = 15 ppm	—	—	15
		Total error	6656.5	10,516.5	45

[a] Output offset voltage and output offset voltage drift are given as RTI figures.

Source: Analog Devices.

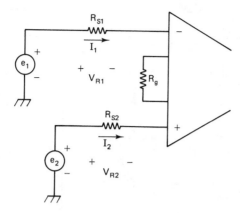

Figure 4–8 Source impedence effects.

currents, *assure that the impedence from the inputs to ground (source impedences) are equal.*

Any difference between the input currents (I_{R1} and I_{R2}) is called the differential input current or the offset current. Even with identical source resistances, this differential input current produces a different voltage at one input than at the other. This is a differential input signal and cannot be separated from the actual differential signal ($e_2 - e_1$). To minimize the effect of offset (differential input) current, *keep the source resistances as low as possible.* Noise and CMRR are also adversely affected by large source impedence and source impedence unbalance.

The input transistors must be biased with current (I_{bias}) and this current comes from the input sources (the sensors). For I_{bias} to flow there must be a complete circuit. This means that there must be a ground return between the instrumentation amplifier (or its power supplies) and the sensors (or their power supply). Without the common connection, no bias current can flow. This is the same as having an infinite R_{S1} or R_{S2}. The instrumentation amplifier's output goes to saturation. *Assure that the instrumentation amplifier and the sensor have a common ground.*

The effects of offset voltage, bias currents, and offset current can be eliminated by properly zeroing the instrumentation amplifier. Refer to Figure 4–9. To eliminate those errors associated with the input amplifier, connect both inputs, through the actual source impedences (if possible), to ground. Set the circuit to give the maximum gain you will use. Adjust the left trim potentiometer to give a zero output. Change the circuit to give a gain of 1. Any voltage at the output is now caused primarily by offset in the output amplifier. Adjust the right potentiometer slightly to give a zero output. Then repeat the high-gain (input amplifier) zero, then the low-gain (output amplifier) zero. Several, increasingly more precise adjustments of both potentiometers may be necessary.

Finally, notice that the AD524 performs more stably with a load of a few kilohms. Decoupling capacitors (0.1 μF ceramic) are also needed, connected as close to each power pin as possible, to analog common.

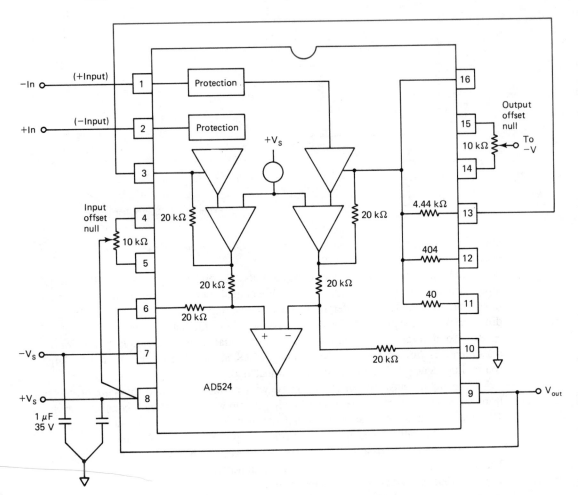

Figure 4–9   AD524 input and output offset adjusts. (Couresty of Analog Devices.)

4–2 ZERO AND SPAN CIRCUITS

The output of a transducer rarely matches the levels you want to provide to the controller, display, or computer. You may need a 0.01-mV/lb input to a digital panel meter, while the load cell provides a 20 μV/lb reading with 18-mV output with no load. Or the A/D converter needs a 0- to 5-V signal, while the temperature transducer outputs 2.48 to 3.90 V. The zero and span circuits of this section will allow you to make this conversion. Running a linear signal through such a span (slope) and zero (y intercept) converter allows you to produce any convenient parameter-to-voltage relationship that you wish. Figure 4–10a illustrates the effect of altering only the span or slope. The slope is inverted (gain of −1) in Figure 4–10b. On the other hand, if you alter the

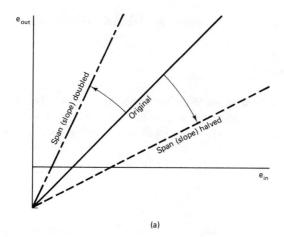

(a)

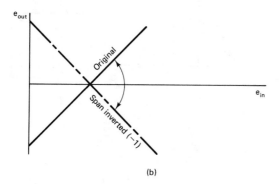

(b)

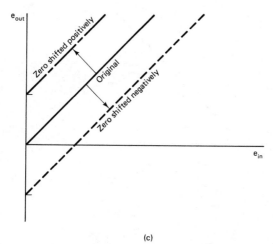

(c)

Figure 4–10 Effects of span and zero
adjustments: (a) varying span (slope); (b)
span (gain) of −1; (c) shifting the zero
(y-intercept).

zero (y intercept), the new line will parallel the original. This is shown in Figure 4–10c.

4–2.1 Inverting Summer

A zero and span converter can be made using the inverting summer. This is shown in Figure 4–11. The signal to be conditioned is a single input, e_{in}. It receives a gain of $-R_f/R_i$. A reference voltage, $\pm V$, is the other input. It receives a gain of $-R_f/R_{os}$. So the output from U_1 is

$$e_{u_i} = -\frac{R_f}{R_i} e_{in} - \frac{R_f}{R_{os}} V$$

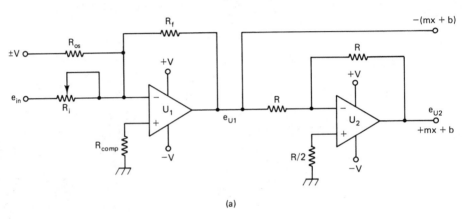

(a)

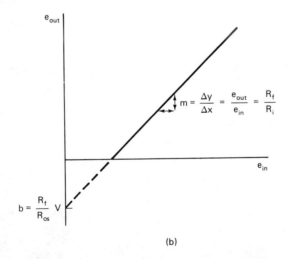

(b)

Figure 4–11   General span and zero converter using an inverting summer: (a) schematic; (b) $mx + b$ definition.

This signal is then fed through an inverting amplifier with a gain of -1.

$$e_{u2} = \frac{R_f}{R_i} e_{\text{in}} + \frac{R_f}{R_{os}} V \qquad (4\text{–}4)$$

Compare this to the equation of a straight line,

$$y = mx + b$$

where y is the dependent variable and x is the independent variable.

For a plot of output versus input voltage, as in Figure 4–11b,

$$m = \frac{R_f}{R_i} \qquad \text{slope or gain or span}$$

$$b = \frac{R_f}{R_{os}} V \qquad y \text{ intercept or offset or zero}$$

EXAMPLE 4–4

When the temperature in a process is at its minimum, the sensor outputs 2.48 V. At maximum temperature, it outputs 3.90 V. The A/D converter used to input these data into a computer has the range 0 to 5 V. To provide maximum resolution, you must zero and span the signal from the transducer so that it fills the entire range of the converter.

Solution   The circuit in Figure 4–11 should be used. The required gain is

$$m = \frac{V_{\text{out}}}{V_{\text{in}}}$$

$$= \frac{V_{\text{out(max)}} - V_{\text{out(min)}}}{V_{\text{in(max)}} - V_{\text{in(min)}}}$$

$$= \frac{5\text{ V} - 0\text{ V}}{3.90\text{ V} - 2.48\text{ V}}$$

$$= 3.52$$

But the gain is set by

$$m = \frac{R_f}{R_i}$$

Pick R_f relatively large, so that a smaller R_i will not load down the sensor.

$$R_f = 330\text{ k}\Omega$$

$$R_i = \frac{R_f}{m}$$

$$= \frac{330\text{ k}\Omega}{3.52}$$

$$= 93.7\text{ k}\Omega$$

Pick R_i as a 47-kΩ fixed resistor with a series 100-kΩ multiturn potentiometer.

This sets the gain (span). To get the offset (zero), substitute the values you have into the circuit equation at one point.

$$y = mx + b$$

or

$$V_{\text{out}} = mV_{\text{in}} + b$$

At $V_{\text{in}} = 2.48$ V, $V_{\text{out}} = 0$ V.

$$0 \text{ V} = (3.52)(2.48 \text{ V}) + b$$

$$b = -(3.52)(2.48 \text{ V})$$

$$= -8.73 \text{ V}$$

But

$$b = \frac{R_f}{R_{os}}(V)$$

Since you need a negative offset, select $V = -12$ V (the negative power supply voltage).

$$R_{os} = \frac{R_f V}{b}$$

$$= \frac{(330 \text{ k}\Omega)(-12 \text{ V})}{-8.73 \text{ V}}$$

$$= 454 \text{ k}\Omega$$

Pick R_{os} as a fixed 220-kΩ resistor with a 500-kΩ multiturn potentiometer.

$$R_{\text{comp}} = R_f \parallel R_i \parallel R_{os}$$

$$= 62.9 \text{ k}\Omega$$

Pick $R_{\text{comp}} = 56$ kΩ.

The resistors in the second stage should be in the kΩ range. This lowers offset without loading the first stage. Pick $R = 2.2$ kΩ. So $R/2 = 1.1$ kΩ.

It is a good idea to check your work at the other specified point.

$$V_{\text{out}} = \frac{R_f}{R_i}V_{\text{in}} + \frac{R_f}{R_{os}}V$$

$$= \frac{330 \text{ k}\Omega}{93.7 \text{ k}\Omega}(3.90 \text{ V}) + \frac{330 \text{ k}\Omega}{454 \text{ k}\Omega}(-12 \text{ V})$$

$$= 13.72 \text{ V} - 8.72 \text{ V}$$

$$= 5 \text{ V}$$

4–2.2 Instrumentation Amplifier

Strain gages, thermocouples, and RTDs all produce very small differential signals. The stable high gain, good common-mode rejection ratio, and large input impedence of the instrumentation amplifier makes it a natural choice to zero and span the signals from these transducers.

The output offset control circuit you saw in Figure 4–5 has been redrawn in Figure 4–12. An external gain-setting resistor, R_g, determines the span. The zero offset is provided by the reference voltage, V_{ref}, through the voltage follower, U_2.

$$V_{out} = Ge_{in} + V_{ref} \qquad (4-5)$$

where G is the gain of the instrumentation amplifier's gain. For an external resistor on the AD524,

$$G = 1 + \frac{40 \text{ k}\Omega}{R_g}$$

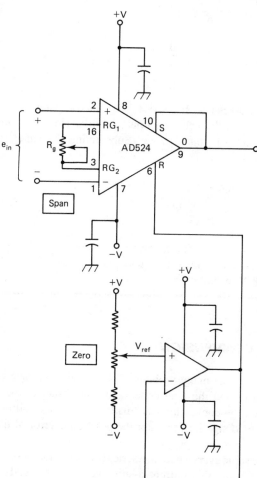

Figure 4–12 Instrumentation amplifier used for zero and span.

EXAMPLE 4–5

The output from a load cell changes 20 μV/lb with an output of 18 mV with no load on the cell. Design a zero and span converter using an instrumentation amplifier which will output 0 V dc when there is no load, and will change 10 mV/lb.

Solution   The required gain is

$$G = \frac{10 \text{ mV/lb}}{20 \text{ μV/lb}}$$

$$= 500$$

Since this is not one of the gains available by pin strapping, you must provide an external gain-setting resistor.

$$R_g = \frac{40 \text{ k}\Omega}{G - 1}$$

$$= \frac{40 \text{ k}\Omega}{499}$$

$$= 80.2 \text{ }\Omega$$

Select R_g as a 100-Ω potentiometer with a series 33-Ω fixed resistor.

When there is no load on the cell, it outputs 18 mV. However, you want the instrumentation amplifier to output 0 V dc. Substituting the values for this point into equation 4–5 gives

$$0 \text{ V} = (500)(18 \text{ mV}) + V_{\text{ref}}$$

$$V_{\text{ref}} = -(500)(18 \text{ mV})$$

$$= -9 \text{ V}$$

So tie one end of the zero potentiometer to ground and the other end to $-V_{\text{supply}}$. Select resistor and potentiometer values that will put approximately -10 V at one end of the pot and -8 V at the other.

4–3 VOLTAGE-TO-CURRENT CONVERSION

Signal *voltage* transmission presents many problems. The series resistance between the output of the signal conditioner and the load depends on the distance, the wire used, the temperature, and how well the connections are made. Even a few millivolts of loss across this series resistance could significantly alter the percentage error of the measurement.

Current, however, is the same everywhere in a series (transmission) loop. Converting the signal to a current and sending that current assures you that the load will receive all of the signal (current) you sent. None will be lost because of line resistance or poor connections.

The type of voltage-to-current conversion you use depends on the load's resistance and whether the load is floating or tied to ground. A floating load is preferable. It allows you to apply common-mode rejection techniques at the receiver to reduce the induced noise. More on this later. However, you may have to drive the signal into a grounded load, either for safety reasons or because the display and control electronics are built that way.

4-3.1 Floating Load

The simplest voltage-to-current converter is shown in Figure 4-13. It is actually only a noninverting amplifier. The transmission loop and remote load into which the signal is being driven form the upper part of the negative feedback loop. Analysis is as simple as the circuit itself. Since the op amp is operating closed loop (with negative feedback), the voltage at the noninverting input also appears at the inverting input. But this voltage is across the lower resistor R. The current through that resistor is I.

$$I = \frac{e_{in}}{R}$$

Since no current (of significance) flows into or out of the inverting input, I must be the current in the current loop.

There are several points you must consider when using the circuit in Figure 4-13. The resistance in the transmission loop ($R_{loop} = R_{wire} + R_{load}$) does not affect the amount of transmitted current at all. The output *voltage* of the op amp is affected by R_{loop}.

$$V_{out} = \left(1 + \frac{R_{loop}}{R}\right) e_{in} < V_{sat} \tag{4-6}$$

You must keep R_{loop} small enough to keep the op amp out of saturation.

Second, the op amp must be able to generate the current required. Many transmission standards call for either 20- or 60-mA currents. Both of these are beyond the capabilities

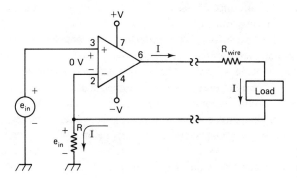

Figure 4-13 Simple voltage-to-current converter.

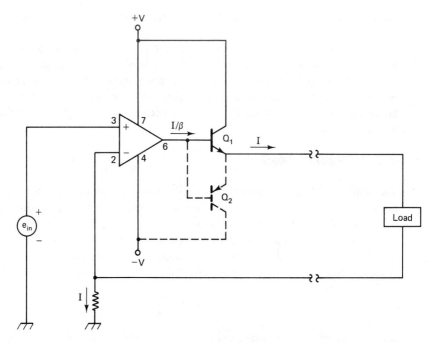

Figure 4–14 Current-boosted voltage-to-current converter.

of most general-purpose op amps. However, you may add a current boost transistor(s) (see Figure 4–14). Because the transistor(s) is within the negative feedback loop, the op amp automatically compensates for its offsets, bias, and nonlinearities. If the signal must go plus and minus, you must add Q_2, a PNP complement of Q_1, to handle the negative current.

Third, notice that current from the load must return along a wire to the op amp (and R). It cannot be driven through the load directly to ground. This is a floating signal and requires two wires to be run. However, since the currents flow in opposite directions, the signal being transmitted is inherently differential. This allows you to use a difference or instrumentation amplifier at the load to reject any common-mode noise picked up on both lines during transmission.

Fourth, the worst-case load is an open. Opening the load removes the negative feedback and sends the op amp into saturation. On the other hand, shorting the load simply turns the circuit into a voltage follower. The signal current is unaffected.

Finally, this noninverting configuration buffers the voltage source, preventing loading. You could build a voltage-to-current converter using an inverter amplifier. However, the current in the transmission loop must then come from the voltage source. Since this could significantly load down the voltage source (sensor), the inverting configuration is not recommended.

The circuit in Figure 4–14 has one additional problem. When

$$e_{in} = 0$$

$$I_L = 0$$

Zero current appears to the load as a valid signal. However, if the current loop opened, or the transmitting electronics failed,

$$I_L = 0$$

the current would fall to zero. The load would respond as if a

$$e_{in} = 0$$

were being transmitted. A method must be devised to allow the load to differentiate between no signal (circuit failure),

$$I_L = 0$$

and the valid input,

$$e_{in} = 0$$

You can do this by providing an offset. With

$$e_{in} = 0 \text{ or } e_{in} = \text{minimum}$$

$$I_L = I(0) > 0$$

A zero minimum input voltage produces a set, nonzero loop current. In this offset circuit, any valid signal would produce some current greater than or equal to $I(0)$. If

$$I_L = 0$$

a circuit failure has occurred.

An offset voltage-to-current converter is shown in Figure 4–15a. The noninverting *amplifier* of Figure 4–14 has been replaced by a noninverting *summer*. The output current now is jointly determined by the input voltage e_{in} and the reference voltage e_{ref}. The two 1-MΩ input resistors must be present (and large) to keep one voltage source from loading down the other.

The input voltage-to-output current transfer curve is shown in Figure 4–15b. It is linear and can be positioned anywhere in the upper two quadrants by specifying $e(A)$, $I(A)$ and $e(B)$, $I(B)$ (the two endpoints of the line). Given that an input voltage of $e(A)$ will produce a current of $I(A)$ and that an input voltage of $e(B)$ will produce a current of $I(B)$, you can determine the needed circuit values by

$$R = \frac{e(B) - e(A)}{2[I(B) - I(A)]} \tag{4–7}$$

and

$$e_{ref} = 2RI(B) - e(B) \tag{4–8}$$

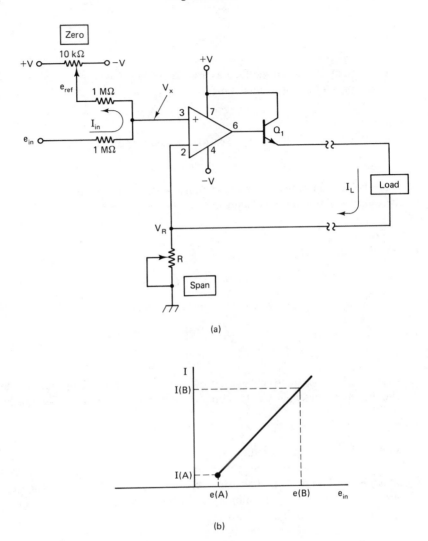

(a)

(b)

Figure 4–15   Offset voltage-to-current converter: (a) schematic; (b) transfer curve.

You can derive these equations as follows. Because the op amp has negative feedback,

$$V_x = V_R$$

$$I_L = \frac{V_x}{R} \tag{4-9}$$

Summing the loop from e_{in} through e_{ref} (and ignoring the 10-kΩ resistance when compared to 1 MΩ) yields

$$e_{in} - I_{in}(1\ M\Omega) - I_{in}(1\ M\Omega) - e_{ref} = 0$$

Solving this for I_{in} gives us

$$I_{in} = \frac{e_{in} - e_{ref}}{2\ M\Omega} \tag{4–10}$$

Summing the loop from e_{in} through V_x, we obtain

$$e_{in} - I_{in}(1\ M\Omega) - V_x = 0 \tag{4–11}$$

$$V_x = e_{in} - \frac{e_{in} - e_{ref}}{2\ M\Omega}(1\ M\Omega)$$

$$\tag{4–12}$$

$$= \frac{e_{in} + e_{ref}}{2}$$

Substituting equation 4–12 into 4–9, we have

$$I_L = \frac{e_{in} + e_{ref}}{2R} \tag{4–13}$$

Equation 4–13 is the transfer equation of the circuit in Figure 4–15a. It is the equation for the line of Figure 4–15b.

At point A,

$$I(A) = \frac{e(A) + e_{ref}}{2R}$$

At point B,

$$I(B) = \frac{e(B) + e_{ref}}{2R}$$

Manipulating these two equations gives us

$$2RI(B) = e(B) + e_{ref} \tag{4–14}$$

$$2RI(A) = e(A) + e_{ref} \tag{4–15}$$

Subtracting equation 4–15 from 4–14 to remove e_{ref} yields

$$2R[I(B) - I(A)] = e(B) - e(A)$$

or

$$R = \frac{e(B) - e(A)}{2[I(B) - I(A)]}$$

Solving equation 4–14 for e_{ref}, we obtain

$$e_{ref} = 2RI(B) - e(B)$$

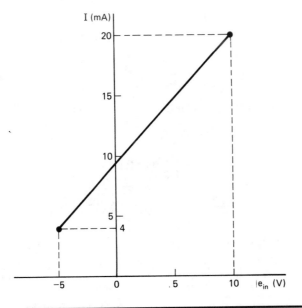

Figure 4–16 Transfer curve (Example 4–6).

EXAMPLE 4–6

Design an offset voltage-to-current converter that will produce 4 mA with an input of −5 V and 20 mA with an input of 10 V.

Solution   The transfer curve is shown in Figure 4–16. The schematic in Figure 4–15a will work. You must select the values of e_{ref} and R.

$$e(A) = -5 \text{ V} \qquad I(A) = 4 \text{ mA}$$

$$e(B) = 10 \text{ V} \qquad I(B) = 20 \text{ mA}$$

$$R = \frac{e(B) - e(A)}{2[I(B) - I(A)]}$$

$$= \frac{10 \text{ V} - (-5 \text{ V})}{2(20 \text{ mA} - 4 \text{ mA})}$$

Be careful not to lose the sign.

$$R = 469 \text{ }\Omega$$

Pick a 430-Ω fixed resistor with a 100-Ω series potentiometer.

$$e_{ref} = 2RI(B) - e(B)$$
$$= 2(469 \text{ }\Omega)(20 \text{ mA}) - 10 \text{ V}$$
$$= 8.8 \text{ V}$$

To calibrate this circuit properly, first set R and e_{ref} to the values calculated. Next apply $e(A)$ and adjust the zero potentiometer *slightly* to get a load current of $I(A)$. Then apply $e(B)$ and adjust the span potentiometer *slightly* to get a load current of $I(B)$. Next reapply $e(A)$ and fine tune the zero potentiometer, then $e(B)$ to fine tune the span. Several iterations of finer and finer adjustments of zero and span will allow you to set both endpoints properly.

4–3.2 Grounded Load

If you need to drive current into a load that is connected to ground, a difference amplifier is needed. This is shown in Figure 4–17. Resistors R_1, R_2, R_3, and R_4 are all equal, giving a gain of 1. A resistor R_s has been placed between the output and the load. Also, R_4 has been connected to the load rather than to ground.

To analyze circuit operation you must first calculate V_{out}. This is most easily done by applying superposition three times to the equivalent circuit shown in Figure 4–18. Turning off (shorting out) two sources and considering the effect of the third gives us

$$V_{out} = V_L + e_2 - e_1$$

This is the amplifier's output voltage in Figure 4–17. The voltage across R_s, then, is

$$
\begin{aligned}
V_{Rs} &= V_{out} - V_L \\
&= (V_L + e_2 - e_1) - V_L \\
&= e_2 - e_1
\end{aligned}
$$

The current through R_s is

$$I_{Rs} = \frac{V_{Rs}}{R_s}$$

$$I_L = I_{Rs} = \frac{e_2 - e_1}{R_s} \tag{4–16}$$

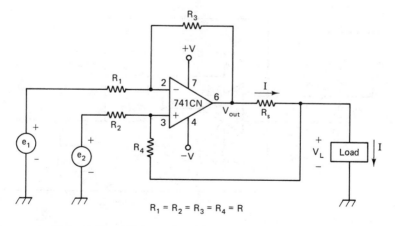

$$R_1 = R_2 = R_3 = R_4 = R$$

Figure 4–17   Voltage-to-current converter driving a grounded load.

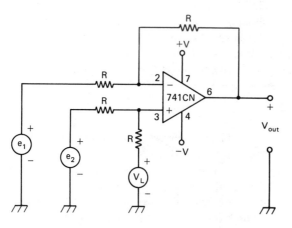

Figure 4–18 Circuit configuration for superposition analysis.

So the load current is set by the difference between e_2 and e_1 and by the sense resistor R_s.

As with the floating voltage-to-current converter, there are several factors to consider. V_{out} must be kept less than V_{sat}, so

$$V_{sat} > IR_{load} + e_2 - e_1 \qquad (4\text{--}17)$$

Second, the op amp's output may be current boosted by either one or two transistors. They are added between the op amp's output and the negative feedback connection. This is just as was done for the floating converter in Figure 4–14.

A difference amplifier is shown. However, you can ground e_1 for a noninverting converter or ground e_2 for an inverting converter. Or you could use one input for the signal, the other for a zero (offset) and R_s for the span adjust. In fact, the difference

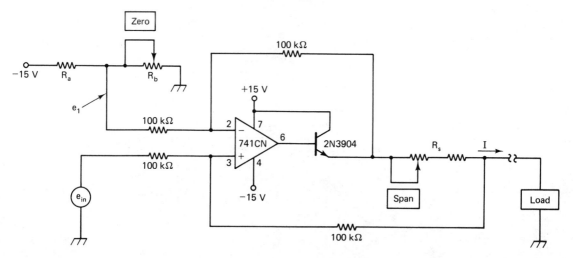

Figure 4–19 Schematic (Example 4–7).

amplifier could be replaced by an instrumentation amplifier. The sense and output terminals are connected to the left side of R_s and the reference terminal to the right.

EXAMPLE 4–7

(a) Design a voltage-to-current converter that will output 4 mA with an input voltage of 0 V and 20 mA with an input voltage of 1.0 V into a grounded load.

(b) For a current 20 mA and ± 15 V supplies, what is the maximum load resistance?

Solution   **(a)** This circuit requires both a zero and a span adjust. Also, a current boost must be added since 20 mA is beyond the guaranteed range for many general-purpose op amps. The schematic to be used is given in Figure 4–19. Resistors of 100 kΩ were selected to minimize loading of e_{in} and e_1. The basic equation is

$$I_L = \frac{e_2 - e_1}{R_s} \qquad e_2 = e_{in}$$

or

$$I_L R_s = e_{in} - e_1$$

At $e_{in} = 0$ V, $I_L = 4$ mA,

$$(4\text{ mA})R_s = -e_1 \tag{4–18}$$

At $e_{in} = 1.0$ V, $I_L = 20$ mA,

$$(20\text{ mA})R_s = 1.0\text{ V} - e_1 \tag{4–19}$$

Substituting equation 4–18 into 4–19 yields

$$(20\text{ mA})R_s = 1.0\text{ V} + (4\text{ mA})R_s$$

$$(16\text{ mA})R_s = 1.0\text{ V}$$

$$R_s = \frac{1.0\text{ V}}{16\text{ mA}} = 62.5\ \Omega$$

Pick a 22-Ω fixed resistor and a 100-Ω potentiometer to allow fine tuning. Substituting the value of R_s into equation 4–18 gives us

$$(4\text{ mA})(62.5\ \Omega) = -e_1$$

$$e_1 = -0.25\text{ V}$$

This can be obtained by selecting

$$R_a = 3.3\text{ k}\Omega$$

$$R_b = 100\text{-}\Omega \text{ potentiometer to allow for zero-point calibration}$$

(b) According to equation 4–17,

$$V_{sat} > I_L R_{load} + e_2 - e_1$$

but you should also take into account the voltage drop across the 2N3904 base–emitter junction:

$$V_{sat} > I_L R_{load} + e_2 - e_1 + 0.6 \text{ V}$$

$$R_L < \frac{V_{sat} - e_2 + e_1 - 0.6 \text{ V}}{I_L}$$

$$< \frac{13 \text{ V} - 1.0 \text{ V} - 0.25 \text{ V} - 0.6 \text{ V}}{20 \text{ mA}}$$

$$< 558 \text{ } \Omega$$

Any larger resistance would cause the op amp to saturate.

4–3.3 Dedicated Integrated-Circuit Voltage-to-Current Converter*

For those who would rather buy a converter than build one, Burr-Brown manufactures the XTR110 precision voltage-to-current converter/transmitter. "The XTR110 is a monolithic precision voltage-to-current converter. It can convert standard 0- to +10-V or 0- to +5-V inputs into 4- to 20-mA or 5- to 25-mA outputs. The required external MOS transistor keeps heat outside the XTR110 package to optimize performance under all output conditions. A precision +10-V reference output can drive 10 mA." Its block diagram is given in Figure 4–20. "The circuit contains four main functional blocks: (1) a precision resistor divider network (R_1–R_5), (2) a voltage-to-current converter (A_1, Q_1, R_6, R_7,), (3) a current-to-current converter (A_2, R_8, R_9, Q_{ext}), and (4) a precision +10-V reference.

"The precision divider network sums three input voltages to the noninverting input of A_1. These are V_{in1} (10-V full scale), V_{in2} (5-V full scale), and V_{ref} in (for offsetting). In the voltage-to-current converter, the op amp, A_1, forces its input voltage across the span setting resistors, R_6 and R_7. Since Q_1 is a high-gain Darlington, base current error is negligible and all current flows to the current-to-current converter (into R_8). The transfer function including input divider is as follows:

$$I_{R8} = \frac{(V_{ref} \text{ in}/16) + (V_{in1}/4) + (V_{in2}/2)}{R_{span}}$$

where R_{span} is the resistance from Q_1 emitter to common.

"The current-to-current converter is the output section of the XTR110 transmitter. The voltage across the 500-Ω resistor (R_8) is forced across the 50-Ω resistor (R_9) by

---

* The quoted material in Section 4–3.3 is from Ref. 2.

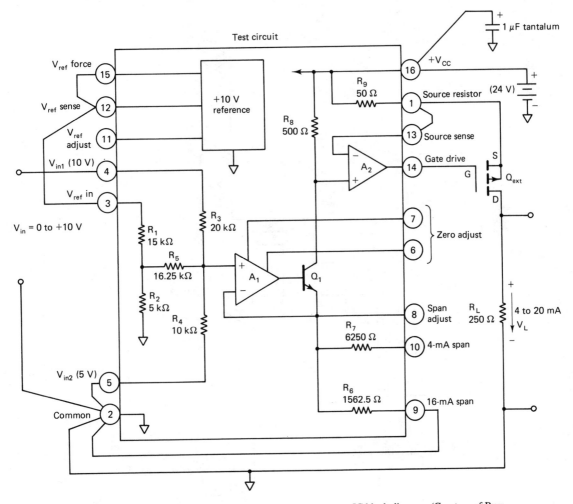

Figure 4–20   XTR110 precision voltage-to-current converter IC block diagram. (Courtesy of Burr-Brown Corporation.)

A_2 and the external MOSFET (Q_{ext}). Since no current flows in the gate of the MOSFET, all current is delivered to the output. This current (I_{out}) is 10 times the internal current through R_8. Use of the external transistor keeps power out of the precision IC to maintain accuracy.

''The overall transfer function for the XTR110 transmitter is

$$I_0 = \frac{10[(V_{ref}\ in/16) + (V_{in1}/4) + (V_{in2}/2)]}{R_{span}}$$

For output currents beyond 40 mA an external resistor can be used in place of R_9.

''The +10-V reference provides input offsetting, e.g., 4-mA offset for the 4- to

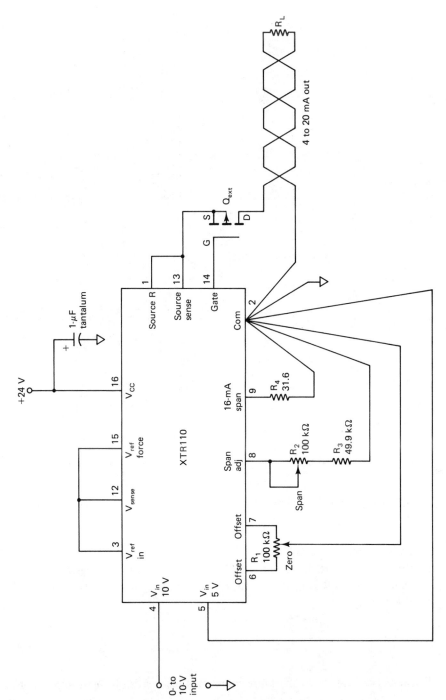

Figure 4-21 Offset and span adjustment circuit for 0- to 10-V input, 4- to 20-mA output. (Courtesy of Burr-Brown Corporation.)

20-mA output configuration. The reference can deliver 10 mA and is protected from shorts to common. Higher current can be provided for other applications by using an external NPN transistor connected to the sense and force pins.

"Connections to the MOSFET are gate drive (pin 14) and source resistor (pin 1). To eliminate errors due to resistance in the connection between pin 1 and the source of the external transistor, connect pin 13 directly to pin 1 as shown in Figure 4–20.

"+V_{cc} may originate at the XTR110 site or may be brought in as part of a three-wire twisted line. Be sure to use sufficient bypassing close to the XTR110 on the +V_{cc} line.

"Careful attention should be directed toward proper connection of the commons. All commons should be joined at one point as close to pin 2 of the XTR110 as possible. The exception is the I_{out} return. It can be returned to any place where it will not modulate the common at pin 2.

"The offset current can be adjusted by using the potentiometer, R_1, shown in Figure 4–21. The procedure is to set the input voltage to zero and then adjust R_1 to give 4 mA at the output. For spans starting at 0 mA, the following special procedure is recommended: Set the input to a small nonzero value and then adjust R_1 to the proper output current. When the input is zero the output will be zero.

"The span is adjusted at the full-scale output current using the potentiometer, R_2, shown in Figure 4–21. This adjustment is interactive with the offset adjustment, and a few iterations may be necessary. For the circuit shown, set the input voltage to +10 V full scale and then adjust R_2 to give 20 mA full-scale output. The values of R_2, R_3, and R_4 for adjusting the span are determined as follows: choose R_4 in series to slightly decrease the span; then choose R_2 and R_3 to increase the span to be adjustable about the center value." Standard input voltage, output current ranges are given in Table 4–3. Also shown there are the required connections to produce the desired transfer relationship.

"For spans beyond 40 mA, the internal 50-Ω resistor (R_9) may be replaced by an external resistor connected between pins 13 and 16. This resistor should have a low thermal coefficient. Also the self heating of this external resistor can cause nonlinearity.

TABLE 4–3 PIN CONNECTIONS FOR STANDARD XTR110 INPUT VOLTAGE/OUTPUT CURRENT RANGES

Input range (V)	Output range (mA)	Pin 3	Pin 4	Pin 5	Pin 9	Pin 10
0–10	0–20	Com	Input	Com	Com	Com
2–10	4–20					
0–10	4–20	+10 V Ref	Input	Com	Com	Open
0–10	5–25	+10 V Ref	Input	Com	Com	Com
0–5	0–20	Com	Com	Input	Com	Com
1–5	4–20					
0–5	4–20	+10 V Ref	Com	Input	Com	Open
0–5	5–25	+10 V Ref	Com	Input	Com	Com

Source: Burr-Brown.

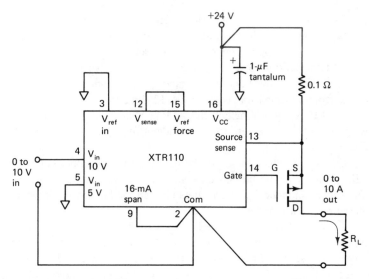

Figure 4–22   0- to 10-A high-current voltage-to-current converter. (Courtesy of Burr-Brown Corporation.)

Choose one with an adequate power rating.'' In fact, a 0- to 10-V to 0- to 10-A (high current!) converter is shown in Figure 4–22.

A full instrumentation channel is shown in Figure 4–23. The input comes from a bridge sensor. This could be a strain gage in a load cell, torque transducer, pressure transducer, or level gage. A sensitivity of ± 1 mV/V has been assumed. So a 10-V excitation will produce a ± 10-mV differential output from the bridge. The excitation voltage necessary to drive the bridge comes from the XTR110 V_{ref}. However, since only 10 mA is available directly from the IC, a 2N3055 has been connected as a emitter follower to provide the required 33 mA. By connecting the V_{sense} (pin 12) at the emitter of the 2N3055, that transistor's base–emitter voltage drop is compensated for, assuring 10 V to the bridge.

The INA101 is an instrumentation amplifier with its gain set to 400 by the 100.25-Ω resistor. Its output will be at $+6$ V when there is no differential input. This is caused by the 40- and 60-kΩ resistors along with the OPA 27 voltage follower.

A full-scale swing of ± 10 mV from the bridge will cause the instrumentation amplifier's output to swing from $+2$ V to $+10$ V. The XTR110 is set as a 0- to 10-V to 0- to 20-mA converter. A minimum input of 2 V will cause an output current of 4 mA.

4–4 *CURRENT-TO-VOLTAGE CONVERTERS*

Once the current signal gets to the place where it is to be used, it must be converted back into a voltage. You can do this very simply with a resistor.

For a ground-referenced load, this is all you need—well, almost. Look at Figure

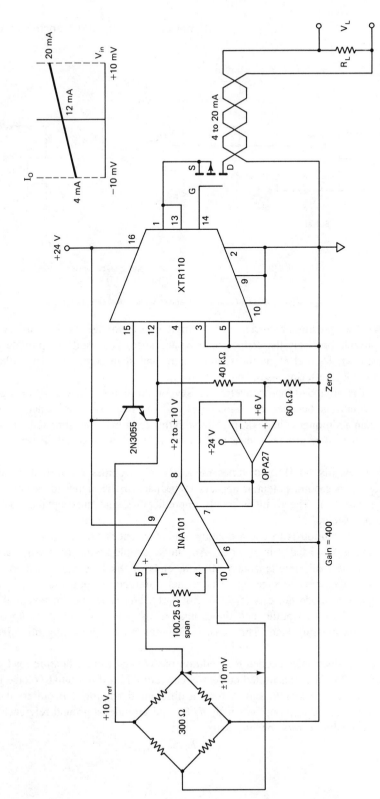

Figure 4-23 Full instrumentation channel. (Courtesy of Burr-Brown Corporation.)

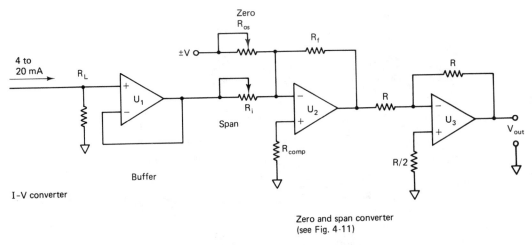

Figure 4-24   Ground-referenced voltage-to-current converter.

4-24. The transmitter current is converted into a voltage by R_L. However, this may not provide precisely the endpoints (zero and span) you want. To provide you with the adjustment, U_2 and U_3 is the standard zero and span converter. The voltage follower U_1 provides buffering, isolating R_L from R_i.

The grounded load converter has several problems. There must be a ground return for the current between the transmitter and receiver. Any resistance in this line will cause an additional voltage drop. Although this error may be calibrated out, any variation in the ground return resistance will cause a variation in signal. Even worse, there is often several volts of difference between ground points in a manufacturing facility. This is usually 60 Hz and varies randomly as machines are turned on and off. This variation in ground potential appears to be part of the signal to the receiver (display and controller). The result is totally unpredictable, and unacceptable, behavior in the control system.

The solution is to use a floating load. Current is sent to, and returned from, the load along a twisted pair of wires. Any noise coupled onto these wires appear at both ends of the load simultaneously. If *both* ends of the load are raised, or lowered, by precisely the same voltage, there is no net difference in potential *across* the load. So the common-mode noise is rejected. Similarly, any difference in potential between the ground of the transmitter and the ground of the receiver will show up on both lines sent to the floating load. This, too, is common mode, producing no *difference* across the load.

The electronics needed to condition the voltage from a floating load are shown in Figure 4-25. The transmitted current is converted to a differential voltage by R_{span}. Op amp U_1 and resistors R_i and R_f form a differential amplifier. It buffers the differential voltage across R_{span}, amplifies it by R_f/R_i, and provides a ground-referenced output. To prevent loading errors, be sure that

$$R_i \gg R_{\text{span}}$$

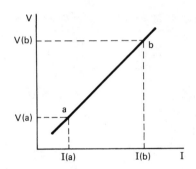

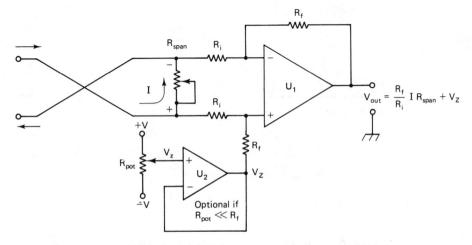

Figure 4–25   Floating current-to-voltage converter.

An offset, or zero adjust, can be injected with R_{pot} and U_2. This is the same configuration that you saw in Section 4–1, output offset control of an instrumentation amplifier (Figure 4–5). The output from U_1, then, depends on the current signal I, the floating load R_{span}, the gain R_f/R_i, and the zero offset voltage V_z.

$$V_{out} = \frac{R_f}{R_i} I R_{span} + V_z \qquad (4\text{–}20)$$

To select the correct zero and span components, look at the transfer curve at the top of Figure 4–25. A point a,

$$V(a) = \frac{R_f}{R_i} I(a) R_{span} + V_z \qquad (4\text{–}21)$$

At point b,

$$V(b) = \frac{R_f}{R_i} I(b) R_{span} + V_z \qquad (4\text{–}22)$$

Subtracting equation 4–21 from equation 4–22 gives

$$V(b) - V(a) = \frac{R_f}{R_i}I(b)R_{span} - \frac{R_f}{R_i}I(a)R_{span}$$

$$= \frac{R_f}{R_i}R_{span}[I(b) - I(a)]$$

Solving for R_{span} yields

$$R_{span} = \frac{V(b) - V(a)}{(R_f R_i)[I(b) - I(a)]} \tag{4–23}$$

Now that you know the value of the span resistor, solve equation 4–21 for V_z.

$$V_z = V(a) - \frac{R_f}{R_i}I(a)R_{span} \tag{4–24}$$

EXAMPLE 4–8

Design a floating current-to-voltage converter that will convert a 4- to 20-mA current signal into a 0- to 10-V ground-referenced voltage signal.

Solution   Use the schematic of Figure 4–25.

$$I(a) = 4 \text{ mA} \qquad V(a) = 0 \text{ V}$$

$$I(b) = 20 \text{ mA} \qquad V(b) = 10 \text{ V}$$

Choose $R_f/R_i = 10$. This seems arbitrary now, but we'll come back to it.
From equation 4–23,

$$R_{span} = \frac{10 \text{ V} - 0 \text{ V}}{(10)(20 \text{ mA} - 4 \text{ mA})} = 62.5 \ \Omega$$

Pick R_{span} as 50-Ω multiturn potentiometer with a series 33-Ω fixed resistor. Since $R_i \gg R_{span}$, pick $R_i = 2.2$ kΩ.

$$\frac{R_f}{R_i} = 10$$

$$R_f = 10R_i = 22 \text{ k}\Omega$$

All that is left is to set V_z. From equation 4–24,

$$V_z = 0 \text{ V} - \frac{22 \text{ k}\Omega}{2.2 \text{ k}\Omega}(4 \text{ mA})(62.5 \ \Omega)$$

$$= -2.5 \text{ V}$$

It is always a good idea to check your work, if possible. At point b,

$$I(b) = 20 \text{ mA}$$

$$V(b) = \frac{22 \text{ k}\Omega}{2.2 \text{ k}\Omega}(20 \text{ mA})(62.5 \ \Omega) - 2.5 \text{ V}$$

$$= 10 \text{ V}$$

It checks!

But why that gain of 10 in the difference amplifier? It is there to lower the necessary voltage across R_{span}. This, in turn, drops the loop power supply voltage requirements. Look at Figure 4–26. The op amp, transistor, and $R_{span\ V-I}$ are in the voltage-to-current converter (Figure 4–15). The resistor $R_{span\ I-V}$ is in the current-to-voltage converter (Figure 4–25). Allowing at least 2 V (saturation) between the op amp's $+V$ pin and its output and summing the voltage drops gives

$$+V = 2 \text{ V} + 0.7 \text{ V} + IR_{span\ I-V} + IR_{span\ V-I} \tag{4–25}$$

The loop supply voltage, back in the voltage-to-current converter, must be at least this large. If this value is inconveniently large, you can lower $R_{span\ I-V}$ and make up for this reduced voltage by putting more gain in the difference amp.

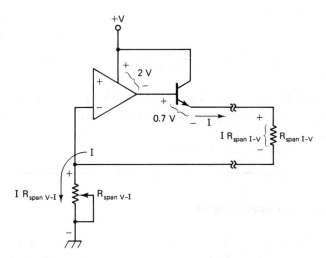

Figure 4–26   Current-to-voltage R_{span} limit.

EXAMPLE 4–9

A voltage-to-current converter, such as in Figure 4–15, has $+V = +12$ V, $R_{span\ V-I} = 312 \ \Omega$, $I_{max} = 20$ mA. What is the maximum size $R_{span\ I-V}$?

Solution   Solving equation 4–25 for $R_{span\ I-V}$, we have

$$R_{\text{span } I-V(\max)} = \frac{+V - 2.7 \text{ V} - IR_{\text{span } V-I}}{I}$$

$$= \frac{12 \text{ V} - 2.7 \text{ V} - (20 \text{ mA})(312 \ \Omega)}{20 \text{ mA}}$$

$$= 153 \ \Omega$$

So the 62.5-Ω resistor of Example 4–8 would work. However, if you had chosen $R_f/R_i = 1$, then $R_{\text{span } I-V}$ would have been 625 Ω, which is way too large. The op amp in the voltage-to-current converter would saturate long before 20 mA would be reached.

EXAMPLE 4–10

A modular transducer outputs 10 to 60 mA of current. The manufacturer indicates that 100 Ω is the maximum allowable floating load. Select a gain (R_f/R_i) and R_{span} for the current-to-voltage converter of Figure 4–25 to give a −10- to 10-V output.

Solution   From equation 4–23,

$$\frac{R_f}{R_i} R_{\text{span}} = \frac{V(b) - V(a)}{I(b) - I(a)}$$

$$= \frac{10 \text{ V} - (-10 \text{ V})}{60 \text{ mA} - 10 \text{ mA}} = 400 \ \Omega$$

So the product of gain times R_{span} is 400 Ω. Since $R_{\max} =$ is 100 Ω, let's set the gain $R_f/R_i = 6$ (or some other convenient value greater than 4).

$$R_{\text{span}} = \frac{400 \ \Omega}{6} = 66.7 \ \Omega$$

4–5 VOLTAGE-TO-FREQUENCY CONVERSION

The transmission of current rather than voltage eliminates error associated with loop resistance. Also, the differential nature of floating current transmission allows you to use an instrumentation amplifier's high common-mode rejection ratio to reduce noise coupled into the loop. However, in industrial environments with heavy loads and large line voltages, even the best instrumentation amplifier may be unable to reduce adequately errors due to noise picked up in the transmission loop.

This noise affects the amplitude of the signal being transmitted, sometimes increasing it, other times decreasing it. To provide the high noise immunity needed, digital transmission may be used. The analog voltage from the sensor and signal conditioner is converted to a pulse train. The pulse width is constant but the *frequency* varies linearly with the voltage applied. This frequency can then be converted to a current and transmitted. Noise coupled into the transmission loop alters the amplitude but not the frequency of the signal. At the load the current is converted to a voltage with a resistor and instrumentation amplifier. The frequency from the instrumentation amplifier is then converted back to the analog voltage originally sent. The effects of large noise and series loop resistance have both been minimized. This is illustrated in Figure 4–27.

The block diagram of a voltage-to-frequency converter IC is given in Figure 4–28. The input comparator, one-shot timer, transistor, and switched current source are inside the chip. You must apply all resistors and capacitors shown, externally.

Capacitor C_L is charged by the switched current source, for a fixed time, determined by R_t and C_t. The source is then switched off and C_L discharges through R_L. When V_x drops below V_1, the comparator triggers the one-shot timer again. The timer drives the output transistor on (output goes low) and connects the current source to charge up C_L. This state continues for a time fixed by external timing components R_t and C_t. The current source is then switched off, the output goes high, and C_L discharges again through R_L. The cycle repeats.

To understand how this cycle produces a frequency proportional to the input voltage, you must notice two facts. The charge is caused by a current source, which produces a fixed rise in V_x independent of the voltage on the capacitor. However, the discharge rate, through R_L, is a simple RC discharge. The discharge rate is directly proportional to the value of V_x. That is, the larger V_x is, the faster it will discharge through R_L.

Look carefully at the diagrams in Figure 4–29. At time 0, the analog voltage is at point a and V_x has just been charged somewhat higher. The output is high and C_L discharges through R_L. When V_x reaches point a (time 1) the comparator triggers the

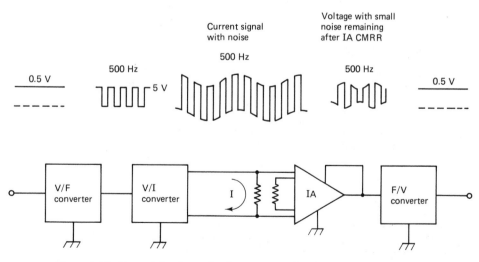

Figure 4–27 Transmission loop using frequency-encoded signal is highly immune to noise.

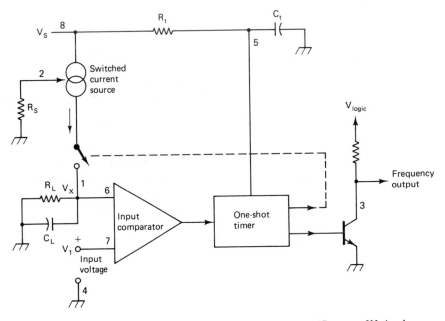

Figure 4–28   Basic voltage-to-frequency converter block diagram. (Courtesy of National Semiconductor.)

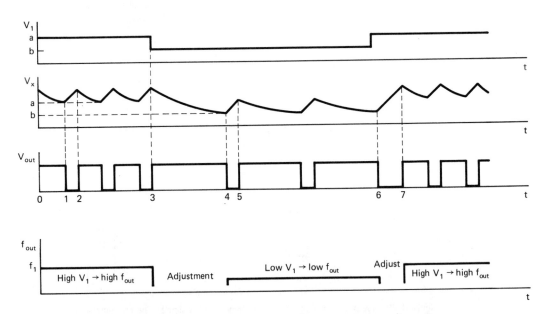

Figure 4–29   Voltage-to-frequency converter operation and waveforms.

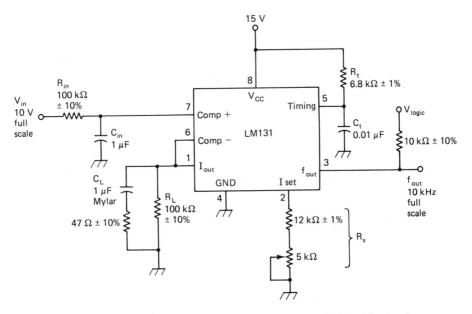

Figure 4–30   Simple voltage-to-frequency converter. (Courtesy of National Semiconductor.)

one-shot. The output goes low and C_L is charged at a fixed rate, for a fixed time by the current source. At time 2 the one-shot goes off and the cycle repeats, producing a frequency f_1.

At time 3, the analog input is cut in half, falling to level b. Capacitor C_L continues to discharge through R_L until its voltage falls just below b as well (time 4). The comparator again triggers the one-shot on and the capacitor is charged by the current source. It charges just as much as it did between times 1 and 2 because it is being charged by a constant current source. At time 5 the one-shot goes off. Capacitor C_L begins to discharge. The discharge rate, now, is slower than before because V_x is lower. The result is a lower frequency. An increase in input voltage (at time 6) causes the comparator to retrigger the one shot continually (between times 6 and 7) until V_x exceeds V_1.

The manufacturer's recommended component values are given in Figure 4–30. That configuration produces an output frequency of

$$f_0 = \frac{1 \text{ kHz}}{\text{volt}} V_{\text{in}}$$

where V_{in} full scale is 10 V. In terms of the components,

$$f_0 = \frac{V_{\text{in}}}{2 \text{ V}} \frac{R_s}{R_L} \frac{1}{R_t C_t} \tag{4–26}$$

Resistor R_t and capacitor C_t set the one-shot time interval. This is the time the output pulse is low.

$$t_{\text{low}} = 1.1R_tC_t \tag{4–27}$$

You must set this to be less than the period of the maximum output frequency.

The 10-kΩ resistor tied to pin 3 is the pull-up for the open-collector output. V_{logic} should be the supply voltage of whatever logic family chip the signal is to be driven into.

The size of the switched current source is set by R_s.

$$i \approx \frac{2V}{R_s} < 200\ \mu\text{A} \tag{4–28}$$

The 5-kΩ cement potentiometer in series with the 12-kΩ resistor allows you to adjust out tolerances in the LM131's gain, R_t, R_L, and C_t.

Resistor R_L and capacitor C_L form the charge and discharge components. The 47-Ω resistor in series with C_L provides hysteresis for the comparator, improving linearity.

Resistor R_{in} is set to equal R_L to minimize the effects of bias currents on the comparator. Capacitor C_{in} forms a low-pass filter with R_{in} to decrease noise effects. In addition, C_{in} should be approximately equal to C_L. This will improve the response time of the converter.

EXAMPLE 4–11

Design a voltage-to-frequency converter that will output 20 kHz when the input is 5 V.

Solution   The circuit in Figure 4–30 will be used. At maximum frequency, the minimum period is

$$T_{\text{min}} = \frac{1}{f_{\text{max}}} = \frac{1}{20\ \text{kHz}}$$
$$= 50\ \mu\text{s}$$

You must set the pulse width no wider than about 80% of the minimum period. Otherwise, at the higher frequencies the pulse width may approach or exceed the period, which will not work.

$$t_{\text{low}} = 1.1R_tC_t$$

Pick $C_t = 0.0047\ \mu\text{F}$ (somewhat arbitrary, but scaled with respect to that suggested by the manufacturer in Figure 4–30).

$$R_t = \frac{t_{\text{low}}}{1.1\ C_t}$$
$$= \frac{(0.8)(50\ \mu\text{s})}{(1.1)(0.0047\ \mu\text{F})} = 7.7\ \text{k}\Omega$$

Since this is not a critical parameter, as long as it is not too big, pick

$$R_t = 6.8\ \text{k}\Omega$$

This give $t_{low} = 35$ μs. From equation 4–26,

$$R_s = \frac{(2\ V)f_0 R_L R_t C_t}{V_{in}}$$

$$= \frac{(2\ V)(20\ kHz)(100\ k\Omega)(6.8\ k\Omega)(0.0047\ \mu F)}{5\ V}$$

$$= 25.6\ k\Omega$$

Pick R_s as a 22-kΩ fixed resistor with a series 10-kΩ potentiometer.

Voltage-to-frequency converters are often also used to provide analog-to-digital conversion. The TTL wave out of the voltage-to-frequency converter can easily be counted by a microprocessor, LSI counter ICs, or counter modules for display or interface with a programmable controller. So, by using a voltage-to-frequency converter, you produce an easily transmitted signal which is very noise immune and which can be directly processed by digital circuits, microprocessors, or computers. You can omit the frequency-to-voltage and analog-to-digital converters.

EXAMPLE 4–12

A pressure transducer measures a pressure from 0 to 100 psig. Its output is 1 V at 0 psig and 5 V at 100 psig. It is desired to produce a count every 16.7 ms. The count produced at 100 psig must be 100 larger than the count at 0 psig.
(a) What frequency span (in hertz) is needed?
(b) What frequency is output at 100 psig? at 0 psig?
(c) What preset could be loaded into an 8-bit binary counter to yield a count that goes from 0 to 100?
(d) Why was a counting period of 16.7 ms chosen?

Solution   (a) The count span is 100 counts in 16.7 ms. That is a frequency span of

$$f = \frac{100\ counts}{16.7\ ms} = 5.988\ kHz$$

(b) This frequency span is produced by a voltage span of

$$V = 5\ V - 1\ V = 4\ V$$

The Hz/volt rating of the voltage-to-frequency converter is

$$\frac{f}{V} = \frac{5.988\ kHz}{4\ V} = 1.497\ \frac{kHz}{V}$$

At 0 psig, $V_{in} = 1$ V. So $f = 1.497$ kHz. At 100 psig, $V_{in} = 5$ V. So $f = 7.485$ kHz.

(c) With an input of 0 psig, 1 V (out of the transducer), the voltage-to-frequency converter outputs 1.497 kHz. In 16.7 ms, this produces

$$\text{counts} = \left(1497 \frac{\text{counts}}{\text{s}}\right) (16.7 \text{ ms})$$

$$= 25$$

So you have to load -25 into the counter. For a binary counter, the preset is

$$\text{preset} = 256 - \text{counts offset}$$
$$= 256 - 25 = 231$$

At the beginning of the 16.7-ms counting period, load 231 into the counter. If the pressure is 0 psig, at the end of the counting period, the counter will have incremented 25 times and will indicate 0.

(d) The counting interval has been set to 16.7 ms for two reasons. That is the period of an 60-Hz cycle. So stable, accurate timing pulses can easily be obtained from the power line. More important, 60-Hz noise can be rejected. If there is any 60-Hz noise on the input to the voltage-to-frequency converter, it will cause the frequency to be too high during its positive half-cycle. But during the negative half-cycle, the converter will run too slowly. The effects of 60-Hz noise are eliminated.

4–6 FREQUENCY-TO-VOLTAGE CONVERSION

The LM131 can also be used to convert an *input frequency* to an *output voltage*. The schematic of the LM131 used as a frequency-to-voltage converter is given in Figure 4–31. Supply voltage, ground, timing, and current set are all connected as they were for the voltage-to-frequency converter (Figure 4–30). The output frequency (open-collector transistor output) is not used, so it should be tied to ground to minimize noise. The output is taken from the switchable current source. The + input of the comparator is tied to a reference level and the comparator's − input is driven by the input frequency.

You will understand the conversion process better by looking at the simplified block diagram of Figure 4–32a. Normally, R_D connected to $+V_{cc}$ holds the comparator's − input at V_{cc}, above the + input. This keeps the one-shot and current source off. A falling edge of the input is differentiated into a spike by R_D and C_D, momentarily pulling the comparator's − input below its + input. The one-shot is fired. It closes the current source, providing I_{out} to the load resistor for

$$t = 1.1 R_t C_t$$

Since the input spike has gone away, at the end of the one-shot's time interval the current source turns off and waits for another trigger pulse. The result is a train of

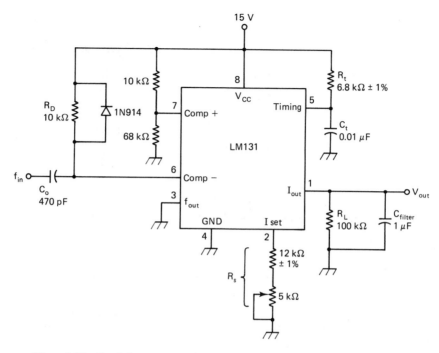

Figure 4–31   Simple frequency-to-voltage converter. (Courtesy of National Semiconductor.)

current pulses to R_L of constant pulse width (t) and with a frequency equal to that of the input. The pulse amplitude is the same as it was for the voltage-to-frequency converter,

$$i = \frac{2\text{ V}}{R_s}$$

The average value (dc) of the current out is proportional to the area under its curve. That is,

$$I_{ave} = \frac{it}{T}$$

$$= \frac{2\text{ V} \times 1.1 R_t C_t}{R_s T}$$

but

$$V_{ave} = I_{ave} R_L$$

$$= 2\text{ V} \times 1.1 R_t C_t \times \frac{R_L}{R_s} \times f_{in} \qquad f_{in} = 1/T \tag{4–29}$$

This pulse waveform must be filtered to remove the ripple, leaving only the dc or average voltage. That is the purpose of C_{filter}. More sophisticated, active filters can be

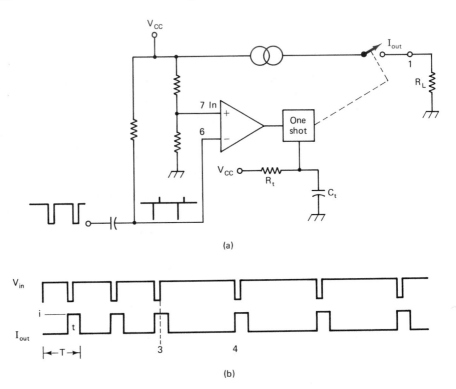

Figure 4–32 Frequency-to-voltage converter operation: (a) simplified block diagram;
(b) waveforms.

built to further reduce the ripple in the output voltage. The more severely you filter the output, the lower the ripple. However, this filtering also slows the response rate of the output dc to a change in input frequency. Also, ripple becomes worse as the input frequency falls. This is indeed unfortunate, since low frequencies should yield small output dc voltages, but also produce the highest ripple. You should try to keep operation above a few hundred hertz.

Frequency-to-voltage converters are also used directly with transducers. Incremental optical encoders, reflective optical sensing, and Hall effect magnetic sensors all output a train of pulses. The frequency of these pulses depends on the speed of rotation of the sensor. To get an analog signal, which is a measure of that speed, requires a frequency-to-voltage converter.

EXAMPLE 4–13

A reflective optical sensor is used to encode the velocity of a shaft. There are six pieces of reflective tape. They are sized and positioned to produce a 50% duty-cycle wave. The maximum shaft speed is 3000 r/min. Design the frequency-to-voltage converter necessary to output 10 V at maximum shaft speed. Provide filtering adequate to assure no more than 10% ripple at 100 r/min.

Solution   The maximum frequency is

$$f_{max} = \frac{6 \text{ counts}}{\text{rev}} \times \frac{3000 \text{ rev}}{\text{min}} \times \frac{1 \text{ min}}{60 \text{ s}}$$
$$= 300 \text{ Hz}$$

$$T_{min} = \frac{1}{300 \text{ Hz}} = 3.33 \text{ ms}$$

$$t_{\text{pulse in}} = 0.5 T_{min} = 1.67 \text{ ms}$$

As you did with the voltage-to-frequency converter, pick

$$t_{\text{out(high)}} \leq 0.8 T_{min} = (0.8)(3.33 \text{ ms})$$
$$\leq 2.664 \text{ ms}$$

Pick $C_t = 0.33 \ \mu\text{F}$.

$$R_t = \frac{t_{\text{out(high)}}}{1.1 C_t} = \frac{2.664 \text{ ms}}{(1.1)(0.33 \ \mu\text{F})}$$
$$= 7.3 \text{ k}\Omega$$

Pick $R_t = 6.8 \text{ k}\Omega$. This set $t_{\text{out(high)}} = 2.47$ ms. You must set $5 R_D C_D \ll 1.67$ ms, so pick $R_D = 10 \text{ k}\Omega$.

$$5 R_D C_D \leq (0.1)(1.67 \text{ ms})$$

$$C_D \leq \frac{(0.1)(1.67 \text{ ms})}{(5)(10 \text{ k}\Omega)} = 3.3 \text{ nF}$$

$$V_{\text{ave}} = \frac{(2 \text{ V})(1.1 R_t C_t) R_L f_{\text{in}}}{R_s}$$

Solving for R_s yields

$$R_s = \frac{(2 \text{ V})(1.1 R_t C_t) R_L f_{\text{in}}}{V_{\text{ave}}}$$
$$= \frac{(2 \text{ V})(1.1)(6.8 \text{ k}\Omega)(0.33 \ \mu\text{F})(100 \text{ k}\Omega)(300 \text{ Hz})}{10 \text{ V}}$$
$$= 14.8 \text{ k}\Omega$$

Pick R_s as a 10-kΩ resistor with a 10-kΩ potentiometer. You should also check the current required out.

$$i = \frac{2 \text{ V}}{R_s} = \frac{2 \text{ V}}{14.8 \text{ k}\Omega} = 135 \ \mu\text{A}$$

This is all right, since it is less than the 200 μA allowed.
At 100 r/min,

$$f = \frac{6 \text{ counts}}{\text{rev}} \times \frac{100 \text{ rev}}{\text{min}} \times \frac{1 \text{ min}}{60 \text{ s}}$$

$$= 10 \text{ Hz}$$

$$T = 0.1 \text{ s}$$

$$t_{\text{pw}} = 0.5 \text{ s}$$

Filtering is accomplished by R_L and C_F:

$$\tau = R_L C_F$$

It discharges according to

$$v_{\text{out}} = V_{\text{pk}} e^{-t/\tau}$$

For 10% ripple,

$$\frac{v_{\text{out}}}{V_{\text{pk}}} = 90\% = e^{-t/\tau}$$

$$\ln (0.9) = -\frac{t}{R_L C_F}$$

$$t = T_{100\text{Hz}} - t_{\text{out(high)}}$$
$$= 10 \text{ ms} - 2.47 \text{ ms} = 7.53 \text{ ms}$$

$$C_F \geq -\frac{t}{R_L \ln (0.9)}$$

$$\geq -\frac{7.53 \text{ ms}}{(100 \text{ k}\Omega)(-0.105)}$$

$$\geq 0.72 \text{ μF}$$

Pick $C_F = 1 \text{ μF}$.

4–7 ISOLATION CIRCUITS

In the most demanding industrial applications the techniques you have seen so far may not prove adequate. Even though you purchase a high-quality instrumentation amplifier, apply proper grounding and cabling techniques, and use current or frequency transmission, there may still be some serious problems. These are ground loops (or common ground connections), extremely high common-mode voltages, and very low failure current requirements. All of these problems can be solved with an isolation circuit.

4–7.1 General Concepts

For proper operation, you have seen that the power supply common of the instrumentation amplifier or converters must be connected to the sensor common. In many industrial and medical applications this presents a major problem. Since common and ground connections are made primarily for personnel safety, the IA common to sensor common connection may be physically very difficult, if not impossible, to make.

A second major problem of instrumentation amplifiers and converters is their inability to handle common-mode voltages that exceed their power supply voltages. In fact, none of the analog ICs you have seen so far will tolerate an input voltage (common mode or differential) that significantly exceeds its power supply voltages. However, in industrial applications, line voltages of hundreds to thousands of volts may be connected accidentally to the signal conditioner's inputs. This type of abuse would not only cause an instrumentation amplifier to fail, but would pass large voltages and currents on to the process control circuitry (often an expensive computer system), causing extensive damage there.

In medical applications such as cardiac monitoring, the conditioner must be able to withstand a defibrillator pulse of 5 kV and continue to process the patient's heartbeat properly. Also, any failure of the conditioner must result in currents in the microampere range.

These three requirements—signal common isolation, extremely high common-mode voltage tolerance, and very low failure currents—cannot be met by op amps or by instrumentation amplifiers. However, the isolation amplifier hybrid integrated circuit meets all three requirements.

TABLE 4–4 ISOLATION-INSTRUMENTATION AMPLIFIER COMPARISON

Key specification	Isolation amplifier	Instrumentation amplifier
CMR for unity gain with 5000 Ω of source unbalance from dc to 100 Hz	115 dB	80 dB
Common-mode voltage range	±2500 V dc (±7500 V, peak)	±10 V
Differential input voltage range	240 V rms (±6500 V, peak)	±10 V
Input-to-ground leakage	Transformer isolated; $10^{11}\ \Omega$ shunted by less than 10 pF	Feedback generated depends upon linear circuit operation
Bias current configuration	Single bias current; amplifier needs only two input conductors	Two bias current; third wire is needed for bias return
Small-signal passband	Dc to 2 kHz	Dc to 1.5 MHz
Gain nonlinearity	0.05%	0.01%
Gain vs. temperature	$\pm0.01\%$/°C	$\pm0.0015\%$/°C
Offset vs. temperature ($G = 1$)	$\pm300\ \mu$V/°C	$\pm150\ \mu$V/°C

Source: Burr-Brown.

A typical isolation amplifier is compared with an instrumentation amplifier in Table 4–4. The isolation amplifier will more strongly reject common-mode voltages while tolerating much higher values of both common-mode and differential input voltages. The isolation amplifier presents much lower leakage, while allowing bias isolation (no bias return needed). However, the instrumentation amplifier has a broader frequency response and is generally more accurate.

4–7.2 Transformer-Coupled Amplifiers

The schematic symbol for a transformer-coupled isolation amplifier is given in Figure 4–33. The amplifier is divided into three separate (isolated) sections. Energy and signal are coupled between these sections by several transformers. There need be no connection between the commons of each section. The power section couples energy into both the input and output sections. The input section may also provide an isolated output voltage to power the sensor. The gain is set by a single resistor on the input side. Two or three additional connections are made to the input section. For two port inputs, the input is applied between V_{in} Hi and common. V_{in} Lo is not present. For three-port input isolation amplifiers, the input is applied between V_{in} Hi and V_{in} Lo. The common connection is then called the guard. It is normally connected through the cable shield to sensor common. It does not have to be referenced to V_{in} Lo. The output signal is an amplified version of the input signal, but is not referenced to the power common or input common.

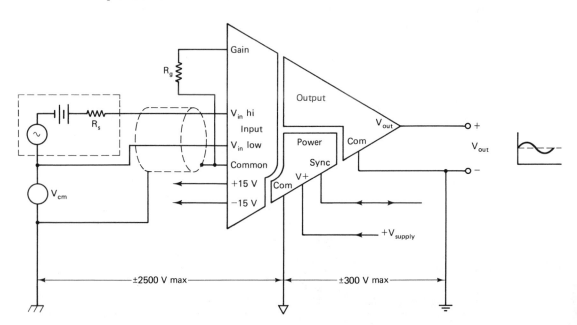

Figure 4–33 Transformer-coupled isolation amplifier schematic symbol. (Courtesy of Analog Devices.)

A very simple block diagram of a transformer-coupled isolation amplifier is given in Figure 4–34. Power voltage is regulated in the power section and then applied to a 100-kHz power oscillator. This ac energy is transformer coupled to the input and the output sections. In each section this ac is rectified, filtered, and regulated to power that section. Such a high-frequency "carrier" was chosen to allow the transformer to be decreased in size and improved in efficiency. Also, the higher this carrier frequency, the broader the amplifier's frequency response.

The input signal also uses the 100-kHz carrier for transmission. Once the input has been filtered and amplified, it amplitude modulates (or in some models, pulse-width modulates) the 100-kHz carrier. This is then transformer coupled into the output section. Here it is synchronously demodulated, filtered, and buffered.

If several transformer-coupled isolation amplifiers are to be operated physically close together, the electromagnetic interference (EMI) produced by the independent oscillators could cause low-frequency beat frequencies, resulting in offset errors. By connecting the power section sync pins together, the oscillators will run in phase.

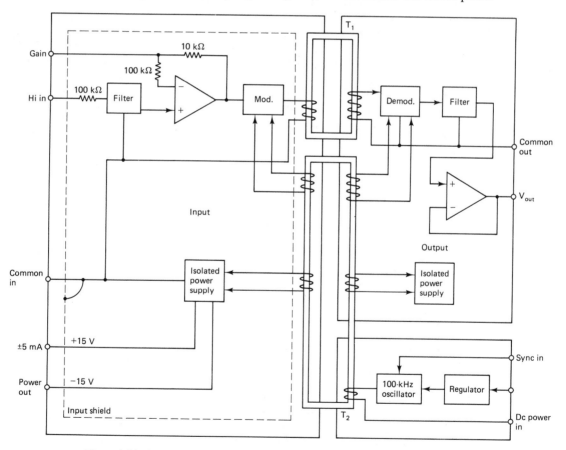

Figure 4–34 Block diagram of the AD289 isolation amplifier. (Courtesy of Analog Devices.)

4–7.3 Optically Coupled Amplifiers

Transformer-coupled isolation amplifiers are expensive and bulky (compared with other IC components). The carrier generates electromagnetic interference if set at a high frequency, but limits the amplifier's bandwidth and response rate if set too low. Optically coupled isolation amplifiers replace the transformer with a LED and a pair of photodiodes. The interference is eliminated and frequency response is increased. Table 4–5 gives a comparison of isolation amplifier characteristics. The transformer-coupled amplifiers have better nonlinearity and isolation characteristics. However, the optically coupled amplifiers have far better frequency response, noise generation (EMI) and susceptibility, much smaller size, and lower cost.

The schematic symbol for an optically coupled amplifier is given in Figure 4–35a. Notice that the symbol does not show a separate, isolated power section. You must provide external, isolated power to the input and output sections. This may be done with a separate dc/dc converter IC. Care must be taken to assure that this circuit can provide adequate isolation. Otherwise, the characteristics of the isolation amplifier will be degraded.

Figure 4–35b gives the simplified internal diagram of an optically coupled amp. The input voltage, V_{in}, causes current to flow through the LED. The light from the LED causes a proportional current, I_2, to flow through D_2. Unfortunately, this LED/D_2 pair is nonlinear. To overcome this, a second photodiode D_1 is placed in the negative-feedback loop of the input amplifier. The characteristics of D_1 and D_2 are carefully matched so that the same light from the LED will cause identical currents I_1 and I_2.

An input voltage V_{in} produces a current,

$$I_1 = \frac{V_{in}}{R_G}$$

TABLE 4–5 TRANSFORMER AND OPTICAL COUPLING COMPARISON

Characteristic	Transformer coupling		Optical coupling
	Amplitude modulation	Pulse-width modulation	Light-intensity modulation
Nonlinearity, max. (%)	0.03–0.3	0.005–0.025[a]	0.05–0.2[a]
Isolation voltage, test (kV)	Up to 7.5	Up to 5	Up to 5
Isolation-mode rejection, at 60 Hz and unity gain (dB)	Up to 120	Up to 120	100
Frequency response (kHz)	2.5	2.5	10–30
Emi generated	Low, if shielded	Low, if shielded	None
High-frequency susceptibility	High	Low	Very low
Size (in.^{3})	5–10	6	Less than 0.5
Price in lots of 100	From $41	From $90	From $26[b]

[a] Burr-Brown products measured at full output-voltage swing.

[b] Without input power supply.

Source: Burr-Brown.

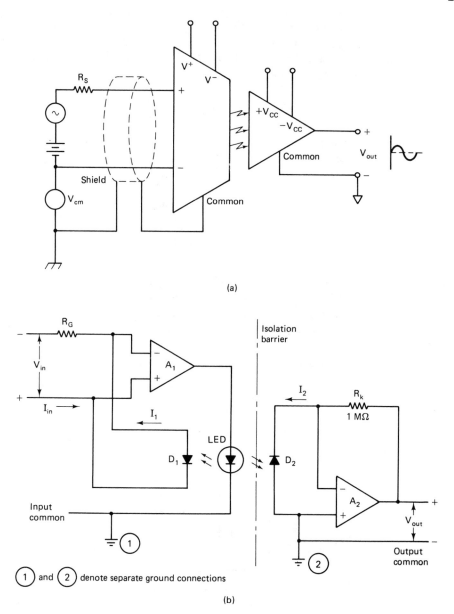

Figure 4–35   Optically coupled isolation amplifier: (a) symbol; (b) simplified internal schematic. (Courtesy of Burr-Brown Corporation.)

because the inverting input of the op amp is held at virtual ground by the negative feedback through the LED and D_1. Because of the extremely high input impedance of the op amp, I_1 must flow through D_1. This is caused by the op amp driving the LED on adequately. But the close match of D_1 and D_2 causes

$$I_1 = I_2 = \frac{V_{in}}{R_G}$$

The input signal has been coupled optically across the isolation barrier. Current I_2 flows through R_K, producing an output voltage.

$$V_{out} = I_2 R_K$$
$$= \frac{V_{in}}{R_G} R_K$$
$$= \frac{R_K}{R_G} V_{in}$$

This technique produces a linear transfer (V_{out}/V_{in}) relationship, eliminates the nonlinearity of the LED/photodiodes and sets the gain with two resistors.

Several examples will clarify the unique advantages of isolation amplifiers. Figure 4–36 depicts an aluminum production process where aluminum oxide is electrolytically

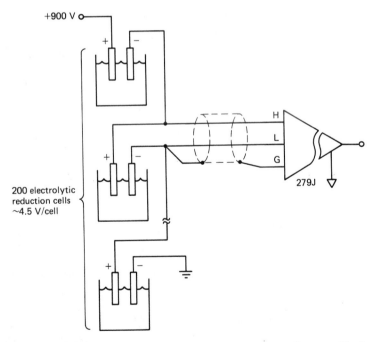

Figure 4–36   Metal processing application of an isolation amplifier. (Courtesy of Analog Devices.)

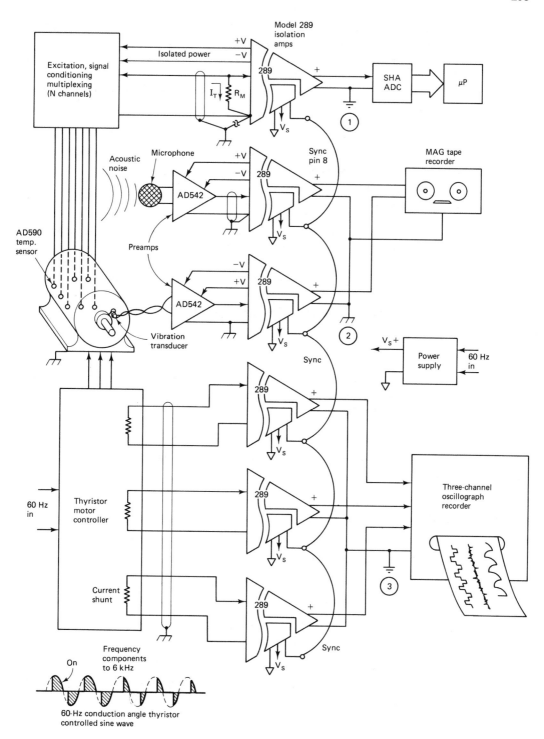

Figure 4–37 Electric machine testing application. (Courtesy of Analog Devices.)

reduced and the aluminum extracted. High voltages in a rather physically harsh environment must be used. However, information concerning the resistivity must be obtained to monitor production rate. An isolation amplifier allows the high CMRR rating and the high voltage/failure mode protection necessary.

In Figure 4–37 several isolation amplifiers are used in electrical machine testing. Their superior common-mode rejection allows very precise signal conditioning, even in the presence of large noise signals generated by the machine under test. Also, the isolation and failure protection safeguards the expensive test instruments in the event of a machine failure. Measurements may be made directly in the main power line with isolation amplifiers to determine voltage and current for thyristor speed control.

When applying isolation amplifiers, there are several factors that you must consider. There is little standardization among models or manufacturers. Isolated power supplies may or may not be present. If they are, outputs and input requirements vary widely. If they are not present, you must use a high-quality dc/dc converter or lose some isolation. Inputs also vary quite a bit. Both two- and three-port (two- or three-wire) inputs are available, as well as low-impedance, high-impedance, and current-input versions. Specifications must be read closely because standards and test conditions vary.

4–7.4 Optical Coupling for On/Off Applications

If the data being processed will eventually be converted into digital form, there is a much simpler and less expensive alternative to isolation amplifiers. The optical coupler is a LED and a phototransistor within a single mini-DIP package. The TIL112 by Texas Instruments is shown in Figure 4–38. When the LED is biased on, its light shines internally onto the phototransistor. This, in turn, allows collector current to flow, even when the base is left open.

Phototransistor current is proportional to LED current. Unfortunately, this relationship is nonlinear. So you cannot transmit analog information accurately through this optical coupler. However, when there is no current flow through the LED, the phototransistor is off. When the LED current is 20 mA or more, the phototransistor is hard on. So you can transmit digital data through this coupler.

A simple scheme is shown in Figure 4–39. Digital data are applied to U_1. U_1

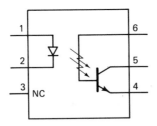

$I_{F\ diode} \leq 100\ mA$

$P_{diode} \leq 150\ mW$

$P_{transistor} \leq 150\ mW$

Figure 4–38 TIL112 optical coupler. (Courtesy of Texas Instruments Incorporated.)

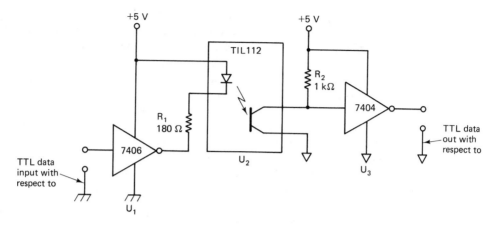

Figure 4–39   Simple optically coupled TTL data transmission.

may be any form of open-collector device capable of sinking 20 mA. Notice that the input signal and U_1 are referenced to a circuit common which is different from the output signal's common. The phototransistor serves as a switch to ground for the input of U_3. U_3 is a buffer. Any gate will work. When no light falls on the phototransistor, it is off. Resistor R_2 pulls the input of U_3 up to a logic high. When the LED adequately illuminates the phototransistor, it saturates placing 0.2 V (a logic low) at the input of U_3. Resistor R_1 limits the current through the LED to between 15 and 20 mA. Resistor R_2 limits the current through the phototransistor to 5 mA while meeting the pull-up and speed requirements of U_3. Finally, notice that the +5-V supply powering U_1 must be entirely separate from the supply powering U_3. Otherwise, the desired ground isolation is void.

EXAMPLE 4–14

Trace the operation of the circuit in Figure 4–39 to determine if the data coming out are the same as the data going in, or if there is an inversion.

Solution   A logic high into U_1 causes its output to go to ground. Summing the voltages through the input of the optical coupler gives us

$$+5 \text{ V} - V_{\text{diode}} - IR_1 = 0$$

$$I = \frac{5 \text{ V} - 1.8 \text{ V}}{180 \ \Omega} = 17.8 \text{ mA}$$

This is enough to saturate the phototransistor. So U_3 receives a logic low input. Since U_3 was chosen as an inverter, the output is high. A logic high in produces a logic high out. The overall circuit is a buffer. It does *not* invert the data.

There are two prevalent ways of using optical couplers to transmit digital data. The first is shown in Figure 4–40. The sensor, amplifiers for signal conditioning, and analog-to-digital converter all sit on the input side of the optical couplers. Excitation, $\pm V_1$, and $+V_{\text{logic 1}}$ must all be provided, referenced to the input common. Each digital line into and out of the A-D converter must have its own optocoupler. Typically, there are 18 or more lines. On the microprocessor or computer side of the isolation barrier are data latches (port IC), address and control decode circuitry, and everything else necessary to make the computer function properly. These chips are powered from a separate $+V_{\text{logic 2}}$, referenced to a different common. Do *not* connect the input common and the microprocessor (computer) common together!

This scheme will provide multichannel, high-resolution (12 bit or more) data acquisition at high data-gathering rates (110 μs per channel or faster). However, to gather such a large amount of data so quickly, you pay a price. First, the A-D converter is expensive. Second, it sits on the input side of the protective isolation barrier. Any fault or failure on the input may destroy all circuits before the optocouplers. This includes the expensive A/D converter. Finally, this scheme requires a separate optocoupler for every digital signal. Although not expensive, they will take up a lot of precious room on your data acquisition board.

If you are able to wait several milliseconds or longer to acquire data, a much simpler isolation scheme is available. Figure 4–41 shows the use of a voltage-to-frequency

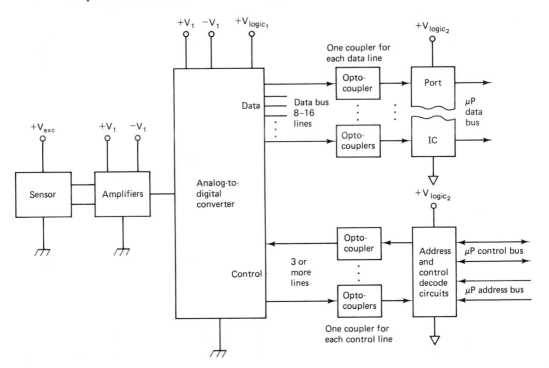

Figure 4–40   Analog-to-digital converter with optical isolation.

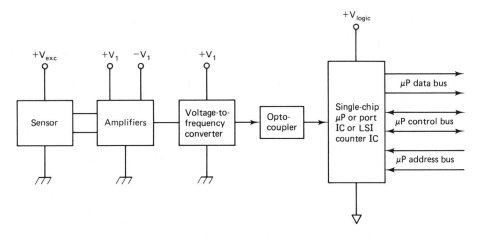

Figure 4–41 Voltage-to-frequency converter with optical isolation.

converter and a single optocoupler. As in the A/D isolation scheme, a sensor, signal conditioner, and appropriate power supplies are all required on the input side of the isolation barrier. However, the expensive A/D converter has been replaced by a much smaller, much cheaper voltage-to-frequency converter. The value of the analog data is now encoded in the frequency of the output from the V/F converter. Since the converter has an open-collector output with adequate current drive, the driver IC (U_1 of Figure 4–39) is not needed. The output of the optical coupler can directly drive the input of a MOS IC (without U_3 of Figure 4–39). This IC may be the microprocessor itself, one bit of a port chip, or one input of a LSI counter.

The simplicity, smaller size, and significantly lower price are all obvious advantages of this system. The AD650 is a voltage-to-frequency converter from Analog Devices which can run at over 200 kHz with greater than 12-bit accuracy. At 200 kHz you can get 4096 counts (12-bit resolution) in 20.48 ms. To improve your resolution, just count longer. If you need only 8-bit resolution, you can get new data every 1.28 ms. So the other big advantage to the V/F isolation technique is the flexibility of being able to trade off speed and resolution. In a control system, when the process variable is far away from the set point and the system is changing quickly to recover, you can count for 1.28 ms to get a quick approximation of the process variable. As the process variable approaches the set point, and change occurs more slowly, you can lengthen the count time to get a higher degree of resolution.

Opto 22 has a line of modular signal conditioners which includes the signal conditioner/amplifier, voltage-to-frequency converter, and optical coupler all within a small, inexpensive module. Although the output frequency may be too slow for some applications, the cost, size, and convenience of the Opto 22 line of voltage-to-frequency optically isolated signal conditioners make them a very attractive solution for many process control data acquisition problems.

Compared to the transformer-coupled and optically coupled isolation amplifiers, the digital optical coupler you have seen in this section appears to be a much more cost-efficient and flexible scheme. However, there are several points of comparison that need to be brought out. At the beginning of this section you saw that isolation had three objectives. They are to allow separate grounds, to allow input voltages well in excess of the supply voltage, and to limit failure currents. Both the transformer-coupled and optically coupled isolation amplifiers accomplish all three objectives.

The digital optical coupler does not perform as well. The input ground and output ground are indeed separate. The coupler itself will tolerate several thousand volts between its input and output sections. However, applying large voltages to the input sections of either the circuit in Figure 4–40 or 4–41 will destroy the sensor, signal conditioner/amplifier, and converter. Only the circuitry on the output of the optical coupler is protected. Finally, there is no failure current limit for the optical coupler itself or for the circuitry in Figures 4–40 and 4–41. Should the input of either of these circuits fail, hundreds of milliamperes of current (or more) may flow. In environments requiring intrinsically safe conditions (explosives, fuels, paint spray, fine particulate), this could lead to an explosion or fire.

4–8 CABLING

Up to this point you have seen how to select a control strategy, accurately measure the process variable, amplify and filter that signal, and transmit it to a remote location. But even with the very best transducers, amplifiers, filters, transmission, and isolation it is entirely possible that the signal received by the controller is junk. *How* you interconnect all of these blocks is just as important as what components you use. Proper cabling can shield against interference from the large magnetic and electric fields produced in all manufacturing environments. *Proper* grounding of the shields, circuits, and power supplies will minimize the impact of differing ground potentials and crosstalk between circuits. Without proper shielding and grounding techniques, even the most expensive data acquisition system will produce erratic results, at best. Proper cabling will allow even a cheap system to realize its full potential.

4–8.1 Magnetic and Electrostatic Shielding

Whenever a current flows, there is an associated magnetic field. The larger the current, the larger the resulting magnetic field. In an industrial facility a single machine may use hundreds of amperes or more. There are tremendous magnetic fields throughout most manufacturing plants.

Whenever the magnetic field cuts a conductor, a current is induced in that conductor. The magnitude of the induced current depends on how rapidly the magnetic field is *changing*. Since the high currents that produced the magnetic fields are usually 60 Hz, the magnetic fields build and collapse at 60 Hz, cutting conductors and inducing noise at 60 Hz onto the signals carried by these conductors. The magnetic fields produced by dc currents do not constantly contract and expand. So they do not continually induce current into your signal conductors. However, switches, relays, electronics, and brushes suddenly switch this current. This *sudden* introduction or collapse in the associated magnetic field induces a significant pulse into any conductor it crosses.

A thoughtful, commonsense layout and routing of circuits and cables is the first step in reducing the effects of magnetic fields. Separate the sensitive, input signal conditioning from the other portions of the electronics. The radio-frequency digital signal of the processor and the high current signals of the power output stages both produce significant magnetic fields *within* the electronic chassis. Place the small-signal analog circuitry on a separate card from the computer and power electronics. Separate this card from the others by a magnetic shield (more on this later). If this is not possible, at least give considerable thought to board layout, grouping sensitive analog processing components together and as far away from sources of magnetic fields as possible. It is not unusual to see a small magnetic shield box covering part of a printed circuit board.

The same procedures hold true for cabling. *Never*, never run 115-V ac power and low-level analog cables in the same raceway or conduit. Plastic conduit, or panduit, does nothing to shield against magnetic fields. Insist on a ferromagnetic material for the power conduit (this keeps the magnetic fields from leaving) and for the low-level analog signal conduit (this keeps the magnetic signals from entering). Do not group your low-level analog signal cables with CATV, broadband, or baseband data communications cables. These radio-frequency, digital signals produce very high frequency noise which is quite difficult to keep out of analog signal cables nearby.

The purpose of magnetic shielding is to divert the field. The shield offers to a magnetic field a path whose reluctance is much lower than air. So the vast majority of the field lines flow through the low-reluctance shield. How effectively a shield contains these magnetic field lines is termed absorption loss, or attenuation. It is expressed in dB. The higher the factor, the better. Keep in mind that dB is a logarithmic relationship. A change of 20 dB is a ratio change of 10. Six dB is a 2:1 change.

Magnetic absorptive loss depends on the type of material used, its thickness, and the frequency of the magnetic field. Look at Table 4–6. At audio frequencies (i.e., 60 Hz) both aluminum and copper have very little ability to shield against magnetic fields.

TABLE 4–6 MAGNETIC SHIELDING EFFECTIVENESS

Frequency	Thickness (in.)	Material		
		Aluminum (dB)	Copper (dB)	Steel (dB)
Audio	0.020	2	3	10
	0.125		10	40
100 kHz	0.020	25	35	>150
	0.125		130	>150

Source: Extracted from Henry W. Ott, *Noise Reduction Techniques in Electronic Systems* (New York: Wiley–Interscience, 1976), Fig. 6–8, p. 147.

Steel is the only effective choice. However, once you enter the radio-frequency bands, both aluminum and copper shields are effective. In fact, there are several coatings that can be sprayed onto plastic cases which shield effectively against high-frequency magnetic fields.

Any difference in potential creates a proportional electric field. Free charges (primarily electrons in conductors) respond to these fields, being attracted or repelled. The larger the potential difference, the larger the resulting electric field, and the more electrons in adjacent carriers rush about in response. But movement of electrons in a carrier is current—current induced into the conductor by some undesired, external voltage.

If you place the sensitive conductor inside another conductor, called a shield, the electrons in the shield should rush about to balance the external electric field. This is shown in Figure 4-42. Each electric field line attracts an electron from the underside of the shield. Although this balances off the external field, it leaves a net charge imbalance on the shield. The top of the box is now negatively charged (all of the electrons have been attracted up there), while the bottom of the box is positively charged (that is where the electrons came from). This imbalance produces an equal and opposite electric field within the shield. Things are just as bad as they were without the shield.

The shield must be tied to an infinite source (and sink) of charge. That is, ground the shield. Once grounded, electrons can flow onto and off the shield to balance any externally produced electrostatic fields without causing a charge imbalance and resulting internal field.

For effective shielding against electrostatic fields, enclose the entire data acquisition channel within a conductive shield. This includes the transducer, the connector leaving the transducer, the cable, the connector entering the analog signal conditioner, the signal conditioner, the power supply, the connection to the computer, display, or controller, and the display or controller itself.

Not only must the signal high be enclosed inside the shield, but the signal common must be as well. Do not use the shield as the signal common. If you do, currents induced in the shield in response to external electric fields become part of the signal

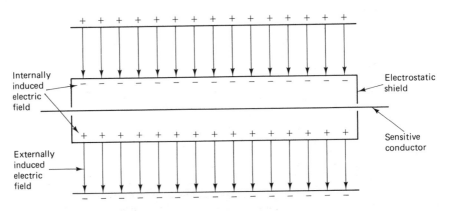

Figure 4-42   Floating electrostatic shield.

common, effectively floating the ground up and down. Instead, carry the signal common inside the shield as well. Cable, then, should be a shielded *pair* or twin-axial, never simple coaxial cable. Be sure that the signal common and the shield are kept completely separate along the entire data acquisition channel.

4–8.2 Grounding

You saw in Section 4–8.1 that to be effective the electrostatic shield must be grounded. But the signal common must not be connected to the shield. This seems contradictory. And what do you do if the transducer is tied to earth, or if the computer is; or worst, if both are? What do you do with power supply grounds, and the chassis safety ground, and the separate analog and digital grounds on converter ICs? These problems are explored and answered in this section.

    To make the shield effective, it must be tied to earth at some point. If grounding at one point is good, why not at several? This common mistake is illustrated in Figure 4–43. The transducer, signal conditioner and computer, and display or controller are all enclosed within a shield, along with the *pair* of leads connecting them. The shield is tied to earth at *both* ends. Unfortunately, there exists a difference in potential between any two earth points. This is shown as v_{noise} in the figure and may be several volts. But the shield provides a low-resistance path, probably 0.5 Ω or less, between these two points. The result is current flow in the shield. Typical numbers suggest

$$I_{\text{shield}} = \frac{v_{\text{noise}}}{R_{\text{shield}}} \approx \frac{2\text{ V}}{0.5\text{ }\Omega}$$

$$\approx 4\text{ A}$$

    Certainly, the shield is not designed to handle so much current. Second, currents of this magnitude will induce significant magnetic fields, very close to the sensitive

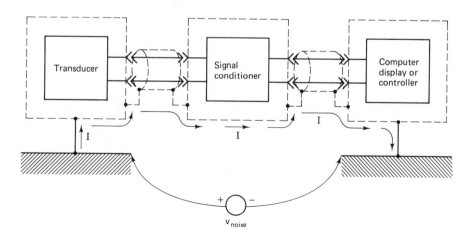

Figure 4–43   Shield improperly grounded at two points.

signals. As you have already seen, these magnetic fields will couple noise into the signal lines.

Certain configurations require that the transducer common be tied to its shield and to earth. This is often the case of temperature transducers attached to a test fixture. The test fixture must be grounded for safety reasons. What do you do with the other shields and the other signal commons?

The correct solution is shown in Figure 4–44. By breaking the shield-to-ground connection at the controller, the current in the shield is limited by the parasitic capacitive reactance between the shield and ground. This is typically on the order of 100 pF. At 60 Hz this parasitic capacitance produces

$$X_c = \frac{1}{2\pi(60 \text{ Hz})(100 \text{ pF})} = 27 \text{ M}\Omega$$

limiting the current to a small part of a microampere.

There are times when the computer's input signal low, from the signal conditioner, is tied to earth. For safety reasons, this connection is usually made by the manufacturer. You are not allowed to remove that ground connection. This puts you back to the problem shown in Figure 4–43, two ground connections to the shield. The simplest solution is to break the shield-to-ground connection, and transducer-to-shield connection, at the transducer. Now you have only one connection between the shield and ground, this time at the computer.

If the transducer–shield–earth connection cannot be broken and the computer–shield–earth connect may not be broken either, there is a significant problem. It is illustrated in Figure 4–45. This configuration suffers from the same problem as that shown in Figure 4–43. There will be large currents flowing through the shield in response to the ground difference voltage v_{noise}. Even worse, since the signal commons are tied to the shields at both ends, this voltage (and resulting current) appears across the common

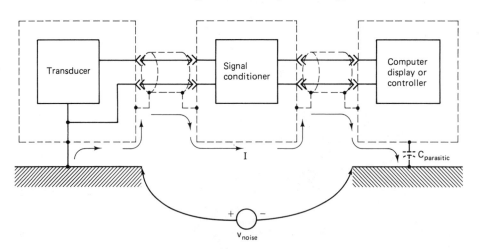

Figure 4–44 Shield properly grounded only at the source.

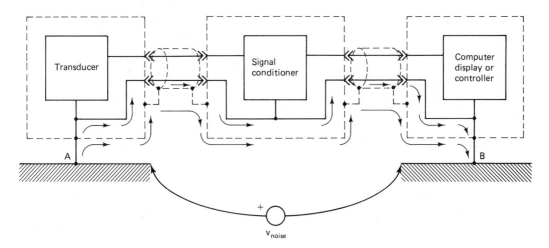

Figure 4–45 Shield and signal common improperly grounded at both ends.

lines of the signal. This floats the signal up and down by v_{noise} randomly as v_{noise} changes. It is probable that the noise voltage will completely bury the signal.

You must break these ground loops. But neither point A nor point B may be disconnected. An isolation amplifier (or digital optical coupler) is needed. Look at Figure 4–46. Both transducer common and computer common are tied to their respective shields and earths. However, the shields between the signal conditioner and the cable to the computer are *not* connected. This breaks the ground loop that had existed along the shield. The isolation amplifier (or digital optical coupler) breaks the ground loop that had existed through the electronics.

In fact, the configuration in Figure 4–46 is probably the best general approach to shielding and grounding. Shields are properly grounded. Equipment may be tied to earth for safety considerations. There is no possible ground loop through the electronics because of the isolation. But just as important is the protection offered by the isolation.

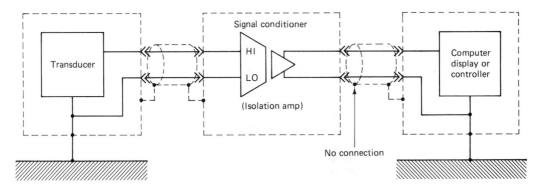

Figure 4–46 Isolation amplifier used to break ground loop.

Without it, any failure or error in wiring could introduce several hundred volts into the front end of the computer. That computer may be damaged, costing thousands of dollars. If the computer is networked to others, the entire computing system of the plant (costing hundreds of thousands of dollars) may be disabled. An isolation amplifier costing less than $100 can prevent all these problems.

The only remaining element in the data acquisition channel to be connected is the power supply. A simplified approach is shown in Figure 4–47. The power supply is also placed within its own shielded enclosure, and the loads, including ground, are taken to the signal conditioner in a shielded cable. You will also need to take power to the transducer and the computer, but for simplicity, those connections have been omitted here.

A problem arises with the center tap and with the parasitic capacitance between the power transformer's primary and secondary. This capacitance is on the order of 0.001 μF. At 60 Hz it presents an impedance of 2.6 MΩ. Any v_{noise} difference between

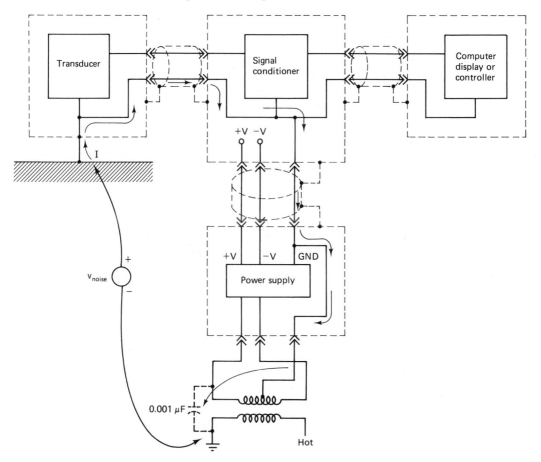

Figure 4–47 Power supply center tap problem.

the transducer ground and the line's neutral will cause current to flow, not along the shield, but along the signal common. Assuming a resistance along this common line of 0.5 Ω and a v_{noise} of 2 V,

$$V_{error} = \frac{0.5\ \Omega}{0.5\ \Omega + 2.6\ M\Omega}(2\ V) = 0.38\ \mu V$$

In very sensitive systems, this 0.38 μV may be a significant part of the signal from the transducer.

The solution is a power supply transformer with a shielded secondary. Its proper use is shown in Figure 4–48. The secondary leads from the transformer are run inside a shielded cable to the power supply. The transformer secondary shield is connected to that cable's shield and on to the rest of the system's shield. In this configuration, any v_{noise} causes current to flow along the shield, not along the signal common.

Now that you have seen how to ground the shield, what do you do with the

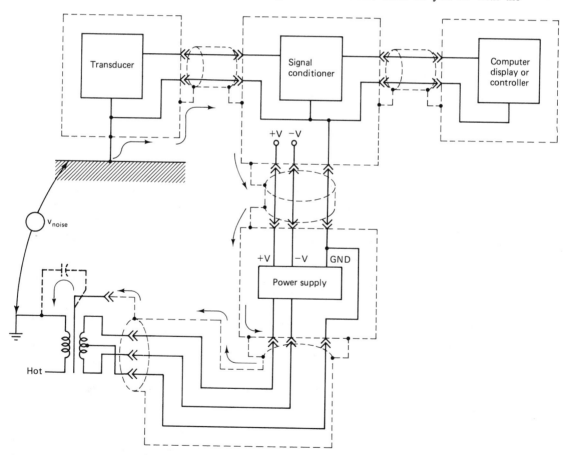

Figure 4–48 Proper connection of a shielded secondary power transformer.

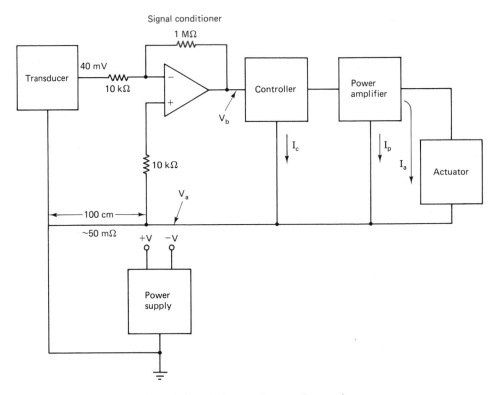

Figure 4–49 Multistage series ground connection.

ground connection for the other electronics? The circuits in Figures 4–42 through 4–48 suggest that they are all tied in series. This is illustrated more clearly in Figure 4–49. The shield connections, which you know should really be included, have been omitted for clarity. At first glance, this looks like a straightforward way of connecting grounds. In fact, this is typical of ground layouts on many printed circuit boards.

EXAMPLE 4–15

Calculate V_a and V_b resulting from the input signal and from the effects of the ground returns current under the following circumstances.
(a) Activator off, $I_c = 5$ mA, $I_p = 20$ mA, $I_a = 0$.
(b) Activator on, $I_c = 8$ mA, $I_p = 35$ mA, $I_a = 1$ A.

Solution The voltage, V_b, is determined by the 40-mV input signal and any voltage developed across the 50-mΩ resistance by the ground return current. To get V_b, apply superposition.

$$V_b = -\frac{1\ M\Omega}{10\ k\Omega}(40\ mV) + \left(1 + \frac{1\ M\Omega}{10\ k\Omega}\right)V_a$$

where $V_a = (I_c + I_p + I_a)(50\text{ m}\Omega)$.

(a) Actuator off

$$V_a = (5\text{ mA} + 20\text{ mA} + 0)(50\text{ m}\Omega) = 1.25\text{ mV}$$

$$V_b = (-100)(40\text{ mV}) + (101)(1.25\text{ mV}) = -3.87\text{ V}$$

Although the correct value should be $(-100)(40\text{ mV}) = -4\text{ V}$, you can compensate for this 3% error with a span adjustment somewhere.

(b) Actuator on

$$V_a = (8\text{ mA} + 35\text{ mA} + 1\text{A})(50\text{ m}\Omega) = 52\text{ mV}$$

$$V_b = (-100)(40\text{ mV}) + (101)(52\text{ mV}) = 1.25\text{ V}$$

The correct value is -4 V. But the large ground return current from the actuator, running through the common 50-mΩ ground bus, has raised the noninverting input of the high-gain signal conditioner by 52 mV. This is more than the transducer signal!

Of course, the results of connecting the activator's ground return along the same path as the low-level signal's return is totally unacceptable. The solution to this problem is simple enough. Provide the high-power signal its own, separate return to power supply ground. This is shown in Figure 4–50. In this configuration, the high return current from the actuator bypasses the sensitive input of the signal conditioner. As it switches on and off, there will be no impact on the signal conditioner's output.

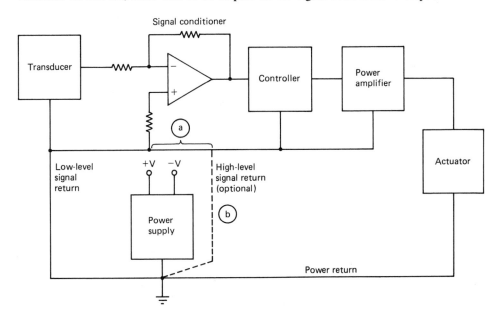

Figure 4–50 Multistage, multireturn ground connection.

If you find that the 3% error caused by the high-level signal return currents (I_c and I_p) is unacceptable, break the ground bus at *a*. Then, provide the controller and power amplifier with their own ground return. This is shown as the dashed line *b* in Figure 4–50. Do not connect both *a* and *b*. This creates a ground loop, with the possibility of some rather large circulating currents. (Remember Figure 4–45?) Also, do not be tempted to run the activator return together with the high-level signal return. The actuator return current may affect the output of the controller and power amplifier just as it did the signal conditioner.

Ideally, every stage throughout the data acquisition and control system would have its own, separate ground return. This is impractical. So group your circuits according to the type and size of signal that each processes, the magnitude of the ground return currents, and the circuit's sensitivity. Then provide a common ground bus for the electronics *within* each group, and a separate return line to the common ground point for each group. A typical grouping is suggested in Figure 4–51.

Notice that the converters are listed in two groups: low level and digital. Most high-resolution converters have two ground connections: an analog ground and a digital ground. Recommendations on how to handle these differ among manufacturers of data acquisition subsystems. Some suggest that the analog ground pin be tied to the low-level analog ground bus and the digital ground pin be tied to the digital bus. These two buses are then returned to the common point ground via their own, separate ground return lines. This is the procedure recommended by Figure 4–51.

An alternative approach suggested by other data conversion IC manufacturers says to tie the analog bus to the analog pin and the digital bus to the digital ground pin of

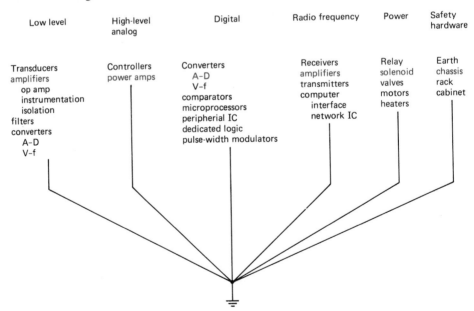

Figure 4–51 Ground-return signal grouping.

the IC. At the converter IC, only, these two buses should be connected by shorting the analog ground pin to the digital ground pin. You then run *one* ground return path from that junction to the common point ground. In this technique there are not separate ground returns for the low-level analog and the digital ground buses. These two buses connect at only one point, the converter IC, and then run jointly to the common ground point through a single lead.

It is important to keep each of the ground return lines separate until they join at the common point ground. Otherwise, as you saw in Example 4–15, there may be major interference. However, the hardware safety ground makes this difficult. Commercial equipment that uses BNC type input or output connectors is the problem. Look at Figure 4–52. The outer conductor is the signal common. But this is tied to the chassis by the BNC connector. Now the signal low has two paths to ground, through its own ground return and through the chassis. So does any interference or fault currents intercepted by the chassis. The signal low and the interference share common paths to ground. This allows the interference, which should have been screened out by the chassis, to float the common point of the signal up and down as it varies. Effectively, the noise picked up by the chassis has become part of the signal. This is similar to the shielding problem in Figure 4–45.

Try to avoid the simple coaxial BNC-type cable and connector. As you saw in the shielding section, using the outer conductor for both shield and signal low defeats the purpose of the shield. If you need the high-frequency characteristics of coaxial cable, insist on an instrument capable of connecting to twin-ax cable. Otherwise, use a shielded pair of leads, with an appropriate connector.

It is unusual to find commercial instruments with twin-ax or MS connectors. However, many vendors will provide an isolated BNC connector as an option. These connectors

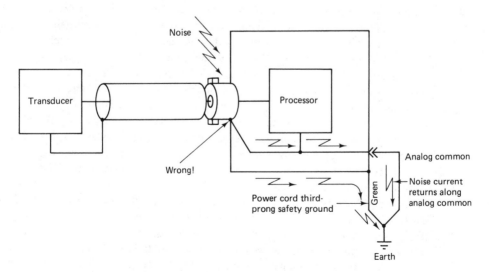

Figure 4–52   Grounded BNC connector problem.

mate to standard BNC cables but do not connect the outer shield to the chassis. A separate input-low connection is brought out, and the shell is insulated from the chassis to which it is mounted. With an isolated BNC front-panel connection, the incorrect signal low-to-chassis connection is broken. It is up to you, then, to cable from the source with twin-ax or shielded pair into a standard BNC cable connector. At that connector, tie the signal high to the center, signal low to the body, and leave the shield open.

SUMMARY

The instrumentation amplifier is a dedicated, closed-loop differential amplifier with extremely high input impedances and a gain that can be set precisely with a single resistor. It is ideal for bridge-type transducers such as strain gages. Normally, the sense pin is tied directly to the output and the reference is grounded. However, other configurations allow you to drive a remote load more accurately, add current boosting, or provide an adjustable offset. The effect of errors can be calculated to produce an error budget. Source impedence balancing, assuring a common ground between the instrumentation amplifier and the sources, zeroing, and supply decoupling are all necessary to assure that the instrumentation amplifier's actual performance matches the manufacturer's specifications.

Zero and span circuits allow you to alter the range and offset of a signal. In graphical terms, you can shift the y intercept (zero) and the slope (span). Using a zero and span circuit, you can alter the output of a transducer so that it precisely fits the input requirements of a display or controller. You may use one or two op amps. If high gain and common-mode rejection are needed, instrumentation amplifiers can be configured to allow easy adjustment of their gain (span) and offset (zero).

Faithful transmission of data from the signal conditioner to the processor that will use it is key to the success of any data acquisition or control system.

The dropping effect that series resistance has on a voltage signal can be overcome by converting the voltage to a current, and transmitting that current. Converters for floating as well as grounded loads are available. Usually, the current is offset, providing a set minimum level at zero input voltage. This allows detection of a broken or shorted current loop. Care must be taken to limit loop resistance and/or to provide adequate loop voltage to prevent saturation. Floating and grounded voltage-to-current converters can be built with op amps or with a special-purpose integrated circuit.

Recovery of the current signal at the receiver is done with a current-to-voltage converter. Although the grounded load converter is simple, it is susceptible to variations in return path resistance, common-mode noise, and differences in potential between earth points. A floating load current-to-voltage converter solves all of these problems. The offset and span of the $I–V$ converter can be adjusted to recover the original signal. The gain within the difference amplifier allows you to lower load resistance.

Added noise immunity is available if you convert the voltage to a frequency.

Noise alters the amplitude of a signal but has little effect on its frequency. Most voltage-to-frequency converters use a charge balancing technique. A capacitor is charged for a fixed time with a constant current. This produces a constant gain in charge and a fixed pulse width. But discharge occurs through a *RC* network. The rate of exponential decay depends on the voltage. So the larger the voltage, the more rapid the discharge and the higher the resulting frequency. In addition to being useful in data transmission, voltage-to-frequency conversion is an effective way to convert analog data to digital. A microcomputer can easily count the frequency of an input logic signal. Establishing a counting period of a multiple of 16.7 ms allows good rejection of 60-Hz noise.

Many voltage-to-frequency converters can be configured to perform frequency-to-voltage conversion. Once each input cycle the converter is tripped and outputs a current pulse of fixed amplitude and duration. The more often the converter is triggered, the more current pulses are output and the higher the output's average value. Of course, you must filter the output, and ripple is still a major problem at low frequencies.

Ground loops, common-mode input voltages that exceed the electronic's power supply, and a requirement for very low currents under failure conditions are all problems that can be solved with isolation amplifiers. Transformer-coupled isolation amplifiers amplitude- or phase-modulate a carrier in the input section. It is coupled to the output section through an internal transformer. There it is demodulated, filtered, and buffered. Transformer-coupled isolation amplifiers are quite accurate and provide isolated power to both sections as well as to the transducer. However, they are sources of electromagnetic noise, are large and relatively expensive, and are slow.

Optically isolated amplifiers use matched photodiodes in the negative-feedback loops of the input and the output amplifiers. This largely overcomes the photodiode/LED's inherent nonlinearity. Although smaller, faster, and cheaper than transformer-coupled amplifiers, optically isolated amplifiers must have isolated power provided externally and are not as accurate.

If the data to be isolated are digital, a simple digital optical coupler may be used. The input is a LED. When turned on, its light causes the output transistor to saturate. When used with a standard analog-to-digital converter, one coupler is needed for each line; or a voltage-to-frequency converter can drive it directly. This technique does allow you to break ground loops. However, it does not protect the *input* circuitry from overvoltage, nor does it limit failure currents.

Along with quality electronics and transmission techniques, proper shielding and cabling are necessary to ensure signal integrity. Magnetic fields are produced by large currents. Effective shielding requires careful routing of signals to keep low-level conductors away from large current carriers. The effectiveness of magnetic shielding also depends on the type and thickness of material. At audio frequencies, steel is required. At radio frequencies, copper or aluminum shields may work.

Electrostatic shields surround the sensitive conductor with a large source or sink of electrons which can easily move to balance any incident electric field. This means that the electrostatic shield must be grounded. To prevent large shield currents, or induced noise in the signal flow, there are a few rules to follow. Ground the shield at only one point. The source is best. Connect the shield to signal low at only one point, again at the source if possible. Never use the shield as your signal low. Break ground loops with an isolation amplifier if necessary.

Power supply grounding may require the use of a transformer with a shielded secondary. To prevent devastating interaction, divide your system signals into groups (low-level, high-level analog, digital, radio frequency, power, and safety). Provide a separate ground return lead for each of these. Avoid the use of grounded BNC connectors and simple coaxial cable.

REFERENCES

1. *Instrumentation and Isolation Amplifiers*, Vol. 1. Norwood, Mass.: Analog Devices, 1982, p. 41.
2. *XTR110 Specifications*. Tuscon, Ariz.: Burr-Brown Corporation, 1984.

PROBLEMS

4-1. For the circuit in Figure 4–5, determine the voltage across the load if e_1 and e_2 are both tied to ground. (*Hint*: $V_{\text{load}} \neq 0$ V.)

4-2. An instrumentation amplifier must amplify a 4-mV differential input and produce a 5-V output. Using an AD524:
   (a) Indicate how to set the gain properly.
   (b) If an input common-mode signal of 2.5 V can produce no more than 10 mV output, calculate the maximum allowable common-mode gain.

4-3. An AD524 is used to amplify a signal of 0 to 5 mV from a differential transducer, unbalanced by 20 Ω. The output of the IA feeds a 12-bit converter with a 5-V input range. The operating temperature range is 0 to 70°C. Determine the effect that errors have on the signal with respect to full-scale input.

4-4. The signal from a controller is 0 V for full off and 10 V for full on. The actuator requires an input of 3 V for full off and 1 V for full on. Design a zero and span converter that will convert the 0- to 10-V signal from the controller into the 3- to 1-V signal needed by the actuator.

4-5. A pressure transducer outputs differential signals of 0 V at −14.7 psig (at full vacuum) and 20 mV at 85.3 psig (full-scale positive pressure). Design a zero and span converter using an instrumentation amplifier such that the IA outputs 0.1 V/psig (−1.47 V at −14.7 psig and 8.53 V at 85.3 psig).

4-6. Explain the advantages of current signals over voltage signals.

4-7. (a) Design a voltage-to-current converter that will drive 60 mA into a floating load when the input voltage is 4 V. The input voltage will never go negative.
   (b) With a ±12-V supply, what is the maximum load resistance?

4–8. Redesign the circuit of Problem 4–7 to produce 60 mA when the input voltage is 4 V, and 10 mA when the input is zero volts. The input voltage will never go negative.

4–9. Design voltage-to-current converters to drive a *grounded* load to meet the following conditions (output current always positive).

  (a) *Differential* voltage of 4 V produces 60 mA.

  (b) Negative voltage of 10 V produces 20 mA.

  (c) Positive voltage of 10 V produces 60 mA, zero volts input produces 10 mA.

  (d) Input voltage of 10 V produces 20 mA, input voltage of 0 V produces 4 mA; use an AD524 instrumentation amplifier.

  (e) For each circuit you designed in parts (a) to (d), what must the minimum power supply voltage be if you are driving a load of 20 Ω?

4–10. Design a voltage-to-circuit converter using a XTR110 which outputs 10 mA for 0 V input and 60 mA for 5 V input.

4–11. For the circuit in Figure 4–23, assuming the output of the bridge is +2.8 mV, calculate the following values.

  (a) $V_{\text{INA 101}}$ pin 9, pin 6, pin 7, pin 8.

  (b) V_{XTR110} pin 12, pin 15, pin 1.

  (c) I_L.

  (d) V_L.

4–12. Design a grounded current-to-voltage converter that will output 0 V with a current of 10 mA and 5 V with an input of 60 mA. (This is the complement of the circuit for Problem 4–10.)

4–13. Design a floating current-to-voltage converter that will output 0 V with a current of 10 mA and 4 V with an input of 60 mA. (This is the complement of the circuit for Problem 4–8.) Set $\pm V$ to ± 12 V. Assure that the gain is set to avoid saturation.

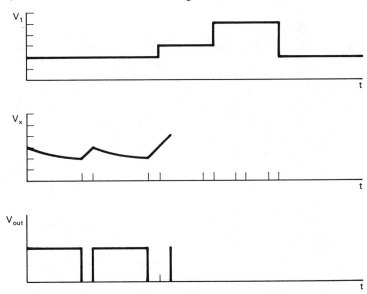

Figure 4–53   Waveforms (Problem 4–14).

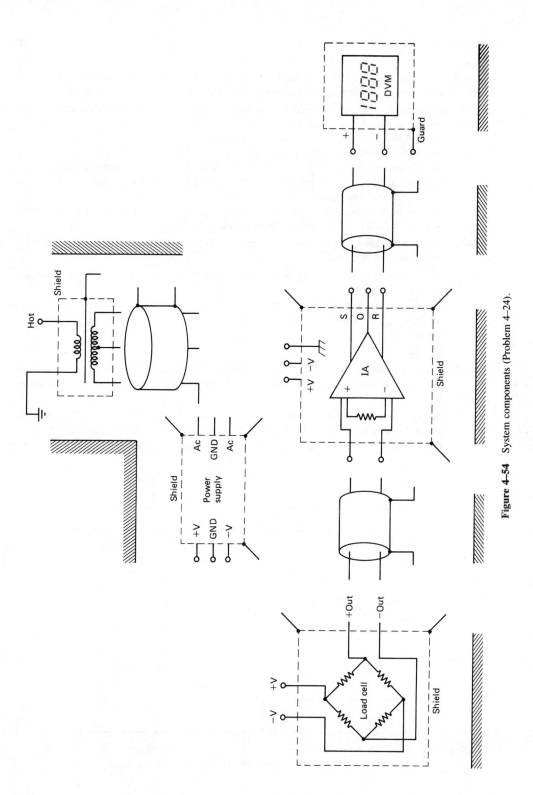

Figure 4-54 System components (Problem 4-24).

TABLE 4–7 SYSTEM CONFIGURATION FOR PROBLEM 4–25

Element	Purpose	Input	Output	Power
1. Reflective optical sensor	Sense shaft speed	None	TTL pulses	+12 V and ground at 50 mA
2. Power supply	Power to nos. 1, 4, and 6	None	±12 V and ground at 500 mA	115 V ac
3. Frequency-to-voltage converter	V_{dc} proportional to speed	TTL from no. 1	0 V dc–10 V dc low current	115 V ac
4. A/D converter	Digital conversion of speed and isolation	0 V dc–10 V dc from no. 3	Plugs directly into no. 5	±12 V dc and ground at 100 mA
5. Programmable controller	Provides control	Data from no. 4	Data to no. 6	115 V ac
6. D/A converter	Converts data from no. 5	Plugs directly into no. 5	0 V dc–10 V dc low current	±12 V dc and ground at 100 mA
7. Power interface module	SCR firing pulses	0 V–10 V dc from no. 6	0 V–2 V pulses at 500 mA	115 V ac
8. SCR bridge	Powers motor armature	Pulses from no. 7	0 V–115 V dc at 10 A	115 V ac
9. Rectifier	Dc motor field power	None	120 V dc at 2 A	115 V ac
10. Motor	turns shaft	None	Shaft speed	Armature from no. 8, field from no. 9

4–14. Complete the waveforms of Figure 4–53 to explain how the voltage-to-frequency converter of Figure 4–28 operates.

4–15. Recalculate component values for the voltage-to-frequency converter of Figure 4–30 for a maximum output frequency of 5 kHz at a maximum input voltage of 5 V. Set the input low-pass filtering at 10 Hz.

4–16. Use the V_{out} waveform you produced in Problem 4–14 as the V_{in} waveform of a frequency-to-voltage converter (Figure 4–31). Draw the I_{out} waveforms and the I_{ave} waveform. Compare these to the V_1 input to the voltage-to-frequency converter of Problem 4–14.

4–17. Design a frequency-to-voltage converter to recover the voltage encoded by the circuit of Problem 4–15.

4–18. List the three characteristics of isolation amplifiers that make then significantly different from instrumentation or operational amplifiers.

4–19. Describe the operation of a transformer-coupled isolation amplifier.

4–20. Describe the operation of an optically coupled isolation amplifier, including the technique used to assure linear response.

4–21. Compare the advantages and disadvantages of transformer-coupled versus optically coupled isolation amplifiers.

4–22. Using an analog-to-digital converter IC with which you are familiar, design an isolated data acquisition system for $0 \text{ V} < V_{in} < 5 \text{ V}$, 8-bit accuracy and resolution, and 100 μs or faster acquisition time. Use a TIL112 for signal isolation. Determine system cost with and without the isolation.

4–23. Modify your solution to Problem 4–15 to provide optical isolation of the output frequency.

4–24. Figure 4–54 contains the elements of a data acquisition channel. Draw a complete wiring diagram. Explain cabling, conduit, shielding, and grounding requirements. Explain how you have properly provided for magnetic and electrostatic shielding.

4–25. It is necessary to control the speed of a 2-hp dc motor. The control system contains the elements indicated in Table 4–7. Repeat Problem 4–24 for this complete control system.

5

Analog Controllers

The controller provides the intelligence of the system. Look again at the block diagram of the parameter control system (Figure 5–1). The controller has two inputs. One indicates the *desired* value of the parameter. This is called the set point (SP). The other input signal indicates the *actual* value of that parameter (as measured by the sensor, conditioned, and transmitted to the controller). This is called the process variable (PV). It is the purpose of the controller to provide a signal that will cause the process to be modified in such a way as to keep the set point and the process variable equal. Any changes in set point or the loads on the process should cause a change in the controller's output, to assure that the PV tracks the SP.

The mathematical analysis of the process/controller loop can be quite extensive. Volumes have been written describing the optimum mathematical relationship for given conditions. How the best controller equation is determined for a given process and design criteria will not be covered here. That is properly the topic of a course (and a text) on control theory. However, in this chapter we show you how to build and analyze a circuit using analog techniques to implement a *given* controller equation.

The simplest controller turns the actuator either hard on or fully off. To prevent excessive cycling or chatter, a dead band (hysteresis) is usually added. To provide finer, smoother control, a proportional band may replace the dead band. Over this proportional band, the output of the proportional controller varies linearly with error. Although capable of tighter control than the on/off controller, the proportional controller cannot *fully* eliminate error. To cause perfect steady-state tracking between the set point and the process variable, an integrator must be added to the proportional controller. This proportional–integral controller will provide good steady-state control but may respond sluggishly to transients. The addition of a derivative element produces a full

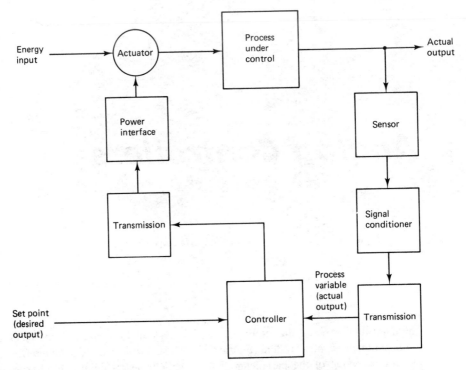

Figure 5-1 Automatic control system.

proportional–integral–derivative (PID) controller. This gives good transient as well as steady-state control.

In the final section you will see two advanced control techniques, feedforward control and cascaded control. These provide even tighter, faster performance than does the three-mode PID controller, with the ability to anticipate errors and begin correction early to overcome the effects of long dead times or process time constants.

OBJECTIVES

After studying this chapter you should be able to do the following:

1. Describe the purpose of the controller in an industrial control system.
2. Given specifications, design two different error amplifiers and describe the advantages and disadvantages of each.
3. For each of these controllers—on/off, proportional, proportional–integral, proportional–derivative, three-mode (PID), cascaded, feedforward—do the following:
   a. Describe operation.
   b. Analyze performance of a given circuit.

c. Design a circuit to meet given specifications.
d. Discuss limitations and advantages, including offset, residual error, and effects of parameter variation on performance.
e. Explain an example of an application that should use this type of controller.

5–1 ERROR AMPLIFIER

All controllers must begin by generating the error signal

$$E = \text{SP} - \text{PV} \tag{5-1}$$

The error is the difference between the set point (desired value) and the actual value. When the actual value is too small, the error is positive. A negative error indicates that the actual value of the controlled parameter is above the desired value.

You can produce the error signal in several ways, two of which are shown in Figure 5–2. The difference amplifier of Figure 5–2a has an output of

$$v_{\text{out}} = \frac{R_2}{R_1}(v_2 - v_1) \tag{5-2}$$

By setting $R = R_2 = R_1$,

$$v_2 = V_{\text{SP}}$$

$$v_1 = V_{\text{PV}}$$

$$v_{\text{out}} = V_{\text{error}} = V_{\text{SP}} - V_{\text{PV}}$$

You must be sure that

$$R \gg R_{\text{pot}}$$

to minimize loading of the potentiometer and bias current problems. Also, all four resistances must be carefully matched to prevent bias and offset problems as well as to enhance common-mode rejection (when $V_{\text{SP}} = V_{\text{PV}}$, $V_{\text{error}} = 0$).

The second error amplifier is an inverting summer:

$$v_{\text{out}} = -\left(\frac{R_3}{R_1}v_1 + \frac{R_3}{R_2}v_2\right) \tag{5-3}$$

By setting $R = R_1 = R_2 = R_3$,

$$v_1 = -V_{\text{SP}}$$

$$v_2 = V_{\text{PV}}$$

$$v_{\text{out}} = V_{\text{error}} = V_{\text{SP}} - V_{\text{PV}}$$

To assure proper operation, you must use the negative of the actual set point desired. This is then inverted by the inverting summer. As with the difference amplifier,

$$R \gg R_{\text{pot}}$$

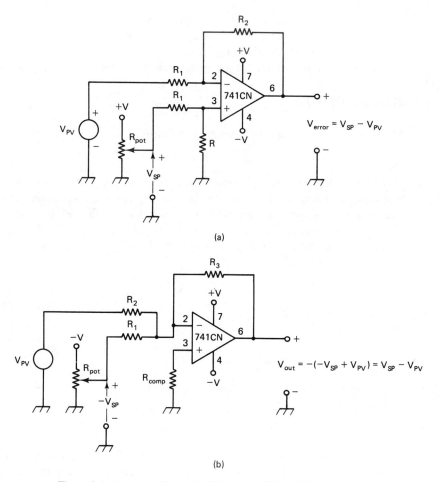

Figure 5–2 Error amplifiers: (a) difference amplifier; (b) inverting summer.

Resistor R_{comp} is to compensate for the effects of bias currents and should equal the parallel combination of all resistance to the inverting terminal. The virtual ground at the inverting pin of the inverting summer isolates each input and the feedback loop. This allows you to tune each of the input resistors without affecting the other input. This is not true for the difference amplifier.

5–2 ON/OFF CONTROLLERS

The on/off controller's output is either fully on or fully off. This causes the actuator either to apply full power to the process or to turn the process power off completely.

A home heating thermostat is a familiar example. Should the temperature fall below the set point, the furnace goes on. Once the temperature has risen above the set point, the controller (thermostat) turns the furnace off again.

To be practical, an on/off controller must have a deadband, or hysteresis. This is illustrated in Figure 5–3. When the *error* is a large negative value, the process variables is much larger than the set point, and the controller is off. This corresponds to the house being too hot. Only after the error has moved positive (from point *a* through *b* to *c*) does the controller output switch to 100%. This condition continues as long as there is any positive error (actual value now below desired value). This corresponds to the house becoming too cold and the furnace turning on. Even when the error falls to zero, point *f*, the controller does not immediately turn off. The controller's output will go off only after the error falls below a certain set negative error at points *g* and *b*.

With such a deadband, the error can never be maintained at zero. At a minimum, it will fluctuate between $\pm \Delta E$ as the controller cycles from full off to full on, and off again, and on again, and off again, ...

To minimize this residual error (distance between $+\Delta E$ to $-\Delta E$) you should decrease the deadband. However, without the deadband, a very small decrease in PV could cause the error to go positive, sending the controller full on. For processes with low-energy storage capacity (inertia), this would immediately raise PV. Any small rise in PV would send the error negative, immediately turning the controller back off. Another minor disturbance, decreasing PV, would begin the cycle over again. Such rapid, full range swings of controller output can seriously damage electromechanical actuators and other system components. The deadband decreases this. Hysteresis, or a deadband, is necessary to prevent cycling. However, it must be minimized to keep residual error small.

An electronic on/off controller is shown in Figure 5–4. Op amp U_1 is the error amplifier. Its output, the error signal, drives the input of U_2. Look carefully at U_2. It is *not* a noninverting amplifier. It is a comparator with hysteresis. When V_{error} is quite

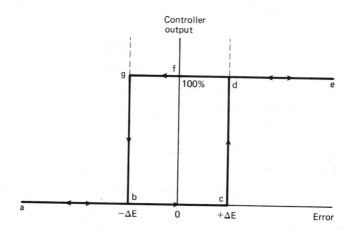

Figure 5–3   On/off controller's transfer curve showing hysteresis.

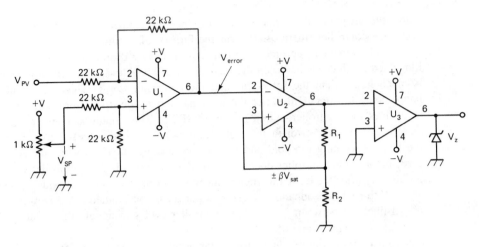

Figure 5–4   On/off controller.

negative, U_2's output goes to positive saturation. Resistors R_1 and R_2 divide this by a factor of β to produce a positive reference voltage.

$$\beta = \frac{R_2}{R_1 + R_2}$$

Only when the error voltage becomes more positive than βV_{sat} will U_2 switch its output to negative saturation.

With negative saturation at the output, the reference voltage (at pin 3 of U_2) has switched to

$$-\beta V_{sat}$$

The error must now become more negative than $-\beta V_{sat}$ before U_2 will switch to a positive output again.

So, U_2 produces the deadband or hysteresis. Referring to Figure 5–3, we see that

$$\pm \Delta E = \pm \beta V_{sat} \tag{5–4}$$

Op amp U_3 inverts the levels from U_2. The zener at the output restricts the output voltage to that specified as the maximum controller output. Often, only positive controller output voltages are allowed. When U_3 tries to go to negative saturation, the zener will forward bias, clamping the output at -0.6 V.

EXAMPLE 5–1

Analyze the operation of the circuit in Figure 5–4 for $R_1 = 100$ kΩ, $R_2 = 10$ kΩ, $\pm V_{sat} = \pm 10$ V, $V_{SP} = 5$ V.
(a) Calculate the size of the deadband.
(b) $V_{PV} = 3$ V.

(c) V_{PV} is increased to 7 V.

(d) V_{PV} is decreased to 5 V.

Solution   **(a)** $\pm\Delta E = \pm\beta V_{sat}$

$$\beta = \frac{R_2}{R_1 + R_2} = \frac{10\ k\Omega}{10\ k\Omega + 100\ k\Omega} = 0.091$$

$$\pm\Delta E = \pm 0.091 \times 10\ V = \pm 0.91\ V$$

This is considered a 1.82-V deadband or hysteresis.

(b) $V_{PV} = 3\ V$

$$V_{error} = V_{SP} - V_{PV} = 5\ V - 3\ V = 2\ V$$

Output of U_2 goes to -10 V and U_2 reference voltage goes to -0.91 V. Op amp U_3 is forced toward positive saturation, but is held at $+V_z$ by the zener diode. This corresponds to point e on Figure 5–3.

(c) As V_{PV} increases to 7 V,

$$V_{error} = 5\ V - 7\ V = -2\ V$$

The circuit moves from point e to d, to f, to g. When

$$V_{error} < -\Delta E = -0.91\ V = -\beta V_{sat}$$

U_2 switches its output to positive saturation. The reference voltage at pin 3 of U_2 goes to $+V_{sat} = +0.91$ V. With V_{PV} at 7 V, the error voltage is -2 V. Op amp U_2 is at positive saturation with a $+\beta V_{sat}$ reference. Op amp U_3 inverts this and tries to go to negative saturation. The zener diode forward biases, clamping the output at -0.6 V. The circuit is at point a in Figure 5–3.

(d) $V_{PV} = 5\ V$

$$V_{error} = V_{SP} - V_{PV} = 5\ V - 5\ V = 0$$

This is at point o on Figure 5–3. Op amp U_2 is still in positive saturation, holding its reference at $+\beta V_{sat} = 0.91$ V. That is point c in Figure 5–3. Only when the error exceeds $+0.91$ V ($V_{PV} > 5.91$ V) will the controller output go back on.

The controller of Figures 5–3 and 5–4 and of Example 5–1 is *inverse* acting. The output moves opposite to the process variable. This is typical of heating control systems. As the temperature falls, the furnace goes on. If the temperature rises too far, the controller goes off.

Refrigeration (and other) systems require a *direct*-acting controller. In a direct-acting controller, the process variable and the controller output move in the same direction. As the temperature rises, the controller's output goes high, turning the compressor on. Lowering the temperature causes the controller's output to fall, turning the compressor off.

The controller in Figure 5–4 can be converted to a direct-acting controller by reversing the inputs of the comparator U_3. Be sure when designing or specifying a controller that you obtain the direction, either direct or inverse, that you want.

5–3 PROPORTIONAL CONTROLLERS

The all-or-nothing response of the on/off controller is adequate for slow systems with significant inertia, when you can tolerate some noticeable error. Often, however, you need a linear region of control. This is provided by the proportional controller. Its transfer curve is shown in Figure 5–5.

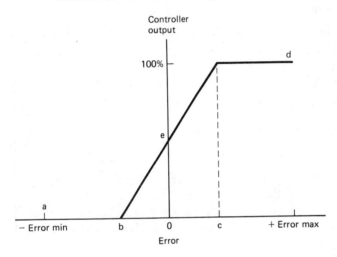

Figure 5–5   Proportional controller transfer curve.

Like the on/off controller, large negative error causes the proportional controller to go full off (point *a*). Large positive error sends the output to 100% (point *d*) just as it did with the two-position controller. Instead of a deadband, however, the proportional controller has a linear response region (points *b* to *c*). Small changes of error, about zero, cause *proportional* changes in the controller output. This gives the controller much finer control over the process.

The proportional controller is described primarily by its proportional band. The proportional band is the change in error (as a percentage of full-scale error) that will cause the output to go from full off to full on.

EXAMPLE 5–2

(a) Draw the transfer curve for a proportional control with (1) a 50% proportional band and (2) a 10% proportional band.

(b) Calculate the slope of the transfer curves.

Solution   (a) (1) A 50% proportional band means that 50% of a full-scale change in error will cause a full-swing output change. This is shown in Figure 5–6a. (2)

A 10% proportional band means that 10% of a full-scale change in error will cause a full-swing output change. This is shown in Figure 5-6b.

(b) The slope is $\Delta Y/\Delta X$ for these transfer curves.

$$m = \frac{\Delta \text{ controller output}}{\Delta \text{ error}}$$

$$(1) \;\; m = \frac{100\%}{50\%} = 2$$

$$(2) \;\; m = \frac{100\%}{10\%} = 10$$

In general, if the input and output of the controller are both expressed in % FSO (full-scale output), then

$$m = \frac{1}{\text{proportional band}}$$

Notice that the tighter the proportional band, the steeper the slope.

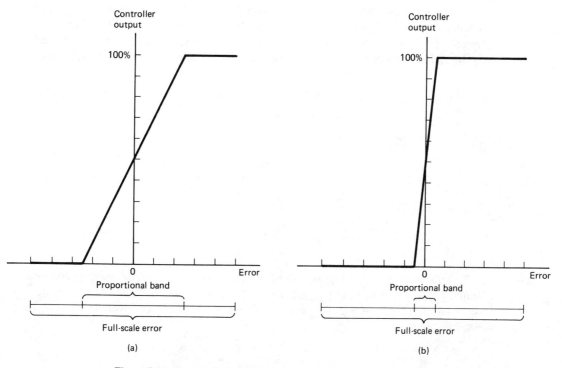

Figure 5-6   Example 5-2 transfer curves for (a) 50% and (b) 10% proportional bands.

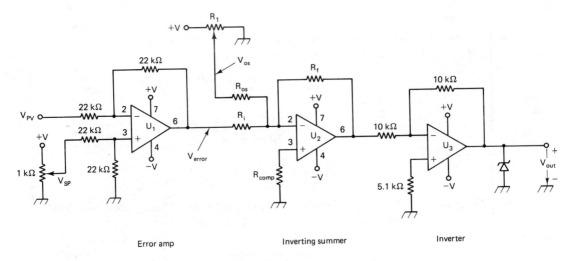

Figure 5–7 Proportional controller.

The schematic for a proportional controller is given in Figure 5–7. Op amp U_1 produces the error signal from the set point (V_{SP}) and process variable (V_{PV}) signals. Op amp U_2 provides the proportional band. U_3 is simply an inverter to compensate for the inversion produced by U_2. The zener diode limits the positive and negative output voltage. The circuit's equation is

$$V_{out} = \frac{R_f}{R_i} V_{error} + \frac{R_f}{R_{os}} V_{os}$$

Usually, $R_f = R_{os}$, so that

$$V_{out} = \frac{R_f}{R_i} V_{error} + V_{os} \qquad (5\text{–}5)$$

With no error,

$$V_{error} = 0$$

$$V_{out} = V_{os}$$

This is point e on Figure 5–5. You can vary V_{os} to set the desired controller output for no error input. Often, it is set to half of the controller's full-scale output.

The slope of the transfer curve is determined by the gain given to V_{error} by the inverting amplifier.

$$m = \frac{R_f}{R_i} \qquad (5\text{–}6)$$

If the axis are scaled in volts, equation 5–6 becomes

$$m = \frac{R_f}{R_i} = \frac{V_{out\ FS}}{\%\ band \times V_{error\ FS}} \tag{5–7}$$

EXAMPLE 5–3

For the circuit in Figure 5–7, with $V_{SP} = 6$ V, $V_{os} = 5$ V, $R_{os} = R_f = 100$ kΩ, $R_i = 22$ kΩ, and $V_z = 10$ V, calculate the following values.

(a) Output voltage with $V_{PV} = 5.5$ V.
(b) Output voltage with $V_{PV} = 4$ V.

Solution   **(a)** $V_{error} = V_{SP} - V_{PV}$
$$= 6\ V - 5.5\ V = 0.5\ V$$

$$V_{out} = \frac{R_f}{R_i} V_{error} + V_{os}$$

$$= \frac{100\ k\Omega}{22\ k\Omega}(0.5\ V) + 5\ V = 7.27\ V$$

(b) $V_{error} = 6\ V - 4\ V = 2\ V$

$$v_{out} = \frac{100\ k\Omega}{22\ k\Omega}(2\ V) + 5\ V = 14\ V$$

However, the output zener will limit the voltage to 10 V:

$$V_{out} = 10\ V$$

In part (a), the controller is still within its proportional band. However, the larger error of part (b) has forced the controller hard on.

EXAMPLE 5–4

Design a proportional controller to meet the following:

Proportional band: 67%
Error maximum: ± 3 V
Full-scale output: 16 V
Zero error causes 25% controller output

Solution   The circuit of Figure 5–7 will work. Drawing the transfer curve first will help with selecting component values. A zero error causes the controller to go to 25% of its maximum output. This means that at $V_{error} = 0$,

$$V_{out} = 0.25 \times 16\ V = 4\ V.$$

This is point a on the curve in Figure 5–8. The slope is

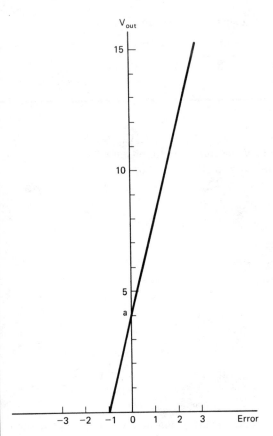

Figure 5–8 Transfer curve for Example 5–4.

$$m = \frac{V_{\text{out FS}}}{\%\ \text{band} \times V_{\text{error FS}}}$$

or

$$m = \frac{16\ \text{V}}{67\% \times 6\ \text{V}} = 4\ \text{V/V}$$

To determine component values, first set $R_{\text{os}} = R_f = 100\ \text{k}\Omega$. The zero error offset can then be provided by

$$V_{\text{os}} = 4\ \text{V}$$

Be sure, however, to pick $R_1 \ll R_{\text{os}}$ to prevent loading down the potentiometer. Pick $R_1 = 5\ \text{k}\Omega$. From equation 5–6,

$$m = \frac{R_f}{R_i}$$

or

$$R_i = \frac{R_f}{m} = \frac{100\text{ k}\Omega}{4} = 25\text{ k}\Omega$$

Pick R_i as 22-kΩ fixed resistor with a series 5-kΩ potentiometer.

$$R_{\text{comp}} = R_f \| R_{\text{os}} \| R_i = 16.7\text{ k}\Omega$$

Pick $R_{\text{comp}} = 16$ kΩ.

Although the proportional controller is better than the on/off controller, error cannot be eliminated completely. For the circuit designed in Example 5–4, no error can occur *only* with a controller output of 4 V. An increase in the process's load may require the controller to output 6 V to bring the controlled variable back in line with the set point (no error). But to get a 6-V controller output, there must be a $\frac{1}{2}$-V error. This is a no-win situation. To reduce the error, the controller must raise its output. But to raise its output, the controller must have some error. This residual error can be reduced by increasing the gain of U_2, and therefore the slope. However, too much gain will cause the system to cycle (oscillate), just as the on/off controller does when given a deadband that is too small. Reduce system error with a proportional controller by increasing gain. But beware of oscillations.

Control engineers normally write system components' equations in Laplace transforms. Equation 5–5 becomes

$$V_{\text{out}} = K_P V_{\text{error}}$$

where V_{out} = controller output
K_P = gain of controller
V_{error} = error

The transfer function of a proportional controller is

$$\text{transfer function} = \frac{V_{\text{out}}}{V_{\text{error}}} = K_p$$

The proportional controller of Figure 5–7 is inverse acting. A rise in the process variable, V_{PV}, is inverted by U_1, back in phase at the output of U_2, and inverted a final time by U_3. This gives the *error* versus output plots of Figures 5–5 and 5–6 a positive slope.

If you want a direct-acting proportional controller, simply omit U_3 in Figure 5–7. The error amp U_1 will cause one inversion, while the proportional amp U_2 reinverts the signal. The output moves in phase with the process variable. For a direct-acting proportional controller, the *error* versus output transfer curve has a negative slope, moving down to the right.

5–4 INTEGRAL AND PROPORTIONAL–INTEGRAL CONTROLLERS

To eliminate residual system error, the controller's response must be changed. The proportional controller's output was proportional to the system error. The integral controller has an output whose *rate of change* is proportional to the error. As long as there is any error at all, the output will continue to change. When the error has been driven to zero, the integral controller's output no longer *changes*. It holds the output which was necessary to produce no error.

In most practical systems this time-variant output, alone, is too slow. It is usually coupled with the proportional controller you saw in Section 5–3. From this proportional–integral controller you get rapid changes in controller output, proportional to the size of the error. But the output will continually adjust itself, in an effort to drive the steady-state error to zero.

5–4.1 Integral Controller

The *rate of change* of the output from a simple integral controller is proportional to the error. Mathematically, this is expressed

$$\frac{dv_{\text{out}}}{dt} = K_I v_{\text{error}} \tag{5–8}$$

where v_{out} = controller output
K_I = integration constant
v_{error} = error

When there is a large error, the controller's output *changes* rapidly to correct the error. As the error gets smaller, the controller's output *changes* more slowly. This minimizes over correction. As long as there is any error, the controller's output will continue to change. Once the error is driven to zero, the controller's output *change* also goes to zero. This means that the controller holds the output which eliminated the error.

This is illustrated in Figure 5–9. A large error between times a and b causes the output to change rapidly. Decreases in the error, between b and d, cause the output to increase more slowly (but the output continues to rise). When the error goes to zero, at time d, the controller's output does not change but holds the output which dropped the error to zero. Negative error, as between times e and f, causes a negative rate of change of the controller's output. That is, the output falls.

To determine the controller output, as a function of error, you must convert the differential equation 5–8 into an integral equation

$$\frac{dv_{\text{out}}}{dt} = K_I v_{\text{error}}$$

$$dv_{\text{out}} = K_I v_{\text{error}} \, dt$$

$$\int d v_{\text{out}} = \int K_I v_{\text{error}}\, dt$$

$$v_{\text{out}} = K_I \int v_{\text{error}}\, dt + V_0 \qquad (5\text{--}9)$$

where V_0 is the initial controller offset. The Laplace transform of equation 5–9 gives

$$V_{\text{out}} = \frac{K_I V_{\text{error}}}{s}$$

and a transfer function

$$\frac{V_{\text{out}}}{V_{\text{error}}} = \frac{K_I}{s} \qquad (5\text{--}10)$$

Figure 5–10 is the schematic of an op amp integrator. Because of the capacitive negative feedback, the op amp's inverting input is held at virtual ground. The input voltage then drives input current into R_i.

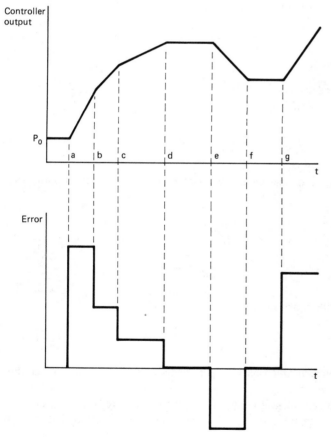

Figure 5–9   Integral controller input/output relationship.

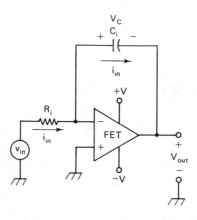

Figure 5–10 Op amp integrator.

$$i_{in} = \frac{v_{in}}{R_i} \tag{5–11}$$

This current cannot flow into the op amp, so it all goes into the capacitor. The voltage/current relationship for the capacitor in Figure 5–10 is

$$\frac{dv_c}{dt} = -\frac{i}{C_i}$$

or

$$dv_c = -\frac{i}{C_i} dt$$
$$v_c = -\frac{1}{C_i} \int i\, dt + V_0 \tag{5–12}$$

where V_0 is the initial charge on the capacitor. Substituting equation 5–11 into 5–12 gives us

$$v_c = -\frac{1}{C_i} \int \frac{v_{in}}{R_i} dt + V_0$$
$$= -\frac{1}{R_iC_i} \int v_{in}\, dt + V_0 \tag{5–13}$$

Compare equation 5–13 with equation 5–9.

$$K_I = -\frac{1}{R_iC_i} \tag{5–14}$$

where K_I is the integration *constant* (units = per second) and R_iC_i is the integration *time* (units = seconds).

The full schematic of an integral controller is given in Figure 5–11. Op amp U_1 produces the error signal. The integrator is U_2. For positive error, its output will go

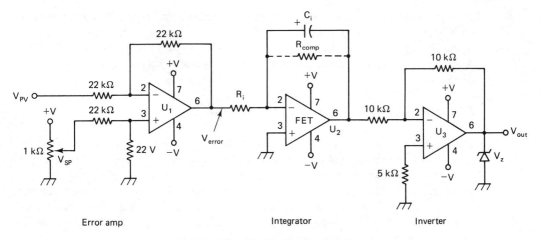

Figure 5–11 Integral controller.

negative (notice the minus sign in equation 5–13). This negative control signal is inverted and limited by U_3 and the zener diode. Resistor R_{comp} allows bias current to bypass C_i. Without R_{comp}, bias currents on *some* general-purpose, bipolar op amps are large enough to charge C_i, even with no error voltage. This causes the output of U_2 to slowly rise until it is saturated. Select

$$R_{comp} > 10 \, R_i$$

if U_2's output rises with $V_{error} = 0$.

Zero error means that there is zero volts on each side of R_i. So no current can flow through it. Therefore, ideally, C_i can neither charge nor discharge. It should hold its voltage. However, when you add R_{comp} to keep bias currents from charging C_i, the capacitor can discharge slowly through R_{comp}. With zero error, then, the output will slowly fall (rather than remaining constant) as C_i discharges through R_{comp}. There is a trade-off to be made. No R_{comp} or a very large R_{comp} allows bias currents to charge C_i. Too small a R_{comp} allows C_i to discharge rather than hold its voltage. Choosing U_2 as an op amp with very low bias currents may be your only solution. A FET or CMOS op amp has bias currents on the order of picoamperes or less. Using a FET or CMOS op amp for U_2 should cause no noticeable change in V_{out} caused by bias currents, even without R_{comp}.

A second nonideal characteristic also threatens the long-term holding ability of the integrator, U_2. All capacitors have a leakage resistance. This is modeled as a resistor in parallel with the plates of the capacitor. So any charge stored on the capacitor will slowly discharge through this leakage resistance. In effect, R_{comp} is being supplied by the capacitor. For aluminum electrolytic the $R_{leakage}$ C time constant is only a few seconds. However, Teflon and film capacitors (polypropylene, polystyrene, polyethylene, and polycarbonate) have a self-discharge time constant formed by $R_{leakage}$ C of typically 1 Ms. Be certain to specify a low leakage capacitor.

In summary, an integral controller will continue to change its output until the error goes to zero. The integration is performed by an op amp with capacitive negative feedback. You will have to control bias currents carefully, or compensate for them. Also, careful selection of the proper type of capacitor is necessary to restrict its self-discharge.

5–4.2 Proportional–Integral Controller

The integral controller alone has very poor transient response. Should the error produce a step input into an integral controller, it will respond by *beginning* to ramp its output. A proportional controller responds to a step in error by stepping its output proportionally. However, the integral controller will continue to change its output until all steady-state error is eliminated. A proportional controller cannot fully eliminate error. The proportional–integral controller is an effort to combine the advantages of both good transient response from the proportional and error elimination from the integral.

A parallel proportional–integral controller is shown in Figure 5–12. Op amp U_1 is the error amplifier, performing the calculation

$$v_{error} = v_{SP} - v_{PV}$$

This error is applied to both the proportional and the integral controllers. In the proportional controller, U_2, the error receives a gain.

$$K_P = \frac{R_2}{R_1}$$

The integral takes the integral of the error, giving

$$v = -K_I \int v_{error}\, dt + V_0$$

where

$$K_I = \frac{1}{R_i C_i}$$

These two signals are combined by U_4, an inverting summer. This gives an overall output of

$$v_{out} = K_P v_{error} + K_I \int v_{error}\, dt + V_0$$

In the Laplace domain this becomes

$$V_{out} = K_P V_{error} + \frac{K_I V_{error}}{s}$$

The transfer function for the circuit in Figure 5–12, then, is

$$\frac{V_{out}}{V_{error}} = K_P + \frac{K_I}{s}$$

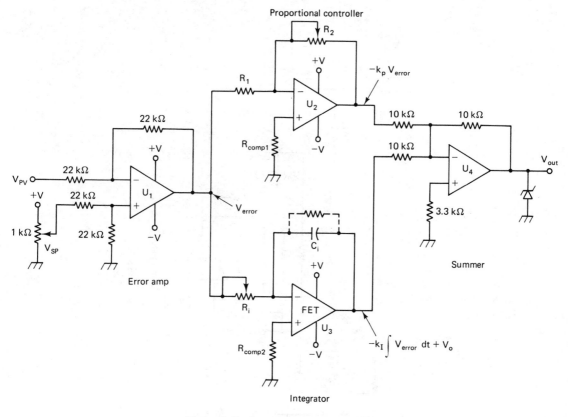

Figure 5–12   Parallel proportional–integral controller.

or

$$\frac{V_{out}}{V_{error}} = \frac{K_P s + K_I}{s}$$

or

$$\frac{V_{out}}{V_{error}} = \frac{s + (K_I/K_P)}{(1/K_P)s}$$

A series proportional–integral controller is shown in Figure 5–13. Op amp U_1 is the error amplifier, performing the calculation

$$v_{error} = v_{SP} - v_{PV}$$

This error is the input to the proportional controller, U_2. Actually, it is only an inverting amplifier. Its gain is the proportionality constant K_P:

$$K_P = \frac{R_2}{R_1}$$

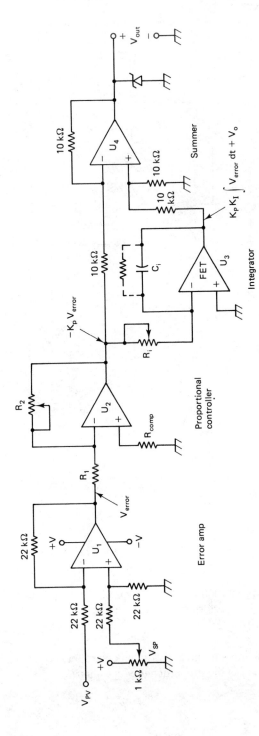

Figure 5-13 Series proportional–integral controller.

Notice two things. The output of U_2 is inverted. Also, this proportional controller has no offset (unlike Figure 5–7).

The input to the integrator, U_3, is the output of the proportional controller, $-K_P V_{error}$. According to equation 5–13,

$$v = -\frac{1}{R_i C_i} \int v_{in}\, dt + V_0 \tag{5–15}$$

or

$$v = -K_I \int v_{in}\, dt + V_0$$

Substituting $v_{in} = -K_P V_{error}$ into equation 5–15 gives us

$$v = -K_I \int (-K_P v_{error})\, dt + V_0$$

$$= K_P K_I \int v_{error}\, dt + V_0$$

The summer U_4 is actually a difference amplifier.

$$v_{out} = \frac{10\ k\Omega}{10\ k\Omega} [(K_P K_I \int v_{error}\, dt + V_0) - (-K_P v_{error})]$$

$$= K_P v_{error} + K_P K_I \int v_{error}\, dt + v_0 \tag{5–16}$$

The Laplace transform of equation 5–16 is

$$V_{out} = K_P V_{error} + \frac{K_P K_I}{s} V_{error} \tag{5–17}$$

for

$$\text{transfer function} = \frac{V_{out}}{V_{error}} = K_P \frac{s + K_I}{s} = K_P \frac{T_i s + 1}{T_i s} \tag{5–18}$$

where

$$T_i = \frac{1}{K_i} = R_i C_i$$

$$K_P = \frac{R_2}{R_1}$$

Control design engineers specify the controller in terms of its transfer function, equation 5–18.

Often, the integration constant, K_I, will be given in terms of resets per minute.

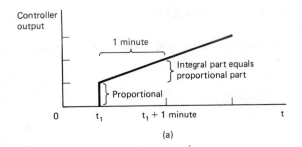

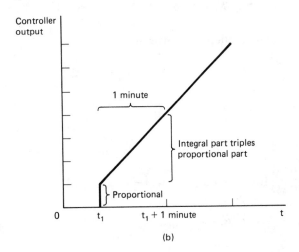

Figure 5–14   Integral constant for (a) 1 and (b) 3 resets per minute.

In Section 5–4.1 you saw that K_I had units of per second. To convert this to resets per minute, you just multiply by 60 s/min.

The electrical significance of K_I is illustrated in Figure 5–14. At time t_1 there is a step in error which causes the proportional part of the controller to step up. Assuming that the error remains constant, the integral part of the controller will now cause the output to ramp up. The ramp *rate* is set by K_I. With an integration constant of 1 reset per minute, in 1 minute the ramp will send the output up the same amount that the proportional part did. This is shown in Figure 5–14a. In Figure 5–14b the integral part of the controller causes a ramp which triples the output produced by the proportional controller. This is caused by an integration constant of 3 resets per minute.

Circuit operation may best be analyzed by examining its response to several step changes in V_{PV} (the process variable).

EXAMPLE 5–5

Determine the response of the circuit in Figure 5–13 to the input, V_{PV}, given in Figure 5–15. Assume that

$$V_{SP} = 5 \text{ V}$$

$$R_1 = 3.3 \text{ k}\Omega$$

$$R_2 = 10 \text{ k}\Omega$$

$$R_i = 10 \text{ k}\Omega$$

$$C_i = 100 \text{ }\mu\text{F}$$

$$V_0 = 0 \text{ (initial charge on capacitor)}$$

$$V_{sat} = \pm 15 \text{ V}$$

Solution

$$V_{error} = V_{SP} - V_{PV}$$

The error voltage is the controlled variable subtracted from 5 V. The error voltage mirrors V_{PV} but is shifted down 5 V.

U_2: The proportional controller is an inverting amplifier with a gain of

$$K_P = \frac{R_2}{R_1} = \frac{10 \text{ k}\Omega}{3.3 \text{ k}\Omega} = 3$$

The output of U_2 is an amplified and inverted version of the error voltage.

U_3: With a fixed input, the integrator is actually a ramp generator.

$$\text{rate} = \frac{V}{RC}$$

$$V = K_P V_{error}$$

$$R = 10 \text{ k}\Omega$$

$$C = 100 \text{ }\mu\text{F}$$

$$\text{rate} = \frac{3V_{error}}{10 \text{ k}\Omega \times 100 \text{ }\mu\text{F}} = \frac{3V_{error}}{\text{second}}$$

Time a–b: $V_{error} = 1$ V, U_3 output will ramp up at a 3-V/s rate.

Time b–c: $V_{error} = 0$ V, U_3 will hold its output constant.

Time c–d: $V_{error} = -2$ V, U_3 will ramp downward at a 6-V/s rate.

The total output is the point-by-point summation of U_3's output and the inversion of U_2's output.

You could build a proportional–integral controller with the same response with fewer op amps. However, the circuit of Figure 5–13 allows you to adjust V_{SP}, $K_P(R_2)$, and $K_I(R_i)$ *independently*. Each component in the controllers with fewer op amps may

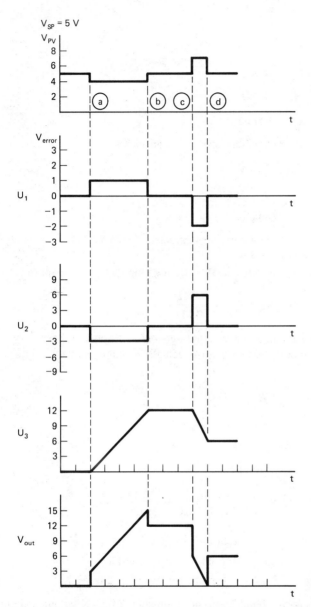

Figure 5–15 Solution to Example 5–5.

affect several parameters. Fine tuning becomes an almost impossible task. Circuit operation is not as straightforward, making testing and troubleshooting rather confusing tasks.

The integral part of this controller may be considered adaptive offset for the proportional controller. The proportional controller provides a constant output for constant error. The integrator then adjusts the ''offset'' to eliminate the error.

When combined with an integrator, the proportional controller's tendency to oscillate increases. You must therefore lower K_P to stabilize the system. However, this, in turn, reduces the controller's ability to respond rapidly. Finally, when used in a system with long process delays, the ever-increasing nature of the integrator may cause the controller to overcorrect before the process's delay can respond.

The proportional–integral controllers of Figure 5–12 and 5–13 are inverse acting. You can easily see this by counting the number of inversions v_{PV} receives as it travels to the output. Op amps U_1, U_2, and U_3 each invert the signal, causing v_{out} to be out of phase with v_{PV}. To produce a direct-acting proportional–integral controller, you must either add or remove an inversion. But you cannot remove U_4 (as you did for the simple proportional controller). It combines the proportional and integral parts. The simplest solution is to add another inverting amplifier after U_4. Set its gain to -1 by letting $R_f = R_i$. Also, you must move the zener diode to the output of this amplifier.

5–5 DERIVATIVE AND THREE-MODE (PID) CONTROLLERS

The proportional–integral controller will remove all steady-state error. In many systems the proportional part will provide adequately fast response to steps in error. However, processes with large inertia need some form of additional kick in response to a step in error. This overcomes the inertia, providing much faster response to error steps than even a proportional controller can give.

This inertia-correcting kick is provided by a derivative controller. Combining a derivative controller with a proportional–integral controller forms the industrial standard three-mode or PID controller.

5–5.1 Derivative Controller

The output of the derivative controller is proportional to the rate of change of the error.

$$v_{out} = K_D \frac{dv_{error}}{dt} \tag{5–19}$$

The Laplace transform of equation 5–19 gives

$$V_{out} = K_D s V_{error} \tag{5–20}$$

for

$$\text{transfer function} = \frac{V_{out}}{V_{error}} = K_D s \tag{5–21}$$

Figure 5–16 illustrates the response of a derivative controller. A step in error, at time a, has a nearly infinite slope, dv_{error}/dt. This sends the controller's output to saturation. Between times a and b, b and c, and e and f, the error is constant (although not zero). The derivative or slope of the error is zero, so the controller's output during these times is also zero. A constant increase in error has a constant slope, producing a constant

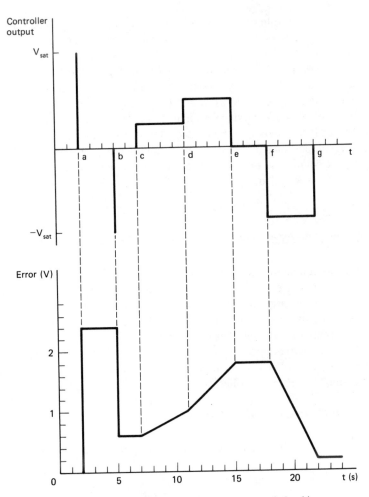

Figure 5-16 Derivative controller input/output relationship.

output (time c to d). Increasing the slope of the error increases the magnitude of the output (time d to e). A decrease in error has a negative slope, which causes a negative output (time f to g).

Figure 5–17 is the schematic of a basic op amp differentiator. Notice that it is just an integrator in which the resistor and capacitor have switched places. Or you could look at it as an inverting amplifier with R_i replaced by C_D. The gain for an inverting amp is

$$\frac{v_{\text{out}}}{v_{\text{in}}} = -\frac{R_f}{Z_c}$$

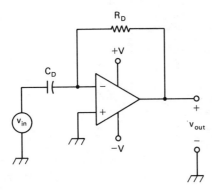

Figure 5–17   Basic op amp differentiator.

In the Laplace domain

$$Z_c = \frac{1}{Cs}$$

$$\frac{V_{\text{out}}}{V_{\text{in}}} = -\frac{R_D}{1/C_D s}$$

$$= -R_D C_D s$$

Compare this with equation 5–21.

$$K_D = R_D C_D = \text{differentiation constant} \tag{5–22}$$

There are two major precautions of which you must be aware. First, for sinusoidal inputs,

$$v_{\text{out}} = \frac{Z_{RD}}{Z_{CD}} v_{\text{in}}$$

$$= \frac{R_D v_{\text{in}}}{1/2\pi f C_D}$$

$$= 2\pi f C_D R_D v_{\text{in}}$$

For low-frequency signals, the output is very small. However, the output goes up with frequency. High-frequency noise receives a large gain. At high frequencies, this large output may feed back through parasitic capacitance, reinforcing itself at the input. High-frequency noise and possible oscillations plague the circuit of Figure 5–17.

This can be solved by adding a series resistor R_i, as shown in Figure 5–18. Resistor R_i, together with C_D, form a low-pass filter at the input. This simple solution to the high-frequency problem increases the complexity of analyzing the circuit. Laplace transforms must be applied from the beginning.

$$\frac{V_{\text{out}}}{V_{\text{in}}} = -\frac{Z_f}{Z_i}$$

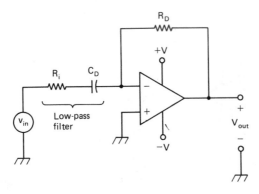

Figure 5–18   Practical differentiator.

where

$$Z_f = R_f$$

$$Z_i = R_i + \frac{1}{C_D s}$$

$$\frac{V_{out}}{V_{in}} = -\frac{R_f}{R_i + 1/Cs}$$

or

$$\frac{V_{out}}{V_{in}} = -\frac{R_f Cs}{R_i Cs + 1}$$

Letting $R_f C = K_D$ and $R_i C = \tau_i$ gives us

$$\frac{V_{out}}{V_{in}} = -\frac{K_D s}{\tau_i s + 1} \tag{5–23}$$

The response of this practical differentiation to the input shown in Figure 5–16 is given in Figure 5–19.

The second major precaution you should observe is that the derivative controller produces an output only for *changes* in error. A system with large *constant* error will have no output from a derivative controller. Derivative controllers must always be used in combination with another type of controller.

Derivative controllers respond to *changes* in error, to overcome process inertia. High-frequency compensate this controller and always use it in combination with other controllers.

5–5.2 Parallel Three-Mode (PID) Controller

Combining the proportional, integral, and derivative controllers produces the three-mode controller. It offers rapid proportional response to error, while having an automatic reset from the integral part to eliminate residual error. The derivative section stabilizes

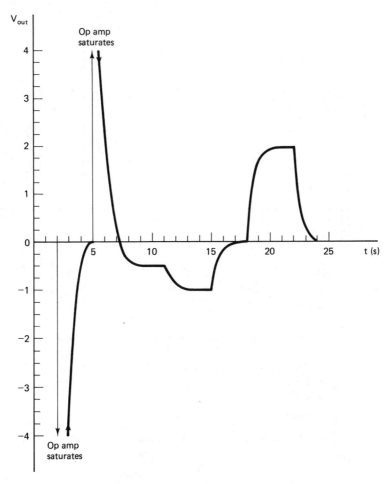

Figure 5–19   Practical differentiator's response.

the controller and allows it to respond rapidly to changes in error. Their individual and combined effects are shown in Figure 5–20.

The schematic for a parallel three-mode (PID) controller is shown in Figure 5–21. As with the integral and proportional integral controllers, you may need to add a large resistor around C_i to compensate for bias currents or use a very low bias current op amp. The derivative limiting resistor R_3 should be kept as small as possible and still assure stability. This will simplify the differentiator's response.

Assuming that the effects of these two "nonideal" resistors are negligible in comparison to the effects caused by the error voltage,

$$v_{out} = K_P v_{error} + K_I \int v_{error} \, dt + K_D \frac{dv_{error}}{dt} + V_0 \qquad (5\text{–}24)$$

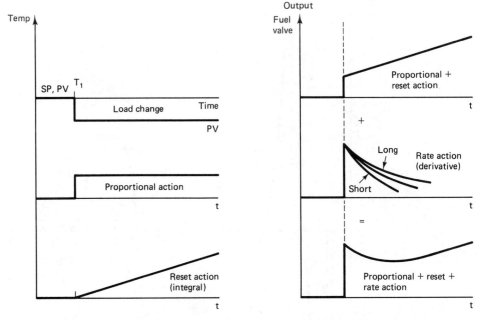

Figure 5–20   PID combined actions. (Courtesy of Texas Instruments Incorporated.)

where $K_P = R_2/R_1$, proportional band (gain)
$\quad K_I = 1/R_iC_i$, integration constant
$\quad K_D = R_DC_D$, derivative constant
$\quad V_o =$ offset integrator initial charge

To get the transfer function, you take the Laplace transform of equation 5–24. That gives

$$V_{\text{out}} = K_P V_{\text{error}} + \frac{K_I V_{\text{error}}}{s} + K_D s V_{\text{error}}$$

$$\frac{V_{\text{out}}}{V_{\text{error}}} = K_P + \frac{K_I}{s} + K_D s$$

$$= \frac{K_D s^2 + K_P s + K_I}{s}$$

or

$$\frac{V_{\text{out}}}{V_{\text{error}}} = K_D \frac{s^2 + (K_P/K_D)s + K_I/K_D}{s} \tag{5–25}$$

This is called the parallel implementation of the three-mode controller. That should be apparent from looking at Figure 5–21. Each term is formed in parallel and then recombined in the summer.

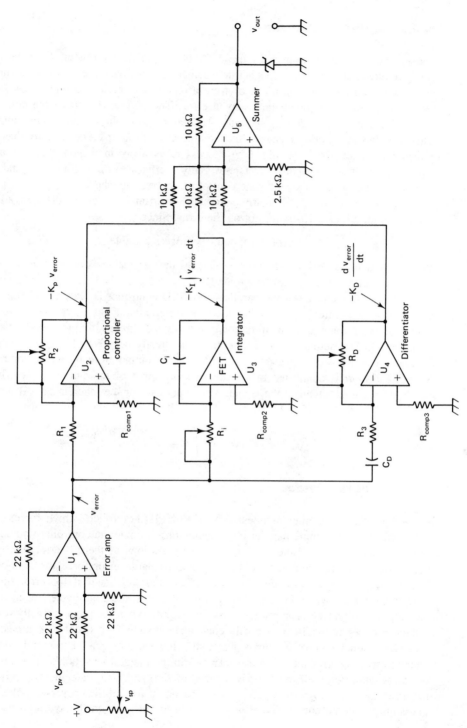

Figure 5–21 Three-mode controller (parallel implementation).

5–5.3 Derivative Overrun

The parallel implementation of Figure 5–21 has a practical problem. Changes in set point are often made in steps. This is true whether you command the controller manually, in cascade with another controller, or from a remote supervisory computer. A step in set point causes a complementary step in error. The derivative part of the controller, responding to the *rate of change*, saturates. This saturates the output (through the summer). This step in set point has caused the controller to lock up. The actuator has been forced wide open (or hard off). The process races away in response to this excess input energy. It will probably overshoot badly, perhaps even ringing back and forth several time before good steady-state control can be reestablished.

The solution to this derivative produced overrun is to allow the derivative to operate on the *process variable*, not on the error. Since

$$\text{error} = \text{set point} - \text{process variable}$$

step changes in set point will not be seen by the derivative controller, and lock-up induced by set-point steps will be avoided.

Making this change in the parallel-mode PID controller is reasonably straightforward. Look at Figure 5–22. The input to the differentiator has been moved from the output of the error amplifier. It is connected instead directly to the process variable signal (v_{PV}). The output of the differentiator is already negative. To provide negative feedback to the process, this must be *added* to the output from the other controllers. So $-K_D \, dv_{PV}/dt$ is connected to the noninverting input of the summer, U_5. The 10- and 5-kΩ resistors attenuate the signal, to compensate for the inherent gain (caused by $R_f = 10 \text{ k}\Omega$ and $R_i = 10 \text{ k}\Omega \parallel 10 \text{ k}\Omega$). The resulting time-domain equation is

$$v_{\text{out}} = K_P v_{\text{error}} + K_I \int v_{\text{error}} \, dt - K_D \frac{dv_{PV}}{dt} \qquad (5\text{–}26)$$

5–5.4 Integral Windup

Integral windup is another nonideal property of PID controllers which forces you to add circuitry to the simple parallel implementation. The integral controller will continue to change its output until the *error* goes to zero. As long as there is error, the voltage out of the integrator continues to build. Should a large error force the controller to saturation, the integral will charge up rapidly, saturating itself if the error does not quickly disappear. When the integral controller saturates, there are two elements holding the output hard on, the proportional and the integral. When the process finally responds and the error begins to fall, you want the controller output to begin to cut back immediately. The proportional controller allows just that. However, to get the integral controller output down, the error must reverse polarity. So the integral term holds the controller's output at saturation until the error is reduced to zero and then undershoots. Only when the error has fallen to zero (where you want to hold it) and then reversed polarity can the controller come out of saturation and begin to cut back on the system's input. So

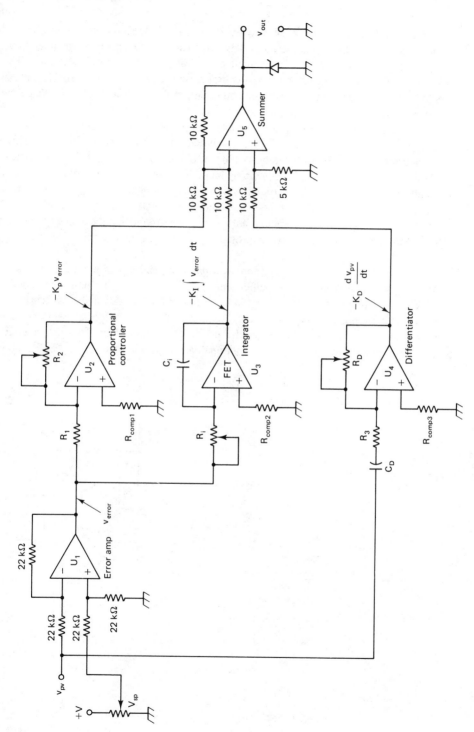

Figure 5–22 Parallel PID controller with derivative correction.

integral windup forces the system to overshoot. Often the process variable rings back
and forth several times before control is fully established and performance stabilizes.

Integral windup can be prevented by monitoring the controller output. When it
reaches 100%, the input error to the integral controller is forced to zero. The integrator
holds its charge until the overall controller output falls below 100%. At that time the
integrator is released, to continue its response.

This method for preventing integral windup may be implemented using the circuit
in Figure 5–23. A comparator U_6 and a switch have been added. The switch may be
either a relay or an analog switch. When the output is below $v_{out(max)}$, the comparator
outputs a high. This keeps the switch open. The integrator functions as it normally
would. However, when the output reaches or just exceeds $V_{out(max)}$, the comparator's
output goes low. This closes the switch placing ground potential at the left end of R_b.
Since the right end of R_b is being held at virtual ground by the op amp, no current
flows through R_b. With no current through R_b, there can be no charge (or discharge) of
C_i. The integrator has been halted.

Resistor R_i has been divided into two parts, R_a and R_b. In practice, this is usually
done anyway since running the potentiometer all the way down would excessively load
the error amplifier. Resistor R_a should be a few kilohms. When the switch is closed,
to stop integration, resistor R_a prevents loading of the error amplifier. This protects the
error signal, which must also go to the proportional controller. This also reduces the
effect of the nonzero on resistance of an analog switch's contacts.

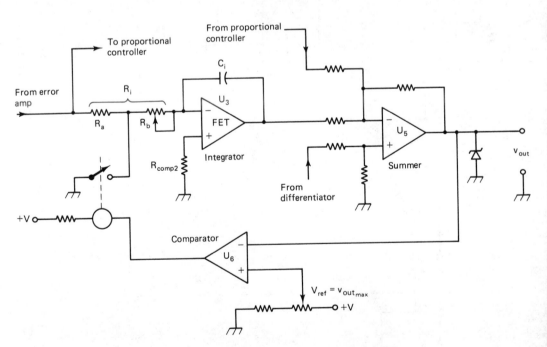

Figure 5–23   Integral windup prevention circuitry.

The exact configuration of the comparator, switch, power, and resistor will depend on precisely which components you use.

5–5.5 Bumpless Auto/Manual Transfer

From time to time it becomes necessary (or at least desirable) to be able to set the controller's output manually. So accommodations for a manual output must be made on any of the PID controllers you have seen.

Having a front-panel control that will directly set the controller output is reasonably simple. However, a problem arises when it is time to transfer from auto to manual, or from manual to auto. If the manual and automatic controllers are not outputting precisely the same voltage when the transfer is made, a step, or bump, will occur. In the worst case, this step may be 100% of the output. Such a bump will cause serious transients when applied through the final actuator to the process.

Bumpless transfer between manual and automatic control prevents these transients. Figure 5–24 is a simplified block diagram showing how bumpless transfer can be accomplished. A manual controller is added to the automatic PID controllers that you have already seen. The desired output is selected with a switch. When in the automatic mode, the manual controller's output is forced to track the output from the automatic controller. Conversely, when in the manual mode, the output of the automatic controller is driven to the value of this manual controller's output. So at the moment before transfer, either way, both controllers have the same output.

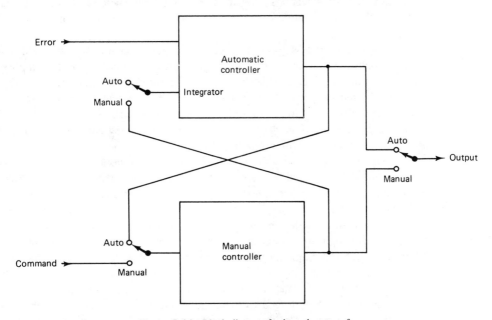

Figure 5–24   Block diagram for bumpless transfer.

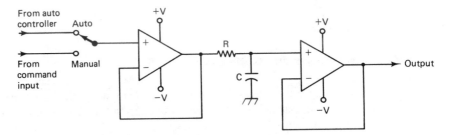

Figure 5-25   Manual controller.

A manual controller is shown in Figure 5–25. The voltage followers at the input and output are to prevent loading. The *RC* time constant is short compared to the integration time of the automatic controller. In the manual mode the capacitor will charge and discharge, following the voltage from the manual control, with a lag on the order of a second or so. This prevents the operator from applying steps to the system by stepping the command input. A step change on the command signal will cause the capacitor to charge exponentially to the new level.

A similar effect is obtained when the switch is made from automatic to manual. While in the automatic mode, the manual controller has been receiving its input from the output of the automatic controller. The voltage on the capacitor has been charged to equal the automatic controller's output. When the switch is made to manual, the manual output is held by the capacitor at the value from the automatic controller. A bumpless transfer has been accomplished. With the input switch in manual, the capacitor beings to charge *exponentially* to the new output, as dictated by the command input signal.

To assure bumpless transfer from manual to automatic, a few modifications of the PID controller are necessary. These are shown in Figure 5–26. To simplify things a bit, the error amplifier and the output summer have been shown as summer circles. The proportional and derivative controllers have been simplified to squares, with the appropriate transfer function inside each. The automatic input to the integrator is through R_i. However, a manual input has been added to the integrator, through R_m. This is driven from a high-gain differential amplifier, U_7.

In the automatic mode, the circuit in Figure 5–26 works as it normally did. The manual controller is forced to track the output of this automatic controller. Since these two outputs are equal, when transfer is made from automatic to manual, there will be no bump.

In the manual mode, the integrator is fed through a small R_m (as compared to R_i). So even though integration occurs as the output ramps from one point to another, it happens much more quickly when the integrator is driven through R_m than when it is in the automatic mode.

At the instant of transfer from automatic to manual, the output of U_7 is zero. The manual control was forced to track the automatic controller. Now, in the manual mode, the automatic controller must be forced to track the output from the manual

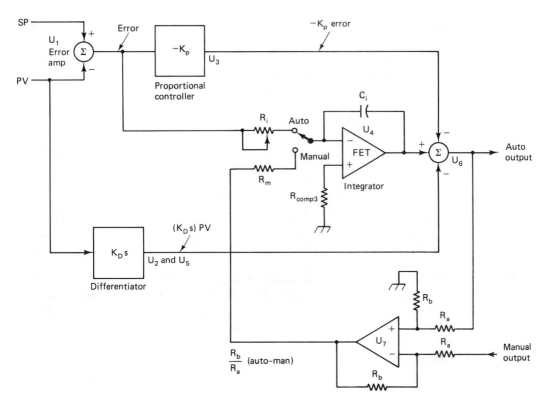

Figure 5–26   PID controller with bumpless transfer.

controller. That is the purpose of U_7. Any difference between the automatic and the manual outputs is amplified and fed to the integrator. The integrator ramps up or down until the auto output equals the manual. This causes a zero input into the integrator. This integrator then holds that voltage. The gain of U_7 must be set high enough to overrule the signals from the proportional and derivative controllers.

The transfer from manual to automatic is bumpless because the output of the auto controller has been forced to equal the manual controller's output. Following the transfer back to automatic control the integrator begins to ramp to the new level dictated by the error signal. Now it is time for the manual controller to track the automatic.

5–6 CASCADED AND FEEDFORWARD CONTROL

You have seen progressively more and more sophisticated control schemes. In Section 5–5 derivative was added to PI to overcome inertia. Circuits to prevent integral windup and to provide bumpless transfer were devised.

But even with all of these techniques, the degree of control may be inadequate.

Two additional controller configurations are available. Either may improve the tightness of your control even further. Cascaded control uses two controllers, one driving the other. Simpler, faster, more precise control may result. Feedforward control anticipates a change in the process variable by sensing changes as they *enter* the process. Long lags and the resulting slow response can be reduced significantly.

5–6.1 Cascaded Control

A general block diagram of a system using cascaded control is shown in Figure 5–27. The overall process you are controlling must be dividible, with some intermediate result available. A secondary controller is placed around this inner, or secondary, loop. The system process variable and system set point drive the primary controller just as they did in the simpler control scheme. However, the output of the primary controller establishes the set point for the secondary controller. The intermediate process result is the process variable for the secondary controller. The output from this controller is used to manipulate the input to the system.

Standard proportional, proportional–integral, or PID controllers may be used for both the primary and secondary controllers. The secondary controller must have a remote set-point capability. That is, instead of determining the set point from a setting on the front panel, the secondary controller must be able to obtain its set point from an externally applied signal.

One advantage of cascaded control is that it may remove the need for an integral term in either controller. That is, a process which required a proportional–integral controller, when controlled by a single controller, may provide much better performance when controlled by two simpler proportional controllers in cascade. In addition, the proportional

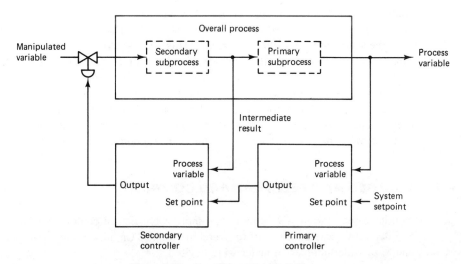

Figure 5–27   Cascaded control block diagram.

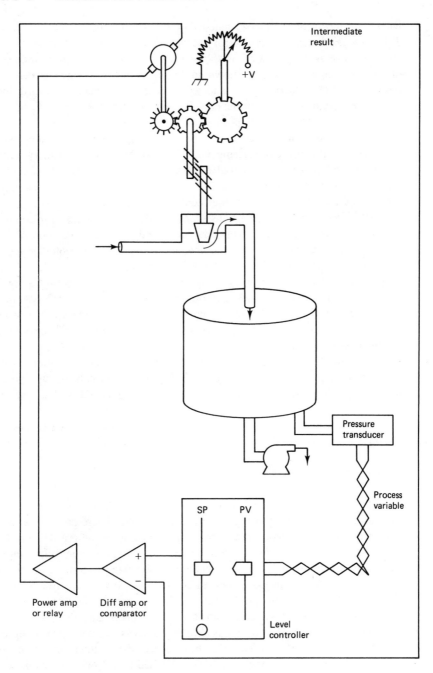

Figure 5–28   Valve position–tank level cascaded control.

band of each controller may be tightened (gain raised) when the integral term is removed. This provides faster, tighter control without the tendency to overshoot.

A valve positioner used as the actuator in a level control system is an example of cascaded control. This is shown in Figure 5–28. The valve is driven in and out through a set of reduction gears and worm gears by a small dc electric motor. Slaved to this gear train is a potentiometer. The voltage from the wiper of the potentiometer is an indication of the valve's position. This is the intermediate result.

The pressure at the bottom of the tank is an indication of the level within the tank. This is the process variable and is transmitted to the primary controller. In a simple control scheme, the output of this level controller would go directly to move the valve. However, in this cascaded arrangement the output of the level controller (primary) drives the set point of the secondary controller.

The secondary controller consists of a difference amplifier (or comparator) and a power amplifier. The level controller output is the desired valve position. This is compared to the actual valve position (the intermediate result) and the motor driven to move the valve until its actual position matches the desired position.

Using cascaded control with this valve positioner can significantly improve the performance of the valve, and therefore of the entire level control system. The effects of nonlinearity, drift, and hysteresis within the valve are reduced. The tendency of the valve to creep open further with increases in fluid pressure, or changes in temperature, is compensated for.

For simple, stable operation the secondary or inner loop should respond much faster than the primary loop. In Figure 5–28 proper level behavior is easier to establish if the valve moves quickly to any new position commanded by the level controller. If the valve positioner responds slowly (as compared to the level), the level may change radically while the valve is trying to move to and settle into a new position. System response mathematics is much more complicated, but absolutely necessary.

5–6.2 Feedforward Control

Even the most sophisticated PID controller, properly tuned and used in cascade, will have a difficult time controlling some processes well. There are several reasons. First, since feedback controllers correct error, there must be some error before the controller begins to change its output. To get a significant change in controller output requires a significant error. Second, for slow processes, the integral term in the controller must be made long, and the proportional "gain" set low. Any change in load will be delayed quite a bit before it begins producing error in the process variable. The controller, also responding very slowly, will compound the problem, taking a long time to effect correction once the error is sensed. All of this time the process has been producing an erroneous product. Finally, load transients that have a period less than three times the resonant period of the system will prevent a PID-controlled loop from ever stabilizing.

These problems can be eliminated, or at least severely reduced, by the proper use of *feedforward* control. "The principal factors affecting the process are measured

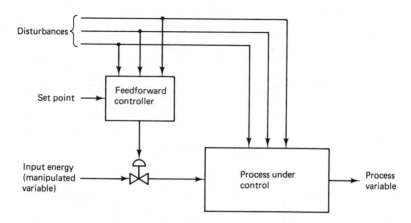

Figure 5-29   Feedforward control block diagram.

and, along with the set point, are used in computing the correct output to most current conditions. Whenever a disturbance occurs, corrective action starts immediately, to cancel the disturbance before it affects the controlled variable'' [1]. A block diagram illustrating feedforward control is shown in Figure 5-29. In a pure feedforward control system, only the loads and disturbances going *into* the system are measured. These are used to calculate the proper signal to the final actuator. If all variables are taken into consideration and measured accurately, and if the feedforward equation is correct and performed accurately by the controller, the process variable will track the set point. There will be no output error.

The equations that relate disturbances and set point to system output and required controller output are often referred to as the system model. This mathematical model must account for the transient behavior of the system as well as its steady-state response. Sophisticated models for highly interactive systems require a great deal of computing power. At least a microprocessor, and often a minicomputer, is required as the feedforward controller.

In simpler loops, analog control modules may be used. Multipliers, dividers, summers, integrators, differentiators, squarers, and root extractors are all available as analog circuits. To some degree you will not be able to account completely for the transient and steady-state effects of all sources of disturbances on your process. This is especially true if individual analog computational modules are used. To tweak out this small remaining error in the process variable, traditional negative feedback is usually added to analog feedforward control systems. It may take the form of cascaded control.

A level control system using only feedback control is shown in Figure 5-30a. This tank is used to mix material *A*, which makes up the majority of the volume, with material *B*. The outlet is fed for further processing by the pump under external command. The level in the tank is sensed and sent to the controller by the level transmitter (LT). The level indicator and controller (LIC) manipulates the main fill valve for material *A*.

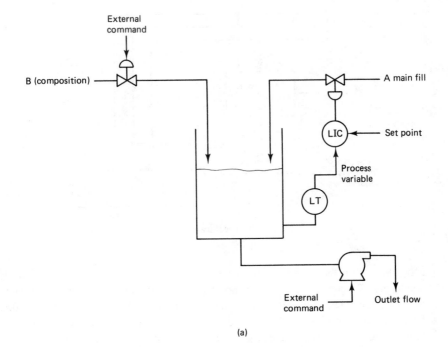

(a)

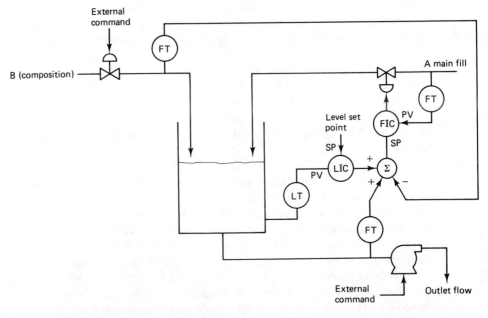

(b)

Figure 5–30   Level control (a) without and (b) with feedforward control.

The material balance equation for this process is

$$\frac{dl}{dt} = k_A q_A + k_B q_B - k_c q_{out} \tag{5-27}$$

where $\qquad\qquad l$ = level

q_a, q_B, q_{out} = flow at A, B, and out

k_A, k_B, k_C = scaling factors

Equation 5–27 states that the rate of change of the level in the tank (i.e., the volume) depends on the flow into and out of the tank.

Since the purpose of the control system is to provide a *steady* level, set

$$\frac{dl}{dt} = 0$$

The main flow, q_A, then becomes

$$k_A q_A = k_C q_{out} - k_B q_B$$

or

$$q_A = \frac{k_C}{k_A} q_{out} - \frac{k_B}{k_A} q_B \tag{5-28}$$

Equation 5–28 points the way for implementing a feedforward control of level. Look at Figure 5–30b. By controlling the main flow, q_A, according to equation (5–28), there will be no change in level. So the flow at B (q_B) and the outlet flow (q_{out}) are measured and sent to a summer. In the summer they are properly scaled and combined. The output of the summer is q_A (equation 5–30). This signal, then, is used as the remote set point for a flow controller (FIC). The actual main flow must be measured and sent to the flow controller as the process variable.

To compensate for errors in the feedforward control and to provide operator adjustment of level, a *feedback* loop must be added. The level transmitter senses the level in the tank and sends that information to a level controller (LIC). The operator may direct the tank level through the set-point input to the level controller. The output of this controller is added into equation 5–28 by the summer to affect the main flow's set point.

Should the tank level rise because of errors in the feedforward calculation, the PV into the LIC goes up. This causes a drop in the output of the LIC, which lowers the output of the summer. The output of the summer is the set point to the main flow control. So q_A is lowered, and the level in the tank falls.

The operator can raise the tank level by driving the level set point up. This raises the output of the LIC and the output of the summer, commanding a higher main flow.

Timing the measurement of the disturbances and the calculated response is important. This is especially true for those systems that exhibit transportation delays. You want to time and scale the correction signal so that it will just cancel the effect the disturbance would have on the output. If the feedforward signal corrects the output too late, the output will sag, since the disturbance arrived first without any offsetting correction. Conversely, if you let the feedforward affect the output too soon, the process will rise (or preshoot), since the process is being driven up in anticipation of a disturbance produced sag which has not yet arrived.

If you are using a computer to produce the feedforward control, adding delay is straightforward. Delays in analog loops are more difficult. Cascading several first-order elements will result in a delay. Such modules are called dynamic compensators or lead-lag modules [2, p. 195].

"Feedforward control reduces the open loop error seen by the feedback loop to the accuracy of the feedforward compensation. If the feedforward compensation accuracy is 10%, the open loop error, and consequently the peak and accumulated errors are reduced by a factor of 10. The accuracy of the feedforward signal depends on the accuracy of the disturbance measurement, the accuracy of the equation that relates the disturbance to the controlled variable, and the accuracy of the arithmetic and dynamic computations" [2, p. 198].

SUMMARY

The controller's purpose is to provide a signal that will cause the process to drive its output (called the process variable) to be equal with the set point. Any change in set point or any disturbances to the process should cause a change in the controller's output, to assure that the process variable tracks the set point.

All controllers begin by generating the error signal

$$E = SP - PV \qquad (5-1)$$

The error signal indicates how far off the process variable is. The controller's purpose is to force this error signal to zero. The error signal may be produced with a difference amplifier, or with a summer. If you use a summer, the process should produce the negative of the process variable. Or $-SP$ could be added to $+PV$, and the error inverted (using an inverting summer).

The simplest control turns the actuator full on or full off. This can be accomplished with a simple op amp comparator. However, unless the process has significant inertia (or energy storage), rapid cycling will occur. This could damage the actuator or process. The introduction of a deadband (hysteresis), by adding positive feedback to the amplifier, reduces this cycling. However, the process variable is now allowed to drift between the comparator's trip points before any control action is taken.

Inverse-acting controllers drive their output down (or off) when the process variable rises. This is typical of heating systems. Direct-acting controllers output a signal that moves in the same direction as the process variable, turning the process harder on as the process variable goes up. Refrigeration systems use direct-acting controllers.

To provide better control than the on/off controller is capable of, the proportional controller outputs a signal that varies linearly with error over some range of error. Small changes of error, about zero, cause *proportional* changes in the controller's output.

The proportional controller may be built with an inverting summer. The error is one input to the summer. The gain given to this error signal sets the proportional band or the proportional gain. An offset is also applied to the summer to allow zero error to cause some nonzero controller output.

A proportional controller will always have some residual error if the actuator must be driven to some position other than that set with the summer's offset input. This error can be reduced by increasing the gain given to the error signal. However, this narrows the proportional band, which leads to oscillations or cycling.

An integral controller changes its output at a *rate* proportional to the error. Large error causes the output to *change* quickly. The output will continue to change until the error is zero. Zero error causes the integral controller to hold its present output (i.e., zero error leads to zero *change* in the output). An integral controller can be built by using a capacitor to provide negative feedback around an op amp. Be sure to use a FET or CMOS op amp to prevent bias currents from charging the capacitor. Also, a film capacitor is recommended to prevent self-discharge (leakage).

Integral controller's alone are too slow to provide adequate control. However, good control may be achieved by combining a proportional with an integral controller. The proportional part of the controller allows rapid changes in the output in response to rapid changes in error. The integral controller replaces the offset of the simple proportional controller. It ramps up and down, tweaking out the residual error the proportional controller cannot remove. This allows you to lower the proportional gain, reducing the tendency to oscillate.

A large response to rapid changes in error requires a derivative controller. Its output is proportional to the rate of change of error. The more *quickly* the error changes, the larger the controller's output. This type of response is achieved by reversing the capacitor and resistor in the op amp integral controller. An op amp derivative controller has an input capacitor and a feedback resistor. However, a series input resistor is also necessary to limit noise.

The derivative controller will produce a zero output for steady-state error, no matter how large. So derivative controllers are seldom used alone. Instead, they are combined with proportional–integral controllers to form the PID or three-mode controller. This is the standard, commercially available controller. Step changes in the set point causes the derivative element to drive the overall controller into saturation. To prevent this, the derivative controller usually operates on the process variable only, rather than on the error.

Integral windup occurs whenever there is a large error and a slowly responding system. This is typical at the startup of a process, when the process variable must be raised from zero. The integrator continues to ramp up until it saturates. This forces the overall controller into saturation. To cause the controller output to drop, the error must go negative. That requires that the process variable be driven past the set point before the controller can even *begin* to lower its output. Integral windup is prevented by turning the integral element off whenever the overall controller output goes to 100%.

Bumpless transfer between automatic and manual operation is necessary to prevent large transients in the process. This is accomplished by forcing the manual controller to track the automatic controller during automatic operation, and vice versa. The manual controller is designed to ramp from one setting to another. This is necessary to smooth out the automatic-to-manual bump and to eliminate operator-induced steps. The automatic controller's integral time constant is radically shortened and an additional feedback loop added during the manual control mode. This assures that the PID controller output will track the manual controller.

Cascaded control uses two controllers. The primary controller drives the set point of the secondary. An intermediate process variable is necessary as the PV input to the secondary controller. Cascaded control often results in faster, more precise performance than with single PID control. In addition, simple proportional, rather than PI or PID, may be used.

Feedforward control measures all disturbances *entering* the process. Their anticipated effect is calculated and the process's input manipulated in order to eliminate any variation in the process variable. Perfect control is limited only by the quality of the measurement and the math. To remove any resulting errors, a *feedback* loop may be cascaded with the feedforward control.

REFERENCES

1. F. G. Shinsky, *Process Control Systems*. New York: McGraw-Hill Book Company, 1979, pp. 166–167.
2. G. K. McMillan, *Tuning and Control Loop Performance*. Research Triangle Park, N.C.: Instrument Society of America, 1983.

PROBLEMS

5–1. Design two different error amplifiers which have an input impedance of 100 kΩ or greater. Specify all component values.

5–2. Design a temperature controller system that
   (a) provides a process variable from 30 to 200°F with a sensitivity of 50 mV/°F.
   (b) provides on/off control.
   (c) sets the deadband to ±5°F.
   (d) provides an adjustable set point from 50 to 150°F.
   (e) provide a switch-selectable direct or inverse operation.

5–3. Draw the transfer curve of a proportional controller and calculate the slope for the following conditions.
   (a) 80% proportional band, 50% output with zero error.
   (b) 25% proportional band, 70% output with zero error.

5–4. For the proportional controller in Figure 5–7, with $V_{SP} = 7.5$ V, $V_{os} = 7.5$ V, $R_f = R_{os} = 100$ kΩ, $R_i = 47$ kΩ, $V_z = 6$ V, ±15 V, calculate the output voltage with
   (a) $V_{PV} = 7.5$ V.
   (b) $V_{PV} = 6.0$ V.

   (c) $V_{PV} = 12$ V.

   (d) $V_{PV} = 3$ V.

5–5. The temperature controller of Problem 5–2 should be replaced with a proportional controller. Set the proportional band to 30% and the full-scale output at 10 V; maximum error is $\pm 10°$, and zero error causes 60% output.

   (a) Convert these specifications to those of Example 5–4.

   (b) Design the controller, specifying all component values.

   (c) Provide switch-selectable direct- or inverse-acting control.

   (d) Draw the transfer curve of the circuit designed with direct action.

5–6. The circuit in Figure 5–31 is a proportional controller. Determine the following.

   (a) Transfer curve.

   (b) Proportional band.

   (c) Controller output equation.

   (d) Controller output with zero error.

   (e) Which components set the (1) set point, (2) proportional band, (3) offset, and (4) output limit?

   (f) How is the error calculated?

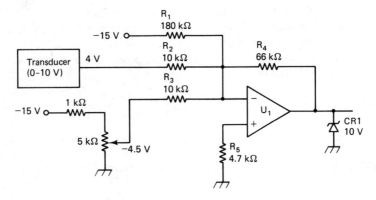

Figure 5–31   Schematic (Problem 5–6).

5–7. Draw the schematic and calculate all component values for an integral controller whose transfer function is

$$\frac{V_{out}}{V_{error}} = \frac{1}{0.3s}$$

5–8. (a) Draw the output from the integral controller of Problem 5–7 whose input is shown in Figure 5–32.

   (b) Redraw the output if K_I doubles.

5–9. Draw the schematic of a parallel PI controller and calculate all component values necessary to satisfy the transfer function

$$\frac{V_{out}}{V_{error}} = \frac{1.5s + 0.2}{0.5s}$$

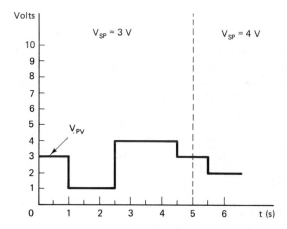

Figure 5–32 Input (Problem 5–8).

5–10. Repeat Problem 5–9 for a series PI controller.

5–11. Determine the response of the circuit in Figure 5–12 to the input given in Figure 5–32 for $R_1 = 10$ kΩ, $R_2 = 15$ kΩ, $R_i = 100$ kΩ, $C_i = 20$ μF.

5–12. Repeat Problem 5–11 for the series PI controller in Figure 5–13. Use the same input and the same component values.

5–13. Draw the schematic and calculate all component values for a derivative controller with a transfer function of

$$\frac{V_{out}}{V_{error}} = \frac{0.8s}{0.1s + 1}$$

5–14. Draw the output from the controller in Problem 5–13 in response to the input shown in Figure 5–32.

5–15. Draw the schematic of a simple parallel PID controller and calculate all component values to meet the transfer function

$$\frac{V_{out}}{V_{error}} = \frac{12s^2 + 7s + 2}{s}$$

5–16. Repeat Problem 5–15 for a parallel PID controller that has been modified to prevent derivative lockup.

5–17. Repeat Problem 5–16, adding the integral windup prevention circuitry. Select a LM311 comparator for U_6 and a specific analog switch instead of the relay. Specify all components, values, and pins.

5–18. Determine the response of the circuit you designed in Problem 5–17 to the input specified in Figure 5–32. However, multiply the horizontal axis by 20. The steps occur at 20, 50, 90, and 110 s.

5–19. A cascaded position control system consists of a motor driving a pulley system. Attached to the motor's shaft are both a potentiometer and a generator. The primary loop is position and the secondary is velocity.
(a) Draw a diagram (see Chapter 1) illustrating how the cascaded control is configured.
(b) Explain, in detail, how this system responds to an increase in set point.

5–20. The cascaded position controller of Problem 5–19 can be implemented using a single quadrature encoder for the sensor(s) and a microprocessor for the controller(s). Explain how both the position and velocity feedback signals are obtained from this single sensor.

5–21. The feedforward control scheme in Figure 5–30 and described by equation 5–27 has the following calibration:

Main fill q_A: 8.4 liters/min = 100% from transmitter

Composition fill q_B: 2.6 liters/min = 100% from transmitter

Outlet flow q_{out}: 15 liters/min = 100% from transmitter

Level: 100 liters = 100% from transmitter

Level controller: proportional $k_p = 3$

    (a) Calculate the scaling constants k_A, k_B, and k_C.

    (b) Assuming 40% level, 40% level set point, 30% composition flow, and 10% outlet flow, calculate the proper main fill flow (q_A).

    (c) Repeat part (b) assuming that the outlet flow changes to 18%.

5–22. The rate at which material is delivered by a conveyor belt depends on the rate that it is dumped on the belt from a hopper, and the speed of the belt. Control is accomplished by varying the speed of the belt. However, the more material there is on the belt, the slower it tends to move.

    (a) Draw a diagram of the conveyor or system with the following: (1) A load cell to measure the amount of material being dropped onto the belt from the hopper. (2) Feedforward control of belt speed based on this weight in signal. (3) A speed sensor. (4) Cascaded feedback of the speed signal to the motor driver. (5) An operator "material out" set-point signal.

    (b) Explain the operation of your system. (1) under steady state, (2) in response to an increase in material in, (3) in response to a decrease in the "material out" set point.

    (c) Explain how you would account for a 3-min transportation dead time between weigh-in and material delivery.

6

Digital Control

The analog controllers you saw in Chapter 5 are adequate for many applications. They provide simple, inexpensive control for loops that do not require high accuracy, flexibility of adjustment, reconfiguration, computation, or dead-time compensation. However, they have many limitations. Analog components that will yield high accuracy at very low drift are expensive. Adjustment of the more sophisticated PID controller is complicated, with tuning constants being highly interdependent. Changing from one controller type to another means that you must replace, and perhaps rewire, the electronics. Computations and delays for feedforward control and for dead-time compensation are difficult, imprecise, clumsy, and expensive with analog electronics—if the computational circuit you need is even available.

Digital control can solve all of these problems inexpensively, while opening up the new field of flexible manufacturing. The introduction of the microprocessor and its successor, the single-chip microcomputer, has allowed wide distribution of intelligence throughout a manufacturing process. You may see a single-chip microcomputer measuring the process variable while performing auto-zero and auto-calibration. A second may be scaling and logging those data while driving a front-panel display. A third could be used for the cascaded controller to position a motor-driven valve using pulse-width modulation or brushless dc servomotor wave synthesis. Each of these ICs costs only a few dollars (or less). All three microcomputers may present data to and receive commands from an 8-bit microprocessor which performs the loop's control algorithm. This processor, along with many others, may communicate to a host 16-bit personal computer. It provides system supervision, directs reconfiguration, provides reports, and allows statistical process control.

During this chapter you will look at three major facets of digital process control.

The first is the data acquisition circuitry. Control can be no better than the data provided to the controlling computer. How those data are converted from analog form and back, and the resolution and speed of that conversion, are critical. An otherwise elegant control scheme may be doomed from the beginning by quanitization errors and aliasing.

Once the data are converted (reliably) into digital, the single-loop digital controller may take over. Its job is to calculate the correct output value. This is done based on present, past, and anticipated errors.

Programmable logic controllers (PLCs) are the topic for the final section of this chapter. An overview of their hardware is presented. Ladder logic is a symbolic programming language used by most PLCs. It is illustrated performing on/off control. A dedicated PLC PID module closes out this chapter.

OBJECTIVES

After studying this chapter you should be able to do the following:

1. Draw the block diagram of a D/A converter.
2. Illustrate the use of D/A converters with a current output, a voltage output, an internal reference, and an external reference.
3. Explain the operation and relative advantages of successive approximation and dual-slope integration analog-to-digital converters.
4. Show how to connect an A/D converter for adjustable zero and span, as well as interfacing to the microcomputer.
5. Calculate the effects of resolution, quanitization error, conversion speed, and sampling rate.
6. List three advantages of digital control over analog control.
7. Describe the three types of digital control. Give the relative advantages and disadvantages of each as compared to the other two types.
8. Draw the block diagram of a single-loop microcomputer-based controller, describing the purpose of each block.
9. Draw the software flowchart of a single-loop microcomputer-based controller, describing the purpose of each block.
10. Discuss microprocessor math precautions, limitations, and techniques used in a single-loop microcomputer-based controller.
11. Explain when an optimum control transfer function is appropriate, how it can be obtained, and its limitations.
12. Derive the output equation for a PID algorithm.
13. Illustrate the derivative problem of a PID digital algorithm.
14. Explain the following output drive techniques:
    a. On/off
    b. Time proportioning

    c. Analog

    d. Phase-angle firing

    e. Pulse-width modulation

15. Describe manual mode, directed self-tuning, and continuous self-tuning of a micro-computer-based single-loop controller.

16. Define the programmable controller.

17. Compare the programmable controller to a standard minicomputer in terms of:

    a. Architecture

    b. Hardware survivability

    c. Software operating system

    d. Language

    e. Math and data handling ability

    In each case, illustrate how the PLC has been optimized for the manufacturing environment.

18. Illustrate relay ladder logic. Use it to solve a given problem, and analyze a given relay ladder diagram.

19. Discuss the variety of I/O modules available for PLCs. Explain how they are different from personal computer interfaces.

20. Explain how the PLC handles programming complex I/O, math, data manipulation, timing and counting, communications, and PID functions.

6–1 DATA ACQUISITION*

"The availability of low-cost computational power (in the form of the microprocessor) has created a wide variety of applications for that power. Since many of these applications involve interfacing of 'real world' analog signals to the digital processor, low-cost IC data converters have become available."

    Section 6–1.1 "deals with D/A converters. The basic function is examined, elementary designs are analyzed, and the strengths of various technologies applied to D/A manufacture are discussed. We will discuss the specifications which apply to D/A converters and how they may be interpreted to determine whether a particular converter is suitable for a particular application. We will also develop selection criteria for D/A converters so the best device for the application can be chosen." Two examples will be presented: a very simple, inexpensive converter that outputs current and requires an external reference; and a higher-resolution, self-contained, microprocessor-interfaced converter.

    Section 6–1.2 "is a discussion of analog-to-digital converters, examining first the relative specifications. . . . Next the different types of IC converters available are examined, with respect to the applications for which they are best suited. The details of interfacing an A/D to a microprocessor are also discussed." Again two specific

---

* The quoted material in Section 6.1 is from Ref. 1 except where noted otherwise.

examples are given. One is an inexpensive 8-bit, successive-approximation A/D with simple zero and span adjustments. The second is a high-resolution, integrating A/D with both parallel and serial communications.

Section 6–1.3 "is a discussion of the practical considerations in using A/D converters and D/A converters. Details of proper power and ground distribution as well as decoupling will also be covered." Resolution, quanitization error, conversion speed, and sampling rate are presented.

6–1.1 Digital-to-Analog Conversion

A digital-to-analog converter "converts digital code to an analog parameter by switching successive-ratio analog bit-weights to a common summing point. The concept of the binary weighting of switched analog levels is illustrated" in Figure 6–1. "The operational amplifier is connected in the inverting 'summing' mode, in which it adds the currents in the binary sequence, $V_{ref}/2R$, $V_{ref}/4R$, etc. The switches shown are simply single-pole, single-throw devices which can connect the desired resistors or 'bits' to the summing node as called for by the digital code."

The diagram in Figure 6–2 "shows the various components that make up a D/A converter. Not all of them are necessarily included in every device available on the market. However, the parts shown inside the dashed-line box are the minimum components needed. Digital switch control is necessary to convert standard logic levels (TTL, CMOS, etc.) to an analog switch-drive level. A reference amplifier is needed in many cases to properly relate the bit weights of the analog switches to an external reference. Many converters also include an analog reference and an output amplifier, which changes the output current of the converter into a voltage. A class of converters includes storage registers and various other digital control functions in the same package. The reason for breaking down converter architecture so finely is that many integrated-circuit converter types have only a few of the above components—trading off complexity for chip size.

"The best known code is natural binary. In a natural binary fractional code having N bits, the MSB has a weight of 1/2: (2^{-1}), the second bit has a weight of 1/4: (2^{-2}), and so forth, down to the LSB, which has a weight of 2^{-N}. The analog output value of the binary number is obtained by adding up the weights of all nonzero bits. The input–output relationship of an ideal 3-bit D/A converter shows exact 1/8-F.S. (1LSB)

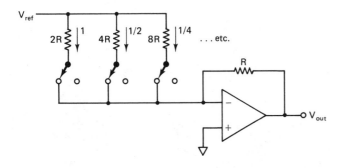

Figure 6–1 Basic D/A conversion technique, continuous binary-weighted. (Courtesy of Analog Devices.)

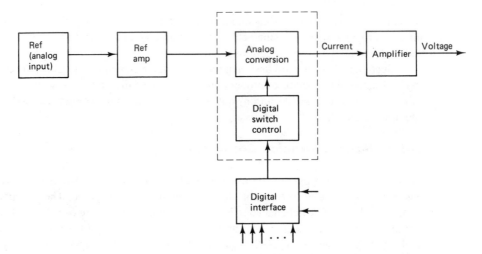

Figure 6–2   D/A converter general functional diagram. (Courtesy of Analog Devices.)

steps at each code change, and no errors at either zero or full scale. Such a converter would also switch between codes infinitely fast with no transient errors and exhibit no change in performance with temperature or time.'' This is shown in Figure 6–3.

"So far, the conversion relationships mentioned have been unipolar: The codes have represented numbers, which in turn represent the normalized magnitudes of analog variables without regard to polarity. A unipolar D/A converter will produce analog

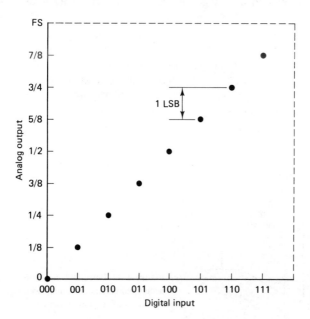

Figure 6–3   Conversion relationship for an ideal 3-bit D/A converter. (Courtesy of Analog Devices.)

signals of only one polarity and D/A converter configured in the bipolar mode will produce signals of either polarity.

"The D/A converter can be thought of as a digitally controlled potentiometer that produces an analog output that is a normalized fraction of its 'full-scale' setting. The output voltage or current depends on the reference value chosen to determine 'full-scale' output. If the reference may vary in response to an analog signal, the output is proportional to the product of the digital number and the analog input.

"The product's polarity depends on the analog signal polarity and the digital coding and conversion relationship. Four-quadrant multiplication is available if the D/A converter accepts reference signals of both positive and negative polarities, and the digital input can represent either a positive or negative number. D/A converters, therefore, may be one quadrant (single polarity of either analog or digital variable) or 4-quadrant. They may even be fractional-quadrant, if the reference has a limited range of variation.

"The specifications for a D/A converter at first glance may seem a little overwhelming; however, they may be easily grouped so that a complete error budget may be done. The specifications can be grouped by first the static accuracy, second the temperature characteristics, and third the dynamic characteristics. Failure to consider any of these specifications may result in poor performance in a given application. The parameters of D/A converters have error specifications which may have any one of four different units of measure associated with it (LSB's, % of FSR, error in volts, ppm)." A comparison of errors and terminology is shown in Figure 6–4.

10-V full scale

8-bit

1 LSB = 39.1 mV = 0.391% FS = 3906 ppm
1/2 LSB = 19.5 mV = 0.2% FS = 1953 ppm

10-bit

1 LSB = 9.77 mV = 0.1% FS = 977 ppm
1/2 LSB = 4.88 mV = 0.05% FS = 488 ppm

12-bit

1 LSB = 2.44 mV = 0.024% FS = 244 ppm
1/2 LSB = 1.22 mV = 0.012% FS = 122 ppm

14-bit

1 LSB = 0.61 mV = 0.006% FS = 61 ppm
1/2 LSB = 0.305 mV = 0.0031% FS = 31 ppm

16-bit

1 LSB = 0.153 mV = 0.0015% FS = 15 ppm
1/2 LSB = 0.076 mV = 0.00076% FS = 8 ppm

LSB = least significant bit's value
% FS = % of full-scale output
      (% of 10 V in this example)
ppm = parts per million
      (directly related to % FS)

Figure 6–4   Data converter error terminology. (Courtesy of Analog Devices.)

"The static accuracy of a D/A converter can be completely described by four error terms: offset, gain (full scale), linearity (relative accuracy), and differential linearity (step size).

"The zero (offset) error is the deviation in the output when the digital input calls for a zero output. It affects all codes by the same additive amount. In a voltage output D/A converter this is the combination of DAC leakage current and the current-to-voltage converter's offset voltage. In a current output DAC the zero error is the DAC leakage current (which is sometimes called leakage current)." This is shown in Figure 6–5.

"The offset (bipolar zero) is the midpoint of a bipolar (e.g., ±10 V output) transfer characteristic which normally falls at zero output. For almost all bipolar converters (e.g., ±10 V output) instead of actually generating negative currents to correspond to negative numbers, a unipolar DAC is used, and the output is offset by half full scale (1MSB). For best results, this offset voltage or current is derived from the same reference supply that determines the gain of the converter.

"The 'gain' of a converter is that analog scale factor setting that establishes the nominal conversion relationship (i.e., full scale). The gain error is an error in the slope of the transfer curve. It affects all codes by the same percentage amount." Look at Figure 6–6.

"The sensitivity of a converter to changes in the power supplies is normally expressed in terms of percent change in analog value (D/A output, A/D input) for a 1% change in power supply (e.g., 0.05%/% V_s). As a rule, for a good converter, the

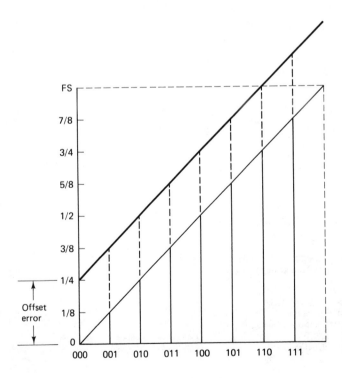

Figure 6–5   Zero (offset) error. (Courtesy of Analog Devices.)

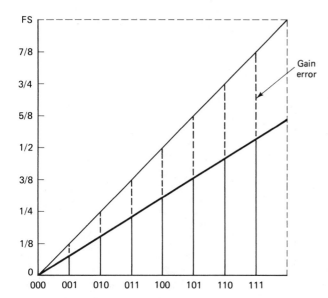

Figure 6–6   Gain error. (Courtesy of Analog Devices.)

fractional change in scale factor should be well below the equivalent of $\pm\frac{1}{2}$LSB for a 3% change in power-supply voltage.

"Linearity error of a converter is the deviation of the analog values, in a plot of the measured conversion relationship, from a straight line. The straight line can be either a 'best straight line,' determined empirically by manipulation of the gain and/or offset to equalize maximum positive and negative deviations of the actual transfer characteristic from this straight line; or, it can be the straight line passing through the endpoints of the transfer characteristic after they have been calibrated. 'Endpoint' nonlinearity is the same as relative accuracy." Linearity error is shown in Figure 6–7.

"In a converter, differential linearity error describes the variation in the analog value of transitions between adjacent pairs of digital numbers, over the full range of the digital input or output. If each transition is equal to its neighbors (i.e., 1LSB), the differential nonlinearity is zero. If a transition differs from one of its neighbors by more than 1LSB (e.g., if at the transition 01111111 to 10000000, the MSB is low by 1.1LSB), a D/A converter can be nonmonotonic, and an A/D converter using it may miss one or more codes.

"Monotonicity requires that a converter always give an increasing (in magnitude) analog value for increasing digital code. Nonmonotonicity is a result of excess differential nonlinearity ($>$1LSB). Monotonicity is essential for many control applications. Notice that a converter which has a differential nonlinearity specifications of $\pm\frac{1}{2}$LSB max is more tightly specified than one which is only guaranteed to be monotonic." An example of nonmonotonicity is shown in Figure 6–8.

"It is important to draw a careful distinction between overall linearity (relative accuracy) and differential linearity (step size between codes). Relative accuracy error describes the deviation of the points along the transfer curve from the ideal true straight

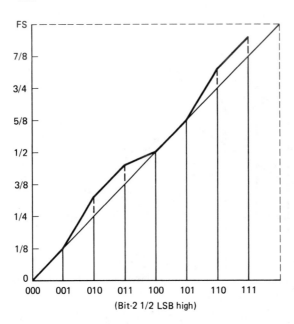

Figure 6–7 Linearity error. (Courtesy of Analog Devices.)

line. Differential linearity describes the equality of the analog steps between adjacent digital codes: If a given step between two codes is not exactly equal to one least significant bit (LSB $= V_{ref}/2^n$, $n =$ number of bits), that step has a differential linearity error.

"Absolute accuracy error of a D/A converter is the difference between the analog output that is expected when a given digital code is applied and the output that is actually measured with that code applied to the converter. Absolute accuracy error can

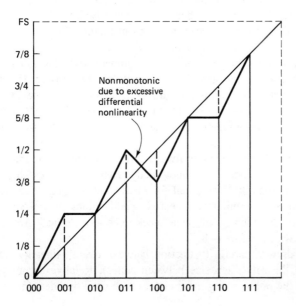

Figure 6–8 Nonmonotonicity. (Courtesy of Analog Devices.)

be caused by gain error, zero error, linearity error, or any combination of the three. Absolute accuracy measurements should be made under a set of standard conditions with sources and meters traceable to an internationally accepted standard.

"The temperature performance of a D/A can be completely described by its offset, gain, and differential-nonlinearity temperature coefficients. Offset or zero temperature coefficient is a 'zero' shift due to temperature. It affects all output readings equally and is expressed as μV/°C or ppm/°C of full scale." The gain temperature coefficient indicates the "gain shift with temperature which causes the slope to change. It is expressed as ppm/°C. (Notice whether the reference is included.) Bipolar offset is affected by both zero and gain temperature coefficients." The differential linearity temperature coefficient "shows the relative change in bit weights with temperature. It is a measure of when a converter can be expected to go nonmonotonic. It is expressed as ppm of full scale/°C.

"The zero stability of a unipolar DAC is almost entirely governed by the output amplifier's zero stability. Since output amplifiers are usually employed essentially as current-to-voltage converters, they operate at low values of closed-loop gain, and the zero TC is not greatly affected by the choice of programmable gain setting (i.e., 0 to 5 or 0 to 10 V). Zero TC is usually expressed in μV/°C.

"Converters that use offset-binary coding are 'zero' set at the all-bits-off point, and their scale factor is set at either all-bits-on or at the MSB transition. However, the zero TC is measured at the MSB transition. It is affected by the reference TC, the tracking of the offset reference, and the tracking of the bipolar-offset and gain-setting resistors.

"The offset or zero TC will behave differently in unipolar and bipolar offset applications. In the unipolar mode, the zero TC depends only on leakage current terms and the offset voltage TC of the output amplifier; these are generally small. However, in the bipolar mode, the zero point occurs at the major carry (code 100 . . .). Both the unipolar offset TC, and gain TC of the device contribute to drift around the zero point. It is important to check this specification closely if bipolar operation will be used." The effects of temperature shifts on the offset zero of a unipolar and bipolar converter are shown in Figure 6–9.

"Monotonic behavior is achieved if the differential nonlinearity is less than 1LSB at any temperature in the range of interest. The differential nonlinearity temperature coefficient may be expressed as a ratio, as a maximum change over a temperature range and/or implied by a statement that the device is monotonic over the specified temperature range."

EXAMPLE 6–1

A 12-bit D/A converter has an initial accuracy of $\frac{1}{4}$LSB and a differential nonlinearity temperature coefficient of 4.0 ppm/°C. The converter is to be used in an environment that goes from $+25°C \leq T \leq 75°C$. Is monotonicity assured?

Solution   From Figure 6–4, for a 12-bit converter 1 LSB = 244 ppm, so

$$\tfrac{1}{4}\text{LSB} = (\tfrac{1}{4})(244 \text{ ppm}) = 61 \text{ ppm}$$

This is the worst-case, initial accuracy. A swing in temperature from +25°C to 75°C causes

$$T = 75°C - (+25°C) = 50°C$$

The 50°C temperature change will cause a differential nonlinearity temperature error of

$$\begin{aligned} \text{error}_{\Delta T} &= (50°C)(4.0 \text{ ppm/}°C) \\ &= 200 \text{ ppm} \end{aligned}$$

Combined with the initial error,

$$\text{error}_{\text{total}} = 61 \text{ ppm} + 200 \text{ ppm} = 261 \text{ ppm}$$

But this is greater than 1LSB. So increasing the digital code 1LSB should cause the output to increase by 244 ppm. But the errors may combine to force the output down 261 ppm. The result of *increasing* the code 1LSB may then be a *decrease* of

$$244 \text{ ppm} - 261 \text{ ppm} = -17 \text{ ppm}$$

The output would drop. This is nonmonotonic!

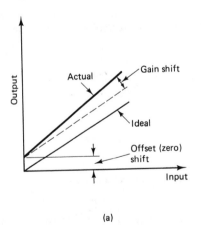
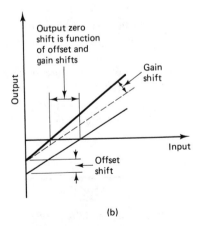

Figure 6–9   Zero offset shifts due to temperature: (a) unipolar; (b) bipolar. (Courtesy of Analog Devices.)

"The previous discussions have covered many of the general issues relating to D/A converters, especially those concerning testing and specification. We will now focus on the implementation of real converter designs using integrated-circuit technologies. We will look at the advantages and limitations of these technologies, with emphasis on the resulting application strengths and weaknesses. We will look in detail at the implementation of each section of the converter and the interconnections between them."

Two older converter techniques are the continuous binary-weighted and successively weighted converters. These are shown in Figure 6–10. "The inverted R-$2R$ or current-

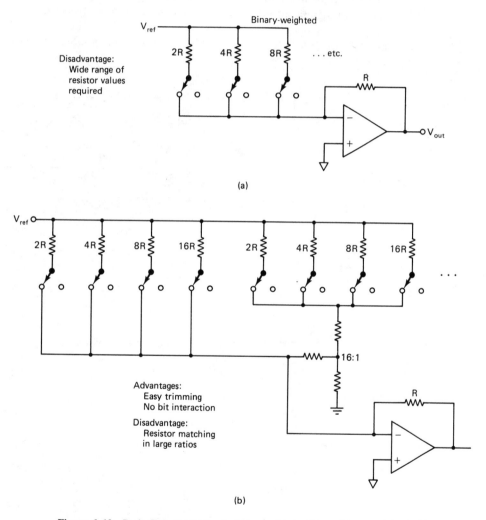

(a)

(b)

Figure 6–10   Basic D/A conversion techniques: (a) continuous binary-weighted; (b) successively weighted binary quads. (Courtesy of Analog Devices.)

switching ladder is being used in most new IC designs. It offers several performance and fabrication advantages: (1) the resistance ladder itself always runs at the same bias—the switches simply steer the current either to ground or to the output through the virtual ground of the amplifier, thus achieving high speed; (2) there is a small (and constant) voltage drop across the switches, thus simplifying circuit design and giving stable, thermal free operation; and (3) only two values of resistance need be fabricated—ideal for monolithic technology.'' The *R-2R* converters are shown in Figure 6–11.

"The inverted *R-2R* ladder can be extended to a 16-bit DAC, however, this requires very tight resistor matching and tracking to guarantee monotonicity. In a 16-bit *R-2R* ladder DAC the tolerance is most critical for the major carry where the 15 LSBs turn off and the most significant bit turns on. If the MSB is more than 0.0015% low, the converter will be nonmonotonic.''

The MC1408 is a D/A converter which has been widely used for many years. It

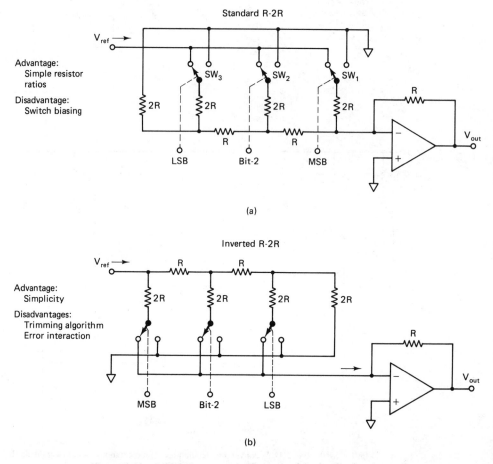

(a)

(b)

Figure 6–11 *R-2R* D/A converter. (Courtesy of Analog Devices.)

consists of a reference current amplifier, R-$2R$ ladder, and eight current switches. For proper operation, you provide the following:

Positive power supply ($+5$ V)

Negative power supply (-5 to -15 V)

Reference current (0.5 to 4 mA)

Eight stable, latched data bits

Current-to-voltage conversion

Compensation capacitor (15 to 75 pF)

Properly configured, the MC1408 then provides an output current that is controlled by the eight binary inputs, and the reference current.

$$I_0 = I_{\text{ref}} \left(\frac{A_1}{2} + \frac{A_2}{4} + \frac{A_3}{8} + \frac{A_4}{16} + \frac{A_5}{32} + \frac{A_6}{64} + \frac{A_7}{128} + \frac{A_8}{256} \right) \tag{6-1}$$

$$A_n = \begin{cases} 1 & \text{for a logic high} \\ 0 & \text{for a logic low} \end{cases}$$

Guaranteed accuracy is $\pm\frac{1}{2}$LSB at 25°C with a reference current of 1.99 mA. Monotonicity is assured for stable reference currents above 0.5 mA. Full-scale settling time is typically 70 ns, to within $\frac{1}{2}$LSB.

A simple circuit using the MC1408 is shown in Figure 6–12. The $+5$-V power is readily available in most digital systems. The V_{EE} supply must be at least 3 V more negative than the voltage connected to $-V_{\text{ref}}$. Since $-V_{\text{ref}}$ has been grounded (more on this shortly), any regulated voltage below -3 V will work.

The capacitor, C_{comp}, provides proper phase margin to assure stable operation (i.e., no oscillations). Its precise value depends on the value of R_{ref} you select. Several recommended pairs of values are given in Table 6–1.

The value of reference current needed to set the output level is

$$I_{\text{ref}} = \frac{V_{\text{ref}}}{R_{\text{ref}}}$$

Since the overall accuracy and drift is directly affected by the reference voltage, it is not recommended that the general-purpose $+5$-V logic power supply be used. However, for very low cost systems, splitting R_{ref} and adding a decoupling capacitor may provide adequate performance. For $I_{\text{ref}} = 2.0$ mA,

$$R_{\text{ref}} = \frac{5 \text{ V}}{2.0 \text{ mA}} = 2.5 \text{ k}\Omega$$

Select one part of R_{ref} as a 1-kΩ resistor, and the other part as a 1-kΩ resistor with a series 1-kΩ potentiometer, for full-scale, span adjustment.

The load resistor converts the output current to a voltage. To meet speed specifica-

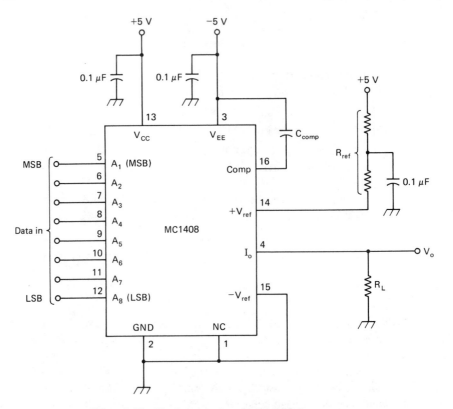

Figure 6–12   Simple connection of MC1408 D/A converter.

tions it must be less than 500 Ω, shunted by less than 25 pF of stray capacitance. Using an R_L of 500 Ω results in a full-scale output voltage of

$$V_{0\,max} = \frac{255}{256}\,(2.0\ \text{mA})(500\ \Omega) = 0.996\ \text{V}$$

There are several ways you can improve the performance of the basic D/A converter in Figure 6–12. The reference should be provided by a highly stable, accurate source,

TABLE 6–1   COMPENSATION CAPACITOR SIZES FOR THE MC1408 D/A CONVERTER

R_{ref} (kΩ)	C_{comp} (pF)
1.0	15
2.5	37
5.0	75

not from the digital power supply. There are many reference diodes and reference ICs available. However, limit reference current to 2 mA for best performance. The temperature coefficient of R_{ref} must be kept low to assure low overall drift specifications and monotonicity.

Output drive can be significantly improved by adding an op amp. It should be configured as an inverting amp. However, there is no need for the input resistor R_i (since its purpose is to convert input voltage to current). The current from the D/A, pin 4, is driven directly into the virtual ground at the op amp's inverting input. Since the output voltage is being produced by the op amp, you may select R_f (the op amp's negative feedback resistor) to produce whatever full-scale output voltage is necessary.

The output op amp amplifier is inverting. If you want a positive output voltage, current must flow *into* the D/A output current pin. This happens when you ground $+V_{ref}$, pin 14, and connect R_{ref} and a negative reference voltage to $-V_{ref}$, pin 15.

Finally, the MC1408 may be used as a multiplying D/A. Instead of supplying a steady reference current (to either $+V_{ref}$, or $-V_{ref}$), you may connect some signal you want controlled. The output, then, is a fraction of that signal. The size of the output is set by the binary bits' values (equation 6–1). If you are applying the input signal through R_{ref}, to $-V_{ref}$, the $+V_{ref}$ must be removed from ground and connected to a stable voltage which equals the positive peak of that input signal.

All of these extra, external components and connections make for a much more complicated and expensive digital-to-analog converter circuit. You may have to add a stable, accurate reference, high-quality op amp, scaling and offsetting components and digital latches to capture and hold the data presented by a microprocessor. All of these extra components, interconnections, and insertion and testing costs will push the overall converter circuit cost up to 5 to 20 times the cost of the MC1408 IC itself.

For a comparable cost, the AD667 from Analog Devices is available. "The AD667 is a complete, voltage output, 12-bit digital-to-analog converter, including a high-stability buried zener voltage reference and double-buffered input latch on a single chip. The converter uses 12 precision high-speed bipolar current steering switches and a laser-trimmed thin-film resistor network to provide fast settling time and high accuracy." A block diagram is given in Figure 6–13.

"Microprocessor compatibility is achieved by the on-chip double-buffered latch. The design of the input latch allows direct interface to 4-, 8-, 12-, or 16-bit buses. The 12 bits of data from the first rank of latches can then be transferred to the second rank, avoiding generation of spurious analog output values. The latch responds to strobe pulses as short as 100 ns, allowing use with the fastest available microprocessors.

"The functional completeness and high performance in the AD667 results from a combination of advanced switch design, high-speed bipolar manufacturing process, and the proven laser wafer-trimming (LWT) technology. The AD667 is trimmed at the wafer level and is specified to $\pm\frac{1}{4}$LSB maximum linearity error (K, B grades) at 25°C and $\pm\frac{1}{2}$LSB over the full operating temperature range.

"The subsurface (buried) zener diode on the chip provides a low-noise voltage reference which has long-term stability and temperature drift characteristics comparable to the best discrete reference diodes. The laser trimming process, which provides the

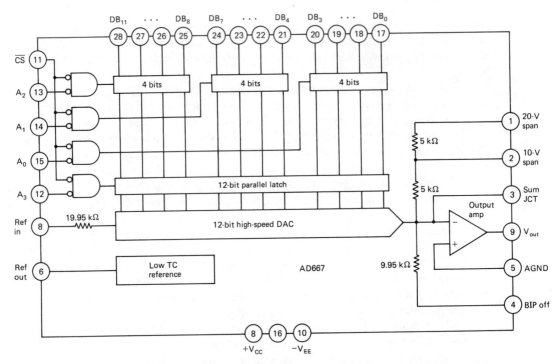

Figure 6–13 AD667 digital-to-analog converter IC functional block diagram. (Courtesy of Analog Devices.)

excellent linearity, is also used to trim both the absolute value of the reference as well as its temperature coefficient. The AD667 is thus well suited for wide-temperature-range performance with $\pm\frac{1}{2}$LSB maximum linearity error and guaranteed monotonicity over the full temperature range. Typical full-scale gain TC is 5 ppm/°C.''

Both positive and negative power supply voltages, as well as ground, are required. A minimum of ±11.4 V dc is required, with ±18 V the absolute maximum. However, if you want to produce ±10 V output, minimum supply voltages must be ±12.5 V. Specifications were tested with ±15-V dc supplies. Unless there is a significant reason to choose another level, ±15 V dc is the logical power supply voltage to use.

Logic levels for both the data (DB_0–DB_{11}) and the addressing (CS, A_0–A_3) may be either TTL or $+5$ V dc CMOS.

The internal reference is laser trimmed for both value and temperature coefficient. Its value is an accurate 5 ppm/°C full-scale temperature coefficient for the entire converter. The reference amplifier can tolerate an indefinite short circuit to ground but only a momentary short to either supply.

The analog output circuitry provides internal, laser-trimmed resistors. So, by proper pin strapping, you can configure the AD667 for full-scale bipolar voltages of ±10, ±5, or ±2.5 V. Unipolar output voltage of 0 to 5 V and 0 to 10 V can also be produced. The proper connections are shown in Table 6–2.

TABLE 6–2   OUTPUT VOLTAGE RANGE CONNECTIONS FOR THE AD667

Output range (V)	Digital input codes	Connect pin 9 to:	Connect pin 1 to:	Connect pin 2 to:	Connect pin 4 to:
±10	Offset binary	1	9	NC	6(through 50-Ω fixed or 100-Ω trim resistor)
±5	Offset binary	2	2	9	6(through 50-Ω fixed or 100-Ω trim resistor)
±2.5	Offset binary	2	3	9	6(through 50-Ω fixed or 100-Ω trim resistor)
0 to +10	Straight binary	2	2	9	5
0 to +5	Straight binary	2	3	9	5

Source: Analog Devices.

The analog output amplifier is capable of sourcing or sinking at least 5 mA. The output impedence is very low, typically 0.05 Ω. A short circuit to ground will be tolerated, indefinitely, and the short-circuit current is limited to 40 mA.

Complete analog connections for unipolar output are shown in Figure 6–14. Gener-

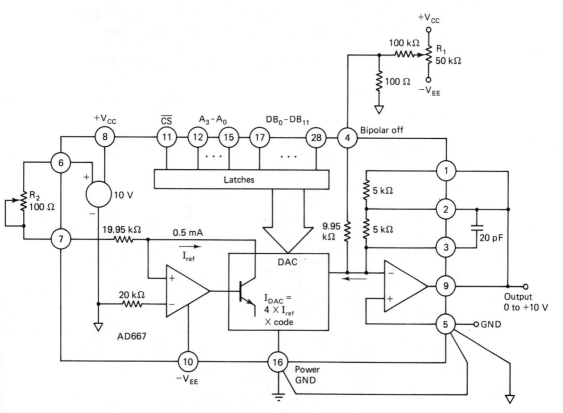

Figure 6–14   AD667 0- to +10-V unipolar voltage output connection. (Courtesy of Analog Devices.)

ally, the internal trimming is good enough to allow you to omit the resistors tied to pin 4. If you do not use the external bipolar offset resistors, just tie pin 4 directly to the analog ground, pin 5. If you choose to use the external bipolar offset, be sure that the temperature coefficients of the resistors and of the voltage at pin 4 are only a few ppm/°C. Also, the supplies from which the pin 4 voltage is derived should be noise free.

Proper bipolar output connections are shown in Figure 6–15. Since a positive *input* offset voltage is needed, you can get it from the reference voltage output at pin 6. This is much cleaner and more stable than the power supply voltage. Be sure that the external offset adjust potentiometer (R_1) and span adjust potentiometer (R_2) have low-temperature coefficients and are low in noise generation.

"The bus interface logic of the AD667 consists of four independently addressable registers in two ranks. The first rank consists of three 4-bit registers which can be loaded directly from a 4-, 8-, 12-, or 16-bit microprocessor bus. Once the complete 12-bit data word has been assembled in the first rank, it can be loaded into the 12-bit register of the second rank. This double-buffered organization avoids the generation of spurious analog output values.

"The latches are controlled by the address inputs, A_0–A_3, and the $\overline{CS}$ input. All control inputs are active low, consistent with general practice in microprocessor systems. The four address lines each enable one of the four latches, as indicated in Table 6–3.

All latches in the AD667 are level-triggered. This means that data present during

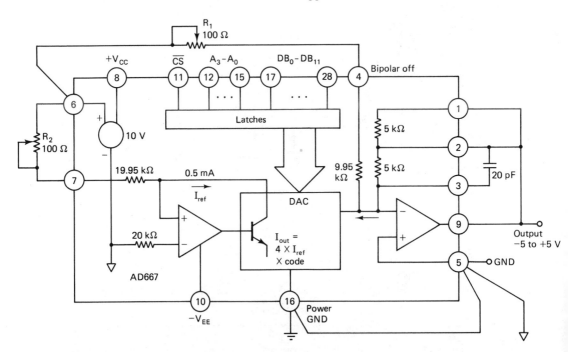

Figure 6–15   AD667 −5- to +5-V bipolar voltage output connection. (Courtesy of Analog Devices.)

TABLE 6–3   AD667 TRUTH TABLE[a]

$\overline{CS}$	A3	A2	A1	A0	Operation
1	X	X	X	X	No operation
X	1	1	1	1	No operation
0	1	1	1	0	Enable 4 LSBs of first rank
0	1	1	0	1	Enable 4 middle bits of first rank
0	1	0	1	1	Enable 4 MSBs of first rank
0	0	1	1	1	Loads second rank from first rank
0	0	0	0	0	All latches transparent

[a] X, Don't care.

the time when the control signals are valid will enter the latch. When any one of the control signals returns high, the data are latched.

"The AD667 interfaces easily to 8-bit microprocessor systems of all types. The control logic makes possible the use of right- or left-justified data formats. Whenever a 12-bit DAC is loaded from an 8-bit bus, two bytes are required. If the program considers the data to be a 12-bit binary fraction (between 0 and 4095/4096), the data are left-justified, with the 8 most significant bits in one byte and the remaining bits in the upper half of another byte. Right-justified data calls for the 8 least significant bits to occupy one byte, with the 4 most significant bits residing in the lower half of another byte simplifying integer arithmetic." These are illustrated in Figure 6–16.

"Figure 6–17 shows an addressing scheme for use with an AD667 set up for left-justified data in an 8-bit system. The base address is decoded from the high-order address bits and the resultant active-low signal is applied to $\overline{CS}$. The two LSBs of the address bus are connected as shown to the AD667 address inputs. The latches now reside in two consecutive locations, with location X01 loading the four LSBs and location X10 loading the eight MSBs and updating the output.

"Right-justified data can be similarly accommodated. The overlapping of data lines is reversed, and the address connections are slightly different. The AD667 still occupies two adjacent locations in the processor's memory map.

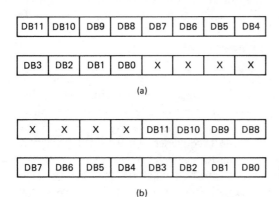

(a)

(b)

Figure 6–16   Twelve-bit data formats for 8-bit systems: (a) left-justified; (b) right-justified. (Courtesy of Analog Devices.)

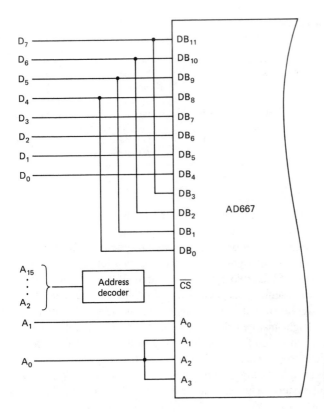

Figure 6–17 Left-justified 8-bit bus interface for the AD667. (Courtesy of Analog Devices.)

"The AD667 is easily interfaced to 12- and 16-bit data buses. In this operation, all four address lines (A_0 through A_3) are tied to low, and the latch is enabled by $\overline{CS}$ going low. The AD667 thus occupies a single memory location. This configuration renders the second rank register transparent, using the first rank of registers as the data latch. The $\overline{CS}$ input can be driven from an active-low decoded address. It should be noted that any data bus activity during the period when $\overline{CS}$ is active will cause activity at the AD667 output. If data are not guaranteed stable during this period, the second rank register can be used to provide double buffering." This is shown in Figure 6–18.

6–1.2 Analog-to-Digital Conversion

"The analog-to-digital converter is at the core of any data-acquisition system designed to transform data in the form of continuous analog variables into a discrete binary code suitable for digital processing. A/D converters take on more varied forms than D/A converters, mainly because of the much wider variety of required characteristics. The discussion here will be limited to A/D converters implemented typically in integrated-circuit or hybrid form. The ideal transfer curve for a 3-bit A/D converter is shown in Figure 6–19 with the analog levels on the horizontal axis and the digital outputs which correspond to those input levels on the vertical axis. Note that a given digital output is

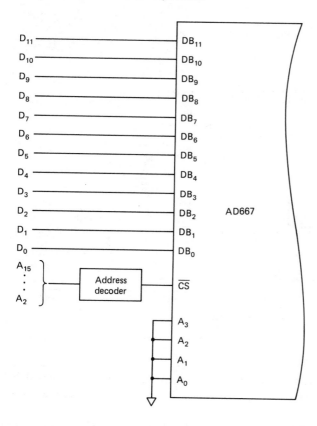

Figure 6–18 Connection for 12- and 16-bit bus interface. (Courtesy of Analog Devices.)

valid over a small range of signal input, not just at a single point; this range is the 'width' of the code. For ideal performance, each code width (except at the extremes) should be one least-significant-bit (LSB) wide; acceptable performance will occur with codes $\frac{1}{2}$ to $1\frac{1}{2}$LSB wide. If a code width becomes so narrow that it disappears, the A/D will never have that code as an output—it will be a 'missed' code. (Observe that integrating A/D converters and V/F converters have inherently uniform code widths which can change significantly only over a large number of counts.)

"The specifications for A/D converters are similar to those for D/A converters. That is, the same concepts of gain error, offset error, and linearity apply with equal importance to A/D converters. The D/A converter output is an analog signal and the input is a digital code which can only represent a finite number of input test conditions. The A/D converter, on the other hand, has an infinite number of input conditions, but a finite number of digital output codes. Thus A/D converter errors are generally the difference between actual and ideal analog inputs that cause a particular code transition to occur. In a D/A converter, differential linearity specifies the size of the analog output change in response to any 1LSB increment in the digital code. In the case of an A/D converter, differential linearity specifies the minimum and maximum limits on the width of any code.

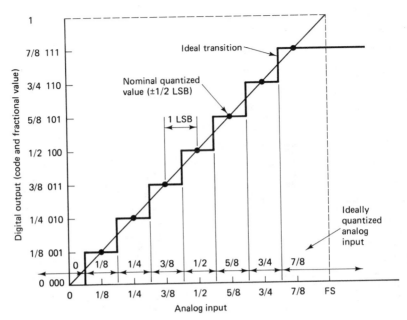

Figure 6–19 Conversion relationship for an ideal A/D converter. (Courtesy of Analog Devices.)

"The problem of missing codes in an A/D converter is generally caused by a nonmonotonic conversion relationship on the part of the internal D/A converter. In the 3-bit example given in Figure 6–20, the DAC's MSB is less than the sum of bits 1 and 2, hence the D/A conversion is nonmonotonic. Since the MSB is always tried first, if it is less than the input value that it is being compared with, it will foreclose the possibility of any lesser code being valid. Since it is turned on first and corresponds to a value less than the analog value of code 011 there is no way 011 can appear. The table shows the results of the trials at various levels in the vicinity of the nonmonotonic bit. It provides verification that code 011 is indeed nowhere to be found—it is a missing code.

"Missing codes in an A/D converter indicate differential nonlinearity more negative than -1LSB. An A/D specified for $\pm\frac{1}{2}$LSB differential nonlinearity will have codes at least $\frac{1}{2}$LSB, and at most $1\frac{1}{2}$LSB wide. As with the D/A converter, it is important to verify that each of the specifications of a particular A/D remain within the system error budget over the full temperature range of interest.

"In order to select the best ADC for a given application, the circuit designer should be familiar with the various types of converters available. In addition, familiarity with the manufacturing process involved will often aid in selection of an ADC. The checklist in Figure 6–21 outlines the proper priorities for selecting an ADC. First and foremost, the required resolution of the converter must be determined. This will determine the number of recognizable quanitization intervals in the ADC transfer function. Since all ADCs exhibit a fundamental quanitization uncertainty of $\pm\frac{1}{2}$LSB, the designer must

What causes missing codes ?

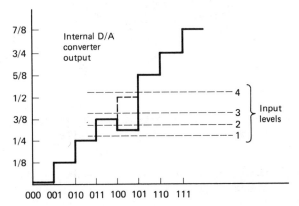

Successive approximations (accept
code if lower than input level)

		Signal		
Code	1	2	3	4
100	No	Yes	Yes	Yes
010	Yes	–	–	–
011	No	–	–	–
110	–	No	No	No
101	–	No	No	No
Answer	010	100	100	100
Correct answer	010	010	011	100
Error	None	2 Bits	1 Bit	None

Missed code = 011

Tracking A/D oscillates

Figure 6-20 Example of missing codes.
(Courtesy of Analog Devices.)

choose an ADC with sufficient resolution to reduce this 'digitizing noise' to an acceptably low value. A useful rule of thumb is that each bit of resolution reduces quanitization noise an additional 6 dB. Thus a 10-bit converter exhibits 'best case' quanitization noise which is approximately 60 dB below full scale.

"Resolution, however, does not imply accuracy. Many A/D converters have been built with far higher resolution than accuracy. Specifications must be examined to ensure that the desired system accuracy can be achieved on a consistent basis. 'Typical' accuracy specs should be avoided whenever possible.

"Of course, all of these errors must be evaluated over the full temperature range of interest. Most manufacturers include temperature coefficients for accuracy specs on their data sheets. It is important that any critical parameters be specified as minimum or maximum values, since 'typical' specs are usually not guaranteed or tested.

"Conversion speed is another important selection factor, since it defines the upper limit on system bandwidth. Generally speaking, the conversion speed requirements will

- Resolution
- Accuracy
    Initial (25°C)
    Drift
- Speed
- Power requirements
- Reference
    Internal
    Ratiometric
- Interfacing
- Cost
- Size   **Figure 6–21** A/D selection features.
- Availability   (Courtesy of Analog Devices.)

dictate the type of converter selected. It is important to recognize that the total conversion speed includes both the ADC conversion time and the aperture and acquisition time of the sample-hold amplifier, if used.

"System power limitations will often dictate the best ADC for the application. Available system supply voltages must be suitable for the converter chosen, and total power dissipation should be held as low as possible in order to minimize heat generation and the attendant drift.

"Applications which use a single ADC can be best satisfied by choosing an ADC with a built-in reference. By using such a converter, one less component must be procured, less board space is required, and the error budget calculation becomes simpler. In systems where the reference must be variable, or where ratiometric operation is desired, or if a master system reference is available, an ADC requiring an external reference can be used to advantage.

"Since most ADCs are interfaced to microprocessors (with the notable exceptions of display-oriented converters and video speed converters), it logically follows that interface logic should be included on-chip. It is important to read manufacturers' claims of 'microprocessor compatibility' with a great deal of caution. An ADC designed for simple interface to one particular processor may be nearly impossible to interface to a different machine.

"Most newer ADCs also include at least a three-state buffer for bus interface. In most cases, direct bus interface is possible. However, high-speed data buses with significant activity during the conversion period may inject noise into the ADC and cause erratic or unstable output data. The solution to this problem (generally encountered only on 12-bit and higher-resolution ADCs) is to use an external three-state buffer. A/D converters designed for voltmeter applications generally provide either multiplexed seven-segment or BCD outputs.

"Let us now address the process by which the optimum ADC can be chosen for a particular application. In order to select an ADC, it is useful to understand exactly what types of ADC are available and how they work. Figure 6–22, a list of A/D converter types, is certainly not complete, but it does include the most popular ones, especially those currently produced in integrated-circuit form. The integrating A/D design, one of the oldest implementations of this function, is still widely used in digital panel meters and digital laboratory instrumentation. It suffers from speed limitation but can achieve

Integrating	High accuracy
	Low speed
	Low cost
Successive approximation	High speed
	Accuracy at cost
	Flexibility
Tracking (counter-comparator)	High speed in track
	Susceptible to noise
Multicomparator "flash"	Highest speed
	High resolution expensive
V/F converter	Fast responding
	Continuous serial output

Figure 6–22 A/D converter types. (Courtesy of Analog Devices.)

high accuracy at relatively low cost. The successive-approximation A/D (which uses a D/A internally) is the most popular for data-acquisition systems because of its moderately high speed and resolution. We will discuss the implementation, application, and specification of this type of converter in considerable detail throughout the remaining discussions. The successive approximation (S/A) converter is very versatile, and recent major cost reductions have made it suitable for increasing numbers of applications; however, it does require some knowledge and experience for successful implementation. The tracking A/D and the voltage-to-frequency converter can be looked upon as variations of the successive-approximation and the integrator design techniques; in these types, the digital data are available on a virtually continuous basis.

"The multicomparator ladder (or parallel) design provides the highest speed, at the expense of limited resolution. Most monolithic parallel converters are limited to 6- or 8-bit resolution." Look at Figure 6–23. "The parallel converter consists of a tapped resistor network and an array of $2^N - 1$ comparators. Each comparator provides a logic output indicating whether the analog input is above or below a particular fraction of the reference voltage. These logic outputs are then decoded to a more useful code (binary or Gray code, for example). The total conversion time for this type of converter is equal to the sum of the propagation delays of the comparators and the decoding logic. This may be as short as a few tens of nanoseconds, translating into conversion rates of tens of megasamples per second.

"The disadvantage of the parallel converter is the limited resolution available. A 10-bit converter would, for example, require 1024 matched precision resistors, 1023 high-speed comparators, and an extensive logic array. Integrating this complex a device remains currently beyond the practical state of the art.

"The concept of the 'dual-slope' integrating A/D is simple. A current proportional to the input signal charges a capacitor for a fixed length of time—the capacitor is then discharged by a current proportional to the reference until the starting point is crossed. The discharge time is then directly proportional to the average value of the input signal. Although good-quality components (especially the capacitor) must be used for reasonable accuracy, only the reference need be an expensive, high-quality component. Speed is an obvious limitation because of the long count time required (for example, you must count to 2000 and do what amounts to 1000 successive comparison tests to achieve a

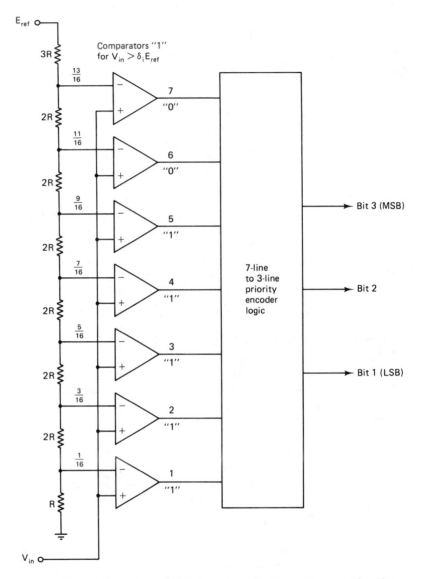

Figure 6–23 Multicomparator, "flash," or parallel converter. (Courtesy of Analog Devices.)

3-digit to 10-bit resolution)." Figure 6–24 is the basic diagram of a dual-slope integrating A/D converter.

"Dual-slope integration has many advantages. Conversion accuracy is independent of both the capacitor value and the clock frequency, because they affect both the up-slope and the down-ramp in the same ratio. Differential linearity is excellent, because

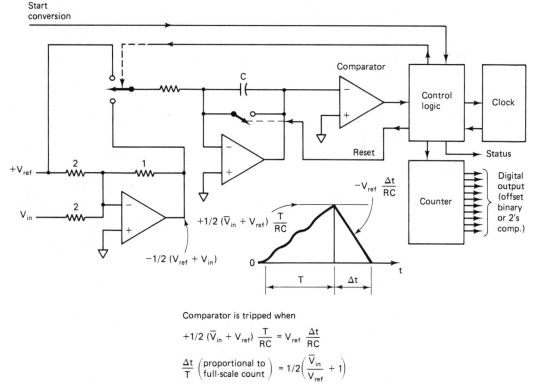

Figure 6–24 Basic diagram of a dual-slope integrating A/D converter. (Courtesy of Analog Devices.)

the analog function is free from discontinuities, the codes are generated by a clock and counter, and all codes can inherently exist. Resolution is limited only by analog resolution, rather than by differential nonlinearity; hence the excellent fine structure may be represented by more bits than would be needed to maintain a given level of scale-factor accuracy. The integration provides rejection of high-frequency noise and averaging of changes that occur during the sampling period. The fixed average period also makes it possible to obtain 'infinite' normal-mode rejection at frequencies that are integral multiples of $1/T$.

    "The throughput rate of dual-slope converters is limited to somewhat less than $\frac{1}{2}T$ conversions per second. The sample time, T, is determined by the fundamental frequency to be rejected. For example, if one wishes to reject 60 Hz and its harmonics, the minimum integrating time is $16\frac{2}{3}$ ms, and the maximum number of conversions is somewhat less than 30/s. Although too slow for fast data acquisition, dual-slope converters are quite adequate for transducers such as thermocouples and gas chromatographs; and they are the predominant circuit used in constructing digital voltmeters. Since DVMs use sign-magnitude BCD coding, bipolar operation requires polarity sensing and reference-polarity switching rather than simple offsetting.

"A shortcoming of conventional dual-slope converters is that errors at the input of the integrating amplifier or the comparator show up as errors in the digital word. Such errors are usually reduced by the introduction of a third portion of the cycle, during which a capacitor is charged with zero-drift errors, which are then introduced in the opposite sense during the integration to (it is hoped) nullify them. Such error-nulling techniques generally entail the addition of more logic. Since CMOS fabrication allows complex digital functions to be integrated without drastically increasing power consumption, it is the first choice for most integrating-type A/D converters.

"One of the most important uses of D/A converters is in the core of certain types of A/D converters. In these A/D converters, the output of the internal DAC is compared to the input level; the logic section of the A/D uses the information from the comparator (internal level above or below input) to modify the code to the DAC until the two levels are brought as close together as possible (within the resolution limit of the DAC). In the simple tracking A/D shown here, an up/down counter drives the DAC in the proper direction to match the input in response to commands from the comparator. The accuracy of the D/A converter directly affects the accuracy of this system as an A/D converter." A tracking ADC is shown in Figure 6–25.

"If the output of the D/A converter is less than the analog input, the counter counts up. If the D/A output is greater than the analog input, the counter counts down. If the analog input is constant, the counter output 'hunts' back and forth between the two adjacent bit values. This converter can follow small changes quite rapidly (it will follow 1LSB changes at the clock rate), but it will require the full count to acquire full-scale step changes. Since it seeks to 'home in' on the analog value, the analogy to a servomechanism is quite evident. The tracking ADC is not often implemented in IC form, since a similar amount of complexity can yield a much more efficient converter—the successive-approximation type.

"This type is more popular for high-speed data acquisition systems since it is always able to complete a conversion with 8, 10, or 12 'counts' or comparisons (for

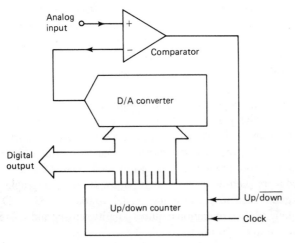

Figure 6–25 Tracking ADC. (Courtesy of Analog Devices.)

8-, 10-, or 12-bit resolution)—whereas the time for a complete conversion with a tracking converter will vary directly with the input signal change. Performance requirements for a DAC to be used inside a successive-approximation A/D will normally be more stringent than for a tracking A/D.''

A successive-approximation A/D converter is shown in Figure 6–26. ''The concept of the successive-approximation converter is directly analogous to that of a beam balance with a set of precision weights in successive binary ratio. One performs the measurement by placing the unknown on one side of the beam, then testing each known weight against the unknown, beginning with the largest. If a given weight tips the scale it is discarded; if not, it remains. This procedure continues down to the smallest weight. If the balance is true and the individual weights all exact, the unknown can be determined to a resolution equal to the smallest weight. (If a weight equal to one-half the smallest weight is added to the unknown side, it can be shown that measurement is always accurate to one-half the smallest weight.)

''The equivalent flow diagram for the successive-decision process and final result indicates that complex logic functions are required. However, complex logic functions can be done fairly rapidly in comparison with analog functions. Note that the successive-approximation A/D lies between the integrating converter and the parallel-comparator type in complexity, speed, and cost. More important, the complexity is not so great as to prevent its implementation in monolithic form.''

The ADC0801 through ADC0805 is a series of 8-bit microprocessor compatible successive approximation analog to digital converters made by National Semiconductor. The schematic of the converter in a typical application is shown in Figure 6–27.

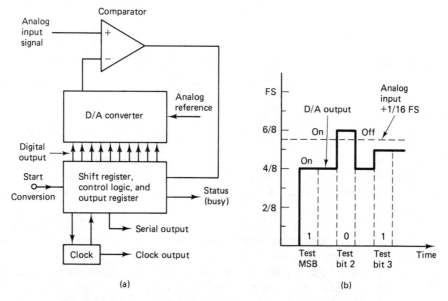

Figure 6–26 Successive-approximation A/D converter: (a) block diagram; (b) three-bit weighing. (Courtesy of Analog Devices.)

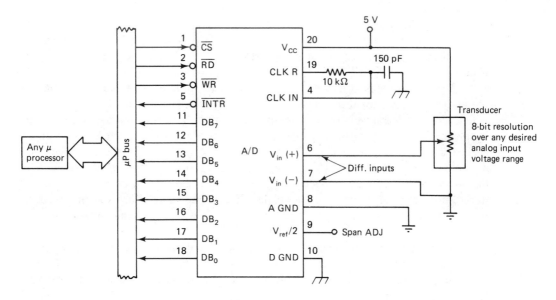

Error specification (includes full-scale, zero error, and non-linearity)			
Part number	Full-scale adjusted	$V_{ref}/2 = 2.500\ V_{dc}$ (no adjustments)	$V_{ref}/2$ = no connection (no adjustments)
ADC0801	±1/4 LSB		
ADC0802		±1/2 LSB	
ADC0803	±1/2 LSB		
ADC0804		±1 LSB	
ADC0805			±1 LSB

Figure 6–27   Typical application of an ADC0801 A/D converter. (Courtesy of National Semiconductor.)

Main power is conveniently set to $+5$ V dc, to coincide with the power available for the other digital circuitry. Addition plus and minus supplies (e.g., ± 15 V) are not required. Separate analog and digital grounds are provided to allow you to minimize noise pickup along a common ground return line. This was explained in detail in Chapter 4. For best performance, these two pins should be returned to the system (power supply) common with separate cables.

An external reference is not required. If you leave $V_{ref/2}$ (pin 9) open, as shown in Figure 6–27, the power supply voltage becomes the reference. This minimizes the number of external components and connections needed. However, any noise present at V_{cc} will affect the measurement. Be certain to severely filter that supply and rigorously decouple the ADC0801 from the other digital circuitry.

An external reference can be applied through the $V_{ref/2}$ pin (pin 9). You may want an external reference for two reasons. First, the V_{cc} supply may be too noisy, causing randomly varying output data for a steady analog input voltage. Second, you may apply a reference that can be varied. This allows you to adjust the analog input voltage, which will produce the output data FF_{hex}. The ability to adjust the full-scale output can be very handy. As the pin's name suggests, the voltage you apply to $V_{ref/2}$ should be half of the intended full-scale input. Often, it is a good idea to put a 1-μF capacitor from the $V_{ref/2}$ pin to ground. This helps remove any noise trying to enter the reference pin. However, when you add this filter capacitor, you must assure that the source driving it has an output impedance of less then 1 kΩ. This is usually done with a voltage follower.

There are two analog inputs, $V_{in(+)}$ and $V_{in(-)}$. The voltage on either must not fall more than 50 mV below ground or rise more than 50 mV above the positive supply. Should either input exceed these limits, the converter may produce erroneous data, or it may refuse to perform a conversion at all. Assuming that the inputs are within limits, the data out are determined by the reference voltage and the difference in potential between these two input pins.

$$\text{data} = 255 \left(\frac{V_{in(+)} - V_{in(-)}}{V_{ref}} \right) \tag{6--2}$$

This gives you quite a bit of flexibility. The input is differential. So the A/D converter will produce an output which is caused by the difference between the inputs while ignoring any voltage common to both inputs. The current from a floating 4- to 20-mA current loop could be converted by placing a 250-Ω resistor in the loop and connecting the two inputs of the converter across the resistor.

A second use of the differential input is to establish an adjustable zero. The voltage supplied at the $V_{in(-)}$ pin is subtracted from the voltage at the $V_{in(+)}$ pin. The data will be 00_{hex} when the input to the $V_{in(+)}$ pin equals the voltage you put on the $V_{in(-)}$ pin. So adjusting the $V_{in(-)}$ voltage will alter the input voltage which produces 00_{hex} data.

"The time interval between sampling $V_{in(+)}$ and $V_{in(-)}$ is $4\frac{1}{2}$ clock periods. The maximum error voltage due to this time difference between input voltage samples is given by

$$V_{e(max)} = (V_P)(2\pi f_{cm}) \left(\frac{4.5}{f_{clk}} \right) \tag{6--3}$$

where $V_{e(max)}$ = error voltage due to sampling delay
     V_P = peak value of the common-mode voltage
     f_{cm} = common-mode frequency

As an example, to keep the error to $\frac{1}{4}$LSB (about 5 mV) when operating with a 60-Hz common-mode frequency, f_{cm}, and using a 640-kHz A/D clock, f_{clk}, would allow a peak value of the common-mode voltage, V_P . . . ~1.9 V" [2].

"Due to the internal switching action, displacement currents will flow at the analog inputs. This is due to on-chip stray capacitance to ground. . . . Bypass capacitors at the inputs will average these charges and cause a dc current to flow through the output resistances of the analog sources. . . . For continuous conversions with a 640-kHz clock frequency with the $V_{in(+)}$ input voltage at $+5$ V, this dc current is at a maximum of 5 μA. Therefore, *bypass capacitors should not be used at the analog inputs or $V_{ref/2}$ pin for high-resistance sources* (>1 $k\Omega$). . . . Large values of source resistance where an input bypass capacitor is not used *will not cause errors*, as the input currents settle out prior to the comparison time. If a low-pass filter is required in the system, use a low-valued series resistor (≤ 1 $k\Omega$) for a passive RC section or add an op amp RC active filter. For low-source-resistance applications (≤ 1 $k\Omega$), a 0.1-μF bypass capacitor at the inputs will prevent pickup due to series lead inductance of a long wire'' [2].

"An example of the use of an adjusted reference voltage is to accommodate a reduced span or dynamic voltage range of the analog input voltage. If the analog input voltage were to range from 0.5 to 3.5 V dc, instead of 0 to 5 V dc, the span would be 3 V. . . ." [2]. This is shown in Figure 6–28a. "With 0.5 V dc applied to the $V_{in(-)}$ pin to absorb the offset, the reference voltage can be made equal to $\frac{1}{2}$ of the 3-V span or 1.5 V dc. The A/D now will encode the $V_{in(+)}$ signal from 0.5 to 3.5 V with the 0.5-V input corresponding to zero and the 3.5-V dc input corresponding to full scale. The full 8 bits of resolution are therefore applied over this reduced analog input voltage range" [2]. The schematic is shown in Figure 6–28b.

The A/D converter requires a clock to sequence its conversion. "Accuracy is guaranteed at $f_{clk} = 640$ kHz. At higher clock frequencies accuracy can degrade. For lower clock frequencies, the duty-cycle limits can be extended as long as the minimum clock high time interval or minimum clock low time interval is no less than 275 ns" [2]. There is an internal clock oscillator. You must supply an external timing resistor and capacitor. Recommended values are shown in Figure 6–27. Or if there is a clock signal already available in your system, just connect it to CLK IN (pin 4).

"The digital control inputs ($\overline{CS}$, $\overline{RD}$, and $\overline{WR}$) meet standard TTL logic levels. These signals have been renamed when compared to the standard A/D Start and Output Enable labels. In addition, these inputs are active low to allow an easy interface to microprocessor control buses. For non-microprocessor-based applications, the $\overline{CS}$ input (pin 1) can be grounded and the standard A/D start function is obtained by an active-low pulse applied at the $\overline{WR}$ input (pin 3) and the Output Enable function is caused by an active-low pulse at the $\overline{RD}$ input (pin 2)" [2].

During the first cycle, during or following power-up an external $\overline{WR}$ pulse must be applied. This will ensure that the converter will start under all subsequent conditions. When both $\overline{CS}$ and $\overline{WR}$ are taken low, the converter resets, and will remain reset until either one goes high. Sometime during the next eight clock pulses, a conversion begins. Sixty-four clock pulses later the conversion is complete, and $\overline{INTR}$ is taken low by the converter as an end-of-conversion signal.

Data are now available. To read them you must take both $\overline{CS}$ and $\overline{RD}$ low. However, the $\overline{RD}$ strobe must occur eight clock periods after the assertion of $\overline{INTR}$ (end-of-conversion) to guarantee reset of $\overline{INTR}$.

Normally, the data pins (DB_0–DB_7, pins 18–11) are open. Two hundred nanoseconds after the falling edge of the $\overline{RD}$ strobe, the data are placed on these pins. They will be held stable on the output pins as long as $\overline{RD}$ and $\overline{CS}$ are low. Two hundred nanoseconds after $\overline{RD}$ goes high the output pins are returned to their high impedance (open) state. It

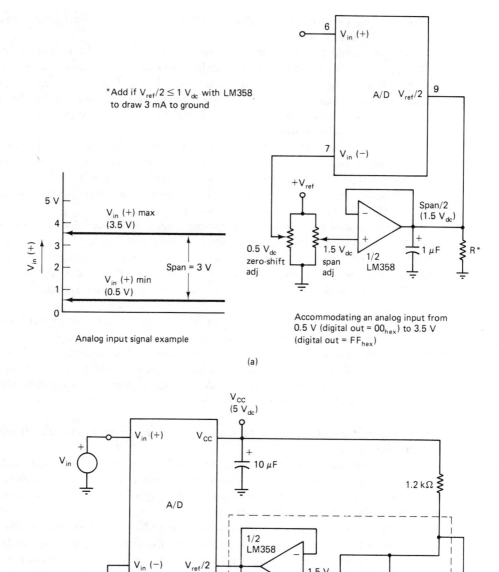

(a)

(b)

Figure 6–28   Adapting the A/D analog input voltages to match an arbitrary input signal range. (Courtesy of National Semiconductor.)

is assumed by the manufacturer that the $\overline{CS}$ pin goes low before $\overline{RD}$ and stays low until after $\overline{RD}$ returns high.

If you would prefer that the converter free-run, then tie $\overline{CS}$ to ground and feed $\overline{INTR}$ to $\overline{WR}$. When $\overline{INTR}$ goes low, signaling the end of a conversion, it immediately triggers another conversion. This is illustrated in Figure 6–29. Don't forget that you must take the $\overline{WR}$ and $\overline{INTR}$ node low once during power-up. So, the START switch has been added. Connecting $\overline{RD}$ to ground causes the data from the previous conversion always to be available at the output pins.

"This converter has been designed to directly interface with derivatives of the 8080 microprocessor. The A/D can be mapped into memory space (using standard memory address decoding for $\overline{CS}$ and the $\overline{MEMR}$ and $\overline{MEMW}$ strobes) or it can be controlled as an I/O device by using the $\overline{I/OR}$ and $\overline{I/OW}$ strobes and decoding the address bit A_0–A_7" [2]. This is illustrated in Figure 6–30a.

"The control bus for the 6800 microprocessor derivatives does not use the $\overline{RD}$ and $\overline{WR}$ strobe signals. Instead, it employs a single $R/\overline{W}$ line and additional timing, if needed, can be derived from the $\phi2$ clock. All I/O devices are memory mapped in the 6800 system, and a special signal, VMA, indicates that the current address is valid" [2]. Figure 6–30b shows how you can combine these signals to drive and read the A/D converter.

The data bus pins (DB_0–DB_7, pins 18–11) may also require a little special handling. "This MOS A/D, like MOS microprocessors and memories, will require a bus driver when the total capacitance of the data bus gets large. Other circuitry, which is tied to the data bus, will add to the total capacitive loading even in TRI-STATE (high-impedance mode). Back plane busing also greatly adds to stray capacitance of the data bus. . . . Basically, the capacitive loading of the data bus slows down the response time, even though dc specifications are still met. . . . If time is short and capacitive loading is high, external bus drivers must be used. . . . High-current bipolar bus drivers with PNP inputs are recommended" [2].

The ADC0801 is ideal for small, inexpensive applications. But many industrial-grade problems demand higher resolution and accuracy. Other required features are a *true* differential input, the ability to measure both a positive and a negative input voltage, and an on-chip reference voltage generator.

Intersil and Maxim manufacture a series of 12-bit (plus sign) A/D converters that meet these requirements. Direct drive of LCD or LED displays, multiplexed BCD output data, and straight parallel or serial data formats are available in the series of converters.

They are all built around the dual-slope integration technique of A/D conversion. However, an auto-zero phase has been added to minimize the effect of drift. This technique provides the required resolution and accuracy in a low-power, cost-effective, CMOS package. However, a maximum of 30 conversions per second can be make. This is much slower than the successive-approximation converters.

"The ICL7109 is a monolithic 12-bit A/D converter designed for easy interface with microprocessors and UARTs. The 12-bit binary plus polarity and overrange outputs can be directly interfaced to a microprocessor bus. In this mode the ICL7109 is controlled by the microprocessor through the chip select and two byte enable inputs. For remote

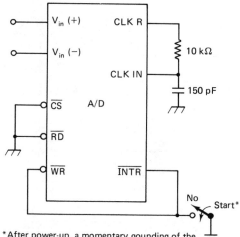

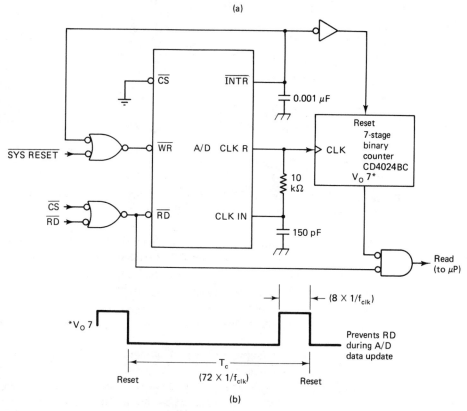

Figure 6–29   Free-run mode: (a) self-clocking; (b) microprocessor interface. (Courtesy of National Semiconductor.)

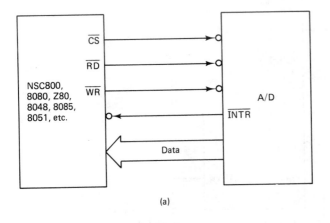

(a)

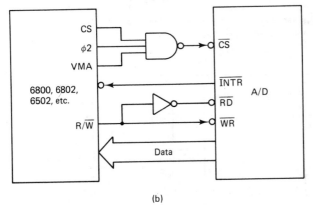

(b)

Figure 6–30 Microprocessor interfaces: (a) 8080 derivative; (b) 6800 derivative. (Courtesy of National Semiconductor.)

data logging applications the ICL7109 outputs are easily converted to a UART handshake mode, working with industry standard UARTs to provide serial data transmission" [3].

"This device offers high accuracy by lowering rollover error less than 1 count and zero reading drift to less than 1 μV/°C. In many data acquisition systems the ICL7109 is an attractive, low-cost, one-per-channel alternative to analog multiplexing due to its low power consumption and input bias current" [3].

Figure 6–31 shows the required external connections. Pins and support components may be arranged into seven groups: power, input, reference, oscillator, integration, data, and control.

The power group consists of $V+$, $V-$, common, and ground. Like the AD0801, the ICL7109 has been designed to use a +5-V positive supply voltage. However, in order to accept negative as well as positive inputs, a negative supply voltage is also required. Performance is tested and specified by the manufacturer with balanced ±5-V supplies.

Pin 1, ground, is the digital ground. Common, pin 33, is analog ground. These

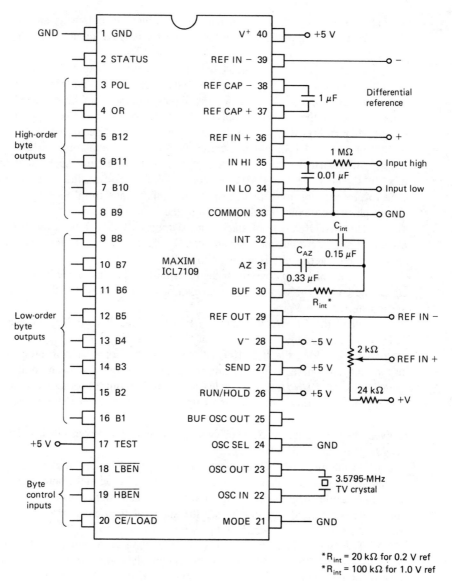

Figure 6–31 ICL7109 typical connections. (Courtesy of Maxim Integrated Products.)

must be kept separate, each having its own return cable to the system's single point ground.

The data conversion equation is

$$\text{data out} = 4096 \times \frac{V_{\text{in}}}{2 \times V_{\text{ref}}} \tag{6–4}$$

An input of $+1$ V will generate the same 12-bit data output as an input of -1 V. However, the POL pin will be at a logic high for positive inputs and at a logic low for negative.

The input pins IN HI and IN LO provide a true differential input with negligible input bias currents and very high input impedance. "Differential input voltages anywhere within the common-mode range of the input amplifier can be accepted (specifically from 1 V below the positive supply to 1.5 V above the negative supply). The system has a CMRR of 86 dB typical in this range. For optimum performance the input voltage of IN-LO and IN-HI should not come within 2 V of either the positive or negative supply" [3]. That is, for ± 5-V dc supplies, you must limit each input to ± 3 V or less. In Figure 6–31 the 1-MΩ resistor and 0.01-μF capacitor at the input pins are used to prevent any noise picked up on the input leads from entering the IC. So you should place these components as close to the IC as practical.

"The ICL7109 has 14 three-state outputs: 12 data bits, 1 polarity bit, and 1 overrange bit. These bits are enabled either by the $\overline{CE/LOAD}$, $\overline{LBEN}$, and $\overline{HBEN}$ control signals or by entering the Handshake mode" [3].

The control group consists of the remaining eight pins. They initiate a conversion, signal the end of the conversion, and control the way in which the two bytes of data are transferred to the processor.

"When the $RUN/HOLD$ input is tied high, the ICL7109 continuously performs A/D conversions with a fixed length of 8192 clock cycles per conversion. When $RUN/HOLD$ is taken low, the ICL7109 will complete the conversion in progress, then wait in the autozero phase. After the minimum autozero time has been completed, a high-going pulse on $RUN/HOLD$ of at least 200 ns is required to start a new conversion; but any pulses during a conversion or up to 2048 clock cycles after $STATUS$ goes low will be ignored. If the ICL7109 is holding at the end of the autozero phase, a new conversion will start and $STATUS$ will go high within seven clock cyles after $RUN/HOLD$ goes high" [3].

"At the end of a conversion cycle the $STATUS$ output goes low, one-half clock period after new data from the conversion have been stored in the output latches. $STATUS$ goes high at the beginning of Signal Integrate. This signal may be utilized as a flag indicating 'data valid' for monitoring the status of the converter or to drive interrupts since data never changes while Status is low" [3].

"The $MODE$ input is used to control the converter output mode. The converter is in its Direct output mode, where the output data are directly accessible under the control of the chip and byte enable inputs when the $MODE$ pin is low or left open. (To ensure a low level when the pin is left open, this input is provided with an internal pulldown resistor.) When the $MODE$ input is pulsed high, the converter enters the UART handshake mode and outputs the data in two bytes, then returns to 'Direct' mode. The converter will output data in the handshake mode at the end of every conversion cycle when the Mode input remains high" [3].

"The ICL7109 is in the Direct mode when the $MODE$ pin is low. In this mode the output interface is a simple parallel interface with a Chip Enable ($\overline{CE/LOAD}$) and two byte enables ($\overline{HBEN}$ and $\overline{LBEN}$). The least significant 8 bits of data are enabled when both $\overline{CE/LOAD}$ and $\overline{LBEN}$ are low. The upper 4 bits of data, polarity, and overrange are enabled whenever $\overline{CE/LOAD}$ and $\overline{HBEN}$ are low'' [3].

"The ICL7109 can be controlled through I/O peripheral ports, as shown in Figure 6–32. These schematics are some practical circuits utilizing the parallel three-state output capabilities of ICL7109. Shown in Figure 6–32a is a straightforward interface to the Intel MCS-48, -80, and -85 systems via an 8255 PPI, where the ICL7109 data outputs are active at all times. The 8155 I/O ports may be utilized in the same way. Although a read performed while the data latches are undergoing updates will lead to scrambled data, this interface can be used in a read-anytime mode'' [3].

Figure 6–32c shows a similar interface to 650X or 680X systems. "The transition of the *STATUS* output from high to low generates an interrupt via the Control Register B CB1 line. Note that CB2 controls the $RUN/\overline{HOLD}$ pin through Control Register B. This application permits software-controlled initiation of conversions'' [3].

The handshake mode is specifically designed to interface the ICL7109 directly to industry standard UARTs, with no external logic required. The ICL7109 is in the handshake mode whenever the *MODE* input is high. In the handshake mode the $\overline{CE/LOAD}$, $\overline{LBEN}$, and $\overline{HBEN}$ pins are outputs and Send is an input. A typical UART to ICL7109 interface is shown in Figure 6–33.

6–1.3 Errors

Even a high-quality data converter with excellent specifications can doom a digital control project to failure if it is not properly matched to the task. This matching must be done in amplitude (resolution and quanitization error) and in speed (conversion rate).

If you want to control a process to within 0.1%, your measurements and commands must be able to resolve 1 part in 1000, or better. A 10-bit converter has a resolution of

$$2^{10} = 1024$$

which just exceeds these requirements. Assuming an analog range of 0 to +10.24 V means that each code change is worth

$$\frac{10.24 \text{ V}}{1024 \text{ bits}} = 10 \text{ mV/bit}$$

There is a $\pm\frac{1}{2}$LSB uncertainty in the data. The code 0111110100 represents 5.00 V. However, even if the converter is perfectly linear, any analog data between 4.995 and 5.005 V will produce that code.

This uncertainty in precisely what analog value the data represent is called quanitization error. Expressed as a percentage of full scale

$$\% \text{ error} = \frac{\text{error}}{\text{converter full scale}} \times 100\%$$

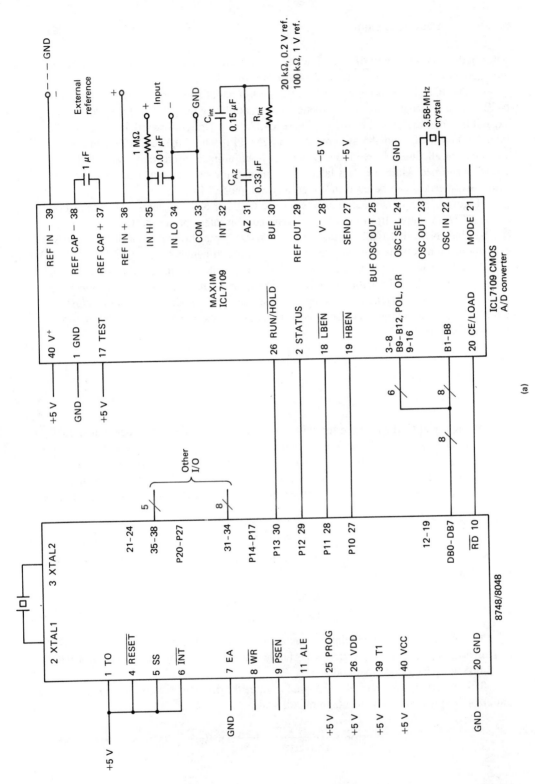

Figure 6-32 Direct-mode microprocessor interfaces: (a) typical connection diagram parallel interface with MCS-48 microcomputer; (b) full-time parallel interface to MCS-48, -80, -85 microcomputers with interrupt; (c) full-time parallel interface to MS680X or MCS650X microprocessors; (d) full-time parallel interface to MCS-48, -80, -85 microcomputer systems. (Courtesy of Maxim Integrated

(a)

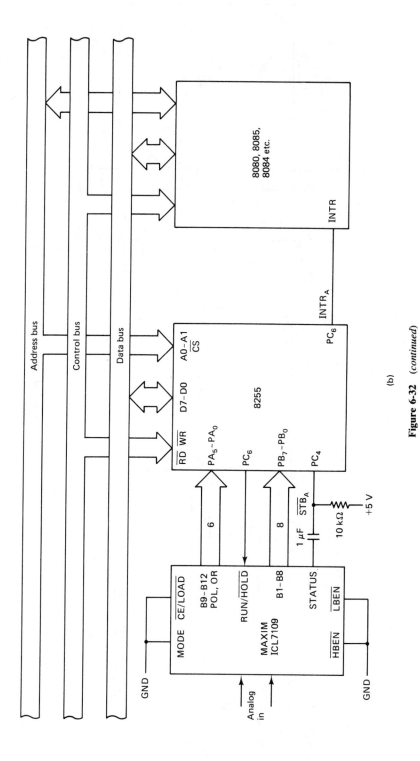

Figure 6-32 (*continued*)

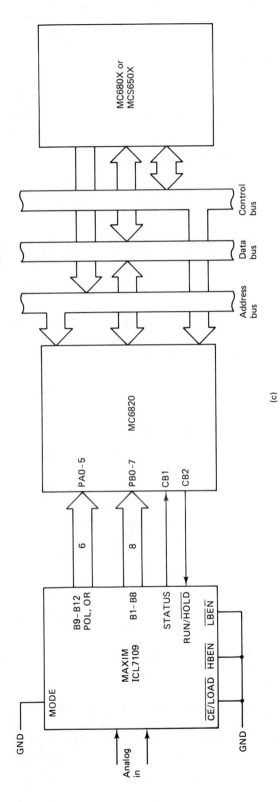

Figure 6-32 *(continued)*

370

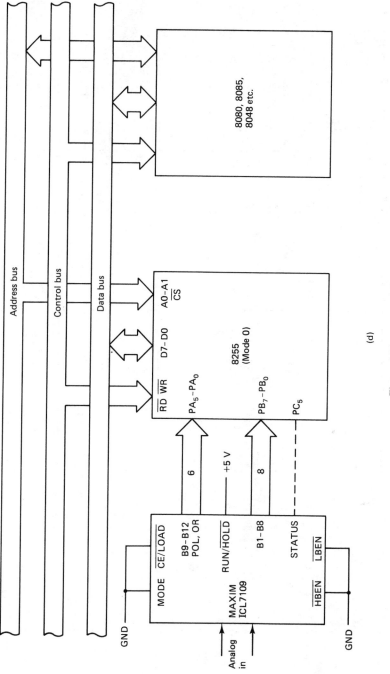

Figure 6-32 (continued)

(d)

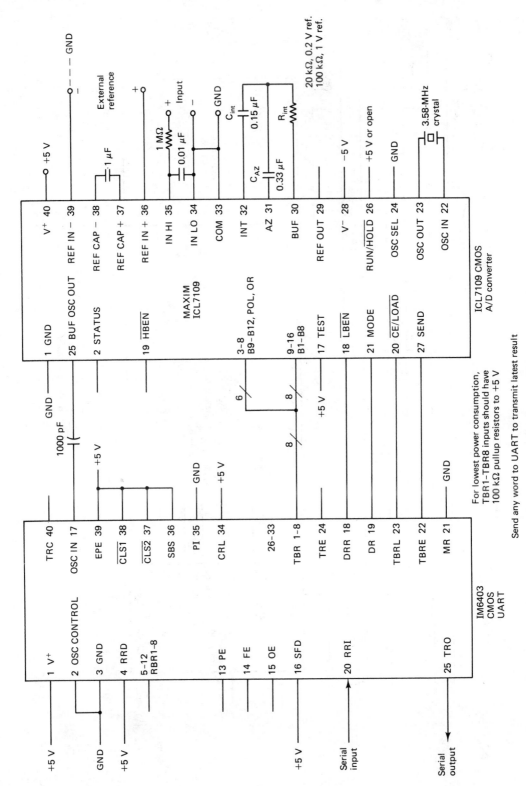

Figure 6–33 UART interface. (Courtesy of Maxim Integrated Products.)

372

or

$$\% \text{ error} = \frac{1 \text{ bit}}{\text{converter resolution}} \times 100\%$$

In analyzing system performance, quanitization error can be modeled as irreducible white noise with an amplitude of 1LSB (value of the least significant bit). In terms of rms voltage

$$\text{error} = \frac{\text{LSB}}{2\sqrt{3}} \text{ V rms}$$

The effect this quanitization error has depends largely on the control algorithm you use. However, systems normally stable when implemented with continuous electronics may have low-level oscillations as the controller jumps back and forth between two adjacent bits, trying to achieve a value or responding to a value that is buried in this quanitization error. A change from 5.005 V to 5.006 V is only a 1-mV change in process variable. But for the 10-bit converter you saw earlier, this will cause the data to jump from 0111110100 to 0111110101. The controller *perceives* a 10-mV jump and drives the output accordingly.

There are two types of speed errors, reconstruction and aliasing. Both are caused by the fact that the digital control system cannot *continuously* convert and process the input (process variable) signal. First, it takes a finite amount of time for the conversion from analog to digital form to take place. This conversion time is also called the aperture time. It depends on the type of A/D converter you have. The successive-approximation converter many take only tens of microseconds. The more-noise-immune integrating A/D may take 33 ms or longer. Once the process variable has been digitized, it must undergo quite a few calculations. These include digital filtering, input scaling, linearization, error calculation, output value calculation (a PID algorithm), and output scaling. After the output value has been computed and sent to the D/A, there are other housekeeping tasks. A front-panel display may need to be updated and a keyboard and switch array inputted and processed. Communication to a supervisory computer may need to be handled. Auto-tuning and self-diagnostics are also features of many modern digital controllers.

All these tasks must be completed before another input sample can be taken. In fact, the larger digital controllers may handle 64 loops or more. So once all of these tasks have been completed for one input channel, it must be repeated for all of the other channels before the computer returns to consider the first signal again.

This time between readings is the sample time. While away computing, the digital controller essentially "thinks" that the process variable is holding steady at the value it obtained from the A/D converter. In reality, this may be far from the truth. Look at Figure 6–34. A rapidly varying input process variable signal is shown in Figure 6–34a. This is sampled and converted at the dots shown in Figure 6–34b. The output from the controller is calculated assuming the input wave shape shown in Figure 6–34c. If this series of numbers (samples) was converted back into an analog voltage, it would have the stair-step shape shown in Figure 6–34c. Certainly, this does not precisely

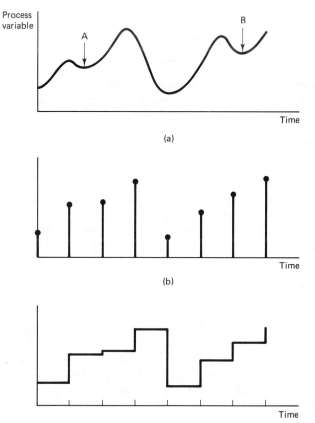

Figure 6-34 Reconstruction error: (a) real-time input; (b) sampled points; (c) reconstructed input.

represent the actual input (Figure 6–34a). The two dips, at points A and B, are completely missed. These errors are examples of reconstruction error.

  Just how good does the reconstructed wave have to be to allow you to maintain control? There has been much research done in sampling theory. The Nyquist criterion states that a repetitive, sinusoidal signal can be completely reconstructed if two samples per cycle (or more) are taken. This certainly does not seem very restrictive. But the two key words are *repetitive* and *sinusoidal*. Given enough cycles, sampling twice a cycle, a sinusoid can be built up.

  However, the process variable is not a repetitive sine wave (we hope). So the two samples per cycle criteria does not provide adequate information to maintain control. "The sampling period can be chosen such that

$$N_r = 2\text{--}4$$

where N_r is the number of samples per rise time of the *closed-loop system*. This means that the sampling period should be chosen in relation to the desired behavior of the closed-loop system. The sampling period can be related to the damped frequency of

TABLE 6–4 PROCESS CONTROL
SAMPLING TIMES

Type of variable	Sampling time (s)
Flow	1–3
Level	5–10
Pressure	1–5
Temperature	10–20

Source: Karl S. Astrom and Bjorn Wittenmark,
Computer Controlled Systems: Theory and Design
(Englewood Cliffs, N.J.: Prentice-Hall, Inc.,
1984).

the closed-loop system. It is convenient to introduce the parameter N. . . . This parameter is the ratio of the damped period and the sampling period. . . . A reasonable rule of thumb is to choose N about 20'' [4, p. 203].

For high-speed servomechanism loops, you should be able to establish a desired closed-loop rise time or bandwidth, or to measure it fairly easily. But many process control loops are inconvenient or difficult to model or measure. Listed in Table 6–4 are suggested sampling times for the more common process control loops using direct digital control. Of course, you must temper these times with what you know of the actual and the desired closed-loop process rise times. "Commercial digital controllers for few loops often have a short fixed sampling interval on the order of 200 ms. This implies that the controllers can be regarded as continuous-time controllers, and the continuous-time tuning rules may be used'' [4, p. 365].

Reconstruction error is one of the two sampling errors. The other is aliasing. Aliasing is caused by sampling a high-frequency signal (noise, perhaps) at a rate below the Nyquist criterion of two samples per cycle. This is illustrated in Figure 6–35. High-

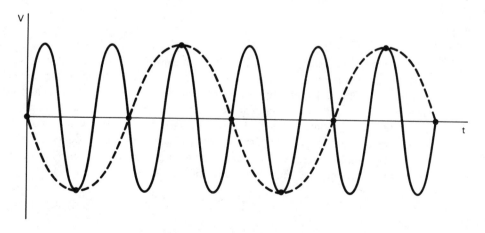

Figure 6–35 Aliasing error.

frequency noise is represented by the solid line. Taking in new data more slowly than twice per cycle makes the controller think that it has a much lower, real input. The controller responds by trying to correct this phantom variation in the process variable.

So noise has caused the controller to try to correct a nonexistent error. The controller output is changed, altering the actuator, driving the process to a new condition. This *really* changes the process variable. The controller must now respond to both the actual process variable change and the aliased noise signal.

The result of all of this is that an otherwise stable system has begun to oscillate because of misinterpreting high-frequency noise as a much-lower-frequency, valid process variable signal.

You have already selected your sampling rate based on the process response time (Table 6–4 and $N_r = 2$ to 4); shortening the sampling time is *not* the solution to aliasing. The signal causing the problem is at a frequency which is too high for it to be a valid process variable signal. It is noise. So the problems of aliasing can be eliminated by removing the high-frequency noise with a low-pass filter.

Since you are working in a system that has digital pulses and steps in the signal, the filter type you choose must be stable, not overshooting or ringing, in response to a square-wave input.

The order of the filter will determine how sharply you attenuate the noise while passing the lower-frequency process variable data. Once you know the type of filter and its order, you must also determine the cutoff frequency, or bandwidth. A useful starting point is [4, p. 365]

$$\omega_{oa} = \frac{k}{h} \tag{6–5}$$

where k is a constant 0.5 to 1 and h is the sampling period in seconds. Of course, in terms of hertz,

$$\omega_{oa} = 2\pi f_{oa}$$

$$f_{oa} = \frac{k}{2\pi h}$$

"For slower sampling rates it is often simpler to sample once per second or faster with an appropriate analog prefilter and apply digital filters to the sampled data" [4, p. 365]. This is largely true because the size and cost of the analog filter capacitors increase significantly as the critical frequencies (ω_{oa}) go down. So use analog filtering down to approximately 0.2 Hz. If it is necessary to filter at a lower cutoff frequency, it is more economical to implement the filter in software (i.e., a digital filter).

The simple first-order low-pass analog filter can be implemented by a discrete data system (computer). The equation for the output is

$$v_{on} = av_i + (1 - a)v_{o(n-1)} \tag{6–6}$$

where v_{on} = present output
         a = constant that sets ω_o

v_i = present input

$v_{o(n-1)}$ = previous output

To implement this equation, you must save the value of the output, so that the calculation during the next cycle can be based on it. The constant, a, is set by the sampling period and the critical frequency you want for the digital filter.

$$a = 1 - e^{-\omega_{od}h} \tag{6–7}$$

where ω_{od} is the critical frequency for the *digital* filter and h is the sampling period.

It has been recommended previously that you let an analog Bessel filter take care of the high frequencies and the digital filter can more economically filter out low-frequency noise. It is recommended that you set the critical frequency of the digital filter at half the analog filter's critical frequency.

$$\omega_{od} = \tfrac{1}{2}\omega_{oa} \tag{6–8}$$

This reduces the effect of an undesired digital filter characteristic referred to a frequency folding.

6–2 Single-Loop Digital Control

The use of a computer to evaluate the desired value of the process's output, its actual value, and then to compute a correction signal has many advantages. Computers do not suffer from the long-term drift effects that analog circuits do. Changes to constants can easily be made without the necessity of actual physical change to the circuitry. In fact, these changes may even be made by the computer itself. So the quality of control improves as the computer "learns" the process. The type of control can be radically altered simply by loading in a new program. No hardware changes are necessary for a radical reconfiguration. Compensation for long dead-time delays or the use of feedforward control requires extensive calculations. These can be implemented directly with a computer. Record keeping, statistical process control, and full, plant-wide computer-integrated manufacturing require that accounting and management computers have access to the results of the manufacturing processes. This is easily done when those processes are themselves under the control of a computer.

6–2.1 Digital Control Schemes

The first attempts at computerized process control was supervisory control. The analog controller was left in the loop. However, a minicomputer was given access to the process variable and was allowed to drive the analog controller's set point. Final control still resided with the analog controller. This is shown in Figure 6–36. This technique realizes *some* of the benefits of computer control. It is easy to install in an existing facility. Control can easily be returned to the analog controllers if the computer fails.

However, the performance of the controlled loops is still restricted by the inherent

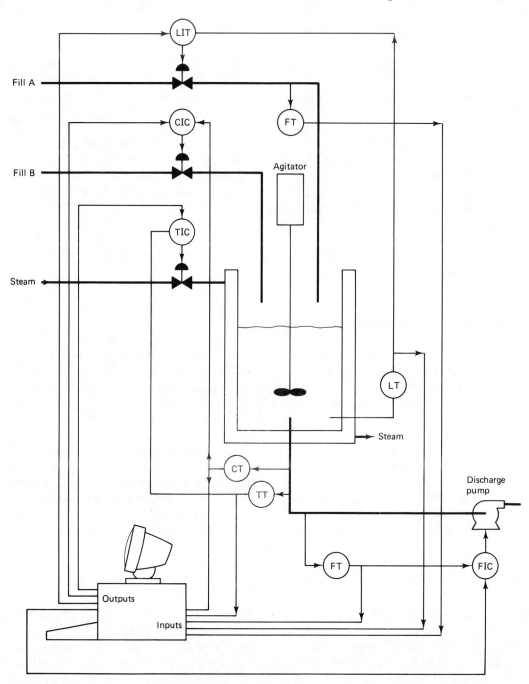

Figure 6–36 Supervisory control.

limitations of the analog controllers. The advantages of self-tuning, radical reconfiguration, dead-time compensation, and feedforward control are all denied to the supervisory computer control scheme.

Once you are prepared to rely on the performance of the computer, the analog controllers can be removed. This allows direct digital control, illustrated in Figure 6–37. In direct digital control, the analog controller has been removed. The minicomputer inputs the process variable directly from the sensor's transmitter. A control algorithm is followed to compute the proper setting of that loop's actuator. This signal is sent directly to the actuator. The computer then goes to the next loop. In a large installation, over 100 loops may be under the direct control of a single minicomputer.

Direct digital control has the potential for realizing all of the benefits of computer control that you saw earlier. However, it, too, has many limitations. Should the computer crash or get "hung-up," all of the loops under its control are now opened. Actuators are stuck and the processes may run away, with expensive and perhaps lethal results. To prevent this, a second minicomputer is used, monitoring and cross-checking the performance of the main control computer. Should a computer failure occur, the backup is ready to take over. But this is expensive and requires very sophisticated software. This backup system will cost you more than the analog controllers you were able to replace.

Also, to be at all economical, the computer must control many loops. To service all the loops two to four times per rise time requires a very fast computer. And there are other alarm, display, communications, self-tuning, and internal housekeeping tasks that the computer must perform. In any significant application it is quite easy to outstrip the performance of even a very fast minicomputer.

The introduction of the microprocessor, and its successor, the single-chip microcomputer, has allowed wide distribution of computing power throughout the manufacturing process. An example of distributed computer control is shown in Figure 6–38. A microcomputer is used as the local controller for each loop. Now, every control loop has its own computer. Long-term stability, self-tuning, remote reprogrammability, and complex algorithms to compensate for dead-time delays and to allow feedforward control are all features that can be provided separately by each microcomputer on each loop. The widespread use of microcomputers (from washing machines to cruise missiles) has lowered their cost to the point that a microcomputer-based controller costs no more (often less) than the analog controller it replaces.

Supervision and integrated plantwide control is accomplished by allowing each microcomputer-based single-loop controller to communicate with a cell supervisor. This minicomputer provides displays, keeps records, issues commands to the loop controllers, and can even program the microcomputer, single-loop controllers. In turn, the cell supervisor reports to and receives commands from a higher-level management computer system.

Communications between each microcomputer, single-loop controller, and its cell supervisor may be over a serial data link, such as the RS-232 or RS-422 standards. Or each loop controller may share a local area network (LAN) with the cell supervisor. A standard assures that physical, electrical, and data structure are all compatible among

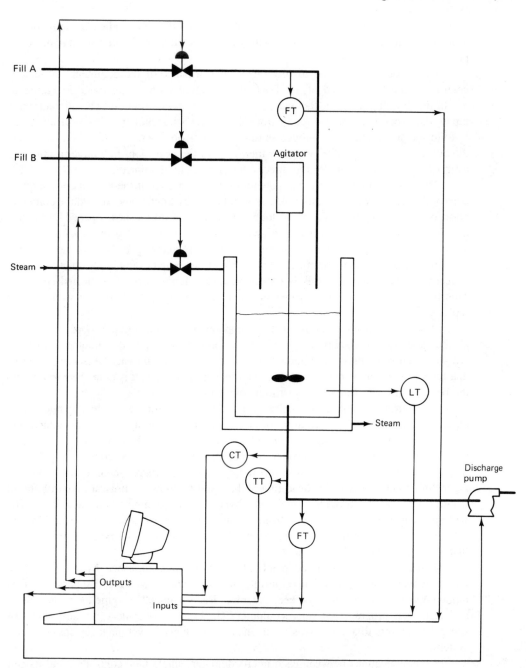

Figure 6–37 Direct digital control.

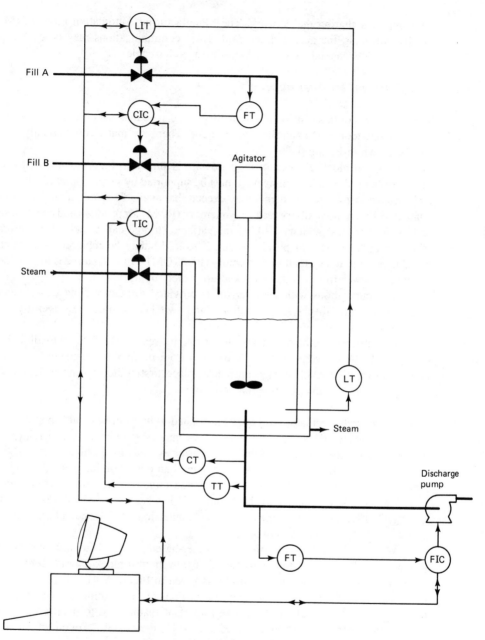

Figure 6–38   Distributed computer control.

the computers sharing the network. The Manufacturing Automation Protocol (MAP) is rapidly becoming the accepted standard. LAN communications may be over a pair of wires, a CATV coaxial cable, or even a fiber optics cable.

6–2.2 Initial Housekeeping

The advantages of this distribution of intelligence can be realized only if a microcomputer-based, single-loop PID controller can be built. There are many commercially available. One is shown in Figure 6–39.

A typical block diagram of the hardware is shown in Figure 6–40. At the core of the controller is the microcomputer. It must be supported by several other blocks. Program and variable storage requirements may exceed that available within a single-chip micro-computer. External, auxiliary read-only memory (ROM) for program and constant storage, and random access memory (RAM) for variable storage can be added to prevent loss of key parameters should power be cut. The RAM may be replaced with electrically erasable programmable read-only memory (EEPROM). An alternative is to provide unin-terruptible power from a battery-backed-up power supply.

Communications with the operator is provided through a front panel. Consisting of LEDs, numeric displays, pushbuttons, and switches, it must be driven by and read by the microcomputer.

The process variable is converted from its real-world form into digital by the analog-to-digital converter block. Conversion from millivolts, frequency, resistance, or current into a high-level voltage must take place first. Filtering and isolation are also included before the analog-to-digital converter.

Similarly, some form of digital-to-analog conversion is required to provide the output signal to the actuator. Although an isolated 4- to 20-mA signal is popular, voltage, time-proportioned triacs, or solid-state relays may be provided. Alarm relays are also energized when the process variable or the error exceeds given limits.

Communications with the host computer is an option on many single-loop control-lers. This may require only a single integrated circuit to translate between the ± 5-V levels of the microcomputer to the higher $\pm V$ levels of RS-232 or RS-422. Or a full set of ICs may be used to provide direct connection to a manufacturing automation protocol (MAP) local area network.

When evaluating or designing a computer-based project, you must give the software as much attention as you do the hardware. A flowchart or block diagram for the program necessary to run a single-loop controller is given in Figure 6–41. There are quite a few blocks, and each block contains many, many lines of programming code. It is tempting to view the PID calculation as the one important feature and to overlook all the other blocks. However, as you can see in Figure 6–41, the actual PID control calculation is only one of over a dozen major tasks that the computer must complete every cycle.

The orderly handling of removal and application of power to the microcomputer is necessary for reliable performance in an industrial environment. The loss of power must be detected and the central processing unit notified. Key parameters and information about the state of the processing must be stored in memory that will not be affected by

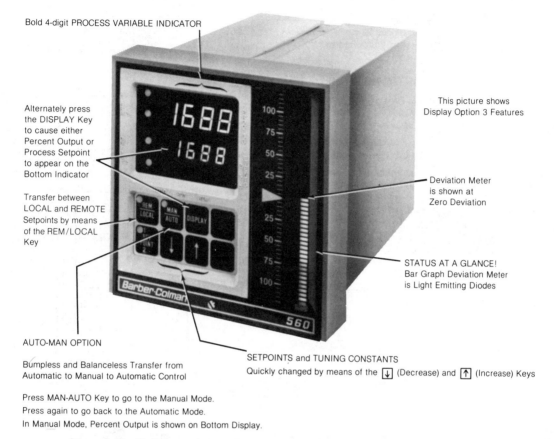

Bold 4-digit PROCESS VARIABLE INDICATOR

Alternately press the DISPLAY Key to cause either Percent Output or Process Setpoint to appear on the Bottom Indicator

Transfer between LOCAL and REMOTE Setpoints by means of the REM/LOCAL Key

This picture shows Display Option 3 Features

Deviation Meter is shown at Zero Deviation

STATUS AT A GLANCE! Bar Graph Deviation Meter is Light Emitting Diodes

AUTO-MAN OPTION

Bumpless and Balanceless Transfer from Automatic to Manual to Automatic Control

SETPOINTS and TUNING CONSTANTS Quickly changed by means of the ↓ (Decrease) and ↑ (Increase) Keys

Press MAN-AUTO Key to go to the Manual Mode.
Press again to go back to the Automatic Mode.
In Manual Mode, Percent Output is shown on Bottom Display.

Figure 6–39   Single-loop microcomputer-based PID controller. (Courtesy of Barbra Coleman.)

power loss. Outputs and alarms must be driven to a safe, predefined condition. When power is restored, these parameters must be retrieved and processing continued from where it was interrupted. This is the function of the Reset on Power-Up block. Be careful to avoid the temptation just to clear all parameters and start over fresh after each power-up. Having to reenter the desired operating parameters from the front panel or host computer after each power interruption would be intolerable in most actual plant operations.

Self-diagnostics is one of the features that sets computer-based equipment apart. At the beginning of operations, the single-loop controller should execute instructions that would allow it to check virtually every block shown in Figure 6–40. A message that this thorough self-test has been completed should be displayed briefly prior to beginning normal operations. In fact, such systems may have more code dedicated to self-testing than to the actual controlling. This is also an ideal time for auto-calibration of the D-A and A-D blocks. Should the self-test be failed, the operator and supervisory host computer should be notified as to the cause. The loop should be powered down,

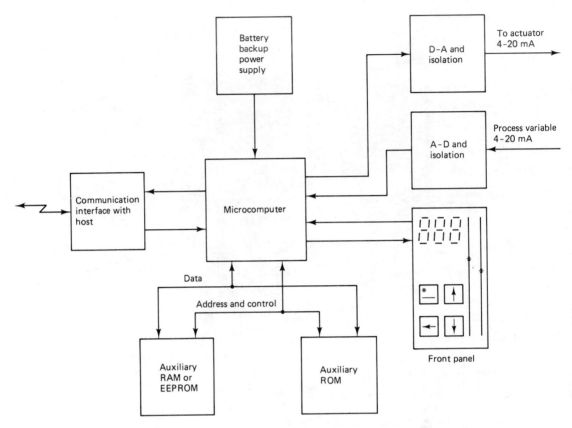

Figure 6–40 Block diagram of a single-loop microcomputer-based controller.

or control transferred to the host. In fact, it would be quite desirable to allow the host
to force the single-loop controller into this self-diagnosis. This would allow routine,
systematic, detailed testing as directed by a central, supervisory host computer. Such
self-testing is well within the power of the microcomputer and would drastically lower
unscheduled maintenance time.

Calculation of the integral and derivative terms of the PID controller requires
that the input be sampled at *uniformly* spaced intervals. To assure this, a timer is used.
The interval is set by several factors. Certainly, the microcomputer must have enough
time to complete all of the required processing. So you would want to set the timer
period (ΔT) reasonably long. However, from the preceding section you saw that sampling
must occur two to four times on the rising edge of the process variable. Table 6–4
also lists recommended process control sampling times. A sampling time of $\frac{1}{2}$ to 1 s is
a typical compromise. (This assumes a system rise time of 1 s or longer.)

When entering the main loop, you must reset this timer. When all goes well, the
program will complete all its processing long before the timer runs down. It then sits
in the diamond-shaped decision loop waiting for the timer to signal it. However, the

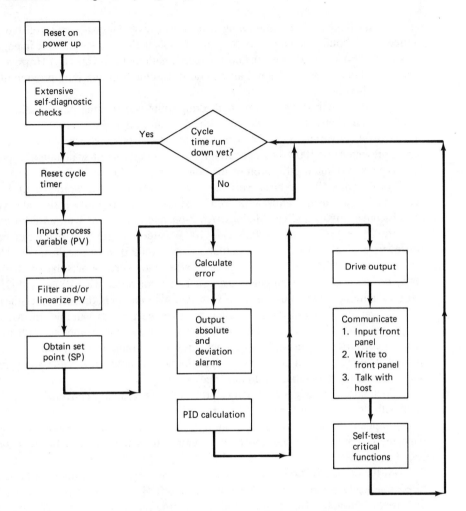

Figure 6–41 Single-loop controller software flowchart.

processor must be able to detect that it has gotten stuck somewhere, or is taking too long to complete all of its processing. This is a fault and must be announced to the operator and/or host computer. The timer should interrupt the microprocessor when it runs down. If the program has not returned to the waiting loop when this interrupt occurs, the fault must be announced and an error-induced shutdown routine entered.

6–2.3 Data Input

The precise code necessary to input the process variable depends on the A/D technique and converter used, as well as the microcomputer. There are several decisions that you must make, independent of these details. First, how is the process variable going to be represented? If you are programming in a higher-level language and you have plenty of time to get around the loop, it is convenient to scale the process variable in engineering units (e.g., °F for temperature, r/min for speed, gallons for level, etc.) However, trying to perform floating-decimal-point arithmetic in assembly or machine programming language is self-abusive.

If you are not going to use engineering units and floating-point math, you must handle all of the subsequent operations with great care. First, the external signal conditioning and A/D converter should be scaled so that at 0% process variable, a data value of zero is presented. At 100% process variable, the converter's full-scale output is produced. This assures maximum utilization of the converter's resolution.

Ideally, this 100% process variable signal just matches the word size of the microcomputer you are using. Otherwise, you must establish this 100% (full-scale) value for all subsequent inputs and calculations. An 8-bit microprocessor with an 8-bit converter will use $2^8 - 1$ (255) as its full-scale 100% value. Single-byte math can be done. However, a 12-bit converter will output $2^{12} - 1$ (4095) at full-scale input. This now represents the 100% level. Over-range calculation and overflow must be checked against 4095. For an 8-bit microcomputer, using a 12-bit converter with 100% = 4095 means that all math operations must be done with two-byte numbers (double precision).

Be careful to avoid the temptation to scale the process variable up. Multiplying the process variable by a constant greater than 1 results in a number with more bits than the converter produced. This implies a resolution (and accuracy) that the converter did not actually give. It appears that you know the process variable more precisely than you actually measured (and converted) it.

Such false accuracy is especially a problem when you have converted to engineering units with floating-point math. Prior to reporting the value, at the front panel, or to the host computer, be sure to round off the number. Report only the number of digits that indicate accurately the resolution (and accuracy) to which the variable was measured and converted.

At the end of Section 6–1.3 you saw that a low-pass digital filter could be applied to economically remove noise that fell below 0.2 Hz but above the response rate of the process variable. This is the point in the program at which to apply the software filtering if it is appropriate. It is recommended that the critical frequency of the digital filter be one-half that of the analog filter. Analog filters are cost-effective down to about 0.2 Hz. This implies that the highest frequency that a digital filter should cut off is 0.1 Hz. Data below this are valid process variable data, while any signals varying faster than 0.1 Hz are considered noise. If your process variable has significant harmonics above 0.1 Hz, you should omit the digital filter. Rely only on the external analog filter for noise removal.

Thermocouples (and a few other types of transducers) are significantly nonlinear. If you know that the process variable is coming from one of these, your program should linearize the signal. This way, the display and control calculations will be performed based on the actual value in the process.

There are two approaches to linearizing a transducer. For either approach you must have a calibration record that relates the transducer's output to the actual process variable. The look-up table approach places this calibration record in ROM (read-only memory). The process variable is used as the address into the table. The correct, linearized value is the data at that address. Using a look-up table is fast and simple. However, it takes up quite a lot of memory. If the entire table is not entered into memory, an interpolation routine must be devised.

The second linearization technique represents the relationship between the transducer output (x) and the true process variable (PV) with a polynomial. The number of terms

$$PV = a_0 + a_1x + a_2x^2 + a_3x^3 + \cdots + a_nx^n$$

determines how accurately the polynomial linearizes the transducer signal. The coefficients (a_0, a_1, a_2, . . .) come from the calibration record and a nonlinear regression statistical calculation. This technique was shown for the thermocouple in Chapter 3 with coefficients given in Table 3–12. A ninth-order polynomial gives linearity of $\pm 1°C$. A nested polynomial can save on execution time, but you must convert the coefficients a_0, a_1, a_2, . . . to b_0, b_1, b_2, ...

$$PV = b_0 + b_1x + b_2(b_1x)x + b_3[b_2(b_1x)x]x + \cdots$$

The polynomial linearization technique requires considerable computing power and speed. But it does not require the extensive ROM memory that the look-up technique does. Polynomial linearization is usually performed by controllers using floating-point math programmed in a high-level language. It is certainly something you would not want to do in assembly language.

The next task for the controller, outlined in Figure 6–41, is to input the set point. This may already be in memory, having been read from the front panel, or from the host, on some previous cycle. If a remote set point is being used, the value must be acquired, scaled, and filtered, just as the process variable was.

There are two additional comments about the set point. First, it must be scaled identically to the process variable. This way, when the process variable matches the set point, the error calculation will give zero. Second, if power is cycled off, then on, the value of the set point must not be lost. So, it must be stored in some form of nonvolatile or battery-backed-up memory.

6–2.4 Control Algorithms

Now it is time to calculate the error. Which equation you use depends on whether the controller is direct or inverse acting. A direct-acting controller will drive its output *up* as the process variable increases. This is typical of cooling systems. For a direct-acting controller,

$$e_{\text{direct}} = PV - SP$$

An inverse-acting controller drives its output *down* as the process variable increases. This is typical of heating systems. For an inverse-acting controller,

$$e_{\text{inverse}} = SP - PV$$

Many single-loop controllers allow you to alter their direction of control (direct or inverse) with a switch behind the front panel, or from the host computer. In performing the error calculation, you must decide which equation to use, as directed by this command read in a previous cycle.

If you are programming in a higher-level language, the subtraction to obtain error is simple. However, in assembly language programming you must be more careful. Typically, a negative number is represented in two's-complement format. But the process variable and set point were input using straight binary. This difference in expressing these numbers will cause confusing and incorrect results. The numbers should all be expressed in the same format. Converters do not work easily in two's complement. Two's complement also cuts the microcomputer's counting range in half (since one bit must represent the polarity). So it is recommended that you convert the result of the error subtraction to the magnitude-plus-sign format. The entire data word is used to represent the magnitude of the error. A bit, in some other word, is set as a flag to indicate that the error is negative.

At this point you can evaluate and drive the alarms. These alarms are of two types, absolute and deviation. If the process variable *exceeds* the absolute *high* alarm limit, the absolute high alarm must be activated. If the process variable falls *below* the absolute *low* alarm limit, the absolute low alarm must be set.

The deviation alarms are based on error. Error more positive than the high-deviation alarm limit will actuate that alarm. Error more negative than the low-deviation alarm limit will activate the low-deviation alarm.

The value of these four alarm limits must have been entered on a previous cycle, from the front panel, or from the host computer. Some controllers fix the deviation alarm limits at ±0.5%. Like the set point, you must be sure that the value of the alarm limits are not lost when power is cycled off, then on again.

Activating an alarm should cause two actions. An output to the real world must be switched. Typically, this is a form C relay (both normally open and normally closed contacts) capable of contact currents of 1 A or more. Providing a set of contacts which change state at an alarm allows the user automatically to activate an emergency procedure to handle the excessive condition.

Second, upon detecting an alarm condition, the microcomputer must set the appropriate flag (a bit). When it is time to service the front panel or to communicate with the host computer, this flag should cause the appropriate front-panel warning display and message to the host computer.

It is now time to calculate the value for the output. Of course, the entire purpose

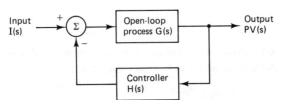

Figure 6-42 Closed-loop control system.

of the controller is to drive the actuator to whatever value is necessary to force the error to zero. There are two approaches used in determining that value.

If you can write the transfer function for the open-loop process control system (actuator, process, transducer, and signal conditioning), optimal control theory can be used. A single-loop system is represented in Figure 6–42. Its closed-loop transfer function is

$$\frac{PV(s)}{I(s)} = \frac{G(s)}{1 + G(s)H(s)} \tag{6–9}$$

There will be more on this in Chapter 8. Assuming that you know how you want the process variable [PV(s)] to respond to a given input variation [I(s)], an optimum function for the controller [H(s)] can be derived. Solving the equation above for H(s) gives

$$H(s) = \frac{I(s)G(s)}{PV(s)} - \frac{1}{G(s)} \tag{6–10}$$

A process called Z transforms allows you to convert this Laplace domain equation for the controller into the Z domain. From this you can write a time-domain equation. The time-domain equation expresses the controller output in terms of present and previous values of the error, coefficients, and the sampling time.

With this controller equation, an input of I(s) will cause on optimum response in the process variable PV(s). Only for this one type of input is the output optimized. Other types of inputs may produce radically (and perhaps unacceptable) outputs. Thorough performance analysis should be completed.

This derivation of an optimum control function, H(s), requires that you know the transfer function of the process, G(s). The less you know about the process, G(s), the more poorly defined its response will be.

The second approach to obtaining a controller equation is the proportional–integral–derivative controller (PID). The PID controller is generic. When properly tuned, it will produce acceptable control for most industrial processes. Also called three-mode, the PID controller allows you to stock one type of controller and use it on flow, level, temperature, velocity, . . . loops. "The three-mode controller represents the ultimate in control of a continuous process for which a specific system transfer function cannot be written" [5].

You saw several analog versions of the three-mode, PID, controller in Chapter 5. In the continuous, analog domain, the controller must have an output that is

$$v_o = K_P e + K_I \int e \, dt + K_d \frac{de}{dt} \tag{6–11}$$

where e is the error and K_P, K_I, K_d are constant. Setting $K_d = 0$ turns off the derivative term, causing a PI controller. Also setting $K_I = 0$ disables the integral part, leaving only proportional control. The precise value of these three constants radically affects the quality of control. Often, they are determined experimentally, by tuning the entire closed-loop system once it is all up and running. There will be more about that in Chapter 8.

To obtain an equation that your microcomputer can implement, the continuous differential equation 6–11 must be converted to a discrete difference equation. First, differentiate both sides of equation 6–11.

$$\frac{dv_o}{dt} = K_P \frac{de}{dt} + K_I \frac{d}{dt}\left(\int e\, dt\right) + K_D \frac{d^2 e}{dt^2}$$

$$\frac{dv_o}{dt} = K_P \frac{de}{dt} + K_I e + K_D \frac{d}{dt}\left(\frac{de}{dt}\right)$$

This equation tells us how much the output must change for each infinitely small change in time, dt. But in your microcomputer-based system, you can look at the real world only once each cycle. The cycle time, T, sets this time interval, dt. So what you are really interested in is how much the output and error must change (Δ) from one cycle to the next (T).

$$\frac{\Delta V_o}{T} = K_P \frac{\Delta e}{T} + K_I e + K_d \frac{\Delta}{T}\left(\frac{\Delta e}{T}\right)$$

where T is the cycle time. Multiplying through by T gives

$$\Delta V_o = K_P \Delta e + K_I e T + K_d \Delta\left(\frac{\Delta e}{T}\right) \tag{6–12}$$

The change in V_o, ΔV_o, is just the difference between its current value and the value you read on the previous cycle.

$$\Delta V_o = V_{on} - V_{on-1}$$

The same is true for the error.

$$\Delta e = e_n - e_{n-1}$$

Rewriting equation 6–12 gives us

$$V_o - V_{on-1} = K_P(e_n - e_{n-1}) + K_I e T + \frac{K_d}{T}(\Delta e_n - \Delta e_{n-1}) \tag{6–13}$$

In the last term, the Δ has been distributed across the two components. These can be expanded as you saw above to give

$$\Delta e_n = e_n - e_{n-1}$$
$$\Delta e_{n-1} = e_{n-1} - e_{n-2}$$

Substituting these into equation 6–13 gives

$$V_o - V_{on-1} = K_P(e_n - e_{n-1}) + K_I e_n T + \frac{K_d}{T}[(e_n - e_{n-1}) - (e_{n-1} - e_{n-2})]$$

or

$$V_o - V_{on-1} = K_P(e_n - e_{n-1}) + K_I e_n T + \frac{K_d}{T}(e_n - 2e_{n-1} + e_{n-2}) \qquad (6\text{--}14)$$

Finally, the current output is

$$V_o = V_{on-1} + K_P(e_n - e_{n-1}) + K_I e_n T + \frac{K_d}{T}(e_n - 2e_{n-1} + e_{n-2}) \qquad (6\text{--}15)$$

You can calculate the current output based on the previous output, the current error, previous errors, the cycle time, and weighting constants.

If you can program this equation using a higher-level language, such as C, Pascal, PL/M, or Fortran, your work will be much easier and less error prone than if you must use assembly language. Such languages allow you to use floating-point math. Negative numbers and overflows are handled for you automatically. Also, many systems that support programming in a higher-level language will also allow you, reasonably easily, to add a math coprocessor. This is an integrated circuit that performs the math operations for you, in hardware. It can evaluate equation 6–15 much more quickly than the control processor can, using math algorithms. For systems that require short cycle times (T), such as position or velocity control, a math coprocessor IC may be a necessity.

If you must program in assembly language, separate equation 6–15 into many steps. Calculate the derivative sum, the weighting constants for each term, and finally the overall output. For each step, check the intermediate result to see if it has gone negative or if it has overflowed.

For negative results, use the sign-plus-magnitude format. A negative term, then, may have the full range of the microcomputer's counting range. However, subsequent steps in your calculation may have to be different for negative terms than for positive.

If you detect an overflow at the end of any of these intermediate steps, set the result of that step to the maximum allowable value. Using double precision (two byte) may be appropriate.

Even with all of this effort, there are still several additional precautions. ". . . although a second-order conventional control system is stable, computer control of the same system can give unstable response for some specific combinations of the proportional gain and the sampling period" [6].

Second, equation 6–15 assumes that the controller cycle time, the time between sampling the process variable, is a constant. However there are several trade-offs. A fast cycle time, small T, is desirable for rapid response to a quickly changing process variable. However, larger values of T are necessary for a stable derivative term. Too small a value for T (in the denominator) would give the derivative term a disproportionately large and jerky action.

Finally, the derivative calculation in a sampled data system may produce unpredicted output jerks. This is because the A/D converter can only pass process variable changes on to the central processor in discrete steps. This is illustrated in Example 6–2.

EXAMPLE 6–2

The process variable begins at 5.000 V and increases 10 mV/s. The set point is 5.000 V. The A/D converter is 8 bits, 10 V full scale. Assuming that $K_d = 3$ s, $T = 1$ s, calculate the derivative output term of equation 6–15.

Solution   Table 6–5 must be completed. PV goes up by 10 mV/s.

$$\text{data in} = \frac{\text{PV}}{10 \text{ V}} \times 256 \text{ (integer value)}$$

$$\text{error} = 128 - \text{data in}$$

$$\text{derivative} = \frac{3 \text{ s}}{1 \text{ s}} (e_n - 2e_{n-1} + e_{n-2})$$

TABLE 6–5   SOLUTION TO EXAMPLE 6–2

n	PV	Data IN	Error$_n$	Derivative
0	5.000	128	0	0
1	5.010	128	0	0
2	5.020	128	0	0
3	5.030	128	0	0
4	5.040	129	1	3
5	5.050	129	1	−3
6	5.060	129	1	0
7	5.070	129	1	0
8	5.080	130	2	3
9	5.090	130	2	−3
10	5.100	130	2	0

The process variable is climbing at a slow, steady rate. In an analog controller this would produce a low, constant derivative term. However, because these data are sampled, and converted, in discrete 39-mV steps, the *data in* column of Table 6–5 shows two discrete steps (at $n = 4$ and $n = 8$). The derivative algorithm, thinking that a 39-mV step has just occurred, responds with a kick, first up, then down.

It is this jerkiness that makes the use of simple digital derivative controllers questionable. A more sophisticated derivative computation may be necessary. Or you may decide to omit derivative action, settling for a proportional–integral control equation.

6–2.5 Command Output

Look back at Figure 6–41, the single loop-controller software flowchart. We have finished the PID calculation block and are now ready to drive the output. This output may be on/off with deadband, time-proportioned, phase-angle-fired, pulse-width-modulated, or analog voltage or current.

For slowly responding processes, an on/off controller works well. When the PID calculation is more positive than a defined positive deadband level, the output (usually 115 V or form C contacts) is turned on. When the PID calculation falls more negative than a defined negative deadband level, the output is turned off. The deadband levels are necessary to prevent actuator and process cycling.

Slowly responding processes that require tighter control than the on/off-type drive can produce may need time proportioning. A time interval that is much longer than one 60-Hz cycle, but much shorter than the process's response time, is chosen. You will need either a hardware timer IC or software timer routine to keep track of this time. At the beginning of the interval, the output is turned on. The value out of the PID calculation determines how long the output is kept on. This technique allows power (115 V ac) to be applied and removed from the actuator only at the zero crossings of the line, minimizing electrical interference caused by switching high-voltage, high-current loads.

In phase-angle firing, the output drive components (both hardware and software) are notified when the line voltage crosses zero volts. Power is removed from the load, turning it off. After a delay, the output drive switches on power to the load (usually through an SCR or triac). Power remains on the load for the rest of that 60-Hz half-cycle. A large value from the PID calculation should cause a short delay, applying power most of that half-cycle. A smaller value from the control calculation results in a proportionally longer delay before firing and a proportionally smaller part of the 60-Hz half-cycle being applied to the load. This drive technique provides much smoother power to the load, but also creates significant electrical interference.

Pulse-width modulation provides a dc output whose frequency is constant and whose pulse width (% duty cycle) varies. A large value from the PID calculation will cause the high time to be large, while a small control output value will cause the high time (% of duty cycle) to be low. A source of dc power is required. The frequency is usually set above the audio range, so a hardware timer IC is usually needed. Severe filtering, just as you would find in a switching power supply, is necessary to make the electrical interference manageable. This type of output drive is appropriate for loads that require significant dc power, such as servomotors.

Most process actuators prefer either 4- to 20-mA or occasionally 0- to 10-V inputs. For this type of output drive you load the value from the PID calculation into a D/A converter. This output must then be converted and scaled to either a 4- to 20-mA current or a 0- to 10-V voltage.

One final comment about output drive must be made. No matter which technique you choose, the electronics must include some form of isolation. This was discussed in more detail in Chapter 4. Without this isolation, an error made in wiring the actuator to the controller, or a failure, could place 115 V ac or more on the ground line of the controller. Of course, this will damage the controller. Even worse, this same fault could run along the communications channel to the host computer, knocking it out as well as anything tied to it.

Once the output has been updated, the program must complete communications with the front panel and the host computer. Sensing and latching front-panel pushbuttons should be done on an interrupt basis. This allows the microcomputer to detect an operator's input at any point in the cycle. However, in writing this routine, be careful that you do not allow the processor to sit and wait for a key closure. If this happened, the processor would become "hung-up" and not complete its cycle. The controller would never get back around to check the process variable and the process would run away, operating open loop.

The same is true with communications with a host computer. However you plan to transmit data between the host and the microcomputer, it must be *completed*. The communication routine must be smart enough not to get "hung up" waiting for the host to respond.

The value of the process variable should be sent from the microcomputer to the host and the microcomputer must be able to receive a new set-point value from the host (called remote set point). The simplest way to do this is through two 4- to 20-mA analog current loops. The microcomputer outputs the process variable through a D/A. The 4- to 20-mA analog current signal from the host commanding the remote set point is read by the microcomputer with an A/D when it reads its process variable.

Digital communications techniques will allow much more information to be exchanged. Standards such as RS-232 or RS-422 may be used, or the microcomputer may be placed on a local area network (LAN). The manufacturing automation protocol (MAP) is evolving as the LAN standard. Data may include self-test results, set point, alarm conditions, output levels, control mode, and controller constants. In fact, an entire new controller algorithm, to replace or supplement the PID equation, may be issued by the host.

Extensive self-testing is necessary when power is first applied to the microcomputer and whenever directed by the host. However, at the completion of every cycle, some self-testing should also be done. Functional testing of the input and output hardware and software, automatic input and output zero and calibration, and a simple check of memory and the communication channel should be undertaken. Should a failure be detected, the operator and perhaps the host computer must be notified. For severe problems, an automatic, orderly shutdown of the process may be directed by the microcomputer.

6–2.6 Modes of Operation

The software flowchart of Figure 6–41 and the discussion to this point have been for the automatic mode of operation. Two other modes may be desired. First is manual operation. In manual, the error calculation, deviation alarms, and PID calculations are removed. Instead, an output command inputted either from the front panel or from the supervisory host computer is sent directly to drive the output. Transfer between automatic and manual control must not allow the output to step. Mode change, at worst, can only cause the output to ramp to a new level at an acceptable rate. This is called bumpless transfer. It was described in more detail in Chapter 5.

The third mode of operation for a single-loop microcomputer-based controller is self-tuning. The simpler version of self-tuning requires operator or host computer initiation.

Once triggered, this type of self-tuning drives its output up and down several times. The algorithm evaluates the process's response to these step changes in the actuator. Based on this information, values for K_P, K_I, and K_D are computed and entered in the PID calculation. The automatic control mode is then reentered. This technique requires operator intervention. It also removes the process from smooth control while the microcomputer experiments with it. This is not always acceptable.

Continuous self-tuning is more sophisticated. It operates in conjunction with the automatic control mode. Whenever an appropriate upset of the set point or the process variable is noticed, the continuous self-tuning algorithm monitors the controller's performance in regulating this change. From this *closed-loop* evaluation, new values of K_P, K_I, and K_D are computed. This procedure happens continuously without operator intervention or interruption of the automatic control. Over time, this type of self-tuning controller "learns" the process, tweaking its own values for optimum control.

6–3 PROGRAMMABLE CONTROLLERS

In this and previous chapters, you have seen several ways of controlling automated manufacturing processes. Dedicated analog circuits were covered in a previous chapter, while the microcomputer single-loop controller was presented in the preceding section. However, the single most widely used industrial controller is the programmable logic controller. "According to the NEMA (National Electrical Manufacturers' Association) Standards, a programmable controller is a digitally operated electronic apparatus that uses a programmable memory for the internal storage of instructions that implement specific functions such as logic, sequence, timing, counting, and arithmetic to control machines and processes" [7].

Originally, the PLC (programmable logic controller) was intended to replace relays in discrete manufacturing operations. Although relays can easily handle the high currents needed to operate actuators and work conveniently on the 115 V ac widely available, they are subject to mechanical fatigue. This leads to failure rates significantly higher than those experienced by electronic components. Interwiring relay contacts and coils to produce the necessary control function is time consuming and very susceptible to errors. Troubleshooting failure in a relay-based control circuit is, at best, very difficult. But most discouraging is when you must scrap the entire relay-based system at the end of every year because the new model of whatever you are making requires a different sequence of manufacturing steps. Driven by these factors, the automotive industry precipitated the development of the programmable logic controller in the mid-to-late 1960s.

Originally, the PLC was used solely for relay logic replacement. But as the capability and reliability of microprocessor components have increased and their cost decreased, the PLC has evolved into "a computer system with a wide assortment of capabilities: arithmetic operations, digital-to-analog conversion, data comparison, word manipulation, complex functions, and equation solving. Two additional capacities include communications with the operator and communications within a distributed control system" [7].

6–3.1 Hardware Overview

The general block diagram for a programmable controller is given in Figure 6–43. Its architecture is just like that of any small computer. All operations are under the direction of the central processing unit. Program instructions are fetched and executed, data manipulated, arithmetic performed, and decisions made. Most central processors today are microprocessor ICs. Program instructions, variables, and constants are stored in memory.

Since it is critical that control not be interrupted by power glitches, and that operation be resumed automatically at the proper place when power is restored, some form of nonvolatile memory is necessary. This is in stark contrast to most traditional computers, which lose part or all of their minds when you turn them off and need your assistance getting started again. For the programmable controller a combination of read-only memory (ROM), battery backed-up random-access memory, and electrically erasable programmable ROM hold *all* instructions and values so that control can easily be reinitiated.

The programmable controller is intensely I/O oriented. Its entire purpose is to drive actuators based on the condition of the sensors connected to its input. A PLC's I/O structure is both very flexible and easy to use. A combination of over 1000 input or output points can be individually examined, stored, used in decision making, or driven. Expanding or changing the input/output configuration is as simple as plugging in the right module or rack. Rarely must the processor even be opened or the program altered. A medium-sized programmable controller with one rack of I/O modules is shown in Figure 6–44. A wide variety of input/output modules are offered by the PLC manufacturer. Line voltage (115 V ac with zero-crossing turn on and off), high-voltage dc, TTL, frequency, analog voltage or current, strain gage, RTD, LVDT, quadrature encoder, stepper motor, thermocouple, real-time clocks, communication interfaces, LAN,

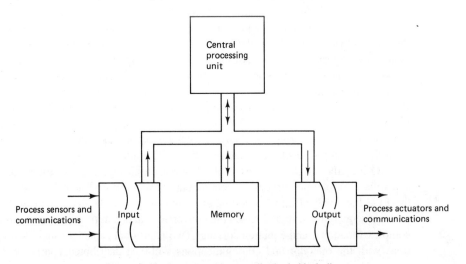

Figure 6–43 Programmable controller basic block diagram.

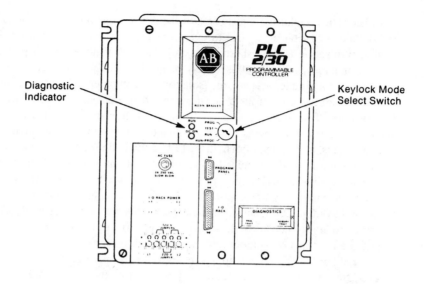

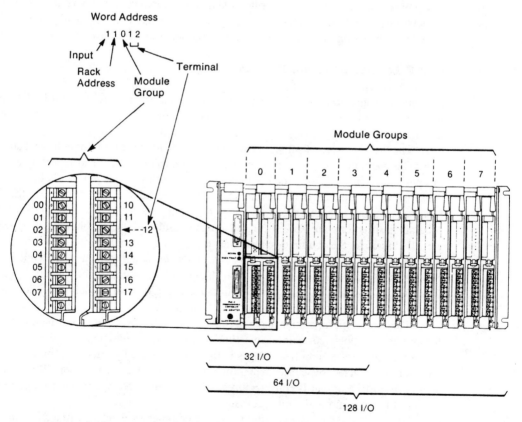

Figure 6–44 AB2/30 programmable controller with one I/O rock. (Courtesy of Allen-Bradley.)

and fiber optics modules are just some of the types of input or output modules available. In addition, isolation of signals to and from the real world through the PLC's I/O is routine. Protection against shorts to as much as 220 V ac at all I/O points is common on most modules. Although this variety of I/O is available for conventional computers, their use is not simple or standard. Isolation for computer I/O boards is unusual.

Programmable controllers are designed to operate in the harsh environment of a factory floor. Temperature extremes from below freezing to well over 100°F must be endured. Electrical transients of several hundred volts or more caused as machines turn on and off must be rejected from both the PLC's power line and its I/O lines. Programmable controllers are normally mounted on a wall or column and forgotten. There they must be able to survive bumps, bangs, occasional collisions with a forklift truck, and vibrations from the machine they are controlling. However, changes to the hardware, either for repair or reconfiguration, must be easy, preferably not requiring tools. The entire unit must be modularly constructed, allowing an electrician to swap every element quickly to locate a malfunction without rewiring and with power on.

Tradition computers require some degree of pampering. A separate computer room isolated from the actual manufacturing floor, with its own air conditioning, ventilation, and power-line protection is the rule. Even those personal computers that have been hardened have some difficulty surviving the "If it doesn't fit, get a bigger hammer" attitude that is commonplace in many high-volume, heavy industries.

6–3.2 Ladder Diagram Programming

As you have just seen, the programmable controller's hardware is optimized to meet the demands of the industrial workplace. However, the success of any computer depends as much on the quality of its software as it does on its hardware.

The PLC has several software features designed to optimize it for industrial automation. The operating system of a programmable controller forces it to repeat a sequence of operations, only part of which is to interpret and follow your program's instructions. This repeated sequence is called the scan. Once placed into the run mode, the PLC repeats this scan without exception. First, all inputs are read. Next, the user-provided program instructions are solved. Based on the results of these solutions, the outputs are all driven to the required states. Self-testing may also be done on both the I/O modules and the processor itself. This scan must be completed in a predefined time. Should the scan take too long, or get "hung up" at some point, an error will be generated. Typically, such an error will cause the processor to halt execution of the scan and notify the operator of the nature of the fault.

This scan-type operation has several implications. All input information used in the program is obtained at the same time, prior to the beginning of the execution of your program. This means that changes in the inputs caused by early steps in the program will not be detected by subsequent program steps until the *next* scan. This is not a significant restriction but is considerably different from standard computer programming and must be kept in mind while programming.

Second, to reduce the possibility of not completing a scan in time, looping and subroutine calls are somewhat limited. Effort is made within the operation system to prevent a user's program from containing an infinite loop; subroutine A calls subroutine B, which calls subroutine A, ... This type of program structure, although allowed in standard computers, would cause a PLC to fail to complete its scan.

Much of the software needed to complete complex input/output operations is also too time consuming to be performed during every scan for all I/O modules by the processor. The more sophisticated input/output modules often have their own microprocessors. Data handling for that module is then very simple for the main processor. It just sends or receives a file of data, then goes on to the next I/O module. It is then up to the microprocessor in the module to figure out how to use these data to drive its outputs, or to assemble data from its inputs for the next main processor's input scan. These intelligent I/O modules also noticeably simplify your programming of complex I/O operations. Analog-to-digital converters, digital-to-analog converters, PID controllers, three-axis motion controllers, communications interfaces, LAN gateways, and intelligent operator panels are examples of I/O with distributing processing power.

From all that you have seen here so far, it would appear that the programmable controller is significantly better than the standard computer. But this enhanced performance has been obtained at the expense of computing power. The math ability of many smaller PLCs is somewhere between clumsy and nonexistent. Data manipulation and communication is crude. For users familiar with programming in a higher-level language, such as BASIC, Pascal, or C, the relay ladder diagram programming language is often frustrating.

Programmable controllers are grouped into four classes based on their I/O capacity. These range from micro (the size of a shoebox), with fewer than 64 input/output points it can read, to large, with the ability to supervise over 893 I/O points. With increasing I/O ability, of course, comes increased size and cost. But more important, math, data-handling ability, and more flexible programming become available as you move to the larger PLCs. Often, a higher-capacity programmable controller will be selected, not because the extra I/O is needed, but because expanded software support is required.

The math operations must be evaluated carefully. On the microPLC there may be none at all. Small PLCs offer only addition, subtraction, multiplication, and division. Medium-sized machines may add square root and a few trig functions. Some large programmable controllers offer most of the functions found on an engineering pocket calculator. However, beware! Even the large, most popular PLCs may not have floating-point arithmetic. Three BCD digits may be all you get; and you may have to keep track of overflow and negative results yourself. For these machines, memory management is not automatic. You must determine where every number is stored, assuring that two operations do not overlap. Even for these large powerful PLCs, math and data manipulation may be only slightly easier than programming in assembly language.

Relay ladder logic is the standard programming language for programmable controllers. It is a highly symbolic, allowing the user to represent the logic as it would be implemented by the electrician if he were wiring relays to accomplish the task at hand.

An example of relay ladder logic is given in Figure 6–45. This is a motor starter circuit. The actual schematic is given in part (a). It consists of the motor itself, represented by the circle, a start button (normally open), a stop button (normally closed), and

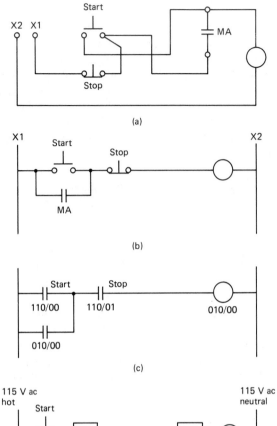

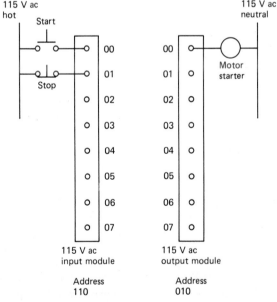

Figure 6–45 Motor starter logic:
(a) electrical schematic: (b) relay ladder
logic diagram: (c) PLC program rung:
(d) PLC wiring electrical schematic.

maintain contacts. These components are wired so that (with 115 V ac applied between X1 and X2) when the start button is pressed the motor begins to spin. Whenever the motor has power applied, the maintain contacts are closed. This places a closed parallel path around the start button. So, once you push it, you can release the start button and the motor will continue to spin. If the stop button is opened, power is removed from the motor. The motor stops. This opens the maintain contacts. To start the motor again, the stop button must be released and the start button must be pushed.

This logic is not obvious. However, redrawing the contacts as they are in Figure 6–45b usually helps. Contacts in parallel form a logical OR operation. Power will be passed if either one OR the other is closed. Contacts in series form a logical AND operation. Power is passed through them only when each AND every one in the series string is closed. It is traditional to show only one load (output) on each rung of the ladder. It is the last item on the right. The rung is TRUE when power is applied through all of the contacts and reaches the load. If something along the rung interrupts power, the rung is FALSE.

This relay ladder logic diagram can be implemented directly on a programmable controller. The PLC program is shown in Figure 6–45c.

There is almost a one-for-one correlation to the relay ladder logic diagram. The numbers above each contact give that input's hardware and memory location. They tell the program which bit on which module to look at. If no voltage is found on that input bit, the contact is considered unoperated, and the logical expression represented by the rung is solved with that contact in the condition shown. If 115 V ac is found on the input bit specified, the contact is considered to be operated. When solving the rung's logic the program will show the contact in the condition opposite to that originally programmed (i.e., normally open contacts will be considered to have closed, normally closed will be considered opened).

If power can be passed all the way along the rung, causing the rung to be true, power is applied to the output module and bit specified by the numbers associated with the load at the right of the rung. These numbers can also be used to represent the condition of the load and can be entered as contacts. Look at the load in Figure 6–45c. It has been given the address 010/00. When the rung is false, no power is applied to that output. Contacts 010/00 represent that fact by remaining open. When the rung goes true, applying power to 010/00, contacts 010/00 are considered to have closed. On subsequent scans, those contacts will be shown as closed, and the rung's logic solved accordingly. The maintain contacts have been implemented logically, without the need for an actual set of hardware contacts.

Wiring to the contacts and load is greatly simplified when using the PLC. Instead of having to interconnect the contacts and loads as shown in the original schematic (Figure 6–45a), the contacts are connected between the 115-V ac hot line and the PLC's input module. Loads are connected between the output module and the 115-V ac neutral. Thats all!

For safety, there is one general practice.

Contacts that *initiate* action should be wired *normally open.*

Contacts that *inhibit* action should be wired *normally closed.*

Following this same scheme, the more advanced functions can be programmed, being activated only when certain conditions make that rung true, or causing some action, when they themselves become true. Moving data from one location to another, comparing data, math, and even subroutine calls and returns all have their special relay ladder logic symbols that you incorporate into your program rungs. The keyboard of a popular programmable controller's CRT programming terminal is shown in Figure 6–46.

More sophisticated operations can easily be handled with fill-in-the-blank programming blocks. Software timers and counters are called up by a single keystroke, followed by filling in requested constants and memory locations. A sample of on-delay timer programming for one PLC is given in Figure 6–47.

The same is true for block data moves, creation and display of messages, communications with peripherals, LANs and external computers, analog-to-digital and digital-to-analog conversions, sequential drum programmers, and even PID control. A representative PID functional programming block is shown in Figure 6–48.

The philosophy in developing programming languages for programmable controllers has been to provide users with code with which they are already familiar. So PLC programming has followed, rather than lead, the computer literacy movement. Initially, most users were electricians, or at least well versed in the relay ladder diagrams used in wiring control relays. So relay ladder logic programming was the natural first choice for a PLC programming language.

With the pervasiveness of personal and home computers (common now even in the lowest elementary school grades) has come a broad base of users who speak BASIC. Consequently, most of the large PLCs now offer some form of higher-level programming

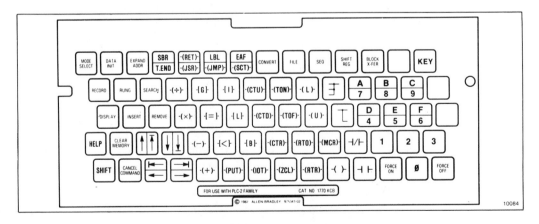

Figure 6–46 PLC programming terminal's keyboard. (Courtesy of Allen-Bradley Company, Inc.)

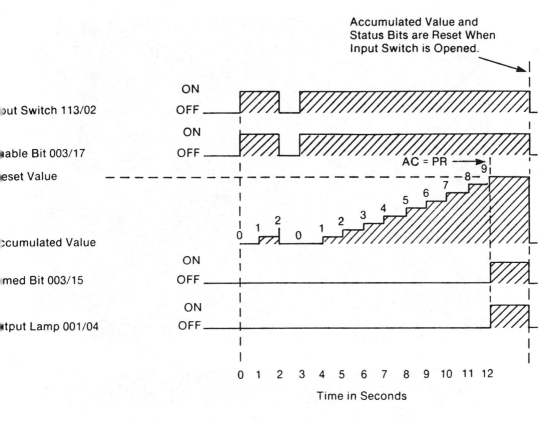

Accumulated Value and
Status Bits are Reset When
Input Switch is Opened.

put Switch 113/02

able Bit 003/17

eset Value

AC = PR

ccumulated Value

med Bit 003/15

tput Lamp 001/04

Time in Seconds

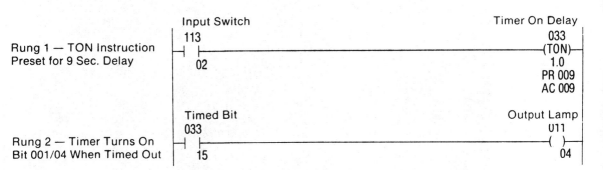

Rung 1 — TON Instruction
Preset for 9 Sec. Delay

Input Switch
113
02

Timer On Delay
033
(TON)
1.0
PR 009
AC 009

Rung 2 — Timer Turns On
Bit 001/04 When Timed Out

Timed Bit
033
15

Output Lamp
U11
( )
04

Figure 6–47 Timer on-delay, timing diagram for a preset value of 9 s. (Courtesy of Allen-Bradley Company, Inc.)

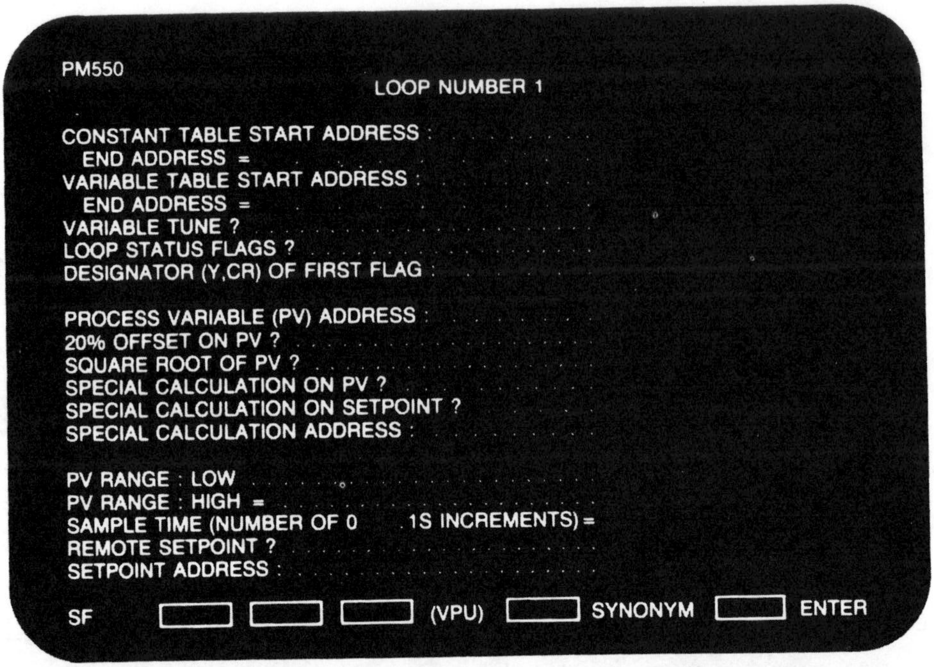

```
PM550
                                          LOOP NUMBER 1

CONSTANT TABLE START ADDRESS :
  END ADDRESS  =
VARIABLE TABLE START ADDRESS :
  END ADDRESS  =
VARIABLE TUNE ?
LOOP STATUS FLAGS ?
DESIGNATOR (Y,CR) OF FIRST FLAG :

PROCESS VARIABLE (PV) ADDRESS :
20% OFFSET ON PV ?
SQUARE ROOT OF PV ?
SPECIAL CALCULATION ON PV ?
SPECIAL CALCULATION ON SETPOINT ?
SPECIAL CALCULATION ADDRESS :

PV RANGE : LOW
PV RANGE : HIGH  =
SAMPLE TIME (NUMBER OF 0      1S INCREMENTS) =
REMOTE SETPOINT ?
SETPOINT ADDRESS :

SF          [    ]  [    ]  [    ]  (VPU)  [    ]  SYNONYM  [    ]  ENTER
```

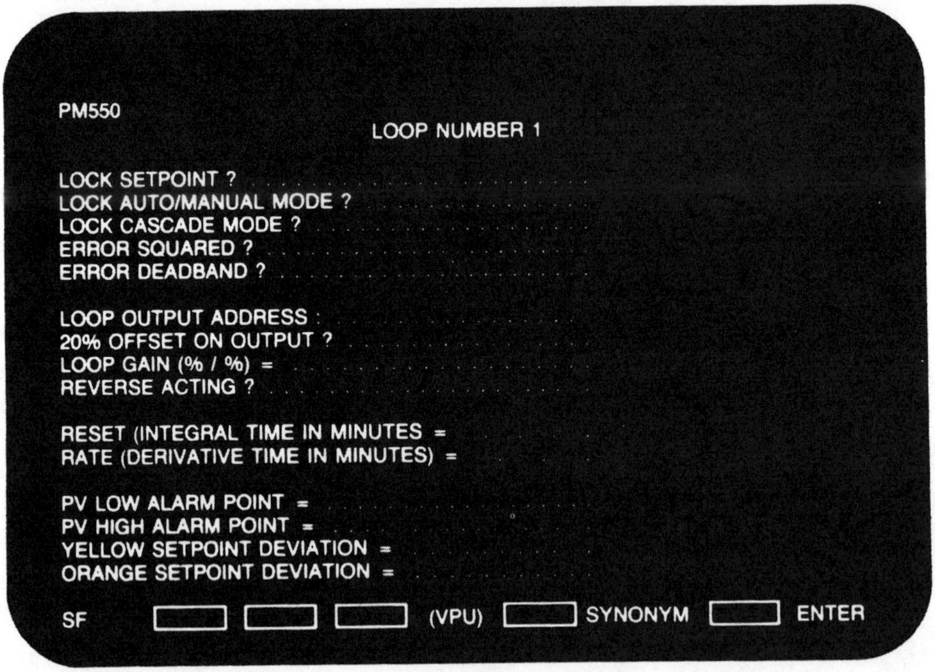

```
PM550
                                          LOOP NUMBER 1

LOCK SETPOINT ?
LOCK AUTO/MANUAL MODE ?
LOCK CASCADE MODE ?
ERROR SQUARED ?
ERROR DEADBAND ?

LOOP OUTPUT ADDRESS :
20% OFFSET ON OUTPUT ?
LOOP GAIN (% / %)  =
REVERSE ACTING ?

RESET (INTEGRAL TIME IN MINUTES  =
RATE (DERIVATIVE TIME IN MINUTES) =

PV LOW ALARM POINT  =
PV HIGH ALARM POINT  =
YELLOW SETPOINT DEVIATION  =
ORANGE SETPOINT DEVIATION  =

SF          [    ]  [    ]  [    ]  (VPU)  [    ]  SYNONYM  [    ]  ENTER
```

Figure 6–48 PID functional programming block. (Courtesy of Texas Instruments Incorporated.)

language. Many provide a BASIC interpreter or compiler. Also available are Fortran, C, PLM, a combination of math and Boolean, or a PLC's own proprietary language.

"We also anticipate . . . much wider use of artificial intelligence. This includes, but is not limited to, actual language processing, expert systems, icons and display manipulation, and most important of all, software productivity for the installer-designer. As is now well known, AI (artificial intelligence) has the capability of delivering high productivity to the software environment, especially in the development mode. There also will be more of the attitude of 'Do what I mean' " [8].

"In the target environment we expect artificial intelligence to help solve the maintenance problem. It must be appreciated that in the future, maintaining large machines will be difficult. With turnover, aging, and reliability of machines it is entirely conceivable that a maintenance person will go down to fix a machine that he has never seen before and will never see again. We also expect simple learning to become embedded into the target machine and that more management by exception will substantially reduce the need for communication bandwidth and make machines much more reliable. . . . In the near future the maximum instruction manual needed, we hope, will be a display on a video screen stating, 'How may I help you?' " [8].

SUMMARY

The analog controllers of Chapter 5 are adequate to provide simple, inexpensive control. However, they suffer from component drift and inaccuracies. They are difficult to adjust or reconfigure. Digital controllers solve all of these problems while opening the field of flexible manufacturing. The personal computer, programmable controller, microprocessor, and microcomputer can be combined in a distributed intelligence system. Each provides control at a progressively simpler level, while communicating with each other, sharing data about process performance, alarm status, instructions, and reprogramming. The nonideal characteristics of the analog circuitry can be largely eliminated. Controller tuning can become automatic. Computations are simple, while entire system reconfiguration is as easy as downloading a series of new programs.

Although these digital controllers offer significant advantages over their analog counterparts, much of the process to be controlled is still analog. Most actuators expect an analog signal to drive them. The digital-to-analog converter takes the data produced by the controller and changes them into a proportional analog signal for these actuators. Many of the transducers output their information about the process variable in analog form. The analog-to-digital converter changes these into digital data that the computer can use. The proper specification of resolution, quanitization error, conversion speed, and sampling rate are as central to successful control as is the transducer's performance, or the tuning parameters of the controller.

The D/A converts a digital code to an analog parameter by switching successive-ratio analog bit-weighted currents to a common summing point. A D/A converter includes analog switches, digital switch control, an analog reference, and an output amplifier.

Outputs may be only positive, or the converter may be configured to produce a bipolar signal.

Static specifications include offset, gain, linearity, and differential linearity. Specifications for the drift of each of these must also be considered. In Section 6–1.1 the performance of two converters was presented in detail. The MC1408 is a popular, simple one-quadrant, current-output D/A. The AD667 is a complete, microprocessor-compatible, four-quadrant D/A with 12-bit resolution.

The specifications for analog-to-digital converters are similar to those for D/A converters. However, there is a wider variety of A/D converters available. The integrating A/D is widely used for panel meters and high-precision applications. It suffers from speed limitations, but provides high accuracy at reasonable cost. The successive-approximation converter is most popular, providing adequate speed and resolution for most control work, at moderate cost. It is susceptible to noise and requires more effort for successful operation. Tracking and flash converters are very fast but have limited resolution and noise immunity.

Two examples of A/D converters were presented in detail in Section 6–1.2. The ADC0801 is an inexpensive series of microprocessor-compatible A/D which use successive approximation. Proper use of its analog reference and differential inputs allows you to zero and span many transducer signals without additional electronics. Digital signal requirements were also presented. The ICL7109 is a 12-bit integrating A/D with parallel output for direct connection to a computer's bus, or serial UART output for remote or stand-alone operation. Like the ADC0801, its analog input pins allow direct zero and span adjustments. To accommodate both serial and parallel outputs, detailed signal requirements and procedures were given.

Converter specifications must be matched to the process under control. Both amplitude (resolution and quanitization error) and speed (conversion speed) must be considered. Resolution sets the minimum-size signal that can be seen. Quanitization error is modeled as white noise with an amplitude of 1LSB. However, systems that are stable with analog electronics may oscillate when converted to digital, as the controller jumps back and forth between two bits. Speed errors include reconstruction and alaising. The A/D converter must sample the data two to four times per process variable rise time to assure that control can be maintained. The input bandwidth must be restricted, to remove the possibility that the controller will mistakenly interpret high-frequency noise as a valid, low-frequency variation in the process variable, which must be corrected. Both analog and digital (software) filters may be applied.

There are three types of digital control. Supervisory control leaves the analog controller in the loop. The computer looks at the process variable and redirects the analog controller's set point. In direct digital control the analog controller is replaced with the computer. It measures the process variable, computes the correct position of the actuator, and drives it directly. Many such single loops are handled, one after the other, by a single direct digital control minicomputer. Distributed computer control places a computer (microcomputer or programmable controller) on each loop. It controls that loop. Communications with a supervisory minicomputer allows integration of the manufacturing effort.

The single-loop digital controller is built around a microprocessor or single IC microcomputer. At its core is the microcomputer itself. This is supported with auxiliary RAM for variable storage, and ROM to hold the program. Battery power as well as line voltage are usually required to assure orderly operation as power is removed and reapplied. Input of the process variable and related analog signals requires an A/D converter with isolation. Output to the actuator uses a D/A converter, also with isolation. Other analog signal conditioning may also be needed to match the signal type required. Communications with the operator are normally done through a front panel that the computer must drive. A communications link to the host (supervisory) computer allows the loop under the control of this micro to be integrated with the rest of the plant.

Software design is at least as critical to a computer's efficient, reliable operation as is its hardware. The single-loop controller computer must be able to check all of its elements upon power-up. Control is performed in an uninterrupted cycle. This cycle must be completed within a specified time. Otherwise, an operational fault has occurred, hanging up the computer. A cycle timer with hardware interrupt keeps watch over this. It must be reset at the beginning of each cycle.

Calculation of the output value begins with inputting, filtering, linearizing, and scaling the process variable. The set point must also be obtained from the front panel, the host computer, or another analog input. Error is calculated, and alarms driven. These alarms may be absolute, based on over or under conditions of the process variable, or they may be deviation, based on the magnitude of the error. The PID calculation is based on present values and past values of the error. Derivative terms may cause instability in a digital controller, although they do not in a comparable analog controller. Be careful. The ease and success you have programming this section of the controller depends on the math level available. A higher-level programming language allows you to work in floating-point arithmetic. A math coprocessor IC speeds operations. If you must work in assembly language, be prepared to exercise extreme care throughout a rather tedious process.

Once the microcomputer has determined the value of the output, it is time to communicate. First, that value must be sent out to the actuator. This may be as simple as a single machine code *out* instruction to a D/A, or it may require a routine to provide pulse-width modulation, phase-angle firing, or time proportioning. Communication also includes interacting with the front-panel display and buttons and exchanging data (and perhaps a new program) with the host computer.

At the completion of each cycle, two additional procedures must be performed. First, a self-test of critical functions must be completed. Second, the cycle timer must be observed. Calculation of integral and derivative terms require a fixed cycle time. So the next cycle cannot be entered until the cycle timer runs down. Also, if the cycle timer runs down before the computer completes its steps, there is a major problem, and emergency procedures must be implemented.

The software described provides automatic control. A single-loop controller must also be able to work in the manual made. In this mode the output is driven, not from an error calculation, but directly from a value input from the front panel or remote computer. Some single-loop controllers also have a self-tuning mode. Under self-tuning the microcomputer calculates the best set of PID constants based on its observations of the process's performance. This allows a controller that "learns" the process, getting better at controlling it with experience.

Programmable controllers are a general-purpose, industrial-grade computer, optimized for direct control of a manufacturing machine. Originally designed to replace relays in a discrete assembly process, their hardware is hardened to survive the extreme temperatures, power spikes and glitches, atmospheric contamination, mechanical vibrations and impacts, input and output overloads, and operator abuse typical on the floor of a heavy-industry manufacturing plant. Under those rare cases when a PLC does fail, it detects its own fault, safely shuts down the machine it is controlling, and notifies the operator what is wrong. Repair is often obvious, simple, and quick, requiring a minimum of skill and no tools or rewiring. There are a variety of I/O modules, allowing easy reading of all variables of interest and the driving of all loads of interest in a manufacturing process.

Programming requirements are as stringent. The language duplicates the relay ladder logic familiar to plant electricians. Advanced I/O, math, data manipulation, timing and counting, communication, and PID algorithms are all available with a minimum of programmer (operator) knowledge. A menu or fill-in-the-box format is best. Artificial intelligence is currently being investigated.

REFERENCES

1. *Data Conversion Seminar*. Norwood, Mass.: Analog Devices, July 1984.
2. *Linear Databook*. National Semiconductor Corporation. Santa Clara, Calif.: 1982, pp. 8–28 to 8–59.
3. *Data Acquisition Catalog*. Sunnyvale, Calif.: Maxim Integrated Products, 1984, pp. 1–29 to 1–45.
4. KARL J. ASTROM and BJORN WITTENMAR, *Computer Controlled Systems: Theory and Design*. Englewood Cliffs, N.J.: Prentice-Hall, Inc., © 1984.
5. CURTIS D. JOHNSON, *Microprocessor-Based Process Control*. © 1984, p. 211. Adapted by permission of Prentice-Hall, Inc., Englewood Cliffs, NJ.
6. PRADEEP B. DESHPANDE and RAYMOND H. ASH, *Elements of Computer Process Control with Advanced Control Applications*. Research Triangle Park, N.C.: Instrument Society of America, 1981, p. 154.
7. MARVIN A. NEEDLER, *Where Do Programmable Controllers Fit in the Engineering Technology Curricula*, 88th Annual Conference, ASEE.
8. RICHARD D. MORLEY, "Tracking the double-diphthong modifier," *Programmable Controls*, March–April 1985.

PROBLEMS

6–1. Draw the block diagram of a D/A converter. Specify the purpose of each block.

6–2. For a D/A converter with a 12-bit resolution, calculate the value of 1LSB in mV, % FSO, ppm, if the range is

(a) 0 to 6 V.

(b) −6 to 6 V.

6–3. A D/A converter has the following static errors:

Zero error: 5 μV

Gain error: 0.03% FSO

Zero error temperature coefficient: 0.7 μV/°C

Gain temperature coefficient: 9 ppm/°C

If the converter has a 6-V FSO and experiences a 20°C temperature change, calculate the range of possible output voltages if the input digital code calls for 3.00-V output.

6–4. A 10-bit D/A converter has an initial accuracy of $\frac{1}{2}$LSB and a differential nonlinearity temperature coefficient of 5.0 ppm/°C. The converter is to be used in an environment that goes from 0 to 80°C. Is monotonicity assured? Prove your answer.

6–5. For the MC1408 D/A converter in Figure 6–12, given that R_{ref} = 4.7 kΩ, R_L = 220 Ω, data in = 01110110, calculate the following values.

(a) I_{ref}.

(b) I_o.

(c) V_o.

6–6. Draw the schematic of a D/A converter using a MC1408 that will output (three separate schematics)

(a) 0 to −10 V.

(b) 0 to +10 V.

(c) a fraction of the input signal, which varies from −5 to 5 V.

6–7. Consider the AD667 shown in Figure 6–14.

(a) How much current flows through the 5-kΩ resistor between pins 1 and 2?

(b) For a full-scale input code, how much current flows in the feedback loop of the output op amp?

(c) Assuming that the external bipolar offsetting resistors are not used, how much current flows through the 9.95-kΩ internal resistor? Explain.

(d) Alter the schematic to give a 5-V full-scale output.

(e) Answer questions (a) to (c) for the 5-V output schematic of part (d).

(f) Answer questions (a) to (c) for the bipolar output in Figure 6–15.

6–8. Draw a timing diagram for the AD667 illustrating the proper sequence, timing, and levels of the chip select, address, and data bits to load in a 12-bit word using right-justified format from an 8-bit microcomputer.

6–9. Explain how conversion is made from an analog voltage to a digital word using the following converters.

(a) Successive-approximation A/D converter.

(b) Dual-slope A/D converter.

6–10. List the advantages of the following converters.

(a) Successive-approximation A/D converter.

(b) Dual-slope A/D converter.

6–11. Draw the schematic of an A/D converter using the AD0801. The input comes from an AD590, which outputs 1 μA/K. Configure the analog input to give 0 at 75°F and 255 at 110°F.

    (a) Draw the schematic.

    (b) Show all of your calculations.

    (c) What must be the voltage at $V_{in(-)}$?

    (d) What must be the voltage at $V_{ref/2}$?

    (e) What is the converter error from full scale, zero, and nonlinearity assuming proper zero and span adjustment using an AD0803 (1) in terms of LSB and (2) in terms of °F?

6–12. (a) Calculate the required clock frequency for the converter of Problem 6–11 to give no more than 0.3°F error in the presence of 5 V peak of 60-Hz noise.

    (b) Alter the schematic of Problem 6–11 to accomplish this.

    (c) Alter the schematic to allow the converter to operate in the free-running mode.

6–13. Draw a timing diagram for the AD0801, illustrating the proper sequence, timing, and levels of the chip select, read, write, interrupt, and data lines to

    (a) trigger the beginning of a conversion.

    (b) signal that a conversion is complete.

    (c) place valid data on the data bus.

6–14. Repeat Problem 6–11 (a)–(d) using the ICL7109. (Set 0 out for 75°F and 4095 out for 110°F.)

    (a) Draw the schematic.

    (b) Show all your calculations.

    (c) What must be the voltage at input low?

    (d) What must be the voltage between the differential reference pins?

    (e) What is the resolution of the data out (in °F)?

6–15. Alter the zero and span values of Problem 6–14 to provide an output of 750 at 75.0°F and 1100 at 110.0°F.

6–16. It is desired to use the AD0801 to control the temperature in a chamber to ±0.1°F.

    (a) What is the quanitization error?

    (b) In Problem 6–11 the converter was zeroed and spanned to fit the range of the temperature. Determine a new % quanitization error equation. Under these conditions, will the AD0801 give an adequately small quanitization error?

    (c) What is the rms error voltage caused by quanitization error?

    (d) Convert this rms error voltage into an error temperature.

6–17. A given closed-loop system was observed to behave as if it were second order. Simulation indicated that it had these characteristics:

Gain: 12

Resonant frequency: 4.69 rad/s

Damping coefficient: 0.65

    (a) For an input step of 0.32, calculate (see Chapter 2) (1) peak overshoot; (2) settling time to 5%; (3) frequency of the damped oscillations.

    (b) How often must the process variable be sampled?

    (c) Can you use an integrating A/D, or must you use successive approximation? Explain.

6–18. (a) An integrating A/D has a conversion time of 16.7 ms. If this is fast enough to measure the process variable properly, what should be the high-frequency cutoff of the antialiasing filter?

    (b) Explain the purpose of that filter.

6–19. Using BASIC, write a program that will implement a digital filter. The cutoff for the antialiasing hardware filter is 5 Hz. The A/D has a 16.7-ms sample time.

6–20. List three advantages of digital control over analog control.

6–21. **(a)** Describe the three types of digital control.
(b) Give the relative advantages and disadvantages of each as compared to the other two types.

6–22. **(a)** Draw the block diagram of a single-loop microcomputer-based controller.
(b) Describe the purpose of each block.

6–23. **(a)** Draw the software flowchart of a single-loop microcomputer-based controller.
(b) Describe the purpose of each block.

6–24. In some versions of BASIC the statement

$$x = \text{TIMER}$$

will set x to the value of time since system reset.
(a) Explain how this could be used to assure uniform cycle times of 2.0 s for proper PID calculations.
(b) Write the BASIC code necessary to do this and indicate how it fits into Figure 6–41.
(c) Will this scheme work as a watchdog timer, to assure that the program does not get hung up? Explain.

6–25. The A/D outputs 1024 when the speed that it is monitoring is 0 r/min, and 2047 when the speed is 3000 r/min clockwise. When the speed is 3000 r/min counterclockwise, the A/D outputs 0. Write the program steps in BASIC needed to calculate the actual speed and to determine the direction of rotation.

6–26. **(a)** Explain the difference between absolute and deviation alarms.
(b) Give an example not given in the chapter for the use of each.

6–27. Write a program in BASIC that will perform a PID calculation. Assume that the value of the process variable and set point are in r/min (from Problem 6–25), and the result of the calculation is in % (0 to 100%).

6–28. Explain the following output drive techniques.
(a) On/off.
(b) Time proportioning.
(c) Analog.
(d) Phase-angle firing.
(e) Pulse-width modulation.

6–29. Describe the following modes of operation for a microcomputer-based single-loop controller.
(a) Manual.
(b) Automatic.
(c) Directed self-tuning.
(d) Continuous self-tuning.

6–30. Define the programmable controller.

6–31. Compare the programmable controller to a standard minicomputer or personal computer. Explain each of the following terms.
(a) Architecture.
(b) Hardware survivability.
(c) Software operating system.

(d) Languages.

(e) Math and data handling ability.

In each case, illustrate how the PLC has been optimized for the manufacturing environment.

6–32. Analyze the relay ladder diagram in Figure 6–49, to answer the following questions.

(a) The STOP button is normally closed, even though it is drawn as normally open. When it is *not* pressed, is power passed on to the START button, or is power removed? Explain.

(b) What is necessary to turn the GRN lamp on?

(c) Once turned on, what holds the GRN lamp on?

(d) While the timer is timing, what is the condition of bit 033/15?

(e) How long does the timer run?

(f) What does it take to get the motor on?

(g) What does it indicate when the WHT lamp is on?

(h) What does a RED lamp on indicate?

(i) When the RED lamp is on, what is the condition of the motor?

(j) When the timer runs down, what happens to bit 033/15?

(k) When the timer runs down, what happens to the: (1) GRN lamp? (2) motor? (3) WHT lamp? (4) RED lamp?

(l) What happens to each of the four outputs if the STOP button is pressed while the timer is running?

6–33. Draw a diagram similar to Figure 6–45 indicating how the hardware of Problem 6–32 should be wired.

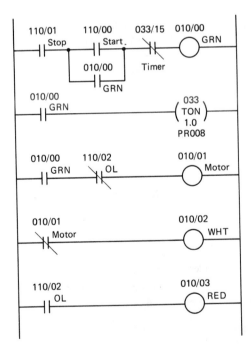

Figure 6–49 Ladder diagram (Problem 6–32).

6–34. Discuss the variety of I/O modules available for PLCs. Explain how they are different from personal computer interfaces.

6–35. Explain how the PLC handles programming complex I/O, math, data manipulation, timing and counting, communications, and PID functions.

7

Power Interfaces

The electronics of the previous chapters have provided a few milliamperes of current at voltage levels that rarely exceeded 10 V dc. However, real industrial loads may require hundreds of amperes at hundreds of volts ac. If this power were simply to be applied, or removed, an electromechanical relay would work adequately. But continuous, proportional power is often required. The precise positioning of a crane moving several tons, the fine tuning of the speed of a several horsepower motor, valve positioning in a high-pressure hydraulic line are only a few examples of the need for precisely adjusted proportional power in the kilowatt range and above.

These power interfaces must meet several criteria. Input is taken from the low-voltage, low-current output of a controller, but the higher-power output must accurately track that input. Second, since the power output often switches 120 V ac, 220 V ac, or more, there must be isolation between the input signal's common and the power line's neutral. Next, switching such large amounts of power certainly can produce significant electrical noise. Proportional control of power must be done in such a way as to reduce this noise to tolerable levels. Finally, the power interface must be highly efficient. When providing 10 kW to a load at an efficiency of 50%, the power interface must itself dissipate 10 kW. This level of waste is just too expensive. Also, any power dissipated by the power interface is normally converted to heat. Unless high efficiencies can be provided, heat sinking of the electronics and heat removal become a real burden.

The simplest way to apply significant power to a load is with a high-power operational amplifier. The OPA512 is presented in Section 7–1 along with operational precautions, heat-sinking calculations, and safe-operating-area evaluation. Much more efficiency can be obtained from a switch-mode power amplifier. The general principle of operation, component selection and limitation, and an example of H-bridge bidirectional switching

414

are given in Section 7–2. Power in the kilowatt range usually requires a thyristor switch. Section 7–3 discusses thyristor-based power supplies. First, the thyristors themselves are presented, followed by trigger devices. Finally, these are combined with other electronics to build an interface that can proportionally apply multiple kilowatts of power.

OBJECTIVES

After studying this chapter you should be able to do the following:

1. Describe the OPA512 high-power op amp.
2. For a circuit using an OPA512, calculate
   a. Current limiting
   b. Power dissipated with resistive or reactive loads
   c. Heat sinking required
   d. Safe operating area
   e. V–I limiter circuit
3. Draw the schematic and explain the operation of two op amps used in
   a. Parallel
   b. Driving opposite ends of a floating load
4. Illustrate how to boost a simple op amp with one or two transistors.
5. Explain the principle of a pulse-width modulation switching amplifier and why it is more efficient than a linear amplifier.
6. Draw the block diagram of a forward converter and explain its operation.
7. Given amplifier specifications, compute and specify all components needed for a simple switch-mode servo amplifier.
8. Discuss the nonideal characteristics of the switch mode servo amp's transistor, diode, inductor, capacitor, and pulse-width modulator IC.
9. Trace the operation of a switch mode servo amplifier, explaining how negative feedback is used to stabilize the output independent of changes in load resistance or supply voltage.
10. Discuss the differences between BJT and VFET switching transistors. Compute power dissipation, speed limitations, and drive-circuit components for each.
11. Draw the schematic and explain the operation of H bridges made with
    a. Bipolar junction transistors
    b. P-channel and N-channel VFETs
    c. All N-channel VFETs
12. Explain the operation of the SCR and the triac, including the definition of significant specifications.
13. Given a thyristor and load, compute the required snubbing components.
14. Draw the schematic for and compute component values for standard and zero-crossing optically isolated thyristor trigger circuits.

15. Draw the schematic of a time-proportioning power interface. Explain its operation. Discuss its advantages and limitations.

16. Use a curve or equation of phase-angle fired voltage versus conduction angle to determine the resulting voltage, given the angle, or vice versa.

17. Draw the schematic for and analyze the operation of a digitally controlled, and an analog voltage-controlled, phase-angle firing circuit.

7–1 POWER OPERATIONAL AMPLIFIER*

Dc loads such as servomotors, relays, solenoids, lamps, heaters, and proportional valves require currents of several hundred milliamperes to several amperes. However, the op amps seen so far will either burn up if presented with such a load, or will current limit at something between 2 and 20 mA. There are several integrated power amplifiers that can deliver the required current. You must, however, be careful in your selection. Integrated audio power amplifiers are optimized for audio applications. They deliver audio signals quite conveniently to speakers, but must be used with caution in any other application.

Many IC manufacturers produce a series of power operational amplifiers. The OPA512 is an example built by Burr-Brown. "The OPA512 is a high voltage, very-high current operational amplifier designed to drive a wide variety of resistive and reactive loads. Its complementary class A/B output stage provides superior performance in applications requiring freedom from crossover distortion. User-set current limit circuitry provides protection to the amplifier and load in fault conditions. A resistor-programmable voltage–current limiter circuit may be used to further protect the amplifier from damaging conditions." A functional block diagram of the OPA512 is given in Figure 7–1.

"The OPA512 employs a laser-trimmed monolithic integrated circuit to bias the output transistors, providing excellent low-level signal fidelity and high output voltage swing. The reduced internal parts count made possible with this monolithic IC improves performance and reliability.

"This hybrid integrated circuit is housed in a hermetically sealed TO-3 package and all circuitry is electrically isolated from the case. This allows direct mounting to a chassis or heat sink without cumbersome insulating hardware and provides optimum heat transfer."

The specifications for the OPA512 are given in Table 7–1. A comparison between the OPA512 and the general purpose 741 op amp is given in Table 7–2. There are several points worth highlighting. All of the nonideal dc characteristics of the powerful OPA512SM are comparable to the 741C. The OP512SM actually has better speed charac-

---

* The quoted material in Section 7–1 is from Ref. 1 except where noted otherwise.

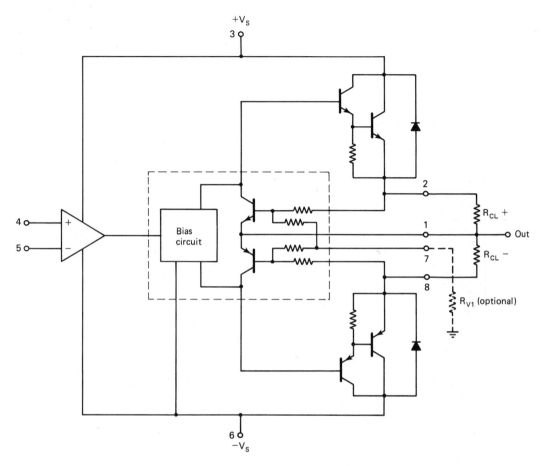

Figure 7–1   OPA512 power op amp block diagram. (Courtesy of Burr-Brown Corporation.)

teristics (gain bandwidth and slew rate) than the 741C. The 741 has an output voltage swing which may approach within 2 V of the power supplies ($V_{\text{saturatuion}}$). The OPA512 must maintain at least a 5-V difference between supply and output. However, this increased difference is compensated for by the ±50-V allowable supply voltage for the OPA512. In fact, you may run the OPA512SM from a single supply of +100 V and ground (or ground and −100 V), or anything in between. For a ground referenced load that requires only a single polarity signal, this allows a drive from the OPA512 of 90 V dc. Finally, the 741C will automatically limit the current in a short circuit to about 20 mA. Distortion of the output voltage signal may begin at load currents of 0.5 mA. In stark contrast, the OPA512SM will allow you to select the short-circuit limit, and can tolerate up to 15 A.

TABLE 7–1 OPA 512 SPECIFICATIONS

ABSOLUTE MAXIMUM RATINGS

```
Supply Voltage, +Vs to −Vs  ........................... 100V
Output Current: source.................................. 15A
                sink ................................. see SOA
Power Dissipation, internal[1] ......................... 125W
Input Voltage: differential ...................... ±(|Vs| − 3V)
               common-mode ........................... ±Vs
Temperature: pin solder, 10s ........................ +300°C
             junction[1]............................. +200°C
Temperature Range: storage[2] ............... −65°C to +150°C
                   operating (case) ........ −55°C to +125°C
```

NOTE: (1) Long term operation at the maximum junction temperature will result in reduced product life. Derate internal power dissipation to achieve high MTTF. (2) OPA512BM, −55°C to +100°C.

SPECIFICATIONS

ELECTRICAL

At T_C = +25°C and V_S = ±40VDC unless otherwise noted.

PARAMETER	CONDITIONS	OPA512BM MIN	TYP	MAX	OPA512SM MIN	TYP	MAX	UNITS
INPUT								
OFFSET VOLTAGE								
Initial Offset			±2	±6		±1	±3	mV
vs Temperature	Specified temp. range		±10	±65		*	±40	μV/°C
vs Supply Voltage			±30	±200		*		μV/V
vs Power			±20			*		μV/W
BIAS CURRENT								
Initial			12	30		10	20	nA
vs Temperature	Specified temp. range		±50	400		*		pA/°C
vs Supply Voltage			±10			*		pA/V
OFFSET CURRENT								
Initial			±12	±30		±5	±10	nA
vs Temperature	Specified temp. range		±50			*		pA/°C
INPUT IMPEDANCE, DC			200			*		MΩ
INPUT CAPACITANCE			3			*		pF
VOLTAGE RANGE								
Common-Mode Voltage	Specified temp. range	±(|Vs| − 5)	±(|Vs| − 3)		*	*		V
Common-Mode Rejection	Specified temp. range	74	100		*			dB
GAIN								
Open-Loop Gain at 10Hz	1kΩ load		110			*		dB
	Specified temp. range, 8Ω load	96	108		*	*		dB
Gain-Bandwidth Product, 1MHz	8Ω load		4			*		MHz
Power Bandwidth	8Ω load	13	20		*	*		kHz
Phase Margin	Specified temp. range, 8Ω load		20			*		Degrees
OUTPUT								
Voltage Swing[1]	BM at 10A, SM at 15A	±(|Vs| − 6)			±(|Vs| − 7)			V
	Specified temp. range, Io = 80mA	±(|Vs| − 5)			*			V
	Io = 5A	±(|Vs| − 5)			*			V
Current, Peak		10			15			A
Settling Time to 0.1%	2V step		2			*		μs
Slew Rate		2.5	4		*	*		V/μs
Capacitive Load	Specified temp. range, G = 1			1.5			*	nF
	Specified temp. range, G > 10			SOA[2]			*	
POWER SUPPLY								
Voltage	Specified temp. range	±10	±40	±45	*	*	±50	V
Current, Quiescent			25	50			35	mA
THERMAL								
RESISTANCE								
AC Junction to Case[3]	Tc = −55°C to +125°C, f > 60Hz		0.8	0.9		*	*	°C/W
DC Junction to Case	Tc = −55°C to +125°C		1.25	1.4		*	*	°C/W
Junction to Air	Tc = −55°C to +125°C		30			*		°C/W
TEMPERATURE RANGE, specified	Tc	−25		+85	−55		+125	°C

*Specification same as OPA512BM.

NOTES: (1) +Vs and −Vs denote the positive and negative supply voltage respectively. Total Vs is measured from +Vs to −Vs. (2) SOA = Safe Operating Area. (3) Rating applies if the output current alternates between both output transistors at a rate faster than 60Hz.

Source: Burr-Brown.

TABLE 7–2 OPA 512 VERSUS 741 SPECIFICATION COMPARISON

	741C	OPA512SM	Unit
Maximum			
Supply voltage $+V_s$ to $-V_s$	36	100	V
Output current	0.025	15	A
Power dissipation	0.085	125	W
Specifications			
Dc			
Input offset voltage (max.)	±6	±3	mV
Bias current (max).	500	20	nA
Offset current (max.)	±200	±10	nA
Ac			
Gain–bandwidth (typ.)	1.5	4	MHz
Slew rate (min.)	0.3	2.5	V/μs
Temperature			
Input offset voltage			
drift (max.)	±15	±65	μV/°C
Θ_{JA} (max.)	100	30	°C/W
Θ_{JC} (max.)	45	1.4	°C/W

Source: Burr-Brown.

"Current-limit resistors must be provided for proper operation. Independent positive and negative current limit values may be selected by choice of R_{CL+} and R_{CL-}, respectively. Resistor values are calculated by

$$R_{CL} = \frac{0.65}{I_{lim}(amperes)} - 0.007 \qquad (7\text{–}1)$$

This is the nominal current-limit value at room temperature. The maximum output current decreases at high temperatures, as shown in the typical performance curve (Figure 7–2). Most wirewound resistors are satisfactory, but some highly inductive types may cause loop stability problems. Be sure to evaluate performance with the actual resistors to be used in production.

"Power amplifiers are rated by case temperature (not ambient temperature). The maximum allowable power dissipation is a function of the case temperature, as shown in the derating curve (Figure 7–3). Load characteristics, signal conditions, and power supply voltage determine the power dissipated by the amplifer. The case temperature will be determined by the heat sinking conditions. Sufficient heat sinking must be provided to keep the case temperature within safe bounds given the power dissipated and the ambient temperature."

Any semiconductor device which carries current will dissipate power. That power is dissipated normally in the form of heat. The heat is generated at the wafer (junction) and must flow through the package to the surrounding air. The package material presents a certain opposition to this flow of heat (thermal resistance Θ_{JA}). The temperature of

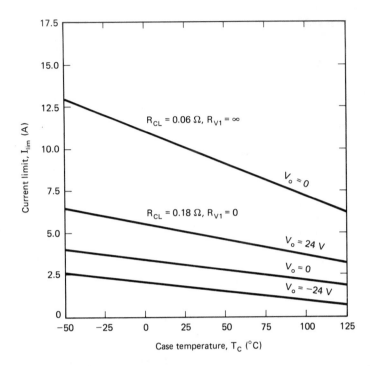

Figure 7–2 Temperature effects on the current-limit characteristics for the OPA512. (Courtesy of Burr-Brown Corporation.)

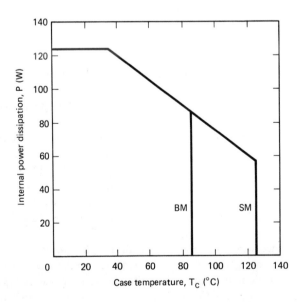

Figure 7–3 OPA512 power derating curves. (Courtesy of Burr-Brown Corporation.)

the junction (wafer) will rise. Should the temperature become too high, the semiconductor will be damaged. Equation 7–2 gives the key relationship.

$$T_J = T_A + \Theta_{JA}P \qquad (7\text{–}2)$$

where T_J = temperature of the junction
T_C = temperature of the ambient
Θ_{JA} = thermal resistance from the junction to ambient
P = power dissipated by the device

It is necessary to keep T_J below the maximum specified by the manufacturer of the device being used. For the OPA512 the maximum allowable junction temperature is 200°C. Caution dictates that you should run the IC at least 10% below this limit. This can be done by minimizing the power dissipated through careful circuit design, by decreasing the temperature (T_A) with a fan, or by decreasing the thermal resistance (Θ_{JA}) with a heat sink.

$$\Theta_{JA}(\text{max}) = \frac{T_J(\text{max}) - T_A}{P} \qquad (7\text{–}3)$$

When a heat sink is used, the junction-to-ambient thermal resistance consists of three terms:

$$\Theta_{JA} = \Theta_{JC} + \Theta_{CS} + \Theta_{SA} \qquad (7\text{–}4)$$

where Θ_{JC} = thermal resistance, junction to case
Θ_{CS} = thermal resistance, case to heat sink
Θ_{SA} = thermal resistance, heat sink to ambient

"The thermal resistance from junction to case, Θ_{JC}, is specified by the power amp manufacturer. Note that some power amps specify a lower thermal resistance for ac signal conditions where the dissipation is shared by both internal power transistors" [2].

"The thermal resistance from the power amp case to the heat sink, Θ_{CS}, depends on heat sink mounting surface flatness. Heat sink compound reduces Θ_{CS} in the presence of small surface imperfections. While it is not a substitute for good heat sink workmanship, it does conduct heat better than the air that would otherwise fill the voids resulting from surface irregularities. Typical values for a TO-3-type package range from 0.1 to 0.5°C/W. Power amps or transistors with electrically hot cases usually require insulating hardware, which adds as much as 1.0°C/W to Θ_{CS}" [2].

The thermal resistance from heat sink to ambient, Θ_{SA}, comes from the heat sink manufacturer's specifications. "Published specifications for heat sinks vary considerably for essentially identical designs. Heat sink performance varies greatly depending on the mounting configuration, surrounding components, airflow, and other environmental factors" [2].

EXAMPLE 7–1

Determine the heat sinking needed for an OP512A operating from ± 40 V dc supplies, driving a 20-Ω load. Hold the junction temperature at or below 150°C. The ambient temperature is 60°C. Calculate the case temperature.

Solution   For dc or low-frequency signals, the power dissipated by the amplifier is

$$P_{\max} = \frac{V_s^2}{4R_{\text{load}}} \qquad (7\text{–}5)$$

where V_s is the supply voltage; one side, not the sum of $+V_S$ and $-V_S$,

$$P_{\max} = \frac{(40 \text{ V})^2}{4 \times 20 \text{ } \Omega} = 20 \text{ W}$$

$$\Theta_{JA}(\max) = \frac{T_J(\max) - T_A}{P} = \frac{150°\text{C} - 60°\text{C}}{20 \text{ W}} = 4.5°\text{C/W}$$

$$\Theta_{JA} = \Theta_{JC} + \Theta_{CS} + \Theta_{SA}$$

so

$$
\begin{aligned}
\Theta_{SA}(\max) &= \Theta_{JA}(\max) - \Theta_{JC} - \Theta_{CS} \\
&= 4.5°\text{C/W} - 1.4°\text{C/W} - 0.5°\text{C/W} \\
&= 2.6°\text{C/W}
\end{aligned}
$$

The maximum case temperature is obtained from

$$
\begin{aligned}
T_{\text{case}} &= T_J - \Theta_{JC}P \\
&= 150°\text{C} - (1.4°\text{C/W})(20 \text{ W}) \\
&= 122°\text{C}
\end{aligned}
$$

The solution of Example 7–1 requires a heat sink that will fit a TO-3 package and have a thermal resistance of 2.6°C/W *or less*. A list of heat sinks is given in Table 7–3.

The calculations of Example 7–1 assume a dc output. A more detailed analysis is necessary if you plan to drive the load with an ac signal of 200 Hz or more. Operation will be along an ac load line which must, at all points, lie within a region of the output transistors' characteristic curve called the safe operating area (SOA). The SOA for the OPA512 is shown in Figure 7–4. The vertical axis is the current through the output transistor, scaled logarithmically. The horizontal axis is the voltage *across* the output transistor. It is very important to realize that the voltage plotted on the horizontal axis is *not* the load voltage. Instead, it is the difference between the load voltage and the op amp's power supply voltage. This axis is also scaled logarithmically.

There are three safe operating areas outlined. The case temperature specifies the area in which you should operate. An increase in case temperature reduces the area

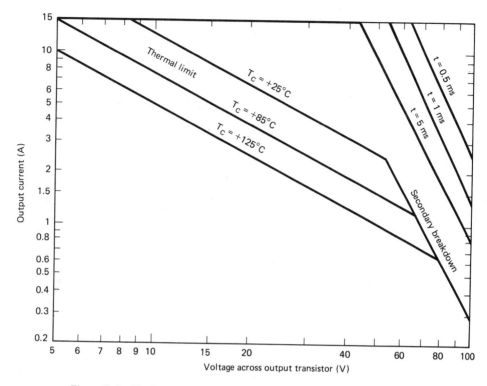

Figure 7–4 OPA512 safe operating area. (Courtesy of Burr-Brown Corporation.)

over which the output transistor's performance can vary. Crossing the applicable boundary will result in damage, reduced life, or failure of the op amp. To assure safe operation when driving a resistive load, plot the ac load line. Keep in mind, however, that the characteristic curve in Figure 7–4 is logarithmic. This means that the load line will be curved. So you may have to plot four or five points before you can sketch in the load curve. As long as this curve falls completely below the applicable case temperature boundary, your circuit is safe. Of course, the closer to the boundary the load curve falls, the more thermal stress the op amp is subject to. Operation under prolonged thermal stress may shorten the life of the power device.

EXAMPLE 7–2

Draw the load curve for the op amp configuration in Example 7–1 on the SOA curve in Figure 7–4. Describe the op amp's operation.

Solution   Several I–V_{ce} points are needed. At 40-V supply and 20-Ω load resistance,

$$V_{ce} = 40 \text{ V} - I(20 \text{ }\Omega) \qquad P_{\text{op amp}} = I \times V_{ce}$$

TABLE 7-3 HEAT SINK SELECTION GUIDE[a]

For TO-202 packages

θ_{SA} approx. (°C/W)	Manufacturer and type
12.5–14.2	Staver V4-3-192
13	Staver V5-1
15.1–17.2	Staver V4-3-128
19	Thermalloy 6106 Series
20	Staver V6-2
25	Thermalloy 6107 Series
37	IERC PA1-7CB with PVC-1B Clip
40–42	Staver F7-3
40–43	Staver F7-2
42	IERC PA2-7CB with PVC-1B Clip
42–44	Staver F7-1

For TO-220 packages

θ_{SA} approx. (°C/W)	Manufacturer and type
4.2	IERC HP3 Series
5–6	IERC HP1 Series
6.4	Staver V3-7-225
6.5–7.5	IERC VP Series
8.1	Staver V3-5
8.8	Staver V3-7-96

For TO-5 packages

θ_{SA} approx. (°C/W)	Manufacturer and type
12	Thermalloy 1101, 1103 Series
12–16	Wakefield 260-5 Series
15	Staver V3A-5
22	Thermalloy 1116, 1121, 1123 Series
22	Thermalloy 1130, 1131, 1132 Series
24	Staver F5-5C
26–30	IERC Thermal Links
27–83	Wakefield 200 Series
28	Staver F5-5B
30	Thermalloy 2227 Series
34	Thermalloy 2228 Series
35	IERC Clip Mount Thermal Link
39	Thermalloy 2215 Series
42	Staver F5-5A
45–65	Wakefield 296 Series
46	Staver F6-5, F6-5L
50	Thermalloy 2225 Series

For TO-3 packages

θ_{SA} approx. (°C/W)	Manufacturer and type
0.4 (9″ length)	Thermalloy (Extruded) 6590 Series
0.4–0.5 (6″ length)	Thermalloy (Extruded) 6660, 6560 Series
0.56–3.0	Wakefield 400 Series
0.6 (7.5″ length)	Thermalloy (Extruded) 6470 Series
0.7–1.2 (5–5.5″ length)	Thermalloy (Extruded) 6423, 6443, 6441, 6450 Series
1.0–5.4 (3″ length)	Thermalloy (Extruded) 6427, 6500, 6123, 6401, 6403, 6421, 6463, 6176, 6129, 6141, 6169, 6135, 6442 Series
1.9	IERC E2 Series (Extruded)
2.1	IERC E1, E3 Series (Extruded)
2.3–4.7	Wakefield 600 Series
4.2	IERC HP3 Series
4.5	Staver V3-5-2
5–6	IERC HP3 Series

θ (°C/W)	Device
9.5	Staver V3-3
10	Thermalloy 6032, 6034 Series
12.5–14.2	Staver V4-3-192
13	Staver V5-1
15	Thermalloy 6030 Series
15.1–17.2	Staver V4-3-128
16	Thermalloy 6106 Series
18	Thermalloy 6107 Series
19	IERC PB Series
20	Staver V6-2
25	IERC PA Series
26	Thermalloy 6025 Series

For TO-92 packages

θ (°C/W)	Device
30	Staver F2-7
46	Staver F5-7A, F5-8-1
50	IERC RUR Series
57	Staver F5-7D
65	IERC RU Series
72	Staver F1-7
85	Thermalloy 2224 Series

θ (°C/W)	Device
50–55	IERC Fan Tops
51	Thermalloy 2205 Series
53	Thermalloy 2211 Series
55	Thermalloy 2210 Series
56	Thermalloy 1129 Series
58	Thermalloy 2230, 2235 Series
60	Thermalloy 2226 Series
68	Staver F1-5
72	Thermalloy 1115 Series

θ (°C/W)	Device
5.2–6.2	Thermalloy 6103 Series
5.6	Staver V3-3-2
5.8–7.9	Thermalloy 6001 Series
5.9–10	Wakefield 680 Series
6	Wakefield 390 Series
6.4	Staver V3-7-224
6.5–7.5	IERC UP Series
8	Staver V1-5
8.1	Staver V3-5
8.8	Staver V3-7-96
8.8–14.4	Thermalloy 6013 Series
9.5	Staver V3-3
9.5–10.5	IERC LA Series
9.8–13.9	Wakefield 630 Series
10	Staver V1-3
13	Thermalloy 6117

Staver Co. Inc.: 41–51 N. Saxon Ave., Bay Shore, NY 11706
IERC: 135 W. Magnolia Blvd, Burbank, CA 91502
Thermalloy: PO Box 34829, 2021 W. Valley View Ln, Dallas, TX
Wakefield Engin Ind.: Wakefield, MA 01880

[a] No attempt has been made to provide a complete list of all heat sink manufacturers. This list is only representative. All values are typical as given by the manufacturer or as determined from characteristic curves supplied by the manufacturer.

Source: National Semiconductor.

I (A)	V_{ce} (V)	P (W)
0	40	0
0.50	30	15.00
0.75	25	18.75
1.00	20	20.00
1.25	15	18.75
1.50	10	15.00
1.75	5	8.75

These points are plotted in Figure 7–5. At no point does this curve cross (or even approach) the 125°C case temperature boundary. This application is acceptable.

"Low-frequency ac signals (less than 200 Hz) should be treated as slowly changing dc as described above, but for higher frequencies (roughly 200 Hz and above) the average power dissipation should be considered. In this situation, the transistors do not instantaneously change temperature in response to the signal waveform but are heated according to the average transistor dissipation." Figure 7–6 "shows the average total

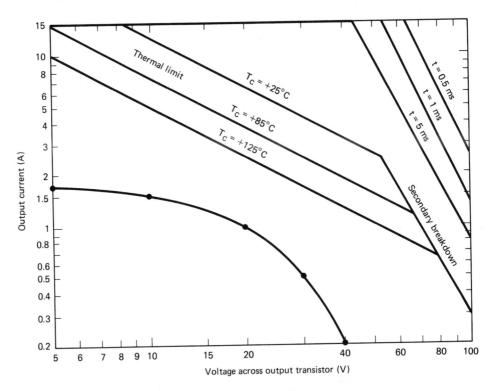

Figure 7–5   SOA load plot for Example 7–2.

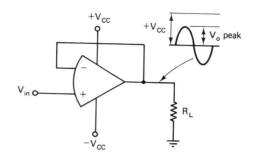

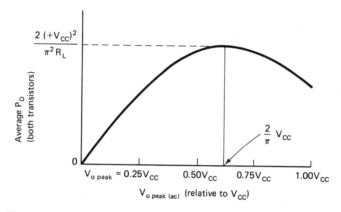

Figure 7–6   AC power dissipation. (Courtesy of Burr-Brown Corporation.)

power dissipation for both transistors as a function of relative output voltage. . . .
The instantaneous dissipation at the worst case of $V_{out} = \pm V_{CC}/2$ is the same for dc,
of course, but with ac, this point is passed for only a brief instant. The output voltage
which causes the greatest average dissipation occurs at a peak at $2V_{CC}/\pi$. This is the
signal level which causes the output to spend the greatest percentage of time near the
instantaneous worst-case points, $+V_{CC}/2$ and $-V_{CC}/2$'' [3].

"It is safest to design the whole amplifier system as if the ac voltage to be handled
is always at the worst-case signal level. Not all systems, however, need or can tolerate
the expense of this over design. If V_{out} peak will always be equal to $0.85V_{CC}$, for
instance, Figure 7–6 shows that the average dissipation will be approximately 25%
less than the worst case" [3].

Figure 7–7 "shows the ac voltage/current waveform for an inductive load. Since
the load current lags the load voltage by 90°, the peak current occurs when the load
voltage is zero. At this instant of maximum current, the voltage across the conducting
transistor is equal to the full supply voltage, $+V_{CC}$ (or $-V_{CC}$ at 180°). This obviously
leads to much greater power dissipation than with a resistive load" [3].

". . . The power dissipated in the amplifier must be equal to the power delivered
by the power supplies less the power delivered to the load. If the load is purely reactive,

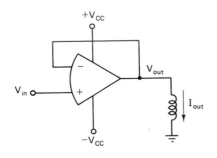

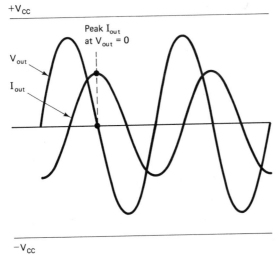

Figure 7–7   Ac voltage/current waveforms
for an inductive load. (Courtesy of Burr-
Brown Corporation.)

the load power is by definition zero. No power can be dissipated by a perfect inductor
or capacitor. For complex load impedances the load power can be measured:

$$P_{out} = (I_{out}\ rms)(V_{out}\ rms)(\cos \theta)$$

where θ is the phase angle between the load voltage and current'' [3].

"The supply power is easily calculated for sine-wave signals and is not sensitive
to the type of load impedance, only the load current. Since the power comes from a
fixed dc voltage supply, it is equal to V_{CC} times the average (not rms) supply current.
For a sine wave this is $2V_{CC}(I_{peak})/\pi$. Each supply provides this for its active half
cycle and 'rests' for the opposite half-cycle" [3].

EXAMPLE 7–3

"A sine wave is applied to a complex reactive load. The peak load voltage is 30
V and the peak load current is 1.75 A. $V_{CC} = \pm 35$ V. A phase angle of 55° is
measured between the load voltage and current. What is the amplifier dissipation?"
[3]

Solution

"Power supply power, $P_S = 2(35 \text{ V})(1.75 \text{ A})/\pi = 39$ W
Load power, $P_{\text{out}} = (0.707)(30\text{V})(0.707)(1.75\text{A}) \cos 55° = 15$ W
Amplifier dissipation, $P_d = P_s - P_{\text{out}} = 24$ W" [3]

"Motor loads can be particularly challenging since they may present a reactive load as well as reverse EMF to the power amp. These situations may be difficult to analyze by the techniques previously described since the power delivered to the load may be converted largely to mechanical power. In fact, sometimes mechanical inertia causes the load to supply power to the amplifier. Consider a dc motor which must be stopped rapidly" (Figure 7–8). "The motor produces a reverse EMF which is proportional to its rotational speed. If the applied voltage is suddenly forced to zero, the full negative power supply voltage, $-V_{CC}$, will appear across the conducting transistor and the load current will be the motor EMF divided by the motor series impedance (assuming no current limit). Such conditions may be difficult to analyze, but can usually be satisfactorily evaluated by empirical tests. Voltage and current measurements can be made under actual load conditions (including mechanical load and inertia to find its duration) to assure operation within the SOA" [3].

"The voltage–current (V–I) limiter circuit [of the OPA512 power op amp] provides a means to protect the amplifier from SOA damage such as a short circuit to ground, yet allows high output currents to flow under normal load conditions. Sensing both the output current and output voltage, this limiter circuit increases the current limit value

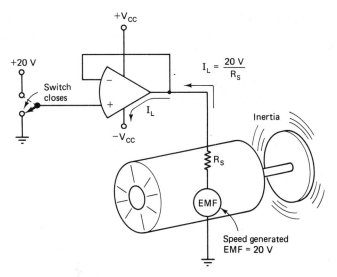

Figure 7–8   High stress caused by CEMF-generated current. (Courtesy of Burr-Brown Corporation.)

as the output voltage approaches the power supply voltage (where power dissipation is low). This type of limiting is achieved by connecting pin 7 through a programming resistor to ground. The V–I limiter circuit is governed by the equation

$$I_{\text{limit}} = \frac{0.65 \text{ V} + [0.28V_o/(20 \ \Omega + R_{VI})]}{R_{CL} + 0.007 \ \Omega}$$

(7–6)

where I_{limit} = maximum current available at a given voltage

R_{VI} = value (kΩ) of the resistor from pin 7 to ground

R_{CL} = current-limit resistor, Ω

V_o = instantaneous output voltage, V

"Reactive or EMF generating loads may produce unusual (perhaps undesirable) waveforms with the V–I limit circuit driven into limit. Since current peaks in a reactive load do not align with the output voltage peaks, the output waveform will not appear as a simple voltage-limited waveform. Response of a load to the limiter, in fact, may produce a 'backfire' reaction producing unusual output waveforms."

There are several ways to increase the power you deliver from the OPA512 to the load. The op amps can be paralleled, as shown in Figure 7–9. Op amp U_1 provides the gain ($-R_f/R_i$) and drives its current through one 0.05-Ω resistor into the load. The output voltage of U_1 is applied to a voltage follower, U_2. This op amp outputs the same voltage and current as U_1, effectively doubling the current to the load. Additional voltage followers can be added in parallel to provide whatever current is required by the load. The 0.05-Ω resistors between each op amp output and the load are to drop any slight differences among op amp output voltages. This technique increases power to the load by providing it with more current.

If the load can be floated (not connected to ground), two op amps can be connected as a bridge amp. This is shown in Figure 7–10. Op amp U_1 provides gain (it may be an inverting or noninverting amp). Its output drives one end of the load. This voltage is also applied to U_2, an inverting amp with gain of -1. The output of U_2, then, is equal in amplitude, but opposite in phase to the output of U_1. So when U_1 drives the left end of the load positive, sourcing current, U_2 drives the right end of the load the same distance negative and sinks the load current. This doubles the voltage across the

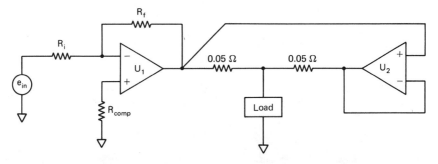

Figure 7–9   Current boosting by paralleling two (or more) op amps.

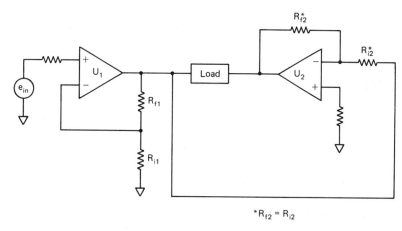

Figure 7-10   Power doubling using a bridge amplifier configuration.

load, doubling the power dissipated by the load. For additional power, U_1 and U_2 could each be paralleled by voltage followers as suggested in Figure 7-9.

For less demanding applications, it may not be necessary to use an expensive power op amp. Using a general-purpose op amp to drive a complementary-symmetry push-pull pair of Darlington transistors may be adequate. Look at Figure 7-11. By connecting the op amp's negative feedback at the load, base–emitter offsets and nonlinearities are automatically compensated for by the op amp. If the output is always going to be of one polarity, the opposite transistor can be eliminated. Moderate effort in matching the characteristics of the two Darlington pairs will yield total harmonic distortion in the order of several percent. For better performance, you must use a more elaborate

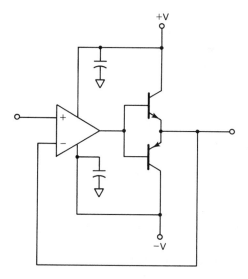

Figure 7-11   Transistor boosting of an op amp.

biasing configuration where the op amp plays only a small role as part of a rather sophisticated discrete power amplifier. But this gets you back to the OPA512.

7–2 SWITCH-MODE SERVO AMPLIFIERS*

The power op amps you saw in Section 7–1 are required to dissipate a significant amount of power. This is because they are operated in their linear region, with considerable voltage across them, while providing many amperes of current to the load. Operation in this linear mode does impart minimum distortion to the signal. However, efficiency is very poor, often well below 50%. It is not at all unusual for the linear power amplifier to dissipate more power than it delivers to the load. This high degree of waste means that the linear power amplifier's power supply is much larger and more expensive than the load demands. Also, wasted power is normally converted to heat. This heat must be dealt with, removed if possible, or its impact on associated electronics taken into account. Power amplifier operation in the linear mode creates problems.

"Switch-mode servo amplifiers are drastically changing the field of power electronics. By using high-frequency digital switching techniques, amplifiers are being built which are much smaller, lighter, cooler, and which consume (waste) considerable less power than the traditional linear amplifier of Section 7–1. In this section you will see the basic principle of operation of a switch-mode power amplifier. The design of a step-down, forward converter will be presented along with a guide to component selection."

7–2.1 Principles of Pulse-Width Modulation

"Switch-mode amplification is based on the principle of pulse-width modulation. The average value (dc) of any wave is determined by the area between the wave and ground. For rectangular (switching) waveforms this is easy to calculate.

$$V_{dc} = \frac{t_{on}}{t_{period}} V_{pk} \qquad (7-7)$$

This is illustrated in Figure 7–12.

"Changing the pulse width (t_{on}) while keeping the period (t_{period}) constant allows you to control the signal's average value (V_{dc}). This is the technique used in switch-mode amplifiers to control the output voltage, compensating for changes in load current or power supply (unregulated) voltage.

"The block diagram for a simple switch-mode amp is shown in Figure 7–13." The input line voltage (typically 115 V ac rms at 60 Hz) is rectified and capacitively filtered. This large-voltage, high-ripple signal is applied to the switching transistor(s), which are driven on and off by the pulse-width modulator IC. The output is a constant

---

* The quoted material in Section 7–2 is from Ref. 4 except where noted otherwise.

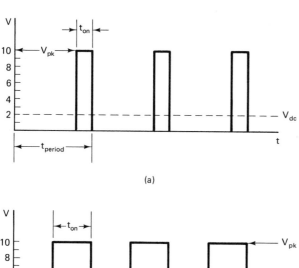

(a)

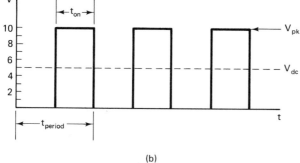

(b)

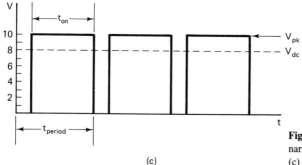

(c)

Figure 7–12 Pulse-width modulation: (a) narrow pulse width; (b) 50% pulse width; (c) wide pulse width.

high-frequency (20 kHz or higher) rectangular wave with a variable pulse width (t_{on}). This high-frequency pulse-width-modulated waveform is applied to a rectifier and *LC* filter, which smooths out the variations, outputting a smooth dc voltage, equal to the average value of the pulse-width-modulated wave. Should some variation in the load cause the output to try to increase, the pulse-width-modulator IC will sense this and reduce the pulse width to the switching transistors. This reduces the pulse width of the signal to the high-frequency rectifier and filter, lowering the output voltage.'' Conversely, an increase in voltage at the low-power input will cause the pulse-width modulator to

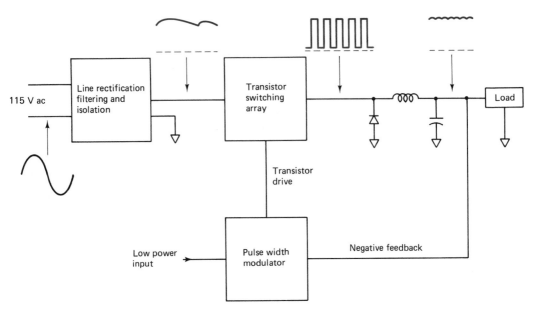

Figure 7–13   Switch-mode servo amplifier block diagram.

increase the pulse width out of the switching transistor array. This raises the voltage to the load. The load voltage tracks the low-power input voltage.

7–2.2 Switch-Mode Filter

"The forward converter is a simple, popular switching configuration. When the transistor is driven on by the pulse-width modulator, it acts as a short, collector to emitter. The large positive voltage from the input filter is applied to the junction of the inductor and diode. The diode is reverse biased. Current begins to increase through the inductor, expanding the magnetic field in the inductor. (Remember, an inductor opposes a change of current through it.) Part of this increasing current goes to charge the output filter capacitor, increasing the output voltage. This part of the operation cycle is shown in Figure 7–14a.

"During the second half of the cycle, the pulse-width modulator drives the transistor off. The almost instantaneous removal of current from the input filter forces the inductor to reverse voltage polarity. It now acts as a generator, sourcing current as the magnetic field collapses. This reversal in polarity places a negative on the cathode of the diode, turning it on. With the diode on, the left side of the inductor is clamped at a few tenths of a volt negative, placing this inductor (more or less) in parallel with the output capacitor and load. As the field in the inductor collapses, the output voltage begins to drop. The output capacitor then discharges, releasing current to the load, in an effort to reduce variation in output voltage. This is illustrated in Figure 7–14b.

"Component selection for switch-mode servo amplifiers is strongly affected by

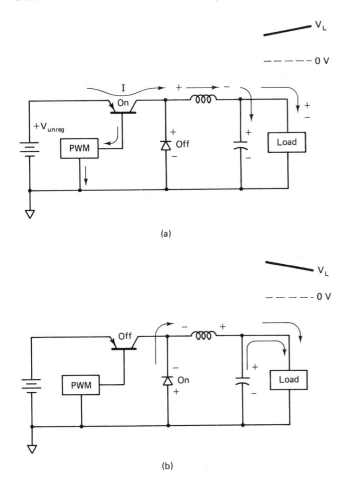

Figure 7–14   Forward converter filter's
(a) charge and (b) discharge cycles.

the nonideal behavior of these components. This is much more severe in switchers than in the linear power amplifiers previously discussed.

"The inductor in the filter stores energy in its electromagnetic field when the transistor is on, slowly releasing it during the transistor's off time. Its purpose is to smooth out the large variations in *current* to the load caused by the on/off, all-or-nothing nature of the switching transistor and diode. The proper value of inductance is given in equation 7–8.

$$L = \frac{V_{out}}{V_{in}} \frac{V_{in} - V_{out}}{2(I_{pk} - I_{out})f} \tag{7–8}$$

where V_{out} = dc regulated output voltage

V_{in} = dc (average) input voltage from the switching transistor (see equation 7–7)

f = switching frequency

I_{out} = dc regulated current provided to the load

I_{pk} = maximum current through the inductor (usually 10 to 40% more than I_{out})

"Practically, there are several other characteristics of the inductor that you must consider besides its inductance. Series resistances, caused by the resistance of the wire in the windings, must be kept low to minimize I^2R power losses across the inductor.

TABLE 7–4   SWITCHING FILTER INDUCTORS (COURTESY OF UNITED TRANSFORMER)

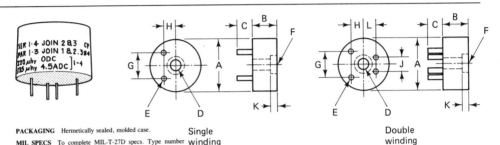

Single winding

Double winding

PACKAGING Hermetically sealed, molded case.

MIL SPECS To complete MIL-T-27D specs. Type number TF5S04ZZ.

APPLICATION These inductors have low losses in the 3 to 100 kHz frequency range, making them ideal for switching regulator and AC filter choke applications.

INDUCTANCE Type numbers correspond to inductance values in microhenries, which are measured at 1 V, 10 kHz, 0 DC with an inductance tolerance of +15%, −5%. Values of inductance other than listed in an existing size are available. Part Number would be: SR(A, B or C)—(inductance in microhy at 0 DC).

CURRENT RATINGS Listing I_1 is for approximately 10% drop in inductance with a typical 20°C temperature rise, and Listing I_2 is for approximately 20% drop in inducatnce with a typical 40°C temperature rise.

Schems.

SRA

Type	No. of Windings	Inductance of 0 DC (μH)	I_1, at 10% drop in L (amps)	I_2, at 20% drop in L (amps)	Max. DCR (ohms)
SRA-1250	1	1250	.8	1.2	.7
SRA-800	1	800	1	1.5	.45
SRA-500	1	500	1.2	1.8	.3
SRA-350	1	350	1.5	2.2	.2
SRA-200*	2	200 (SER)	2	3	.12
		50 (PAR)	4	6	.03
SRA-88*	2	88 (SER)	3	4.5	.052
		22 (PAR)	6	9	.013
SRA-32*	2	32 (SER)	5	7.5	.02
		8 (PAR)	10	15	.005

SRC

Type	No. of Windings	Inductance at 0 DC (μH)	I_1, at 10% drop in L (amps)	I_2, at 20% drop in L (amps)	Max. DCR (ohms)
SRC-10000	1	10,000	.84	1.1	2.1
SRC-6400	1	6400	1	1.35	1.4
SRC-2500	1	2500	1.6	2.2	.55
SRC-1600	1	1600	2.1	2.8	.34
SRC-1000	1	1000	2.6	3.5	.21
SRC-640*	2	640 (SER)	3.3	4.5	.13
		160 (PAR)	6.6	9	.033
SRC-400*	2	400 (SER)	4	5.4	.088
		100 (PAR)	8	10.8	.022
SRC-240*	2	240 (SER)	5	6.8	.056
		60 (PAR)	10	13.6	.014

SRB

Type	No. of Windings	Inductance at 0 DC (μH)	I_1, at 10% drop in L (amps)	I_2, at 20% drop in L (amps)	Max. DRC (ohms)
SRB-3000	1	3000	.8	1.2	1.2
SRB-2000	1	2000	1	1.5	.8
SRB-1200	1	1200	1.25	1.88	.5
SRB-780	1	780	1.6	2.4	.3
SRB-520	1	520	2	3	.2
SRB-320	1	320	2.5	3.75	.13
SRB-220*	2	220 (SER)	3	4.5	.08
		55 (PAR)	6	9	.02
SRB-120*	2	120 (SER)	4	6	.05
		30 (PAR)	8	12	.013
SRB-80*	2	80 (SER)	5	7.5	.032
		20 (PAR)	10	15	.008

SRD

Type	No. of Windings	Inductance at 0 DC (μH)	I_1, at 10% drop in L (amps)	I_2, at 20% drop in L (amps)	Max. DCR (ohms)
SRD-500	1	500	9.5	13	.033
SRD-900	1	900	7.3	10	.057
SRD-2500	1	2500	4.4	6	.15
SRD-5000	1	5000	3.1	4.2	.33
SRD-10000	1	10,000	2.2	3	.60
SRD-22000	1	22,000	1.4	2	1.4
SRD-40000	1	40,000	1.1	1.5	2.4
SRD-90000	1	90,000	.73	1	5.4
SRD-360000	1	360,000	.36	.50	22
SRD-1.4	1	1.4 Hy	.18	.25	88
SRD-5.6	1	5.6 Hy	.09	.125	352

Source: TRW.

Parasitic capacitance within the inductor must also be kept low. Large capacitance within the inductor converts it into a parallel tank circuit with a definite possibility of resonance and unwanted oscillations.

"The magnetic characteristics of the inductor must also be considered. In order to provide adequate electromagnetic energy storage in a small space, the core should be ferromagnetic. However, excessive currents through the transistor or diode may be produced if the core saturates. An air gap is needed. It can be provided by actually breaking the core. Or, an effective air gap can be made by distributing nonferromagnetic material evenly throughout the core."

The traditional procedure has been for you to custom design the high-frequency, high-current inductors needed for the switching servo amplifier. However, there are now available a wide assortment of stock inductors specifically designed for the high-current, high-frequency requirements of switchers. Table 7–4 is a sample of these.

The purpose of the capacitor is to restrict changes in output voltage (ripple) caused by the switching. Select the value of the capacitor as

$$C = \frac{I_{pk} - I_{out}}{4\,\Delta V_o f} \tag{7–9}$$

where ΔV_o is the peak output ripple voltage. In terms of the inductor already chosen in equation 7–8,

$$C = \frac{V_o}{V_{in}} \frac{V_{in} - V_o}{8\,\Delta V_o L f^2} \tag{7–10}$$

"However, a real filter capacitor is not pure capacitance. Equivalent series resistance (ESR) and equivalent series inductance (ESL) are significant. A typical capacitor model is given in Figure 7–15. Resistance and inductance of the leads and the foil of the plates convert the capacitor into a series resonant circuit. The frequency impedence characteristic of a series resonant circuit is given in Figure 7–16.

"At the resonant frequency of the capacitor (f_r) the capacitive reactance cancels

Figure 7–15   Simple model of a capacitor.

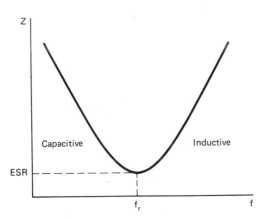

Capacitive   Inductive

ESR

f_r f

Figure 7–16   Frequency response of the capacitive model.

the reactance of the ESL and the device appears as a resistor whose value is ESR. This resonance frequency is

$$f_r = \frac{1}{2\pi\sqrt{\text{ESL} \cdot C}} \tag{7–11}$$

Below the resonance frequency, the capacitor behaves, more or less, as an ideal capacitor. However, above resonance, the impedence is primarily inductive, causing the real capacitor's overall impedence to *increase* with frequency.

"A value for ESR can be obtained either from the manufacturer, or from measurement of the capacitor's dissipation factor and capacitance with a capacitance meter.

$$\text{ESR} = \frac{D}{2\pi f_m C} \tag{7–12}$$

where D is the dissipation factor and f_m is the meter's test signal frequency (usually either 60 or 1000 Hz but should be the frequency at which the capacitor will be used). The lower the ESR, the lower the losses across the capacitor. The ESL must be obtained from the manufacturer's specifications. However, it is critical, because it sets the capacitor's resonance frequency, above which impedance increases. The rectangular waves in the switcher are rich in high-frequency harmonics. Careful thought must be given in selecting the capacitor's ESR and f_r (and therefore ESL) to allow adequate attenuation of the fundamental frequency and all significant harmonics. These must be traded-off against cost, since ultralow ESR and ESL capacitors are quite expensive. Finally, wide, short connections should be made to the filter capacitor to decrease interwiring inductance. Treat the switching servo amp as a high-power, radio-frequency circuit.

"Finally, the capacitor's ripple current rating must be considered. Assuming a triangular-shaped ripple current from the inductor,

$$I_{\text{ripple}} \text{ rms} = \frac{I_{\text{ripple}} \text{ peak-peak}}{2\sqrt{3}} \tag{7–13}$$

This ripple current causes power dissipation by the capacitor's ESR, heating up the capacitor. This heat, in turn, adversely affects the mortality of the capacitor. Also, ESR is inversely proportional to the capacitor's temperature, causing performance to drift during operation if the heat is not properly removed. This accounts for the switcher's poorer performance at low temperatures.

"At the present time it is customary to use either aluminum or tantalum electrolytics and bootstrap them in either a series or parallel configuration in order to overcome the difficulties associated with high ESR, capacitance drop-off with frequency, and most of all, current-carrying limitations that are associated with these types of devices" [5].

"These problems become compounded still further when the switching power supply and switch mode servo amplifier is required to operate over wide temperature ranges commonly experienced in military and commercial airborne applications" [5].

"When considering that the present high-frequency switching power supplies are operating primarily in the 20- to 40-kHz region, it is evident that new approaches must be attempted when considering higher-efficiency switching supplies that will be required to operate in excess of 100 kHz" [5].

"In meeting this challenge film capacitors can play a major role since their basic loss characteristics and current-carrying capabilities are far superior to those of the highest-quality electrolytics" [5].

"If a switching power supply were required to operate at −55°C (which is typical for airborne applications)—and at frequencies of 100 kHz and above, it would require the electrolytic capacitors to be at least three to four times the size of a metallized film device. This is due to the large losses of capacity, the increased ESR, and the capacitance falloff with frequency. This is reflected in Table 7–5, which compares the relevant characteristics of film versus electrolytics" [5].

"When combining this with the ability of film capacitors to carry at least five

TABLE 7–5 COMPARISON OF CAPACITOR'S NONIDEAL CHARACTERISTICS

Type 20 MF 50 V dc	ESR 100 kHz (Ω)		Maximum rms ripple current (A) at +25°C	Capacitance change vs. frequency 1000 Hz through 100 kHz (%)	Cap. change at −55°C (%)
	−55°C	+25°C			
Metallized polycarbonate type 5MC	<0.0010	<0.0010	>12.7	< 1	± 2
Wet-slug tantalum	>2.0	>0.07	< 1.2	> −25	> −20
Aluminum electrolytic	>3.0	>0.09	< 0.60	> −25	> −30

Source: Bernard Laverne, *Improving High Frequency Converted Performances and Efficiency with Film Capacitors* (Eatontown, N.J.: Electronic Concepts.)

times the ripple current of typical electrolytics (either the higher-quality tantalum or average aluminum type), it is foreseeable that in order to compensate for overall stability plus current-handling limitation, a 200-μF electrolytic capacitor can be replaced with a reliable film type of only 20 μF'' [5].

"Further reliability factors stem from the fact that film capacitors can take 200% overvoltage spikes and voltage reversals of 100%, where electrolytics are normally limited to voltage reversal of no greater than 1 V and overvoltage stress to a maximum of 130% for those of the highest qualities'' [5].

"Film capacitors have defined and distinct advantages over electrolytics for use in high-frequency switching power supplies. These include the following:

1. Maximum capacity change ±2% from −55 to +125°C
2. No capacitance falloff with frequency
3. Low ESR (high power efficiency)
4. Low ESL (higher resonant frequency)
5. No fluids that can leak
6. Temperature range −55 to +125°C
7. ESR not affected over operating temperature range
8. Self-healing properties
9. Overvoltage protection of 200%'' [5]

A sample data sheet for a series of metallized polycarbonate film capacitors designed for switching power applications is given in Table 7–6.

7–2.3 Switching Diodes

"The four parameters of major importance for the diode(s) in the switching section of the regulator are forward current (peak and average), speed, forward bias voltage drop, and reverse bias voltage drop. The speed of conventional diodes is limited primarily by the reverse recovery time. That is the length of time it takes to remove the minority current carriers from near the junction when reverse bias is applied, to establish the depletion region (stopping current flow). Reverse recovery time is directly proportional to the forward (load) current. The longer reverse recovery is, the longer it takes for the diode to turn off, and the more power the switching components must dissipate. Efficiency drops.

"There are two types of diodes whose speeds and forward current ratings are adequate for switching regulators. One process adds gold during the diffusion. Those gold-diffused fast recovery diodes have adequately low reverse recovery times at high forward currents. The second, high-speed power diode is called the Schottky diode. There is no semiconductor junction. The diode is formed entirely of N-type material, with one metal to semiconductor connection formed in such a way as to allow current flow in only one direction. Rectification is achieved without minority carriers and so the inherent reverse recovery time is eliminated.

TABLE 7-6 TYPE 5MC SWITCHER FILM CAPACITORS

Voltage (V dc)	Capacitance (μF)	ESR (mΩ) 100 kHz	Maximum ripple current (A)					I_{peak}	DVDT	Resonant frequency (kHz) 5MC22 5MC26 5MC27	Resonant frequency (kHz) 5MC28 5MC29
			25°C	50°C	85°C	105°C	125°C				
50	1.0	18	7.8	5.1	4.0	1.9	1.0	383	383	890	
	3.0	15	9.8	6.4	4.8	2.3	1.2	1148	383	550	
	5.0	13	10.6	6.9	5.1	2.8	1.3	1221	244	375	
	10.0	11	12.6	8.2	5.9	3.1	1.4	2441	244	265	318
	20.0	10	14.8	9.6	6.8	3.3	1.8	3583	179	178	214
	50.0	6	23.5	14.9	10.7	4.4	2.1	7067	141	108	130
75	1.0	19	7.9	5.1	3.8	1.9	1.0	575	575	840	
	3.0	15	10.3	6.7	4.9	2.5	1.2	1098	366	560	672
	5.0	13	11.6	7.5	5.6	2.8	1.4	1343	269	356	427
	10.0	12	13.5	8.8	6.5	3.2	1.6	2686	269	251	301
	20.0	11	16.5	10.7	7.9	4.0	2.0	4243	212	171	205
	50.0	6	24.2	15.7	11.6	4.6	2.2	7462	149	100	120
100	1.0	20	8.0	5.2	3.8	1.9	1.0	671	671	780	684
	3.0	15	10.6	6.9	5.1	2.5	1.3	941	314	570	427
	5.0	13	12.4	8.1	6.0	3.0	1.5	1567	313	356	290
	10.0	12	14.6	9.5	7.0	3.5	1.8	2208	221	242	192
	20.0	11	17.1	11.1	8.2	4.1	2.1	3483	174	160	115
	50.0	6	23.6	15.3	11.3	4.5	2.2	7584	152	96	

Source: Electronic Concepts.

"The forward bias voltage drop across the Schottky diode is approximately half that of a conventional silicon diode. This means that when biased on, the Schottky diode will have to dissipate half of the power of a gold-diffused high-speed power diode. However, the reverse voltage break down rating of Schottky diodes is on the order of 30 V. This restricts their use to lower voltage."

7–2.4 Pulse-Width-Modulation IC

"Most regulator integrated-circuit manufacturers offer a pulse-width-modulator IC. Which to buy depends largely on the features you need, availability, and cost. National Semiconductor's LM3524 is fairly representative of the pulse-width-modulator ICs available. Its block diagram is given in Figure 7–17.

"Several characteristics and features of this particular IC should be pointed out. The maximum input (supply) voltage is 40 V. So you must reduce the rectified line voltage before applying it to this IC. The output transistors are driven with complementary signals with a definite off period for each before either goes on. Each is capable of 100 mA output. The on-chip oscillator's frequency is controlled by an external resistor and capacitor (pins 6 and 7). Maximum frequency is 350 kHz.

"The duty cycle is a function of the voltage at the compensation pin (pin 9). The relationship is shown in Figure 7–18." Notice that the relationship is both direct and linear as the voltage on pin 9 is varied from 1 V to 3 V. The two output transistors are driven on alternately. On one cycle, the upper transistor is enabled through its NOR gate by a logic low at Q of the toggle flip-flop. $\overline{Q}$ is high, disabling the lower transistor. The next pulse from the oscillator flips the toggle flip-flop, setting Q to a logic high and $\overline{Q}$ to a logic low. These, in turn, enable the lower power transistor and disable the upper.

This alternate action of the output transistors serves two purposes. First, each transistor rests for half the time, cooling down. Second, it allows push-pull operation if you should need to drive alternate halves of a power transformer primary.

The key to the LM3524's performance is the comparator. To get one of the transistors on, its base must be driven high. This requires that *all* inputs to that NOR gate be at a logic low. The comparator's output goes low when the voltage on pin 9 (the compensation pin) is above the oscillator's ramp. Conversely, whenever the voltage on the oscillator's ramp rises above the voltage on the compensation pin, the comparator's output goes high, disables the NOR gate, and drives the transistors off.

$$V_{\text{oscillator}} < V_{\text{comp}} \implies Q \quad \text{on}$$
$$V_{\text{oscillator}} > V_{\text{comp}} \implies Q \quad \text{off}$$

This is illustrated in Figure 7–19. The higher the voltage on pin 9 is, the longer each cycle it exceeds the oscillator's ramp, and the longer each cycle one of the output transistors stays on. Driving V_{pin9} to 3 V should keep the output transistors on virtually the entire cycle. Conversely, pulling V_{pin9} below 1 V will force the transistors off.

This is the purpose of the shutdown transistor. A logic high on the shutdown pin

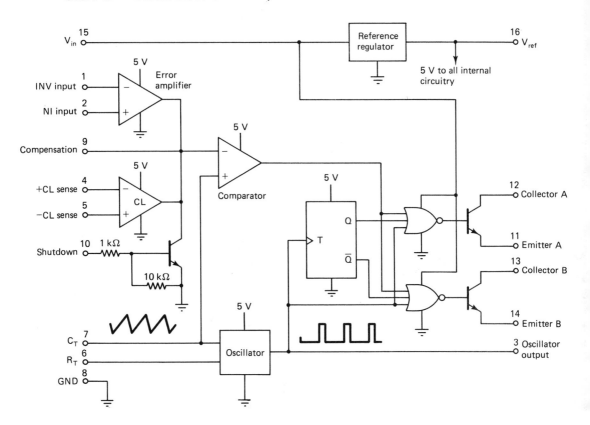

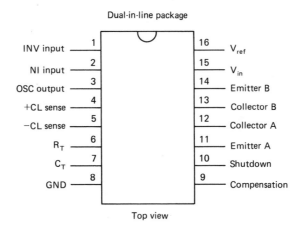

Figure 7–17   LM3524 pulse-width-modulator IC block diagram. (Courtesy of National Semiconductor.)

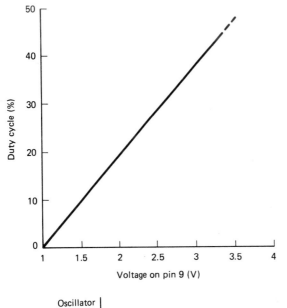

Figure 7–18 Compensation pin voltage versus pulse width for the LM 3524. (Courtesy of National Semiconductor.)

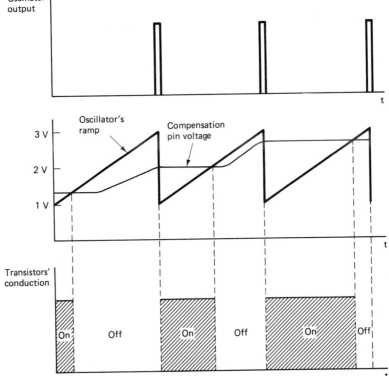

Figure 7–19 Pulse-width-modulator operation.

turns its transistor on. This shorts the compensation pin (pin 9) to ground (pulling it below 1 V). The ramp *always* exceeds the voltage on pin 9, so the output transistors are always off.

The comparator labeled CL has a similar function. When the voltage on +CL, pin 4, exceeds the voltage on −CL, pin 5, by 0.2 V, the CL comparator sends its output to ground. This, in turn, pulls $V_{\text{pin}9}$ below 1 V, shutting down the pulse-width modulator's outputs. This feature is used for current limiting.

$$V_{+\text{CL}} - V_{-\text{CL}} \geq 200 \text{ mV} \implies Q \quad \text{off}$$

The error amplifier is a general-purpose, high-gain difference amplifier. Its output impedance is high enough to allow any voltage (or short) impressed at pin 9 to override its output without damage. The error amplifier is normally used to allow the pulse-width amplifier to provide negative feedback.

The LM3524 pulse-width modulator IC in a simple forward converter amplifier is shown in Figure 7–20. Unregulated power is provided to both the switching transistor and the pulse-width modulator. This voltage must be at least 2 V greater than the largest output wanted. This provides saturation headroom for the transistor. However, the unregulated power must stay below 40 V, the chip's maximum supply voltage. With power and ground applied to the LM3524, +5 V dc will appear at pin 16, V_{ref}. This powers the internal electronics as well as making 20 mA available for external use.

Connecting R_T and C_T between ground and their pins on the IC will enable the oscillator. Sharp TTL-compatible spikes will appear at the oscillator output (pin 3). A sawtooth-shaped voltage, from 1 to 3 V, is available across C_T. These signals were illustrated in Figure 7–19. The frequency is

$$f_{\text{osc}} \approx \frac{1}{R_T C_T}$$

$$1.8 \text{ k}\Omega \leq R_T \leq 100 \text{ k}\Omega$$

$$0.001 \text{ }\mu\text{F} \leq C_T \leq 0.1 \text{ }\mu\text{F}$$

The two output transistors are wired in parallel. When either transistor goes on, it grounds the base bias circuit of the main pass transistor. This establishes base current, saturating the power transistor. Power is passed to the filter and load. When both transistors are off, no base current flows in the main switching transistor, and it goes off. Base bias resistor R_{b1} should be chosen large enough to limit current into the ICs outputs to below 100 mA. However, it must assure enough base current to saturate the pass transistor. Resistor R_{b2} improves performance by allowing the charge of parasitic capacitance and swamping out the effect of base leakage current. It is usually selected about 10 times larger than R_{b1}.

The rectifier, inductor, and capacitor convert the pulse-width-modulated switching signal from the transistor into a steady (more or less) dc signal for the load. Their operation and selection were discussed in previous sections.

The voltage at the load is sampled by R_f and R_i and fed back to the inverting

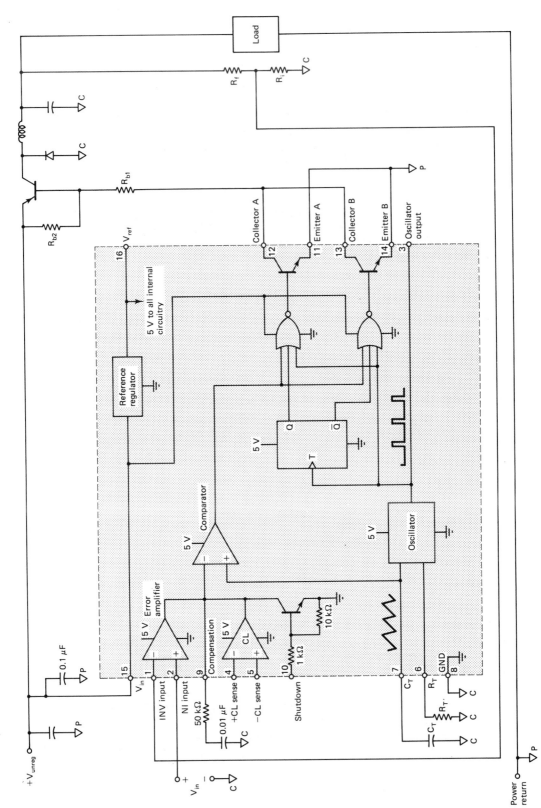

Figure 7–20 LM3524 in a sample forward converter amplifier.

input of the error amplifier. Because of its high open-loop gain, this amplifier will drive its output to whatever voltage is necessary to minimize the difference in potential between its two inputs. This sounds a lot like an op amp. In fact, you can view this entire circuit as a rather complex noninverting (op) amp. The output voltage, at the load, will be

$$V_L = V_{in}\left(1 + \frac{R_f}{R_i}\right)$$

However, the error amp's common-mode input voltage is between 1.8 and 3.4 V. So you may need to add a zero and span circuit in front of V_{in}, to assure that the range of your control signal is converted to match these limits.

EXAMPLE 7–4

(a) For the circuit in Figure 7–20, with $R_f = 9$ kΩ, $R_i = 1$ kΩ, and $V_{in} = 2$ V, $V_{unreg} = 30$ V, determine (1) V_{load}; (2) $V_{inv\,input}$; (3) % duty cycle.
(b) Explain what happens if V_{in} is raised to 2.5 V.
(c) Explain the effects if V_{unreg} is raised to 40 V.

Solution   (a) $V_{load} = V_{in}\left(1 + \frac{R_f}{R_i}\right)$

$$= 2\,V\left(1 + \frac{9\,k\Omega}{1\,k\Omega}\right)$$

$$= 20\,V$$

$V_{inv\,input}$ is the voltage at the junction of R_f and R_i. So by the voltage-divider law,

$$V_{inv\,input} = \left(\frac{R_i}{R_i + R_f}\right)V_{load}$$

$$= \left(\frac{1\,k\Omega}{1\,k\Omega + 9\,k\Omega}\right)20\,V$$

$$= 2\,V$$

This is the same voltage as at V_{NI} (i.e., V_{in}). Since the error amplifier is going to drive its output as necessary to minimize the difference between its inputs, this result makes sense.

$$\%\ \text{duty cycle} = \frac{V_{load}}{V_{unreg}}$$

This is another way of writing equation 7–7.

$$\%\ \text{duty cycle} = \frac{20\,V}{30\,V} = 67\%$$

(b) When the input voltage rises, V_{NI} goes up. This drives the voltage on pin 9 up. Raising the voltage on pin 9 means that the ramp will be below $V_{pin\,9}$ longer each cycle. Since the transistors are on when the ramp is below $V_{pin\,9}$, these transistors will stay on longer each cycle. This increases the % duty cycle, which produces a larger dc voltage out of the filter. The voltage fed back through R_f and R_i is increased proportionally until $V_{load} = 25$ V, producing $V_{inv\,input} = 2.5$ V $= V_{NI}$. There the circuit's performance stabilizes.

(c) When the unregulated input (V_{pk}) rises to 40 V, the output from the filter goes up (see equation 7–7). This pushes the voltage on $V_{inv\,input}$ up to 4 V, because of the divider relationship of R_f and R_i. Raising the inverting input into the error amplifier drives its output (pin 9) down. Lowering the voltage on pin 9 reduces the time that the ramp stays below that voltage. So the time that the transistors stay on is reduced. This, in turn, lowers the average voltage to the load. This process continues until the duty cycle is reduced enough to lower the load voltage back to 25 V, sending V_{inv} to 2.5 V, where it matches V_{NI} and V_{in}.

7–2.5 The Transistor Switch

The power switching device may take one of two forms, the bipolar junction transistor (BJT) or the vertical field-effect transistor (VFET). The bipolar junction transistor is more familiar to most. However, the VFET dominates applications that run over 100 kHz. The advantages of each will be investigated at greater length later.

Both devices have several common characteristics of which you must be aware, when used in a switching servo amplifier. Ideally, each would switch as shown in Figure 7–21. "From time zero to t_1, the transistor is hard on, passing current to the load. Ideally, there is no voltage dropped across the transistor, so it dissipates no power.

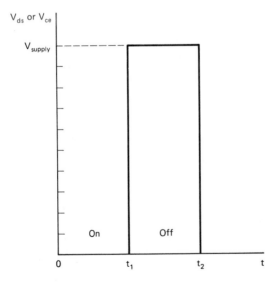

Figure 7–21   Ideal switching waveform.

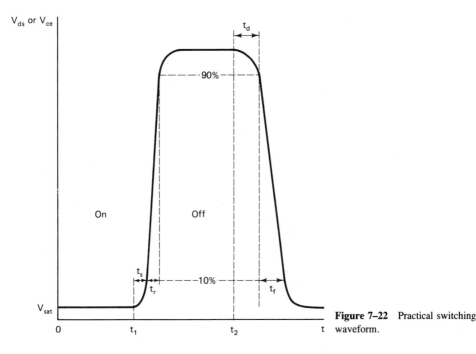

Figure 7–22 Practical switching waveform.

At time t_1, the transistor is turned off. It responds instantaneously, taking no significant time to go off. Between times t_1 and t_2, the transistor is off, completely off. No current leaks through, so even though full supply voltage is across the transistor, it dissipates no power. At time t_2, the transistor is turned on again. Ideally, the transistor's voltage falls instantaneously to zero.

"Of course, no such ideal transistor switch exists. A more practical response is illustrated in Figure 7–22. Between time zero and t_1 the transistor is saturated (on). The actual saturation, collector to emitter, voltage varies from 0.2 V to over 1 V, increasing with current. At reasonable load current levels, several watts of power must be dissipated by the transistor. At t_1, the transistor is switched off. However, current continues to flow during the storage time (t_s) and the rise time (t_r). During the rise time, the transistor has both significant voltage across it and significant current through it. Considerable power must be dissipated during this period. A similar problem occurs at t_2 when the transistor is turned on. The delay time (t_d) slows response, while power must be dissipated during the fall time (t_f). Manufacturers specify the delay, storage, and rise and fall times for their transistors at various collector current levels. A good rule of thumb is to assure that the total response time ($t_s + t_r + t_d + t_f$) is less than 10% of the minimum pulse width at rated load current."

$$t_s + t_r + t_d + t_f < 0.1 t_{min}$$

In fact, the power dissipated by the switching device is strongly affected by the type of load being driven. Figure 7–23a shows a VFET driving a resistive load. A

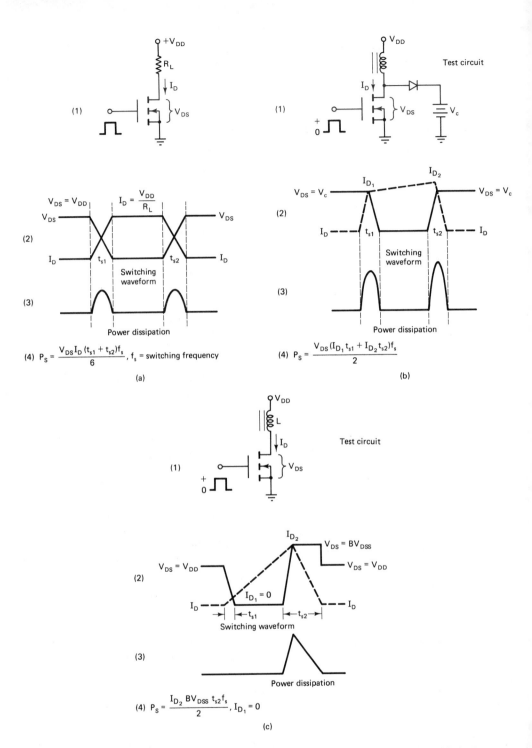

Figure 7–23 Switching losses: (a) resistive, (b) clamped inductive, and (c) unclamped inductive load switching waveforms. (Courtesy of Siliconix.)

TABLE 7-7 SWITCHING LOSS COMPARISON

Figure 7-23	V_{DS} (V)	I_{D1} (A)	I_{D2} (A)	t_{s1} (nS)	t_{s2} (nS)	f_s (kHz)	P_s (W)
a	100	1	1	100	100	100	0.33
b	100	1	1	100	100	100	1
c	150	0	2	100	400	100	6

Source: Siliconix.

clamped inductive load is shown in Figure 7-23b, and an unclamped inductive load in Figure 7-23c. Their relative losses are given in Table 7-7.

The safe operating area (SOA) outlines those combinations of collector-to-emitter voltage and collector current (or drain-to-source voltage and drain current) which the transistor can simultaneously provide. You saw these curves for the OPA512 power op amp in Figures 7-4 and 7-5. For the 2N3055, a NPN bipolar transistor, the SOA curves are given in Figure 7-24. "Although the 2N3055 is rated at 15 A collector current, 60 V collector to emitter, and 115 W power dissipation, all three ratings cannot be maximized at the same time. To assure that the transistor does not fail, you must keep the operation (V_{ce} versus I_C) point below the dc line. Normally, in saturation you

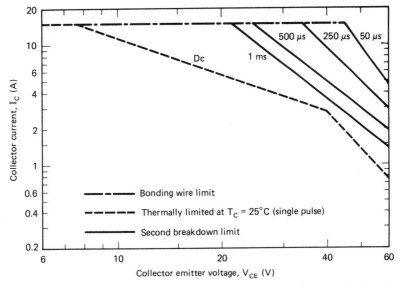

There are two limitations on the power-handling ability of a transistor: average junction temperature and second breakdown. Safe operating area curves indicate I_C–V_{CE} limits of the transistor that must be observed for reliable operation; that is, the transistor must not be subjected to greater dissipation than the curves indicate.
The data are based on $T_C = 25°C$; $T_{J(pk)}$ is variable depending on the power level. Second breakdown pulse limits are valid for duty cycles to 10% but must be derated for temperature.

Figure 7-24 2N3055 safe operating area. (Courtesy of Motorola Semiconductor.)

will be operating in the upper left corner (low V_{ce}, high I_c) or in the lower right corner when the transistor is off (high V_{ce}, low I_c). Switching between these two points will follow a straight line defined by the load. The entire load line, as well as both endpoints, should exist entirely within the safe operating area.

''The second breakdown limit lines (1 ms, 500 μs, 250 μs, 50 μs) may be a bit misleading. They indicate that if the transistor is to be pulsed on for only a limited time each cycle, higher current at higher voltage is available. Carefully read the note. Those lines are valid only if the on time is 10% of the period. Your switcher may require considerably larger duty cycle.

TABLE 7–8 POWER TRANSISTOR SPECIFICATIONS.

ELECTRICAL CHARACTERISTICS (T_C = 25°C unless otherwise noted).

Characteristic		Symbol	Min	Max	Unit
OFF CHARACTERISTICS (1)					
*Collector-Emitter Sustaining Voltage	2N3055A, MJ2955A	$V_{CEO(sus)}$	60	–	Vdc
(I_C = 200 mAdc, I_B = 0)	MJ15015, MJ15016		120	–	
Collector Cutoff Current		I_{CEO}			mAdc
(V_{CE} = 30 Vdc, $V_{BE(off)}$ = 0 Vdc)	2N3055A, MJ2955A		–	0.7	
(V_{CE} = 60 Vdc, $V_{BE(off)}$ = 0 Vdc)	MJ15015, MJ15016		–	0.1	
*Collector Cutoff Current	2N3055A, MJ2955A	I_{CEV}	–	5.0	mAdc
(V_{CEV} = Rated Value, $V_{BE(off)}$ = 1.5 Vdc)	MJ15015, MJ15016		–	1.0	
Collector Cutoff Current	2N3055A, MJ2955A	I_{CEV}	–	30	mAdc
(V_{CEV} = Rated Value, $V_{BE(off)}$ = 1.5 Vdc,	MJ15015, MJ15016		–	6.0	
T_C = 150°C)					
*Emitter Cutoff Current	2N3055A, MJ2955A	I_{EBO}	–	5.0	mAdc
(V_{EB} = 7.0 Vdc, I_C = 0)	MJ15015, MJ15016		–	0.2	
*SECOND BREAKDOWN					
Second Breakdown Collector Current with Base Forward Biased		$I_{S/b}$			Adc
(t = 0.5 s non-repetitive)	2N3055A, MJ2955A		1.95	–	
(V_{CE} = 60 Vdc)	MJ15015, MJ15016		3.0	–	
*ON CHARACTERISTICS (1)					
DC Current Gain		h_{FE}			–
(I_C = 4.0 Adc, V_{CE} = 2.0 Vdc)			10	70	
(I_C = 4.0 Adc, V_{CE} = 4.0 Vdc)			20	70	
(I_C = 10 Adc, V_{CE} = 4.0 Vdc)			5.0	–	
Collector-Emitter Saturation Voltage		$V_{CE(sat)}$			Vdc
(I_C = 4.0 Adc, I_B = 400 mAdc)			–	1.1	
(I_C = 10 Adc, I_B = 3.3 Adc)			–	3.0	
(I_C = 15 Adc, I_B = 7.0 Adc)			–	5.0	
Base-Emitter On Voltage		$V_{BE(on)}$	0.7	1.8	Vdc
(I_C = 4.0 Adc, V_{CE} = 4.0 Vdc)					
*DYNAMIC CHARACTERISTICS					
Current-Gain—Bandwidth Product	2N3055A, MJ15015	f_T	0.8	6.0	MHz
(I_C = 1.0 Adc, V_{CE} = 4.0 Vdc, f = 1.0 MHz)	MJ2955A, MJ15016		2.2	18	
Output Capacitance		C_{ob}	60	600	pF
(V_{CB} = 10 Vdc, I_E = 0, f = 1.0 MHz)					
*SWITCHING CHARACTERISTICS (2N3055A only)					
RESISTIVE LOAD					
Delay Time	(V_{CC} = 30 Vdc, I_C = 4.0 Adc,	t_d	–	0.5	μs
Rise Time	I_{B1} = I_{B2} = 0.4 Adc,	t_r	–	4.0	μs
Storage Time	t_p = 25 μs Duty Cycle ≤ 2%)	t_s	–	3.0	μs
Fall Time		t_f	–	6.0	μs

(1) Pulse Test: Pulse Width = 300 μs, Duty Cycle ≤ 2%.
*Indicates JEDEC Registered Data (2N3055A)

Source: Motorola Semiconductors.

"The note also indicates that this safe operating area is valid for a case temperature of 25°C. Unfortunately, most power devices operate with their case much hotter. Figure 7–24 must be derated for temperature by a factor of 0.64 W/°C. This factor is the inverse of the junction-to-case thermal resistance of the transistor." Table 7–8 contains the specifications for the 2N3055 (NPN) and MJ2955 (PNP) transistors.

$$P_{\text{derate}} = P_{25°C} - \frac{1}{\Theta_{Jc}}(T_c - 25°C)$$

For a case temperature of 125°C and a $P_{25°C}$ of 115 W,

$$\begin{aligned}
P_{\text{derate}} &= 115 \text{ W} - (0.64 \text{ W/°C})(125°C - 25°C) \\
&= 115 \text{ W} - 64 \text{ W} \\
&= 51 \text{ W}
\end{aligned}$$

So to operate the 2N3055 at a case temperature of 125°C, you must decrease the power of the transistor by more than half. The derated SOA curve is a constant power line where

$$I_{ce} \times V_{ce} = 51 \text{ W}$$

This is drawn parallel to the dc line up to $V_{ce} = 40$ V. Above 40 V, the derated SOA line is continued, at a steeper angle, also parallel to the dc line. This is shown in Figure 7–25. Remember, both quiesent endpoints (hard on and hard off) and the entire transition center of the load line must lie beneath the derated SOA curve.

Whether to use a bipolar junction transistor (BJT) or a vertical power field-effect

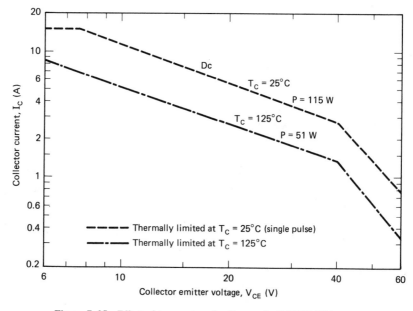

Figure 7–25   Effect of temperature derating on the 2N3055 SOA curves.

transistor (VFET) depends on several characteristics of the switching servo amplifier. The output voltage determines the required blocking voltage rating of the transistor. The frequency used sets the size, efficiency, and cost of filter components as well as affecting the transistor switch selection. The drive circuitry is significantly different for the BJT and the VFET. Both complexity and efficiency of the drive circuit are determined by the choice of the transistor switch.

"The basic single transistor flyback and forward converter switches must block *twice* the maximum supply voltage plus a spike caused by leakage and layout inductance and the forward recovery transient of the clamp diode" [6].

This suggests that the transistor switch you chose should be able to block a voltage which is several times (two or three) the peak input voltage. There are available VFETs which can block up to 500 V when off while passing over 100 A when saturated. Bipolar transistors are noticeably better; blocking over 1400 V when off and passing up to 300 A when on. Of course, operation at these extremes is exceptional. However, in general, there are more high-voltage, high-current BJTs available than VFETs. In either case, caution is highly advised when removing and applying this amount of energy in a fraction of a microsecond.

One major reason for using a *switching* servo amplifier is increased efficiency. Ideally, the switch should dissipate no power. However, when saturated there is a definite voltage drop across the transistor, a nonzero ON resistance. Using typical values, for the BJT,

$$\begin{aligned} P_{\text{on}} &= V_{ce} \times I_c \\ &= (0.75 \text{ V})(100 \text{ A}) \\ &= 75 \text{ W} \end{aligned}$$

and for the VFET,

$$\begin{aligned} P_{\text{on}} &= I_d^2 R_{ds} \\ &= (100 \text{ A})^2 (0.07 \ \Omega) \\ &= 700 \text{ W} \end{aligned}$$

So, at low frequency, the BJT clearly produces a much more efficient switch. However, as the frequency rises, a larger percentage of the duty cycle is spent going on or going off. While the switch is turning on or off there may be 50 V or more across the switch with 50 A or more through it. Much power is dissipated during these rises and falls. At low frequencies the percentage of the cycle spent on these edges is small and the energy wasted there negligible. However, at higher frequencies the switch turns on and off more often, wasting a proportionally larger amount of energy. A VFET generally switches much more quickly than a BJT with comparable current and voltage ratings. So for applications switching at or above 100 kHz, the VFET is more efficient. For lower frequencies, choose the BJT.

For both power handling and efficiency, it appears that the BJT is a better choice than the VFET. But these switches must be driven on rapidly, held on, and then driven off just as rapidly. The complexity, cost, and efficiency of the drive circuit must also be considered.

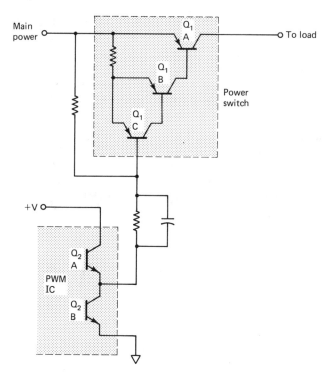

Figure 7–26   Simple BJT drive circuit.

One possible base drive circuit is shown in Figure 7–26. Since it may be necessary to deliver 100 A or more to the load, as dictated by the pulse-width modulator IC, a double Darlington configuration is often needed. These may be available in a single package. At the instant that the PWM IC switches, the capacitor acts as a short, allowing very high base currents during turn on. This speeds up the flooding of the three base–emitter junctions with current carriers. The base resistor limits steady-state current, assuring that the power switch is saturated, while keeping the PWM IC output transistor's current at a safe level.

To turn the BJT off, its base–emitter region must be depleted of current carriers. The higher the collector current, the more current carriers there are, and the longer this process takes. An active-high driver transistor, Q_{2A}, speeds this process. When Q_{2B} turns off, Q_{2A} goes on. A positive step is immediately applied to the base of the power switch through the base capacitor. This significantly speeds the removal of the current carriers in the base–emitter junctions, turning the BJTs off rapidly. Unfortunately, many PWM ICs do not have an active-high driver transistor (Q_{2A}). When Q_{2B} goes off, these PWM ICs leave the bases open, to float up as parasitic capacitances are charged. Turn-off time for these circuits is noticeably slower.

At first glance, driving a VFET seems much simpler than switching and maintaining a BJT. Whenever the gate-to-source voltage exceeds the threshold voltage, the depletion-mode VFET saturates. For an N-channel device, $V_{GS(th)}$ is positive. For a P-channel

VFET, $V_{GS(th)}$ is negative. A typical threshold voltage is 7 V, well within the range of CMOS or open-collector TTL logic. No current is needed, since the channel's resistance is controlled by the *voltage*-produced field at the gate. The gate appears as an open. Virtually no power is required to hold the transistor saturated.

But driving a VFET quickly is not as simple as driving its gate directly from a logic chip. The maximum gate-to-source voltage must not be exceeded. Usually, a zener diode and series resistor are enough to limit any peaks and protect the transistor's input.

Although the gate looks open to dc, there is capacitance between gate and source and between gate and drain. When the device is off, the driving circuit sees C_{iss}, the common source input capacitance. This is the sum of the gate-to-source and gate-to-drain capacitance and may total 500 pF or more. To begin to turn the VFET on, this capacitance must be charged up to $V_{GS(th)}$.

For a capacitor,

$$I = C \frac{dv}{dt}$$

For a typical driver,

$$dv = V_{GS(th)} \sim 7 \text{ V}$$

$$dt = \text{time delay prior to device beginning}$$
$$\text{to turn on} \sim 20 \text{ ns}$$

$$C = C_{iss} \sim 500 \text{ pF}$$

$$I = \text{current needed from driver}$$
$$= (500 \text{ pF}) (7 \text{ V/20 ns})$$
$$= 175 \text{ mA}$$

To drive the gate up 7 V in 20 ns, to start turning the VFET on requires 175 mA (during that 20 ns).

Once the VFET begins to turn on, its drain voltage drops rapidly. Although the gate voltage is being held constant, C_{dg} (C_{rss}) must be charged as its drain-side voltage drops. The current to charge this "feedback" or Miller effect capacitance also must come from the gate drive circuit. Assuming a

$$V_{DD} = 100 \text{ V}$$

$$V_{on} = 1 \text{ V}$$

$$dt = 30 \text{ ns}$$

$$C = C_{ds} = C_{rss} \sim 100 \text{ pF}$$

$$I = (100 \text{ pF}) [(100 \text{ V} - 1 \text{ V})/30 \text{ ns}]$$
$$= 330 \text{ mA}$$

So to drive the VFET's output down, the driver circuit must provide 330 mA for the 30 ns that the drain voltage is falling. Once the VFET is on, with the associated capacitances charged, little, if any, current is needed to hold the device saturated.

Turning the VFET off requires the reverse polarity currents, to discharge the C_{iss} below $V_{GS(th)}$, then to charge up the C_{dg}, as the drain voltage again rises to V_{DD}.

The gate driver circuit then needs to be able to source and sink significant amounts of current actively, very rapidly, but for only a brief time each cycle. This is *not* what logic gates or even traditional pulse width modulation ICs are good at.

The D469 is a quad CMOS driver designed specifically to meet these requirements. Its schematic symbol and package are given in Figure 7–27. There are four independent buffers, each which can be either inverting or noninverting. Being CMOS, it is directly compatible to low-power CMOS logic or microprocessors. Each driver can sink or source a peak of 500 mA of current, or drive a 500-pF load with a 20-ns rise time. The buffers may be paralleled to increase drive current if necessary. Although the output voltage levels are

$$HI = V_{DD} - 4 \text{ V}$$

$$LO = 4 \text{ V}$$

these levels nicely match the $V_{GS(th)}$ requirements of a VFET.

Look back at the forward converter filter in Figure 7–14, and then the full schematic in Figure 7–20. These circuits work well if you always want to *source* load current. The load voltage is always positive. But in servo control you must be able to reverse

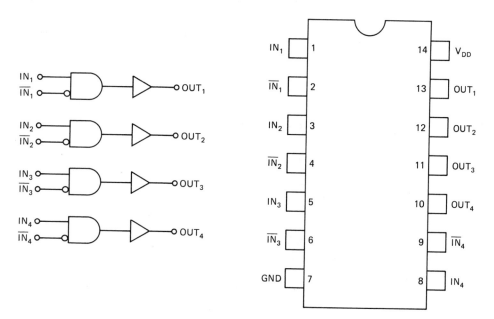

Figure 7–27 D469 quad CMOs MOSFET driver. (Courtesy of Siliconix.)

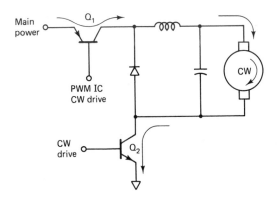

Figure 7–28 H-bridge clockwise drive.

the direction of load current, applying voltage of either polarity to the motor. The forward converter must be modified.

Bidirectional, proportional power can be produced using an H bridge. The first step in converting the forward converter into an H bridge is to replace the load's ground connection with a NPN power transistor. This is, shown in Figure 7–28. To drive the motor clockwise, Q_2 is saturated, grounding the bottom of the motor and the filter components. Current is sourced through Q_1 as controlled by the PWM IC and smoothed by the forward converter filter.

Counterclockwise rotation requires that current flow *up* through the motor. This is accomplished by adding a second set of transistors and filter components. Look at Figure 7–29. Clockwise drive and control transistors Q_1 and Q_2 are turned off. The counterclockwise drive transistor, Q_4, is turned on. Power is proportionally controlled with the PWM IC CCW drive into Q_3. Current now flows up through the motor, opposite

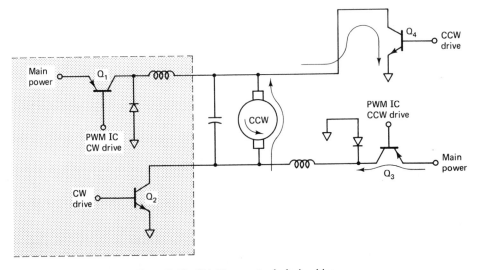

Figure 7–29 H-bridge counterclockwise drive.

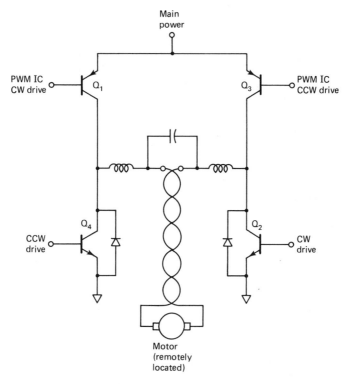

Figure 7–30 Complete H bridge.

to its direction when the motor turned clockwise. By making the filter capacitor nonpolarized, it can be used in either direction. Finally, the flyback diodes have been tied directly to ground. This breaks a parallel path across the motor through the disabled (clockwise) forward converter.

A more traditional schematic for the H bridge is given in Figure 7–30. Notice that the two transistors, which work together, are placed on opposite sides of the bridge. So for clockwise motion Q_1 and Q_2 are used. Current flows down through Q_1, *left to right* through the filter and motor, and down through Q_2 to ground. Counterclockwise motion used Q_3 and Q_4. Current flows down through Q_3, *right to left* through the motor and down through Q_4 to ground.

There is one major precaution. *Never* allow both transistors on one side of the bridge (Q_1 and Q_4 or Q_3 and Q_2) to be on at the same time. Should this happen, the main power would be shorted to ground. In fact, this is so important that overlapping off-time logic may be added. Its purpose is to assure that *all* transistors are off prior to turning either Q_2 or Q_4 on.

Building an H bridge with VFETS requires isolated drive circuitry for the upper transistors. An H bridge made with two P-channel and two N-channel transistors is shown in Figure 7–31. Notice that the upper, P-channel transistors have their sources tied to the main power $V+$. Since $V_{GS(th)}$ for a P-channel VFET is negative, you must

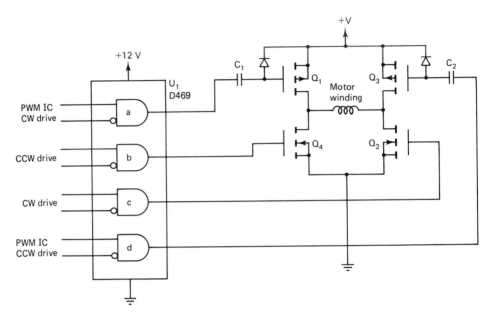

Figure 7–31 H bridge using capacitive isolation for P-channel MOSFETs. (Courtesy of Siliconix.)

pulse the gate voltage about 7 V below $V+$ to saturate that transistor. When the driver IC (U_{1a} or U_{1d}) outputs a step down to a logic low, this falling edge is coupled through C_1 or C_2 and rapidly charges the associated C_{iss} to a level far enough below $V+$ to hold the associated transistor saturated.

When the driver IC (U_{1a} or U_{1d}) steps from a low to a high output, a pulse of current is sent through C_1 or C_2. This rapidly reverses the charge on the transistor's C_{iss}, pulling the gate up to $V+$, turning the transistor off. The gate-to-source diodes prevent driving the gate above $V+$, which might damage the VFET.

Driver ICs U_{1b} and U_{1c} drive the lower N-channel VFETs directly. A logic high turns on the associated VFET, a low turns it off. As with the BJT H bridge, you must provide the logic signals and assure proper timing. Q_1 must be completely off and the associated rise time completed prior to beginning to turn on Q_4. The same is true for Q_3 and Q_2.

This all seems simple enough. Unfortunately, manufacturing a fast, high-voltage, high-current P channel VFET is much more expensive than manufacturing its N-channel complement. So drive circuits that allow N-channel transistors to be used in the upper half of the H bridge have been designed.

These are all based around transformer coupling. A single-ended transformer-coupled VFET switch is shown in Figure 7–32a and its performance waveforms in Figure 7–32b. The UC1706 is a MOSFET driver IC made by Unitrode. When its inverting input is driven to a TTL low, its outputs drive high. This positive step is differentiated

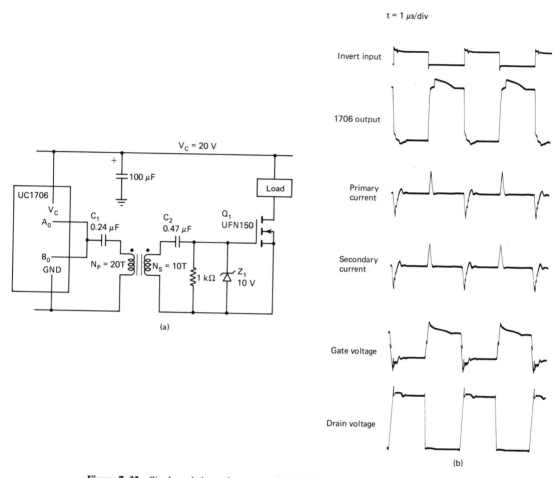

Figure 7–32 Single-ended transformer-coupled VFET switch (a) schematic; (b) waveforms. (Courtesy of Unitrode.)

into a current pulse by C_1 and passed through the primary of the coupling transformer. This pulse transformer steps up current to the secondary, rapidly charging the transistor's C_{iss} and turning it on. The zener assures that the maximum gate voltage rating of the VFET is not exceeded.

When the invert input of the UC1706 is driven to a TTL high, its outputs go low. This step down reverses the direction of current through the primary, producing a negative current pulse out of the secondary. This negative pulse rapidly discharges the transistor's C_{iss}, turning it off.

A full H bridge using transformer-coupled N-channel VFETS is illustrated in Figure 7–33. A logic high from any one of the four driver IC gates will turn on the associated transistor. Remember to drive the transistors in pairs (Q_1 and Q_2 on, Q_3 and Q_4 off, or

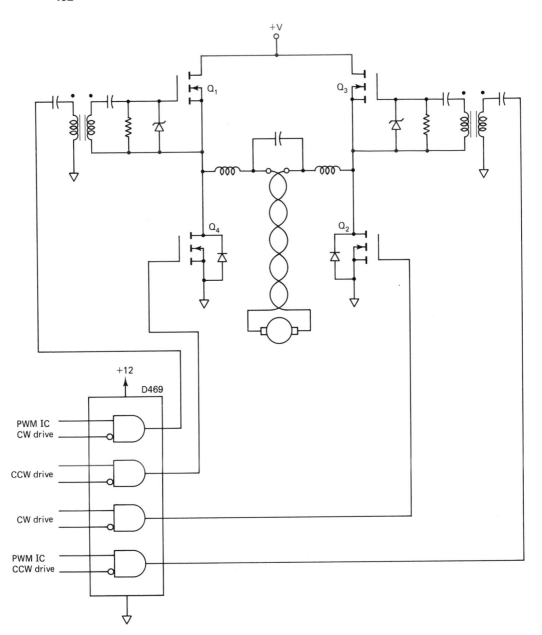

Figure 7–33 Transformer-coupled VFET H bridge.

vice versa), and to allow enough delay time that all transistors are fully off before any are driven on.

7–3 THYRISTOR-BASED POWER INTERFACES

Thyristors are a family of high-power semiconductor switches. Unlike transistors, they are pulsed on and will then remain on after the switching pulse is removed. This means that you can switch large amounts of power on with very little energy.

Isolation of the control electronics must be provided because the thyristor is connected in series with the line (often 440 V or more). Firing pulses must be provided with respect to that line, not necessarily the line's neutral. Transients and faults may generate spikes nearing 1000 V, certainly more than any traditional electronics could survive without the protection of circuit common isolation.

With proper transformer or optical isolation, triggering a thyristor as a switch is relatively simple. But in this mode, full power is applied to the load, or the load is turned fully off. As you have seen in previous chapters, this on/off control is often not adequate. Applying proportionally more or less power to the load, as directed by a low-voltage, low-current control signal is not simple for a thyristor. Both phase-angle firing and time proportioning circuits allow proportional power to be delivered to the load through thyristors. Each has its relative advantages and disadvantages.

7–3.1 Thyristor Devices

The silicon-controlled rectifier (SCR) is the most widely used thyristor. It comes in a broad assortment of current and voltage ratings, as shown in Figure 7–34. The SCR schematic symbol is given in Figure 7–35. As the symbol suggests, the main current path is one direction, from anode to cathode. Normally, the SCR is off and presents a very high impedance between anode and cathode. However, if the gate is made several volts more positive that the cathode, and adequate gating current (tens to hundreds of milliamperes) is provided, the SCR will switch on when the anode becomes positive with respect to the cathode. Main path current (a few amperes to thousands of amperes) can then flow from anode to cathode. This current will continue to flow even after the gating voltage and current are removed. To turn the SCR off (commutate) the anode-to-cathode *current* (I_{AK}) must fall below a small value called the holding current (I_H). Once I_{AK} is below I_H, the SCR goes off and can only be turned on again by positive gating voltage and current when the anode-to-cathode voltage is positive.

There are several specifications of which even the casual user must be aware.

1. *Repetitive forward blocking voltage, V_{DRM}.* At or below this voltage, the SCR will be turned on only by the proper gate signal. You should assure that the V_{DRM} is greater than the peak repetitive voltage applied to the SCR.

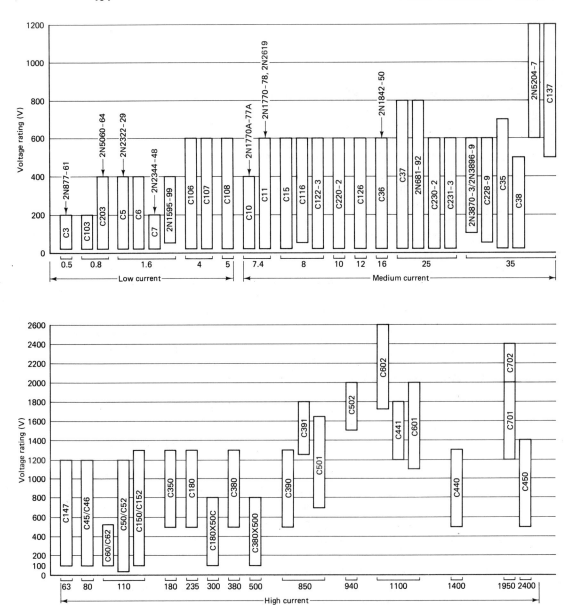

Figure 7–34   Silicon-controlled-rectifier selection guide. (Courtesy of General Electric.)

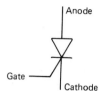

Anode

Gate

Cathode   **Figure 7–35**   SCR schematic symbol.

2. *Breakover voltage,* $V_{(BO)}$. At this anode-to-cathode voltage, the SCR may spontaneously turn on, even without a gating signal. This is highly undesirable. Assure that $V_{(BO)}$ is greater than the peak voltage applied to the SCR.

3. *Repetitive peak reverse voltage,* V_{RSM}. This is the same as the peak-inverse-voltage rating of a conventional diode. Keep the peak negative voltage below V_{RSM}.

4. *Forward voltage drop,* V_F. This is the anode-to-cathode voltage drop when the SCR is conducting.

5. *Conducting rms current,* I_{rms}. This is the maximum forward (anode-to-cathode) rms current the SCR can handle.

6. *Surge current,* I_{TSM}. This is the maximum peak current the SCR can pass repeatedly, cycle after cycle.

7. *Holding current,* I_H. This is the minimum forward current the SCR will pass and remain latched on. You must be able to lower the anode current below I_H to turn the thyristor off.

8. *Gate trigger voltage,* V_{GT}. The voltage applied between gate and cathode must exceed this value while providing adequate gate current to turn the SCR on.

9. *Peak reverse gate voltage,* V_{GRM}. This is the maximum negative voltage you can apply between gate and cathode without damaging the SCR.

10. *Gate trigger current,* I_{GT}. You must provide at least this much gate current to turn the SCR on.

11. *Peak gate power,* P_{GM}. This is the largest value of instantaneous gate voltage times gate current you can drive into the gate without damaging the SCR.

The triac can conduct or block equally well in either direction. It can be pulsed on with either a positive or a negative trigger pulse (gate to MT_1). This makes the triac ideal for controlling ac loads. Like the SCR, however, once on it will continue to conduct until its main path current falls below I_H. The schematic symbol for the triac is given in Figure 7–36.

Operation, specifications, and most performance features of the triac are very

MT_2

Gate

MT_1 **Figure 7–36**   Triac schematic symbol.

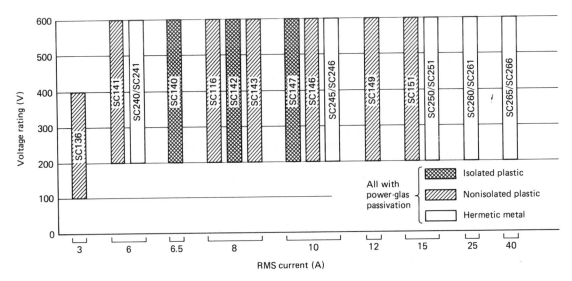

Figure 7-37 Triac selection guide. (Courtesy of General Electric.)

similar to those of the SCR. But you can see by comparing Figure 7–34 with Figure 7–37 that there is currently a much wider selection of SCRs. Also, the triac is usually limited to 60- or 400-Hz applications. At higher frequencies, stored charge does not have adequate time to recombine before the opposite polarity voltage is applied and conduction continues. So, once fired, the triac may not turn off at higher frequencies. Since SCRs only conduct every other half-cycle, they can be operated (and successfully turned off) at much higher frequencies.

There are several precautions that you should observe when working with thyristors. The only way to turn a thyristor off is to reduce the current below the holding current. For circuits driven from the line, this occurs automatically 120 times a second. However, for dc-powered applications you will have to design a commutator. Often a power NPN switching transistor is placed in parallel with the SCR and pulsed on just long enough to steal I_{AK} and turn the SCR off.

How rapidly the anode-to-cathode voltage rises is

$$\frac{dv}{dt}$$

If this rate of rise of main path voltage is too fast, high-frequency harmonics may couple through parasitic junction and lead capacitances to the gate. At the gate, this noise may falsely trigger the thyristor on.

Once the thyristor is turned on, current is determined by line voltage and load impedance. If this current tries to increase more rapidly than conduction can actually spread across the crystal from the region of the gate, localized overheating will occur, damaging the device. This critical rate of rise of anode current (di/dt) should be anticipated and an appropriate SCR specified. Series inductance will also help.

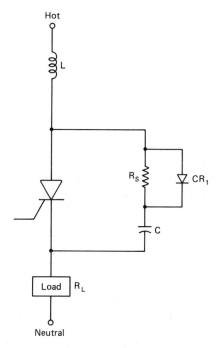

Hot

Neutral

Figure 7-38 SCR snubbing.

When large voltage and currents are switched from off to on, radio-frequency interference (RFI) is generated. This is a major problem when the thyristor is fired at or near 90° (when the line is near peak voltage). RFI can spread throughout a system, particularly along the power lines, causing much trouble.

Snubbing is a technique of placing inductance, capacitance, and resistance around the thyristor to limit the critical rate of rise of voltage (dv/dt) to which the thyristor is subjected. Lowering these sharp edges usually lowers the radio-frequency interference to acceptable levels as well.

A simple SCR snubber is shown in Figure 7-38. The series inductor (L) is used to limit the rate of rise of current (di/dt). A basic inductor's performance is described by

$$v_L = L \frac{di}{dt}$$

The worst case occurs when the SCR is fired at the peak of the line voltage. This entire voltage is impressed across the inductor. So

$$L = \frac{v_{\text{line}}(\text{peak})}{(di/dt)_{\text{SCR max spec}}} \tag{7-14}$$

The voltage across the capacitor in an RC circuit rises exponentially.

$$v_c = V_{\text{pk}}(1 - e^{-t/RC})$$

The rate of rise of voltage across this capacitor is

$$\frac{dv_c}{dt} = \frac{V_{pk}}{RC} e^{-t/RC}$$

This dv/dt is at its maximum at $t = 0$:

$$\left(\frac{dv_c}{dt}\right)_{max} = \frac{V_{pk}}{RC} \tag{7-15}$$

A positive step, anode to cathode, will forward bias the diode, CR_1. This places the capacitor C in parallel with the SCR. The capacitor then limits the rate of rise of voltage across the SCR. The R in equation 7–15 is the minimum load resistance, R_L. For a heater this is its cold resistance. For a motor, it is the locked rotor resistance of the armature.

$$C = \frac{V_{DRM}}{R_{L(min)}(dv/dt)_{SCR\ spec}} \tag{7-16}$$

V_{DRM} is substituted for V_{pk} because that is the largest positive voltage the SCR is guaranteed to be able to block. Any larger spike, step, or level may falsely trigger the SCR because of its magnitude, not its rate of rise.

The diode, CR_1, must be able to handle the full current, limited only by R_{Lmin}. However, this happens only when the snubber is called into service to short out a random spike.

$$I_{CR1(pk)} = \text{diode's repetitive peak current}$$

$$I_{CR1(pk)} = \frac{V_{SCR\ DRM}}{R_{L(min)}}$$

The snubbing capacitor charges when the SCR is off and a positive voltage appears between the SCR's anode and cathode. This occurs for any random noise pulses that may be impressed across the SCR and on every positive cycle of the line voltage. During these line-voltage positive cycles the capacitor charges to the peak of the line's voltage.

When the SCR is fired, it acts as a short. The capacitor then rapidly discharges through the turned-on SCR, anode to cathode. Unless limited, this capacitor discharge current, combined with the load current, may exceed either the SCR's surge current or the di/dt of the SCR. The capacitor charges through the diode, CR_1, but discharges through R_S. This resistor is used to keep the discharge current's peak to a safe limit.

$$I_{SCR} = I_{load} + I_{discharge}$$

$$I_{discharge} < I_{TSM} - I_{load}$$

$$I_{discharge} = \frac{V_{cap\ charge}}{R_S}$$

$$I_{\text{discharge}} = \frac{V_{\text{line}}(\text{peak})}{R_S}$$

$$\frac{V_{\text{line}}(\text{peak})}{R_S} < I_{TSM} - I_{\text{load}}$$

$$R_S > \frac{V_{\text{line}}(\text{peak})}{I_{TSM} - I_{\text{load}}}$$

Since the purpose of R_S is to protect the SCR by limiting the capacitor's discharge current, it is prudent to convert the inequality to an equation by increasing the value of R_S. A rather conservative value is

$$R_S \cong \frac{10 V_{\text{line}}(\text{peak})}{I_{TSM} - I_{\text{load}}} \qquad (7\text{--}17)$$

The SCR snubbing technique of Figure 7–38 will not work for a triac. For ac triac snubbing, current must flow in both directions, and the capacitor must charge and discharge equally well either way. This means that paralleling the resistor with a diode for rapid charge but current-limited discharge will not work.

The simplest solution is just to remove the diode, as shown in Figure 7–39. As long as $R_S \leq 0.1 R_{L\text{min}}$, the series resistor, R_S, will not detrimentally affect the exponential charging of C.

If a larger R_S is needed, two snubbing networks can be used. Look at Figure 7–40. Network 1 is active when the hot terminal is positive with respect to neutral. Network 2 is active during the negative half-cycle.

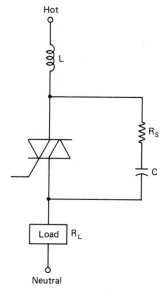

Figure 7–39 Simple triac snubbing.

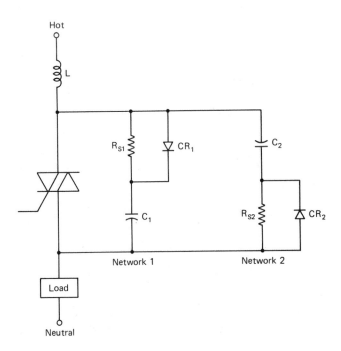

Figure 7–40   Double network triac snubber.

7–3.2 Thyristor Triggers

The circuit to fire the SCR or triac is not trivial. It must be able to provide adequate gate voltage and current without exceeding the maximum gate power dissipation. It should limit the energy required from the driver. Also, it should provide isolation from the line so that the control circuit common need not be tied to line neutral.

However, it is necessary that the thyristor be triggered with a pulse referenced to its cathode or MT_1. This suggests that the cathode and the control common both be tied to power line neutral. This is considered dangerous. A single incorrect connection or reversed wire would apply line voltage to the common of the control (or computer) network. Isolation between control common and any power lead is recommended with the SCR trigger pulse coupled to the SCR with either a pulse transformer or an optical coupler.

As important is the need to tie the load to power line neutral and use the thyristor to switch the hot (as shown in Figures 7–38 through 7–40). With this configuration, turning the thyristor off removes power from the load. It is safe. If you tie the load to power line hot and switch the neutral (to make triggering simpler), a very real hazard exists. When the thyristor is off, it is inactive. However, it has hot on both sides of it. Touching a lead on either side of this inactive load is grabbing the power line hot. Electrocution may result.

So for both personnel and equipment safety it is mandatory to tie the load to

TABLE 7–9 OPTICALLY COUPLED THYRISTOR TRIGGERS[a]

Package	Device type	Minimum isolation voltage (V)	Typ. LED trigger current IFT (mA)	Peak blocking voltage (V)
Plastic DIP	MOC633A[b]	7500	15	400
case 730A-01	MOC634A[b]	7500	8	400
	MOC635A[b]	7500	5	400
	MOC640A[b]	7500	15	400
	MOC641A[b]	7500	8	400
	MOC3009	7500	30	250
	MOC3010	7500	15	250
	MOC3011	7500	10	250
	MOC3020	7500	30	400
	MOC3021	7500	15	400
	MOC3030[a,c]	7500	30	250
	MOC3031[a,c]	7500	15	250
	MOC3040[c]	7500	30	400
	MOC3041[c]	7500	15	400

[a] Underwriters' Laboratories Recognition File E54915.

[b] VDE couplers.

[c] With zero-crossing detector.

Source: Motorola Semiconductors.

neutral. Switch the hot with the thyristor. Couple the thyristor triggering pulse between gate and cathode (or MT_1) with some form of isolation.

For years, unijunction transistors (UJT) were matched with pulse transformers to trigger the thyristors. The unijunction transistor shaped level variations into a sharp high-energy pulse. This pulse drove the primary of a pulse transformer. Its secondary was connected between the SCR's gate and cathode. The UJT had to be matched to the transformer, which was matched to the thyristor's gating requirements. Size, cost, and availability of these triggering components are all problems.

Motorola produces a series of *optically* isolated triac drivers. They meet all of the requirements outlined above, are small, inexpensive, and can be fired directly by comparator or by digital logic. They are listed in Table 7–9.

The schematic and pin diagram are given in Figure 7–41. The device consists of a light-activated silicon bilateral switch optically coupled to a light-emitting diode. When the LED is turned on, the silicon bilateral switch is activated. By driving the LED at 60 Hz with an on time of 80 μs, trigger currents of over 600 mA can be supplied to gate a SCR or triac on.

A typical firing circuit is shown in Figure 7–42. To fire the silicon bilateral switch (and therefore the triac or SCR), you must turn the LED on. Although this takes only about 8 mA, at 1.8 V across the LED, maximum output current to the thyristor's gate requires a forward current through the LED of 30 mA, with a drop across the LED of

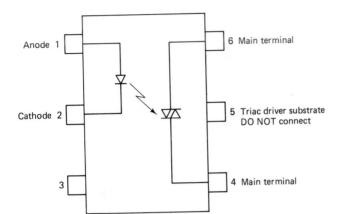

Anode 1

Cathode 2

3

6 Main terminal

5 Triac driver substrate
DO NOT connect

4 Main terminal

Figure 7–41 Optically coupled triac driver schematic. (Courtesy of Motorola Semiconductor.)

about 4 V. This occurs when the output of the comparator goes to a logic low. Current flows through the LED. Its value is set by the supply voltage, the drop across the LED (2 to 4 V), and the size of the limiting resistor, R_a. As soon as the thyristor is gated on by the MOC3010, the voltage across the thyristor falls to about 1.5 V. This is too small to keep the MOC3010 bilateral switch on, so it turns off. This is very convenient, allowing large gate current pulses from the MOC3010 without requiring any pulse-shaping networks.

The MOC3010 can be directly driven by open-collector logic. Several applications

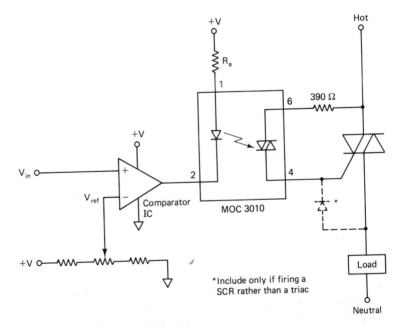

Figure 7–42 Comparator–triac driver interface circuit.

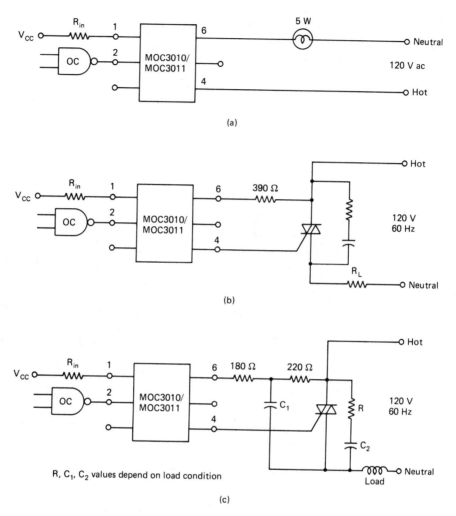

Figure 7–43 Logic-activated triac driver circuits (a) lamp driver; (b) resistive load; (c) inductive load. (Courtesy of Motorola Semiconductor.)

are shown in Figure 7–43. As with the comparator-driven versions, the load is activated when pin 2 of the driver (LED cathode) is pulled down to ground. Resistor R_{in} should be selected to set the LED forward current between 8 and 50 mA.

All of the triggers listed in Table 7–9, except the last four, will apply a firing pulse to the thyristor as soon as the LED is turned on, whether the line voltage is near zero or near its peak. Turning a thyristor on near the line voltage peak may be necessary for *proportional* control of power to the load. However, if you simply want to apply full power to the load, it is far better to trigger the thyristor near the zero crossing. This drastically reduces the *di/dt* problems of switching large load currents, prolongs the life of the load and the thyristor, and drastically reduces RFI generation.

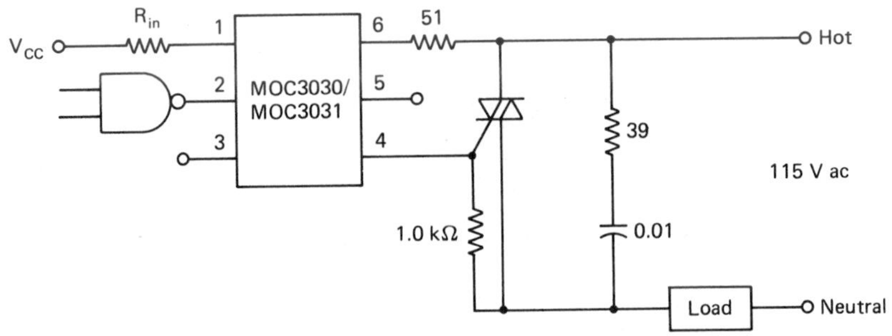

Figure 7–44 Zero-crossing optically coupled triac driver. (Courtesy of Motorola Semiconductor.)

The MOC3030 is a zero-crossing optically isolated triac driver from Motorola Semiconductors. To the user it appears very similar to the MOC3010. However, to trigger a thyristor, the LED must be on *and* the line voltage must be near the zero crossing. Should the LED be turned on when the line voltage is high, less than 200 µA gating current is provided.

A typical application is shown in Figure 7–44. The logic gate must be open collector, capable of sinking at least 15 mA. When the gate's output goes low, the LED turns on. Resistor R_{in} should be selected to assure adequate LED current and to limit it below 50 mA.

On the output side, the 51-Ω resistor limits peak gating current (and current through the silicon bilateral switch) to less then 1 A to protect the MOC3030 and the triac. Larger, but not small, resistance can be used to further limit the gating current. The 1-kΩ resistor provides a path for the small current that occurs when the LED is turned on and the line voltage is away from the zero crossing.

7–3.3 Proportional Power Circuits

The thyristor is a *switch*. When it is off, no power is passed to the load. When it goes on, the load receives full line voltage. This is fine for simple on or off operations. But to provide proportional control of power to the load, you must be a bit more sophisticated.

Two proportional power thyristor circuits are discussed in this section. The first is time proportioning. This technique applies power to the load in whole half-cycles. Over a 1-s interval, for 50% power out, 60 half-cycles would be passed to the load. To reduce power to 25%, only 30 half-cycles would be passed to the load each cycle. This technique is simple to implement and reasonably free from radio-frequency interference. However, a trade-off must be made between resolution of control and smoothness.

The other proportional power thyristor technique is phase-angle firing. This scheme allows high resolution and smooth power application. During each half cycle the thyristor is triggered on. Firing later each cycle lowers the power that the thyristor can apply to the load. Firing the thyristor early every cycle allows it to conduct current to the load for a longer phase angle each cycle, raising the power to the load. Firing away from

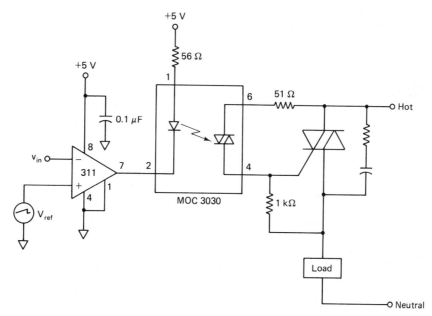

Figure 7-45   Simple time-proportioning circuit.

the zero crossings is necessary, but this creates significant RFI. Also, simpler versions of phase-angle firing circuits are noticeably nonlinear.

Now that you have been introduced to the two types of proportional power thyristor circuits, let's look more carefully at each. The circuit in Figure 7-45 is a simple version of time proportioning. The reference voltage is a slow ramp. The input voltage is the dc level which is to direct the power applied to the load. When the ramp is lower than the input, the comparator saturates, grounding the cathode of the MOC3030's LED. This fires the triac at every zero crossing. When the ramp exceeds v_{in}, the comparator's output opens. This turns the MOC3030 and the triac off.

Figure 7-46 is a timing diagram for this circuit. The upper trace is the 115-V (or higher) line voltage. The second trace shows two signals. The ramp goes typically from 0 to 10 V. This is V_{ref}. The other line in the center trace is the input voltage. It is shown undergoing three changes. The bottom trace is the time-proportioned voltage applied to the load.

At time 0, the ramp falls below v_{in}. This turns on the MOC3030, triggering the triac and applying power to the load at every zero crossing until time 1. At time 1 the reference ramp exceeds v_{in}. The comparator turns off, as does the MOC3030's LED. When the triac goes off at the next zero crossing, it is *not* triggered back on. Power continues to be removed from the load for the rest of that ramp's period. For the first 30% of the ramp's period power was applied to the load. For the remainder it was removed.

Raising the input voltage, v_{in}, should cause a proportional increase in the power

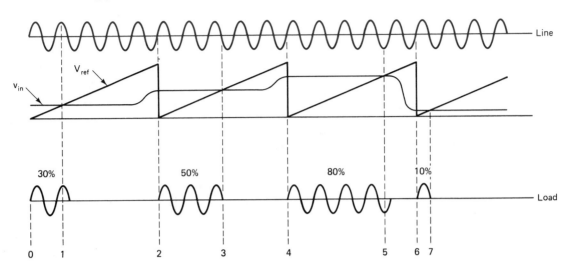

Figure 7–46 Time-proportioning waveforms.

out. At time 2 the ramp falls back below the input voltage. The MOC3030's LED is again driven on, causing the triac to be fired at every subsequent zero crossing. But since v_{in} has increased, it takes the ramp longer to exceed this new level. Consequently, the triac is fired at the first five zero crossings. This yields an increase in output power.

Raising v_{in} further, between times 3 and 4, causes the load to receive power for even more half-cycles, until the ramp finally exceeds v_{in} at time 5. Similarly, lowering v_{in}, between times 5 and 6 causes the load to receive only one half-cycle before the ramp exceeds v_{in}, at time 7.

This scheme of half-cycle time proportioning must apply power in an integer number of 8.3-ms half-cycles. The illustration in Figure 7–46 only controlled 10 half-cycles before the ramp reset. So power was applied in 10% increments. To improve your resolution to 1% requires 100 half-cycles. Therefore, you must lengthen the ramp's period to

$$T_{ramp} = 100 \text{ half-cycles} \times \frac{8.33 \text{ ms}}{\text{half-cycle}} = 833 \text{ ms}$$

This sets the basic time at 0.83 s, far too slow a response for servo systems, but probably just fine for larger inertia process systems.

The second limitation of this time-proportioning technique is its smoothness. To apply 50% power with 1% resolution, the load will receive 50 half-cycles, consecutively, for 415 ms. Then for the next 415 ms, no power at all is applied. The load coasts. This alternate power and coast, power and coast results in rather jerky operation in any low-inertia loads.

The solution to both limited resolution and jerky operation is to apply power to the load some part of every half-cycle. This is done with phase-angle firing. Look at Figure 7–47. Between times a and b, the SCR is off, so no voltage is passed to the

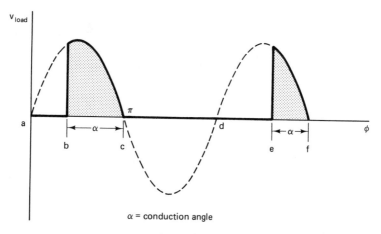

Figure 7–47   Phase-angle-firing waveform. (α = conduction angle.)

load. At time *b*, the SCR is fired, applying full line voltage to the load. The SCR continues to conduct (even after the trigger pulse is removed) through the remainder of the positive cycle. This (time *b* to *c* measured in degrees) is called the conduction angle.

At time *c*, the line voltage and current fall to zero and begin to reverse polarity. Anode current falls below I_H, so the SCR goes off. The SCR must be fired on again in the next positive half-cycle. Lowering the conduction angle by firing the SCR later in the cycle (point *e* to *f*) lowers the power applied to the load.

There are two ways to analyze this phase-angle-fired waveform. If it is to be applied to a load that requires dc, such as a dc motor, you want to determine the average value of the waveform. If, however, the phase-angle firing is to be done to a triac, with the load expects an ac signal, the rms value must be determined.

First look at the average value.

$$V_{ave} = \frac{1}{T} \int_0^T e(t)\, dt \tag{7–18}$$

where T is the period of the full wave and $e(t)$ is the instantaneous value of the voltage. In terms of angle, rather than time,

$$e(\theta) = \begin{cases} 0 & 0 \le \theta \le \phi \\ V_{pk} \sin \theta & \phi < \theta \le \pi \end{cases}$$

where ϕ is the firing angle. The conductor angle α is

$$\alpha = \pi - \phi \qquad \text{or} \qquad \phi = \pi - \alpha$$

Substituting these into the equation above yields

$$e(\theta) = \begin{cases} 0 & 0 \le \theta \le \pi - \alpha \\ V_{pk} \sin \theta & \pi - \alpha < \theta \le \pi \end{cases} \tag{7–19}$$

To determine the average value of the phase-angle-fired waveform (Figure 7–47) as the conduction angle is varied, substitute equation 7–19 into equation 7–18.

$$V_{ave} = \frac{1}{\pi} \int_0^\pi e(\theta)\, d\theta$$

$$= \frac{1}{\pi} \left(\int_0^{\pi-\alpha} 0\, d\theta + \int_{\pi-\alpha}^\pi V_{pk} \sin\theta\, d\theta \right)$$

$$= \frac{V_{pk}}{\pi} \left(-\cos\theta \, \Big|_{\pi-\alpha}^{\pi} \right)$$

$$= \frac{V_{pk}}{\pi} [\cos(\pi - \alpha) + 1] \qquad (7\text{–}20)$$

Not surprisingly, there is *not* a linear relationship between the average value passed to the load and the conduction angle. Changing the conduction angle does not produce a proportional change in the average voltage applied to the load. The nonlinearity of this V_{ave} versus α relationship is about 10% FSO, using a best-fit, least-squares analysis (see Chapter 3).

To determine the root-mean-squared value of the phase-angle-fired waveform, you must apply

$$v_{rms} = \sqrt{\frac{1}{T} \int_0^T e^2(t)\, dt} \qquad (7\text{–}21)$$

This is the standard rms formula. In terms of the phase-angle-fired voltage, equation 7–19,

$$v_{rms} = \sqrt{\frac{1}{\pi} \left(\int_0^{\pi-\alpha} 0^2\, d\theta + \int_{\pi-\alpha}^\pi V_{pk}^2 \sin^2\theta\, d\theta \right)}$$

$$v_{rms} = \sqrt{\frac{V_{pk}^2}{\pi} \int_{\pi-\alpha}^\pi \sin^2\theta\, d\theta}$$

But

$$\int \sin^2 x\, dx = \tfrac{1}{2}x - \tfrac{1}{4}\sin 2x$$

so

$$v_{rms} = \frac{V_{pk}}{\sqrt{\pi}} \sqrt{(\tfrac{1}{2}\theta - \tfrac{1}{4}\sin 2\theta)\, \Big|_{\pi-\alpha}^{\pi}}$$

A little algebra yields

$$v_{rms} = \frac{V_{pk}}{\sqrt{\pi}} \sqrt{\tfrac{1}{2}\alpha + \tfrac{1}{4}\sin 2(\pi - \alpha)} \qquad (7\text{–}22)$$

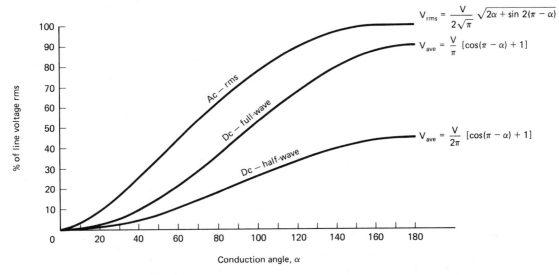

Figure 7–48 Phase-angle-fired voltages versus conduction angle.

This relationship between the conduction angle, α, and the resulting v_{rms} is even more nonlinear than that for the average value. Least-squares nonlinearity analysis gives about 19% FSO nonlinearity.

In Figure 7–48 are three plots of voltage to the load versus conduction angle. The top curve gives the v_{rms}, the center gives v_{ave}, assuming full-wave rectification. If only half-wave rectification is used, the v_{ave} is also cut in half.

EXAMPLE 7–5

Phase-angle firing is used to control power applied to a load from a $120V_{rms}$ line. Calculate the V_{rms} and V_{ave} for the following conduction angles.
(a) 45°.
(b) 90°.
(c) 135°.

Solution   (a) From Figure 7–48, at 45° conduction the load receives

$$v_{rms} = 30\% \times \text{line voltage}$$
$$= 0.30 \times 120 \text{ V} = 36V_{rms}$$

The average value is

$$v_{ave} = 13\% \times \text{line voltage}$$
$$= 0.13 \times 120V = 15.6V_{dc}$$

(b) At 90° conduction angle

$$v_{rms} = 70\% \times 120 \text{ V} = 84V_{rms}$$
$$v_{ave} = 45\% \times 120 \text{ V} = 54V_{dc}$$

(c) At 135° conduction angle

$$v_{rms} = 95\% \times 120 \text{ V} = 114V_{rms}$$
$$v_{ave} = 77\% \times 120 \text{ V} = 92.4V_{dc}$$

From Example 7–5 there are several points to be noted. First, the voltage response is *very* nonlinear. The vast majority of control lies between conduction angles of 60 and 120°. Second, the vertical axis is scaled in % of line voltage rms. To obtain actual load voltage you must multiply the ordinate (*y* value) by the line's voltages's rms value. Finally, even at full conduction ($\alpha = 180°$), the average value of a full sine wave is only 90% of the applied rms.

For good response under open-loop or feedforward control, every element must perform linearly. Phase-angle firing, as shown in Figure 7–48, certainly would *not* be acceptable. You are left with several alternatives. First, for open-loop applications use some other form of power interface which has a more linear response. A second alternative is to add additional electronics to the phase-angle-firing circuit to linearize its response. For analog control, you may add in front of the power interface a circuit whose transfer curve is the *complement* of the phase-angle-firing circuit. Together the two will respond linearly. Or you may run the input through a cosine generator (for V_{ave} response). For digital applications, a PROM look-up table or algorithm within a microcomputer can be used to compensate for the phase-angle-firing circuit's nonlinearity.

Closed-loop negative-feedback control applications are not nearly as critical. The controller (which drives this phase-angle-firing power interface) will change its output to whatever value is necessary to produce the desired process variable. So mild nonlinearities in the power interface and the process itself are *automatically* compensated for by the closed-loop negative-feedback controller.

Circuits to control phase-angle firing have several elements in common. First, the circuit must be able to detect when the line voltage crosses zero. The input signal then determines how long after that zero crossing the firing must delay. A low input, requesting small output power, must cause a long delay. A larger input, signifying more output power, must cause a shorter delay. Following the delay, an isolated pulse must be coupled to the thyristor's gate. The tyristor turns on and continues to conduct until the next zero crossing is approached. There it turns itself off ($I_{ak} < I_H$) and awaits another firing pulse.

The schematic for a digitally controlled phase angle firing circuit is given in Figure 7–49. The 25.2-V transformer followed by the resistor and diodes produces a square wave at the input of U_{1a}, which is synchronized with the line but restricted to legal TTL levels. The *RC* and diode networks around U_{1a} and U_{1b} form positive differentiators. These produce a <u>positive</u> *spike* at every zero crossing of the line. Inverter U_{1c} inverts this, holding the load pin of the counters U_2 and U_3 high most of the time. At each zero crossing U_{1c} pulls these pins to ground for a few microseconds. The 7405 open collector is needed to assure adequate drive current for the differentiator and the MOC3010.

Integrated circuits U_2 and U_3 are parallel load counters. Cascaded together by

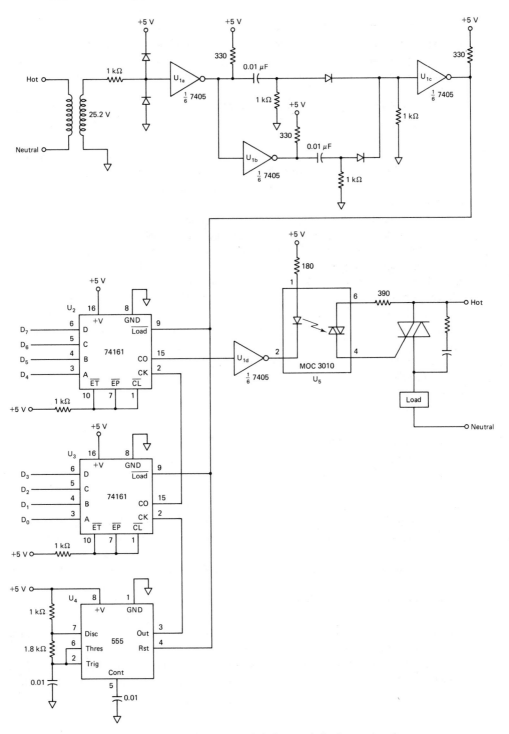

Figure 7–49 Digitally controlled phase-angle-fired power interface.

tying the carry out (CO) of U_3 (lower byte) to the clock (CK) of U_2 (upper byte), they may be viewed as a single 8-bit parallel-load up counter. At each zero crossing of the line, U_{1c} pulses their load pin low, causing the counters to load whatever data are presented at D_0–D_7. The counters then begin to count up, at a rate dictated by the 555 clock.

The 555 clock, U_4, is also reset by U_{1c}, to assure proper line synchronization. The frequency has been set to 30.8 kHz. This frequency will allow 256 steps during a single line voltage half-cycle.

The counters, U_2 and U_3, increment at every clock pulse until they overflow (at a count of 256). When U_2 overflows, it sets its CO, pin 15, high. This drives the output of U_{1d} low, turning on the MOC3010. The triac is fired and power is applied to the load.

Presenting a small number at D_0–D_7 means that the counters must increment many times before they overflow, firing the triac. Power is applied to the load late in the cycle, causing a small conduction angle and very little power to the load.

Conversely, a large binary value of D_0–D_7 means that the counters will increment only a few times before overflowing. The triac is fired early in the cycle. This produces a large conduction angle and a large output voltage to the load.

To compensate for the nonlinearity of the phase-angle-firing circuit, a PROM could be inserted between the data inputs, D_0–D_7, and the counter inputs. The PROM would contain a look-up table. The D_0–D_7 inputs would be the address into the PROM while the PROM's output data would be loaded into the counters. When 128 is presented to the PROM, it would output the binary data necessary to cause 50% rms output voltage.

If you are driving the triac from a microcomputer, counters U_2 and U_3 and the clock U_4 can be replaced with a single LSI timer chip. Zero-crossing pulses from U_{1c} interrupt the microcomputer, as does the counter's overflow. The microcomputer directly fires U_{1d} and the triac.

Figure 7–50 is the schematic for a phase-angle-firing circuit whose conduction angle is controlled by an input analog voltage. It is divided into four major blocks: zero-crossing pulse generator (U_{1a} and U_{1b}), synchronized ramp generator (U_{2A}), zero and span signal conditioner (U_{2B}), and comparator with trigger (U_{1c} and U_3).

As with the digitally controlled circuit discussed previously, the operation of this analog-controlled trigger must be synchronized to the line voltage's zero crossing. This is the purpose of the transformer, U_{1a} and U_{1b} comparators, the RC shapers, and the diodes. The two comparators produce 30-V p-p square waves which switch as the line voltage crosses ground. Since one is inverting and the other is noninverting, opposite-polarity square waves are produced. The RC networks shape these square waves into positive and negative spikes of about 100 μs. The diodes pass only the positive pulses: at one zero crossing from U_{1a}, at the other zero crossing from U_{1b}.

The ramp is produced by U_{2A}, its feedback capacitor, and input potentiometer. Because of negative feedback, the op amp's inverting input is held at virtual ground.

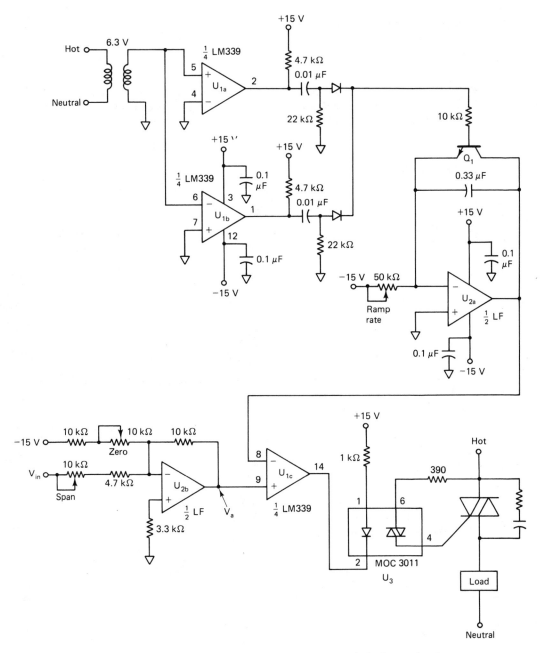

Figure 7–50 Analog voltage-controlled phase-angle-fired power interface.

A constant current of

$$I = \frac{15 \text{ V}}{R_{\text{ramp rate}}}$$

flows from the op amp's output, through the capacitor, through $R_{\text{ramp rate}}$, to -15 V. Since this current is constant, the capacitor will charge at a constant rate, producing a ramp. Setting

$$R_{\text{ramp rate}} = 37.7 \text{ k}\Omega$$

produces a charging current of

$$I = \frac{15 \text{ V}}{37.7 \text{ k}\Omega} = 398 \text{ }\mu\text{A}$$

Charging of 0.33-μF capacitor with 398 μA of current produces a ramp rate of

$$i = C \frac{dv}{dt}$$

$$\text{ramp rate} = \frac{\Delta v}{\Delta t} = \frac{I}{C}$$

$$= \frac{398 \text{ }\mu\text{A}}{0.33 \text{ }\mu\text{F}} = 1206 \text{ V/s}$$

At every zero crossing, a pulse from either U_{1a} or U_{1b} saturates Q_1. This shorts out the ramp capacitor, forcing it to discharge rapidly. So at every zero crossing of the line, the ramp drops to ground, then starts climbing again. This ramping continues for one half-cycle of the line, 8.3 ms. During the 8.3 ms the capacitor has to charge, it will ramp up

$$\Delta v = (\text{ramp rate}) \Delta t$$
$$= (1206 \text{ V/s})(8.3 \text{ ms}) = 10 \text{ V}$$

Out of U_{2A} is a ramp beginning at 0 V at the zero crossing and increasing linearly to 10 V during the 8.3 ms of a line half-cycle.

The zero and span amplifier has the equation

$$V_a = -\left(\frac{10 \text{ k}\Omega}{R_{\text{span}} + 4.7 \text{ k}\Omega}\right) V_{\text{in}} - \left(\frac{10 \text{ k}\Omega}{R_{\text{zero}} + 10 \text{ k}\Omega}\right)(-15 \text{ V})$$

with

$$R_{\text{span}} = 5.3 \text{ k}\Omega$$

$$R_{\text{zero}} = 5 \text{ k}\Omega$$

$$V_{\text{out}} = -V_{\text{in}} + 10 \text{ V}$$

This linearly inverts and offsets the input voltage. The first two columns of Table 7–10 illustrate this. As long as the ramp is below V_a, the output of the comparator (U_{1c}) is

TABLE 7–10 ANALOG-VOLTAGE-CONTROLLED PHASE-ANGLE-FIRING POWER INTERFACE PERFORMANCE

V_{in} (V)	V_a (V)	Time to firing (ms)	Percent cycle applied
0	10.0	8.2	0
2.5	7.5	6.2	25
5.0	5.0	4.1	50
7.5	2.5	2.1	75
1.0	0	0	100

open and the triac is off. However, as soon as the ramp climbs above V_a, the output of U_{1c} shorts to -15 V. This lights the LED in the MOC3011 and turns on the triac.

Look at Table 7–10 again. A low voltage at V_{in} causes a proportionally high voltage at V_a. It takes quite a while from the zero crossing for the ramp to exceed this reference. So the firing pulse is long delayed, delivering only a small voltage to the load. Increasing V_{in} lowers V_a. A smaller reference on the comparator means that less time must be delayed before the ramp exceeds this level and fires the triac. The triac conducts for much more of the cycle, passing a larger voltage to the load.

SUMMARY

The simplest way to deliver significant power to an actuator is with a power op amp. The OPA512 is capable of operating with a total difference in supply voltages of 100 V and can provide currents up to 15 A. Simple op amps current limit at 20 mA. At these high levels of voltage and current, power dissipation and heat-sinking calculations are critical. For ac operation the safe operating area must be defined and performance restricted to well within its borders. The reactance of the load must also be considered. It may produce quite unexpected stress on the power op amp. The OPA512 also has a voltage–current limiter circuit which increases the current limit as the output voltage approaches the supply.

Additional power can be driven into the load by paralleling two op amps. Do not forget a small series resistor to drop any slight difference in voltage, prior to connecting the two outputs. If you can float the load, one end can be driven with a noninverting amp, while the other is driven to the opposite voltage with an inverting amp. This doubles the voltage across the load. Placing one or two transistors inside the negative feedback loop of a low-power op amp boosts the power it can deliver to the load, without adding any offsets.

A linear power amplifier is typically very inefficient, often dissipating more power than it can deliver to the load. For high-power applications this is unacceptable. In a switch mode servo amplifier the main-pass transistor is operated as a switch, driven either hard off or hard on. In either case, little or no power must be dissipated. To smooth the resulting square wave, a forward converter uses an *LC* filter and a flyback diode. The transistor switch is driven by a pulse-width-modulation IC.

The value of the inductor and capacitor can be calculated, based on input and output voltages, currents, and frequency. However, the capacitor's ESL and ESR must be minimized for proper operation. A film capacitor is usually required. High-speed, high-power, low-forward-voltage ratings are needed for the flyback diode. These may be provided by either a fast-recovery diode or a Schottky diode.

The pulse-width-modulator IC drives the main-pass transistor. The frequency is set by an internal oscillator, and the pulse width is varied in response to a noninverting input, an inverting input, and several shutdown options. Properly configured, the forward converted switching servo amplifier can be viewed as a sophisticated, highly efficient noninverting op amp.

Both high-power bipolar junction transistors and vertical field-effect transistors can be used as the main switch. The BJT performs more efficiently at switching frequencies below 100 kHz.

However, the BJT requires more sustained power and a more complex circuit to drive it. Power dissipation and SOA must be considered for these transistors as they were for the OPA512 op amp. Although the VFET's gate appears as a dc open, there is significant capacitance. This requires several hundred milliamperes of current to alter its charge quickly. The simplest VFET drives uses a special MOSFET driver IC.

Bidirectional output current from a single polarity supply can be produced by floating the load across the middle of a bridge. Transistors are driven by the PWM IC in diagonally opposite pairs. Both BJT and VFET versions of the H bridge may be made.

Providing power above a few 100 W to a load requires a thyristor. Proper triggering to accomplish proportional control over output power, transient snubbing, and control circuit isolation must all be addressed. Snubbing is accomplished with a resistor–capacitor– diode network in parallel with the thyristor. Component values are determined by the line voltage, *di/dt*, load resistance, *dv/dt*, and diode current ratings.

A series of light-activated bilateral switches greatly simplifies the triggering and isolation of thyristors. Isolation voltage of over 7000 V is provided. A trigger pulse of an amp or so is available with only 30 mA of input, LED current. With some versions of this trigger a pulse will be applied to the thyristor as soon as the LED is lit. However, other models will trigger the thyristor only at the zero crossing. Zero-crossing triggering assures minimum electrical interference and shock to the thyristor and load. But power is passed to the load for the entire half-cycle.

To provide proportional power to a load using a thyristor switch requires either time proportioning or phase-angle-firing circuitry. Time proportioning compares a slow ramp to the control (input) voltage. During the portion of the period that the ramp is below the input the zero-crossing trigger is enabled. Power is applied for a number of full half-cycles. When the ramp exceeds the input, no further power is applied to the load. Time proportioning produces very low RFI but may be jerky or have problems with adequate resolution.

Phase-angle firing causes the thyristor to conduct some portion of every cycle.

The firing pulse is delayed following the zero crossing. Once fired, the thyristor conducts for the remainder of that half-cycle. This delay, and therefore the conduction angle, can be related directly to both the average value of the load voltage and its rms value. Unfortunately, there is a noticeable nonlinearity between conduction angle and output voltage.

Phase-angle firing can be controlled digitally. At every zero crossing the digital word is loaded into a counter. It is incremented until it overflows. At overflow, the thyristor is triggered. A large digital input means a short delay before overflow and a long conduction angle.

Analog-voltage-controlled phase-angle firing compares the input control voltage to a 8.3-ms ramp (synchronized with the line voltage's zero crossings). The firing pulse is delayed until the ramp exceeds the input. An inverting zero and span amplifier is required before the comparator.

REFERENCES

1. *OPA512 Specifications*. Tucson, Ariz.: Burr-Brown Corporation.
2. *How to Determine What Heat Sink to Use*, Application Note AN83A. Tucson, Ariz.: Burr-Brown Corporation, 1985.
3. *Understanding Power Amplifier Specifications*, Application Note AN123. Tucson, Ariz.: Burr-Brown Corporation, 1983.
4. S. R. Cheshier, *Electronic Communications Technology Handbook*. New York: Prentice-Hall, Inc., in press, Chap. 14.
5. Bernard Lavene, *Improving High Frequency Converter Performances and Efficiency with Film Capacitors*. Eatontown, N.J.: Electronic Concepts.
6. Bill Roehr and Frank Cathell, "High voltage MOSFET and bipolar switches," *Power Conversions International*, January 1984.

PROBLEMS

7–1. From the specifications of the OPA512, determine the following values.
   (a) Typical supply voltages ($\pm V$).
   (b) Maximum current drawn from the supply to bias the OPA512.
   (c) Case temperature range for the OPA512BM, OPA512SM.
   (d) Maximum output voltage ($\pm V = \pm 30$ V, $I = 15$ A).
   (e) Power dissipated, under the conditions of part (d).
   (f) Typical upper frequency for full output voltage.
   (g) Maximum output voltage with $+30$ V on both $+$input and $-$ input.
   (h) Worst-case shift in offset voltage for a maximum variation in case temperature for the OPA512SM. (Assume that the output was zeroed at 25°C.)

7–2. It is necessary to limit the OPA512's output current to 4 A sink and 7 A source. Draw the schematic and determine appropriate component values.

7–3. Determine the heat sink needed for an OP512A operating from ± 30-V dc supplies, driving an 8-Ω load. Hold the junction temperature at or below 125°C. The ambient temperature is 40°C. Also calculate the case temperature.

7–4. For Problem 7–3, draw the load line on Figure 7–4. Is the op amp operating safely? Explain.

7–5. For $V_{cc} = \pm 30$ V, $R_L = 8$ Ω, what is the worst-case peak input ac voltage (that input peak voltage which would cause maximum op amp power dissipation)? How much power must the op amp dissipate?

7–6. A sine wave is applied to a complex reactive load. The peak voltage is 25 V and the peak load current is 3 A. $V_{cc} = \pm 30$ V. A phase angle of 30° is measured between the load voltage and current. What is the op amp's dissipation?

7–7. Draw the schematic of two OPA512s used to drive a total of 10 A through a 2-Ω load. If one amplifier outputs a 5% higher voltage than the other, calculate the following values.
    (a) v_{out} for each op amp.
    (b) I_{out} for each op amp.
    (c) Power dissipated by the series resistors.
    (d) Power dissipated by the op amps ($\pm V = \pm 30$ V).

7–8. Draw the schematic of two OPA512s used to drive opposite ends of a load. Load current is 10 A, and load resistance is 8 Ω. Calculate the following values.
    (a) v_{out} for each op amp.
    (b) I_{out} for each op amp.
    (c) $\pm V$ required.

7–9. It is desired to drive an 1-Ω load using an op amp (maximum $I \cong 2$ mA). (*Hint*: Power transistors rarely have $\beta > 20$.)
    (a) Draw a schematic illustrating how you would deliver 8 A to the load.
    (b) Calculate $I_{\text{op amp}}$, $P_{\text{op amp}}$, I_Q, P_Q, β, V_{load}, $V_{\text{out op amp}}$.

7–10. A pulse-width-modulated signal has a peak of 30 V and a frequency of 80 kHz.
    (a) If the pulse width is 9 μs, calculate % duty cycle and the average value out.
    (b) If the desired output average value is 5 V, calculate the required % duty cycle and the pulse width (μs).

7–11. Consider the switching servo amplifier run by the PWM described in Problem 7–10.
    (a) Calculate a range of minimum acceptable inductors for an average dc output of 5 V and an average current of 10 A. Select an appropriate inductor from Table 7–4.
    (b) Assuming the peak-to-peak ripple must be held to 0.15 V, calculate a range of acceptable capacitances. Select an appropriate capacitor from Table 7–6.

7–12. The switching servo amplifier of Problems 7–10 and 7–11 has a rise and fall time of 90 ns. The frequency of the highest significant harmonic is

$$f_H = \frac{0.35}{t_r}$$

    (a) Calculate this harmonic's frequency.
    (b) The resonant frequency of the capacitor's C and ESL should be significantly (about 10 times) above the harmonic's frequency calculated in part (a). Select an appropriate capacitor from Table 7–6.
    (c) For the capacitor you selected, calculate its ESL.

TABLE 7–11   IRF 543 VFET SPECIFICATIONS

Absolute Maximum Ratings

Parameter		IRF540, IRF541	IRF542, IRF543	Units
I_D @ T_C = 25°C	Continuous Drain Current	28	25	A
I_D @ T_C = 100°C	Continuous Drain Current	20	17	A
I_{DM}	Pulsed Drain Current ①	110	100	A
P_D @ T_C = 25°C	Max. Power Dissipation	150		W
	Linear Derating Factor	1.0		W/K ⑤
V_{GS}	Gate-to-Source Voltage	±20		V
E_{AS}	Single Pulse Avalanche Energy ②	230 (See Fig. 14)		mJ
I_{AR}	Avalanche Current ① (Repetitive or Non-Repetitive)	28 (See E_{AR})		A
E_{AR}	Repetitive Avalanche Energy ①	15 (See I_{AR})		mJ
dv/dt	Peak Diode Recovery dv/dt ③	5.5 (See Fig. 17)		V/ns
T_J T_{STG}	Operating Junction Storage Temperature Range	−55 to 175		°C
	Lead Temperature	300 (0.063 in. (1.6mm) from case for 10s)		°C

Electrical Characteristics @ T_J = 25°C (Unless Otherwise Specified)

Parameter		Type	Min.	Typ.	Max.	Units	Test Conditions
BV_{DSS}	Drain-to-Source Breakdown Voltage	IRF540 IRF542	100	—	—	V	V_{GS} = 0V, I_D = 250 µA
		IRF541 IRF543	80				
$R_{DS(on)}$	Static Drain-to-Source On-State Resistance ④	IRF540 IRF541	—	0.060	0.077	Ω	V_{GS} = 10V, I_D = 17A
		IRF542 IRF543	—	0.080	0.100		
$I_{D(on)}$	On-State Drain Current ④	IRF540 IRF541	28	—	—	A	V_{DS} > $I_{D(on)}$ X $R_{DS(on)}$ Max. V_{GS} = 10V
		IRF541 IRF543	25				
$V_{GS(th)}$	Gate Threshold Voltage	ALL	2.0	—	4.0	V	V_{DS} = V_{GS}, I_D = 250µA
g_{fs}	Forward Transconductance ④	ALL	8.7	13		S (℧)	V_{DS} ≥ 50V, I_{DS} = 17A
I_{DSS}	Zero Gate Voltage Drain Current	ALL	—	—	250	µA	V_{DS} = Max. Rating, V_{GS} = 0V
			—	—	1000		V_{DS} = 0.8 x Max. Rating V_{GS} = 0V, T_J = 150°C
I_{GSS}	Gate-to-Source Leakage Forward	ALL	—	—	500	nA	V_{GS} = 20V
I_{GSS}	Gate-to-Source Leakage Reverse	ALL	—	—	−500	nA	V_{GS} = −20V
Q_g	Total Gate Charge	ALL	—	40	61	nC	V_{GS} = 10V, I_D = 28A
Q_{gs}	Gate-to-Source Charge	ALL	—	8.6	13	nC	V_{DS} = 0.8 x Max. Rating See Fig. 16
Q_{gd}	Gate-to-Drain ("Miller") Charge	ALL	—	32	48	nC	(Independent of operating temperature)
$t_{d(on)}$	Turn-On Delay Time	ALL	—	15	23	ns	V_{DD} = 50V, I_D = 28A, R_G = 9.1Ω
t_r	Rise Time	ALL	—	72	110	ns	R_D = 1.7Ω
$t_{d(off)}$	Turn-Off Delay Time	ALL	—	40	60	ns	See Fig. 15
t_f	Fall Time	ALL	—	50	75	ns	(Independent of operating temperature)
L_D	Internal Drain Inductance	ALL	—	4.5	—	nH	Measured from the drain lead, 6mm (0.25 in.) from package to center of die.
L_S	Internal Source Inductance	ALL	—	7.5	—	nH	Measured from the source lead, 6mm (0.25 in.) from package to source bonding pad.
C_{iss}	Input Capacitance	ALL	—	1500	—	pF	V_{GS} = 0V, V_{DS} = 25V
C_{oss}	Output Capacitance	ALL	—	500	—	pF	f = 1.0 MHz
C_{rss}	Reverse Transfer Capacitance	ALL	—	90	—	pF	See Fig. 10

Source-Drain Diode Ratings and Characteristics

Parameter		Type	Min.	Typ.	Max.	Units	Test Conditions
I_S	Continuous Source Current (Body Diode)	ALL	—	—	28	A	Modified MOSFET symbol showing the integral Reverse p-n junction rectifier.
I_{SM}	Pulsed Source Current (Body Diode) ①	ALL	—	—	110	A	
V_{SD}	Diode Forward Voltage ④	ALL	—	—	2.5	V	T_J = 25°C, I_S = 28A, V_{GS} = 0V
t_{rr}	Reverse Recovery Time	ALL	97	210	460	ns	T_J = 25°C, I_F = 28A, di/dt = 100 A/µs
Q_{RR}	Reverse Recovery Charge	ALL	0.42	0.95	2.1	µC	
t_{on}	Forward Turn-On Time	ALL	Intrinsic turn-on time is negligible. Turn-on speed is substantially controlled by L_S + L_D.				

Thermal Resistance

Parameter		Type	Min.	Typ.	Max.	Units	
R_{thJC}	Junction-to-Case	ALL	—	—	1.0	K/W ⑤	
R_{thCS}	Case-to-Sink	ALL	—	0.50	—	K/W ⑤	Mounting surface flat, smooth, and greased
R_{thJA}	Junction-to-Ambient	ALL	—	—	80	K/W ⑤	Typical socket mount

Source: International Rectifier.

(d) Assuming a I_{ripple} peak-peak = 1.8 A, (1) calculate the I_{ripple} rms and (2) for the capacitor you selected, calculate the power that must be dissipated due to its ESR.

7–13. Draw a complete schematic such as in Figure 7–20 to implement the design completed in Problems 7–10 through 7–12.

   (a) Indicate all component values assuming that V_{in} = 2.08 V.

   (b) Select a flyback diode and defend your choice.

   (c) To output 10 A, a Darlington configuration is necessary. Modify the schematic accordingly.

   (d) Select the transistors and defend your choices.

7–14. For the circuit you just designed, explain in detail (see Example 7–4) how the circuit responds to the following conditions.

   (a) The load demands more current, causing the load voltage to dip to 4.0 V.

   (b) The input, V_{in}, is lowered to 1.8 V.

   (c) The power input, $+V_{unreg}$, is lowered to 20 V.

7–15. Make a table comparing advantages and limitations of the following power switches.

   (a) Bipolar junction transistor.

   (b) Vertical field-effect transistor.

7–16. Can a MJ2955A be used as the main switching transistor in the switching servo amplifier of Problems 7–10 through 7–14? To justify your answer you must consider voltage, current, and power ratings, SOA, and speed.

7–17. Draw a schematic showing how you would replace the BJTs of Figure 7–26 with an N-channel VFET. Explain how your circuit works correctly.

7–18. The IRF543, N-channel VFET (see Table 7–11) has been suggested as a replacement for the MJ2955A (of Problem 7–16) to be used in the schematic you draw in Problem 7–17.

   (a) Are the voltage and current ratings satisfactory? Explain.

   (b) Will the circuit from Problem 7–17 be able to provide adequate theshold voltage without exceeding the gates' maximum? Explain.

   (c) When driven on, at I_{load} = 10 A, how much power must the transistor dissipate?

   (d) Assuming that $+V_{unreg}$ = 30 V and V_{load} = 5 V, what is the average power dissipation of the transistor. (Careful here!)

   (e) Assuming adequate drive, can this transistor meet the speed requirements? Prove your answer.

   (f) How much current must be sourced (or sunk) to drive the transistor's gate to the threshold voltage in 100 ns?

   (g) What must you do to the circuit in Problem 7–17 to provide this current?

7–19. To drive the H bridge of Figure 7–31, you are given the PWM IC waveform and a direction bit (low = CW, high = CCW). Design the necessary circuitry that will provide the signals indicated in Table 7–12. Also assure that Q_2 and Q_4 drive circuitry is capable of sourcing 400 mA, while Q_1 and Q_3 drive circuitry can sink at least 400 mA.

TABLE 7–12 LOGICAL OPERATION FOR PROBLEM 7–19

Direction bit	Q_1	Q_2	Q_3	Q_4
0	PWM pulses	High	Open	Open
1	Open	Open	PWM pulses	High

7–20. Design the logic necessary to drive the eight inputs of U_1 (D469) in Figure 7–31 to meet the requirements of Table 7–12.

7–21. Explain in *detail* how each of the waveforms in Figure 7–32 is produced.

7–22. Modify your answer to Problem 7–20 to drive the upper N-channel VFETs of Figure 7–33.

7–23. A thyristor is to be powered from the 120-V rms line. The load has an initial, minimum resistance of 2 Ω. The thyristor available has $I_{TSM} = 500$ A. The thyristor's ratings are

$$V_{DRM} = 300 \text{ V}$$

$$I_{rms} = 100 \text{ A}$$

$$\frac{dv}{dt} = 500 \text{ V/}\mu\text{s}$$

$$\frac{di}{dt} = 800 \text{ A/}\mu\text{s}$$

(a) Design the needed snubbing network.
(b) If the thyristor is a triac, must two networks be used? Justify your answer.

7–24. The circuit in Figure 7–42 has failed. List six possible causes if the load is always
(a) on.
(b) off.

7–25. Explain why the resistor in series with the bilateral switch of the MOC3030 is so much smaller than the same resistor for the MOC3010.

7–26. Can time proportioning be accomplished using a triangle wave with equal ramp-up and ramp-down time? Construct a diagram similar to Figure 7–46 to defend your answer.

7–27. Draw the complete schematic of a time-proportioning circuit needed to apply power proportionally to a 1.5-kW heater. Power to the heater is to be proportional to a control input voltage with a range of 0 to 10 V. Assure 2% resolution. Compute all component values.

7–28. **(a)** Complete equation 7–20 for a conduction angle of 180°. Compare this value to the traditional V_{pk}-to-V_{ave} relationship.
(b) Complete equation 7–22 for a conduction angle of 180°. Compare this value to the traditional V_{pk}-to-V_{rms} relationship.

7–29. Using phase-angle firing, what conduction angle is necessary to produce the follwing V_{rms} to the load, using a 220-V_{rms} line?
(a) 55 V.
(b) 110 V.
(c) 165 V.

7–30. Repeat Problem 7–29 for a V_{ave} to the loads specified.

7–31. Complete a timing diagram for the circuit in Figure 7–49. Include the following: line voltage, U_{1c} output, data-in-counters, U_4 output, U_{1d} output, load voltage. Assume that D_0–D_7 is 250.

7–32. Using the diagram you drew for Problem 7–31, explain the effects of changing D_0–D_7 to 80 on each of the six items entered in the timing diagram.

7–33. For the proportional power interface in Figure 7–50, compute the following values.
(a) Total positive pulse width of the spike out of U_{1a}.

    (b) Total negative pulse width of the spike out of U_{1b}.

    (c) Positive pulse amplitude at the cathodes of the diodes out of U_{1a} and U_{1b}'s pulse-shaper network. (Careful! Assume C fully charged to -15 V when the positive step occurs.)

    (d) Peak base current for Q_1.

    (e) Value needed for the ramp rate resistor if the supply voltage changes from -15 V to -12 V.

    (f) Value needed for the zero and span resistors if the supply changes from -15 V to -12 V, and V_{in}(max) changes to $+5$ V. [Still want V_a(max) $= 10$ V.]

    (g) Voltage out of U_{1c} when the MOC3011 LED is on. (Assume that $V_{LED} = 2.5$ V.)

7–34. Complete a timing diagram such as that in Figure 7–46 for the circuit in Figure 7–50. Include the following: line voltage, voltage out of pulse shapers (U_{1a} and U_{1b} with R, C, and CR), voltage out of U_{2A}, V_a for $V_{in} = 2$ V, voltage out of U_{1c}, and the load voltage.

7–35. Repeat Problem 7–34 for

    (a) $V_{in} = 5$ V.

    (b) $V_{in} = 7$ V.

8

System Response

In Chapters 2 through 7 you have been studying the characteristics of the individual blocks of a control system. You should now be able to design any of these system components, given appropriate specifications. Or, given a complete control system, you should be able to determine the performance of any of the elements, separately.

As long as the system is run open loop, its overall performance is simply the sum of the response of its elements. However, you have seen repeatedly that a significant improvement in overall system performance can be obtained if you close the loop, providing negative feedback.

Entire volumes have been written on closed-loop system design and analysis. Still more engineering texts are available on how to determine the *optimal* controller transfer function. No serious effort will be made in this chapter to duplicate the rigor, nor fully summarize the conclusions of these many books.

Instead, in this chapter you will find an introduction to the mathematical analysis of closed-loop systems. The precise format depends on whether you want to evaluate the system as a process or as a servo. Examples of the derivations, and analysis of first- and second-order elements with proportional and proportional–integral controllers are presented. The systems' time-domain transient response and final value will be computed. If you are not already familiar with Laplace operations, you should review Appendix A carefully before beginning this chapter.

Bodé plots give you a graph of the system's frequency response. Properly plotted, gain and phase margin can be derived. These, in turn, allow you to predict how stable a system will be prior to bringing it "on-line." With large, powerful, expensive, potentially lethal elements this is more than a good idea. Since there are many good personal computer programs available to provide a system's Bode' plot, emphasis will be on the use of the information available from the plots, not in the generation of these plots.

Selecting the best values for your controller's constants often appears to be as much black magic as science. The last section of this chapter will present three techniques. The Bodé plot of the full system will allow you to select controller constants. The step response of the process, along with all instrumentation and actuators, can be tested open loop. From this process reaction rate plot, values for the PID controller's constants can be obtained. If you cannot run the process open loop, tuning constants can still be obtained using the ultimate cycle tuning technique.

OBJECTIVES

After studying this chapter, you should be able to do the following:

1. Define a process control transfer function and a servo control transfer function.
2. Given the transfer function for the element under control and the controller, derive the transfer function for a closed-loop process control system and a closed-loop servo control system.
3. Given appropriate transfer functions, determine the time-domain response to a step input of:
   a. The element under control, run open loop.
   b. The element with servo-control-type negative feedback.
   c. The element with process-control-type negative feedback.
4. Apply the final value theorem to the three cases stated above.
5. Draw the Bodé plots necessary to analyze the stability of a negative feedback system containing some combination of gain, derivative, integral, first-order lead, first-order lag, and second-order underdamped lag elements.
6. Use the Bodé plots drawn in objective 5 to determine the gain margin and phase margin of a negative feedback system.
7. Illustrate the impact of proportional, integral, and derivative constants on the open-loop Bodé plot of a negative-feedback system.
8. For the process reaction and the ultimate cycle tuning techniques:
   a. Describe in detail how to test a system to obtain required data.
   b. Given test results, calculate constants for proportional, P-I, or three-mode controllers.

8–1 SYSTEM TRANSFER FUNCTIONS

Every element in an industrial setting can be described, more or less, by an equation. This equation gives the output of the element in terms of its inputs and constants. When converted to the Laplace domain, complex behavior can usually be analyzed using algebra rather than differential equations. This is presented in Appendix A.

The output of a control system is the process variable. If you are analyzing the system as a process, energy input or load disturbances are considered to be the input.

$$PV(s) = F(s) \times R(s) \tag{8–1}$$

where PV = system's output, process variable

F = function describing the performance of the system

R = energy input or load disturbance

Since the transfer function of a system is defined as

$$\text{transfer function} = \frac{\text{output}(s)}{\text{input}(s)}$$

for a system analyzed as a process, its transfer function is

$$\frac{PV(s)}{R(s)} \tag{8–2}$$

A system may also be evaluated as a servo. The output of a servo is still the process variable. However, a servo's input is considered to be the set point.

$$PV(s) = F(s) \times SP(s) \tag{8–3}$$

The transfer function of a servo is given by

$$\frac{PV(s)}{SP(s)} \tag{8–4}$$

In this section of the chapter, you will derive the general transfer function for a closed-loop process and for a closed-loop servo. You will apply these to determine the transfer functions for first- and second-order elements with proportional and proportional–integral controller negative feedback.

8–1.1 Process Control

The purpose of a *process* is to *regulate* its output. The set point is considered to be fixed. Negative feedback, when used, is to alter the system's input energy in such a way as to eliminate or reduce the effects of variations in that energy or in the loads on the process variable. Ideally, there would be no change in the process variable (system output) for any change in input (energy or load disturbance). Examples of a process are a home heating system, a level control system, or flow control.

The traditional block diagram of a process control system is given in Figure 8–1. The system elements' transfer functions are given by $G(s)$. This includes the power interface and actuator (Chapter 7) and the element under control itself (Chapter 2). The transducer (Chapter 3), the signal conditioning and transmission (Chapter 4), any filtering, and the controller's transfer function are given by $H(s)$. You saw three types of analog controllers in Chapter 5, culminating in the three-mode PID controller. Since the set point is considered fixed in process analysis, it is not shown separately.

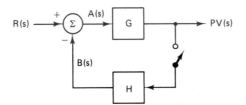

Figure 8–1 Traditional process control closed-loop block diagram.

For open-loop operation, the switch is left open. The process variable then becomes

$$PV(s) = G(s) \times R(s)$$

So any changes in the input, $R(s)$, directly affect the process variable.

However, by closing the switch, closed-loop operation is enabled. The controller should now alter the amount of energy, $R(s)$, as needed to keep the process variable, $PV(s)$, constant. Under closed-loop control,

$$PV(s) = G(s) \times A(s) \tag{8–5}$$

but

$$A(s) = R(s) - B(s) \tag{8–6}$$

and

$$B(s) = H(s) \times PV(s) \tag{8–7}$$

So, substituting equation 8–7 into equation 8–6 yields

$$A(s) = R(s) - H(s) \times PV(s) \tag{8–8}$$

and substituting equation 8–8 into equation 8–5, we have

$$PV(s) = G(s)[R(s) - H(s) \times PV(s)]$$

$$PV(s) = G(s)R(s) - G(s)H(s)PV(s)$$

Solving for PV(s) gives us

$$PV(s) + G(s)H(s)PV(s) = G(s)R(s)$$

$$PV(s)[1 + G(s)H(s)] = G(s)R(s) \tag{8–9}$$

The transfer function for the overall system when negative feedback is used is $PV(s)/R(s)$. Solving equation 8–9 for the system transfer function gives us

$$\frac{PV(s)}{R(s)} = \frac{G(s)}{1 + G(s)H(s)} \tag{8–10}$$

This form may look familiar. When applying negative feedback around an op amp,

$$A_{cl} = \frac{A_{ol}}{1 + \beta A_{ol}}$$

where A_{cl} = closed loop (with feedback) gain of the amp
      A_{ol} = op amp's open-loop gain
       β = attenuation ratio of the feedback network

EXAMPLE 8–1

Given a first-order element with a steady-state gain of 6, a time constant $\tau = 20$ s, and a proportional controller with $K_p = 10$, determine the following:
(a) System closed-loop transfer function.
(b) Response of the output to a unit step in input energy in (1) the Laplace domain and (2) the time domain.
(c) Steady-state value of the process variable.

Solution   (a) The transfer function is

$$\frac{PV}{R} = \frac{G}{1 + GH}$$

where

$$G = \frac{A}{1 + \tau s}$$

$$= \frac{6}{1 + 20s} \qquad \text{(time is in seconds)}$$

$$H = K_p = 10$$

Substituting these into the transfer function gives

$$\frac{PV}{R} = \frac{6/(1 + 20s)}{1 + [60/(1 + 20s)]}$$

Finding a common denominator for the denominator yields

$$\frac{PV}{R} = \frac{6/(1 + 20s)}{(1 + 20s + 60)/(1 + 20s)}$$

Simplifying, we obtain

$$\frac{PV}{R} = \frac{6}{61 + 20s}$$

But the standard form is $A_{\text{system}}/(1 + \tau_{\text{system}}s)$. To get to this form, the numerator and denominator must be divided by 61:

$$\frac{PV}{R} = \frac{6/61}{1 + (20/61)s}$$

$$\frac{PV}{R} = \frac{0.0984}{1 + 0.328s}$$

(b) The output is

$$PV = \frac{0.0984}{1 + 0.328s} R(s)$$

The Laplace transform for a unit step is

$$R(s) = \frac{1}{s}$$

Substituting this into the equation for the process variable gives us

$$PV = \frac{0.0984}{s(1 + 0.328s)}$$

Look at Table A-1, line 17a. This gives the transform pair

$$\frac{A}{s(\tau s + 1)} \quad \longleftrightarrow \quad A(1 - e^{-t/\tau})$$

This means that the system steady-state gain A_{system} = 0.0984 and that the system time constant τ_{system} = 0.328 sec. In the time domain,

$$PV(t) = 0.0984(1 - e^{-t/0.328sec})$$

Without negative feedback, the output would have responded to a unit step with a steady-state gain of 6 and a time constant of 20 sec. Adding negative feedback with a proportional controller gain of 10 has reduced the steady-state gain by 61 and sped the response up by the same factor. Figure 8–2 contains plots of the open-loop response to a unit step and the closed-loop response. Since the purpose of a closed-loop *process* control system is to keep the output steady, this system is performing well.

(c) The steady-state value of the process variable is

$$PV_{steady\ state} = \lim_{t \to \infty} [0.0984(1 - e^{-t/0.328})]$$

$$= 0.0984(1 - 0)$$

$$= 0.0984$$

    Looking carefully at the results of Example 8–1 may lead you to the conclusion that to improve performance, all you have to do is to increase the proportional controller's constant, K_p (the feedback gain). This gain certainly appears in the denominator of both the closed-loop system steady-state gain (A_{system}) and the system's time constant (τ_{system}). This division by the controller's gain does indeed reduce the amplitude of the change in the process variable. It also forces that change to settle out much more quickly.

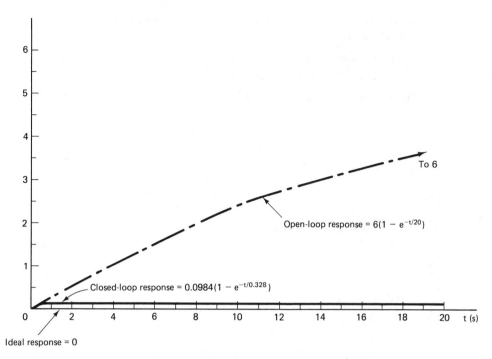

Figure 8–2   Responses (Example 8–1).

However, Laplace analysis assumes that all of the elements are both linear and unbounded. In reality, no hardware performs perfectly linearly. More of a problem is the fact that there is an upper and a lower limit to the values that an element can actually output. Laplace operations ignore this minor detail. Because a controller saturates for outputs above 10 V (rather than giving you 250 V, like the Laplace equations may expect), a process predicted to be stable by Laplace techniques may alternately drive its output all the way up, then all the way down, back and forth. This limit cycling may be caused by having the gain of the proportional controller too high. Any small error drives the controller's output either on or off.

So even though the analysis you have so carefully followed in Example 8–1 predicts good results, when you actually fire-up the process, it may appear to oscillate. In reality it is limit cycling.

To stop limit cycling you must lower the proportional controller's gain. But this slows down the speed of response of the closed-loop process and allows the process variable to change more in response to a change in the system's input. The solution is to lower the proportional controller's gain and to add integral to the controller. The error that the proportional controller is unable to step out, the integral will slowly ramp away.

EXAMPLE 8–2

Derive the closed-loop process control transfer function for a first-order element with a series proportional-integral controller.

Solution   The transfer function for a closed-loop system analyzed as a process is

$$\frac{PV}{R} = \frac{G}{1 + GH}$$

For a first-order element,

$$G = \frac{A}{1 + \tau s}$$

A series proportional–integral controller's transfer function is

$$H = K_p \left(\frac{s + K_i}{s} \right)$$

Combining these gives

$$\frac{PV}{R} = \frac{A/(1 + \tau s)}{1 + \left(\dfrac{A}{1 + \tau s} \right) K_p \left(\dfrac{s + K_i}{s} \right)}$$

Finding a common denominator, we have

$$\frac{PV}{R} = \frac{A/(1 + \tau s)}{\dfrac{s(1 + \tau s) + K_p A(s + K_i)}{s(1 + \tau s)}}$$

Simplifying yields

$$\frac{PV}{R} = \frac{As}{s(1 + \tau s) + K_p A(s + K_i)}$$

Distributing and grouping terms in the denominator gives

$$\frac{PV}{R} = \frac{As}{\tau s^2 + (AK_p + 1)s + AK_i K_p}$$

But all standard forms have the coefficient of s^2 set to 1. So dividing the numerator and the denominator by τ gives

$$\frac{PV}{R} = \frac{(A/\tau)s}{s^2 + \left(\dfrac{AK_p + 1}{\tau} \right) s + \dfrac{AK_i K_p}{\tau}}$$

The system will have a second-order response. The standard second-order denominator is

$$s^2 + 2\zeta\omega_n s + \omega_n^2$$

where ζ is the damping coefficient and ω_n is the resonant frequency in radians/second. Equating coefficients gives

$$\omega_n^2 = \frac{AK_p K_i}{\tau}$$

or

$$\omega_n = \sqrt{\frac{AK_p K_i}{\tau}} \tag{8–11}$$

The damping coefficient comes from

$$2\zeta\omega_n = \frac{AK_p + 1}{\tau}$$

Solving for ζ yields

$$\zeta = \frac{AK_p + 1}{2\tau\omega_n} \tag{8–12}$$

These equations can be rearranged to give the values of the controller's constants in terms of system constants and desired response parameters.

$$K_p = \frac{2\zeta\omega_n \tau - 1}{A} \tag{8–13}$$

$$K_i = \frac{\omega_n^2 \tau}{AK_p} \tag{8–14}$$

Use equations 8–11 and 8–12 to determine the response of a given system. Or, if you are designing or altering the controller's constants, equations 8–13 and 8–14 may be used.

EXAMPLE 8–3

The first-order system of Example 8–1 was found to cycle when controlled by a proportional controller with $K_p = 10$. Determine the following if a proportional–integral controller with $K_p = 4$ is substituted.

(a) Natural resonant frequency in rad/s and in hertz.
(b) Integral controller's K_i, T_i, and resets/min settings to cause an overall closed-loop process response as a critically damped system.
(c) Laplace domain and time-domain process variable equations with a unit step input.
(d) Plot of the time-domain response. Compare this to Figure 8–2.
(e) Steady-state value of the process variable.

Solution   First write all of the constants that you have been given.

$$\tau = 20 \text{ sec}$$

$$A = 6$$

$$K_p = 4$$

$$\text{critically damped } \zeta = 1$$

(a) Rearranging equation 8–12 to determine the resonant frequency yields

$$\omega_n = \frac{AK_p + 1}{2\zeta\tau}$$

$$= \frac{(6)(4) + 1}{2 \times 1 \times 20 \text{ sec}}$$

$$= 0.625 \text{ rad/sec}$$

$$f_n = \frac{\omega_n}{2\pi}$$

$$= \frac{0.625 \text{ rad/sec}}{2\pi}$$

$$= 0.1 \text{ Hz}$$

So if the system is going to oscillate, it will be at a frequency of about 0.1 Hz. In testing, be prepared to wait several periods (tens of seconds) to verify stable operation.

(b) Once K_p and the resonant frequency have been defined, the integral controller's constant can be adjusted to set the damping. From equation 8–14,

$$K_i = \frac{\omega_n^2 \tau}{AK_p}$$

$$= \frac{(0.625 \text{ rad/sec})^2(20 \text{ sec})}{6 \times 4}$$

$$= 0.326/\text{sec}$$

$$T_i = \frac{1}{K_i}$$

$$= \frac{1}{0.326/\text{sec}}$$

$$= 3.07 \text{ sec}$$

The reset/min rating is just K_i expressed per minute rather than per second.

$$\text{resets/min} = 0.326/\text{sec} \times 60 \text{ sec/min}$$
$$= 19.6 \text{ resets/min}$$

(c) The complete closed-loop transfer equation was developed in Example 8–2. It is

$$\frac{PV}{R} = \frac{(A/\tau)s}{s^2 + \left(\dfrac{AK_p + 1}{\tau}\right)s + \dfrac{AK_iK_p}{\tau}}$$

Substituting the values given yields

$$\frac{PV}{R} = \frac{0.3s}{s^2 + 1.25s + 0.3912}$$

The denominator is indeed a perfect square, as it should since this was designed to be critically damped.

$$\frac{PV}{R} = \frac{0.3s}{(s + 0.625)^2}$$

or

$$PV = \frac{0.3sR}{(s + 0.625)^2}$$

A unit step in the Laplace domain is

$$R = \frac{1}{s}$$

so

$$PV = \frac{0.3s(1/s)}{(s + 0.625)^2}$$

$$= \frac{0.3}{(s + 0.625)^2}$$

Look at Table A-1, line 15b.

$$\frac{A}{(s + a)^2} \quad \longleftrightarrow \quad Ate^{-at}$$

So, in the time domain, by equating coefficients, we have

$$PV = 0.3te^{-0.625t}$$

(d) The plot of the time-domain response is given in Figure 8–3. The vertical and horizontal axes have both been expanded to display the effects better. Keep in mind that without feedback, a unit step applied to the input will result in a charging exponential at the output. Eventually, the output will reach 6. This rise would occur with a time constant of 20 s, taking 100 s to be considered stable. The desired result of a process control system is to keep the output from responding at all to changes on its input. The proportional controller in Example 8–1 did reasonably well, holding the output variation to 1.6% and settling in about 1.6 s.

The proportional–integral controller's results are also shown in Figure 8–3. Following the input step, the output does rise, but peaks out at about 0.177 (3.0% of the open-loop output) in 1.6 s. Following that, the output is driven to zero by the controller. This is precisely what you want.

(e) From the plot in Figure 8–3 you can see that the steady-state response of a first-order process with a critically tuned proportional–integral controller is zero.

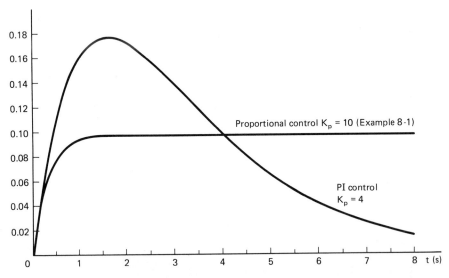

Figure 8–3 Response (Example 8–3).

8–1.2 Servo Control

The process controller's purpose is to keep the process variable *regulated*. Changes in input energy or loads are shown as the input function. The controller should keep the output constant, despite input changes. Since the set point is constant, it is included inside the controller block, not shown separately.

A system may also be evaluated as a servo. The output of a servo is still the process variable. However, a servo's input is considered to be the set point.

$$PV(s) = F(s) \times SP(s) \qquad (8–3)$$

The transfer function of a servo is given by

$$\frac{PV(s)}{SP(s)} \qquad (8–4)$$

The servo control system's purpose is to cause the process variable to *track* the set point. Under perfect servo control, the process variable would always equal the set point as the set point is varied through its range. It is assumed that the input energy and loads remain constant, so they are not shown in the servo control block diagram of Figure 8–4. As in the process control block diagram in Figure 8–1, the actuator, power interface, and element under control are grouped in the block labeled G. The remaining electronics and the controller are in the feedback block H. Since the effects of changes in set point must be evaluated, the set-point input has been added at the input of the feedback block.

The controller actually operated on the error signal. This is

error = set point − process variable

Figure 8–5 shows this difference calculation being accomplished. A summer block is used, with one positive and one negative input. But Figure 8–5 does not look quite right. Standard block diagrams have their input on the left. The signal is operated on by a series of blocks, proceeding from left to right. The output is the last thing on the right. Figure 8–6 shows this rearrangement completed. This diagram gives an entirely different view of a servo control loop. The controller is no longer in the feedback. Instead, it is the first block that the input (i.e., the set point) encounters. The controller

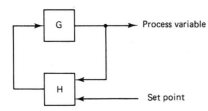

Figure 8–4   Initial servo control block diagram.

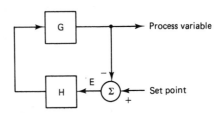

Figure 8–5   Servo controller with error block.

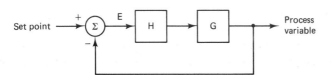

Figure 8-6   Traditional servo control block diagram.

is in series with the element under control. There appears to be no negative feedback element. All of the output (process variable) is treated as negative feedback. This is also called 100% negative feedback.

There are several key features of servo loops. These are worth repeating. The purpose of a servo control loop is to cause the process variable (i.e., the output) to track the set point (i.e., input). Input energy and loads are considered to be constant.

Without negative feedback, any change in the set point is passed to the output through the transfer functions of $H(s$ and $G(s)$.

$$PV(s) = SP(s)[H(s) \times G(s)]$$

So the *open-loop servo control* transfer function becomes

$$\frac{PV(s)}{SP(s)} = H(s) \times G(s)$$

When negative feedback is applied, this changes significantly. Look at Figure 8–6 again.

$$PV(s) = G(s) \times H(s) \times E(s) \qquad (8\text{–}15)$$

where E is the error produced by subtracting the feedback (the process variable) from the input (set point).

$$E(s) = SP(s) - PV(s) \qquad (8\text{–}16)$$

Substituting equation 8–16 into equation 8–15 gives

$$PV(s) = G(s) \times H(s)[SP(s) - PV(s)]$$

or

$$PV(s) = G(s) \times H(s) \times SP(s) - G(s) \times H(s) \times PV(s)$$

A little algebra is necessary to solve this for PV.

$$PV(s) \times [1 + G(s) \times H(s)] = G(s) \times H(s) \times SP(s)$$

$$PV(s) = \frac{G(s) \times H(s) \times SP(s)}{1 + G(s) \times H(s)}$$

The transfer function for *closed-loop servo control* is

$$\frac{PV(s)}{SP(s)} = \frac{G(s) \times H(s)}{1 + G(s) \times H(s)} \qquad (8\text{–}17)$$

Compare this to equation 8–10, the transfer function for closed-loop process control. The servo closed-loop transfer function has the controller's transfer function in the numerator. The process closed-loop transfer function does not. As you will see in the following example, this will make quite a difference in the system's performance.

EXAMPLE 8–4

Given a first-order element with a steady-state gain of 6, a time constant $\tau = 20$ s, and a proportional controller with $K_p = 10$, determine the following.
 (a) System servo closed-loop transfer function.
 (b) Response of the output to a unit step in set point in (1) the Laplace domain and (2) the time domain.
 (c) Steady-state value of the process variable.
      Notice that this is a repeat of Example 8–1, but analyzing the system's response to a change in set point.

Solution   (a) The transfer function is

$$\frac{PV}{SP} = \frac{GH}{1 + GH}$$

where G is the transfer function for the element under control,

$$G = \frac{6}{1 + 20s}$$

and H is the transfer function for the proportional controller.

$$H = 10$$

Substituting these into equation 8–17 gives

$$\frac{PV}{SP} = \frac{\dfrac{6}{1 + 20s} \times 10}{1 + \dfrac{6}{1 + 20s} \times 10}$$

Next you must obtain a common denominator.

$$\frac{PV}{SP} = \frac{\dfrac{60}{1 + 20s}}{\dfrac{1 + 20s + 60}{1 + 20s}}$$

Simplifying gives

$$\frac{PV}{SP} = \frac{60}{61 + 20s} \qquad (8\text{–}18)$$

But the standard form is

$$\frac{A}{1 + \tau s}$$

So equation 8–18 must have its numerator and denominator both divided by 61.

$$\frac{PV}{SP} = \frac{0.984}{1 + 0.328s}$$

(b) The output is

$$PV = \frac{0.984}{1 + 0.328s} SP(s)$$

The Laplace transform of a unit step at the input is

$$SP = \frac{1}{s}$$

Substituting this into the equation yields

$$PV = \frac{0.984}{s(1 + 0.328s)}$$

Look at Table A-1, line 17a. This gives the transform pair

$$\frac{A}{s(\tau s + 1)} \quad \longleftrightarrow \quad A(1 - e^{-t/\tau})$$

This means that the system steady-state gain $A_{system} = 0.984$ and that the system time constant $\tau_{system} = 0.328$ sec. In the time domain,

$$PV(t) = 0.984(1 - e^{-t/0.328 sec})$$

Without negative feedback, the output would have responded to a unit step with a steady-state gain of 6 and a time constant of 20 sec. Adding negative feedback with a proportional controller gain of 10 has reduced the steady-state gain to almost 1, and sped the response up by 61. Figure 8–7 contains plots of the open-loop response to a unit step and the closed-loop servo response. Since the purpose of a closed-loop *servo* control system is to force the output to equal the set point, this system is performing well.

(c) The steady-state value of the process variable is

$$PV_{steady\,state} = \lim_{t \to \infty} [0.984(1 - e^{-t/0.328})]$$

$$= 0.984(1 - 0)$$
$$= 0.984$$

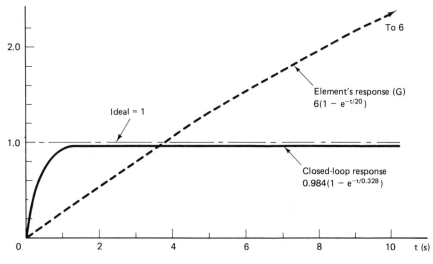

Figure 8–7   Response (Example 8–4).

Proportional control alone was not capable of completely removing the error in closed-loop *process* control. The same is true in closed-loop *servo* control. Without closed-loop servo control the process variable overshoots the set point's unit step by 600%. Adding proportional closed-loop servo control causes the process variable to settle within 1.6% of the set point.

You may be able to get better performance with a higher proportional controller gain (K_p), but risk system cycling. As with closed-loop *process* control, better performance can be obtained by going to a proportional–integral controller.

8–2 FINAL VALUE THEOREM

The value that the process variable eventually settles into is an important measure of the system's performance. This is called the final value. In Example 8–1 the final value was obtained by

$$\text{final value} = \lim_{t \to \infty} [0.0984(1 - e^{-t/0.328s})]$$

This was straightforward enough.

However, in Example 8–2, when the integral controller was added, the answer is not quite so simple. The time-domain equation for the process variable is

$$PV = 0.3te^{-0.625t}$$

Taking the limit of this as time (t) goes to infinity is not obvious. The first t causes the value of PV to increase without bound. However, the $-t$ in the exponent drives that term, and therefore the value of PV, to zero. It is necessary to evaluate the equation at several values to determine which phenomenon is dominant.

Taking the limit as time goes to infinity, or worse, evaluating several values of the time-domain equation of PV, requires that you first have that time-domain equation. The systems and coefficients shown in examples in this chapter were selected because the transforms back into the time domain were reasonably simple. But most real elements under control are much more complicated than simple first order. Full proportional–integral–derivative control, or cascaded control, is the rule. Although the transfer functions for these systems are not too difficult to obtain, transforming the result into the time domain may be very tedious (and as a result, error prone). In fact, most control engineers work predominantly in the Laplace domain, rarely, if ever, transforming into the time domain.

So, how, then, can you determine the final value of the process variable in the time domain? It is done with the *final value theorem*. This theorem states that

$$\lim_{t \to \infty} f(t) = \lim_{s \to 0} sF(s)$$

Instead of having to transform into the time domain and then taking a limit as time goes to infinity, you just take the limit of the function multiplied by s in the Laplace domain as s goes to zero.

EXAMPLE 8–5

Apply the final value theorem to the following equations.

(a) $PV = \dfrac{0.0984}{s(1 + 0.328s)}$ Example 8–1   process control (proportional)

(b) $PV = \dfrac{0.3}{(s + 0.625)^2}$ Example 8–3   process control (proportional–integral)

(c) $PV = \dfrac{0.984}{s(1 + 0.328s)}$ Example 8–4   servo control (proportional)

(d) $PV = \dfrac{1.2s + 0.391}{s(s + 0.625)^2}$ Example 8–4   servo control using a proportional–integral controller

Solution

(a) $\lim\limits_{t \to \infty} PV(t) = \lim\limits_{s \to 0} s \times PV(s)$

$$= \lim_{s \to 0} s \, \frac{0.0984}{s(1 + 0.328s)}$$

$$= \lim_{s \to 0} \frac{0.0984}{1 + 0.328s}$$

$$= \frac{0.0984}{1 + 0.028 \times 0}$$

$$= 0.0984$$

This matches the result obtained in Example 8–1. A process controlled with a proportional controller will reduce the output change, but cannot eliminate it.

(b) $\lim_{t \to \infty} \text{PV}(t) = \lim_{s \to 0} s \times \frac{0.3}{(s + 0.625)^2}$

$$= 0 \times \frac{0.3}{(0 + 0.625)^2}$$

$$= 0$$

This also matches the results obtained in Example 8–3. A process controlled with a proportional–integral controller can eliminate any effect of the input on the output. Notice that this conclusion was reached without having to take an inverse transform or having to calculate any time-domain values.

(c) $\lim_{t \to \infty} \text{PV}(t) = \lim_{s \to 0} s \times \frac{0.984}{s(1 + 0.328s)}$

$$= \lim_{s \to 0} \frac{0.984}{(1 + 0.328s)}$$

$$= \frac{0.984}{1 + 0.328 \times 0}$$

$$= 0.984$$

This matches the result obtained in Example 8–4. A servo system with a proportional controller will cause the output to change, but cannot make it fully track the set point.

(d) $\lim_{t \to \infty} \text{PV}(t) = \lim_{s \to 0} s \times \frac{1.2s + 0.391}{s(s + 0.625)^2}$

$$= \lim_{s \to 0} \frac{1.2s + 0.391}{(s + 0.625)^2}$$

$$= \frac{1.2 \times 0 + 0.391}{(0 + 0.625)^2}$$

$$= \frac{0.391}{0.391}$$

$$= 1$$

Controlling a servo system with a proportional–integral controller allows the process variable, at least eventually, to track the set point perfectly.

In summary, use of the final value theorem allows you to determine the steady-state value of a system's output without having to solve the time-domain equation at several points. In fact, you do not even have to transform the Laplace solution into the time domain.

8–3 STABILITY: THE BODÉ PLOT

A system is said to be *stable* when a change at its input causes its output to, eventually, settle at some level. The key word here is *settle*. There are two types of instability. If the output is driven up or down until something in the system saturates, the system is unstable. The system may respond to the change at its input by driving its output up and down, up and down, up and down. . . . The amplitude of this oscillation may be constant, or it may grow, until the system is driven from one saturation limit to the other, back and forth. Look at Figure 8–8. Several examples of both stable and unstable system responses are given.

Certainly, it is desirable to have a stable system. Instabilities may cause inconvenience, manufacturing of out-of-spec product, wasted time and money, and in the extreme, catastrophic failure and the loss of life. With something as important as this, it is often critical to be assured, prior to starting up a system, that it will be stable. Testing and adjusting a system for optimum performance is fine. However, trying to adjust an unstable system, to prevent it from oscillating, saturating, or blowing up, while the system is in the process of an unstable response is ill advised.

8–3.1 An Overview

To predict and prevent unstable operation, you need to know its cause. Instability, especially the type illustrated in Figure 8–8g, is caused by improper amplitude and phase feedback. Look at Figure 8–9. This is a simplified diagram of a feedback system, either process or servo. There is a 180° phase shift across the summer. This simply means that negative feedback is being applied. The reactive characteristics of the element under control [$G(s)$] and the controller [$H(s)$] cause the problem. For any real element, its gain varies, more or less, with the frequency of the signal. Along with a change in gain amplitude comes a shift in phase. Second-, third-, or higher-order elements are often used. So it is quite conceivable that at some frequency there will be another 180° phase shift, this shift across the $G(s)H(s)$ block.

This phase reversal, in itself, does not present a problem. For example, if the

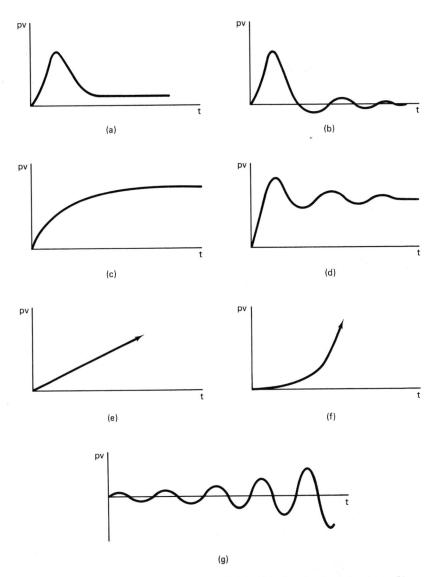

Figure 8–8 Examples of system responses: (a) stable, heavily damped process; (b) stable, lightly damped process; (c) stable, heavily damped servo; (d) stable, lightly damped servo; (e) unstable, integral response; (f) unstable, exponential response; (g) unstable, increasing oscillations.

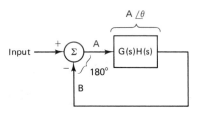

Figure 8–9 Simple stability illustration.

$G(s)H(s)$ block has a gain of 0.5 at the frequency which produces 180° phase shift, a unit step at the input of Figure 8–9 will cause the following:

point A to 1,	point B goes down to -0.5,	this sends
point A to 1.5,	point B goes down to -0.75,	this sends
point A to 1.75,	point B goes down to -0.88,	this sends
point A to 1.88,	point B goes down to -0.94,	this sends
point A to 1.94,	point B goes down to -0.97,	this sends
point A to 1.97,	point B goes down to -0.99,	this sends
point A to 1.99,	point B stays at -0.99	

The system stabilizes.

On the other hand, if the $G(s)H(s)$ block has a gain of 2 at the frequency which produces a 180° shift, the following results from a unit step at the input:

point A to 1,	point B goes down to -2,	this sends
point A to 3,	point B goes down to -6,	this sends
point A to 7,	point B goes down to -14,	this sends
point A to 15	. . .	

Things are getting out-of-hand very quickly. This system is unstable.

Clearly, the gain of the $G(s)H(s)$ block at the frequency that causes 180° phase shift is the critical factor. Without a lot of math, if that gain is less than 1, the system will be stable. A gain of greater than 1 will cause an unstable system.

So to predict, or correct, system stability, you need to determine the frequency response of the $G(s)H(s)$ block. Both the amplitude variation with frequency and the phase variation with frequency are important. Notice, you are not trying to determine the frequency response of the entire closed-loop system

$$\frac{G(s)}{1 + G(s)H(s)} \quad \text{or} \quad \frac{G(s)H(s)}{1 + G(s)H(s)}$$

All you want is the frequency response of $G(s)H(s)$, to determine if those elements provide the critical gain and phase shift.

The rigorous determination of the frequency response of a block, given its transfer function, requires several steps.

1. Substitute $j\omega = s$, in the transfer function, where ω is frequency in rad/sec. This gives you a complex expression, having both real and imaginary parts.

2. Separate this complex expression into a real part and an imaginary part. Usually, this requires that you multiply both the numerator and the denominator by the complex conjugate of the denominator.

3. The magnitude or gain equation, then, is

$$\text{gain} = \sqrt{\text{real}^2 + \text{imaginary}^2}$$

   This gives you an equation for gain as a function of frequency. To get a plot, substitute values for ω and solve the equation repeatedly for gain.

4. The phase equation is given by

$$\text{phase} = \arctan \frac{\text{imaginary}}{\text{real}}$$

Again, to get a plot, you must substitute values for ω and solve the equation repeated for the phase.

"The horizontal axis on frequency response plots is normally scaled logarithmically. A log scale horizontal axis is shown in Figure 8–10. Each decade (factor of 10) increase or decrease moves you the same distance along the scale. There are two other points that you should notice. First, the starting point is not at zero. If you went farther left, each increment would lower the scale by 10 (to 0.1, then 0.01, then 0.001, etc.), but you would never reach zero. So start your log scales at the lowest-frequency decade of interest, not at zero. Second, the divisions between decades are not uniform (linear). This is easily seen in Figure 8–10(b). Be careful about this when interpolating between major divisions" [1].

"Gain plotted on the vertical axis is normally expressed in decibels.

$$\text{dB} = 20 \log_{10} \frac{\text{output}}{\text{input}}$$

You can readily convert ratio gain (output/input) to dB gain with most scientific calculators. Notice that log base 10 is used, not the natural log (ln or log base e). It is handy to

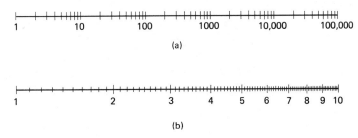

Figure 8–10 Logarithmically scaled frequency axis: (a) 5 decade (cycle) log scale; (b) one logarithmic deside expanded.

TABLE 8–1 RATIO-TO-DB
CONVERSIONS

$\dfrac{v_o}{v_{\text{in}}}$	dB	$\dfrac{v_o}{v_{\text{in}}}$	dB
1000	60	0.707	−3
100	40	0.5	−6
10	20	0.1	−20
2	6	0.01	−40
1	0	0.001	−60

know several dB and ratio gain points. These are listed in Table 8–1. Decreasing the ratio gain by 10 subtracts 20 dB; increasing by 10 adds 20 dB. Doubling the gain adds 6 dB; halving it subtracts 6 dB. Cutting the gain by $\sqrt{2}$ gives −3 dB. A ratio gain of 1 (output = input) is a gain of 0 dB'' [1].

The procedures outlined above are rigorously correct but rarely necessary. A frequency response or Bodé plot can be *sketched* fairly simply. First, the transfer function must be factored into the simplest terms possible. Then the response of each term is drawn separately on a semilog graph. Both gain (dB) and phase graphs are sketched. Finally, the composite Bodé plot is formed by adding the individual lines, point by point. On the phase plot this is possible because phases add. The individual terms can also be added on the gain plot. In the transfer function the terms are multiplied. However, the gains are expressed in dB, a logarithm. Multiplication of the ratio gains means that you should add their dB gains.

This technique is illustrated in Figure 8–11. This is the Bodé plot for a transfer function of

$$G(s) = \frac{6}{1 + 20s}$$

and

$$H(s) = 10s$$

This gives

$$G(s)H(s) = \frac{60s}{1 + 20s}$$

There are three separate terms here.

$$A = 60 \quad \Longrightarrow \quad 20 \log (60) = 35.6 \text{ dB}$$

$$B = s$$

$$C = \frac{1}{1 + 20s}$$

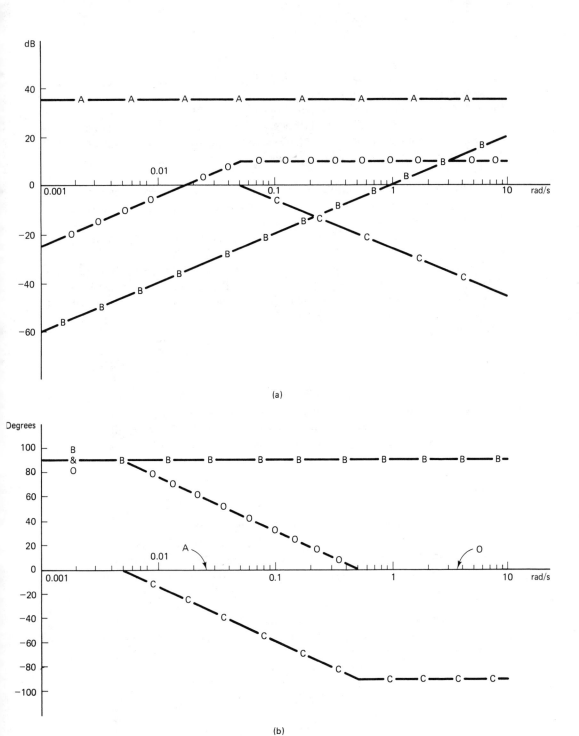

Figure 8–11 Sample Bodé (a) gain and (b) phase plots.

Now, look at the Bodé gain plots in Figure 8–11a. Term A is constant with frequency. Its level is 35.6 dB. Term B is a derivative. Its Bodé gain plot is a straight line that crosses 0 dB at 1 rad/s. It has a slope of +20 dB/decade (more on this later). Term C is called a first-order lag. Its Bodé gain plot is at 0 dB until 0.05 rad/s. After that point, it drops at a rate of −20 dB/decade. The overall Bodé gain plot is the point-by-point summation of these three lines. It is shown marked with an o in Figure 8–11a.

The Bodé phase plot is given in Figure 8–11b. Term A does not shift the phase at all, so it coincides with the x axis. The derivative term, B, causes a constant 90° shift, independent of frequency. The first-order lag term, term C, causes a −45° shift at 0.05 rad/s, varying linearly to 0° at lower frequencies and shifting on to −90° as the frequency increases.

A glance at the gain and phase Bodé plots in Figure 8–11 is enough to predict a stable system. Even though the gain exceeds 1 (0 dB), at no time does the phase shift across $G(s)H(s)$ approach 180°. So oscillations will not occur. However, even though the Bodé plot analysis of this system predicts that it will be stable, limit cycling may still occur.

8–3.2 Gain

The Bodé plot of a block that shows simple gain is a horizontal line. The gain does not vary with frequency. The amplitude of the line is the dB value of the block's gain. A simple gain block does not shift the phase of a signal. So the phase Bodé plot of a simple gain block is a horizontal line at 0°. The gain and phase Bodé plots for a gain block are shown in Figure 8–12.

8–3.3 Derivative

A derivative term is some power of s in the numerator. For a first-order derivative, s is only raised to the first power. Its gain Bodé plot consists of a straight line rising at 20 dB/decade. It crosses the 0-dB axis at 1 rad/s. A first-order derivative shifts the phase 90° independent of frequency. A first-order derivative's Bodé plots are shown in Figure 8–13.

A second-order derivative has s raised to the second power. Its gain Bodé plot is a straight line passing through 0 dB at 1 rad/s. However, its slope is 40 dB/decade. The phase shift of a second-order derivative is a constant 180°. This same progression follows as the order of the derivative term increases. In general, for an nth-order derivative, the gain is a straight line passing through 0 dB at 1 rad/s. The

$$\text{slope} = n \times 20 \text{ dB/decade}$$

The phase shift for an nth-order derivative is constant with frequency. It is

$$\text{phase} = n \times 90°$$

Several different order derivatives' Bodé plots are shown in Figure 8–14.

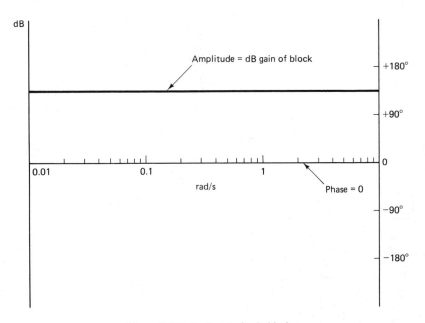

Figure 8–12 Bodé plot of gain block.

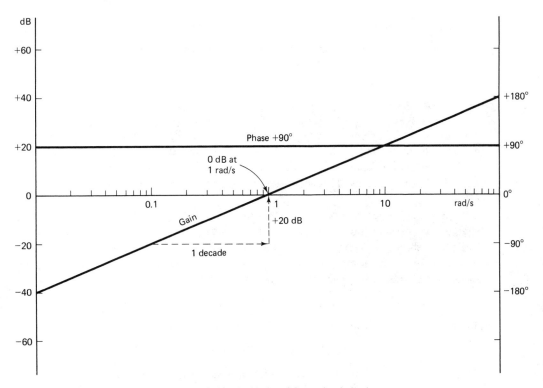

Figure 8–13 Bodé plot of first-order derivative.

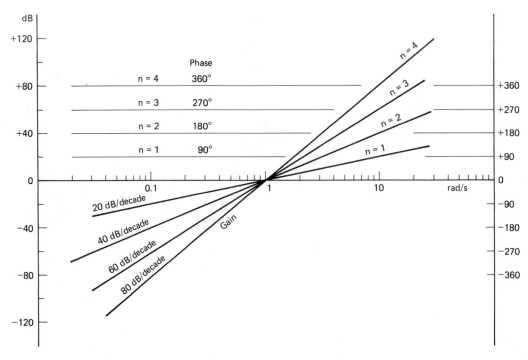

Figure 8–14 Bodé plot for general *n*th-order derivative.

8–3.4 Integral

An integral term is some power of *s* in the denominator. For a first-order integral, *s* is only raised to the first power. Its gain Bodé plot consists of a straight line falling at −20 dB/decade. It crosses the 0-dB axis at 1 rad/s. A first-order integral shifts the phase −90° independent of frequency. A first-order integral's Bodé plots are shown in Figure 8–15.

A second-order integral has *s* raised to the second power. Its gain Bodé plot is a straight line passing through 0 dB at 1 rad/s. However, its slope is −40 dB/decade. The phase shift of a second-order integral is a constant −180°. This same progression follows as the order of the integral term increases. In general, for an *n*th-order integral, the gain is a straight line passing through 0 dB at 1 rad/s. The

$$\text{slope} = -n \times 20 \text{ dB/decade}$$

The phase shift for an *n*th-order integral is constant with frequency. It is

$$\text{phase} = -n \times 90°$$

Several different order integrals' Bodé plots are shown in Figure 8–16.

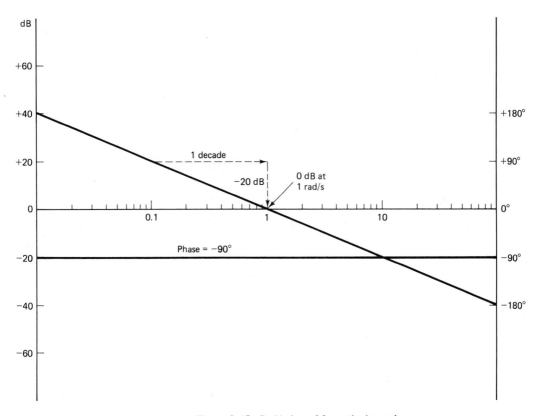

Figure 8–15   Bodé plots of first-order integral.

8–3.5 Lead

An element that is said to have a *lead* transfer function is of the form

$$(1 + \tau s)^n$$

where τ is the element's time constant and n is the order of the element.

The Bodé plot of a first-order lead element is shown in Figure 8–17. Since the Laplace variable, s, is in the numerator, the gain plot rises at a rate of 20 dB/decade. There is, at least eventually, a $+90°$ phase shift. The curves, however, are not simple straight lines. For the gain Bodé plot, the curve follows the 0-dB axis. As the critical frequency is approached, the curve begins to rise, nonlinearly at first, but eventually at 20 dB/decade. The critical frequency, ω_c, is set by the element's time constant:

$$\omega_c = \frac{1}{\tau}$$

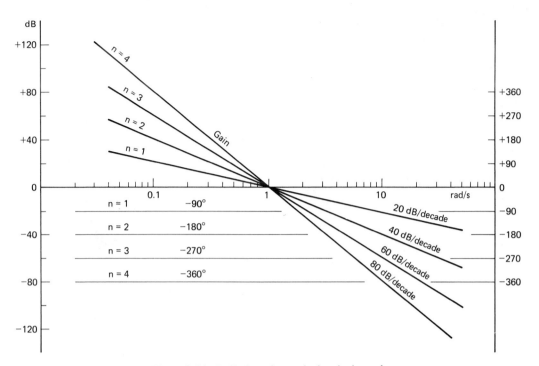

Figure 8–16 Bodé plots of general nth-order integral.

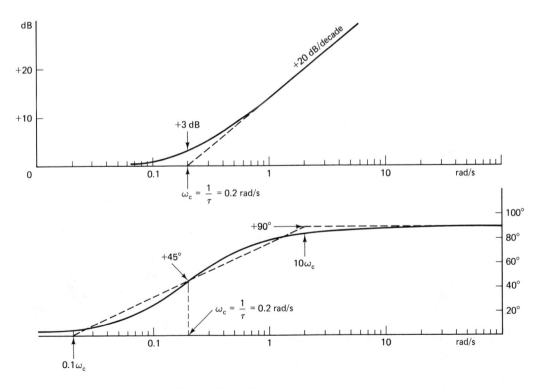

Figure 8–17 Bodé plots for first-order lead.

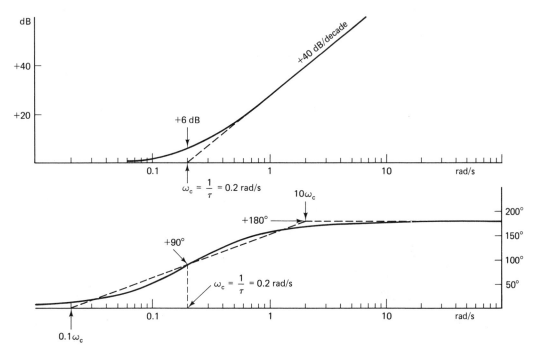

Figure 8–18   Bodé plots for second-order lead.

In Figure 8–17 the time constant is 5 s, setting the critical frequency to 0.2 rad/s. For the first-order lead element, the actual gain is at 3 dB at the critical frequency.

To simplify sketching the Bodé plot, you can draw a straight line, beginning at the critical frequency and rising at 20 dB/decade. The actual gain plot is 3 dB above this line at the critical frequency. At half the critical frequency, the actual gain is about 1 dB. At twice the critical frequency, the actual gain is about 1 dB above the straight 20-dB/decade line.

The phase shift of a first-order lead can also be sketched with the help of the critical frequency and a straight line. At the critical frequency, the phase is shifted 45°. At $0.1\omega_c$ the phase shift is 0°. At $10\omega_c$ the phase shift is complete at 90°. Above $10\omega_c$ the phase shift is essentially constant.

Now look at Figure 8–18. It is the Bodé plot of a second-order lead. It looks very similar to the plots for a first-order lead. The critical frequency is determined the same way. The rise of the gain plot is 40 dB/decade, not 20 dB/decade. The eventual phase shift is 180°, not 90°.

Now look at Figure 8–19. It is the Bodé plot of a third-order lead. It looks very similar to the plots for a first-order lead, too. The critical frequency is determined the same way. The rise of the gain plot is 60 dB/decade, not 20 dB/decade. The eventual phase shift is 270°, not 90°. Table 8–2 indicates the numerical differences among various order lead Bodé plots.

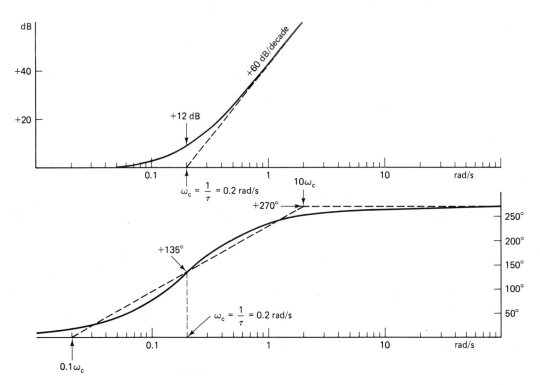

Figure 8–19 Bodé plots for third-order lead.

8–3.6 Lag

An element that is said to have a *lag* transfer function is of the form

$$\frac{1}{(1 + \tau s)^n}$$

where τ is the element's time constant and n is the order of the element.

The Bodé plot of a first-order lag element is shown in Figure 8–20. Since the Laplace variable, s, is in the denominator, the gain plot falls at a rate of -20 dB/ decade. There is, at least eventually, a $-90°$ phase shift. The curves, however, are not simple straight lines. For the gain Bodé plot, the curve follows the 0-dB axis. As the critical frequency is approached, the curve begins to fall, nonlinearly at first, but eventually at -20 dB/decade. The critical frequency, ω_c, is set by the element's time constant:

$$\omega_c = \frac{1}{\tau}$$

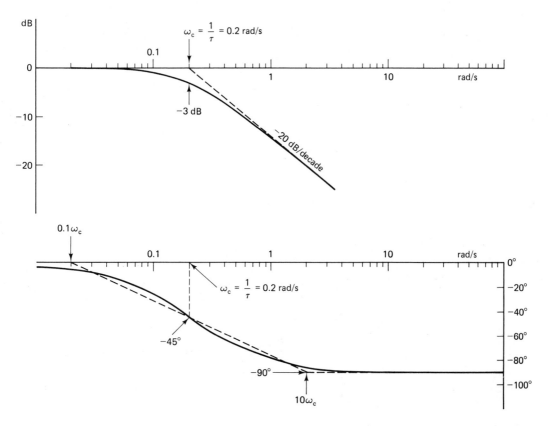

Figure 8–20 Bodé plots for first-order lag.

TABLE 8–2 CONSTANTS FOR LEAD ELEMENTS' BODE PLOTS

	Order			
	1	2	3	n
Gain at $0.5\omega_c$	1	2	3	n
Gain at ω_c	3	6	9	3n
Gain at $2\omega_c$ above slope	1	2	3	n
Phase at ω_c	45°	90°	135°	$n \times 45°$
Phase at $10\omega_c$	90°	180°	270°	$n \times 90°$

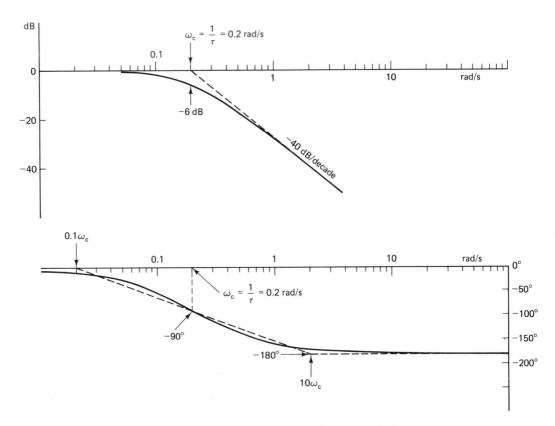

Figure 8–21　Bodé plots for second-order lag.

The phase shift of a first-order lag can also be sketched with the help of the critical frequency and a straight line. At the critical frequency, the phase is shifted $-45°$. At $0.1\omega_c$ the phase shift is $0°$. At $10\omega_c$ the phase shift is complete at $-90°$. Above $10\omega_c$ the phase shift is essentially constant.

These plots are fully complementary to the lead elements' Bodé plots you saw in Figures 8–17 through 8–19. The lead elements boost gain as frequency goes up, and the phase is shifted positively. The lag elements cut the gain as the frequency rises. The phase is shifted negatively. The Bodé plots for second- and third-order lag elements are given in Figures 8–21 and 8–22. Compare these to the first-order lag in Figure 8–20 and the lead elements' plots in Figures 8–17 through 8–19. In fact, the constants in Table 8–2 can be applied to lag elements. Just keep in mind that the lag element cuts gain and shifts the phase negative.

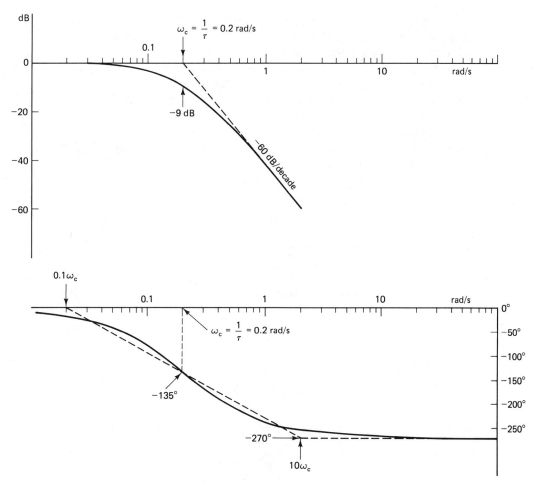

Figure 8–22 Bodé plots for third-order lag.

8–3.7 Second-Order Lag, Underdamped

The transfer function for a second-order lag element can be written in the form

$$\frac{A_0 \omega_n^2}{s^2 + 2\zeta\omega_n s + \omega_n^2}$$

where A_0 = steady-state gain
ζ = damping coefficient
ω_n = resonance frequency, rad/sec

For $\zeta \geq 1$ the denominator can be factored in two *real* terms. These you can then treat as separate first-order lag elements. Their Bodé plots can be drawn according to the procedures described in Section 8–3.6.

However, for $\zeta < 1$, the factors of the denominator are complex, having imaginary parts. This means that the element is underdamped.

The Bodé gain plots for a collection of second-order underdamped elements is given in Figure 8–23. There are several lines, each for a different damping coefficient. The horizontal, frequency, axis has been normalized. That is, it has been divided by the resonant frequency, ω_n. So to scale this axis in terms of frequency (either hertz or rad/s), simply multiply every point by ω_n.

The vertical axis has also been normalized. The actual gain is

$$db_{actual} = 20 \log A_0$$

To obtain the actual Bodé plot from Figure 8–23, you must calculate the dB_{actual} and *add* this value to each point on the vertical axis.

There are several other items to consider. Damping coefficients below 0.707 causes the gain Bodé plot to peak up near the resonant frequency. The lower the damping

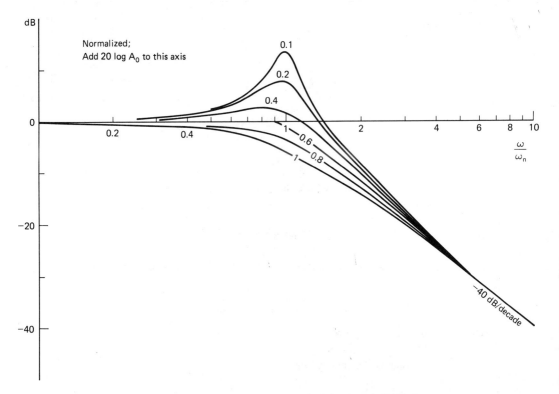

Figure 8–23 Normalized second-order gain Bodé plots.

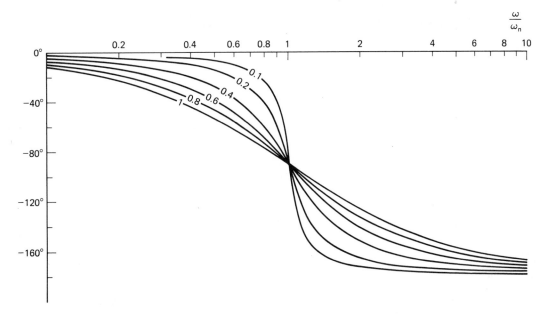

Figure 8–24 Normalized second-order phase Bodé plots.

coefficient, the higher the peak becomes. However, at two octaves above the resonant frequency ($\omega_n \times 4$) the gain rolls off at -40 dB/decade, regardless of the damping coefficient. Similarly, at two octaves below the resonant frequency ($\omega_n/4$) the gain is flat, regardless of the damping coefficient. The damping coefficient affects the gain Bodé plot only within 2 octaves below and above the resonant frequency.

The phase Bodé plots for second-order underdamped elements are shown in Figure 8–24. As with the gain Bodé plots, the horizontal axis has been normalized. To obtain a denormalized plot, multiply the horizontal axis scale by ω_n. Since these plots are all second order, they share several characteristics. First, at the resonant frequency (1 on the normalized plot) *all* plots pass through $-90°$. At $0.1\omega_n$ the plots are approaching zero phase shift. At $10\omega_n$ the plots are approaching $-180°$. The initial and final flatness and the steepness of the plot as it crosses $-90°$ are determined by the damping coefficient.

EXAMPLE 8–6

Draw the Bodé plots for a negative-feedback system consisting of an element under control, second-order lag, underdamped:

$$A_0 = 1.25$$

$$\zeta = 0.4$$

$$\omega_n = 4 \text{ rad/s}$$

Controller proportional with a series low-pass filter:

$$K_p = 10$$

$$A_{filter} = 2$$

$$\omega_{filter} = 3 \text{ rad/s}$$

Solution   The transfer function for the element under control is

$$G = \frac{20}{s^2 + 3.2s + 16}$$

For the controller

$$H = K_p \times \frac{A_{filter}}{s + \omega_{filter}}$$

$$= \frac{20}{s + 3}$$

This is a first-order lag. However, it is in the wrong form. First-order lag elements should be in the form

$$H = \frac{A}{1 + \tau s}$$

To put the controller equation into this form, 3 must be factored out.

$$H = \frac{20}{3(1 + 0.33s)}$$

This gives

$$H = \frac{6.7}{1 + 0.33s}$$

So the overall transfer function that you have to plot is

$$G \times H = \frac{20}{s^2 + 3.2s + 16} \times \frac{6.7}{1 + 0.33s}$$

Now look at the top of Figure 8–25. It is the gain Bodé plot for this example. The constant term 6.7 is plotted as a straight line.

$$dB = 20 \log (6.7) = 16.5 \text{ dB}$$

The first-order lag starts as a straight line along the 0-dB axis. At the critical frequency, ω_c, it breaks and falls at a rate of -20 dB/decade.

$$\omega_c = \frac{1}{\tau}$$

$$= \frac{1}{0.33} = 3 \text{ rad/s}$$

Although the actual curve is a little off of these straight lines, generally the straight-line approximations are accurate enough.

The second-order element must come from denormalizing the curve in Figure 8–23. You denormalize the vertical axis by adding

$$dB = 20 \log A_0 = 20 \log 1.25 = 1.9 \text{ dB}$$

So, at low frequencies, the 0.4 damping coefficient curve starts at 1.9 dB. It peaks up to above 4.5 dB before beginning to fall. To denormalize the frequency

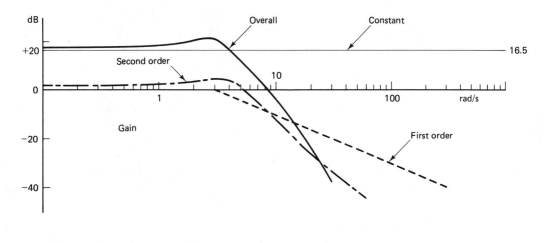

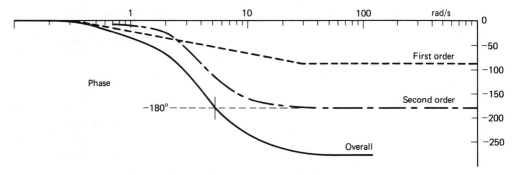

Figure 8–25   Bodé plots (Example 8–6).

axis, you must multiply the horizontal coordinate by ω_n, 4 rad/s. Several points were picked from Figure 8–23, denormalized, and plotted on Figure 8–25. The second-order lag term was then sketched in.

The phase plots are shown in the lower half of Figure 8–25. The constant term presents no shift in phase. The first-order lag element causes a $-45°$ shift at ω_c. At $0.1\omega_c$ the shift is $0°$. At $10\omega_c$ the shift is $-90°$. The second-order element's phase starts at $0°$, passes through $-90°$ at ω_n, and ends at $-180°$. These points are sketched in from Figure 8–24. The overall phase shift is a point-by-point summation of these curves.

8–3.8 Gain and Phase Margins

Gain margin and phase margin give a quantitative measure of how stable or unstable a negative-feedback system is. To determine gain margin the point of interest is the frequency which causes the phase to shift $\pm180°$. At that frequency the gain margin is the distance that the overall gain is *below* the 0-dB axis. The farther below the 0-dB axis the gain is, the larger the gain margin is, and the more stably the negative-feedback system will behave. It is not at all unusual to find gain margin as one of the major specifications in a negative-feedback-system design.

Of course, if there is more than 0-dB gain at the frequency which causes the phase to be shifted $\pm180°$, the negative-feedback system will be unstable. Look carefully at Figure 8–26. This is an expansion of the middle two decades of Figure 8–25, the Bodé plots for Example 8–6. The phase passes through $-180°$ at about 5.3 rad/s. Projecting this frequency up to the gain plot, you can see that there is a gain of about $+10$ dB. This negative-feedback-system example will be unstable. To assure stable operation, the overall gain must be dropped at least 10 dB. To provide a 15-dB gain margin, you must reduce the overall gain by 25 dB. This can be done by lowering the gain in the low-pass filter to 1 (0 dB) and dropping the proportional controller's gain.

To determine phase margin, first find the frequency at which the overall gain has dropped to 0 dB. In Figure 8–26 this is approximately 8.5 rad/s. Project this frequency onto the phase plot. At that frequency, determine the distance between the overall phase shift and $\pm180°$. If the overall phase has not yet shifted $180°$, the remaining distance is the phase margin. If there has been more than $180°$ phase shift, the negative feedback system is unstable.

For the system plotted in Figure 8–26, at 8.5 rad/s, there is a $-220°$ shift. The negative-feedback system is unstable. The phase has shifted $40°$ beyond what is necessary to assure stable operation. This conclusion is consistent with the gain margin analysis, which also predicted instability. To make this system stable, you must reduce the phase shift at 8.5 rad/s by at least $40°$. To provide a $15°$ phase margin, the phase shift must be lowered by $55°$, making it $165°$ at 8.5 rad/s.

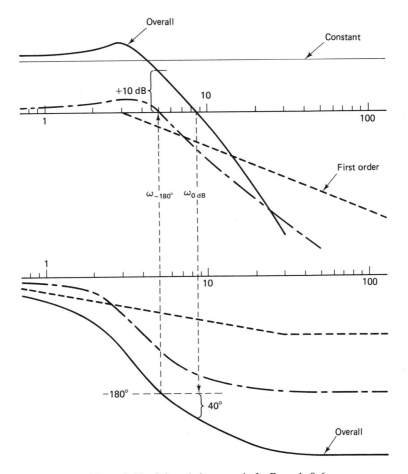

Figure 8–26   Gain and phase margin for Example 8–6.

EXAMPLE 8–7

Determine the stability, gain margin, and phase margin of the negative feedback system in Example 8–6, if the low-pass filter in the controller is altered to have

$$A_{\text{filter}} = 1 \qquad \omega_{\text{filter}} = 8 \text{ rad/s}$$

Solution   The transfer function for the element under control is

$$G = \frac{20}{s^2 + 3.2s + 16}$$

For the controller

$$H = K_p \times \frac{A_{\text{filter}}}{s + \omega_{\text{filter}}}$$

$$= \frac{10}{s + 8}$$

This is a first-order lag. However, it is in the wrong form. First-order lag elements should be in the form

$$H = \frac{A}{1 + \tau s}$$

To put the controller equation into this form, 8 must be factored out.

$$H = \frac{10}{8(1 + 0.125s)}$$

This gives

$$H = \frac{1.25}{1 + 0.125s}$$

So the overall transfer function that you have to plot is

$$G \times H = \frac{20}{s^2 + 3.2s + 16} \times \frac{1.25}{1 + 0.125s}$$

Now look at the top of Figure 8–27. It is the gain Bodé plot for this example. The constant term 1.25 is plotted as a straight line.

$$dB = 20 \log (1.25) = 1.9 \text{ dB}$$

The first-order lag starts as a straight line along the 0-dB axis. At the critical frequency, ω_c, it breaks and falls at a rate of -20 dB/decade.

$$\omega_c = \frac{1}{\tau}$$

$$= \frac{1}{0.125} = 8 \text{ rad/s}$$

Although the actual curve is a little off of these straight lines, generally the straight-line approximations are accurate enough.

The second-order element has not changed at all, so it is copied directly from Figure 8–25. The overall gain plot is the point-by-point summation of these three curves. As compared to the overall gain plot in Figure 8–25, it has the same shape but a lower amplitude.

The phase plots are shown in the lower half of Figure 8–27. The constant term presents no shift in phase. The first-order lag element causes a $-45°$ shift at ω_c. At $0.1\omega_c$ the shift is $0°$. At $10\omega_c$ the shift is $-90°$. The second-order element's phase starts at $0°$, passes through $-90°$ at ω_n, and ends at $-180°$. These points are sketched in from Figure 8–24.

The overall phase plot is a point-by-point summation of these curves. As compared to the phase plot of Figure 8–25, it has the same general shape but is not as steep, and is shifted to the right (higher frequencies).

Now it is time to determine the gain margin. First, you must find the frequency at which the phase passes through $-180°$. From the Figure 8–27 phase plot, this is at 7 rad/s. Now look at the gain plot, 7 rad/s. The overall gain is below the 0-dB axis! This modified negative feedback system will be stable. The gain margin is the distance between the overall gain plot and the 0-dB axis. It is about 3 dB.

To determine the phase margin, find the frequency at which the overall gain falls to 0 dB. From Figure 8–27 that is 6 rad/s. Project this frequency down to the phase plot. At that frequency the distance from the overall phase shift down to $-180°$ is the phase margin. The phase margin is about $15°$.

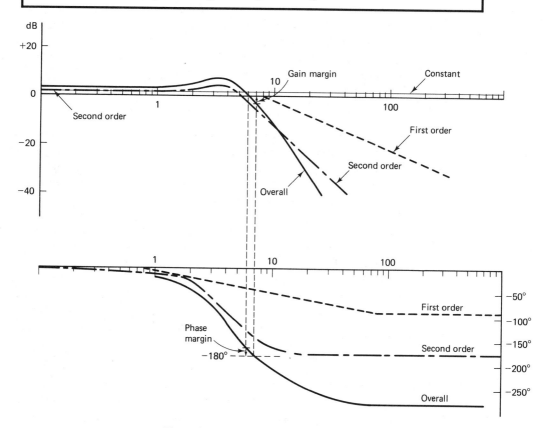

Figure 8–27   Bodé plots (Example 8–7).

8–4 CONTROLLER TUNING

There are two approaches to determining the transfer function for the controller in a negative-feedback system. The first technique allows you to calculate the controller's transfer function directly. You must know the transfer function of the element under control accurately, $G(s)$. Then you must define the output desired, $V_{out}(s)$, for a given input, $V_{in}(s)$. With this information you can calculate the required transfer function of the controller, $H(s)$.

$$\frac{V_{out}}{V_{in}} = \frac{G(s) \times H(s)}{1 + G(s) \times H(s)}$$

Solving this equation for $H(s)$ yields

$$H(s) = \frac{V_{out}/V_{in}}{G(s)(1 - V_{out}/V_{in})}$$

In fact, matrix operations can be set up to calculate the controller's transfer function in response to a combination of input stimuli.

To be able to select the controller's transfer function this way requires that you know the transfer function of the element under control. For servo loops (such as in robotics or military aeronautics) the element is often that well defined, or is worth spending the time to define rigorously. Second, the response to the *specified* input is assured. However, how the closed-loop system responds to other types of inputs is not guaranteed. Thorough testing and simulation is in order to assure that the output will at least be acceptable for all practical types of inputs.

Rarely are manufacturing processes so neatly defined. It is unusual to have an accurate transfer function for an element you want to control. Even if you do know its transfer function today, its behavior may change significantly with time, temperature, humidity, and so on. Custom designing a controller for each of the hundreds of controlled loops in a manufacturing plant is undesirable, even if it could be done. Maintenance, calibration, and spare parts would be unmanageable.

What is needed is a generic controller that has the potential to work acceptably in almost all applications. This is the three-mode, or PID, controller. You can stock a very limited number of models and still be able to cover most of the controller requirements for a plant. It will do a good job at controlling most traditional process loops if its three constants are properly selected. This procedure of selecting the controller's constants is called tuning. In the worst case you may need to retune the controller periodically. Microprocessor-based controllers have the ability to receive new constants from a supervisory computer, to tune themselves upon command, or to retune themselves continuously.

8–4.1 Tuning with the Bodé Plot

During the initial configuration of the control loop you may sketch a Bodé plot of the system's open-loop [$G(s) \times H(s)$] frequency characteristics. The primary reason for this analysis is to assure that when you power the real system up, as a closed loop, it will behave stably.

In Section 8–3 you saw how to use the gain margin or the phase margin to predict this stability. But how much gain margin or phase margin must you have to provide *good* control? The standard answer is that a gain margin of 6 dB or a phase margin of 40° produces a slightly underdamped closed-loop system.

$$\text{gain margin} \geq 6 \text{ dB}$$
$$\text{phase margin} \geq 40°$$

The greater the gain or phase margin, the more stably, but more slowly, the closed-loop system will respond.

To achieve the margin desired, you must alter the constants in the controller, $H(s)$. This is simplest for a proportional controller. Its transfer function is

$$H(s)_{\text{proportional}} = K_p$$

The proportional controller provides a constant gain, independent of frequency. Its phase shift is 0°. So the composite open-loop Bodé gain can be shifted up or down by proportionally changing the controller's gain. The phase plot will not be affected.

Have care when adjusting the controller's gain based solely on the Bodé plots. Lowering the gain K_p certainly will make the closed loop more stable. However, residual error gets worse as the proportional controller's gain goes down. With a low proportional gain the process variable will settle at some place different from the set point. Picking a large gain (low gain margin) reduces this residual error but also causes problems not predicted by the Bodé plots. As the proportional controller's gain goes up, its proportional band gets narrower. Errors outside the proportional band drive the controller either hard on or hard off. Bodé plots, based on Laplace transforms, assume a linear unbounded system. Even though the Bodé plot may predict a stable system (with no oscillations), any significant error may cause the controller to jump back and forth across a narrow proportional band. The actuator is driven from stop to stop. This is limit cycling, unpredictable by the Bodé plots, but caused by the narrow band (high gain) of the proportional controller.

The integral function is added to the proportional controller to eliminate residual error. The transfer function of a proportional–integral controller is

$$H(s) = \frac{K_p(s + K_i)}{s}$$

where K_p is the proportional controller gain and K_i is the integral constant in resets/s or resets/min. Arranging this in a form more convenient for Bodé plots, we have

$$H(s) = \frac{(K_p/T_i)(1 + T_i s)}{s}$$

where T_i is the integral time,

$$T_i = \frac{1}{K_i}$$

With the proportional–integral controller the Bodé plot has gotten a bit more complicated. Look at Figure 8–28a. It is the Bodé plots of a proportional–integral controller

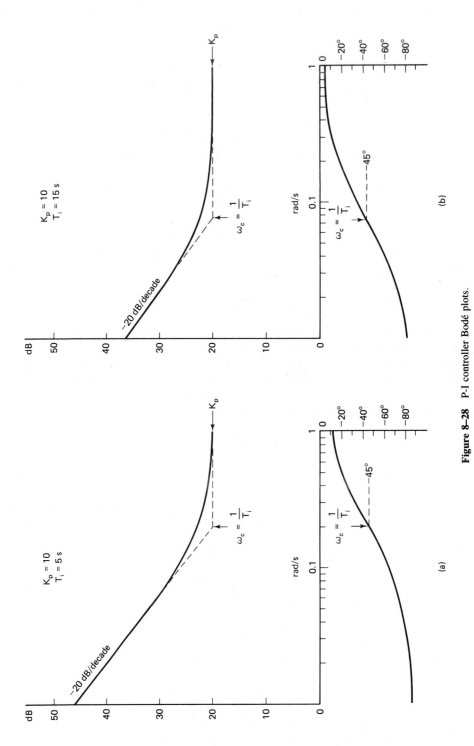

Figure 8-28 P-I controller Bodé plots.

with $K_p = 10$ and $T_i = 5$ s. The ultimate gain is set only by K_p. So changing K_p of the P-I controller in your closed loop will shift its overall open-loop Bodé plot proportionally up or down.

However, there is a low-frequency boost, caused by the integral term. It is this increased gain at low frequencies that assures that a P-I controller will eliminate the residual error and still have a chance of being stable.

The first-order lead term $(1 + T_i s)$ produces the break in the gain plot. That break occurs at

$$\omega_c = \frac{1}{T_i}$$

or

$$\omega_c = K_i$$

Below this break (critical) frequency, the gain is falling at -20 dB/decade. Above, the gain has settled at K_p. Also, at the break frequency, the phase has been shifted by $-45°$. Below, the shift slopes to $-90°$, and goes to $0°$ about one decade above ω_c.

So how do you use this information to choose a value for K_p and K_i? The problem with the proportional controller alone is that it exhibits residual error. The constant K_p is usually adjusted as high as possible while still providing 6-dB gain margin. This reduces the residual error. However, since the low-frequency boost of the integral part of the P-I controller will eliminate the residual error, you can drop K_p, to assure better gain margin.

Well above the P-I controller's break frequency (K_i), the controller's gain is set solely by K_p. This indicates that the P-I controller's break frequency should be set considerably below the frequency at which the gain margin is determined. This way, the boosting effect of the integral part of the controller will not affect the gain at the frequency where the gain margin is determined.

Also, notice that the integral part of the P-I controller shifts the phase negatively. This hurts you, forcing the frequency at which the total frequency shift is $-180°$ to a lower value. At lower frequencies there is more gain, narrowing the gain margin. However, at a decade above the P-I controller's break frequency (K_i) the shift across the controller is almost back to zero. This, too, suggests that the controller's break frequency (which is also the integral constant) should be set at one decade below the frequency that would otherwise cause the phase to be shifted $-180°$.

Proportional–Integral Controller Constants

K_p *slightly below that value needed to assure 6-dB gain margin without the integral portion of the controller*

K_i $= 1/T_i = $ *integral's break frequency set to* $0.1\omega_{-180°}$

where $\omega_{-180°}$ is the frequency at which the phase shift of the open loop (excluding the integral controller) goes to $-180°$

EXAMPLE 8-8

For the system described in Example 8–7, determine the controller settings if a P-I controller were to be used.

Solution   From the solution of Example 8–7, and Figure 8–27, the gain margin is only 3 dB. This is too close to instability for comfort. To provide a little room for error, drop the overall gain another 6 dB. This should give a 9-dB margin.

$$\text{ratio} = \text{antilog} \frac{-6\,\text{dB}}{20} = 0.5$$

The controller's proportional gain should be reduced by 0.5 to yield a 9-dB gain margin. Since the original proportional controller had a gain of 10, set

$$K_p = 5$$

The frequency at which the phase is shifted $-180°$ is 7 rad/s. This is where the gain margin is taken.

$$\omega_{-180°} = 7 \text{ rad/s}$$

Set the integral's break frequency one decade below that.

$$K_i = 0.7/\text{s} \qquad 0.7 \text{ reset/s} = 42 \text{ resets/min}$$

This means that the integral time is

$$T_i = \frac{1}{K_i}$$
$$= 1.42 \text{ s} = 0.024 \text{ min}$$

Of course, these values must be treated as initial settings. Further adjustment once the loop is closed and running is certainly in order.

Derivative is added to the proportional–integral controller to improve both speed and stability. Its transfer function is

$$\text{simple PID} = \frac{K_d s^2 + K_p s + K_i}{s}$$

Actually, this form is impractical. The derivative element causes the gain to increase without bound as frequency goes up (look at Figure 8–13). This gives high-frequency noise too much gain. Practical PID controllers limit this high-frequency gain with a first-order lag element (low-pass filter). The time constant of this filter is usually set to about one-tenth of the derivative time.

$$\text{practical PID} = \frac{K_d s^2 + K_p s + K_i}{s\,(1 + 0.1 K_d s)}$$

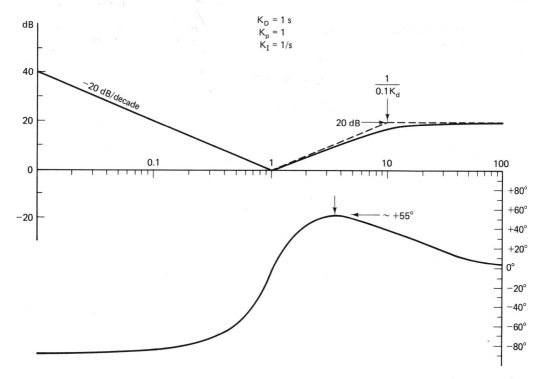

Figure 8-29   PID controller Bodé plots.

The Bodé plot for a PID controller is shown in Figure 8-29. All three constants have been set to 1. The low-frequency response looks just like the proportional–integral Bodé plots, with a -20-dB/decade rolloff and a phase shift which begins at -90° and then shifts toward zero. The derivative element has a critical frequency at

$$\omega_d = \frac{1}{K_d}$$

At that frequency, the derivative term drives the gain plot upward at a slope of +20 dB/decade. This continues for one decade. The high-frequency limiter term $1/(1 + 0.1\ K_d s)$ then comes into play, canceling the derivative roll-up. The gain levels off at +20 dB. Phase is shifted positively by the derivative term, about 55°, before being driven back to zero by the high-frequency limiter term.

The boost in high-frequency gain improves the speed of a loop controlled by a PID controller. The positive phase shift cancels some of the shift toward -180° produced by $G(s)$, filters, and the integral controller. This improves the phase margin.

The exact frequency where the phase peaks, and the size of the peak, depend, in part, on the value of K_d and the fact that the high-frequency limiter's frequency has been set to $1/(0.1K_d)$. This combination of values places the phase peak at the geometric mean of the derivative's critical frequency ($1/K_d$) and the high-frequency limiter's frequency.

$$\text{phase peak's frequency} = \frac{3.16}{K_d}$$

To tune the derivative part of the PID controller, set this phase peak at the frequency that would have caused $-180°$ phase shift (where you measure the gain margin) if the derivative controller had not been used. Don't forget that the derivative term is going to add gain at and above this frequency, so you may need to lower K_p to compensate. Set K_d so that

$$\omega_{-180°} = \frac{3.16}{K_d}$$

Actually, this is a rather simplistic approach. It seems to work fine for a PID controller with all three constants set to 1 (Figure 8–29). However, the PID controller has a second-order lead element, a gain term, a first-order lag element, and an integral term. How the three constants affect the steady-state gain, damping and resonant frequency of the second-order term, as well as the overall PID Bodé plot is rather involved.

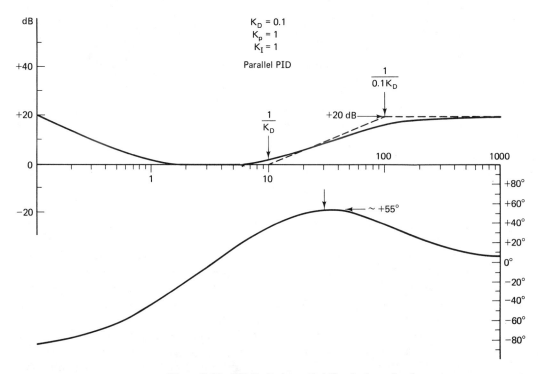

Figure 8–30   PID Bodé plots with $1/K_d$ raised one decade.

Figure 8–30 is the Bodé plot of a PID controller with K_d lowered to 0.1 s. The other two constants have been left at 1. The entire graph has been shifted one decade higher in frequency. Otherwise, there seems to be little difference between this plot and Figure 8–29, with K_d set to 1 s. This certainly makes sense. However, raising K_d lowers the derivative's critical frequency. The derivative term of the PID controller begins to interact with the low-frequency boost of the integral element. Figure 8–31 shows the Bodé plots of the same PID controller with K_d raised to 10. This lowers the derivative's critical frequency to 0.1 rad/s. The phase is still boosted but only by about 45°. Although this boost happens within one decade above $1/K_d$, it is not at the predicted frequency.

The point to all of this is that interaction between elements within the PID controller may produce rather unexpected results, depending on the controller type and how close the parameters are set to each other. In general, interaction can be minimized by keeping the derivative critical frequency ($1/K_d$) equal to or above the integral constant (K_i). A frequency analysis of your final design is a good idea, prior to implementing and running the loop. There are several programs available commercially for personal computers which will output the Bodé plots of a system, given its transfer function.

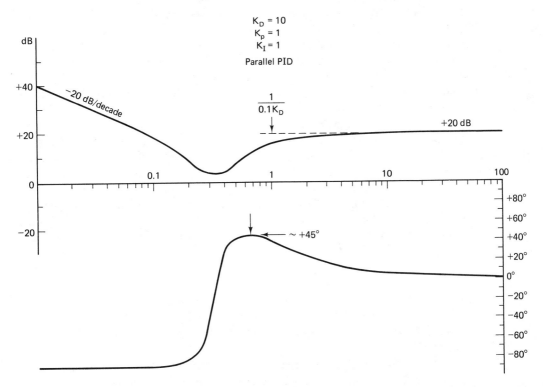

Figure 8–31 PID Bodé plots with $1/K_d$ lowered one decade.

8–4.2 Process Reaction Tuning

Tuning with Bodé plots gives you an initial setting for the controller's constants. With it you may have some confidence that the loop will behave stably when it is first brought up. But the accuracy of tuning with Bodé plots depends on having correct transfer functions for each element in the loop. Even if this were possible for most manufacturing processes (dream on!), how the equipment is installed and adjusted may vary quite a bit from the control engineer's design. What you need is a way to test the loop, as installed, and derive tuning constants from this *actual* loop performance.

Process reaction is one technique which allows you to do just that. The loop is allowed to stabilize somewhere near the middle of its operational range. The controller is switched to manual and the actuator is changed. The response of the *open* loop is plotted. From this plot tuning constants for simple proportional, proportional–integral, or PID control can be derived.

Process reaction runs the system open loop. Certainly, if you are going to run the process open loop, it must respond stably to a change in the actuator's input. That is, the process must be self-regulating. The element under control is modeled as a first-order plus dead-time process. For many process control loops this is appropriate. But the less the element actually matches this model, the poorer the accuracy of the tuning constants.

There are several advantages to process reaction tuning. You really do not need any mathematical description of the loop. In many loops an accurate transfer function may be impossible to obtain. A minimum of time and interference is required. Since the tuning data are obtained with the loop running, any efforts will disturb the production staff and will probably result in out-of-spec product. For large, high-volume manufacturing facilities, this is a major concern.

This tuning technique has several disadvantages. The element under control must be self-regulating. It must not run away when the negative feedback is removed. There are many loops that require negative feedback to operate at all. Position control and level control in a pumped tank both demand negative feedback to operate at all. Process reaction tuning cannot be used on those loops. Since the loop is measured without the controller, any nonideal performance of that controller is not considered. Finally, to the degree that the element under control does not fit the first-order-plus-dead-time model assumed, inaccurate tuning constants will result.

To perform process reaction tuning, perform the following steps:

1. First assure that the process variable (PV) and the controller output (CO) are expressed in percent full-scale output. This may be the normal mode of operation for the controller. Otherwise, some measurements may be necessary before going any further.

2. Monitor the controller output and the process variable with an instrument that is fast enough to catch and expand a step change in the process variable but has enough storage ability to hold all of the data as the process variable rises. For a

process, this may be a strip-chart recorder or *X-Y* plotter. A servo loop may require a digital storage scope. Be suspicious of data on a process variable reported by a supervisory computer over a network. This monitoring system may not respond fast enough to give you all of the points needed.

3. Alter the set point in the closed-loop system to produce a 50% process variable. Allow the system to stabilize.

4. Change the controller's mode to manual. Assure that the process variable settles down from any bump this transfer may have created.

5. Determine the value of the controller's output (CO) in % full-scale output.

6. Step the output of the controller 10% (e.g., if CO was 45%, step it to 55%).

7. Continue recording the value of the process variable until it stabilizes. For a first-order-plus-dead-time process you will get a plot similar to the one shown in Figure 8–32.

8. You are now finished with the process, so it can be put back into the automatic control mode and returned to production.

9. On the process variable curve, draw a tangent through the inflection point (where the slope goes from increasing to decreasing). Extend it far enough to intersect the projections of the initial process variable value (point *A*) and the final process variable value (point *B*).

10. Measure the lag time *L* and the rise time *T* from the plot, as shown in Figure 8–32.

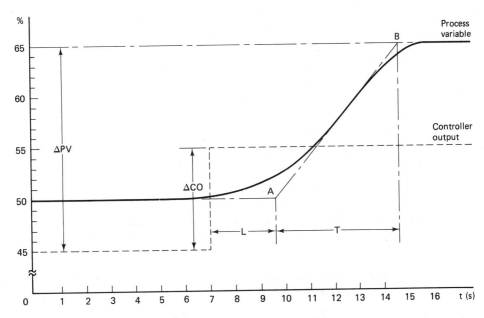

Figure 8–32 Process reaction tuning.

11. Compute the controller's constants from the following equations:
    a. Reaction rate:

$$N = \frac{\Delta PV}{T} \qquad \frac{\%}{\sec}$$

    b. Proportional controller:

$$K_p = \frac{\Delta CO}{N \times L}$$

    c. Proportional–integral controller:

$$K_p = 0.9 \times \frac{\Delta CO}{N \times L}$$

$$T_i = 3.33L$$

    d. Proportional–integral–derivative controller:

$$K_p = 1.2 \times \frac{\Delta CO}{N \times L}$$

$$T_i = 2L$$

$$K_d = 0.5L$$

Some controllers require that the proportional band be specified instead of the proportional controller's gain. Assuming that the input to the controller and its output are expressed in the same units (percent in the discussion above),

$$\text{proportional band} = \frac{100\%}{K_p}$$

Some controller designs require the integral constant.

$$K_i = \frac{1}{T_i}$$

EXAMPLE 8–9

For the element illustrated in Figure 8–32, determine the tuning constants that should be used for a PID controller.

Solution   From the process reaction in Figure 8–32, the controller output is stepped from 45% to 55% at $t = 7$ s.

$$\Delta CO = 55\% - 45\% = 10\%$$

The tangent line is drawn through the inflection point and projected up and down. It intersects the original process variable value (50%) at point A at 9.6 s.

$$L = 9.6 \text{ s} - 7 \text{ s} = 2.6 \text{ s}$$

The tangent line intersects the final process variable value (65%) at point B at 14.6 s.

$$T = 14.6 \text{ s} - 9.6 \text{ s} = 5.0 \text{ s}$$

The reaction rate is

$$N = \frac{\Delta PV}{T} = \frac{65\% - 50\%}{5.0 \text{ s}} = 3.0\%/\text{s}$$

For a PID controller, the proportional gain is

$$K_p = 1.2 \times \frac{\Delta CO}{N \times L} = \frac{1.2 \times (55\% - 45\%)}{3.0\%/\text{s} \times 2.6 \text{ s}} = 1.54$$

This gives a proportional band of

$$\text{proportional band} = \frac{100\%}{K_p} = \frac{100\%}{1.54} = 65\%$$

The integral time is

$$T_i = 2 \times L = 2 \times 2.6 \text{ s} = 5.2 \text{ s}$$

This gives an integral constant of

$$K_i = \frac{1}{T_i} = \frac{1}{5.2 \text{ s}} = 0.19/\text{s}$$

The derivative time

$$K_d = 0.5 \times L = 0.5 \times 2.6 \text{ s} = 1.3 \text{ s}$$

Process reaction tuning sets the derivative constant at $0.5 \times L$ and the integral time at $2 \times L$. Bodé plot tuning suggests that the derivative critical frequency ($1/K_d$) be kept above the integral constant K_i. If you did a Bodé plot analysis on a process reaction tuned controller, you would find that

$$\omega_d = \frac{1}{K_d} = \frac{1}{0.5 \times L} = \frac{2}{L}$$

$$K_i = \frac{1}{T_i} = \frac{1}{2 \times L} = \frac{0.5}{L}$$

or

$$\omega_d = 4 \times K_i$$

A process reaction tuned controller sets the derivative critical frequency two octaves ($\times 4$) above the integral constant. This is completely consistent with what was suggested by Bodé plot tuning.

8–4.3 Ultimate Cycle Tuning

The ultimate cycle tuning technique derives the controller's constants while the process under control is running *closed* loop. This allows you to use this method on position control systems and integral processes which could not be run open loop for process reaction tuning. Ultimate cycle tuning also provides better results in loops which are dominated by dead time [2].

The controller gain in the loop to be tuned is raised until the process variable oscillates with a steady amplitude. You must push the loop right to the edge of instability. This may be hazardous, both to equipment and to personnel. During the time that you are experimentally adjusting the controller's gain to get these stable amplitude variations in the process variable, the process may be producing out-of-spec product. The gain adjustment is trial and error. Since the speed of some processes may be measured in significant parts of an hour, ultimate cycle tuning may be a lengthy procedure, taking the loop you are tuning out of service for quite some time.

To perform an ultimate cycle tuning, perform the following:

1. Assure that the process variable is displayed in % full scale.
2. Monitor the process variable with a recording device, fast enough to follow system oscillations, but with enough storage capacity to allow you to catch and hold several cycles.
3. Establish stable control with the process variable and controller output near the middle of their ranges.
4. Lower the proportional gain and alter the integral and derivative constants to eliminate their contributions. If the controller has the proportional constant expressed as proportional band, set it to the widest % PB available. The integral constant in resets/minute should be set to zero. If integral time is used with the controller being tuned, set it to the largest value available. Set the derivative time to zero.
5. Increase the proportional gain (lower the % proportional band) until the process variable begins to oscillate. Carefully tweak the gain further to assure that those oscillations are of relatively constant amplitude. If the process variable does not break into spontaneous oscillations, you may jog the set point to cause a small perturbation in the system.
6. The ultimate gain, K_{p-u}, is the proportional gain necessary to cause steady-state oscillations in the process variable. The ultimate period, T_u, is the period of those oscillations, as recorded by the digital scope, supervisory computer, or strip-chart recorder.
7. Compute the controller's constants from the equations below.
   a. Proportional controller:

$$K_p = 0.5 \times K_{p-u}$$

b. Proportional–integral controller:

$$K_p = 0.45 \times K_{p-u}$$

$$T_i = 0.83 \times T_u$$

c. Proportional–integral–derivative controller:

$$K_p = 0.6 \times K_{p-u}$$

$$T_i = 0.5 \times T_u$$

$$K_d = 0.125 \times T_u$$

If the controller requires the % proportional band to be entered instead of the proportional gain, then as long as the process variable, set point, and controller output are expressed in %,

$$\% \text{ proportional band} = \frac{100\%}{K_p}$$

If the controller wants the integral constant (resets/s or resets/min) to be entered instead of the integral time (seconds or minutes), then

$$K_i = \frac{1}{T_i}$$

As with the process reaction tuning technique, the PID controller's derivative time (K_d) is set to one-fourth of the integral's time. Again, this sets the derivative's critical frequency two octaves ($\times$ 4) above the integral constant, consistent with the suggestions of Bodé plot tuning.

SUMMARY

The performance of a negative-feedback system depends both on the performance of each element and on how the negative feedback is applied. When you analyze a system as a process the input is considered to be the energy applied to the element under control, or disturbances applied to that element. The objective of the negative feedback is to minimize the effect of any variation of the input on the process variable. Given that the transfer function of the element under control is $G(s)$ and the electronics and controller have a transfer function of $H(s)$, the overall closed-loop transfer function for a process with negative feedback is

$$\text{process transfer function} = \frac{G}{1 + G \times H}$$

With this transfer function, a step at the input will produce a small, rapid change at the output. If proportional control alone is used, the output will settle at some small but nonzero value. This is called residual error. The larger the proportional gain, the lower the residual error. Changing the controller to proportional–integral allows the residual error to be driven to zero.

A servo system is one in which the output (process variable) should track the input (set point). Ideally, any variation on the set point will immediately be duplicated at the output of the element under control. For this type of negative-feedback system, the input is the set point, and input energy and load disturbances are considered negligible. A little looking will show you that for a servo system, the controller and the element under control are actually in series, with 100% negative feedback applied. The overall closed-loop transfer function for a servo with negative feedback is

$$\text{servo transfer function} = \frac{G \times H}{1 + G \times H}$$

With this transfer function, a step at the input will cause a rapid rise at the output, to a new level. This rise is much more rapid than the element under control would have produced by itself. If proportional control alone is used, the output cannot settle at exactly the level placed on the input. However, proportional–integral control will eliminate this residual error.

If you are interested primarily in the process variable's steady-state value, you do not actually have to transform the Laplace domain equation for the process variable back into the time domain. The final value theorem states that

$$\text{final value} = \lim_{t \to \infty} f(t) = \lim_{s \to 0} sF(s)$$

So once you have the equation for the output $[F(s)]$ you simply multiply that by s and take the limit as s goes to zero.

The stability of a negative-feedback system can be predicted using its Bodé plot. A Bodé plot consists of two frequency response plots, gain (in dB) versus frequency and phase shift versus frequency. The horizontal, frequency axis is normally plotted in radians/second on a logarithmic scale. Although a rigorous numerical analysis can be completed to determine the frequency responses, usually amplitude and phase sketches can be made directly from the transfer function's terms. Simple gain produces a constant amplitude plot and no phase shift. An nth-order derivative has a gain plot which passes through 0 dB at 1 rad/s. That line has a slope of $+n \times 20$ dB/decade. The phase shift is a constant $+n \times 90°$. The nth-order integral is the inverse of the derivative. Its gain plot also passes through 0 dB at 1 rad/s. The line's slope is $-n \times 20$ dB/decade, sloping downward as frequency increases. The nth-order integrator shifts the phase a constant $-n \times 90°$.

An nth-order lead is of the form

$$(1 + \tau s)^n$$

Its gain plot follows the horizontal axis until it reaches the critical frequency, ω_c.

$$\omega_c = \frac{1}{\tau}$$

At the critical frequency, the gain plot breaks and rises at a $+n \times 20$ dB/decade rate. The phase shift for an nth-order lead is at $0°$ at $0.1\omega_c$, $+n \times 45°$ at ω_c and levels off at $+n \times 90°$ at $10\omega_c$.

The nth-order lag is the complement of the lead. The term is in the denominator. The gain plot breaks at the critical frequency and falls as frequency increases. The phase shift is negative.

A second-order underdamped lag term requires a little more work. The steady-state gain is

$$\text{steady-state gain} = \frac{A_0}{\omega_n^2}$$

At two octaves below the resonant frequency ($\omega_n/4$) the gain is level at the steady-state gain and independent of the damping coefficient. At two octaves above the resonant frequency ($\omega_n \times 4$) the gain falls off at -40 dB/decade, also independent of the damping coefficient. However, near ω_n, the gain peaks up for values of $\zeta < 0.707$; the smaller ζ is, the higher the gain's peak. All of the phase plots pass through $-90°$ at ω_n. Large values of damping cause the phase to shift relatively linearly. Lower damping produces a flat phase shift away from ω_n, with a steep drop through $-90°$ at ω_n.

Once you have plotted each gain and phase curve for each term in the open-loop transfer function $G(s) \times H(s)$, the overall Bodé gain plot is produced by adding the gain plots point by point. The same is done to get the overall phase plot.

Gain margin is measured at the frequency which causes a $180°$ phase shift. If there is less than 0 dB gain at that frequency, the system is stable. Adequate gain does not exist for oscillations to be self-sustaining. The distance below the 0-dB axis the gain plot falls at the $180°$ phase frequency is the gain margin. The phase margin is measured at the frequency that causes the gain to drop to 0 dB. If there has not been $180°$ phase shift, the system will be stable. The distance down from the phase shift plot to $-180°$ at the 0-dB frequency is the phase margin.

If you know the transfer function for every element in a system precisely and can define the response you want for a particular stimulus, the transfer function for the controller can be derived. The response of the system to other inputs is not guaranteed. Also, it is rare to know the total system transfer function accurately for a manufacturing system. So, although optimum control is possible, it is not practical for most manufacturing systems.

Instead, a generic controller is used. Its constants can be adjusted well enough to provide adequate control of most loops found in a plant. There are three ways to adjust these parameters. Bodé plot tuning involves adjusting the proportional gain, integral time, and derivative time to provide at least a 6-dB gain margin or a $40°$ phase margin. The proportional gain shifts the gain plot up or down without affecting the phase plot. Lower this gain makes the closed-loop system more stable, but increases the residual error.

Residual error is tweaked out with the integral part of the controller. It provides an integral term which boosts low-frequency gain. This eliminates the residual error. There is a first-order lead term in the integral part of the controller. As frequency increases, this term cancels the drop in gain of the integral, allowing the gain plot to level off at K_p. At the integrator's critical frequency,

$$\omega_c = \frac{1}{T_i} = K_i$$

the phase is shifted $-45°$. At lower frequencies it shifts toward $-90°$.

So, how do you choose a value for K_p and K_i? Set K_p slightly below that value needed to assure 6-dB gain margin without the integral portion of the controller. Set K_i to $0.1 \times \omega_{-180°}$ (where $\omega_{-180°}$ is that frequency at which the phase shift of the open-loop controller without the integral term produces a $-180°$ phase shift). This assures that the negative phase shift of the integral term does not seriously affect $\omega_{-180°}$, where the gain margin is determined.

Adding derivative to the proportional–integral controller causes the gain to boost as frequency increases. To some degree this is desirable to improve the transient response of the system. However, too much high-frequency gain will make any system unstable because of high-frequency noise. A limiter is usually added in practical PID controllers. It is a first-order lag term, set to come into play at $1/(0.1 \times K_d)$. This cancels the roll-up of the derivative and sets the high-frequency gain at 20 dB (ratio gain of 10).

The derivative critical frequency is

$$\omega_c = \frac{1}{K_d}$$

This sets the frequency where the gain boost begins. In addition to boosting the gain, the derivative term also shifts the phase positively. This improves the phase margin by canceling some of the shift toward $-180°$ caused by the process and the integral controller. This shift peaks at about $+55°$ and then drops back to $0°$. The precise location of this peak depends on the type PID controller you have and the setting of the integral constant. When the integral critical frequency is below the derivative critical frequency, the phase peak occurs at

$$\frac{3.16}{K_d}$$

To tune the derivative part of the PID controller, set this phase peak at the frequency that would have caused $-180°$ phase shift if the derivative controller had not been used.

Process reaction tuning allows you to derive the controller parameters from a quick open-loop dynamic response test. This makes the measurement simple, removes the loop from production a minimum of time, and consequently, produces a minimum of out-of-spec product. However, the loop must be able to run stably open loop. It must be inherently self-regulating. This eliminates position servo loops and integral processes. Also processes with long dead times cannot be well tuned with the process reaction tuning technique.

To accomplish process reaction tuning, first assure that the controller output and the process variable are expressed in % FSO. Monitor each on an appropriate recorder. While in manual mode, step the controller output (CO) about 10%. The plot of the process variable's response should be "S" shaped. Draw a tangent that runs through the inflection point of this curve, projecting it until it intersects both the previous and the final values of the process variable. The lag, L, is the time from the controller output step to the lower intersection. The rise time, T, is the time from that intersection to the tangent's intersect with the final process variable value.

Reaction rate:

$$N = \frac{\Delta PV}{T}$$

Proportional controller:

$$K_p = \frac{\Delta CO}{N \times L}$$

Proportional–integral controller:

$$K_p = 0.9 \times \frac{\Delta CO}{N \times L}$$

$$T_i = 3.33L$$

Proportional–integral–derivative controller:

$$K_p = 1.2 \times \frac{\Delta CO}{N \times L}$$

$$T_i = 2L$$

$$K_d = 0.5L$$

If your controller requires either proportional band or K_i, then

$$\text{proportional band} = \frac{100\%}{K_p}$$

$$K_i = \frac{1}{T_i}$$

With ultimate cycle tuning you can obtain adequate controller parameters for most processes. The loop is tested while closed, so position control, integral processes, and other non-self-regulating elements can be evaluated. However, the controller must be adjusted to the point of loop instability. This may be quite hazardous, take the loop out of production for a long time, and produce out-of-spec product.

As with the process reaction technique, the process variable value must be recorded in % FSO. Begin by setting the parameters as ineffectively as possible. Slowly increase the proportional gain until the process variable oscillates with a steady amplitude. You may have to jog the set point to begin the oscillations. The value of the proportional gain that causes steady amplitude oscillations is called K_{p-u}. The period of these oscillations is T_u.

Proportional controller:

$$K_p = 0.5 \times K_{p-u}$$

Proportional–integral controller:

$$K_p = 0.45 \times K_{p-u}$$

$$T_i = 0.83 \times T_u$$

Proportional–integral–derivative controller:

$$K_p = 0.6 \times K_{p-u}$$

$$T_i = 0.5 \times T_u$$

$$K_d = 0.125 \times T_u$$

REFERENCES

1. J. Michael Jacob, *Applications and Design with Analog Integrated Circuits*, © 1982, pp 312–313. Reprinted by permission of Prentice-Hall, Inc., Englewood Cliffs, New Jersey.
2. Gregory K. McMillan, *Tuning and Controller Loop Performance*. Research Triangle Park, N.C.: Instrument Society of America, 1983, pp. 14–15.

PROBLEMS

8–1. Describe a process control system. Indicate types of variables controlled, relative speed of response, variable for which the analysis is performed (tracing of a set point or regulation of load disturbances), and the transfer function for the closed-loop system response in terms of the element's transfer function (G) and the controller's transfer function (H).

8–2. Repeat Problem 8–1 for a servo control loop.

8–3. Derive the closed-loop response of a process with the transfer function

$$G = \frac{A}{s}$$

and a proportional controller with a gain of K_p.

8–4. Repeat Problem 8–3, replacing the proportional controller with a series proportional–integral controller with a proportional gain of K_p and an integral time of T_i.

8–5. Write the transfer function of the element under control and proportional controller from Problem 8–3 to allow analysis of the closed-loop response to a change in set point.

8–6. Write the transfer function of the element under control and series proportional–integral controller from Problem 8–3 to allow analysis of the closed-loop response to a change in set point.

8–7. Write the closed-loop transfer function of a second-order element with a transfer function of

$$G = \frac{A\omega_n}{s^2 + 2\zeta\omega_n s + \omega_n^2}$$

controlled by a proportional controller with a gain of K_p, analyzed as a servo system.

8–8. Repeat Problem 8–7, replacing the proportional controller with a series proportional–integral controller with a proportional gain of K_p and an integral time of T_i.

8–9. A first-order element under control has a steady-state gain of 6 and a time constant of 20 s. It is combined with a proportional controller with a gain of 10. The closed-loop process control transfer function is

$$\frac{PV}{IN} = \frac{0.54}{1 + 1.82s}$$

(a) Calculate the time-domain response of this closed-loop process to a unit step of the input (IN).

(b) Plot this response.

(c) On the same graph, plot the process variable's response if the element had been operated open loop, without the controller.

(d) Indicate on the graph the ideal response of the process to the step in input energy (IN).

8–10. The element under control in Problem 8–9 has its controller changed to a proportional–integral controller with $K_p = 16.7$ and $K_i = 2/s$. This change produces a closed-loop servo transfer function of

$$\frac{PV}{SP} = \frac{100s + 200}{20s^2 + 101s + 200}$$

Repeat problem 8–9 for a unit step in the set point.

8–11. The closed-loop servo system in Problem 8–10 is underdamped. Calculate the values of K_p and K_i which will cause the loop to be critically damped with a time constant of 5 s (resonant frequency of 0.2 rad/s).

8–12. Apply the final value theorem to the systems of Problems 8–9 and 8–10. Compare the results predicted by the final value theorem to the results obtained from working Problems 8–9 and 8–10.

8–13. Draw the open-loop Bodé plot of the integral element (Problem 8–3) with a series proportional–integral controller for $A = 5$, $K_p = 10$, and $K_i = 0.1/s$.

8–14. Repeat Problem 8–13, adding a simple RC low-pass filter between the process (G) and the PI controller. $R = 80$ kΩ; $C = 100$ μF.

8–15. Draw the open-loop Bodé plot of a second-order lag element (G) with a series proportional–integral controller (H) for $A = 6$, $\zeta = 0.6$, $\omega_n = 0.5$ rad/s, $K_p = 4$, and $K_i = 0.8/s$.

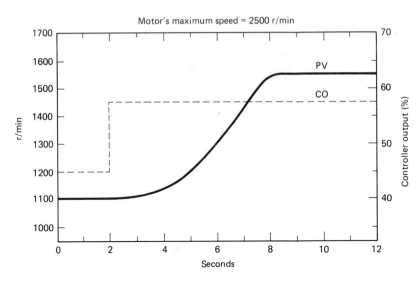

Figure 8–33 Process reaction tuning (Problem 8–18).

8–16. For the open-loop Bodé plots of Problems 8–13 through 8–15, determine the stability; specify both gain and phase margins.

8–17. Use Bodé plot tuning to determine the controller constants for an element with a transfer function of

$$G = \frac{5}{s(1 + 8s)} \qquad \text{(see Problem 8–14)}$$

(a) Simple proportional controller.
(b) Series proportional–integral controller.
(c) Parallel PID controller.

8–18. The plot in Figure 8–33 is from a process reaction test of a motor's speed. Select the controller tuning parameters for the following controllers.
(a) Proportional controller.
(b) Proportional–integral controller.
(c) PID controller.

8–19. An ultimate cycle test was performed on a system. When steady-state oscillations occurred, the controller was set to

Proportional band: 23%

Integral time: 999 s

Derivative time: 0 s

The process variable oscillated with a period of 35 s. Determine the proper proportional band, integral time, and derivative time for

(a) proportional control only.
(b) proportional–integral control.
(c) PID control.

Appendix A

Laplace Transforms

The solution of a differential equation requires that you find some function which when substituted into the differential equation, differentiated, multiplied by constants, and added to other derivatives of itself makes the original equation true. Sound complicated? Entire texts and multiple semesters can be dedicated to solving differential equations.

However, don't give up. The Laplace transform allows you to manipulate and solve differential equations with a table and some algebra. That's all. Take a look at Figure A-1. Differential equations, theorems, and techniques could be applied to obtain the solution directly. Or, you could apply Laplace transform techniques. By use of a table, the differential equation, which is a function of time (t), is moved into the frequency domain. Here it is a function of the dummy Laplace variable (s). All you have to do to perform this transformation is to look up each term of the differential equation in a table.

Now that the equation is in the frequency domain, you simply apply *algebra* to solve for V in terms of constants and s. The solution must then be converted back into the time domain. You do this by using the same table that allowed the first transformation.

The key to this algebraic solution of differential equations is the transformations between the time and frequency domains. Mathematically, the transformation of a function in the time domain, $f(t)$, into a function in the frequency domain, $F(s)$, is accomplished using the Laplace transform.

$$\mathcal{L}\{f(t)\} = F(s)$$

$$\mathcal{L}\{f(t)\} = \int_0^\infty f(t)e^{-st}\,dt$$

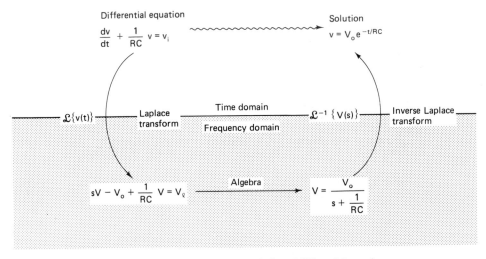

Figure A–1   Laplace transform solution of differential equation.

The inverse transformation, from a frequency-domain function, $F(s)$, to a time-domain function, $f(t)$, is

$$\mathcal{L}^{-1}\{F(s)\} = f(t)$$

$$f(t) = \int_{a-i^\infty}^{a+i^\infty} F(s)e^{st}\, dt$$

Fortunately, a table of useful functions, with their transformations, has been developed. So you do not have to perform any integrations. Just use the table. Table A-1 gives those transforms that are found most often in process control applications. You can find much more extensive tables in any handbook of mathematical tables. The following examples illustrate how to use the techniques of Laplace transforms to solve differential equations.

TABLE A-1   LAPLACE TRANSFORMS

No.	$F(S)$	$f(t)$	Comments
1.	1	$\delta(t)$	Unit impulse
2.	$\dfrac{A}{s}$	$A(t) = \begin{cases} 0 & t < 0 \\ A & t \geq 0 \end{cases}$	Step
3.	$\dfrac{1}{s}$	$U(t) = \begin{cases} 0 & t < 0 \\ 1 & t \geq 0 \end{cases}$	Unit step
4.	$\dfrac{A}{s^2}$	At	Ramp
5.	$\dfrac{2A}{s^3}$	At^2	Parabola
6.	$\dfrac{A\omega}{s^2 + \omega^2}$	$A \sin \omega t$	Sine

TABLE A-1 (continued)

No.	$F(S)$	$f(t)$	Comments
7.	$\dfrac{As}{s^2 + \omega^2}$	$A \cos \omega t$	Cosine
8.	$aF(s)$	$af(t)$	
9.	$\dfrac{n!}{s^{n+1}}$	t^n	
10.	$sF(s) - f(0)$	$\dfrac{df(t)}{dt}$	
11.	$s^2 F(s) - sf(0) - \dfrac{df(0)}{dt}$	$\dfrac{d^2 f(t)}{dt^2}$	
12.	$\dfrac{F(s)}{s}$	$\displaystyle\int f(t)\, dt$	
13a.	$\dfrac{A}{\tau s + 1}$	$\dfrac{A}{\tau} e^{-t/\tau}$	Free response of first-order system
13b.	$\dfrac{A}{s + a}$	Ae^{-at}	
14a.	$\dfrac{A}{(\tau_1 s + 1)(\tau_2 s + 1)}$	$\dfrac{A}{\tau_1 - \tau_2}(e^{-t/\tau_1} - e^{-t/\tau_2})$	Free response of second-order system ($\zeta > 1$)
14b.	$\dfrac{A}{(s + a)(s + b)}$	$\dfrac{A}{b - a}(e^{-at} - e^{-bt})$	
15a.	$\dfrac{A}{(\tau s + 1)^2}$	$\dfrac{At}{\tau^2} e^{-t/\tau}$	Free response of second-order system ($\zeta = 1$)
15b.	$\dfrac{A}{(s + a)^2}$	Ate^{-at}	
16.	$\dfrac{A\omega_n^2}{s^2 + 2\zeta\omega_n s + \omega_n^2}$	$\dfrac{A\omega_n e^{-\zeta\omega_n t}}{\sqrt{1 - \zeta^2}} \sin(\omega_n\sqrt{1 - \zeta^2}t)$	Second-order system, free response ($\zeta < 1$)
17a.	$\dfrac{A}{s(\tau s + 1)}$	$A(1 - e^{-t/\tau})$	First-order system response to a step input
17b.	$\dfrac{A}{s(s + a)}$	$\dfrac{A}{a}(1 - e^{-at})$	
18a.	$\dfrac{A}{s^2(\tau s + 1)}$	$A\tau\left(e^{-t/\tau} + \dfrac{t}{\tau} - 1\right)$	First-order system response to a ramp input
18b.	$\dfrac{A}{s^2(s + a)}$	$\dfrac{A}{a^2}(e^{-at} + at - 1)$	

TABLE A-1 (*continued*)

No.	$F(S)$	$f(t)$	Comments
19a.	$\dfrac{A\omega}{(s^2 + \omega^2)(\tau s + 1)}$	$\dfrac{A\omega\tau}{1 + \omega^2\tau^2}e^{-t/\tau} + \dfrac{A}{\sqrt{1 + \omega^2\tau^2}}\sin(\omega t - \psi)$ where $\psi = \tan^{-1}\omega\tau \quad (0 < \psi < \pi)$	First-order system response to a sine input
19b.	$\dfrac{A\omega}{(s^2 + \omega^2)(s + a)}$	$\dfrac{A\omega e^{-at}}{\omega^2 + a^2} + \dfrac{A}{\sqrt{\omega^2 + a^2}}\sin(\omega t - \psi)$ where $\psi = \tan^{-1}\omega/a \quad (0 < \psi < \pi)$	
20a.	$\dfrac{A}{s(\tau_1 s + 1)(\tau_2 s + 1)}$	$A\left(1 + \dfrac{\tau_1 e^{-t/\tau_1} - \tau_2 e^{-t/\tau_2}}{\tau_2 - \tau_1}\right)$	Second-order system response to a step input ($\zeta > 1$)
20b.	$\dfrac{A}{s(s + a)(s + b)}$	$\dfrac{A}{ab}\left(1 + \dfrac{ae^{-bt} - be^{-at}}{b - a}\right)$	
21a.	$\dfrac{A}{s(\tau s + 1)^2}$	$A\left(1 - \dfrac{\tau + t}{\tau}e^{-t/\tau}\right)$	Second-order system response to a step input ($\zeta = 1$)
21b.	$\dfrac{A}{s(s + a)^2}$	$\dfrac{A}{a^2}[1 - (1 + at)e^{-at}]$	
22.	$\dfrac{A\omega_n^2}{s(s^2 + 2\zeta\omega_n s + \omega_n^2)}$	$A\left[1 + \dfrac{e^{-\zeta\omega_n t}}{\sqrt{1 - \zeta^2}}\sin(\omega_n\sqrt{1 - \zeta^2}\,t - \psi)\right]$ where $\psi = \tan^{-1}\dfrac{\sqrt{1 - \zeta^2}}{-\zeta} \quad (0 < \psi < \pi)$	Second-order system response to a step input ($\zeta < 1$)
23a.	$\dfrac{A}{s^2(\tau_1 s + 1)(\tau_2 s + 1)}$	$A\left(t - \tau_1 - \tau_2 - \dfrac{\tau_2^2 e^{-t/\tau_2} - \tau_1^2 e^{-t/\tau_1}}{\tau_1 - \tau_2}\right)$	Second-order system response to a ramp input ($\zeta > 1$)
23b.	$\dfrac{A}{s^2(s + a)(s + b)}$	$\dfrac{A}{ab}\left[t - \dfrac{a + b}{ab} - \dfrac{(b/a)e^{-bt} - (a/b)e^{-at}}{b - a}\right]$	
24a.	$\dfrac{A}{s^2(\tau s + 1)^2}$	$A[t - 2\tau + (t + 2\tau)e^{-t/\tau}]$	Second-order system response to a ramp input ($\zeta = 1$)
24b.	$\dfrac{A}{s^2(s + a)^2}$	$\dfrac{A}{a^2}\left[t - \dfrac{2}{a} + \left(t + \dfrac{2}{a}\right)e^{-at}\right]$	
25.	$\dfrac{A\omega_n^2}{s^2(s^2 + 2\zeta\omega_n s + \omega_n^2)}$	$A\left[t - \dfrac{2\zeta}{\omega_n} + \dfrac{e^{-\zeta\omega_n t}}{\omega_n\sqrt{1 - \zeta^2}}\sin(\omega_n\sqrt{1 - \zeta^2}t - \psi)\right]$ where $\psi = 2\tan^{-1}\dfrac{\sqrt{1 - \zeta^2}}{-\zeta} \quad (0 < \psi < \pi)$	Second-order system response to a ramp input ($\zeta < 1$)

TABLE A-1   (continued)

No.	$F(S)$	$f(t)$	Comments
26a.	$\dfrac{A\omega}{(s^2 + \omega^2)(\tau_1 s + 1)(\tau_2 s + 1)}$	$A\left[\dfrac{\tau_1^2\omega e^{-t/\tau_1}}{(\tau_1 - \tau_2)(1 + \omega^2\tau_1^2)} + \dfrac{\tau_2^2\omega e^{-t/\tau_2}}{(\tau_2 - \tau_1)(1 + \omega^2\tau_2^2)}\right.$ $\left. + \dfrac{\sin(\omega t - \psi)}{[(1 + \omega^2\tau_1^2)(1 + \omega^2\tau_2^2)]^{1/2}}\right]$ where $\psi = \tan^{-1}\omega\tau_1 + \tan^{-1}\omega\tau_2$	Second-order system response to a sine input $(\zeta > 1)$
26b.	$\dfrac{A\omega}{(s^2 + \omega^2)(s + a)(s + b)}$	$A\left[\dfrac{\omega e^{-at}}{(b - a)(\omega^2 + a^2)} + \dfrac{\omega e^{-bt}}{(a - b)(\omega^2 + b^2)}\right.$ $\left. + \dfrac{\sin(\omega t - \psi)}{[(\omega^2 + a^2)(\omega^2 + b^2)]^{1/2}}\right]$ where $\psi = \tan^{-1}\dfrac{\omega(a + b)}{ab - \omega^2}$ $(0 < \psi < \pi)$	
27a.	$\dfrac{A\omega}{(s^2 + \omega^2)(\tau s + 1)^2}$	$\dfrac{A}{1 + \omega^2\tau^2}\left[\dfrac{\omega t + 2\omega\tau}{1 + \omega^2\tau^2}e^{-t/\tau} + \sin(\omega t - \psi)\right]$ where $\psi = 2\tan^{-1}\omega\tau$	Second-order system response to a sine input$(\zeta = 1)$
27b.	$\dfrac{A\omega}{(s^2 + \omega^2)(s + a)^2}$	$\dfrac{A}{\omega^2 + a^2}\left[\dfrac{a\omega(at + 2)e^{-at}}{\omega^2 + a^2} + \sin(\omega t - \psi)\right]$	
28.	$\dfrac{A\omega\omega_n^2}{(s^2 + \omega^2)(s^2 + 2\zeta\omega_n s + \omega_n^2)}$	$\dfrac{A\omega_n^2}{[(\omega_n^2 - \omega^2)^2 + 4\zeta^2\omega^2\omega_n^2]^{1/2}}$ $\cdot\left[\sin(\omega t - \psi_1) + \dfrac{\omega e^{-\zeta\omega_n t}\sin(\omega_n\sqrt{1 - \zeta^2}\,t - \psi_2)}{\omega_n\sqrt{1 - \zeta^2}}\right]$ where $\psi_1 = \tan^{-1}\dfrac{2\zeta\omega\omega_n}{\omega_n^2 - \omega^2}$ $0 < \psi_1 < \pi$ and $\psi_2 = \tan^{-1} - \dfrac{2\zeta\omega_n^2\sqrt{1 - \zeta^2}}{\omega^2 - \omega_n^2(1 - 2\zeta^2)}$ $0 < \psi_2 < \pi$	Second-order system response to a sine input $(\zeta < 1)$

Source: Floyd E. Nixon, *Handbook of Laplace Transformation: Fundamentals, Applications, Tables and Examples*, 21e, © 1965, Referenced and adapted by permission of Prentice-Hall, Inc., Englewood Cliffs, New Jersey.

EXAMPLE A-1

Given a charged capacitor circuit with an initial charge of 5 V, $R = 10\ \text{k}\Omega$, and $C = 0.1\ \mu\text{F}$, plot the voltage versus time.

$$\frac{dv}{dt} + \frac{1}{RC}v = 0 \left.\right|_{v(t = 0) = v_o}$$

Solution

$$R = 10 \text{ k}\Omega, \qquad C = 0.1 \mu\text{F}, \qquad v_o = 5 \text{ V}$$

You must take the Laplace transform of each term of the equation.

$$\mathcal{L}\left\{\frac{dv}{dt}\right\} + \mathcal{L}\left\{\frac{1}{RC}v\right\} = \mathcal{L}\{0\} \qquad \text{(A-1)}$$

Now look at Table A-1. From line 10,

$$\mathcal{L}\left\{\frac{df(t)}{dt}\right\} = sF(s) - f(0)$$

so

$$\mathcal{L}\left\{\frac{dv}{dt}\right\} = sV - v_o$$

where v_o is the initial charge on the capacitor $v_0 = 5$. From line 8,

$$\mathcal{L}\left\{af(t)\right\} = aF(s)$$

so

$$\mathcal{L}\left\{\frac{1}{RC}v\right\} = \frac{1}{RC}V$$

From line 2,

$$\mathcal{L}\left\{A\right\} = \frac{A}{s}$$

so

$$\mathcal{L}\left\{0\right\} = \frac{0}{s} = 0$$

Substituting these transformations into equation A-1 yields

$$sV - v_o + \frac{1}{RC}V = 0$$

You must now solve for V.

$$sV + \frac{1}{RC}V = v_o$$

$$V\left(s + \frac{1}{RC}\right) = v_o$$

$$V = v_o\left(\frac{1}{s + 1/RC}\right)$$

This is the solution in the frequency domain, in terms of constants and the dummy variable, s. Now it must be transformed back into the time domain.

$$\mathscr{L}^{-1}\{V\} = \mathscr{L}^{-1}\left\{v_o\left(\frac{1}{s + 1/RC}\right)\right\}$$

From line 13b of Table A-1,

$$\mathscr{L}^{-1}\left\{\frac{A}{s + a}\right\} = Ae^{-at}$$

Let $a = 1/RC$, $A = v_o$:

$$v(t) = v_o e^{-t/RC}$$

Substituting the values given at the beginning of the example, we obtain

$$v(t) = 5e^{-t/1\text{ ms}} \tag{A-2}$$

To obtain the plot, just substitute values of t into equation A-2, tabulate the results, and then plot. The result is given in Figure A-2.

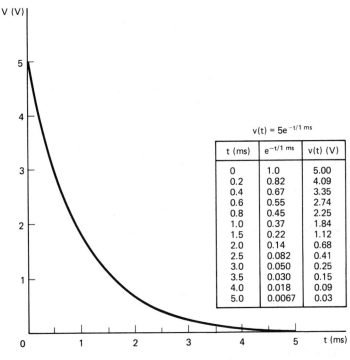

$$v(t) = 5e^{-t/1\text{ ms}}$$

t (ms)	$e^{-t/1\text{ ms}}$	v(t) (V)
0	1.0	5.00
0.2	0.82	4.09
0.4	0.67	3.35
0.6	0.55	2.74
0.8	0.45	2.25
1.0	0.37	1.84
1.5	0.22	1.12
2.0	0.14	0.68
2.5	0.082	0.41
3.0	0.050	0.25
3.5	0.030	0.15
4.0	0.018	0.09
5.0	0.0067	0.03

Figure A–2 Plot (Example A–1).

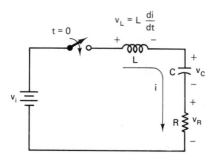

Figure A–3 Schematic (Example A–2).

Example A-1 showed the solution of a first-order differential equation. The *RLC* circuit of Figure A-3 produces a second-order equation.

EXAMPLE A-2

Given the *RLC* circuit of Figure A-3, with $R = 6.32$ kΩ, $C = 0.002$ μF, $L = 20$ mH, and $V = 10$ V, plot the current versus time. Also, assume that there is no initial current or charge. The differential equation for the circuit is

$$\frac{d^2i}{dt^2} + \frac{R}{L}\frac{di}{dt} + \frac{1}{LC}i = \frac{1}{L}\frac{dv_i}{dt} \tag{A-3}$$

Solution From line 11 of Table A-1,

$$\mathscr{L}\left\{\frac{d^2f(t)}{dt^2}\right\} = s^2F(s) - sf(0) - \frac{df(0)}{dt}$$

so

$$\mathscr{L}\left\{\frac{d^2i}{dt^2}\right\} = s^2I - sI_o - \frac{di(t=0)}{dt}$$

Since there is no initial current,

$$I_o = 0$$

An inductor cannot change its current instantaneously, so

$$\frac{di}{dt}(t=0) = 0$$

$$\mathscr{L}\left\{\frac{d^2i}{dt^2}\right\} = s^2I - sI_o - \frac{di}{dt}(t=0)$$

$$= s^2I$$

The input is a step

$$\mathscr{L}\left\{\frac{dv_i}{dt}\right\} = s\mathscr{L}\left\{v_i\right\} - v_o$$

where v_i is a step of height V. At $t = 0$, v_o (the initial value of the step) $= 0$, and

$$\mathscr{L}\left\{step\right\} = \frac{V}{s}$$

Taking the Laplace transform of equation A-3 gives us

$$s^2I + \frac{R}{L}\left(sI - I_o\right) + \frac{1}{LC}I = \frac{1}{L}s\left(\frac{V}{s}\right)$$

But since $I_o = 0$,

$$s^2I + \frac{R}{L}sI + \frac{1}{LC}I = \frac{V}{L}$$

$$I\left(s^2 + \frac{R}{L}s + \frac{1}{LC}\right) = \frac{V}{L}$$

$$I = \frac{V}{L}\left[\frac{1}{s^2 + (R/L)s + 1/LC}\right]$$

Substituting the values given at the beginning of the example, we have

$$I = \frac{10\ V}{20\ mH}\left[\frac{1}{s^2 + \dfrac{6.32\ k\Omega}{20\ mH}s + \dfrac{1}{(20\ mH)(0.002\ \mu F)}}\right]$$

$$= 500\left(\frac{1}{s^2 + 3.16 \times 10^5 s + 2.5 \times 10^{10}}\right)$$

It just happens that this becomes

$$I = 500\left[\frac{1}{(s + 1.58 \times 10^5)^2}\right] \tag{A-4}$$

From line 15b of Table A-1,

$$\mathscr{L}^{-1}\left\{\frac{A}{(s + a)^2}\right\} = Ate^{-at}$$

Compare this to equation A-4.

$$a = 1.58 \times 10^5$$

so

$$i(t) = 500te^{(-1.58 \times 10^5)t} \tag{A-5}$$

You obtain a plot of $i(t)$ by substituting different values of t into equation A-5, tabulating, and then plotting the results. This is shown in Figure A-4. From the plot you can see that the current starts at zero but peaks at about 6 μs. It then decreases and becomes insignificant after 50 μs.

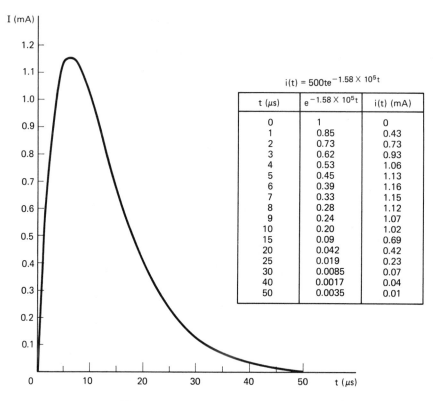

I (mA)

$i(t) = 500te^{-1.58 \times 10^5 t}$

t (μs)	$e^{-1.58 \times 10^5 t}$	i(t) (mA)
0	1	0
1	0.85	0.43
2	0.73	0.73
3	0.62	0.93
4	0.53	1.06
5	0.45	1.13
6	0.39	1.16
7	0.33	1.15
8	0.28	1.12
9	0.24	1.07
10	0.20	1.02
15	0.09	0.69
20	0.042	0.42
25	0.019	0.23
30	0.0085	0.07
40	0.0017	0.04
50	0.0035	0.01

Figure A–4 Plot (Example A–2).

The values in Example A-2 were arranged to cause the denominator to be a perfect square, $1/(s + a)^2$. A more realistic example follows.

EXAMPLE A-3

Given a mass–spring–damper system with $R = 4$, $m = 10$, $k = 12.5$, and a unity step for the input force, plot the position of the mass versus time. Also, assume that the mass begins from rest. The differential equation for the system is

$$\frac{d^2x}{dt^2} + \frac{R}{m}\frac{dx}{dt} + \frac{k}{m}x = \frac{f_i}{m} \tag{A-6}$$

Solution   Taking the Laplace transform of both sides of the differential equation gives

$$\mathcal{L}\left\{\frac{d^2x}{dt^2}\right\} + \mathcal{L}\left\{\frac{R}{m}\frac{dx}{dt}\right\} + \mathcal{L}\left\{\frac{k}{m}x\right\} = \mathcal{L}\left\{\frac{f_i}{m}\right\}$$

$$s^2X - sx_o - \frac{dx(0)}{dt} + \frac{R}{m}sX - \frac{R}{m}x_o + \frac{k}{m}X = \frac{1}{sm} \qquad \text{(A-7)}$$

Since the mass begins from rest,

$$x_o = 0$$

$$\frac{dx(0)}{dt} = 0$$

Equation A-7 becomes

$$s^2X + \frac{R}{m}sX + \frac{k}{m}X = \frac{1}{sm}$$

Factoring out X leaves

$$X\left(s^2 + \frac{R}{m}s + \frac{k}{m}\right) = \frac{1}{sm}$$

$$X = \frac{1}{ms[s^2 + (R/m)s + k/m]} \qquad \text{(A-8)}$$

Equation A-8 is the solution to the differential equation in the frequency domain. You now must substitute values for the constants and transform the result back to the time domain.

$$R = 4 \qquad m = 10 \qquad k = 12.5 \qquad X = \frac{0.1}{s(s^2 + 0.4s + 1.25)}$$

From line 22 of Table A-1,

$$\mathcal{L}^{-1}\left\{\frac{A\omega_n^2}{s(s^2 + 2\zeta\omega_n s + \omega_n^2)}\right\} = A\left[1 + \frac{e^{-\zeta\omega_n t}}{\sqrt{1 - \zeta^2}}\sin\left(\omega_n\sqrt{1 - \zeta^2}\,t - \psi\right)\right]$$

where

$$\psi = \tan^{-1}\frac{\sqrt{1 - \zeta^2}}{-\zeta} \qquad 0 < \psi < \pi$$

$$\omega_n^2 = 1.25 \qquad \text{so} \qquad \omega_n = 1.12$$

$$2\zeta\omega_n = 0.4 \qquad \text{so} \qquad \zeta = \frac{0.4}{2\omega_n} = \frac{0.4}{2(1.12)} = 0.179$$

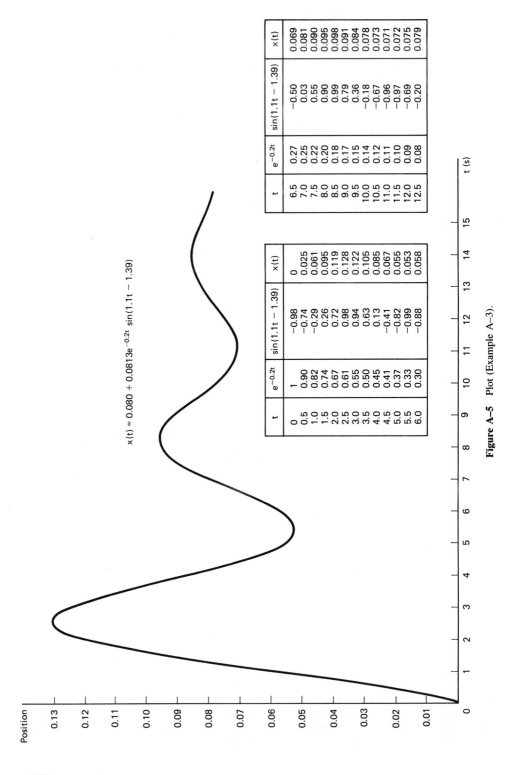

$$x(t) = 0.080 + 0.0813e^{-0.2t}\sin(1.1t - 1.39)$$

t	$e^{-0.2t}$	$\sin(1.1t - 1.39)$	x(t)
0	1	-0.98	0
0.5	0.90	-0.74	0.025
1.0	0.82	-0.29	0.061
1.5	0.74	0.26	0.095
2.0	0.67	0.72	0.119
2.5	0.61	0.98	0.128
3.0	0.55	0.94	0.122
3.5	0.50	0.63	0.105
4.0	0.45	0.13	0.085
4.5	0.41	-0.41	0.067
5.0	0.37	-0.82	0.055
5.5	0.33	-0.99	0.053
6.0	0.30	-0.88	0.058

t	$e^{-0.2t}$	$\sin(1.1t - 1.39)$	x(t)
6.5	0.27	-0.50	0.069
7.0	0.25	0.03	0.081
7.5	0.22	0.55	0.090
8.0	0.20	0.90	0.095
8.5	0.18	0.99	0.098
9.0	0.17	0.79	0.091
9.5	0.15	0.36	0.084
10.0	0.14	-0.18	0.078
10.5	0.12	-0.67	0.073
11.0	0.11	-0.96	0.071
11.5	0.10	-0.97	0.072
12.0	0.09	-0.69	0.075
12.5	0.08	-0.20	0.079

Figure A–5 Plot (Example A–3).

$$A\omega_n^2 = 0.1 \quad \text{so} \quad A = \frac{0.1}{\omega_n^2} = \frac{0.1}{1.25} = 0.080$$

$$\psi = \tan^{-1}\frac{\sqrt{1-(0.179)^2}}{-(0.179)} = \tan^{-1}(-5.50) = +1.39 \text{ rad}$$

$$x(t) = 0.080\left[1 + \frac{e^{-(0.179)(1.12)t}}{\sqrt{1-(0.179)^2}}\sin\left[(1.12)\sqrt{1-(0.179)^2}\,t - 1.39\right]\right]$$

$$= 0.080 + 0.0813e^{-0.200t}\sin(1.10t - 1.39) \tag{A-9}$$

The argument of sin is in radians. To obtain the plot, just substitute values of t into equation A-9, tabulate the results and then plot (Figure A-5). Notice that this second-order system, with the constants given, rings, oscillating several cycles before it settles to its new position.

Appendix B

Process Transfer Functions

B-1 INTEGRAL PROCESS ELEMENT

To obtain the transfer function, you must transform equation 2–1 into the Laplace domain. This is done with Table A-1. From line 12,

$$\mathcal{L}\left\{\int f(t)\,dt\right\} = \frac{F(s)}{s}$$

so

$$V_o = K\,\frac{V_i}{s}$$

$$\frac{V_o}{V_i} = \frac{K}{s} \tag{B-1}$$

There are three standard test signals that are used routinely when evaluating a process element's response. They are the step, the pulse, and the ramp. The most common is the step. To determine the response of an integral-type element to a step input using equation B-1, you have

$$V_o = K\,\frac{V_i}{s} \tag{B-2}$$

From line 2 of Table A-1, the Laplace domain equation for a step is

$$V_i = \frac{A}{s}$$

where A is the height of the step. Substituting this into equation B-2 gives

$$V_o = \frac{K}{s}\frac{A}{s}$$

$$V_o = \frac{KA}{s^2}$$

To transform this back into the time domain, again look in Table A-1. Using line 4,

$$v(t) = KAt \tag{B-3}$$

which is the equation for a ramp. The slope, or rate of increase of the output, is KA per second.

Since applying a step input to an integral-type process element may saturate the system, will changing the input to a ramp be any better? From line 4 of Table A-1, the Laplace domain equation for a ramp input is

$$V_i = \frac{A}{s^2}$$

Substituting this into equation B-2 gives you

$$V_o = \frac{K}{s}\frac{A}{s^2}$$

$$V_o = \frac{KA}{s^3}$$

Transforming back into the time domain requires line 5 from Table A-1:

$$\frac{2A}{s^3} = At^2$$

so

$$v(t) = \frac{KA}{2}t^2 \tag{B-4}$$

The output changes as time *squared*. This is much more rapid than the first case (step input; ramp output).

B-2 FIRST-ORDER PROCESS ELEMENT

The transfer function for a first-order process element is

$$\frac{V_o}{V_i} = \frac{A}{\tau s + 1} \tag{B-5a}$$

or

$$\frac{V_o}{V_i} = \frac{A}{s+a} \tag{B-5b}$$

where A is the steady-state gain and τ is the time constant.

When evaluating the response of an integral process element, three standard test inputs were used: the step, the ramp, and the pulse. These same signals will be applied to the first-order element of equation B-5.

The step input is the most traditional test input, and all response parameters are obtained from it.

$$V_o = \frac{A_1}{\tau s + 1} V_i$$

$$V_i = \frac{A_2}{s}$$

which is the Laplace domain equation for a step of height A_2 (Table A-1, line 2).

$$V_o = \frac{A_1 A_2}{s(\tau s + 1)} \tag{B-6}$$

To transform this back into the time domain, again look in Table A-1. Line 17a indicates that

$$\mathscr{L}^{-1}\left\{\frac{A}{s(\tau s + 1)}\right\} = A(1 - e^{-t/\tau})$$

so

$$V_o(t) = A_1 A_2 (1 - e^{-t/\tau}) \tag{B-7}$$

The second standard test signal is a ramp. How will a first-order element respond to a ramp? The output in the Laplace domain is

$$V_o = \frac{A_1}{\tau s + 1} V_i$$

From line 4 of Table A-1, the equation for a ramp input is

$$V_i = \frac{A_2}{s^2}$$

where A_2 is the slope of the ramp, so

$$V_o = \frac{A_1 A_2}{s^2(s\tau + 1)}$$

To convert this back into the time domain, again refer to Table A-1, this time line 18a.

$$v_o(t) = A_1 A_2 \tau \left(e^{-t/\tau} + \frac{t}{\tau} - 1\right) \tag{B-8}$$

The third standard input is the pulse or impulse. As with the other first-order elements,

$$V_o = \frac{A_1}{\tau s + 1} V_i$$

From line 1 of Table A-1,

$$V_i = 1$$

so

$$V_o = \frac{A}{\tau s + 1}$$

You can convert this into the time domain by using line 13a of Table A-1,

$$V_o(t) = \frac{A}{\tau} e^{-t/\tau} \tag{B-9}$$

B-3 DEAD TIME

The transfer function for a simple dead-time element is

$$\frac{V_o}{V_i} = A e^{-t_d s} \tag{B-10}$$

where A is the element's steady-state gain, and t_d is the dead time.

B-4 SECOND-ORDER PROCESS ELEMENT

The general transfer function for a second-order element is

$$\frac{V_o}{V_i} = \frac{A\omega_n^2}{s^2 + 2\zeta\omega_n s + \omega_n^2} \tag{B-11}$$

where A = element gain
  ω_n = natural or resonant frequency
  ζ = damping coefficient

B-4.1 Overdamped Response

The denominator of the second-order transfer function is

$$s^2 + 2\zeta\omega_n s + \omega_n^2$$

If the element is overdamped, $\zeta > 1$, then this denominator can be separated into two *real* roots.

The overall transfer function for two first-order elements is

$$\frac{A_1}{\tau_1 s + 1} \frac{A_2}{\tau_2 s + 1}$$

$$\frac{A_1 A_2}{(\tau_1 s + 1)(\tau_2 s + 1)}$$

It is clear that the denominator can be separated into two real factors. But what are A, ζ, ω_n, τ, and k_p? Figuring that out takes a little algebra. Multiplying the two factors in the denominator gives

$$\frac{A_1 A_2}{\tau_1 \tau_2 s^2 + (\tau_1 + \tau_2)s + 1}$$

Dividing through by $\tau_1 \tau_2$ yields

$$\frac{A_1 A_2 / \tau_1 \tau_2}{s^2 + [(\tau_1 + \tau_2)/\tau_1 \tau_2]s + 1/\tau_1 \tau_2} \tag{B-12}$$

Compare Equation B-12 with the general form of the second-order element, equation B-11.

$$\frac{A\omega_n^2}{s^2 + 2\zeta\omega_n s + \omega_n^2} \tag{B-11}$$

$$\omega_n^2 = \frac{1}{\tau_1 \tau_2}$$

$$\omega_n = \frac{1}{\sqrt{\tau_1 \tau_2}} \tag{2-6}$$

$$\tau_{\text{system}} = \frac{1}{\omega_n} = \sqrt{\tau_1 \tau_2} \tag{2-7}$$

$$k_p = A\omega_n^2 = \frac{A_1 A_2}{\tau_1 \tau_2} \tag{2-8}$$

$$2\zeta\omega_n = \frac{\tau_1 + \tau_2}{\tau_1 \tau_2}$$

$$\zeta = \frac{\tau_1 + \tau_2}{2\omega_n(\tau_1 \tau_2)}$$

$$\zeta = \frac{\tau_1 + \tau_2}{2(1/\sqrt{\tau_1 \tau_2})(\tau_1 \tau_2)}$$

$$\zeta = \frac{\tau_1 + \tau_2}{2\sqrt{\tau_1 \tau_2}} \tag{2-9}$$

EXAMPLE B-1

Given a $\frac{1}{4}$-in.-long bare RTD followed by appropriate signal-conditioning electronics ($A = 0.255$ V/Ω), and a simple RC filter ($R = 4.7$ kΩ and $C = 220$ μF).

(a) Determine the second-order transfer function for those cascaded first-order elements.

(b) Determine ζ.

(c) Write the Laplace-domain and time-domain equations for the element's response to a 75°C step in temperature.

Solution   For the RTD, as you saw in Example 2–2,

$$A = 0.3925 \ \Omega/°C$$

$$\tau_1 = 5.5 \text{ sec}$$

You saw a simple RC filter in examples and problems in Chapter 2. It has

$$A_1 = 1$$

$$\tau_1 = RC = (4.7 \text{ k}\Omega)(220 \text{ μF}) = 1.03 \text{ sec}$$

The electronics is a simple gain stage with $A_3 = 0.255$ V/Ω. You can assume that at T_{nominal} the electronics have been adjusted to give an output of zero volts.

The overall transfer function for the probe, the electronics, and the filter is

$$\frac{A_1 A_2 A_3}{(\tau_1 s + 1)(\tau_2 s + 1)}$$

or

$$\frac{A \omega_n^2}{s^2 + 2\zeta\omega_n s + \omega_n^2}$$

$$\zeta = \frac{\tau_1 + \tau_2}{2\sqrt{\tau_1 \tau_2}}$$

$$= \frac{1.03 \text{ sec} + 5.5 \text{ sec}}{2\sqrt{(1.03 \text{ sec})(5.5 \text{ sec})}}$$

$$= 1.37$$

So the overall transfer function is

$$\frac{V_o}{V_i} = \frac{(0.3925 \ \Omega/°C)(1)(0.255 \text{ V}/\Omega)}{[(1.03 \text{ sec})s + 1][(5.5 \text{ sec})s + 1]}$$

$$= \frac{0.100 \text{ V}/°C}{[(1.03 \text{ sec})s + 1][(5.5 \text{ sec})s + 1]}$$

For a 75°C step in temperature,

$$V_i = \frac{75°C}{s}$$

Substituting this into the transfer function gives

$$V_o = \frac{(75°C)(0.100 \text{ V/°C})}{s[(1.03 \text{ sec})s + 1][(5.5 \text{ sec})s + 1]}$$

$$= \frac{7.5 \text{ V}}{s[(1.03 \text{ sec})s + 1][(5.5 \text{ sec})s + 1]}$$

Look in Table A-1, line 20a:

$$\mathcal{L}^{-1}\left\{\frac{A}{s(\tau_1 s + 1)(\tau_2 s + 1)}\right\} = A\left[1 + \frac{\tau_1 e^{-t/\tau_1} - \tau_2 e^{-t/\tau_2}}{\tau_2 - \tau_1}\right]$$

where $\tau_2 > \tau_1$. $A = 7.5$ V, $\tau_1 = 1.03$ sec, $\tau_2 = 5.5$ sec,

$$v_{out}(t) = 7.5 \text{ V}\left[1 + \frac{(1.03 \text{ sec})e^{-t/1.03 \text{ sec}} - (5.5 \text{ sec})e^{-t/5.5 \text{ sec}}}{4.47 \text{ sec}}\right]$$

$$= 7.5 \text{ V}\,(1 + 0.230e^{-t/1.03 \text{ sec}} - 1.23e^{-t/5.5 \text{ sec}})$$

There are several points illustrated by this example. The response is two exponentials, each decaying at its own rate. If one of the time constants is significantly longer than the other, it dominates the response. After $5\tau_1$ (i.e., 5.15 sec) the first exponential (from the filter) has died out. The output now follows the first-order response of the slower time constant. As far as the damping is concerned, this means that if $\tau_1 \ll \tau_2$, then ζ becomes large. The element is heavily damped and its behaves like a first-order element with $\tau = \tau_2$. This holds true for all inputs, steps, ramps, or pulses.

B-4.2 Critically Damped Response

The denominator of the second-order transfer function is

$$s^2 + 2\zeta\omega_n s + \omega_n^2$$

For a critically damped element, with $\zeta = 1$, the denominator becomes

$$s^2 + 2\omega_n s + \omega_n^2$$

This is factorable into two, *real, equal* roots. That means that the denominator is

$$(s + \omega_n)^2$$

Cascading two first-order elements with equal (or nearly equal) time constants produces a critically damped second-order system.

$$\frac{A_1}{\tau s + 1}\frac{A_2}{\tau s + 1} = \frac{A_1 A_2}{(\tau s + 1)^2}$$

B-4.3 Underdamped Response

The denominator of the second-order transfer function is

$$s^2 + 2\zeta\omega_n s + \omega_n^2$$

For an underdamped, second-order element with $\zeta < 1$, that denominator cannot be factored. Applying the quadratic equation produces imaginary or complex roots. Cascading two first-order elements *cannot* produce an underdamped second-order system.

When a step is applied to an underdamped element,

$$V_o = \frac{A_1\omega_n^2}{s^2 + 2\zeta\omega_n s + \omega_n^2} V_i$$

$$V_i = \frac{A_2}{s}$$

$$V_o = \frac{A_1 A_2 \omega_n^2}{s(s^2 + 2\zeta\omega_n s + \omega_n^2)}$$

From line 22 of Table A-1,

$$\mathscr{L}^{-1}\left\{\frac{A\omega_n^2}{s(s^2 + 2\zeta\omega_n s + \omega_n^2)}\right\} = A\left[1 + \frac{e^{-\zeta\omega_n t}}{\sqrt{1 - \zeta^2}}\sin\left(\omega_n\sqrt{1 - \zeta^2}\,t - \psi\right)\right]$$

Index